CONTRIBUTIONS
TO
ANTHROPOLOGY

A. Irving Hallowell, 1892–1974

CONTRIBUTIONS
TO
ANTHROPOLOGY

Selected Papers of
A. Irving Hallowell

With Introductions by
Raymond D. Fogelson
Fred Eggan
Melford E. Spiro
George W. Stocking
Anthony F. C. Wallace
Wilcomb E. Washburn

University of Chicago Press
Chicago and London

346182

c̆

The University of Chicago Press, Chicago 60637
The University of Chicago Press, Ltd., London

©1976 by The University of Chicago
All rights reserved. Published 1976
Printed in the United States of America
80 79 78 77 76 9 8 7 6 5 4 3 2 1

Library of Congress Cataloging in Publication Data

Hallowell, Alfred Irving, 1892–1974.
    Contributions to anthropology.

    "Supplementary bibliography of works by A. Irving
Hallowell": p.
    1. Ethnology—Collected works. 2. Indians of North
America—Collected works. 3. Anthropology—History—
Collected works. 4. Chippewa Indians—Collected works.
I. Title.
GN304.H34 1976   301.2   75-20890
ISBN 0-226-31414-6.

CONTENTS

PUBLISHER'S NOTE

Because of the prohibitive cost of resetting so much material, most of the articles in this book have been photoreproduced from earlier publications. This accounts for discrepancies in type, style, and format between chapters. Articles were reprinted from the following sources, with permission of the publishers:

Chapter 7—"Cross-Cousin Marriage in the Lake Winnipeg Area." In *Twenty-fifth Anniversary Studies*, ed. D. S. Davidson, pp. 95–110. Philadelphia: Philadelphia Anthropological Society, 1937.

Chapter 9—"Ojibwa Ontology, Behavior, and World View." In *Culture in History: Essays in Honor of Paul Radin*, ed. Stanley Diamond, pp. 19–52. New York: Columbia University Press, 1960.

Chapter 10—"Ojibwa World View and Disease." In *Man's Image in Medicine and Anthropology*, ed. Iago Galdston, pp. 258–315. New York: International Universities Press, 1963.

Chapter 11—"The Role of Dreams in Ojibwa Culture." In *The Dream and Human Societies*, ed. G. E. von Grunebaum and Roger Caillois, pp. 267–92. Berkeley: University of California Press, 1966.

Chapter 12—"The Impact of the American Indian on American Culture." *American Anthropologist* 59 (April 1957): 201–17.

Chapter 13—"American Indians, White and Black: The Phenomenon of Transculturalization." *Current Anthropology* 4 (1963): 519–31.

GENERAL INTRODUCTION

Raymond D. Fogelson

A. Irving Hallowell died on 10 October 1974. He was justly renowned in his lifetime as one of the world's most distinguished
anthropologists; and his work, influence, and inspiration live
on. The publication of this collection of his essays was intended not to memorialize his passing from the discipline with
which he so closely identified, but rather to make available to
interested scholars certain of his less accessible and later papers that are still relevant to modern anthropology. Thus, this
volume supplements and complements his earlier collection
of essays, *Culture and Experience* (Philadelphia: University
of Pennsylvania Press, 1955).[1]

In the decade following the appearance of *Culture and Experience*, which honored his sixtieth birthday, Hallowell's vig-
orous academic and scholarly career continued unabated. Until
his official retirement at age seventy, he remained a vital presence at the University of Pennsylvania, where he maintained
a full teaching schedule, advised a new generation of graduate
students, and freely bestowed the benefits of his accumulated
wisdom on colleagues near and far. He served as a visiting
professor at the University of Washington, the University of
Wisconsin, Bryn Mawr College, the University of Chicago,
Temple University, and Chatham College, and he had a significant influence on students at all these institutions. He was
invited to Nigeria to witness the installation of a former student, N. Azikwe, as governor-general.[2] In 1965 he was presented a festschrift, *Context and Meaning in Cultural Anthropology* (edited by Melford E. Spiro and published by the Free
Press), which contained important essays by former students
and colleagues. During this active period he also participated

Raymond D. Fogelson is associate professor of anthropology at the
University of Chicago.

in numerous major conferences. His contributions to them
formed the basis for many of the articles in the present collection. His last years were marked by severe illness and considerable suffering; as a result he was unable to complete
many projects that he had planned and begun, including publication of the present collection of essays.[3]

Negotiations for this volume were started in the spring of
1969. Emanuel Geltman, then senior social science editor for
the University of Chicago Press and a long-time admirer of
Hallowell's work, encouraged the project, and after requisite
refereeing a contract was signed and an advance payment
made. Hallowell had submitted an outline listing the papers he
wished to include. He had planned to make revisions and up-
date many of the essays, as well as to provide introductions to
the major sections and a general introduction.

In resurrecting the project, I have tried to remain faithful to
Professor Hallowell's original outline. Some modifications
were made, however. The autobiographical statement, "On Being an Anthropologist," originally an appendix, was relocated
to a more prominent position in order to serve in place of the
general introduction that Hallowell was unable to complete.
The essay "Psychology and Anthropology," originally placed in
the "History of Anthropology" section, was coupled with "Personality, Culture, and Society in Behavioral Evolution," and the
new section was labeled "Psychology and Culture"; this
change met with Hallowell's approval before his death. In the
original outline all five papers dealing specifically with the Ojibwa were grouped together in one large section. It seemed reasonable to divide this section into two: "Ojibwa Ecology and
Social Organization" and "Ojibwa Culture and World View"
(Hallowell's original title for the whole section). The essay
"Northern Ojibwa Ecological Adaptation and Social Organization," the only previously unpublished article in this collection,
was unavailable when the original outline was submitted. Fortunately, Mrs. Maude Hallowell was able to locate a draft of the
paper, and we are able to include it as originally planned. This
essay has received only minimal editing by Professor Eggan,
Robert Brightman, and myself and thus retains a draftlike quality that contrasts sharply with the gloss and high scholarly stand-

ards characteristic of Hallowell's published work (e.g., there is nary a footnote and no references!). Nevertheless, the essay contains useful new information and reflects Hallowell's mature conceptualization of the essential nature of Ojibwa social organization.

The only radical departure from the original plan was to invite selected scholars to provide short introductory commentaries on the major sections of the volume. Although these introductions in no way substitute for commentaries that Hallowell himself might have written, they nevertheless help assess Hallowell's crucial contributions to specific subareas of anthropology and thereby enhance the overall value of the volume. An unscheduled bibliography of Hallowell's later writing, supplementing and updating those provided in *Culture and Experience* and *Context and Meaning*, completes the volume.

I will conclude this introduction with some brief observations of my own on the general significance of this new collection of Hallowell essays. This volume can profitably be compared with the collection of essays in *Culture and Experience*. The latter work is certainly continuous with the present one in the sense that many of the themes and basic orientations set forth there are elaborated and more fully developed in the present collection. However, *Culture and Experience* focused primarily on one aspect of Hallowell's lifework—his immense contribution to a widely ramifying psychological anthropology, or as he preferred to conceive of it, "Psychology and Culture." As a result, other major aspects of his contributions to anthropology were underrepresented in *Culture and Experience*.

As George Stocking implies, Hallowell can be acknowledged as the legitimate father of modern scholarly interest in the history of anthropology. His major writings pertaining to this area, mostly postdating *Culture and Experience*, are reproduced in sections III and IV. In a sense, his entry into the intellectual history of anthropology reflected something of a new career; the only essay of this sort appearing in *Culture and Experience* is his informative article "The Recapitulation Theory and Culture."

Another major thrust in Hallowell's later work was his constantly growing interest in evolutionism, particularly behavioral evolution. Stocking notes that "an underlying (or over-arching) evolutionary perspective" informed much of Hallowell's work, and Lewis Langness, in his review of *Context and Meaning in Cultural Anthropology (American Anthropologist* [1965]: 722–73) predicts that Hallowell's ultimate place in the history of science will be defined in terms of the reintegration of anthropology that he encouraged through his conceptualization of behavioral evolution. Although I don't agree entirely with these assessments—certainly much of Hallowell's earlier work has an antievolutionist flavor, as might be expected of a student of Franz Boas via Frank Speck, and his later ethnographic work tended to stress cultural uniqueness and particularism—certainly Hallowell's attention to general and long-term behavioral evolution, as seen from many perspectives, intensified toward the end of his career and has been influential to physical anthropologists, linguists, archeologists, and nonanthropological specialists in human evolution. This developing concern is first signaled in his presidential address to the American Anthropological Association, "Personality Structure and the Evolution of Man" (reprinted as the lead essay in *Culture and Experience*), and is carried through in a brilliant series of papers culminating in the essay "Personality, Culture, and Society in Behavioral Evolution," republished here.

Another important part of the Hallowell legacy was his contribution to the fields of social organization and ecology. His discoveries in these areas have been appreciatively summarized by Fred Eggan, both here and elsewhere.[4] These contributions, however, scarcely surface in *Culture and Experience*, and thus we feel that the reprinting of the 1937 paper "Cross-Cousin Marriage in the Lake Winnepeg Area," which was the end product of more than ten years of investigation and is now a rare collector's item, performs a real service. As Eggan also notes, Hallowell, following Speck, can also be regarded as a pioneer cultural ecologist. This emphasis was apparent in his doctoral dissertation, published as "Bear Ceremonialism in the Northern Hemisphere" (and perhaps prefigured still earlier in his 1920 M.A. thesis, "The Problem of Fish Nets in North America"). Although some of his work in ecology was based on the kind of hard empirical data favored by many present-day cultural ecologists (e.g., "The Size of Algonkian Hunting Territories, A Function of Ecological Adjustment," *American Anthropologist* 51 [1949]: 35–45), he was more interested in how human beings perceived nature and acted within a culturally constituted behavioral environment (as Anthony Wallace rightly emphasizes), a subbranch of ecological studies that is now being increasingly referred to as ethno-ecology.[5]

I regard the section "Ojibwa Culture and World View," insightfully introduced by Melford Spiro, as containing the most germinal essays in the present collection. I am pleased that they will now be available to a wider audience. These essays clearly articulate with several of the papers in *Culture and Experience*, particularly those dealing with Ojibwa concepts of space, time, and measurement and the ones concerned with the self and its behavioral environment. Here prominence is given to the Ojibwa concept of person, and Hallowell demonstrates brilliantly how such a fundamental understanding helps elucidate whole ranges of cultural behavior. I have often wondered why such seemingly central concepts as the notions of self and person have been so long neglected by anthroplogists, despite promising starts in this direction made by Paul Radin, Marcel Mauss, Dorothy Lee, and others. Even with the incessant anthropological preoccupation with the formal properties of kinship systems—systems insecurely anchored to a mysterious, usually triangular, symbol referred to as "ego"— it is interesting to note how little we know about the differential characteristics of this shadowy ego personage as he becomes manifest in different cultures. Some of this deficiency shows signs of being corrected in the recent work of Meyer Fortes, Clifford Geertz, Louis Dumont, and David Schneider. However, I think it is to Hallowell that we must turn to discover the foundations for a comparative and researchable study of ethno-personality theory.[6]

Hallowell maintained an abiding interest in investigating processes of culture change. This concern emerges as early

as the late 1920s in his groundbreaking papers on historical
changes in kinship terminology, but he is probably best known
for his research on the psychological dimensions of acculturation, in which he made innovative use of the Rorschach Test.
This latter work is well represented by the papers in part IV of
Culture and Experience.[7]

In his later years Hallowell became concerned with certain
neglected topics in the history of American Indian–white
relationships. The overwhelming thrust of acculturation studies
of the American Indian emphasized induced changes in Indian
society and culture wrought by Euro-American contact. The
Social Science Research Council's "Memorandum for the Study
of Acculturation" (*American Anthropologist* 38 [1936]: 149–52),
an influential document written by Robert Redfield, Ralph
Linton, and Melville Herskovits, served as a kind of "charter"
to legitimize the study of acculturation in American anthropology. This document clearly specified that acculturation
comprehended phenomena resulting "from continuous first-
hand culture contact" that led to "subsequent changes in the
original culture patterns of either or *both* [my emphasis]
groups." Despite the phrasing, virtually no one examined the
impact of the Indian on Euro-American culture. It is true, of
course, that at least since Clark Wissler's time, every school-
child could recite a grocery list of Indian "gifts" to Western
culture: such items as corn, tobacco, turkeys, tomatoes, and
potatoes, and so forth, and, if the child were truly precocious,
the Jerusalem artichoke. However, the broader and less evident
assimilation of Indian culture into American lifeways was never
charted until Hallowell's informative essays on this topic.
Moreover, Hallowell was able to see this as a dynamic process
honed on the whetstone of the frontier. His emphasis on the
fact that many whites, from the colonial period to the present,
voluntarily gave up the "blessings" of civilization to become
transculturalized Indians has (as Wilcomb Washburn correctly
points out) stimulated American historians to reevaluate the
moral history of Indian-white relations.

These, then, are some of my reflections on the significance
of this new collection of Hallowell essays. Given the breadth

of Hallowell's anthropological vision and his astounding erudition, other readers will doubtless discern other themes and arrive at different evaluations of what is significant. I feel that the essays permit an expanded view of the Hallowell legacy. Like Franz Boas, who was presented a festschrift in 1906 and continued to be a productive scholar until his death in 1942, or A. L. Kroeber, who was similarly honored in 1936, when many of his important contributions lay ahead, Hallowell accomplished much of his most enduring work in his later years, long after he had firmly established himself as a major anthropologist and received most of the honors recognizing his achievements. Hallowell was a genuinely creative scholar, ever reaching out in new directions to forge new links within anthropology and to make meaningful connections across traditional disciplinary lines. Despite these incursions and excursions, his work reveals discernible threads of continuity, a remarkable sense of integration, and rare authenticity. His career possesses a definite identity that is clearly generative.[8]

NOTES
1. This introduction in no way purports to be a definitive assessment of Hallowell's work and life. In addition to the valuable autobiographical statement reprinted here and the introductions to the different sections of this book, the interested reader might consult Hallowell's preface to *Culture and Experience* and the new preface he prepared for the Schocken paperback edition; the introduction (written by Melford Spiro and myself) to *Context and Meaning in Cultural Anthropology*; and the several obituaries that appeared in journals of learned societies. At the time of this writing, Dennison Nash has organized two sessions for the 1975 American Anthropological Association Annual Meetings that will be devoted to Hallowell's work. I hope these papers will soon find their way into the published record.
2. Hallowell's Nigerian experiences are delightfully recounted in a brief article, "To Nigeria!" published in the *Philadelphia Anthropological Society Bulletin* 14, no. 1, (January 1961): 7–11. I am indebted to Jean Adelman, librarian at the University Museum, for locating this reference.
3. Hallowell was commissioned to write a short general monograph on the Ojibwa for the Holt, Rhinehart and Winston

series Case Studies in Anthropology. He completed the monograph, but unfortunately the only copy was lost in the mails; his deteriorating health prevented his reconstructing the book from his notes. There also is a manuscript draft of a late paper reconsidering Bear Ceremonialism; Frederica de Laguna hopes to publish this essay, along with several others, together with a reprinting of Hallowell's 1926 monograph on Bear Ceremonialism. There may be more unfinished manuscripts among Hallowell's papers, but as yet these have not been thoroughly searched.

4. See especially, "Social Anthropology: Methods and Results," in *Social Anthropology of North American Tribes,* ed. F. Eggan, enlarged ed. (Chicago: University of Chicago Press, 1955); F. Eggan, *The American Indian* (Chicago: Aldine, 1966), pp. 86–89; and F. Eggan, "Northern Woodland Ethnology," in *The Philadelphia Anthropological Society: Papers Presented on Its Golden Anniversary*, ed. Jacob W. Gruber (Philadelphia: Temple University Press, 1967).

5. The term ethno-ecology appears in Bruce Cox, ed., *Cultural Ecology: Readings on the Canadian Indians and Eskimos* (Toronto: McClelland and Stewart. 1973). An interesting illustration of the utility of an ethno-ecological approach to complement more materialistic interpretations is provided by Edward Rogers in an essay in which he compares two Cree communities, one tightly nucleated and the other having a dispersed settlement pattern. After factoring out numerous ecological facts that might account for the differences, he concludes that strength of witchcraft belief (i.e., a feature of the *behavioral* environment rather than the *physical* environment) appears to be the decisive factor (in D. Damas, ed., *Ecological Essays*. Contributions to Anthropology, Ethnology 7, [Ottawa: National Museum of Canada, 1968]).

6. Two scholars whose research builds directly on Hallowell's study of Ojibwa ontology are Mary Black, whose 1967 Stanford doctoral dissertation and several stimulating papers attempt to apply ethnoscientific procedures to study Ojibwa ontology and world view,. and Anne S. Straus, whose 1976 University of Chicago doctoral dissertation provides a thorough and brilliant analysis of Northern Cheyenne concepts of self, person, and ethnopersonality theory.

7. The best summary of Hallowell's Rorschach works appears in his ninety-page article "The Rorschach Technique in Personality and Culture Studies," in *Developments in the Rorschach Technique*, vol. 2, ed. Bruno Klopfer et al. (Yonkers, N.Y.: World Publishing Co., 1956). This source is seldom

cited; it is even omitted in Gardner Lindzey's otherwise comprehensive survey, *Projective Techniques and Cross-Cultural Research* (New York: Appleton-Century-Crofts, 1961).

8. Special thanks go to the contributors of the introductory sections, who rose magnificently to the occasion and also managed to meet deadlines promptly; to Mrs. Maude Hallowell for helpful advice and cheerful encouragement; to Emanuel Geltman, who helped conceive the project; and last but not least to the cooperative staff at the University of Chicago Press who skillfully served as midwives in nursing the project through to completion.

I | AUTOBIOGRAPHICAL NOTES

ONE

On Being an Anthropologist

1972

BECOMING AN ANTHROPOLOGIST

The social scientists of her sample, comments Anne Roe (1953), often show a sense of rebellion against traditional family values. I think this was true of me. Since I had no outstanding talents and evinced no special interest in any of the professions, my conservative parents assumed I would take up a business career. Therefore, after a three-year course in a manual-training high school, I was sent to the Wharton School of Finance and Commerce of the University of Pennsylvania.

In those days, before World War I, the Wharton school had a much more flexible curriculum. It was also then the home of social sciences (economics, sociology, and political science), but anthropology was in the College of Liberal Arts. The school permitted its students to take many electives in the college; so in addition to the required business-oriented courses, I sampled chemistry, history, English literature, and Italian Renaissance painting, though I did not look into anthropology. Above all, I discovered social science and took all the courses in economics and sociology that were offered. I had work with Scott Nearing, and in my senior year I was admitted to a seminar given by Simon N. Patten, a singular economist of that time who is now almost forgotten. In rebellion against classical economics, Patten attempted to deal with problems of change and evolution and tried to open up a perspective emphasizing abundance rather than scarcity (see Patten, 1924).

Soon I gave up all thought of a business career. The social sciences and ideas of social reform absorbed my interest. I wanted to go ahead with graduate studies, but because there were no family funds, and fellowships with stipends were scarce in those days, I entered social work and took some graduate courses in sociology on the side. Since I had been brought up in a protected environment, social work opened my eyes to how "the other half" lived. As a representative of the Family Society, I went into the homes of unfamiliar ethnic groups—Poles, Italians, Negroes. Casework among people with such

3

diverse backgrounds provided me with a wide experience in interviewing.

It was also at this time—the late 1910's and early 1920's—that I was first introduced to psychoanalysis. Psychoanalysis was then a novel, exciting, and controversial topic among American intellectuals, especially in New York. A. A. Brill, the first American psychiatrist to become a member of Freud's group in Vienna, published his translation of Freud's *Interpretation of Dreams* in 1913. It almost immediately stirred up tremendous interest. Many social workers eagerly turned to psychoanalysis for a new illumination of social theory and interpersonal relations. In Philadelphia the Pennsylvania School of Social Work engaged A. A. Goldenweiser, an anthropologist, to give a series of lectures on psychoanalytic theory. Goldenweiser was one of the first social scientists in this country to attempt to apply Freudian psychology to the elucidation of social facts. His lectures had nothing to do, however, with personality and culture studies as they subsequently developed.

During my undergraduate days I had met Frank G. Speck. We were both members of the same fraternity. At the fraternity house I had often listened to his stories about his experiences with Indians. (Speck was a gifted raconteur.) I had also dropped in to hear him lecture. Casting around for courses which were given at a time that would fit my social-work schedule, I signed up for several of his.

I found the general anthropological approach very stimulating as compared with the approach of sociology. I thought the anthropologists' rejection of a unilineal theory of cultural evolution very progressive. The idea of "culture," too, was rather new and it was not in the sociologists' kit. Anthropology opened a vista far beyond the ethnic groups in my own backyard. Abstract and theoretical social problems now had a very broad base.

Another feature that impressed me was the political attitude which characterized the anthropologists of that period. If I may use so old-fashioned a label, it was very "liberal." Perhaps this was due to the dominant influence of Franz Boas. My own attitudes were on the liberal side. I was very doubtful, for instance, about our entry into World War I, and I had socialistic inclinations.

Since I already knew Speck and since his classes were small, we quickly became well acquainted. I became a candidate for a master's degree in anthropology, dropped my courses in sociology, and decided to leave social work for a career in anthropology. At the time I thought this was a radical shift, but now I see a continuity: my move was well within the broad boundaries of the social sciences, theoretical and applied.

Speck helped me to obtain a Harrison Fellowship so that I could devote full time to graduate work. During one semester I made a weekly trip to New York to attend Boas' seminar at Columbia University. All the members of the group, which included Ruth Benedict and Melville Herskovits, were assigned books for seminar reports and discussion. My assignment consisted of Edward Westermarck's *History of Human Marriage* and John Dewey's *Human Nature and*

Conduct, which had only recently been published. A group of us from Boas' seminar also met privately each week with Goldenweiser for anthropological discussions.

With my interests ranging over broad social problems, it may seem paradoxical that the people in whom I became most interested were the American Indians. But these were the primitive, aboriginal people of America—and they were Frank Speck's pets. At this time, he was engaged in "salvage anthropology" among the Indians of the eastern United States.[1] Speck's self-involvement with the study people and their problems was perhaps greater than that of other anthropologists of the period. He was always extolling the sovereign virtues of the Indians and proclaiming the intrinsic values of their culture. Current political events and problems in American life held little interest for him; he was critical in general of the values of American culture. This attitude Speck shared with other anthropologists, for these were the days of Harold Stearns' *Civilization in the United States,* to which both Robert H. Lowie and Elsie Clews Parsons contributed.[2] It was also the time when many American writers and artists were going abroad to do their work.

Speck was about as detached from American culture as one could be. He would not, for instance, buy a car, and he never read newspapers. In a sense, he was also detached from the university and its affairs. I never remember his serving on a committee; his thoughts and energies were entirely devoted to his research among Indians. And I imitated my mentor for a long while. I, too, identified myself with the Indians, and tried to avoid serving on university committees. Anthropology in all its aspects was the overarching thing and Boas was king, for Speck had been not only a student of Boas but also a deeply rooted follower. Boas had said the last word. What one strove for was to follow Boas in his ubiquitous interests—ethnology, archeology, physical anthropology, and linguistics. Anthropology, despite broad areas of specialization, was regarded as an all-embracing study of man which should be conceptualized and pursued as a whole even while the individual engaged in specialized investigations.[3]

FIELD WORK IN THE 1920's

It was in this spirit, following Speck, that I began my field work among an acculturated group of Indians in eastern Canada, the St. Francis Abenaki. These Abenaki, who were related to the Penobscot of Maine whom Speck had studied intensively, lived on a reservation sixty miles east of Montreal on the south side of the St. Lawrence River. They were bilingual but they lived much as the French Canadians did who surrounded them. I set out to recover for the record the remnants of their aboriginal culture. It did not occur to me to study their "community" or any problems of "acculturation." In fact, this latter approach was not articulated in anthropology until the 1930's. These were the days when the major emphasis was on "culture traits" and "trait complexes," such information to be reconstructed from fast-disappearing native cultures (see Beals, 1953).

Thus I collected Abenaki objects of material culture for the Museum of the American Indian (Heye Foundation) in New York. There were more of these to collect than one might suppose—the last birchbark canoe, for example, and a native "slow match." I made a series of physical measurements (unpublished). I also studied the native language, which was still spoken by everyone, made a collection of loan words, and secured some folktales in text.[4] I collected information on their hunting customs and particularly on their hunting territories, a special interest of Speck's, and wrote a paper (unpublished) on the subject. I became interested in the Abenaki kinship system, and I was able to document changes unknown to the Indians themselves. This was made possible through my discovery of an eighteenth-century manuscript dictionary on the reservation. Melville Herskovits (1938) pointed out that my paper (1928) was one of the earliest attempts to demonstrate changes in a kinship system from documentary sources. (Incidentally, the Abenaki system does not belong to the Northern Algonkian pattern, which reflects cross-cousin marriage.)

Although I made quite a few brief trips to the Abenaki, this kind of field work did not satisfy me. A number of years went by while I fretted for an opportunity to work in a really "primitive" culture. Meanwhile, there was the problem of a thesis, and nothing appropriate had emerged from the Abenaki investigations.

Finally, with a lead from J. G. Frazer and with Speck's encouragement, I began research in what I would later call "bear ceremonialism." In the course of studying the variety and detail of local ceremonies, I was soon led to evidence of the occurrence of related ceremonies in the Old World as well as the New. There appeared to be a nucleus of common ceremonial traits suggesting historical connections from Lapland to Labrador. If one took this finding, along with a somewhat similar distribution of other culture traits commonly shared by the peoples of Eurasia and northern North America, an old culture stratum seemed indicated (see Hatt, 1933; Lowie, 1934). With respect to antiquity, I drew attention to the peculiar disposal of bear skulls and long bones at Drachenloch, Switzerland, during paleolithic times and the crudely modeled figure of a bear in the cave of Montespan. Other archeological evidence of an ancient bear cult has since turned up. I realized that there was a local setting for bear ceremonialism everywhere—involving mythology, world view, the hunting of other animals, and so on—but I chose to be selective and to consider the geographical distribution of the associated features of bear ceremonialism in a broad cultural-historical setting.

Incidentally, Bertold Laufer at first discouraged me by questioning my ability to handle the Eurasian data. But things worked out somehow, and later he was extremely complimentary about the final product.[5] The monograph which ultimately emerged (Hallowell, 1926) has created more reverberations in Europe than anything else I have written. At first it was taken up by the Kulturkreise School. Then it helped focus further field work among the Russians. More recently it has been discussed by those interested in prehistoric religion (see Campbell, 1959; Maringer, 1960; Lissner, 1961).

KINSHIP, CULTURE, AND PSYCHOLOGY

Meanwhile, my interest in kinship was further stimulatèd by the residence in Philadelphia of an Araucanian Indian, J. Martin Collio, with whom both Speck and I had personal contact. I obtained a set of kinship terms from him as early as 1922. At first they were very puzzling to me. Eventually, they turned out to be the Omaha pattern, an ill-defined type at the time. I hesitated to publish my information, partly because the data were obtained from a single informant, but also because I half-hoped that someday I might be able to go to South America and do field work among the Araucanians. Then, stimulated by an article by A. Lesser (1929), I presented my material at a meeting of the American Anthropological Association in 1929. It met with little or no discussion so I put the paper aside. More than a decade later, in 1943, at a lecture he gave before the Philadelphia Anthropological Society, G. P. Murdock remarked that in his survey of social organization and kinship throughout the world, he was struck by the absence of the Omaha pattern in South America, although he suspected its presence among the Araucanians. So I sent my paper, in its original form, to the *American Anthropologist* and it was published (Hallowell, 1943).

Long before this, however, I had made some other excursions into the relations between kinship pattern and social behavior, which led directly to my study of the Northern Ojibwa. In Montreal, in the late 1920's, I discovered some old dictionaries which suggested that cross-cousin marriage had once existed among the North-Central Algonkians. While this finding would excite very little interest today, in the United States in the 1920's the prevailing view, supported by such influential anthropologists as Kroeber and Truman Michelson, was that kinship terms were to be considered as purely linguistic phenomena. Thus, one aspect of the problem was the traditional attitude of American anthropologists toward the study of the functional ramifications of kinship in its total sociocultural setting. At any rate, at the International Congress of Americanists in 1928, I read a paper raising the question of the existence of cross-cousin marriage among the Algonkian (Hallowell, 1930). As I recall now, I received no support for my hypothesis but a rather critical appraisal from Michelson. It was not until shortly after the congress that I learned that W. D. Strong, who had recently spent fifteen months in Labrador, reported the practice of cross-cousin marriage among the Barren Ground band of the Naskapi. So I made plans to go into the field in order to discover whether the kinship pattern together with the practice of cross-cousin marriage actually existed in any contemporary North-Central Algonkian group.

I went into the field both "functionally" and "problem-oriented." My first trip was made in 1930 to the Algonkians of the Lake Winnipeg region. Pursuing my search for cross-cousin marriage among the Ojibwa of the Berens River, I well remember an early conversation with William Berens, my closest collaborator. I hesitatingly asked him whether a man could marry a woman he called *ninəm*. His reply was, "Who the hell else would he marry?" In a sense, the problem I had come to investigate was solved: the Ojibwa of the Berens River did practice cross-cousin marriage and used the appropriate terminology. The situation among the Northern Algonkians was more complicated, however, because historical circumstances had led to differential changes in terminology and social practice among different groups. Later I concluded that "Northern Algonkian kinship systems are . . . intelligible as variants of a basic pattern that has undergone modifications as the result of acculturative processes and differences in local conditions" (Hallowell, 1937).

My field work among the Cree and Ojibwa of the Lake Winnipeg region had hardly begun when I was drawn into a newly emerging area of research in anthropology: the psychological interrelations of individuals and their culture. From its beginnings anthropology has been influenced by developments within the academic tradition in psychology; but around 1920 it was psychoanalysis with its psychiatric background, its concepts of individual psychodynamics and personality, that challenged anthropologists.[6] This was another facet of the great impact of psychoanalytic theories on the thinking of the modern world, particularly on the sciences of human behavior. As I have said, I first met psychoanalysis burgeoning in social-work circles in Philadelphia. The anthropologists' interest, however, was on a directly professional level, and there was much discussion and many thoughtful reviews of the writings of Freud and other analysts. All of this interested me very much. All through the 1920's I followed the various new developments in psychoanalysis and in psychological anthropology.

Now, in the 1930's I became directly involved in psychological anthropology through Edward Sapir. After Sapir went to Yale in 1931, we became better acquainted and had some stimulating discussions on psychoanalysis and anthropology. Sapir had long been interested in psychoanalysis. As early as 1917 he had reviewed Freud's *Delusion and Dream* and Oskar Pfister's *The Psychoanalytic Method* for *The Dial*. Any and all new ideas in the field he welcomed, so that, for example, he gave C. G. Jung's *Psychological Types* an appreciative and thoughtful review in *The Freeman* (1923). More recently he had been listening to Harry Stack Sullivan expound his ideas on the collaboration of social scientists in the testing of his interpersonal-relations theory. Sapir had also explored various methods of getting at such information in different cultures.[7] It was to be expected, therefore, that when Sapir became chairman of the Division of Anthropology and Psychology of the National Research Council he would set up a committee on "Personality in Relation to Culture." Sapir invited me to be a member. Among the others were Ruth Benedict, Harry Stack Sullivan, Adolf Meyer, and A. A. Brill.

There was strong resistance among professional anthropologists to this psychological approach. There were also many real problems, including the question of how far psychoanalytic concepts were to be used as compared to behavioristic or Gestalt concepts. Another basic question was: From what sources were psychological data, apart from ethnological data, to be derived?

The Rorschach test was relatively new at this time. It had many advantages over other psychological tests of personality: it was a subtle means of probing many of the complexities of personality and it was "culture-free." The scoring system also made comparisons possible on either an individual basis or a group basis. From the scanty literature on the Rorschach, I learned enough to be able to try my hand at administering and scoring the test. On my next trip to the Berens River I stopped in Chicago hoping to see the Rorschach expert, Samuel J. Beck, but I missed him. So on my own I collected a large sample of protocols from both adults and children.

It was after this field trip in 1937 that I met Bruno Klopfer, who became very interested in my Indian Rorschach records. We had several conferences to discuss my material and then decided to collaborate on joint papers to be presented at the 1938 meetings of the American Anthropological Association in New York (Hallowell, 1938; Klopfer, 1938). There was a greal deal of curiosity (a large audience came to hear the papers), and while there was some interest, there was more derision. Who could take playing with ink blots seriously? However, I went ahead with my research in personality and culture among the Ojibwa using the Rorschach test (see Hallowell, 1956).

In recent years there has been a lessening of interest in personality and culture. Anthropologists are busy cultivating other fields, and psychologists have been critically evaluating the Rorschach test (see Lindzey, 1961). However, I should say that my own conception of psychological anthropology has always been a broad one that transcends the study of personality and culture in the narrow sense. There are many psychological areas that should be dealt with. It may surprise some when I say that I never gave a course myself under that rubric; my course was called "Culture and Psychology." Consequently, I fully agree with John Fischer's remarks and the shift he made in the 1965 *Biennial Review of Anthropology* by changing the title of his section from "Culture and Personality" to "Psychology and Anthropology."

Within this broad framework my interests expanded still further. Using my Ojibwa investigations for specific illustrations, I explored such topics as acculturation processes and personality changes (Chaps. 18–19 in Hallowell, 1955), culture and perception (Hallowell, 1951), and the nature and concept of the self (Chaps. 4 and 8 in Hallowell, 1955).

THE OJIBWA

My Ojibwa experience in the early 1930's was a plunge into a new world and involved problems I was little prepared to face. Since Alanson Skinner's preliminary survey in 1911, nothing had been done in the area. It was an

immense region and I had to choose a locale. As a matter of fact, I started with
the Cree and then shifted to the Ojibwa after discovering that, while there was
plenty of evidence everywhere for acculturation, up the Berens River there
were some pagan Indians. These Ojibwa had retained attitudes and a world
view which were "primitive," even though their tools, clothing, and diet were
not. This fact involved the acculturation problem in a modified form, one quite
different from the situation in eastern Canada. I think it was not until about
this time, however, that I realized there were no completely unacculturated
Indians in the United States and Canada. Before anthropologists were professionally trained in field work, Indians everywhere had been transferred to
reservations when the frontier was closed in 1890.

My original attitude toward the Indians nevertheless persisted. I deeply
identified myself with the Berens River Ojibwa. To the small number of white
people in the area I paid practically no attention. I never made friends with
the personnel of the Hudson's Bay Company posts and became only casually
acquainted with the missionaries, among whom I was more friendly with the
Catholics than with the Protestants. Since I was completely oriented toward
Indians and their culture rather than the total community, I did not at first
realize what the basic pattern of relationship was between whites and Indians.
Actually, it exemplified all the basic features of the pattern in the South
between whites and Negroes; for example, the use of first names for Indians
(my friend Chief Berens was "Willie"); a tabu on eating together; the use of
the back door by Indians when visiting whites (missionaries included); dis-
countenance of intermarriage; "passing." I have always regretted not making
a serious study of this relationship pattern. At the time I did not think of it,
for my exclusive concern was the Indians.[*]

Although the Ojibwa I worked with were not "primitives" in the sense of
having a fully functioning aboriginal culture, they were closer to it than I had
thought. There was a graded spectrum on the Berens River, those at the mouth
of the river being the most acculturated and those inland the least. As I found
out later, when I spent the summer of 1946 with a group of students on the
Ojibwa reservation at Lac du Flambeau, Wisconsin, this was only one segment
of a wider acculturation problem. Here I found myself in the position of being
an authority for these highly acculturated Ojibwa on the really old-fashioned
Ojibwa "up north."

It was the gradual realization of this broader acculturation problem that led
me in the end to attempt to interpret and expound the world view of the most
conservative Ojibwa (see Chap. 18 in Hallowell, 1955; Hallowell, 1960). This
became an excursion into ethnoscience—or ethnosemantics, if you will—for
I became aware of how sharply different the Ojibwa world was from our own
and of the necessity for testing the meaningfulness of familiar conceptual
dichotomies, such as natural-supernatural, for example. This process meant
the reintegration of ethnographic material collected under separate and quite

different categories on another level. In short, it involved an attempt to see the Ojibwa world as they saw it—an *emic* as contrasted to an *etic* viewpoint. Ecologically, it led me to the concept of a behavioral environment—a concept borrowed from Gestalt psychology—an environment culturally constituted in such a way that it structures the major psychological field in which individuals act, forming their basic cognitive orientation.

THE LATER YEARS: EXPLORATIONS IN BEHAVIORAL EVOLUTION

All these investigations in psychology and culture inevitably led to a general consideration of the psychological dimension of human evolution (Hallowell, 1950; Hallowell, 1963; Hallowell, 1965). In this endeavor I assumed a more inclusive perspective than the one provided by physical anthropology and archeology alone, one that emphasizes the continuities as opposed to the discontinuities in behavioral evolution between man and the nonhominid primates. I tried to bring together as an integral whole the organic, psychological, social, and cultural dimensions of the evolutionary process as they relate to the underlying conditions necessary for human existence. As Dobzhansky (1962) has pointed out, "Human evolution cannot be understood as a purely biological process, nor can it be adequately described as a history of culture. There exists a feedback between biological and cultural processes" (see also Menaker, 1965). And we may add, there is a feedback between specifically psychological processes and cultural ones: the emergence of ego processes, the development of self-objectification, the socialization of symbolic forms, and the rise of sociocultural systems. In this development there was no "critical point" at which culture emerged, as Kroeber maintained (see Geertz, 1964).

Beyond the world views of man, basic to his life everywhere, there is another evolutionary problem: how man has so fully assimilated subjective and unconscious experiences and integrated them with the acquisition and accumulation of pragmatic knowledge about the external world, in a manner difficult to disentangle. David Beres, a psychoanalyst, departing from the restricted meaning of the term "imaginative" as the obverse of "realistic," extends its psychological connotation to include "a process whose products are images, symbols, fantasies, dreams, ideas, thoughts and concepts." Imagination in this sense is a complex function entering into "all aspects of psychic activity—normal mentation, pathological processes, and artistic creativity." His point is that "imagination is not opposed to reality, but has as one of its most important applications, adaptation to reality." In other words, reality can best be understood, not only as a relatively indeterminate concept, but as one which is *always* infused with imaginative processes. Symbolic representations, derived from such processes, involve mediating ego functions between the external world and the inner drives of man. "To be aware of reality it becomes necessary to have two points of reference—one is the perception of the external world, the other the internal image, the mental representation."[9]

From this perspective, dreams, fantasies, myth, art, and the world views of man, as articulated in cultural traditions, may be interpreted as making positive use of psychological resources in cultural adaptation and personal adjustment. Reliable knowledge of reality in any scientific sense need not be assumed to be a necessary condition for either biological adaptation or cultural adjustment to the actualities of human existence. Man is an animal who has been able to survive by making cultural adaptations in which his own imaginative interpretations of the world have been fed back into his personal adjustment to it.

What I have tried to do in this chapter, in semiautobiographical fashion, is to outline a personal record of my own experience in anthropology, of my changing values and problems in field work. How this personal experience is related to the wider picture of the basic changes and emphases in the anthropological tradition and to changing values in the wider world, I leave to others.

NOTES

1. "It was not an uncommon experience and considered quite a *coup* for a student of Boas to catch the dying gasp of an American Indian language and culture. Sapir in the field of language and Speck in that of natural history exemplify the tradition. Speck, beloved by the Indians and learned beyond most men, sometimes managed to reconstruct a society and its culture from the merest fragments, approaching the feats of psycho-analysts in his study of Delaware ceremonies, which rank among those of the first class in American ethnology" (Fenton, 1953).

2. According to Hoffman (1962), Stearns' book, "which appeared early in 1922, was a historical landmark of the post-World War I years, a curious document of disaffection, pointing to and reiterating the failure of culture, entertainment, family life, religion—of everything but science, and even it scored only a partial success in the survey of American life and institutions" (p. 21). "The twenties were marked by a disrespect for tradition and an eager wish to try out any new suggestions regarding the nature of man—his personal beliefs, convictions, or way to salvation" (p. 33).

3. I am writing, of course, as an American anthropologist. But see Hultkrantz (1968) and the commentaries on that article.

4. The St. Francis Abenaki dialect is still spoken today and presents some interesting problems; see Day (1964; 1967).

5. In his presidential address to the American Oriental Society, Laufer (1931) said: "We owe a model investigation to Dr. A. I. Hallowell . . . into the bear ceremonialism in northern Asia and America where the worship of the bear is widely distributed and practically alike in form and content."

6. For a historical summary of the influence of psychology on anthropology, see Hallowell (1954).

7. For a more extended discussion of the seminal influence of Edward Sapir on personality and culture studies, see Hallowell (1954, pp. 203ff.).

8. As a matter of fact, there is a racial problem in Canada that has been little studied; see the novel by Bodsworth (1960).

9. All quotations in this paragraph are from Beres (1960a, 1960b).

REFERENCES

BEALS, RALPH. 1953. "Acculturation." In A. L. Kroeber, ed., *Anthropology Today: An Encyclopedic Inventory.* Chicago: University of Chicago Press.

BERES, DAVID. 1960a. "Perception, Imagination and Reality." *International Journal of Psycho-Analysis,* vol. 41.

1960b. "The Psychoanalytic Psychology of Imagination." *Journal of the American Psychoanalytic Association,* vol. 8.

BODSWORTH, FRED. 1960. *The Strange One.* New York: Dodd, Mead.

CAMPBELL, JOSEPH. 1959. *Masks of God: Primitive Mythology.* New York: Viking.

DAY, GORDON M. 1964. "A St. Francis Abenaki Vocabulary." *International Journal of American Linguistics,* 30: 371–392.

1967. "Historical Notes on New England Languages." *Contributions to Anthropology: Linguistics I.* Bulletin 214. Ottawa: National Museum of Canada.

DOBZHANSKY, T. 1962. *Mankind Evolving: The Evolution of the Human Species.* New Haven: Yale University Press.

FENTON, W. N. 1953. "Cultural Stability and Change in American Indian Societies." *Journal of the Royal Anthropological Institute,* 83: 169–170.

GEERTZ, C. 1964. "The Transition to Humanity." In Sol Tax, ed., *Horizons of Anthropology.* Chicago: Aldine.

HALLOWELL, A. IRVING. 1926. "Bear Ceremonialism in the Northern Hemisphere." *American Anthropologist.* 28: 1–175.

1928. "Recent Historical Changes in the Kinship Terminology of the St. Francis Abenaki." *Proceedings of the Twenty-second International Congress of Americanists,* pp. 97–145. Rome.

1930. "Was Cross-Cousin Marriage Practiced by the North-Central Algonkian?" *Proceedings of the Twenty-third Congress of Americanists,* pp. 519–544. New York.

1937. "Cross-Cousin Marriage in the Lake Winnipeg Area." *Twenty-fifth Anniversary Studies,* 1:95–110. Publications of the Philadelphia Anthropological Society, ed. D. S. Davidson.

1938. "An Experimental Investigation of a Series of Berens River Indians." Unpublished.

1943. "Araucanian Parallels to the Omaha Kinship Pattern." *American Anthropologist,* 45: 489–491.

1950. "Personality Structure and the Evolution of Man." *American Anthropologist,* 52:159–173. (Presidential address to the American Anthropological Association, 1949; also Chap. 1 of Hallowell 1955.)

1951. "Cultural Factors in the Structuralization of Perception." In J. H. Rohrer and M. Sherif, eds., *Social Psychology at the Cross-Roads.* New York: Books for Libraries.

1954. "Psychology and Anthropology." In John Gillin, ed., *For a Science of Social Man.* New York: Macmillan.

1955. *Culture and Experience.* Philadelphia: University of Pennsylvania Press.
Chap. 4, "The Self and Its Behavioral Environment."
Chap. 8, "The Ojibwa Self and Its Behavioral Environment."
Chap. 18, "Background for a Study of Acculturation and the Personality of the Ojibwa."
Chap. 19, "Acculturation and the Personality of the Ojibwa." (Presidential address to the Society for Projective Techniques, 1950.)

1956. "The Rorschach Test in Personality and Culture Studies." In Bruno Klopfer *et al.,* eds., *Developments in the Rorschach Technique.* New York: Harcourt Brace Jovanovich. Vol. 2.

1960. "Ojibwa Ontology, Behavior and World View." in S. Diamond, ed., *Culture in History.* New York: Columbia University Press.

1963. "Personality, Culture and Society in Behavioral Evolution." In S. Koch, ed., *Psychology: A Study of a Science.* New York: McGraw-Hill. Vol. 6.

1965. "Hominid Evolution, Cultural Adaptation and Mental Dysfunctioning." In A. V. S. de

Reuck and Ruth Porter, eds., *Ciba Foundation Symposium on Transcultural Psychiatry,* London. Boston: Little, Brown.

HATT, G. 1933. "North American and Eurasian Culture Connections." *Proceedings of the Fifth Pacific Congress.* Canada. 4:2755–2768.

HERSKOVITS, MELVILLE. 1938. *Acculturation.* New York: J. J. Augustin.

HOFFMAN, FREDERICK J. 1962. *The Twenties,* rev. ed. New York: Viking.

HULTKRANTZ, A. 1968. "The Aims of Anthropology: A Scandinavian Point of View." *Current Anthropology,* 9: 289–310.

KLOPFER, BRUNO. 1938. "Personality Investigation and Its Variables as Shown by Tests of Berens River Indians." Unpublished.

LAUFER, BERTOLD. 1931. "Columbus and Cathay, and the Meaning of America to the Orientalist." *Journal of the American Oriental Society,* 51:99.

LESSER, A. 1929. "Kinship Origins in the Light of Some Distributions." *American Anthropologist,* 31:710–730.

LINDZEY, GARDNER. 1961. *Projective Techniques and Cross-Cultural Research.* New York: Appleton.

LISSNER, IVAR. 1961. *Man, God and Magic.* New York: Putnam.

LOWIE, R. H. 1934. "Religious Ideas and Practices of the Eurasiatic and North American Areas." In E. E. Evans-Pritchard, Raymond Firth, B. Malinowski, and I. Schapera, eds., *Essays Presented to C. G. Seligman.* London: K. Paul, Trench, and Trubner.

MARINGER, JOHANNES. 1960. *The Gods of Prehistoric Man.* New York: Knopf.

MENAKER, E. AND W. 1965. *Ego in Evolution.* New York: Grove.

PATTEN, SIMON N. 1924. *Essays in Economic Theory,* ed. by R. G. Tugwell. New York: Knopf.

ROE, ANNE. 1953. *The Making of a Scientist.* New York: Dodd, Mead.

II | HISTORY OF ANTHROPOLOGY

INTRODUCTION

George W. Stocking, Jr.

As a graduate student in American civilization at Pennsylvania in the late 1950s, I ventured twice into the Anthropology Department, both times to take courses with Pete Hallowell: one on "Psychology and Culture," the other on "The History of Anthropology." Both of them opened up new intellectual vistas: the one, as it were, of anthropology in being; the other, of anthropology in becoming. Focusing largely on Ojibwa materials, the former was an attempt from the outside to provide a framework for understanding an alien self in its culturally constituted behavioral environment; the latter was an attempt from within the tradition of professional anthropology to investigate the emergence of a particular form of scientific understanding in Western European culture. And yet the two had a great deal in common. My notes on the history of anthropology start with the concepts of "world view," of "cognitive orientation," of "folk-science": "In all cultures [there are] certain categorical questions which in [an] abstract way are legitimate anthro[pological] questions—*apply [the] same technique to western civil[ization] & world view.*" From there we proceeded to the analysis of the Christian medieval world view and to the "two large axes of empirical observation [which] had to be established as [a] condition for anthro[pological] progress"—the broadened spatial orientation growing out of the age of discovery, and the progressive temporal orientation resulting from the secularization of the Christian linear view of history in the context of the scientific revolution.

It is hardly surprising that the two courses had much in common, since they were both products of the same mind. But from another point of view, the unity is worthy of comment,

George W. Stocking, Jr., is professor of anthropology at the University of Chicago.

since the anthropologist as historian of his own enterprise
often seems to shed certain fundamental aspects of the anthropological world view and to abandon the attempt at "emic"
understanding of the anthropological past in its own terms
for an ostensibly "etic" account of the true line of anthropological progress. Hallowell himself had of course a definite
notion of progress in anthropology. If medieval "folk-anthropology" was one among many similar "folk anthropologies," modern professional anthropology was a unique emergent within a
specific cultural tradition. Here, as in other areas of his work,
there was an underlying (or overarching) evolutionary perspective that became explicit in his later work. But Hallowell never
lost sight of the "categorical questions" that linked modern
anthropology to "folk-anthropologies" in general and that took
different forms in different historical or cultural contexts. At
its best, his history of anthropology is informed by a sense of
the way these questions posed themselves to particular groups
of historical actors—even when, as in his history of nineteenth
century American anthropology, the essential structure is provided by the subdisciplines of the professional anthropology
in which he had been trained.

The fact that it was informed by an anthropological attitude
was not all that distinguished Hallowell's history of anthropology from that of some of his confreres. Somehow he had
acquired along the way the bibliographic bent, the archival
interests, and the delight in specific historical detail which
are the hallmarks of the historical scholar—as his "discoveries"
of old dictionaries and his extensive footnote apparatus testify.
At times this expressed itself in a slightly antiquarian style.
He himself was conscious, in his account of Philadelphia anthropology, that it was to some extent "odd bits of historical
information" he had "patched together." On the other hand,
the same historical bent led him to eschew the oral anecdotalism that so often characterizes the "history" of anthropological elders. And at its best, his history was of thoroughly
professional quality. The essay "The Beginnings of Anthropology in America" is still the best published account available.

His own published researches, however, were only one

aspect of Hallowell's contribution to the history of anthropology. He was the leading spirit behind the Social Science Research Council Conference of 1963, a major milestone in the recent interest in the field. His essay "The History of Anthropology as an Anthropological Problem" provides a model for an approach that is in the best sense both historical and anthropological. Several of his students, inspired by that model, have gone on to do important work in the field. I hope that the republication of these essays will stimulate others to pursue the inquiry in the same interdisciplined spirit.

TWO

The History of Anthropology
as an Anthropological Problem

1965

In thinking about the history of anthropology, it is desirable in the first place to focus upon anthropological questions, rather than upon labeled disciplines, or groups of disciplines, as we now find them conventionally defined.[1] By anthropological questions I mean any of those to which we would now seek answers in a professionally recognized tradition: in the literature of physical anthropology, archaeology, cultural or social anthropology and linguistics. For these areas of specialized knowledge only emerged after anthropological questions had been articulated, answers to them consciously pursued, and organized data and concepts embodied in a professionally transmitted tradition. In this respect anthropology is a very recent development in the intellectual history of western culture.

At the same time, the broadly gauged comparative and historical framework of inquiry which we now assume in anthropology has led to a consideration of all kinds of data relevant to man in a universally human perspective. In this frame of reference we may ask: How far did the cultures of non-western peoples provide answers to anthropological questions? Were there any conditions present which motivated a search for answers to them? What observational data were available to the people of these cultures? What quantitative and qualitative differences existed in the kind of anthropological knowledge available? What circumstances and events promoted, or retarded, the accumulation of such knowledge in different cultures? If we were in a position to answer questions of this kind we would be better able to appraise the cultural and historical background of the interest in anthropological questions which became articulated and reached fruition in the organized inquiry with which we are familiar.

The history of anthropology considered as an anthropological problem supplements an exclusive concern with the history of organized inquiries and any attempt to arbitrarily isolate their development from its roots in a wider cultural context. On the contrary, it directs attention to the cultural context and historical circumstances out of which formulations of anthropological questions must have developed and suggests that, at this level, one may find parallels in early western culture to non-western cultures. The history, then, of what is now labelled anthropology in western culture is linked with the study of the sociology of knowledge, "ethnoscience" and the study of man and his behavior from many different points of view, humanistic and scientific, in the modern period of western culture. If we look for the most authoritative answers to anthropological questions in both societies other than our own and in the earliest phase of western culture[2] we are most likely

---

[1]Based upon a paper with the same title read at a Symposium on the History of Anthropology, Annual Meeting, American Anthropological Association, (Chicago) November, 1962. A background paper ("Anthropology and the History of the Study of Man"), prepared for the Conference on the History of Anthropology, sponsored by the Social Science Research Council (N. Y.: April, 1962) also has been drawn upon. Since many of the problems alluded to in this paper have not been studied, documentation is chiefly illustrative.

[2]*I.e.*, the period subsequent to the fall of Rome in the West in 476, A. D.

to find them embedded in the cognitive orientation of a people, in their culturally constituted world view, from which they have not been abstracted and articulated. Questions related to man and his nature are an integral part of mythology and religion. The persons most concerned with such matters are priests, theologians, philosophers, or their equivalents. The kind of knowledge possible in this type of tradition is limited by its dogmatic character, in the absence of any motivations which encourage independent or objective inquiry. In western culture we know that radical changes occurred in the course of a few centuries and that this level of knowledge was transcended: A secular view of the world based on independent inquiry arose to challenge the traditionally sanctioned one—"La crise de la conscience européenne" of Paul Hazard. The class of persons to whom one could turn for authoritative answers to anthropological questions began to shift. The criteria for evaluating the reliability of anthropological knowledge became transformed as independent, objective inquiry expanded.

The significance of these historic events, which were only part of the revolutionary intellectual changes which occurred in Europe, are unique in their anthropological implications. For in their total range and sweep, they have no precise parallel in the cultural development of any other society. Western culture, among other things, is distinctive as the theatre of a continuing and accelerating effort by man to obtain increasingly reliable knowledge about his own nature, behavior, his history and varying modes of life, as well as his place in the universe. The labels which ultimately emerged to discriminate varying facets of the professional study of man sometimes obscure the enduring and characteristic intellectual preoccupation with himself that became so ramified, and so persistent in the history of western culture.

Besides this, the concomitant historical events which occurred have a dual interest for anthropology today. On the one hand, they involve on a large scale what have now become familiar problems of inquiry to anthropologists on a smaller scale: cultural changes and radical social readjustments, movements of population; cultural borrowing and the effects of contacts with other cultures; economic transformation and radical changes in value systems. On the other hand, it was during this same period in western culture that new anthropological questions came to the fore, while older ones were more sharply focused.

While in western culture the rise of the conscious pursuit by specialists of answers to anthropological questions is unique, at the same time this only expresses in a highly developed form a universal interest in himself exemplified by man everywhere. For man's capacity for becoming an object to himself and contemplating his existence as a being living in a world conjunctively with beings other than his kind is concomitant with his distinctive mode of cultural adaptation itself.[3] Consequently, it is not surprising to find man's ideas of his own nature reflected in the traditional world views of human societies. All cultures provide answers to some anthropological questions which are considered to be authoritative and final. Traditional knowledge of this kind may be characterized as folk anthropology, i.e., a body of observations, beliefs, and socially sanctioned dogmas which parallel folk knowledge about other aspects of the phenomenal world. What we have in the case of western culture is an opportunity to *document* an intellectual shift from the level of

---

[3]See Hallowell, 1963.

folk anthropology to a level of systematic observations and inquiry detached from traditional beliefs, and inspired by values giving prime emphasis to the search for more reliable knowledge of all aspects of human phenomena.

Unfortunately, the reliability of different areas of folk knowledge has not yet been as carefully studied as it might be. In some areas where direct observation and experience is involved, such as ethnobotany, animal and human anatomy, its level may be much higher than once supposed. Laughlin, e.g., goes so far as to say that:

> "We may consider the likelihood that man was always aware of his affinity with other animals and consequently did not need to 'discover' this obvious relationship any more than he discovered his stomach or eyeballs, or than the female of our species discovered that she was bearing the young. The early apprehension of a working knowledge of anatomy, human and non-human, was indispensable to man's survival. This was crucial in an animal form that was liquidating various physical abilities and instincts in exchange for the use of tools, who had both to defend himself from predators and to hunt and utilize other animals and who required assistance for the birth of his young . . . Though varying greatly around the world, the anatomical information possessed by most peoples has probably been consistently underestimated."[4]

On the other hand, we know that there were many anthropological questions which could neither be posed nor answered in terms of the personal experience of men cognitively oriented in the provincial traditions of non-literate, or even early literate, cultures. Among the most obvious of these is any knowledge of the total range in the physical types of mankind throughout the world, or the actual antiquity of man. Furthermore, even if we grant that man recognized his anatomical affinities with other animals at a very early period, was this the only kind of affinity recognized or the primary one emphasized? Did animals have "souls", like men, or were they only "machines"? And, in the case of the Greeks, if it is said, as Kluckhohn does, that they "saw man as a part of nature and to be naturalistically understood",[5] can we say that "nature" has an equivalent meaning at all periods of European culture, to say nothing of its meaning in other cultures?[6] The conceptual framework in which observations are ordered and the explanation of phenomena must be considered in their cultural and historical context before significant comparison can be made. To recognize that man has animal-like characteristics had a different meaning in a nineteenth century evolutionary context than it had for the Greeks, or in earlier periods of European culture, or for non-literate peoples. Further investigation in the area of "ethnoscience" may provide a more satisfactory basis for making detailed comparisons of the limits and range of reliable knowledge possessed by non-European peoples both with respect to its pragmatic aspect, and the way in which such knowledge is classified and ordered in relation to the premises of different world views.[7] It would be interesting to know in how many cultures where close observation of any order of phenomena led to knowledge of more or less immediate pragmatic value this level was transcended and what steps led to this

---

[4]Laughlin, pp. 150, 172.
[5]Kluckhohn, p. 42.
[6]Collingwood.
[7]French and Sturtevant.

later development.[8] For a very limited knowledge of man may be pragmatically adequate within a particular sociocultural system. There may be no need to question its validity. Incentives stimulating the acquisition of new, or more reliable knowledge, may never arise. Essential anthropological questions, of limited scope, can be answered in meaningful fashion by appeal to tradition and personal experience.

In early western culture the level of knowledge represented in the traditional Christian world view is equivalent to folk anthropology. It was culturally constituted, untested knowledge about man and his world, reinforced by socially sanctioned religious values which gave it the stamp of ultimate truth. This traditional world view of the West is the historical backdrop against which changes in the answers to anthropological questions may be plotted. It is the known cultural base line against which shifts from a level of folk anthropology in the direction of more reliable, objective, tested knowledge about man can be documented. It is in this respect that the culture history of the West provides the record of a unique experience in the history of man's awareness of himself.

Thus an anthropological approach to the history of anthropology in western culture suggests that this history should be set squarely within the cultural context of western civilization. Relationships should be sought between historical events, changing intellectual currents and other factors having a bearing on the kind of anthropological questions that were being asked and the answers that were being sought at successive periods. This would supersede the historical chronicle in which lip service is given to Herodotus as the "father" of anthropology, an oversimplified linear chronology of name-dropping passes for history and a causual leap is made from western culture to that of Greece in the fifth century B. C. The actual historical process is more complicated and devious than can be represented in any straightaway linear scheme of ideas or "influences".[9] Classical writers and the classical tradition do enter the picture, of course, but within the context of the intellectual history of western culture itself as part of its literature. What in anthropological terminology we might call "literary acculturation" was actively promoted, including the attempt to reconcile this pagan heritage with the Bible and the Christian world view. One example of this heritage was Pliny's uncritical collection of material concerning fabulous races and peoples. "If theologians ever doubted these tales," says Hodgen, "they were restrained by a traditional classicism and scholastic logic from refuting their existence. As for man as a whole, the Fathers desired less to know him than to save him."[10] Belief in the existence of fabulous races was actually reinforced: they appeared on maps right up to the discovery of the New World and

---

[8]Goodenough, e.g., (p. 110) points out that, " . . . . practical and empirical in their approach, the Carolinian people belie the frequent assumption that man everywhere is awed by the marvels of nature and, stirred to speculate thereon, seeks to formulate a coherent theory as to the origin and meaning of the cosmos . . . . Rooted in navigation, aimed at determining directions and predicting the weather, native astronomy is perhaps too important for personal safety to permit its being removed from an empirical context."

[9]cf. Butterfield (Man . . . . , p. 32) who writes: "The history of science could never be adequately reconstructed by a student who confined his attention to the few men of supreme genius. We should produce a misleading diagram of the whole course of things if we merely drew direct lines from one of these mighty peaks to another. The great books are undoubtedly preferable to the reader, more serviceable in education, and more enriching to the mind; but, if we restrict ourselves to these, the result is likely to be a rope of sand; and in any case this is not the way in which to make discoveries in the history of any science. In reality, the technical historian, bent on discovery—proceeding therefore from the known to the unknown—tends to find himself drawn rather in the opposite direction."

[10]Hodgen, p. 50 and Chapter 1, The Classical Heritage.

after.[11] The answers to anthropological questions given by the Greeks themselves, or other peoples of the ancient Near East, would require independent studies. Such investigations would illuminate the differences between the cultural historical situation in these societies as compared with the West in the development and fruition of anthropological ideas.[12]

The first chapter, then, in the history of anthropology may be conceived as a history of the conditions, events, activities and ideas which undermined the provincial folk anthropology of early western culture and, at the same time, laid the groundwork for independent observation and the ultimate accumulation, ordering and interpretation of a body of knowledge which provided more reliable answers to a wide range of anthropological questions. To those of us working in the field today, for example, it seems obvious that anthropology should make use of a comprehensive spatio-temporal frame of reference which embraces all living varieties of *Homo-sapiens*, as well as extinct cultures and peoples of the distant past and more ancient hominid types besides. This basic frame of reference is essential to the ordering of our wide-ranging empirical data. The interesting historical question, then, is how this inclusive spatio-temporal "grid" came into being. The answer, I think, is that it only became possible to employ systematically such a conceptual frame of reference after a long and complex series of historical events had occurred in Europe which were, to begin with, quite extraneous to the study of man.

So far as a world-wide geographical perspective is concerned, this could not emerge until the entire globe had been explored. It began, of course, with the great Age of Discovery. And what is significant for the history of anthropology is that this was a unique achievement of the people of western Europe. Even in the absence of organized anthropological inquiry it had a profound impact upon their thought. The broadening of the base thus provided for the direct empirical observation of the physical characteristics, languages and cultures of the living peoples of the world was one of the necessary conditions required for answering vital anthropological questions. It was logically analogous to the broadening of the base of visual observation of objects in outer space after the invention of the telescope. The growing acquaintance with the peoples of distant, almost semi-fabulous lands, through the proliferation of *Narratives, Descriptions* and *Collections* of the reports of travelers of all kinds, brought home to the peoples of Europe the inescapable fact that their own outlook was, after all, extremely parochial. The idea of cultural relativity did not have to await the development of cultural anthropology. "It is perfectly correct to say,'" writes Hazard, "that all the fundamental concepts, such as Property, Freedom, Justice and so on, were brought under discussion again as a result of the conditions in which they were seen to operate in far-off countries, in the first place because, instead of all differences being referred to one universal archetype, the emphasis was now on the particular, the irreducible, the individual; in the second, because notions hitherto taken for granted could now be checked in the light of facts ascertained by actual experience, facts readily available to all inquiring minds. Proofs, for which an opponent of this dogma or that had laboriously to rum-

---

[11]For further details see Wittkower.
[12]See, e.g., Lutz, who points out that the Sumerians entertained the idea of progressive stages in the cultural development of man. Yet there is no evidence of empirical research. *Cf.* the Three Age concept.

mage about in the storehouses of antiquity, were now reinforced by additional ones, brand-new and highly coloured. See them just arrived from abroad, all ready for use!''[13]

In many respects an adequate temporal dimension relevant for the study of man lagged far behind a global geographical perspective. It could not become significant until the traditional view that the whole of creation and man's entire history could be encompassed within the span of 6000 years was displaced. It was contingent upon a reconsideration of the chronology of human history,[14] a revitalization, linked with material evidence, of the Three Age system of man's industrial development, (stone, bronze, iron ages),[15] the periodization of the history of the earth, in terms of geological and paleontological evidence,[16] and the empirical demonstration of man's "prehistory", a term used for the first time in 1851.[17] It will be recalled that John Frere, who sent some flint hand axes to the Secretary of the Society of Antiquaries of London in 1797, remarked in his accompanying letter that the situation in which they were found tempted one "to refer them to a very remote period indeed; *even beyond that of the present world*". (Italics ours.) But these remarks were ignored. Although modern archaeologists would place these tools in the Lower Paleolithic, no one took Frere's speculations seriously.[18] At this time there was no temporal frame of reference into which they could be fitted. But more than this was involved: there was no archeological frame of reference, either. As Heizer points out, certain preconditions had to be met, "stone tools had to be admitted as having

[13]Hazard, p. 10. *Cf.* Butterfield (*Origins* . . . . , pp. 183-184), who makes the point that changes in European thought and value towards the end of the seventeenth century were not only due to developments in physical science but were affected by widely read books of travel that reported discoveries in distant lands. See also Shapiro.

[14]Haber recalls (p. 33) that Joseph Justus Scaliger (1540-1609) revolutionized chronology in his *De emendatrione temporum* (1583). "He showed that ancient history was not confined to that of the Greeks and Romans, but should include Persian, Bablylonian, Egyptian, and the secular Jewish history. He gathered extant fragments of ancient history, succeeded in reconstructing the lost *Chronicle* of Eusebius . . . and studied the ancient systems of time keeping. He was thus able to compile for the first time in the modern period a sound—though sometimes erroneous—universal chronology of profane history, as distinguished from the uncritical and somewhat mythological sacred history of traditional chronology." The attempt of B. G. Niebuhr (1776-1831) to substitute historical scholarship (in his *History of Rome*, 1811-1832, see Stern, p. 46 ff.) for the folk history of Livy, is comparable in principle to the transcendence of the level of folk anthropology which had scarcely begun. But historical scholarship was not prepared to deal with such large questions as "universal" or "general" history. (See Butterfield, *Man* . . . . , chapter 2, "The Rise of the German Historical School"). "In reality", he writes, (p. 103) "the work of providing a rational account of man on the earth would seem to have been taken over from the theologians by the general philosophers in the eighteenth century. The need to know how mankind had come from primitive conditions to its existing state would appear to have been felt before the historians were in a condition to supply what was wanted. Man's reflection on the matter marched ahead of his researches; and it was the *philosophes*—the 'general thinkers' as we might call them—who attempted to map out the course of things in time. And this would appear to be the reason why the philosophy of history, as it was called, came to its climax before the study of history had reached its modern form. The Göttingen school resented the facile generalizations which the men of the enlightenment produced without research, and imposed upon human history from the outside." General history, of course, did not include archaeological prehistory; the necessary temporal frame of reference had to be radically expanded.

[15]See Daniel (1943, 1950) and, in particular, Heizer, (1962). Also Sanford.

[16]See Gillispie. Charles Lyell (1797-1875) published the first volume of his *Principles of Geology* in 1830. Despite resistance in orthodox circles, by the middle of the next decade the age of the earth had been extended to millions of years. "With Lyell's *Antiquity of Man*, [1863] and Lubbock's *Pre-Historic Times* [1865]" says Haber (p. 287), "the last step had been taken in the overthrow of Biblical chronology as an all inclusive time span for the work of creation". For a concrete example of how the Mosaic Time Scale hindered and distorted the development of a temporal framework required for an intelligible interpretation of racial and cultural events, see Mulvaney's discussion of the Australian material.

[17]By Daniel Wilson. See Daniel (1964), p. 9.

[18]See Daniel (1964), pp. 40-41. Heizer (1959) publishes Frere's letter.

been made by man. The correction of the idea that flaked and polished stone tools were thunderbolts which fell from the sky came about slowly through the discovery and awareness of savage peoples, particularly those of the New World following its discovery by Columbus, and the realization that these peoples who used stone tools lived in a pre-metal stage and were living as modern man once had lived."[19] In other words, sixteenth century published accounts of the manufacture of stone tools by living American aborigines, circulated as a consequence of the Age of Discovery, provided an initial clue relevant to the question of man's antiquity. These revelations planted the seeds of the classical "comparative method", for in the sixteenth and seventeenth centuries, Montaigne, Hobbes and Locke were already expressing the view that American Indians were existing representatives of an earlier general stage of human cultural development. However tentative and extraneous, at first, to anthropology as we think of it now, this line of thought anticipated the establishment of a firm spatio-temporal framework as a necessary foundation for the orderly investigation and solution of anthropological questions that were to become more and more clearly focused in the future.

While the Age of Discovery and the expansion of European peoples provided an essential condition for the direct, first-hand observation of the living peoples of the world, this was not a sufficient condition for the accumulation of reliable information of a high order. What has not been carefully investigated are the factors that retarded the reliability of observation and the motives, techniques, concepts, and other factors which promoted reliability. What seems to have happened is that for a considerable time the new observational facts concerning man's physical traits, cultures and languages, continued to be rationalized in relation to the persisting tradition of folk anthropology or other concepts. Besides this, European ethnocentrism created fictitious images of native peoples—the image of the Noble Savage on the one hand, and the ignoble or bestial savage on the other. Seen in modern anthropological perspective these images are the kind of phenomena which might be expected to be one of the consequences of superficial contact with, or secondhand knowledge of, exotic peoples prior to any systematic or scholarly study of them.[20] Although lack of written records and pictorial material makes the problem difficult to study, the images of primitive man projected by Europeans are counter-balanced by the images of civilized man and European culture for which we have evidence

---

[19]Heizer (1962), p. 260.

[20]In the 4th century B. C. Theopompus (born ca. 378), a Greek historian, wrote about the E-truscans in a manner which reminds us of some of the early reports of the people of the South Pacific. According to him sexual promiscuity existed, sexual intercourse sometimes occurred publicly, and children did not know their own parents. For quotation see Hus (pp. 157-158). The first work to present the sexual mores of the people of the South Seas for the English reader was Hawkesworth's *Account of the Voyages . . . in the Southern Hemisphere . . . Drawn up from the Journals which were kept by the Several Commanders . . . etc.* 1773. He was a man of letters and had not been on any of the voyages. As a matter of fact, his book was condemned for inaccuracy and indecency, yet it obtained wide circulation. Boswell met Capt. Cook at dinner in 1776 and asked him about the book. Boswell reports in his *Journal* (p. 308) that Cook said, "Hawkesworth made in his book a general conclusion from a particular fact, and would take as a fact what they had only heard . . . . . He said that a disregard of chastity in unmarried women was by no means general at Otaheite, and he said Hawkesworth's story of an *initiation* he had no reason to believe." "Why, Sir," Boswell goes on to say, "Hawkesworth has used your narrative as a London tavern keeper does wine. He has *brewed it* (i.e. mixed other ingredients with it)". Boswell also says (p. 341) that Cook "candidly confessed to me that he and his companions who visited the South Sea Islands could not be certain of any information they got, or supposed they got, except as to objects falling under the observations of the senses, their knowledge of the language was so imperfect they required the aid of their senses, and anything which they learnt about religion, government, or traditions might be quire erroneous."

among some non-literate peoples. Lips published a fascinating collection of photographs of museum specimens in his book, *The Savage Hits Back*, and cargo cults offer interesting material. Like Europeans, non-literate peoples made use of what knowledge they had of other peoples' cultures for their own purposes.

Anthropologists have paid little attention to the images of the "savage" in European culture—possibly because some of the best examples are found in the humanist tradition, in literature and the pictorial arts.[21] Recently Wilcomb Washburn, an historian, referring to the American Indians, has pointed out that "it has become fashionable for twentieth-century critics to ridicule the 'noble savage' presumably 'created' by such writers (as Rousseau), but it is evident that the assumptions of twentieth-century writers about seventeenth—or eighteenth century Indians must be examined as critically as the assumptions of the earliest writers."[22] He has also pointed out that changing images may, in part, prove to be a function of changing power relationships.[23] There is a nice problem here because once anthropology entered the phase of an organized discipline, some of the travel literature that was previously used to create what some have thought to be fictitious images of primitive man became source material in ethnography.

Direct observation of the non-literate peoples of the world did, of course, dispel some ancient fictions of folk anthropology. But the process was sometimes slow. The final disappearance of some of the fabulous races took several centuries. The *monopoli*—with no heads, but with faces in their chests—were included in Pliny's inventory, referred to by John Mandeville in his reputed fourteenth century travels and reported by Sir Walter Raleigh as living in the New World (Guiana) in the sixteenth century, although the latter did not claim to have seen them himself. A picture of one of these individuals, associated with several perfectly decent Indians, is to be found in a plate in Lafitau's *Moeurs des sauvages Amériquains* (1724).[24]

How indeed was it possible to evaluate the reliability of observations on distant races and cultures of the world, particularly when observers sometimes disagreed? John Mandeville's travels were read in eleven languages and for five centuries before it became known that they never took place at all, but were compiled from other

---

[21]See Fairchild, Pearce and Smith. An example of how the circulation of pictorial material created confusing and undiscriminating racial images, even relating to the ancestors of Europeans themselves, is the intricate connection between John White's drawings of *Indians* of Roanoke, made on the spot in the late sixteenth century, De Brys' engravings of *Picts* (1590) and "The Portraiture of the Ancient Britaines", published by John Speed in 1611 (See Kendrick, pp. 123-125 and Plates XII-XV). Kendrick comments: "Speed . . . . . seems to have realized that it was no use quoting classical authors to the effect that the ancient Britons wore few, if any, clothes, and painted themselves, if at the same time one refused to recognize that the picture of a naked and painted person would give some idea of the probable appearance of an Ancient Briton. There was no question of any disgrace here, but rather an occasion for pride; for nakedness implies hardiness, and painting oneself is, after all, art. Where an Ancient Briton was concerned, there could be no doubt that savagery must include the idea of nobility."

[22]Washburn, 1964, p. 415.

[23]Washburn (1957, p. 54): "Perhaps the 'idea of the noble savage' developed its greatest force when the white man was dependent on the Indian for his safety and sustenance (as in the early years of exploration and settlement), perhaps the 'idea of the treacherous savage' represents a period when both groups were powerful and a threat to each other. Finally, the 'idea of the filthy savage' may well have developed its greatest force when the Indian came to be dependent on the will of the White man (as in the late eighteenth century). Frederick J. Dockstader of the Museum of the American Indian in New York has suggested a most recent idea: that of the 'incompetent savage' which he suggests has arisen because of the growing economic rivalry between Indians and Whites in recent years." Smith (p. 244) points out that in the early nineteenth century pictorial material from the South Pacific was used in missionary propaganda to create an image of the ignoble savage.

[24]Reproduced in Hodgen, opposite p. 335.

authorities back to Pliny. In the sixteenth century it was even thought by some that Mandeville was more reliable than Marco Polo, Columbus and Cortez.[25] Banks and Cook did not find giants in Patagonia. Yet their more reliable observations were not, at the time, considered superior evidence to the testimony of others. One of the interesting factors here is that, in support of the existence of giants, pictorial material had appeared plainly showing the difference in height between Europeans and Patagonians.[26] The question of the validity of observations is of anthropological interest both with respect to the steps by which a higher level of reliability was achieved and the role played by persistent traditions of any kind which retarded the progress of objective knowledge.[27] Even in this century overtones of this old problem—although in a more refined form—are sometimes heard. A decade ago Kluckhohn said: "In cultural anthropology we are still too close to the phase in linguistics when non-European languages were being forcibly recast into the categories of Latin grammar".[28]

Among the positive contributions that emerged from the Age of Discovery was the fact that, it became more and more apparent that many of the anthropological observations reported could not be reconciled with traditional folk anthropology. While all the many revolutionary new questions which arose could not be satisfactorily answered or, if they were, do not seem adequately treated to us today, nevertheless, many of them were legitimate anthropological questions: the influence of climate, the diffusion of customs and social and cultural development. We still are faced with many of the same questions today and the answers are controversial. In order to place some of these questions in their historical context, I wish to quote here a passage from an unpublished manuscript of Katherine George who some years ago systematically surveyed the African travel literature from the fifteenth through the eighteenth century.

Among other things, Dr. George points out that "The Age of Discovery not only confronted the travellers with an astonishing array of cultural diversities which

---

[25]For information on Mandeville consult Letts and particularly Bennett, cf. Hodgen, pp. 69-71.
[26]"Making faithful records of the native peoples of the Pacific proved to be more difficult than making accurate records of plants, animals, or landscapes", writes Smith (pp. 20-21). "There was, for example, the question of size . . . . there had accumulated by 1768 a formidable body of evidence that the natives of Patagonia were giants. The Captains, Harrington and Carmen, had come back in 1704 with stories of giants. Byron, in 1764, only four years before Cook sailed in the Endeavour, corroborated their story . . . . . Byron's meeting with this chief was illustrated in Hawkesworth's *Voyages*, the chief being made, in accordance with Byron's description, to tower above the Englishman." However, since Byron had no professional artist with him, this was "simply an illustration based on a written statement". Banks, accompanying Cook, did have artists and was anxious to correct misconceptions about the size of the Patagonians. He wrote in his *Journal* that the men were from five feet eight inches to five feet ten inches in height, while the women were smaller, seldom exceeding five feet. Furthermore, Buchan and Parkinson both made drawings of the Fuegians showing them to be normal in height. Nevertheless, a belief in the giantism of the Patagonians persisted. Lord Monboddo claimed that Hawkesworth's summary weighed heavily in this direction and even after the publication of the latter's *Voyages*, there was an English collection which illustrated a giantess and a French collection showing a giant Fuegian receiving Commodore Byron. See Smith (p. 255 and Plates 167, 168, 169 for the transformation wrought after the invention of photography by Daguerre (1789-1851) and the use of instrumentation and modelling. See Smith, too, for example of the articulation of the general need for more precise observation on men by such eighteenth century writers as Ferguson, Monboddo and Herder, as well as the more detailed and explicit instructions given La Pérouse (1785) as compared with Cook (pp. 100-102).
[27]According to Smith (see pp. 30, 34) the acceptance of the idea of giants in Fuegia probably reflects a long tradition in Europe of *antipodal inversion* i.e., "the long-standing belief that things in the southern hemisphere were somehow invested or at least governed by laws which differed from those governing the northern parts of the world."
[28]Kluckhohn, 1953, p. 508.

seemed to call for explanation, but after these had been considered and somewhat assimilated, it also disclosed the presence of cultural correspondences or parallels; correspondences such as that between a familiar homeland society and one in Africa, between a custom or culture and a similar trait or condition among the Old Testament Hebrews, or between African society and the social life of the classical peoples of European antiquity. Often these parallels, which were recognized as both contemporary and historical, were merely noted but not explained. But occasionally in early reports, and more frequently in later, notation was accompanied by efforts on the part of travellers to place them in broader context of theory. In other words, such parallels were accounted for as the outcome of either diffusion or development. The travellers who adopted the diffusionist position emerged with explanations inferring contact at some period in past time; while those who ascribed similarities to a uniformly operative process of social development noted correspondences between existing African custom and earlier cultural conditions among European or other historical peoples. The latter assumed, in short, that the primitive folk encountered in Africa were an early stage of progressive or developmental change like that which was once manifested during the course of the history of some civilized people".[29]

In addition to the posing and answering of anthropological questions which Dr. George documents in the African travel literature, she also notes a radical shift in attitude towards *Africans* in the eighteenth century. The concept of "the bestial African primitive," and "the lawless, promiscuous society peculiarly associated with him," disappears. "The institutions and customs of the African primitive are not merely accepted with a new tolerance by the eighteenth century traveller; they are even fairly often upheld as models to be admired and emulated by the civilized world. For the 'noble savage' is indubitably a personage in these acounts." Admittedly a romanticism which, "in its extremer forms, at least, can and does distort objectivity." George concludes that the errors "to be chalked up against this new positive prejudice in favor of the African primitive are as nothing beside the almost countless errors of commission and omission attributable to the earlier negative prejudice." Consequently, she thinks that the concept of the "noble savage" "became of necessity a friend rather than an enemy to the advance of knowledge about the primitive. A bias it might remain, with capacities to distort . . . . ., (nevertheless) it introduced a compulsion to go forth and observe." It may have been "a door to objectivity," if not objectivity itself.[30]

So far as genuine anthropological concepts are concerned, there are clearly defined historical links with a past which long antedated the rise of any variety of anthropological discipline. Radcliffe-Brown found that his distinction between ethnology and social anthropology had its roots in seventeenth and eighteenth century writers. These two interests, he says, were clearly recognized by William Robertson in his *History of America* (1777) where this author "gives one of the earliest definitions of the study that later came to be called social anthropology, and distinguished from the investigation of the origins of peoples which we now call

[29]*Social Theory in the early literature of voyage and exploration in Africa.* Doctoral Dissertation, Dept. of Social Institutions, Univ. of California, Berkeley, 1944. Katherine B. Oakes (Mrs. H. C. George).
[30]George (1958), pp. 71-72..

ethnology."[31] It was Robertson, it may be added, who explicitly stressed parallel development, rather than migration or historical contacts, as the explanation of cultural similarities.[32] Hoebel, who has also studied Robertson's work, finds that he anticipates Tylorian and Morganian anthropology. More intensive research will no doubt turn up other links with the past which will enable us to appraise current anthropological ideas in better historical perspective.

While a comprehensive temporal frame of reference, although slow in developing, ultimately provided a convenient means of integrating facts about hominid evolution and prehistoric man with human history and events in the natural world, its most vital significance did not lie in its chronological usefulness. It was, rather, because the conception of time characteristic of western culture embodied distinctive qualitative features which made it possible to order the dynamics of human evolution, changes in socio-cultural systems, linguistic forms and other phenomena of change in an orderly linear form. In this temporal frame of reference, too, persistent, enduring, and unchanging properties of phenomena could be distinguished from variable ones. What is significant, then, is that anthropology arose and developed in a culture whose world view embodied the archetype of a conception of human events in time which differed radically from that of the more ancient civilizations. In contrast with Greek culture, for example, where the passage of time was conceived as cyclical and not rectilinear, a number of scholars have pointed out that the Christian world view embodied the notion of a universal history of mankind moving along a linear course between Creation and the Last Judgment.[33] It comprised a unique series of historical events which were irreversible. It now appears that, more and more widely applied and secularized, a linear, rather than a cyclical, conception of time, vital because it was seen as the ground for the generation of novel configurations of events and developmental sequences, eventually became the model in western culture for the interpretation of the dynamics of historical events in all orders of phenomena.

Since cosmogenesis found its explanation in folk cosmogony, physical science (mechanics, astronomy), at first, was not at all concerned with the "history" of the universe. For Newtonian physics the world was the same today as yesterday and

---

[31]Radcliffe-Brown, p. 146.
[32]See Hallowell, 1960, pp. 13-14.
[33]See, e.g., Brandon, Eliade, Peuch, Haber.
    Butterfield (*Man* . . . , Preface, ix-x) writes: "Philosophy and religion in many parts of the world, and even in ancient Greece . . . . too often led to the depreciation of history—the feeling that time's changes are meaningless, the notion that events move in aimless, ever-recurring cycles . . . . . Yet the Christian could not turn his back on history, for his very religion was 'historical': it was essential for him to regard Christ as an actual historical figure. In view of the Incarnation and the Crucifixion, it was impossible for him to take the line that events in time are really of no significance or that history offers the pattern of aimless, repeating cycles. Perhaps it was the pull of the Old Testament which, in the last resort, kept him close to earth—close to history—when he was in danger of moving away from reality. Perhaps it was as a result of the influence of the Old Testament, which began its story of mankind with the Creation, that there developed so remarkably under Christianity the notion of a 'universal history'—that is, a single story of all mankind . . . . . Other factors, such as the Scientific Revolution of the seventeenth century . . . . . affected the course of historical inquiry, and in the subsequent period, the growing currency of the idea of progress seemed to give new point, new meaning, to history itself—new reason for discovering the course of man's development in the antecedent age." Haber (p. 25) says that it was St. Augustine who placed "the conception on a unique, concrete, course of time in the mainstream of Christian eschatology", and if, "in the eighteenth century, the time scale of Biblical chronology became an onerous barrier to scientific progress, it had served an heroic role during the Patristic period in establishing the archetype of progress itself which science so readily borrowed."

in the distant past. Physical science concentrated upon what Simpson has called immanent, or nonhistorical processes and principles, inherent in the very nature of matter-energy (gravity, energy, radiation). However, "the actual state of the universe, or any part of it at a given time, its configuration, is not immanent and is constantly changing . . . . . History may be defined as configurational change through time, a sequence of real, individual, but interrelated events."[34] Simpson points out that before the eighteenth century most people thought that the configurational aspects of natural phenomena were likewise unchanging (the hills are "everlasting") both aspects being simply given, "probably by the creative acts of gods."[35] And, since until Darwin living species were thought to be immutable, each occupying its assigned niche in the Great Chain of Being, a time dimension in early observationable and classificatory biology was not of central importance.

What is of special interest historically, and particularly from an anthropological point of view, are the two main sources from which the knowledge and intellectual stimulus came which required an explicit differentiation between immanent and configurational characteristics. These were geology and human history. "No matter what they thought of causes," Simpson points out, "the pioneer geologists learned that the configuration of the earth is constantly changing, that it has a history. Hence it follows that the structure of the earth—and, by an extension quickly made, that of the whole physical universe—is not immanent but is at any moment a transient state within a historical sequence." And, "in the field of human history, change in social structure and the human condition were generally evident, so that a thoroughgoing belief in static configuration was hardly possible to even the earliest historians."[36] Thus a linear conception of a sequence of irreversible events in time more and more deeply permeated the thinking of western man not only in the humanities, but in the physical and biological sciences and the incipient social sciences from the eighteenth century onward.

While there are traces of cyclical theories in the Middle Ages and later, as a consequence of the influence of Arabic and Classical learning, they did not prove viable. In the sixteenth and early seventeenth centuries the belief that a general process of degeneration was taking place had its vogue.[37] But, from the seventeenth century forward, writes Eliade, "linearism and the progressivistic conception of history assert themselves more and more, inaugurating faith in an infinite progress, a faith already proclaimed by Leibniz, predominent in the century of 'enlightenment' and popularized in the nineteenth century by the triumph of the ideas of the evolutionists."[38] It was within the intellectual climate engendered by the early phase of the conceptualization of the history of man as progressive that the cultural data already accumulated in the Age of Discovery began to be fitted into this new frame of universal temporal reference. General stages, or grades, of cultural development were discerned and articulated, notably by the Scots of the eighteenth century, in terms of "conjectural history."[39] Associated with the reconstruction of cultural stages in the development of mankind, without the benefit of prehistoric archaeology,

---

[34]Simpson, 1964, p. 122 in chapter 7, "The Historical Factor in Science."
[35]Simpson, 1960, p. 118.
[36]*Ibid*, p. 118.
[37]See Harris and Hodgen, p. 263 *ff*.
[38]Eliade, pp. 145-146.
[39]See Bryson. The term "conjectural history" was introduced by Dugald Stewart.

we find the emergence of the "comparative method" in its earliest form.[40] Although used by, and sometimes identified with, nineteenth century anthropologists it was far from being original with them. In fact, Auguste Comte (1798-1857) considered it integral to his positive philosophy and sociological method. A whole constellation of ideas, too, which defined a distinctive level of primitive mentality—a child-like quality, a concrete rather than an abstract mode of thought, a capacity for myth making, with even a tincture of madness—not only antedate organized anthropological inquiry, but date back to the earliest phase of the progressive philosophy of human development.[41]

By the time the question of the mutability of species had been settled by Darwin in the middle of the nineteenth century, all human phenomena could be considered diachronically in a linear scheme of temporal reference. The Biblical age of the World had been transcended and the way was cleared for a more objective approach to anthropogensis, and an increasing precision in ordering and interpreting human phenomena in time and space.

All I have tried to do here is to give emphasis to the fact that the events and conditions which led up to the period when anthropological questions became the concern of specialists and organized disciplines, require exploration as an anthropological problem—as a significant chapter in man's pursuit of knowledge about himself as part of his cultural adaptation. At the same time, this chapter in man's history in western culture is as much a part of the history of anthropology as the subsequent chapters concerned with the techniques, methodologies, concepts and theories developed. The primary historical question is not when anthropology began but, how did it come about that in western culture thinkers were increasingly motivated, not only to search for more reliable knowledge about their surrounding world, but to intensify their efforts to collect and analyze data that would provide more and more reliable answers to anthroplogical questions. Even a superficial consideration of this problem directs attention to distinctive features of western culture, to unique historical events, which made the rational and empirical study of man possible in a manner unparalleled in any other culture: the expansion of the European peoples beginning with the Age of Discovery, the development of modern science as a rational approach to the study of phenomena which transcends folk knowledge on all fronts. Furthermore, Butterfield has stressed the fact that "we do not always remember that it [western civilization] is similarly distinguished for its 'historical mindedness' . . . . . For a long time we have been coming to realize that we must study the history of science if we wish to understand the character and development of our civilization. We have been much slower in realizing the importance of the history of history."[42] We have been even slower in undertaking the

---

[40]For the seventeenth and eighteenth century use of the comparative method see Bock and Teggart (pp. 92 ff.).

[41]See Manuel pp. 43-44; 141-142. Fontenelle (1657-1757) "revived the Augustinian analogy between the history of mankind and the development of the child to maturity, and envisioned the historical process as the gradual elimination of puerile myth and its replacement by adult mathematical-physical reasoning. Fontenelle defined primitive mentality, but he did not admire it; this was a stage of human consciousness which mankind was fortunate enough to have outgrown. In comparing the ancients, the savages, the peasants, and the children, Fontenelle allowed them the attributes of humanity, even a rudimentary capacity to reason, but he regarded them as incapable of exercising those higher powers of abstraction so remarkably concentrated among members of the French academies. For every event, Fontenelle believed, the primitive like the peasant, demanded a concrete specific cause." (p. 44)

[42]Butterfield, Man . . . . . , New Preface, VII.

detailed investigation of the history of the study of man. Yet, it has been in western culture that man has become most completely aware of his own unique being and the possibility of making himself the subject of rational objective inquiry. The historical and cultural factors that led to this type of inquiry are an important part of the history of anthropology. However, as Margaret T. Hodgen has observed recently,[43] we have not yet probed far enough, nor deeply enough into the past. Particularly at a time, too, when there is such an upsurge of interest in the history of science, the history of anthropology should not be viewed as antiquarianism, or even marginal to current interests. A historical orientation to the development of anthropological knowledge should provide a point of departure for a sounder appraisal of current trends of thought and further research, as well as clarifying our professional role in relation to other disciplines concerned with the study of man.

BIBLIOGRAPHY

History of Anthropology

BENNETT, JOSEPHINE W. *The Rediscovery of Sir John Mandeville.* New York: Modern Language Association of America, 1954.

BOCK, KENNETH E., "The Acceptance of Histories." *Uni. of Cal. Pub. in Sociology and Social Institutions*, 3(1956), 1-132.

BOSWELL: *The Ominous Years, 1774-1776*, ed. by C. Ryskaup and F. A. Pottle. New York: McGraw-Hill, 1963.

BRANDON, SAMUEL G. F., *Time and Mankind, an Historical and Philosophical Study of Mankind's Attitude to the Phenomena of Change.* London: Hutchinson, 1951.

BRYSON, GLADYS. *Man and Society: The Scottish Inquiry of the Eighteenth Century.* Princeton: Princeton University Press, 1945.

BUTTERFIELD, HERBERT. *The Origins of Modern Science.* New York: Macmillan (paperback ed.), 1960.

BUTTERFIELD, HERBERT. *Man on His Past. The Study of the History of Historical Scholarship.* Boston: Beacon Press, 1960.

COLLINGWOOD, R. G. *The Idea of Nature.* Oxford: Clarendon Press, 1945.

DANIEL, GLYN E. *The Three Ages.* Cambridge: The University Press, 1943.

DANIEL, GLYN, E. *A Hundred Years of Archaeology.* London: Duckworth, 1950.

DANIEL, GLYN E. *The Idea of Prehistory.* London: Watts, 1962 (Penguin, 1964).

ELIADE, MIRCEA. *Cosmos and History, The Myth of the Eternal Return.* New York: Harper Torch Books, 1959.

FAIRCHILD, HOXIE N. *The Noble Savage, a Study in Romantic Naturalism.* New York: Columbia University Press, 1928.

FRENCH, DAVID. "The Relationship of Anthropology to Studies in Perception and Cognition." In *Psychology: A Study of a Science*, ed. Sigmund Koch, Vol. 6, *Investigations of Man as Socius*, pp. 388-428. New York: McGraw-Hill, 1963.

GEORGE, KATHERINE. "The Civilized West Looks at Primitive Africa: 1400-1800. A Study in Ethnocentrism," *Isis*, 40(1958), 62-72.

GILLISPIE, CHARLES C. *Genesis and Geology. A Study in the Relations of Scientific Thought, Natural Theology, and Social Opinion in Great Britain, 1790-1850.* New York: Harper Torch Books, 1959.

GOODENOUGH, WARD H. "Native Astronomy in Micronesia: A Rudimentaty Science", *Scientific Monthly*, August, 1951.

GUY, B. *The French Image of China Before and After Voltaire*, 1963. (*Studies on Voltaire and the Eighteenth Century*, ed. Theodore Besterman).

HABER, FRANCIS C. *The Ages of the World—Moses to Darwin.* Baltimore: Johns Hopkins Press, 1959.

HALLOWELL, A. IRVING "The Beginnings of Anthropology in America", in *Selected Papers from the American Anthropologist 1888-1920*, ed. by Frederica deLaguna. Evanston, Ill.: Row, Peterson, 1960.

HALLOWELL, A. IRVING. "Personality, Culture and Society in Behavioral Evolution, in *Psychology: A Study of a Science*, ed. Sigmund Koch, Vol. 6, *Investigations of Man as Socius*, pp. 429-509. New York: McGraw-Hill, 1963.

[43]Forword, p. 7.

HARRIS, VICTOR. *All Coherence Gone.* Chicago: University of Chicago Press, 1949.

HAZARD, PAUL. *La Crise de la Conscience Européenne.* Paris: Boiven & cie 1935. (Translated as *The European Mind. The Critical Years (1680-1715).* New Haven: Yale University Press, 1953).

HEIZER, ROBERT F. *The Archaeologist at Work.* New York: Harper, 1959.

HEIZER, ROBERT F. "The Background of Thomsen's Three-Age System," *Technology and Culture,* 3(1962), 259-266.

HODGEN, MARGARET T. *Early Anthropology in the Sixteenth and Seventeenth Centuries.* Philadelphia: University of Pennsylvania Press, 1964.

HOEBEL, E. ADAMSON. "Willian Robertson: An 18th Century Anthropologist-Historian," *American Anthropologist,* 62(1960), 648-655.

HUS, ALAIN. *The Etruscans.* New York: Evergreen Press, 1961.

KENDRICK, T. D. *British Antiquity.* London: Methuen, 1950.

KLUCKHOHN, CLYDE. "Universal Categories of Culture," in *Anthropology Today,* prepared under the chairmanship of A. L. Kroeber. Chicago: University of Chicago Press, 1953.

KLUCKHOHN, CLYDE. *Anthrolology and the Classics.* Providence, R. I.: Brown University Press, 1961.

LAUGHLIN, WILLIAM S. "Acquisition of Anatomical Knowledge by Ancient Man," in *Social Life of Early Man,* ed., Sherwood L. Washburn. New York: Viking Fund Publications in Anthropology, No. 31 (Wenner-Gren Foundation for Anthropological Research), 1961.

LETTS, MALCOLM. *Sir John Mandeville. The Man and His Book.* London: Batchworth, 1949.

LIPS, JULIUS E. *The Savage Hits Back.* (With an introduction by B. Malinowski.) New Haven: Yale University Press, 1937.

LUTZ, HENRY F. "The Sumerian and Anthropology," *American Anthropologist,* 29 (1927), 202-209.

MANUEL, FRANK E. *The Eighteenth Century Confronts the Gods.* Cambridge: Harvard University Press, 1959.

MULVANEY, D. J. "The Australian Aborigines 1606-1929," *Historical Studies: Australia and New Zealand,* 8 (1958), 150-151.

PEARCE, ROY H. *The Savages of America. A Study of the Indian and the Idea of Civilization.* Baltimore: Johns Hopkins Press, 1953.

PEUCH, HENRI-CHARLES. *Gnosis and Time,* in *Man and Time, Papers from the Eranos Yearbooks.* New York: Pantheon Books, 1957.

RADCLIFFE-BROWN, ALFRED R. *Method in Social Anthropology.* Selected Essays, ed. by M. N. Srinivas. Chicago: University of Chicago Press, 1958.

SANFORD, EVA M. "The Study of Ancient History in the Middle Ages," *Journal of History of Ideas,* 5 (1944), 21-43.

SHAPIRO, HARRY L. "Anthropology and the Age of Discovery," in *Process and Pattern in Culture, Essays in Honor of Julian H. Steward,* ed. by R. A Manners, pp. 337-348. Chicago: Aldine Publishing Co., 1964.

SIMPSON, GEORGE GAYLORD. "The History of Life," in *Evolution After Darwin,* ed. Sol Tax. Vol. 1. *The Evolution of Life,* pp. 117-180. Chicago: University of Chicago Press, 1960.

SIMPSON, GEORGE GAYLORD. *This View of Life. The World of an Evolutionist.* New York: Harcourt, 1964.

SMITH, BERNARD. *European Vision and the South Pacific 1768-1850. A Study in the History of Art and Ideas.* Oxford: Oxford University Press, 1960.

STERN, FRITZ, ed. *The Varities of History. From Voltaire to the Present.* New York: Meridian, 1956.

STURTEVANT, WILLIAM C. "Studies in Ethnoscience," *American Anthropologist,* 66, No. 3, Part 2, *Special Publication* 1 (1964), 99-131.

TEGGART, FREDERICK J. *Theory and Process of History.* Berkeley: University of California Press, 1945.

WASHBURN, WILCOMB E. "A Moral History of Indian-White Relations: Needs and Opportunities for Study," *Ethnohistory,* 4 (1957), 47-61.

WASHBURN, WILCOMB E., *The Indian and the White Man.* ed. (Documents in American Civilization Series.) New York: Anchor Books, Doubleday & Co., Inc., 1964.

WITTKOWER, RUDOLPH. "Marvels of the East: A Study in the History of Monsters," *Journal of the Warburg and Courtauld Institutes,* 5 (1942), 159-91.

THREE

The Beginnings of Anthropology in America

1960

INTRODUCTION

THE history of anthropology, writ large, is rooted in the search by man for increasingly reliable knowledge about himself and his place in the universe. As a scientific discipline, anthropology as we know it is a recent and highly distinctive achievement of modern western civilization. It represents a unique and continuing effort to substitute tested, objective knowledge about man—his origins, nature, and history—for what in other cultures may be called folk-anthropology. For in these cultures, as well as in the earliest phases of European civilization, what we find is a body of observations, beliefs, and socially sanctioned dogmas about man which parallel common-sense knowledge and traditional beliefs about other aspects of the phenomenal world. It is only with the revolution in world-view that has occurred in western culture that the level of folk-anthropology has been transcended.

This change was stimulated by the rise of rationalism, the development of scientific aims and methods in the study of natural phenomena and, in particular, by rapidly increasing information about the aborigines of remote parts of the world during the Age of Discovery. With the disappearance of the parochialism of the Middle Ages, surrounded by a realm of fable which had distorted and cramped the empirical foundation necessary for a scientific anthropology, it became possible for the first time for man to think about himself in terms of world geography and a more reliable body of information about the peoples of the world. This, of course, was a large step forward in relation to the past. It was only a small beginning in relation to the future. Four centuries more were to pass before a coordinate time perspective emerged, the result of archeological and paleontological discoveries which, when conjoined with richer biological knowledge, firmly set man in an evolutionary framework inconceivable within the world view of European peoples of the Age of Discovery.

Anthropology as an organized discipline was not born in a cultural and historical vacuum. Its mature stage is not fully intelligible unless considered as the result of earlier ideas about man and his history, with the accumulation of relevant data, which preceded it. During the long period when the contemporary framework of anthropology was slowly developing, and long before there was any conscious recognition of the need for an articulated body of knowledge that would be the foundation of a distinctive discipline with a trained personnel,[1] questions were being raised that posed what were essentially anthropological problems. During the same period, too, more and more empirical data were accumulating. Even in the twentieth century we still turn to the information recorded by untrained observers—missionaries, explorers, travelers and traders—collected during the Age of Discovery and later.

The anthropological significance of the intellectual impact exerted by the fresh and more inclusive geographical and human perspective that followed the expansion of western European peoples is exemplified by the discovery of the Western Hemisphere and its inhabitants. The full implication of this discovery was not grasped by Columbus himself who, still medieval in much of his thinking, was convinced that he was close to the Earthly Paradise when he reached the mouth of the Orinoco on his third voyage.[2] But when Amerigo Vespucci gave the name *Mundus Novus* to the discovered territory, thus emphasizing its separateness from the known world even though the geographical fact was not to be demonstrated fully for two centuries, the phrase itself imbued the Western Hemisphere with an aura it has never lost.[3] The distinctive physical appearance of the aborigines, their peculiar lang-

---

[1] Writing in 1904 Boas said: "Up to ten years ago we had no. trained anthropologists. . . ." "The History of Anthropology," *Science* 20:522.

[2] Louis Weckmann, "The Middle Ages in the Conquest of America," *Speculum* 26:131-132, 1951; Howard Rollin Patch, *The Other World According to Descriptions in Medieval Literature*, Chap. 5, "Journeys to Paradise" (Cambridge: Harvard University Press, 1950).

[3] Vespucci (1451-1512) has been a controversial figure. For a recent appraisal, see German Arciniegas, *Amerigo and the New World. The Life and Times of Amerigo Vespucci* (New York: Knopf, 1955). This author (p. 226), referring to the famous letter entitled *Mundus Novus* which Vespucci addressed to Lorenzo di Pier Francesco de Medici in 1503, and which was translated and circulated throughout Europe, states: "None of those who read it failed to grasp its importance." In it Amerigo wrote: "In days past I wrote you of my return from those lands that we have sought and discovered . . . and which I can licitly call the New World" and farther on: "We learned that that land is not an island, but a continent, because it extends along far-stretching shores that do not encompass it and it is populated by innumerable inhabitants." Amerigo spoke of it as a "fourth part" of the world, thus specifically differentiating the Western Hemisphere from Europe, Asia, and Africa. Arciniegas comments (p. 227) that "this was not *a* new world; it was *the* New World, to be written not in small letters, but in capitals. After he

uages and highly diverse cultures immediately became a focal point
in discussions of what were vital anthropological problems of immense
scope—questions involving the human status and capabilities of the
Indians, questions of their origin and migrations, questions concerning
possible linguistic and cultural connections with people of the Old
World. As Prescott wrote in 1843, in his *Conquest of Mexico*: "When
the Europeans first touched the shores of America, it was as if they
had alighted on another planet . . . everything there was so different
from what they had before seen. They were introduced to new varieties
of plants, and to unknown races of animals; while man, the lord of all,
was equally strange in complexion, language, and institutions. It was
what they emphatically styled it, a New World. Taught by their faith
to derive all created beings from one source, they felt a natural per-
plexity as to the manner in which these distant and insulated regions
could have obtained their inhabitants. The same curiosity was felt by
their countrymen at home, and European scholars bewildered their
brains with speculations on the best way of solving this interesting
question."[4] These learned men raised many questions which, although
they could not be answered at the time on the basis of what we now
consider reliable knowledge, persisted into the later period when
anthropology became an organized discipline.

We are still faced with the problem of establishing sound criteria
for the determination of a thoroughly human status, psychologically
and biologically, but this problem no longer arises with respect to living
peoples. Early explorers, however, were not sure about the humanity
of the Hottentots; in the eighteenth century, Lord Monboddo, one of
the most learned men of his time, held that speech was not a necessary
human trait. When the Spanish first came in contact with the Indians
it was not assumed without debate that they were thoroughly human,
that they possessed reason, that they could be brought into a state of
grace and acquire a Christian civilization. In more modern terminology,
it was not assumed that they had endowments that equaled those of
Europeans and could therefore become acculturated. Ginés de Sepúl-
veda (1490-1573) thought them to be "as inferior to the Spaniards in
prudence, ingenuity, virtue, and humanity as children are to adults,
and women to men. The difference between them was as great as that
between fierce and cruel persons and those who are merciful and
humane; as between the intemperate and the temperate; and he was

---

had thus baptized it, the term passed into general use as something never
before thought of. Even today, when we wish to refer to this hemisphere in
words conveying its uniqueness, we say the New World." *See also* Chap. 22,
"The Name America."

[4] Appendix, Part I.

inclined to judge it as great as between monkeys and men."[5] On the other hand Bartolomé de Las Casas (1474-1566) has gained in stature over the centuries because of his insistence that all the peoples of the world were men. "To him," says Lewis Hanke, "the Indians discovered in Spain's onward rush through the New World were not beasts, not slaves by nature, nor childlike creatures with a limited or static understanding, but human beings with all the responsibilities, capabilities, and potentialities of men everywhere."[6]

Granted that the Indians were human in the sense of being descendants of Adam, the question of their origin and migration became a persistent and controversial issue for several centuries. They could hardly be considered authochthones, descendants of a Tertiary ape of Patagonia as in Ameghino's post-Darwinian theory, since, according to Christian tradition, there had been a universal flood which only Noah and his immediate family survived. The question was: How and when did descendants of Noah reach the New World? Attempts to answer this question inspired the collection and comparison of an enormous amount of complex linguistic and cultural data, used to support varying hypotheses. Although the use of these data was less sophisticated, nevertheless the kind of problem attacked cannot fail to remind us of the contemporary search for linguistic and cultural connections between New World natives and Old World peoples.

Beginning in the sixteenth and continuing into the nineteenth century, the most popular theory of Indian origins was that they were descendants of the Ten Lost Tribes of Israel.[7] In seventeenth century

---

[5] Silvio Zavala, *New Viewpoints on The Spanish Colonization of America* (Philadelphia: University of Pennsylvania Press, 1943), p. 33.
[6] Lewis Hanke, *Bartolomé de Las Casas. Bookman, Scholar and Propagandist* (Philadelphia: University of Pennsylvania Press, 1952), p. 97. *See also Aristotle and the American Indians. A Study in Race Prejudice in the Modern World* (Chicago: Regnery, 1959).
[7] As early as 1607 Gregorio Garcia (*Origen de los Indios de el nuevo mundo*), who had been a missionary in South America for two decades, reviewed all the theories of the peopling of the Western Hemisphere advanced up to that time and evaluated the tenability of them as well. He thought the Jewish theory had some merit but did not adhere to it. (See Don Cameron Allen, "The Legend of Noah. Renaissance Rationalism in Art, Science and Letters," *Illinois Studies in Language and Literature*, Vol. 33, Nos. 3-4, 1949, pp. 121-122.) Allen remarks (p. 122): "most of the historians writing in the early part of the 17th century were so overwhelmed by the multiplicity of theories about the plantation of America that they were ready, like Acosta, to cut the Gordian knot by accepting all of them." Indeed, there is scarcely an Old World people to whom, at one time or another, some share in the peopling of America has not been attributed: Icelanders, Celts, Welsh, Norsemen, Romans, Phoenicians, Carthaginians, Egyptians, Abyssinians, East Indians, Tartars, Scythians, Chinese, Polynesians, Australians. The Jewish theory, however, was extremely persistent and illustrates the problem that was posed in its classical form. The old "Tartar" derivation, broadly inter-

Europe treatise after treatise dealing with this theory was published
by learned men. One of these authors, Georgius Hornius (1652), tells
us that the problem of the origin of the Indians was so vexed at the
time "that a girl possessed by the devil is said to have asked constantly,
'Quomode insulae animalia acceperint, et eo homines post Adamum
pervenerint?' " [x] Thomas Thorowgood's *Jewes in America, or Proba-*
bilities that the Americans are of that Race (1650) listed fifty or more
parallels between Indian and Jewish culture traits, besides discussing
linguistic ones. The author corresponded with Roger Williams who,
along with Thomas Mayhew, John Eliot, and Cotton Mather, seems to
have agreed with his thesis, as did Samuel Sewell, William Penn and
others.[9]

The Jewish theory of Indian origin was widely accepted in the
United States in the eighteenth century. Its major proponent was James
Adair.[10] In the nineteenth century this theory was canonized in the
Book of Mormon; in England, Edward King, Viscount Kingsborough,
devoted almost a lifetime in an attempt to demonstrate it.[11] Yet, Isaac

---

preted, represents the nearest approximation to modern views. Samuel F.
Haven, the librarian of the American Antiquarian Society, discussed the
various theories in what was virtually the first attempt to write a history of
American anthropology despite the title he used. ("Archaeology of the
United States, or Sketches Historical and Bibliographical, of the Progress of
Information and Opinion Respecting Vestiges of Antiquity in the United
States," *Smithsonian Contributions to Knowledge*, Vol. 8, Washington, 1856.)
By the time that Justin Winsor published his *Narrative and Critical History*
of America, Vol. 1 (Boston and New York, 1889), which contained his richly
annotated bibliographical essay, "The Progress of Opinion Respecting the
Origin and Antiquity of Man in America" (pp. 369-412), we are at the
threshold of academic anthropology, so that references to the early theories
occupy a very small space. Since that time Don Cameron Allen (*op. cit.*) has
provided the most comprehensive and detailed account of seventeenth
century theories in his chapter, "The Migrations of Men and the Plantation
of America" (pp. 113-137). For references in particular to the Jewish theory
see Justin Winsor, *op. cit.*, pp. 115-116; the Bibliographical note, Appendix
A, in Lewis Hanke, *The First Social Experiments in America* (Cambridge,
1935); "Tribes, Lost Ten" in the *Jewish Encyclopedia* (12:249-253, 1906);
Allen Godbey, *The Lost Tribes, Suggestions Towards Rewriting Hebrew*
History (Durham: Duke University Press, 1930); a brief article ("Lost Ten
Tribes of Israel") by A. F. Chamberlain in *The Handbook of American*
Indians 1:775.

[x] Allen, *op. cit.*, p. 128.

[9] *Ibid.*, p. 126. Cf. Haven, *op. cit.*, p. 5; Justin Winsor, *op. cit.*, p. 115.

[10] James Adair, *The History of the American Indians, particularly those*
Nations Adjoining to the Mississippi, East and West Florida, Georgia, South
and North Carolina, and Virginia (London: 1775). (Reprinted Johnson City,
Tenn.: Watauga Press, 1930, ed. by Samuel C. Williams.)

[11] *Antiquities of Mexico*, 9 vols. (London, 1830-48). For other nineteenth
century titles, particularly those written by "learned religionists," see Roy
Harvey Pearce, *The Savages of America. A Study of the Indian and the Idea*
of Civilization (Baltimore: Johns Hopkins Press, 1953), p. 62, note.

de la Peyrere in 1665 had already cut the Gordian knot, vilified as he was for it and taken firmly in hand by the Church. He maintained that the Bible referred only to a flood in Jewish history, not a universal flood. He thought that the first creation had taken place long before Adam and that the American Indians were not the descendants of Adam. Don Cameron Allen says that "in every sense of the word . . . he was the father of modern prehistory." [12]

Despite the limitations set by the inevitable Biblical framework in which the problem was set, we can plainly see that attempts to investigate the question of the origins of American man was a legitimate anthropological problem and that it likewise involved, in turn, the question of the origin and dispersal of mankind as a whole. We can also appreciate the complexity of the methodological issues involved insofar as evidence was sought in linguistic and cultural parallels. The same kind of methodological issues arose in later discussions of diffusion. Bock has pointed out that Sir Matthew Hale, a seventeenth century monogenist, "unlike many of his successors in the diffusionist tradition . . . was not content to establish historical connection simply with evidence on similarities. Historical evidence of migration was required. This, unfortunately, was not available, but at least Hale took great pains to demonstrate how the descendants of Noah might have reached America after the flood."[13]

Another broad anthropological problem concerning the American Indians was that of the effect of environmental surroundings. This problem concerned the human, as well as the animal, population of the New World as compared with the Old World. Initiated by the great naturalist Buffon, "the pope of eighteenth century zoologists," and followed by the even more dogmatic pronouncements of De Pauw and Raynal, the question was dramatized by Jefferson's entrance into the controversy in his *Notes on the State of Virginia*.[14]

Buffon maintained that "There is some combination of elements and other physical causes, something that opposes the amplification of animated Nature" in the New World. The animals are smaller and even domesticated species transported to the Western Hemisphere decline in size. In the American savage "the organs of generation are small

---

[12] Allen, *op. cit.*, p. 133.

[13] Kenneth E. Bock, "The Acceptance of Histories. Toward a Perspective for Social Science," *University of California Pub. in Sociology and Social Institutions*, Vol. 3, No. 2, pp. 1-132 (Berkeley and Los Angeles: University of California Press, 1956), p. 72.

[14] See, in particular, Gilbert Chinard, "Eighteenth Century Theories on America as a Human Habitat," *Proceed. Amer. Philosophical Society* 91:27-57, 1947; and Antonello Gerbi, *La Disputa Del Nuovo Mondo. Storia di una polemica, 1750-1900* (Milano-Napoli, 1955).

and feeble. He has no hair, no beard, no ardor for the female . . . . His sensations are less acute; and yet he is more cowardly and timid. He has no vivacity, no activity of mind." In short, the Indians "have been refused the most precious spark of Nature's fire." Although it is sometimes overlooked, Buffon was not arguing for inherent racial differences. His central point was that nature is not everywhere salubrious and that, generally speaking, the New World was not equal to the Old as a natural habitat for either animals or man.

Jefferson was indignant and, as Chinard has suggested, just as Buffon's remarks about the absence of large animals may have stimulated Jefferson's interest in all discoveries made here of gigantic bones in order to refute the French naturalist, "it may also be that it [Buffon's view] incited him to make every possible effort to encourage philosophical and 'literary' study of the natives, which later he evidenced in his investigations on the Indian dialects and in his instructions written on the occasion of the Lewis and Clark expedition."[15] At any rate, Jefferson vigorously defended the Indians. He found Buffon's characterization "an afflicting picture indeed, which, for the honor of human nature, I am glad to believe has no original." He said he could speak to some extent from his personal knowledge of the Indians, and, while admitting that "more facts are wanting," expressed the opinion that "we shall probably find that they are formed in mind as well as in body, on the same module with the 'homo sapiens Europaeus.' "[16] Jefferson was referring here to one of the four varieties which Linnaeus recognized within the species *sapiens* of his genus *Homo*. To Jefferson and men of his circle, whose thinking was set within the framework of the "great chain of being," the term "species" did not have precisely the meaning it assumed in later biological connotation. There were characteristic qualities inherent in all "species" from the time of creation, for they had undergone no transformation. This was the basis of the unity and equality of mankind as a "species"; it did not imply that individuals, considered as such, were born equal. The equality they possessed stemmed from their membership in a "species." One

[15] Chinard, *op. cit.*, p. 56, note.
[16] *Notes on the State of Virginia*, ed. with an Introduction and Notes by William Peden. Pub. for the Institute of Early American History and Culture at Williamsburg, Va. (Chapel Hill: University of North Carolina Press, 1955), pp. 59, 62. As one of Jefferson's biographers has pointed out [Marie Kimball, *Jefferson: War and Peace, 1776-1784* (New York: Coward-McCann, 1947), p. 286], he had consorted with the Indians since childhood and "he had an understanding of them that was vouchsafed to few of his contemporaries. As he wrote John Adams: 'In the early part of my life I was very familiar with the Indians, and acquired impressions, attachment, and commiseration for them which have never been obliterated.' " This biographer has an excellent chapter on the *Notes on Virginia*.

of the distinctive characteristics of man, as compared with other species of animals, was his adaptability to all climates and geographical conditions.[17]

Jefferson was also acquainted, at first hand, with a variety of authors who had discussed the origin of the Indians. He knew the writings of Acosta and Herrera who, along with others, did not agree with those who thought the Indians were descended from the Ten Lost Tribes.[18] Jefferson did not commit himself to this hypothesis, either, and he rejected the theory of a universal deluge; his views on this subject, in the political arena, were used as ammunition against him.[19]

Long before Jefferson's time, as far back as the discovery of the New World, native languages, customs, and beliefs were the subject of direct inquiry by many men who were closely associated with the Indians and whose persistent curiosity about aboriginal life, even though it transcended their immediate practical aims, led them to record valuable factual material and comments which sometimes strike a modern note. Such ethnographic and linguistic observations played an important role in laying much of the empirical foundation for the anthropology of a later day. Thus Lewis Hanke observes that "one may say that the founder of American Anthropology was Friar Ramon Pane, who accompanied Columbus on his second voyage (1493) for the express purpose of observing the natives and reporting on their ways" (in addition to performing his priestly duties).[20] Hanke also appraises

----

[17] Cf. Daniel J. Boorstin, *The Lost World of Thomas Jefferson* (New York: Holt, 1948), pp. 59-60, 63-64.

[18] Kimball, *op. cit.*, p. 301. Acosta's thinking probably was congenial to Jefferson on another point. In his *Natural and Moral History of the Indies* (1590), Jose de Acosta explicitly opposes as false the opinion of others that "the Indians are a brutal and bestial people without understanding, or with so little that they scarcely merit the name of men." What he asserts, on the contrary, is that "they have a natural capacity to be taught, more so than many of our own people." See Hanke, *Aristotle and the American Indians, op. cit.*, p. 90. Acosta had observed the Indians in both Mexico and Peru.

[19] See Peden's Introduction to the *Notes* (*op. cit.*, pp. xxiii, xxiv). The *Notes* were scrutinized by his political opponents. "For his interest in philosophy and science Jefferson was labelled 'howling atheist' and 'confirmed infidel'; his speculations concerning the origin of the earth's surface or the ancestry of the American Indian, for example, were said to be part of his determined campaign to undermine the Bible."

[20] Lewis Hanke, *Bartolome de Las Casas. An Interpretation of His Life and Writings* (The Hague: M. Nyhoff, 1951), pp. 63-64. We owe to Pane a brief account of the religious beliefs and folklore of the long extinct Tainos (Haiti). For a translation see Edward G. Bourne, "Columbus, Ramon Pane and the beginnings of American Anthropology," *Proceed. Amer. Antiquarian Society*, N.S. 17:310-348, 1906. *See also* Robert Streit, "Fr. Ramon Panes, der erste Ethnograph Amerikas," *Zeitschrift für Missions Wissenschaft* 10: 192-193, 1920.

Bartolomé de Las Casas as an anthropologist, pointing out that his right to be called so rests "upon his approach to the study of cultures so alien to his own. He did not automatically assume that the Indians should be measured by a Spanish yardstick but on the contrary tried to understand the importance of their customs and beliefs within the framework of their own culture. He looked at all peoples, the ancient Greeks and sixteenth century Spaniards as well as the newly discovered New World natives, as human beings in different stages of development from rude beginnings to a higher stage of culture."[21] He "concluded that the civilization of the strange beings brought to the notice of the world by the Spanish conquest was a culture not only deserving of study but also worthy of respect. Las Casas advanced the idea that Indians compared very favorably with the peoples of ancient times, and maintained that the Maya temples in Yucatan were not less worthy of admiration than the pyramids of Egypt. Most startling of all his views was the statement that in some respects Indians were superior to Spaniards. But the world was not able to learn that Las Casas was an anthropologist, because the *Apologetic History* was not printed until 1909. Few read it even today, for its text runs to 704 double-columned pages in small type, and often it is confused with the *History of the Indies*."[22]

The classic contributions of Bernardino de Sahagún and Bishop Diego de Landa, so familiar to all Meso-American scholars, need only passing mention here, as do the great quantities of linguistic material collected by missionaries. In the field of South American ethnography, the straightforward descriptive account of Jean de Lery of what he saw and heard among the Tupinamba (1557-58) may be cited as an example of the permanent usefulness of the account of an early observer. A translation of it is incorporated in the *Human Relations Area Files*. In the field of North American ethnography, according to Perry Miller, Roger Williams' *A Key into the Language of America* (1643) was "the nearest approach to an objective, anthropological study that anyone was to achieve in America for a century or more"; Miller adds that Williams was "the only Englishman of his generation" who "could treat Indian culture with respect."[23]

---

[21] Hanke, *op. cit.* (1951), p. 62. In a footnote, p. 64, the author gives bibliographical references to the use made of Las Casas by some modern anthropologists.
[22] Lewis Hanke, *op. cit.*, pp. 9-10.
[23] Perry Miller, *Roger Williams: His Contributions to the American Tradition* (New York: 1953), pp. 52-53. Another writer, Ola E. Winslow [*Master Roger Williams* (New York: Macmillan, 1957), p. 162], has pointed out that, "this *Key* is the first comprehensive book-length attempt in English to put the Indian language into print."

Coming from the same century, the *Jesuit Relations* has well-recognized ethnographic value.[24] In view of the debates about the degeneracy of the New World peoples initiated over a century later by Buffon and the early discussions by the Spanish, it may be noted that these French missionaries, despite their personal hardships, entertained no doubt about the capabilities and intelligence of the Indians. And, in the area with which they were familiar, this conclusion could not have been inferred from any dramatically visible cultural achievements. Nevertheless, in the *Relation* of 1634 it is stated that, despite the better education of the French peasants, "I have not seen anyone so far of those who have come to this country who does not confess and admit frankly that the savages have more wit than our ordinary peasants."[25]

Jefferson, in concluding his plea in defense of the capabilities of the Indians, laid particular stress upon their talent for oratory. He used Logan's speech, which he compared with the oratory of the ancients, as his prime example. From the beginning there has been much controversy about the authenticity of this speech.[26] However, it is a matter of record that Father Rale had been equally impressed with Indian oratory much earlier. In this case there was no question of different versions, or translation, or postponed recording. Yet Rale, too, made a direct and favorable comparison with European oratory. Referring to his reception by the Illinois in 1691, he wrote: "Then the chief rose and commenced his harangue. I confess to you that I admired his flow of words, the aptness and the force of the arguments which he set forth, the eloquent turn which he gave them, the choice and delicacy of the expressions with which he adorned his discourse. I am persuaded that, if I had put down in writing what this savage said to us offhand and without preparation, you would readily agree that the most capable Europeans, after much meditation and study, could scarcely compose an oration more solid or well turned."[27]

In view of the relativistic attitude towards cultural data that emerged in later professional writing by American anthropologists, it may be noted that J. H. Kennedy calls attention to the fact that a number of the Jesuits introduced a relativistic note into their commentary. Lallemant concluded that "men are men everywhere, at the ends

---

[24] Joseph D. McGuire, "Ethnology in the 'Jesuit Relations,'" *AA* 3:257-269, 1901.

[25] Quoted J. H. Kennedy, *Jesuit and Savage in New France* (New Haven: Yale University Press, 1950), p. 135.

[26] For a detailed review, see E. D. Seeber, "Critical Views on Logan's Speech," *Journal of American Folk-Lore* 60:130-146, 1947.

[27] Quoted by Kennedy, *op. cit.*, p. 139.

of the earth as well as in the middle" and that "this new world has the same nature as the old; it has its virtues and vices just like Europe." "The relator of 1657-58 felt that the French and the Indians differed mainly in taste and customs, and agreed with Le Jeune and Lallemant that they were similar in temperament. Everything, he wrote, after considering the Indian use of musk, the favorite songs of the two lands, their ways of seasoning meat, using cosmetics, dressing their hair, and clothing their bodies, was relative. But at the same time the relator took the opportunity to preach to his readers: 'The world is full of variety and inconsistency, and one will never find permanence. If someone went up on a very high tower whence he could see at his ease all the nations of the earth, he would have trouble in telling those who are wrong or right, foolish or wise, in such strange varieties and such confusion.' "[28]

One statement made by Le Jeune in 1633 is a particularly interesting example of relativism because he implies that there are cultural constituents that are of functional significance in the perception of individuals of different groups. After pointing out that the Indians he knows dislike the odor of musk "while an old piece of fat would seem to them to have a pleasant odor," he says: "Now you may judge if certain things are not more accepted to the smell of some people than others, *and whether our fancies and customs have not great power over us*." (Italics mine.)[29]

In his review of the history of the study of social organization, Sol Tax has pointed out two early observations that are of special interest since they may be taken in the nature of discoveries. John Lederer, writing about the eastern Siouan-speaking Tutelo in 1672, was the first to mention sibs, matriliny and exogamy, although not, of course, by these names. And Father Lafitau, in the eighteenth century, describing the kinship system of the Iroquois, explicitly puts his finger on "the archetype of the classificatory system which was to become a catch phrase in the infant science a century and a half later."[30] Besides this,

---

[28] Kennedy, *op. cit.*, p. 103. One of Le Jeune's explicit observations quoted by Kennedy (p. 103) will serve to illustrate the nature of Jesuit relativism. In 1633 he wrote:
"Oh, how feeble is the judgment of men. Some find beauty where others see only ugliness. The most beautiful teeth in France are the whitest, in the Maldive Islands whiteness of the teeth is a deformity, they redden them to be beautiful. And in Cochin China, if I recall aright, they paint them black. Who is right?"
[29] *The Jesuit Relations and Allied Documents*, ed. by R. G. Thwaites, Vol. 5 (Cleveland: The Burrows Co., 1896-1901), p. 153.
[30] Sol Tax, "From Lafitau to Radcliffe-Brown, A Short History of the Study of Social Organization," in *Social Anthropology of North American Tribes*, ed. Fred Eggan (Enlarged Edition, Chicago: University of Chicago

Wilhelm Schmidt sees Lafitau as "the founder of scientific ethnology," the central question of which, for Schmidt, is the reconstruction of the cultural history of primitive peoples. The chief methodological problem, then, is how to arrive at reliable chronological sequences for nonliterate peoples where archeological data or written documents are unavailable. Lafitau is important because he "laid down and developed the fundamental principle that existing uncivilized races show us the stagnant remains of earlier stages of civilization, through which the ancestors of the more advanced race passed thousands of years ago, leaving us vestiges of these earlier stages to be found among the discoverers of prehistory. Thus the still existing uncivilized races could give us the earliest image of the life of primitive man. But it was the fate of ethnology that the widespread application of this principle in the nineteenth century was unduly influenced by the dominant evolutionist and materialist theories of the time."[31] Schmidt is referring, of course, to the beginnings of the use of the "comparative method." Associated with the idea of cultural stages in the development of mankind and the notion of progress, it was used widely by the Scottish exponents of "conjectural history," as well as other eighteenth century thinkers.[32] Adam Ferguson thought that the culture of contemporary American Indians reflected "as in a mirror, the features of our own progenitors."[33] Herder said that the Germans had once been Patagonians![34] And in the early nineteenth century Auguste Comte (1798-1857) was convinced that a scientific sociology could be based on the "historical" or "comparative" method.[35] The latter was far from being an invention of cultural evolutionists in the post-Darwinian period.

Press, 1955), p. 445. Many eighteenth century writers, like David Zeisberger, recognizing unilateral descent groups, referred to them as "tribes," a terminology that we find persisting in Morgan.

[31] Wilhelm Schmidt, S.V.P., *Primitive Revelation*, trans. by Rev. Joseph J. Baierl, S.T.D. (St. Louis: B. Herder Book Co., 1939), p. 96.

[32] The term "conjectural history" was introduced by Dugald Stewart. See G. Bryson, *Man and Society*, p. 88. For the seventeenth and eighteenth century use of the "comparative method," see Kenneth E. Bock, *op. cit.*, and particularly F. J. Teggart, *Theory and Process of History* (Berkeley: University of California Press, 1945), pp. 92 ff.

[33] Quoted by Bock, *op. cit.*, p. 78.

[34] "A few centuries only have elapsed since the inhabitants of Germany were Patagonians." See selection from "Outlines of a Philosophy of the History of Man" in *The Idea of Progress. A Collection of Readings*, selected by Frederick J. Teggart, with an Introduction by George H. Hildebrand (Revised Edition, Berkeley: University of California Press, 1949), p. 313.

[35] He described it "as forming the very core of his positive philosophy and comprising the sociological method *par excellence*. . . [it aims] at the construction of a developmental social series. If we are to discern this series, if we are to avoid the confused descriptions offered by ordinary historians, if we are not to be lost in a sterile empiricism, then we must *begin* with a

There were writers, too, in the eighteenth century who, like nine-teenth century cultural evolutionists, explicitly stressed parallel devel-opment, rather than migration or historical contacts, as the explana-tion of cultural similarities. One of these was William Robertson whose *History of America*, published in London in 1777, was serialized in one hundred and fifty issues of the *Boston Weekly Advertiser*. With respect to the peopling of America he said, "it is vain either to reason or inquire because it is impossible to come to any decision. . . . Nothing can be more frivolous or uncertain than the attempts to discover the original of the Americans, merely by tracing the resemblance between their manners and those of any particular people in the ancient continent. If we suppose two tribes, though placed in the most remote regions of the globe, to live in a climate nearly of the same temperature, to be in the same state of society, and to resemble each other in the degree of their improvement, they must feel the same wants, and exert the same endeavours to supply them. The same objects will allure, the same passions will animate them, and the same ideas and sentiments will arise in their minds. The character and occupations of the hunter in America must be little different from those of an Asiatic, who depends for subsistence on the chase. A tribe of savages on the Danube must nearly resemble one upon the plains washed by the Mississippi. Instead, then, of presuming from this similarity, that there is any affinity be-tween them, we should only conclude, that the dispositions and man-ners of men are formed by their situation, and arise from the state of society in which they live."

"In every part of the earth," Robertson goes on to say, "the progress of man hath been nearly the same; and we can trace him in his career from the rude simplicity of savage life, until he attains the industry, the arts, and the elegance of polished society." Robertson then adds an acute qualification. He observes that among every people there are some customs like a seventh day consecrated to religious worship and rest, which, "as they do not flow from any natural want or desire pe-culiar to their situation, may be denominated usages of arbitrary in-stitution." Consequently, "if between two nations settled in remote parts of the earth, a perfect agreement with respect to any of these should be discovered, one might be led to suspect that they were connected

'leading rational conception' of human development or social evolution. Some broad view of history must be adopted, Comte insisted, if the different periods of civilizational growth are to be seen as stages in a general evolution. In fact, it was the rational subordination of humanity to a single law of continuous development that gave to positivism its 'exclusive and spontaneous char-acter.'" (Bock, *op. cit.*, p. 8; cf. Teggart, *op. cit.*, chaps. 9 and 10.)

by some affiinity."[36] At a later date, writers of the *Kulturkreislehre* made the same point. Robertson thinks, however, that since instances of such "arbitrary" customs, "common to the inhabitants of both hemispheres, are, indeed, so few and so equivocal, no theory concerning the population of the New World ought to be founded upon them."[37] For him, the greatest importance of the discovery of the New World natives lay in the fact that it "enlarged the sphere of contemplation, and presented nations to our view, in stages of their progress, much less advanced than those wherein they have been observed in our continent." With the exception of the "Mexican and Peruvian empires," he writes, "we behold communities just beginning to unite, and may examine the sentiments and actions of human beings in the infancy of social life, while they feel but imperfectly the force of its ties, and have scarcely relinquished their native liberty. That state of primeval simplicity, which was known in our continent only by the fanciful description of poets, really existed in the other."[38] We have here a statement, I think, which clearly parallels the attitude of the pioneer anthropologists of the nineteenth century who were motivated to learn at first hand, and to record everything possible, not only about the American Indians, but the primitive peoples of the world because the latter represented the antithesis of "civilized" man. It was the task of anthropology, particularly at a period when prehistoric archeology was in its infancy, to identify and study nonliterate peoples who typified the early steps in human progress. "Conjectural history" in the eighteenth century had already set the framework for this kind of inquiry. And the word "civilization," which only came into general use in the same century,[39] gave linguistic embodiment to the culminating stage, which was identified, of course, with the cultural attainments and values of Europe. Robertson's thinking was already set in this frame of reference. For him, nowhere in the New World had a civilized stage been fully attained. "When compared with other parts of the New World, Mexico and Peru may be considered as polished states," he writes. "But if the comparison be made with the people of the ancient continent, the inferiority of America, in improvement, will be conspicuous, and neither

---

[36] *The Works of William Robertson, D.D.*, to which is prefixed an account of the life and writings of the author by Dugald Stewart, F.R.S. Edin., *History of America*, Vol. 5 (London, 1851), pp. 225-255.

[37] *Ibid.*, p. 256.

[38] *Ibid.*, pp. 269-270.

[39] See e.g. Morris R. Cohen, *The Meaning of Human History* (La Salle: Open Court, 1947), p. 231; *Civilization—Le Mot et L'Idée*, exposés par Lucien Febvre, Émile Tonnelat, Marcel Mauss, Alfredo Niceforo, Louis Weber (Paris: Alcan, 1930); Henry Nash Smith, *Virgin Land, the American West as Symbol and Myth* (Cambridge: Harvard University Press, 1950), p. 218.

the Mexicans nor Peruvians will be entitled to rank with those nations which merit the name of civilized."[40]

It is interesting to note how Jefferson applied the eighteenth century scheme of "conjectural history" to the cultural variability he observed within the newly expanded boundaries of the United States. What he saw exhibited, following a latitudinal axis across the country from west to east, was a cultural gradient that roughly exemplified the stages in the whole cultural history of mankind. In a letter to a friend, written in his later years, he said: "Let a philosophic observer commence a journey from the savages of the Rocky Mountains, eastwardly towards our seacoast. These he would observe in the earliest stage of association living under no law but that of nature, subsisting and covering themselves with the flesh and skin of wild beasts. He would next find those on our frontiers in the pastoral state, raising domestic animals to supply the defects of hunting. Then succeed our own semi-barbarous citizens, the pioneers of the advance of civilization, and so in his progress he would meet the gradual shades of improving man until he would reach his, as yet, most improved state in our seaport towns. This, in fact, is equivalent to a survey, in time, of the progress of man from the infancy of creation to the present day."[41] Jefferson's synthesis of cultural difference in space with a temporal schema of cultural development suggests, in principle, the later "age and area" theory of Wissler and others, but on a more grandiose scale.

Jefferson emerges as a significant figure in early anthropological thinking in this country not only because of his enduring interest in the Indian, his personal investigations, and expressed opinions. Through his attitude toward rational inquiry, his active association with learned men of his time, and his role in our national government, he personifies, in a sense, the distinctive historical context in which anthropology in the United States was nourished in its infancy. He was something of a relativist and "gives the savage his due as one whom circumstances, for good and for bad, have held him in an early state of society."[42] Of fundamental importance is the fact that Jefferson's broad intellectual grasp of the science of his time enabled him to envisage specialized lines of inquiry that were open to empirical investigation by scholars

[40] Robertson, *op. cit.*, Vol. 6 (Book VII), pp. 1-2.
[41] Quoted by Roy Harvey Pearce, *op. cit.*, p. 155. Henry Nash Smith, *op. cit.*, p. 219, points out that, "when the theory of civilization became current in this country many observers were struck by its applicability to the actual state of affairs in the West. The comment was frequently made that in America one could examine side by side the social stages that were believed to have followed one another in time in the long history of the Old World." Several early nineteenth century examples are cited.
[42] Pearce, *op. cit.*, p. 94.

in the United States. In a letter (1789) to Reverend Joseph Williard, President of Harvard, he said: "What a field have we at our doors to signalize ourselves in! The Botany of America is far from being exhausted, its Mineralogy is untouched, and its Natural History or Zoology, totally mistaken and misrepresented. . . . It is for such institutions as that over which you preside so worthily, Sir, to do justice to. our country, its productions and its genius. It is the work to which the young men, whom you are forming should lay their hands."[43] While Jefferson does not mention any discipline explicitly devoted to the study of man in his letter, his own pioneer work in the collection of Indian vocabularies, his descriptive and statistical data on Indian tribal groups tabulated in the *Notes*, his excavation of a mound, and the memorandum he prepared for the Lewis and Clark expedition concretely demonstrate, in principle, the kind of inquiry that he thought could be profitably carried on in America. Thus, without an academic label, he himself and others of his circle set an example by accumulating new knowledge regarding "*Homo sapiens Americanus.*" This was anthropology, without portfolio, pursued on our own frontiers.[44]

Later recognition of this fact is on record. A. F. Chamberlain contributed an article on "Thomas Jefferson's Ethnological Opinions and Activities" to the *American Anthropologist* in 1907; Karl Lehmann-Hartleben, considering Jefferson as archeologist, says that he anticipated by a century the aims and methods of modern archeology;[45] and

---

[43] Quoted by Dumas Malone, *Jefferson and the Rights of Man* (Boston: Little, Brown, 1951), pp. 84-85. A century later (1890), instruction in anthropology actually has been initiated at Harvard.

[44] A somewhat comparable situation existed in other sciences even though their content had been more exactly defined. Writing about science in general in the days of the early republic, A. Hunter Dupree [*Science in the Federal Government* (Cambridge: Belnap Press of Harvard University Press, 1957), p. 7] says: "Science was not separate from philosophy, the arts, or literature in either organization or personnel. Within the framework of natural philosophy and natural history, the particular fields of physics and chemistry, botany, zoology, and mineralogy were clear, but nobody imagined that a man should devote his whole time to one of them. Indeed, almost none of the members [of the American Philosophical Society or the American Academy of Arts and Sciences] were even professional scientists. Many were doctors, lawyers, or clergymen, making their living and spending much of their time in ways unconnected with science."

[45] "The excavation is made, not to find objects, but to resolve an archeological problem. Every smallest detail of the evidence is observed for its own sake with painstaking minuteness, but always with the major problem in mind. Most amazing of all, a brief exploration immediately shows the inadequacy of surface excavation and leads to the establishment of the method of 'trial ditching' down to the virgin soil and to the observation of successive archeological strata which reveal the inner structure of the mound." Karl Lehmann-Hartleben, "Thomas Jefferson, Archeologist," *Amer. J. Archaeology* 47:161-3, 1943.

Jefferson as a pioneer student of American Indian languages has been reviewed several times.[46] As for the memorandum which he drew up for the Lewis and Clark expedition, in which he probably received the assistance of Benjamin Rush and others,[47] it anticipates the "Notes and Queries" approach. Wissler says: "He gave full directions for the recording of ethnographic data, surprisingly modern in tone, which might even now serve as a guide to a field worker. This document is not famous like Jefferson's draft of the Declaration of Independence but it shows the same masterful grasp of fundamentals, for he fully sensed the modern field worker's job. He went even farther in anticipating the practical value of such knowledge in promoting the acculturation of the Indians. Every graduate student of anthropology should be required to read these memoranda of Jefferson if for no other reason than to knock some of the conceit out of him."[48]

The importance of Jefferson's instructions does not lie solely in the comprehensiveness of their categories, nor in the effective use that the

---

[46] H. C. Montgomery, "Thomas Jefferson as a Philologist," *Amer. J. Philology* 65:367-371, 1944; Mable Morris, "Jefferson and the Language of the American Indian," *Modern Language Quarterly* 6:31-34, 1945.

[47] Pearce, *op. cit.*, p. 107.

[48] Clark Wissler, "The American Indian and the American Philosophical Society," *Proceed. Amer. Philosophical Society* 86:196, 1943. There is considerable rhetorical exaggeration, of course, in this statement of Wissler's. What he apparently had in mind was not simply the general categories of inquiry pertaining to Indians in Jefferson's well-known instructions, e.g., the extent and limits of their possessions; their language, traditions, and monuments; their ordinary occupations in agriculture, fishing, hunting, war, etc., and the implements for these; their food, clothing, and domestic accommodations, and so on, which have often been reprinted [e.g., in Pearce, *op. cit.*, p. 106; *The Journals of Lewis and Clark*, ed. by Bernard De Voto (Boston: Houghton Mifflin, 1953)]. Of more contemporary interest than these is the list of almost a hundred more specific topics arranged under six general headings, including morals, religion, and amusements. [See *Original Journals of the Lewis and Clark Expedition*, ed. by Reuben Gold Thwaites, 8 vols. (New York, 1904-1905), Appendix, vol. 7, pp. 283-287, entitled "Ethnological Information Desired." Although the manuscript which survives is in the handwriting of Clark, it is considered by the editor to be "a transcript of instructions from Jefferson."] Samples of these topics are: How long do the women usually suckle their children? Do they ever resort to suicide under the influence of their passions, particularly love? Do they use animal sacrifices in their worship? Do they eat the flesh of their prisoners? Have they any music, and what are their musical instruments? Do they ever adopt their prisoners as members of their Nation? The Jewish theory of American Indian origins still persisted because one question was: What affinity is there between their religious ceremonies and those of the ancient Jews?

In their paper, "The Contributions of Lewis and Clark to Ethnography," Verne F. Ray and Nancy O. Lurie (*Journal of the Washington Academy of Sciences* 44:358-370, 1954) point out that while practically all of the topics listed "were dealt with at some point in the journey. . . no one tribe was described completely in terms of these specific subjects. . . ." (p. 359.)

explorers made of them. Their wider significance is due to the fact that they established a precedent.[49] Later exploring expeditions were also instructed to secure linguistic and ethnographic information.

Jefferson's historic role was decisive in forging a link between anthropological inquiry, government enterprise, and responsibility for Indian affairs. During his lifetime a shift from decentralization to centralization of responsibility for our formal relations with the Indians came about.[50] By the late seventeen eighties the new American government had developed a policy which recognized Indian titles to western lands which had to be extinguished before the whites moved in. It was of great practical importance, then, for the government to have reliable knowledge about the western tribes. Wissler has emphasized the point that Jefferson not only saw the need for ethnographic information in relation to guiding the administration of Indian affairs but that "the acculturation of the Indians would be more effective if based upon knowledge of the aboriginal tribal culture."[51] Jefferson said in his instructions to Lewis and Clark that "considering the interest which every nation has in extending and strengthening the authority of reason and justice among the people around them, it will be useful to acquire what knowledge you can of the state of morality, religion and information among them, as it may better enable those who endeavor to civilize and instruct them, to adapt their measures to the existing nations and practices of those on whom they are to operate." Wissler's comment is: "Those wise counsels of Jefferson's were unheeded at the time, to be revived by our contemporaries as ideas original to our own era."

By the time we enter the early decades of the nineteenth century the outlines of the broad areas of anthropology as we know it today begin to emerge—linguistics, ethnology, archeology, physical anthropology—with the Indians as the chief subject of investigation. Specialization in research begins. Individual scholars can be identified as contributors to early developments in specialized fields of inquiry. There is a definition of problems, and continuity with subsequent research can be clearly discerned. Of course, all areas of investigation did not progress at the same rate; the physical measurement of the living Indians lagged far behind the study of their languages. The investigation of linguistics and ethnology was stimulated by the realization that the aboriginal languages and cultures were dying out or rapidly changing. This led to an emphasis upon the need for observations among the western tribes during the period of exploration as the frontier moved farther and

---

[49] Pearce, *op. cit.*, p. 107; Wissler, *op. cit.*, pp. 196-197.
[50] See Walter H. Mohr, *Federal Indian Relations, 1774-1778* (Philadelphia, 1933), p. 54.
[51] Wissler, *op. cit.*, p. 197.

farther west. As a consequence of the Louisiana Purchase and the
acquisition of Florida, our national territory more than doubled and
the population increased from about four million in 1790 to seventeen
million in 1840.

In addition to the sober investigations already begun by scholars
—dramatists, poets, novelists, and painters also became absorbed in
the Indian as a subject of interest, and the work of many of them
achieved great popularity. This impact of the American Indian on
American culture is one aspect of what I have characterized elsewhere
as the "backwash of the frontier."[52] Between 1820 and 1840, for
example, there were at least thirty plays with Indian themes that
appeared on the American stage. Among novelists, James Fenimore
Cooper is, of course, the prime example of an author who, in the early
eighteen-twenties, began to exploit the Indian as a subject in American
literature, although he knew nothing of Indians at firsthand. His major
source of information was the writings of the scholar-missionary John
Heckewelder.[53] At the same time, horror stories of Indian captivity,
which had captured the public fancy in the eighteenth century, continued to be popular and some became best sellers. Recently Marius
Barbeau has re-examined these accounts with reference to their value
as ethnographic documents.[54]

Thus, intricate relations soon developed between the work of
scholarly writers on the one hand, and literary artists and painters on
the other. Henry R. Schoolcraft, for instance, wrote a narrative poem on
the Creek Wars about 1821, although it was not published until 1843,[55]
and he dedicated his *Algic Researches* to Lieutenant Colonel Henry
Whiting, an army officer who had served on the frontier and was likewise the author of two narrative poems about the Indians.[56] Lewis Cass,
Governor of Michigan Territory, who was also considered an authority
on Indians at the time, joined with Schoolcraft in contributing notes to
these poems and vouched for their general fidelity to Indian usages.

---

[52] A. Irving Hallowell, "The Backwash of the Frontier: The Impact of
the Indian on American Culture," in *The Frontier in Perspective*, ed. by
Walker D. Wyman and Clifton B. Kroeber (Madison: University of Wisconsin
Press, 1957), p. 254. (Reprinted in *Annual Report of the Smithsonian Institution, 1958*, Washington, 1959.)

[53] See Paul A. W. Wallace, "John Heckewelder's Indians and the Fenimore Cooper Tradition," *Proceed. Amer. Philosophical Society* 96:496-504,
1952, who says: "Cooper poured the prejudices of John Heckewelder into the
Leather-Stocking mold, and produced the Indian of nineteenth-century con-
vention."

[54] Marius Barbeau, "Indian Captivities," *Proceed. Amer. Philosophical
Society* 94:522-548, 1950.

[55] *Alhalla* . . . (New York: Wiley and Putnam, 1843). He used the
pseudonym, Henry Rowe Colcraft.

[56] *Ontwa, the Son of the Forest*, 1822, and *Sannillac*, 1831.

Henry W. Longfellow, in turn, found in the Ojibwa myths and tales collected by Schoolcraft, the inspiration for *Hiawatha* (1855), a character which achieved world-wide fame as *the* Indian of poetry. The painters of the Western Indians, unlike most of the dramatists, poets, and novelists who achieved the greatest literary distinction in the handling of Indian themes, enjoyed firsthand contacts with their subjects. Besides rendering visual impressions of the aborigines of this newly explored region, they frequently supplied documentary details of permanent ethnographic value.

On some of its official exploring expeditions, the government employed painters, as it later employed photographers. On the Long Expedition (1819-1820), charged with the exploration of the country between the Mississippi and the Rocky Mountains, there were two artists, Samuel Seymour and Titian Peale, although only the former had official status. In the instructions issued to members of the expedition, Major Long stated: "Mr. Seymour, as painter for the expedition, will furnish sketches of landscapes. . . . He will also paint miniature likenesses, or portraits if required, of distinguished Indians, and exhibit groups of savages engaged in celebrating their festivals or sitting in council, and in general illustrate any subject, that may be deemed appropriate in his art."[57] Seymour, therefore, has been credited with being the first artist to visit this unknown country, but his paintings and sketches are somewhat disappointing as compared with the work of later artists, despite their historical importance. One of Peale's drawings is probably the earliest picture of a Plains tipi.

An artist of quite a different category, who worked independently, was George Catlin (1796-1872). He journeyed to St. Louis in 1830, made friends with William Clark, the associate of Meriwether Lewis a quarter of a century before but now Superintendent of Indian Affairs, and soon embarked on the journeys which were to bring him distinction as a painter of the western Indians in their aboriginal state. "As historical documents," writes John Ewers, "George Catlin's paintings offer a broad panorama of the Wild West as it appeared a century and a quarter ago. Indians were then as independent as their aboriginal ancestors had been when they met the first white explorers. The Great Plains were still Indian country. The few white men who entered it

---

[57] J. F. McDermott, "Samuel Seymour: Pioneer Artist of the Plains and Rockies," *Annual Report of the Smithsonian Institution, 1950,* Washington, 1951, pp. 497-509. In David I. Bushnell, Jr., *Villages of the Algonquian, Siouan, and Caddoan Tribes West of the Mississippi, Bulletin 77 of the Bureau of American Ethnology,* Washington, 1922, will be found two reproductions of paintings by Seymour as well as drawings and paintings which have been proved of ethnographic value by such men as Catlin, Bodmer, Kane, Kurz, Stanley, Rindisbacher, Wimar, etc., along with brief biographical notes.

were mostly traders and trappers. Cowboys, prospectors, land survey-
ors, and homesteaders were unknown there in the 1830's. . . . Indeed
Catlin traveled almost alone through the country of the warlike Sioux
before either Sitting Bull or Custer were born." At this period "the
average easterner and the interested European had only a vague and
confused impression of the country beyond the Mississippi and the
people who lived there. Indians appeared in the popular art of the
time as lovely dark-skinned maidens or tall handsome hunters beside
some cool forest stream. They were the romantic creations of sentimental
landscape painters, as unreal as James Fenimore Cooper's poetic red-
men in Leatherstocking Tales. On the other hand, in the widely read
horror stories of the period—the Indian captivities—Indians were presented as blood-thirsty savages who enjoyed torturing helpless
prisoners. One extreme view of the Indian was as false as was the
other."[58] In 1837 Catlin opened his Indian Gallery in New York. It included almost five hundred paintings and specimens of clothing and
handicrafts he had collected. Later he exhibited in Boston, Philadelphia
and Washington and then took his gallery to Europe in 1839. "No one
had brought the Wild West to civilization in pictorial form for everyone
to see before," says Ewers.

From this time on, graphic images of the western Indians became
more and more familiar to the American public through various sources.
When the English translation of *Travels in the Interior of North America* by Maximilian, Prince zu Wied, was published (1843), the aqua
tints of the Swiss artist Karl Bodmer (1809-1893), who had accompanied Maximilian, became known. These were based on painstaking
water colors the artist had made during a stay of eleven months on the
Upper Missouri in 1833-1834.[59] More than half a dozen of them are
used by Robert H. Lowie to illustrate his *Indians of the Plains* (1954).[60]
And the recent scholarly edition of John Treat Irving's *Indian Sketches*
(1955)[61] makes effective illustrative use of the work of Catlin, Bodmer,

[58] John C. Ewers, "George Catlin, Painter of Indians and the West,"
Annual Report of the Smithsonian Institution, 1955, Washington, 1956, pp.
494, 502.

[59] For further information of anthropological interest on early painters of
the West, see Bernard De Voto, *Across the Wide Missouri* (Boston: Houghton
Mifflin, 1947), Appendix 2, "The First Illustrators of the West." He says (pp.
404-405): "If Catlin has the priority of having first painted the West, Bodmer
was the first artist who did it justice." In 1955 the United States National
Museum exhibited more than one hundred water colors of Bodmer never
before shown.

[60] *Anthropological Handbook No. 1*, American Museum of Natural History (New York: McGraw-Hill, 1954).

[61] Edited and annotated by John Francis McDermott (Norman: University of Oklahoma Press, 1955).

and Charles Bird King (1785-1862).[62] The latter, a portrait painter who
had studied abroad under Benjamin West, was encouraged to paint
Indian chiefs visiting Washington by Thomas L. McKenney, U.S. Superintendent of Indian Trade. The first portraits were painted as early as
1821 when a formal delegation from the Pawnee, Omaha, Kansa, Oto,
and Missouri tribes came to Washington. King's portraits formed the
nucleus of a growing collection, first in the War Department, then the
Department of the Interior, and finally, greatly augmented by the work
of another prolific painter of the western Indian, John M. Stanley
(1814-1872),[63] at the Smithsonian Institution in 1858. Here it was almost completely destroyed by fire in 1865.[64] But these paintings,
especially the work of King, became world-renowned when reproductions of 120 portraits, in color, became the chief feature of the monumental triology, *The Indian Tribes of North America*, by Thomas L.
McKenney and James Hall. The first volume in the folio edition of this
book was published in 1836, followed by succeeding volumes in 1838
and 1844.

The shadow of the Indian loomed almost as large in these early
decades of the new republic as it had in the Colonial period. In so far
as scholarship was concerned, the Indian was a natural anthropological
subject for Americans even though anthropology as a discipline had not
yet been clearly defined. During the same decades when the West was
being explored and when many of the eastern Indians were being
forced beyond the Mississippi, the study of American Indian languages
began to be more systematically pursued through the contributions of
Gallatin, Duponceau, and Pickering. In archeology, although mounds
and earthworks had long been noticed, Caleb Atwater's pioneer work
was subsidized and published under the auspices of the newly founded
American Antiquarian Society. In physical anthropology, new ground
was broken by John C. Warren, soon to be followed in the eighteen
thirties by the more important work of Samuel G. Morton. Comment
already has been made on the important impetus given by Jefferson
to the collection of ethnographic data by those who began to penetrate
the vast expanse of the trans-Mississippi region. In 1822, Henry R.
Schoolcraft was appointed Indian Agent at Sault Ste. Marie where the
government had just established a fort. Here he was to marry an Ojibwa

[62] See John C. Ewers, "Charles Bird King, Painter of Indian Visitors to
the Nation's Capital," *Annual Report of the Smithsonian Institution, 1953,*
Washington, 1954, pp. 469-472, 8 pl.
[63] See W. Vernon Kinietz, *John Mix Stanley and his Indian Paintings*
(Ann Arbor: University of Michigan Press, 1942).
[64] See Frederick Webb Hodge, "The Origin and Destruction of the
National Indian Portrait Gallery," *Holmes Anniversary Volume* (Washington,
1916).

girl, master the language, and obtain the material for his pioneer collection of Indian myths and tales.

All these early efforts, then, led to the intimate association that prevailed, until recently, between American anthropology and the study
of the aborigines of this country, a fact which gave a distinctive coloring
to the early history of anthropology here as compared with its development in countries where no comparable conditions existed. Perhaps the
underlying unity implied in the study of the inhabitants of a single
great continent, despite their great diversity in many respects, accounts,
in part, for the traditional emphasis later given in the United States
to anthropology as the unified study of man. For convenience in treatment, however, I shall deal with the early history of American linguistics, ethnology, physical anthropology, and archeology separately.
Nevertheless, I hope it will be apparent that, while there was a
division of labor in personnel as well as in subject matter and the
promotion of research, the boundaries between these areas were loosely
drawn.

LINGUISTICS

Missionary enterprise in the New World demanded some mastery
of aboriginal languages. From the earliest period of contact with the
Indians, vocabularies or dictionaries were compiled, grammatical
sketches written, and parts of the Scriptures translated into Indian languages. In North America John Eliot has achieved special fame because,
in the seventeenth century, he translated the entire Bible into an
Algonkian language and wrote *The Indian grammar begun: or, An
Essay to bring the Indian language into rules, for the help of such as
desire to learn the same. . .* (1666). Eliot is representative of other,
less famous individuals who contributed to our knowledge of native
languages through description, analysis, and the compilation of word
and phrase lists. There were also those who became interested in
linguistic data because they sought supporting evidence for some particular theory of Indian origins.

Before the eighteenth century had come to an end, two events
took place in linguistic studies abroad that had vital repercussions in
this country. Both of them stimulated an interest in the languages of
the New World within the new framework of comparative and historical linguistics. The first of these events was the promotion by Catherine
the Great (1729-1796) of the systematic collection and publication of
selected vocabularies on a world-wide scale. The second was the dis-

covery by Sir William Jones (1746-1794) that Sanskrit was structurally related to Greek and Latin. He thought that all three languages must have "sprung from some common source which, perhaps, no longer exists."[1] Thus the modern era of linguistic study, which began to flourish in the nineteenth century, was foreshadowed. It was recognized, too, that America provided a great natural reservoir of linguistic information.

In connection with the enterprise initiated by Catherine, but which she soon turned over to P. S. Pallas (1741-1811), both Franklin and Washington had been asked to secure Indian vocabularies for a second edition. The later compilation by J. C. Adelung and J. S. Vater, *Mithridates, oder allgemeine Sprachenkunde,* published between 1806 and 1817, was in effect the culmination of Catherine's original plan. In this work more than eight hundred pages are devoted to the languages of the New World.[2]

At first, the great linguistic diversity of American speech forms, differing widely from each other as well as from languages of the Old World, was not fully grasped. What was looked for were similarities, some fundamental unifying characteristics. It also seemed astonishing to those who were familiar only with the languages of literate peoples that the unwritten speech of the savages of America could manifest comparable regularities. Thus, when Everett Hale wrote his Introduction to J. H. Trumbull's *Natick Dictionary* (1903), he took occasion to point out that "the linguists of the continent of Europe took it for granted, almost, that Eliot's statement regarding the grammar of the Indian tribes could not be true. It seemed to them impossible that languages so perfect in their systems and so carefully precise in their adaptations of those systems could maintain their integrity among tribes of savages who had no system of writing." Yet, later studies "have proved that the elaborate system of grammar was correctly described by Eliot, and, to the surprise of European philologists, that it is fairly uniform through many variations of dialect and vocabulary."[3] On all sides, however, it was apparent that more data were required. So the history of the study of American Indian languages at the scholarly level reflects an increasing awareness of the need for securing more reliable and carefully

[1] Holger Pedersen, *Linguistic Science in the Nineteenth Century* (Cambridge: Harvard University Press, 1931), p. 18. "Until the close of the eighteenth century," says Pedersen, "European linguistic science had advanced but little beyond the knowledge of linguistics achieved by the Greeks and Romans." (p. 1.)

[2] See Pedersen, *op. cit.;* and particularly Thomas A. Kirby, "Jefferson's Letters to Pickering," in *Philologica: The Malone Anniversary Studies,* ed. by Thos. A. Kirby and Henry B. Woolf (Baltimore: The Johns Hopkins Press, 1949).

[3] James Hammond Trumbull, *Natick Dictionary, Bulletin 25 of the Bureau of American Ethnology,* Washington, 1903, x.

recorded linguistic data before comparison, classification, and other problems could be satisfactorily investigated.

Thomas Jefferson, early in his career, sensed the need for salvaging information on American Indian languages. He was not directly influenced by events abroad. In the *Notes*, written before 1785, he says: "It is to be lamented then, very much to be lamented, that we have suffered so many of the Indian tribes already to extinguish, without our having previously collected and deposited in the records of literature, the general rudiments at least of the languages they spoke. Were vocabularies formed of all the languages spoken in North and South America, preserving their appelations of the most common objects in nature, of those which must be present to every nation, barbarous or civilized, with the inflections of their nouns and verbs, their principles of regimen and concord, and these deposited in all the public libraries, it would furnish opportunities to those skilled in the languages of the old world to compare them with these, now, or at a future time, and hence to construct the best evidence of the derivation of this part of the human race."[4] While Jefferson is convinced that the comparative study of languages is the high road to the discovery of "the affinities of nations," and his personal interest in the collection of vocabularies is always emphasized, at the same time he appreciated the need for information on linguistic structure. Over a century ago Haven pointed out that Jefferson's remarks "contain the idea that Schlegel (1808) subsequently made productive," that is, "the decisive importance and precedence which grammatical forms ought to have over single words in proving the affinities of languages."[5] Besides this, Jefferson saw the need for placing linguistic data on record so that it could be studied in the future. His own personal efforts over three decades were devoted to this end. He had hoped to publish comparative material on about fifty tribes. No one else in America had attempted anything so extensive.[6] But Jefferson was elected President in 1801 and served two

[4] *Notes on the State of Virginia, op. cit.,* p. 101.
[5] Haven, *op. cit.,* pp. 55-56.
[6] Another early student of American Indian languages was Benjamin Smith Barton (1766-1815), Professor of Materia Medica, Natural History and Botany in the University of Pennsylvania. His *New Views of the Origin of the Tribes and Nations of America* (1798) was stimulated by Pallas and dedicated to Jefferson. It contains comparative vocabularies from Indian languages and a few Asiatic languages. He thought the Indians came from Asia and expressed the view that "many hundred, perhaps three or four thousand, years have been necessary to produce the difference of dialects which we observe between many American and Asiatic nations." Barton's interest in the Indians included "antiquities" as well as linguistics; he urged the exploration of mounds and published briefly on articles taken from them. See Francis W. Pennell, "Benjamin Smith Barton as Naturalist," *Proceed Amer. Philosophical Society* 86:108-122, 1943, and Mitra, pp. 36-37.

terms. He took his linguistic manuscript to Washington, and, having learned of the work of Pallas about this time, sought to obtain a copy of the latter's book. But the pressures of the high office he had assumed interfered with his plans. The story of the loss of Jefferson's linguistic manuscript is familiar. Sent to Monticello in 1809 in a trunk, the latter was stolen and the papers scattered. Some of them were recovered and later deposited in the American Philosophical Society,[7] which Jefferson served as President from 1797 to 1815.

One of his first acts in this capacity was to consider "a plan for collecting information respecting the antiquities of North America." At the end of 1798 a formal report was presented which stated that "the first object of the committee was to invite communications from distant places and with that view the annexed circular letter has been extensively distributed." Included in the document were suggested inquiries "into the Customs, Manners, Languages, and Character of the Indian Nations, Ancient and Modern, and their migrations," as well as the solicitation of detailed information on archeological remains.[8]

Wissler, writing about the pioneer work done by members of the American Philosophical Society in studying the Indians, says that in 1815 the Society recognized linguistics by creating the "Historical and Literary Committee when Duponceau had succeeded Jefferson,"[9] who was asked to serve on this committee. However, Chinard has pointed out that while Wissler quotes from the earlier circular mentioned he "does not seem to have noticed the part played by Jefferson in the organization of the committee" that was responsible for it. Chinard's point is of prime historical importance because he concludes that "the Jeffersonian touch is easily recognized" in the late eighteenth century circular. Its subject matter, so far as the Indians were concerned, far transcended linguistics. It was truly anthropological in scope. It is, in fact, the earliest link in a chain of more and more systematic and detailed questionnaires, the purpose of which was to secure information of all kinds on the Indians. For subsequent to Jefferson's instructions to Lewis and Clark we have the questionnaires prepared by Lewis Cass, Schoolcraft, and the Smithsonian Institution, long prior to the organization of the Bureau of American Ethnology in 1879. In Chinard's words, the eighteenth century circular of the Philosophical Society may be said to "constitute the charter of American ethnology, and as such would deserve to be better known." Although amateurs by present day standards, the learned men of the Philosophical Society who were active in

---

[7] See Kimball, op. cit., pp. 291 ff.
[8] See Gilbert Chinard, "Jefferson and the American Philosophical Society," Proceed. Amer. Philosophical Society 87:263-276, 1943.
[9] Wissler, op. cit., p. 192.

promoting the study of the American Indians included pioneers in American linguistics as well as in other areas of incipient anthropological inquiry. Barton (physician), Duponceau and Pickering (lawyers), Zeisberger, Heckewelder, and Jonathan Edwards (clergymen), Jefferson and Gallatin (statesmen), Schoolcraft and Powell were all members of this Society.

In the nineteenth century, the linguistic horizon of European scholars began to broaden and historical and comparative linguistics in the modern sense got underway. As Edgerton has pointed out: ". . . scholars began to learn something of many exotic languages such as Chinese, Malayo-Polynesian and American Indian. Thus doubts were raised as to the validity of earlier notions of 'philosophical' grammar and supposed laws of language structure, which in fact were usually based chiefly on classical languages or on nothing but fancy. The great German scholar Wilhelm von Humboldt (1767-1835) was one of the first to emphasize the necessity of profound practical knowledge of as many languages as possible as a basis for linguistic generalizations. His point of view was shared by the best American linguists of his time, Pickering and Du Ponceau, who corresponded with him."[10]

John Pickering (1777-1846) made older works on American Indian languages more generally available. Among these were John Eliot's *Indian Grammar* (1822), Roger Williams' *Key* (1827), Rale's *Dictionary of the Abenaki Language* (1833), and other items, which he edited with linguistic notes and comments of his own. He wrote an article on Indian languages for the *Encyclopedia Americana* (1831); at the suggestion of Humboldt he collaborated with Vater on the section devoted to American languages in *Mithridates;* and in 1820 he published an *Essay on a Uniform Orthography for the Indian Languages of North America.* Edgerton says that this was "nothing more nor less than a start towards an international phonetic alphabet. It is, of course, crude and rudimentary when judged by modern standards. But it is highly creditable to Pickering that he saw what was needed. His alphabet was adopted by missionary societies, and it exerted an important and useful influence. . . . In fairness to the author it should be emphasized that he did not expect his symbols to suffice for all, or even fully for any Indian language. He hoped it would be taken as basic for the 'fundamental sounds,' and recommended that additions and diacritical marks be used as needed. He was merely making a praiseworthy attempt to introduce a minimal degree of order into the dreadful confusion which had prevailed up to then, and which still makes it so hard to know

---

[10] Franklin Edgerton, "Notes on Early American Work in Linguistics," *Proceed. Amer. Philosophical Society* 87:25, 1943.

what sounds those early writers were trying to represent by the letters they used."[11] Even in the early twentieth century the transcription problem persisted. In 1913 the American Anthropological Association appointed a committee "charged with the drawing up of a phonetic system of transcribing Indian languages" (Boas, Goddard, Sapir, Kroeber), which published a report in 1916.[12]

Peter Stephen Duponceau (1760-1844), French born, came to America and served in the Revolution. Just as Pickering promoted the publication or republication of early works on Indian languages, Duponceau translated and had published in the Transactions of the American Philosophical Society (1830) the Delaware grammar of David Zeisberger (1721-1808)[13] and some material collected by John G. E. Heckewelder (1743-1823).[14] Wissler points out that "he identified the Osage language as of the Siouan family" and "recognized the languages of eastern Siberia as of American Indian type and distinct from other Asiatic languages."[14a] His treatise, *Mémoire sur le système grammatical des langues de quelques nations indiennes de l'Amérique du Nord*, was published by the French Academy in 1838 and won the Volney Prize, a high distinction. He invented the term "polysynthetic" to describe the incorporating aspects characteristic of many Indian languages; first used in print in 1819, it is still employed although no longer so categorically for aboriginal American tongues.[15]

Henry Rowe Schoolcraft (1793-1864), while his knowledge of Ojibwa was thorough, did not make any distinctive contribution to the study of American linguistics—although Duponceau made use of his material in his *Mémoire*. However, "we owe to him," as Edgerton has said, "a pair of linguistic terms which have passed into general scholarly use, *inclusive* and *exclusive*, as applied to first-person plural terms of

[11] Edgerton, *ibid.*, p. 27. Pickering was an excellent classical scholar and an authority on Roman law. He declined a professorship of Greek at Harvard as he had previously declined one in Hebrew at the same institution. He was also the first president of the American Oriental Society (1842).

[12] "Phonetic Transcription of Indian Languages," *Smithsonian Miscellaneous Collections*, Vol. 66, No. 6, Washington, 1916.

[13] Zeisberger was a Moravian missionary who was adopted by the Onondaga with whom he lived in central New York (1752-1755). He wrote a grammar and dictionary of their language. His association with the Delaware began in 1762 and resulted in a dictionary and grammar.

[14] Heckewelder was another Moravian missionary, particularly notable for his *Account of the History, Manners, and Customs of the Indian Nations who Once Inhabited Pennsylvania* (1819).

[14a] Wissler, *op. cit.*, p. 193.

[15] Edgerton, *op. cit.*, p. 29. Haven, *op. cit.*, p. 67, points out that Humboldt had used the term "agglutination," Schoolcraft suggested that "holophrastic" best conveyed the idea, and others thought "encapsulated" and "coalescence" appropriate, but these terms never came into general use.

reference."[16] Schoolcraft identified this distinction as used in Ojibwa in 1834.[16a]

Albert Gallatin (1761-1849), Swiss born, a teacher of languages as a young man, later active in American business and politics, Secretary of the Treasury under Jefferson, and subsequently minister to France and England, simultaneously carried out a program of productive scholarship. He was responsible for the first systematic comparative treatment and classification of the native languages of North America. In 1836 he published *A Synopsis of the Indians within the United States east of the Rocky Mountains and in the British and Russian Possessions in North America* which, in addition to the text, contains a map showing the distribution of the Indian population according to tribes and linguistic groups.[16b] "Not only did he use all material that had been printed, and a good deal in manuscript, notably from Du Ponceau's extensive collection, but also the United States Secretary of War, at his request, sent out a printed questionnaire containing a vocabulary of six hundred words, selected sentences, and grammatical queries, which recipients were asked to answer."[17] Here we see evidence of the continuing role which the government was to play in facilitating the collection of anthropological data of various kinds. In 1842 Gallatin helped to organize the American Ethnological Society and was its first president. His final summation of data on North American Indian languages, published by the Society in 1848 when he was eighty-seven years of age, is to be found in the 188-page Introduction he wrote to Horatio Hale's *Indians of North-West America*.[17a] In his tabulation, thirty-two linguistic families are distinguished. In 1891, J. W. Powell said that Gallatin was the Linnaeus of "systematic philology relating to the North American Indians. Before his time much linguistic work had been accomplished, and scholars owe a lasting debt of gratitude to Barton, Adelung, Pickering and others. But Gallatin's work marks an era in American linguistic science from the fact that he so thoroughly introduced comparative methods, and because he circumscribed the boundaries of so many families, so that a large part of his work remains and is still to be considered sound. There is no safe

---

[16] Edgerton, *op. cit.*, p. 30.
[16a] "Lectures on the Chippewa Substantive," p. 173, Appendix II, in Henry R. Schoolcraft, *Narrative of an Expedition Through the Upper Mississippi to Itasca Lake, etc.* (New York: Harper, 1834).
[16b] *Trans. and Collections,* American Antiquarian Society, Vol. 2, 1836, pp. 1-422.
[17] Edgerton, *op. cit.*, p. 30.
[17a] "Hale's Indians of North-West America, and Vocabularies of North America," with an Introduction by Albert Gallatin, *Trans. of the Amer. Ethnological Society,* Vol. 2, 1848.

meeting place anterior to Gallatin, because no scholar prior to his time had properly adopted comparative methods of research, and because no scholar was privileged to work with so large a body of material. It must further be said of Gallatin that he had a very clear conception of the task he was performing, and brought to it both learning and wisdom."[18] Later, Goddard (1913), in the article reprinted in this volume, said that "considering the small amount of material at the time available, Mr. Gallatin's conclusions are sound and accurate." Gallatin himself once remarked that, except for his linguistic studies, all his writings were only of a "local and ephemeral importance."

After Gallatin's death a considerable period elapsed before the classification of Indian languages that he had initiated was carried further by Powell. In the interim, however, the Smithsonian Institution promoted the collection of vocabularies and other linguistic information. A pamphlet prepared by George Gibbs (1815-1873) was issued in 1863.[18a] It was entitled *Instructions for research relative to the Ethnology and Philology of America.* Its philology section includes the phonetic alphabet recommended (presumably based on Pickering), as well as a standard vocabulary of 211 words. "It is mainly the one prepared by the late Hon. Albert Gallatin, with a few changes made by Mr. [Horatio] Hale [1817-1896], the Ethnologist of the United States Exploring Expedition [1838-1842], and is adopted as that upon which nearly all the collections hitherto made for the purpose of comparison have been based. For the purpose of ascertaining the more obvious relations between the various members of existing families, this number is deemed sufficient. The remote affinities must be sought in a wider research, demanding a degree of acquaintance with their languages beyond the reach of transient visitors." In other words, it was clearly recognized that, since linguistic data at this time could not be secured in the field by experts, some standardized and comparable material collected by amateurs was better than none at all.

A new chapter in American linguistics opened when Major John Wesley Powell (1834-1902) entered the field. Although he was not a trained linguist, his interest long antedated the founding of the Bureau of American Ethnology which, under his direction, became such an effective instrument in promoting the collection and publication of basic material in the linguistic field. Powell's original interests were in geography and geology, and even in his later life (1881) he assumed the directorship of the United States Geological Survey without re-

---

[18] J. W. Powell, *Indian Linguistic Families of America North of Mexico, Seventh Annual Report of the Bureau of Ethnology*, Washington, 1891, pp. 9-10.
    [18a] *Smithsonian Miscellaneous Collections*, No. 160, 33 pp.

linguishing his post in the Bureau. But under the stimulus of his good friend Joseph Henry (1797-1878), Secretary of the Smithsonian Institution at the time of his western explorations, Indian cultures and languages became one of his primary and enduring concerns.

To understand the influence of Henry on Powell, we must look briefly at the former's part in the development of anthropology at this time. Previous to his election as the first secretary of the Smithsonian Institution in 1846, Joseph Henry, professionally a physicist, had submitted a plan of organization. Among other things, he envisaged the collection of data on the Indians which he considered part of *anthropology*. Henry's use of this term in its broadest sense in his 1877 *Report* is of considerable historic interest to us now, as is the contemporary interest in the study of man reflected in his remarks. He says that "anthropology, or what may be considered the natural history of man is at present the most popular branch of science. It absorbs a large share of public attention and many original investigators are assiduously devoted to it. Its object is to reconstruct, as it were, the past history of man, to determine his specific peculiarities and general tendencies." He then goes on to say that "American anthropology early occupied the attention of the Smithsonian Institution" and that "to collect all the facts which could be gathered in regard to the archeology of North America, and also of its ethnology, or, in other words, an account of its present Indian inhabitants, was considered a prominent object in the plan of operations of the establishment."[19] It was no accident then that Henry was responsible for the preparation of questionnaires on subjects such as language, ethnography and archeology which, printed and distributed to missionaries, army men, teachers, engineers, government officials and factors at trading posts, solicited information which could then be filed in the Smithsonian Institution. One of these pamphlets has been mentioned. Another, issued in 1867, was entitled, "Circular relating to Collections in Archeology and Ethnology."

Thus, when Powell consulted Henry about his original western explorations in 1867, the latter suggested that he pay some attention to the Indians of the area. As one writer has said: "The request could not have been made to a more responsive student. All of the western surveys except that of King studied the Indians to some extent, only

---

[19] *Annual Report of the Smithsonian Institution, 1877*, Washington, 1878, p. 22. In a much earlier *Report* (1857, p. 36), he had said: "It is the sacred duty which this country owes to the civilized world to collect everything relative to the history, manners and customs, the physical peculiarities and, in short, all that may tend to illustrate the character and history of the original inhabitants of North America."

Powell studied them with passion."[20] Powell seized every opportunity
for firsthand contact with the Indians in order to collect linguistic and
ethnographic data.[21] Because of this, his experience more closely parallels
that of later anthropological field workers than it does that of his predecessors who studied the native languages. He gained a "tolerable
speaking acquaintance," as he himself says, with several Shoshonean
languages,[22] and there is plenty of evidence to show that he respected
the Indians and gained their respect. On a preliminary trip to northeastern Utah the year before his famous exploration of the canyon of
the Colorado River in 1869, he came into intimate contact with a band
of Utes camped near his own cabins on the White River. He not only
made friends with these Indians; he established a tie with them which
probably is unique in the annals of field work. Since they were entirely
dependent upon their bows and arrows because they had acquired no
firearms, Powell's party supplied these Utes with game during the winter. He spent evening after evening with them, making linguistic and
ethnographic inquiries. No one else had studied these people, and his
biographer says: "Powell's vocabularies of Ute words were the first that
were ever recorded, and his systematic collections of their handicraft
were a revelation to the Smithsonian Institution."[23] This pioneer plunge
into anthropological field work had a lasting effect upon the Major's
subsequent career. In 1876 Powell obtained permission from Joseph
Henry to examine and publish the 670 Indian vocabularies which had
been accumulated by the Smithsonian.[23a] The following year his first
linguistic publication, *Introduction to the Study of Indian Languages*,
appeared, which fitted into the program of systematic inquiry already

[20] Wallace Stegner, *Beyond the Hundredth Meridian. John Wesley
Powell and the Second Opening of the West,* with an Introduction by
Bernard De Voto (Boston: Houghton Mifflin, 1954), p. 134.
    [21] In his *Report of the Survey of the Colorado River of the West*, 42nd
Congress, 3rd Session, House Misc. Document, No. 76 (1873), pp. 7-8, Powell
says: "It has been my habit to have two or three intelligent Indians ride
with me wherever I have gone. This has afforded a rare opportunity for
talking with them on the journey and in camp, and I have made it available
in the study of their language, having collected more than 2,000 words, and
obtained some knowledge of the grammar of their language, such as the
declension of the pronoun and noun, conjugation of the verb, modification
of the adjectives, their use of numerals, and many idiomatic expressions. I
have also discovered among them a very elaborate system of mythology,
which is their explanation for the origin of things, their authority for habits
and customs, and their common or unwritten law. I have also collected a
number, perhaps three or four score, of their simple songs. Their marriage and
burial customs have been noted and many other interesting facts observed."
    [22] *Indian Linguistic Families, op. cit.,* p. 140.
    [23] William Culp Darrah, *Powell of the Colorado* (Princeton: Princeton
University Press, 1951), pp. 105-106.
    [23a] See *Annual Report of the Smithsonian Institution, 1876*, p. 35.

initiated by Henry. Powell's publication was undertaken as a revised edition of the Gibbs pamphlet already mentioned, and was designed as a guide for those who were interested in recording Indian languages; it contained a word list and instructions for recording, spelling, and grouping vocabularies.[24]

J. G. Shea, in the sixties and seventies, may be said to have promoted the study of Indian linguistics independent of government through the initiation of his *Library of American Linguistics;* and D. G. Brinton, among the first to appreciate the value of texts,[25] began the publication of his *Library of American Literature* later. Yet the determinative role which Powell played in stimulating the collection and publication of linguistic data can scarcely be overestimated. When he assumed the directorship of the Bureau of American Ethnology in 1879, he established a tradition which gave high priority to linguistic studies, many of which appeared in the *Bulletins.* When his own epochal *Indian Linguistic Families* was published in the *Seventh Annual Report* in 1891, it was presented with scholarly modesty. He reviewed the work of his predecessors; he referred to the assistance he had received from his associates (James C. Pilling and Henry W. Henshaw); and he explicitly called attention to the fact that the accompanying map was to be regarded as tentative, "setting forth in visible form the results of investigation up to the present time, as a guide and aid to future effort."[26] So far as Bureau publications are concerned, Powell's linguistic program may be said to have culminated long after his death when the last volume of the *Handbook of American Indian Languages,* edited by Franz Boas, was issued in 1938.[27] So far as any final classification of

---

[24] Darrah, *ibid.*, p. 260. The volume was originally planned as the first part of a more general manual of ethnology. It was "used by all the amateur and part-time workers who collaborated in Powell's studies of the Indian languages." (Stegner, *op. cit.*, p. 398, note 15.) Powell's biographer (Darrah, p. 261) says that: "It was on the basis of this monograph and the promise it held that Secretary Baird sponsored Powell for the directorship of the new bureau."

[25] Wissler, *op. cit.*, p. 194.

[26] Powell, *op. cit.*, p. 26.

[27] In the Preface to the first volume (1911), Boas says that it "had its inception in an attempt to prepare a revised edition of the 'Introduction to the Study of Indian Languages' by Major J. W. Powell." He goes on to say that: "During the first twenty years of the existence of the Bureau of American Ethnology much linguistic material had been accumulated by filling in the schedules contained in Major Powell's Introduction and in this manner many vocabularies had been collected while the essential features of the morphology of American languages remained unknown. It seemed particularly desirable to call attention in a new edition of the Introduction, to the essential features of the morphology and phonetics of American languages, and to emphasize the necessity of an analytic study of grammar." Part 1 of the *Handbook* was published as the *Bulletin 40 of the Bureau of American*

the languages of the New World is concerned, whether in North America or southward, this problem still awaits solution.[28]

ETHNOLOGY

Following the discovery of the New World, as already has been mentioned, cultural as well as linguistic facts were put on record by those whose contact with the Indians had other major aims. Later, led by Jefferson and the Philosophical Society, an attempt was made to promote the collection of ethnographic, archeological, and linguistic information on a wider scale by interested amateurs.

There was one eighteenth century educator, however, who suggested a radically different plan for securing reliable information about the aborigines. While it was not acted on at the time, it was thoroughly modern in conception. The suggestion was that someone fully prepared for the task (i.e., a philosopher) should make it his *primary* business to go out and live with the Indians, studying on the spot the manners and customs of those groups which we should now call totally unacculturated. The man who advanced this idea was Samuel Stanhope Smith (1750-1819), a clergyman who first served as professor of moral philosophy at the College of New Jersey (Princeton), and was president of this institution from 1795 to 1812. In a letter written in 1784 he says: "As the character, and manners, and state of society among the savages, would make a very important part of the history of human nature, it appears to me to be an object that merits the attention of literary societies, not less than the discovery of new islands and seas. Hitherto the Indians have been observed, chiefly within the compass of the United States, and by traders or soldiers, who had objects very different from philosophy in their view. The character of the observers has necessarily confined their observations, in a great measure, to that part of the Indian tribes that has been corrupted by our interests, or intimidated by our injuries. . . . But I conceive it would not be unworthy of societies established for extending human knowledge, to employ good philosophers, who should be hardy enough for the undertaking, to travel among their remotest nations, which have never had any intercourse with Europeans; to reside among them on a familiar footing; to dress and live as they do; and to observe them when

---

Ethnology, 1911; Part 2 followed in 1922. Between 1933 and 1938 additional linguistic sketches were separately published. These were combined (1938) and published as Part 3 under the imprint of J. J. Augustin, New York.

[28] See J. Alden Mason, "Introduction," *The Languages of South American Indians, Bulletin 143 of the Bureau of American Ethnology*, Vol. 6 (Washington, 1950), pp. 157-317.

they should be under no bias or constraint. We should then see whether there be any essential difference between them and the tribes with which we are already acquainted. We should discover, in the comparison of their languages, their different degrees of improvement; their affinities with one another; and, at the same time, the objects with which each has chiefly conversed, that have occasioned a variety in their terms and phrases. But above all, we should discover the nature and extent of their religious ideas, which have been ascertained with less accuracy than others, by travellers who have not known to set a proper value upon them."[1]

At this time, Smith was thinking about the American aborigines in the anthropological frame of reference that was characteristic of much of eighteenth century thought: circumstances and way of life are the major determining factors to be considered. Man everywhere shares a common human nature, and common potentialities.[2] Man has never been confined, "like the inferior animals to a bounded range beyond

---

[1] Michael Kraus, "Charles Nisbet and Samuel Stanhope Smith—Two Eighteenth Century Educators," *The Princeton University Library Chronicle* 6:22-23, 1944. It would be interesting to know whether Smith had read Rousseau. The latter made a similar suggestion, in a footnote to his *Dissertation on the Origin and Foundation of the Inequality of Mankind*, published in 1755. [*The Miscellaneous Works of Mr. J. J. Rousseau*, 5 vols., ed. C. E. Vaughn (French Edition, London, 1767), I, pp. 292 ff. *The Political Writings of Jean Jacques Rousseau*, 2 vols. (Cambridge, England, 1915), I, note on pp. 211-12.] Rousseau points out that despite the fact that Europeans have been "employed in running over the other parts of the world. . . the people of Europe are the only men upon earth we are as yet well acquainted with. . . ." This is due to the fact that "there are but four kinds of people who make long voyages; there are seamen, merchants, soldiers, and missionaries. Now, it is hardly to be expected that the three first should be very good observers; and with respect to the last, even were they not, like the rest, subject to the prejudices of their occupation, we may conceive they are too much taken up by the immediate duties of their sublime vocation to descend to engage in researches which may seem calculated merely to gratify curiosity; and which would interfere with the more important labors to which they are devoted." Rousseau goes on to say that he can hardly conceive "how it is, that in an age wherein useful and polite literature are so much affected, there are not two men properly connected and rich, the one in money, and the other in genius, both fond of glory and aspiring after immortality; one of which should be willing to sacrifice 20,000 crowns of his fortune, and the other ten years of his life, to make a justly celebrated voyage around the world; not to confine their observations in such a voyage to plants and minerals, but for once to study men and manners, and, after so many ages spent in measuring and surveying the house, to make themselves really acquainted with those who live in it."

[2] Smith argued in his *Essay on the Causes of the Variety of Complexion and Figure in the Human Species*, 1787 (Second Edition, Enlarged, 1810, p. 244), that only when "the whole human race is known to compose only one species," is it possible for "the science of human nature" to become "susceptible of system."

which he could not pass either for the acquisition of science, or, the enlargement of his habitation. . . . The lower animals have no defense against the evils of a new climate but the force of nature. The arts of human ingenuity furnish a defense to man against the dangers that surround him in every region."[3] Smith was a thoroughgoing environmentalist.[4] He viewed the Indians in their total setting; physical environment and culture were the major variables to be considered. The "state of society, which may augment or correct the influence of climate. . .is itself a separate and independent cause of many conspicuous distinctions among mankind. These causes may be infinitely varied in degree; and their effects may likewise be diversified by various combinations. And, in the continual migrations of mankind, these effects may be still further modified, by changes which have antecedently taken place in a prior climate, and a prior state of society."[5] Thus when Smith, in his letter, says that the kind of approach to the study of the Indians he proposes "would make a very important part of the history of human nature" it must be understood that he advanced his idea with a definite anthropological hypothesis in mind. He was not concerned at all, as were others later, with the collection of ethnographic information with any practical or ap-

---

[3] Quoted by Daniel J. Boorstin, *The Lost World of Thomas Jefferson* (New York: Holt, 1948), p. 64.
[4] Referring to instances of "persons who have been taken captive in infancy from Anglo-American families and grown up in the habits of savage life," he says (*op. cit.*, p. 172): "These descendents of the fairest European universally contract such a resemblance of the natives, in their countenance, and even in their complexion, as not to be easily distinguished from them; and afford a striking proof that the differences in physiognomy between the Anglo-American, and the Indian depend principally on the *state of society.*" Generalizing further (p. 174), he asserts his conviction that "if the Anglo-American, and the Indian were placed from infancy in the same state of society, in this climate which is common to them both, the principal differences which now subsist between the two races, would in a great measure, be removed when they should arrive at the period of puberty."
With this hypothesis in the forefront of his thinking, it is intelligible why it was that in the second edition of his *Essay* he "annexed some strictures on Lord Kames' dissertation *On the Original Diversity of Mankind,*" (p. 6), for the latter has been characterized as "the first of the 'racialists' in the interpretation of human society" [Gladys Bryson, *Man and Society: The Scottish Inquiry of the Eighteenth Century* (Princeton, 1945), p. 66]. Since there was no way of settling such issues at the time, what is of historic interest is Smith's emphasis upon what he called "the state of society" (i.e., "diet, clothing, lodging, manners, government, arts, religion, agricultural improvements, commercial pursuits, habits of thinking, and ideas of all kinds naturally arising out of this state, infinite in number and variety," p. 176) in *"multiplying the varieties of mankind."* (p. 6.) He notes in the "advertisement" to the second edition that whereas Blumenbach has laid some stress on climate he has "wholly omitted the second type [i.e., the state of society] which I have endeavoured to illustrate." (p. 6.)
[5] *Op. cit.*, p. 244.

plied ends in view. This kind of detachment was long in abeyance after his time despite the increase in the quantity and quality of ethnographic data.

We can also appreciate why it was that Smith wanted his ideal ethnologist to study unacculturated Indians.[6] By the time trained anthropologists did enter the scene they were compelled, for the most part, to study Reservation Indians and what, at a later period, some invidiously called "memory cultures." For it is an historic fact that the frontier in Turner's sense (i.e., the existence of vast reaches of free arable land) was closed by 1890 and governmental relations with the Indians had become stabilized. This, incidentally, was just a few years before Boas became professor of anthropology at Columbia and began training anthropologists there.

The preacademic period of the nineteenth century presents the same general picture in the study of ethnology as was the case in linguistics. Until the founding of the Bureau of American Ethnology in 1879, investigations were carried on by individuals whose pursuit of the subject was not primarily vocational. What is remarkable is the immense amount of material that was accumulated under these conditions, the quality of so much of it, the emergence and definition of basic problems, and the impetus given to later investigations in the academic period when the scope of American anthropology far transcended the study of American Indians.

Meriwether Lewis and William Clark demonstrated on their famous expedition (1804-1806) that it was possible for untrained men, guided only by the instructions with which they had been provided by Jefferson, and continually faced with linguistic barriers in direct communication with their informants, to collect an immense and valuable body of ethnographic fact. Verne F. Ray and Nancy Oestreich Lurie, in their article "The Contributions of Lewis and Clark to Ethnography,"[7] have been generous in their praise. They characterize these explorers as "good social scientists. . .unappreciated forerunners in a tradition of field research that led to the recognition of the superiority of American field work and the establishment of a sound science of ethnology."

---

[6] Referring to the Brotherton Indians, the remnants of the Pamunkey in Virginia, and other specific cases, Smith observes (p. 271) that "they afford a proof of the deterioration of the mental faculties which may be produced by certain states of society, which ought to make a philosopher cautious of proscribing any race of men from the class of human beings, merely because their unfortunate condition has presented to them no incentives to awaken genius, or afforded opportunities to display its powers." Previously he took Jefferson to task for his relatively unfavorable judgment of the potentialities of Negroes, observed only as slaves.

[7] *Journal of the Washington Academy of Sciences* 44:358-370, 1954.

Lewis "was a man who on the one hand had a mind geared to social scientific analysis and on the other was capable of 'applying' anthropology in its most modern sense. The nascent development of a purposeful social science was present in the researches carried out by him and his co-leader, Clark." Considering the fact that "most of the data in the journals were gathered through the unsatisfactory mediums of sign language, the Chinook jargon, or interpretation through two or more languages before reaching English," this is, indeed, high praise. It is based on the attitude with which the explorers approached their subjects, the nature of their basic assumptions, the discrimination with which they recorded their data and the caution with which they made generalizations. Ray and Lurie point out that as social observers in the field they showed intellectual respect for the Indians, as well as for their rights and property, "even at the cost of the objectives of the expedition." They "consistently identified sources of their information and distinguished between data obtained from a member of a subject tribe as compared to that given by neighboring tribesmen." Moreover, "the explorers' descriptions of aspects of material culture are time and again equal or superior to accounts in modern ethnographies." Besides this, they seem to have been at one "with modern social scientists in judging cultural differences to be the result of learning, not the consequence of innate characteristics of intellect varying from race to race. They also recognized individual traits of personality to be due to training, not biological inheritance."

Although Lewis and Clark did indulge in some generalizations about Indians, they were alert to regional differences which they characterized in terms of what we now would call cultural values, but which they called "personality" characteristics. In effect, they set up three culture areas: "the Plains, Plateau, and Northwest Coast. These are, of course, physiographic as well as culture areas, but Lewis and Clark established them as the latter, categorizing on the basis of cultural personality or character. . . .The Plains people were suspicious, treacherous, warlike; the Plateau, mild, generous, happy, and hospitable; the Northwest Coast, untractable, sharp, and competitive—given to driving hard bargains." Since the handsomely printed and carefully edited Thwaites Edition of the journals and related materials was not published until a century after the expedition, effective use of the anthropological data collected by Lewis and Clark was difficult. In the opinion of Ray and Lurie this information has even now been unduly neglected.

Lewis and Clark, of course, had no time to settle down and become intimately acquainted with a single tribal group or to master any Indian language. Nor was any one ethnic group completely described in

terms of their questionnaire. Consequently their material differs considerably in form and content from the pioneer work that had been
done in the East by David Zeisberger (1721-1808) and John G. E.
Heckewelder (1743-1823). Wissler calls these latter men "the first great
leaders in American ethnography."[8] Both had ranged less widely than
Lewis and Clark, had a practical knowledge of the languages of the
people among whom they worked, and were, in addition, held in high
scholarly repute by their contemporaries. Zeisberger lived with the
Onondaga for several years and wrote a monumental dictionary. In
1762 he began a long sojourn with the Delaware. His *History of the
North American Indians,* translated and edited by Archer B. Hulbert
and William N. Schwarze, was published by the Ohio State Archaeological and Historical Society (1910).[9] Heckewelder was long associated
with the Delaware and was a correspondent of Peter Duponceau who
translated his influential work, *An Account of the History, Manners
and Customs of the Indian Nations Who once Inhabited Pennsylvania
and the Neighboring States* (1819), into French.[10] Wissler says that
since Heckewelder "regarded the beliefs and mythologies of Indians
worth recording as a part of their social histories" and insisted that "the
Indian was not a beast," "that he had intelligence, ability and moral
worth," he met some opposition in the Philosophical Society which
published his book, because certain members "considered no Indian
beliefs and traditions of value because they were pagan and further
because not susceptible of documentary proof."[11] Mitra says that
"Heckewelder was rearing the scaffolding by which the philological
structures of Pickering, Du Ponceau and Gallatin on the one hand, and
the ethnographic monuments of Schoolcraft on the other were later
built up."[12]

At the same time, it should not be forgotten that, in the early
decades of the nineteenth century, the need for the immediate collection of ethnographic facts on one frontier other than the Far West, was
appreciated by an individual far removed from scholarly circles. The

---

[8] Wissler, *op. cit.,* p. 197.
[9] Edmund de Schweinitz published *The Life and Times of David
Zeisberger* in 1870. For further information see Erminie Wheeler-Voegelin,
"Some Remarks and Annotations concerning the Traditions, Customs, Lan-
guages, etc. of the Indians in North America from the Memoirs of the
Reverend David Zeisberger, and other Missionaries of the United Brethren,"
Ethnohistory 6:42-69, 1959.
[10] For an example of the Heckewelder-Duponceau correspondence, see
Erminie Wheeler-Voegelin, "John Heckewelder to Peter S. Du Ponceau,"
Ethnohistory 6:70-81, 1959.
[11] Wissler, *op. cit.,* p. 197.
[12] Panchanan Mitra, *A History of American Anthropology* (University of
Calcutta, 1933), p. 95.

influence of Lewis Cass, Governor of Michigan Territory (1813-1831) and *ex officio* Superintendent of Indian Affairs, should not be overlooked. Later Secretary of War under Jackson, when he dealt chiefly with Indian affairs, Senator from the new state of Michigan (1845-1847), and Secretary of State (1857-1860), Cass achieved fame not as a scholar, but rather as one of the influential political figures of his time. Nevertheless, because of his personal contacts with Indians on the old northwest frontier, who nicknamed him "Big-Belly," and his role in the negotiation of many treaties, he achieved a considerable reputation as an authority on the Indians.[13] Because of its rarity, the 64-page questionnaire on ethnology and linguistics that Cass published in 1823 under the title, *Inquiries Respecting the History, Traditions, Languages, Manners, Customs, Religion, Etc. of the Indians, living within the United States*, has receded into obscurity.[14] Yet historically, it is important as a chronological link between Jefferson's instructions to Lewis and Clark, as well as Pickering's *Essay on a Uniform Orthography* (1820), and the questionnaire circulated by Schoolcraft when he began his monumental survey under government auspices. As has been noted, Gallatin used the same technique in collecting linguistic data and Morgan later used it in securing schedules of kinship terms. Thus, this method was well established by the time the Smithsonian Institution was in full operation and Joseph Henry initiated his questionnaires.

Lewis Cass prepared his questionnaire after returning from the government expedition he led through the Great Lakes to the headwaters of the Mississippi River in 1820 because, as he says in the Preface: "The time for collecting materials to illustrate the past and

---

[13] See Frank B. Woodford, *Lewis Cass, The Last Jeffersonian* (New Brunswick: Rutgers University Press, 1950), pp. 138-139; 146-147. Cass gained particular notoriety by charging that Cooper had idealized his Indians after the manner of Heckewelder. See his reviews of books dealing with the Indians in *North American Review* 22:53-119, 1826; 24:357-403, 1828.

[14] Generous excerpts from this questionnaire and an outline of its categories may be found in Appendix B (1) in Mentor L. Williams, *Schoolcraft's Indian Legends* (East Lansing: Michigan State University Press, 1956). For the history of this pamphlet, see Vernon Kinietz, *Delaware Culture Chronology*, Prehistory Research Series, Vol. 3, No. 1, Indiana Historical Society (Indianapolis, 1946), p. 15. An original questionnaire of 30 pages was printed in 1821 and was supplemented by another a short time later. Kinietz says: "In 1823, both pamphlets were reprinted and bound together with continuous paging. The queries were widely distributed among Indian agents, traders, and others who might be able to furnish information on specific tribes." He was unable to locate a copy of the questionnaire in its original form. [Foreword to C. C. Trowbridge, *Meeãrmeear Traditions*, ed. Vernon Kinietz, Museum of Anthropology, University of Michigan, Occasional Contributions, No. 7 (Ann Arbor, 1938).] Of the 1823 edition Kinietz was able to locate only three extant copies (*Shawnee Traditions;* C. C. Trowbridge's *Account;* Vernon Kinietz and Erminie W. Voegelin, eds.,

present conditions of the Indians is rapidly passing away."[15] It was on this expedition that Cass first met Schoolcraft, who was engaged by Calhoun, then Secretary of State, as an expert in mineralogy and geology.[16] The ethnological section of the *Inquiries* included more than twenty general categories covering "Statistical Information" as well as "Astronomy-Mathematics" and "Music and Poetry." The questions themselves number upwards of three-hundred fifty, many more than are to be found in Jefferson's instructions. The linguistic section runs to 36 pages. Cass sent his *Inquiries* to traders, military men, and Indian agents within his jurisdiction, requesting replies. He evidently intended to collate the returns himself, since Schoolcraft, writing in 1825, says that the public is justified in "anticipating from his pen an elementary work upon the aborigines which every person who has directed his thoughts to the subject has admitted to be a desideratum in our vernacular literature."[17]

Apparently Cass was not altogether satisfied with the quality of the data.[18] At any rate, no over-all treatment of the information collected ever appeared. But some manuscripts embodying ethnographic data organized on the plan of the *Inquiries* of Cass have been discovered and published in this century. A report on the Sauk and Fox, prepared by Thomas Forsyth in 1827 for William Clark, then Superintendent of Indian Affairs in St. Louis, was published in 1912.[19] Still later, two manuscripts by C. C. Trowbridge, who was associated with Cass on the 1820 expedition, were published. The one on the Miami [Meeãrmeear] was sent to Cass in 1825.[20]

Occasional Contributions, op. cit., No. 9, 1939, note p. xix). Kinietz does not say where these are to be found, but Dr. Wheeler-Voegelin informs me (letter, April 2, 1959) that the Clements Library, University of Michigan, has one, and another is in the library of the American Antiquarian Society. In the Foreword to *Meeãrmeear Traditions,* Kinietz remarks (p. vi): "The distribution of questionnaires may not have originated with Cass, but it is interesting to note that the same technique was subsequently used by Schoolcraft, Morgan, and Powell."

[15] Mentor L. Williams, *op. cit.,* p. 289.
[16] Schoolcraft wrote the semiofficial report of this expedition. See *Narrative Journal of Travels Through the Northwestern Region of the United States Extending from Detroit through the Great Chain of American Lakes to the Sources of the Mississippi River in the Year 1820,* ed. by Mentor L. Williams (East Lansing: Michigan State College Press, 1953).
[17] Quoted by Williams, *Schoolcraft's Indian Legends,* p. 288.
[18] See letter to Schoolcraft quoted by Williams, *op. cit.,* p. 288.
[19] See Emma H. Blair, ed., *Indian Tribes of the Upper Mississippi Valley and Region of the Great Lakes,* 2 vols. "An Account of the Manners and Customs of the Sauk and Fox Nations of Indians" (2:183-245), (Cleveland: Clark, 1912).
[20] See the *Occasional Contributions* from the Museum of Anthropology of the University of Michigan No. 7 and 9, *op. cit.*

Henry R. Schoolcraft (1793-1864), first associated with Cass on the 1820 expedition and again on a treaty-making party in 1821, achieved fame as a pioneer in American anthropology. But H. R. Hays' recent characterization of Schoolcraft as "America's first social anthropologist and the first genuine field anthropologist in the world"[21] somewhat exaggerates his actual historical position. In 1822, through the influence of Cass, Schoolcraft was appointed Indian agent at Sault Ste. Marie, where Ft. Brady had just been established. Schoolcraft referred to it as "that remote outpost" in his memoirs. He retained this position until 1841, the agency moving to Mackinac in 1833. Schoolcraft met Thomas McKenney during this period when the latter was negotiating a treaty at Fond du Lac and spoke to him about collecting information on "literary topics." In 1832 he discovered the true source of the Mississippi in the lake he named Itasca.[22]

Immediately upon arriving at Sault Ste. Marie, Schoolcraft began collecting linguistic and ethnographic material along the lines suggested in the *Inquiries* of Cass. In the same letter in which the latter complained about the quality of the material that had come in, he said to Schoolcraft: "I may safely say that what I received from you is more valuable than all my other stock . . . . The result of your inquiries into the Indian language is highly valuable and satisfactory. . . . I should be happy to have you prosecute your inquiries into the manners, customs, etc. of the Indians. You are favorably situated and have withal such unconquerable perseverance, that I must tax you more than other persons."[23] Thus Schoolcraft was launched upon a future career which, beginning with an unrivaled firsthand acquaintance with the Great Lakes region and a particularly intimate association with the Ojibwa, since his first wife was an educated woman of mixed blood, culminated in his six-volume encyclopedia, *Historical and Statistical Information Respecting the History, Condition, and Prospects of the Indian Tribes of the United States,* compiled under government auspices and published in Washington (1851-1857).

It may be significant that, among the questions under the heading of "Music and Poetry" which Cass included in his *Inquiries,* there was one which ran: "Do they relate stories, or indulge in any work of imagination? Have they any poetry?" At any rate, less than a month after

---

[21] H. R. Hays, *From Ape to Angel. An Informal History of Social Anthropology* (New York: Knopf, 1958), p. 5.

[22] For biographical data on Schoolcraft, consult Chase S. Osborn and Stellanova Osborn, *Schoolcraft—Longfellow—Hiawatha* (Lancaster: Jacques Cattell Press, 1942), Part III. This book also contains a bibliography of the writings of Schoolcraft.

[23] Williams, *op. cit.,* p. 288.

Schoolcraft took up his post as Indian Agent in 1822, he wrote in his journal: "The fact, indeed, of such a fund of fictitious legendary matter is quite a discovery and speaks more for the intellect of the race than any trait I have heard. Who would have imagined that these wandering foresters should have possessed such a resource? What have all the voyagers and remarkers from the days of Cabot and Raleigh been about, not to have discovered this curious trait, which lifts up indeed a curtain, as it were, upon the Indian mind, and exhibits it in an entirely new character."[24] Schoolcraft had discovered the existence of traditional oral narratives—the myths and tales of the Ojibwa. By the time he published his own collection, he asserted that such narratives were "also found among some of the tribes west of the Mississippi"; and, since he thought they must be found elsewhere too, he says "it becomes a question of interest to ascertain how far a similar trait can be traced among the North American tribes" and asks whether "the South American aborigines possessed, or still possess, this point of intellectual affinity with the tribes of the North."[25]

Schoolcraft made his discovery long before the term "folklore" was introduced by William J. Thoms in 1846[26] and more than half a century before the English Folk-Lore Society (1878) or the American Folklore Society (1888) were founded. The active collection of oral narratives among European peoples had been initiated in the early nineteenth century, but there is no evidence to show that Schoolcraft knew about this.[27] As a matter of fact, the Grimms, in their later search for comparative material, discovered Schoolcraft's work. What amazed Schoolcraft was not only the novelty of the fact that "savages" possessed a native "literature" but that these narratives had a social function and threw a great deal of light upon the savage mind. In 1824, two

---

[24] *Personal Memoirs of a Residence of Thirty Years with the Indian Tribes of the American Frontiers: with Brief Notices of Passing Events, Facts, and Opinions, A. D. 1812 to A. D. 1842* (Philadelphia: Lippincott, 1851), p. 109.

[25] Since *Algic Researches, Comprising Inquiries Respecting the Mental Characteristics of the North American Indians. First Series. Indian Tales and Legends.* 2 vols., 248 and 244 pp. (New York: Harper, 1839) is not easily accessible, my references are to the reprinting edited by Mentor L. Williams, *Schoolcraft's Indian Legends*, 1956. The passage quoted is from the section entitled "Preliminary Observations," p. 18.

[26] See Melville J. Herskovits, "Folklore after a hundred years: A problem in redefinition," *JAFL* 59:89, 1946.

[27] See Guiseppe Cocchiara, *Storia del folklore in Europa* (Torino: Edizioni Scientifiche Einaudi, Collezione di studi religiosi, ethnologici epsicologici, XX, 1952), p. 622; Richard M. Dorson, "The First Group of British Folklorists," *Journal of American Folk-Lore* 68:1-8, 333-340, 1955; T. F. Crane, "The External History of the Kinder—und Hausmärchen of the Brothers Grimm," *Modern Philology* 14:577-610, 1916-17; 15:65-76, 355-83, 1917-18.

years after he had become aware of the myths and tales, he wrote in his journal that nothing he had ever heard about the Indians had prepared him for what he had found. He says: "I had always heard the Indian spoken of as [a] revengeful, bloodthirsty man, who was steeled to endurance and delight in deeds of cruelty. To find him a man capable of feelings and affections, with a heart open to the wants and responsive to the ties of social life, was amazing. But the surprise reached its acme when I found him whiling away a part of the tedium of his long winter evenings in relating tales and legends for the amusement of the lodge circle. These fictions were sometimes employed, I observed, to convey instruction or impress examples of courage, daring, or right action. But they were, at all times, replete with the wild forest of notions of spiritual agencies, necromancy, and demonology. They revealed abundantly the cause of his hopes and fears, his notions of a Deity, and his belief in a future state."[28]

Algic Researches was intended to make Schoolcraft's discovery known. On a visit to Gallatin in 1838, before his book appeared, the latter warned him to "take care that, in publishing your Indian legends, you do not subject yourself to the imputation against [James] MacPherson"[29] who, it will be recalled, published poems (1759) attributed to Ossian based upon oral traditions which he claimed he had collected in the Scottish Highlands but which did not bear critical scrutiny. *Algic Researches* was widely reviewed and favorably appraised. But the total unfamiliarity of the general public with Indian folklore at this time is reflected in the statement of one reviewer that the legends "will at least establish the fact of an oral imaginative lore among the aborigines of this continent."[30] And Stith Thompson, referring in passing to a few tales collected by the Jesuits, says: "It was not until the time of Henry Rowe Schoolcraft that any serious efforts were made to learn about Indian tales."[31] Even after the publication of *Algic Re-*

---

[28] *Personal Memoirs, op. cit.*, pp. 196-197; Williams, *op. cit.*, p. 309. Cf. *Algic Researches* (Williams Ed.), p. 5.

[29] *Personal Memoirs, op. cit.*, p. 596.

[30] *Ibid.*, p. 650.

[31] Stith Thompson, *The Folktale* (New York: Dryden Press, 1946), p. 298. J. G. Kohl, (*Kitchi-Gami. Wanderings Round Lake Superior*, London, 1860, p. 87), a German traveler who spent some time among the Ojibwa, paid tribute to Schoolcraft's discovery. "The Canadian voyageurs, traders, and 'coureurs des bois,'" he writes, "are as delighted with these stories as the Indians themselves. But it says little for the poetic feeling and literary taste of the old Missionaries, and the other innumerable travellers who have described these countries, that the outer public has only learned so little, and at so recent a date, of this memorable treasure among these savage tribes. Of the old authors, hardly one alludes to this subject, which the Missionaries probably thought too unholy for them to handle, and which other travellers overlooked through their ignorance of the language and want of leisure. Mr.

searches, decades elapsed before any other collection of tales from an Algonkian people was published.[31a] The collection and comparative treatment of such material was well under way, however, before the academic period in American anthropology had begun.

Although Schoolcraft had said that "the value of these traditionary stories appeared to depend, very much, upon their being left, as nearly as possible, in their original forms of thought and expression,"[32] he did not follow his own better judgment. He molded them, to some extent, to suit his own literary taste: "excrescences" were lopped off because the Indians were so prolix, vulgarisms were weeded out, sometimes a legend was broken in two or cut off.[33] Nevertheless, besides being known to the public, Schoolcraft's collection was used by subsequent generations of scholars. He had many followers, says Stith Thompson— "Indian agents, doctors, missionaries and teachers who heard tales which interested them and who refurbished them for a generation of romantic readers. But it was not until the last quarter of the nineteenth century that we begin to receive faithful recordings of American Indian tales. With the development of the Bureau of American Ethnology and

Schoolcraft was the first, in his 'Algic Researches,' to make an attempt to collect the fables and stories of the Indians; and Longfellow in his 'Hiawatha,' has submitted some graceful specimens to the European world of letters." There was no demand for a second edition of *Algic Researches,* but the material was used under many different titles in subsequent years. See A. Irving Hallowell, "Concordance of Ojibwa Narratives in the Published Works of Henry R. Schoolcraft," *Journal of American Folk-Lore* 59:136-153, 1946. Longfellow's indebtedness to Schoolcraft is set out in detail in Part Two of Osborn and Osborn, *op. cit.*

[31a] Charles G. Leland's *The Algonquin Legends of New England* was not published until 1885 and *Legends of the Micmac* by Silas T. Rand did not appear until 1894. The dates for other nineteenth century collections were: Eskimo (Rink, 1875); Athabascans (Petitot, 1886); Ponca and Omaha (J. O. Dorsey, 1888); Klamath (Gatschet, 1890); Sioux (Riggs, 1893). See Bibliography, Stith Thompson, *Tales of the North American Indians* (Cambridge: Harvard University Press, 1929).

[32] *Algic Researches* (Williams Ed.), p. 19; and *Personal Memoirs,* p. 514.

[33] "They required pruning and dressing, like wild vines in a garden. . . . The attempts to lop off excrescences are not, perhaps, always happy. There might, perhaps, have been a fuller adherence to the original language and expression; but if so, what a world of verbiage must have been retained. The Indians are prolix, and attach value to many minutiae in the relations which not only does not help forward the denouement, but is tedious and witless to the last degree. The gems of the legends—the essential points—the invention and thought-work are all preserved." (*Personal Memoirs, op. cit.,* p. 655; cf. p. 585 and Preface to *The Myth of Hiawatha,* 1856.) In all fairness it should be noted that the editing Schoolcraft did was not unique. Speaking of Europe, Thompson (*op. cit.,* p. 407) points out that until the nineteenth century no one knew "what the traditional oral folktale actually sounded like." Although the Grimms "took down their stories as they heard them," they "had no scruples against reworking them from edition to edition. But by 1840 or thereabouts a number of scholars were making serious attempts to publish authentic oral texts. . . ."

the influence of such scientists as J. W. Powell there begin to appear an increasing number of first-rate collections, some of them even accompanied by the original text."[34]

By the time Schoolcraft, in 1841, gave up his post as Indian agent and acting Superintendent of Indian Affairs for the State of Michigan (1836-1841), he already had become a distinguished man. He not only had been discharging his day-to-day duties as a government official as well as actively participating in the negotiation of treaties; in 1833 he had been invited to be a member of a party attending President Jackson on a tour of New England; he had served two terms as a member of the Legislative Council of Michigan Territory, and four years as a regent of the University of Michigan; he had been president of the Michigan Historical Society. In addition to publishing *Algic Researches,* poems and articles in the *North American Review* and other periodicals, he had written a book describing his discovery of the source of the Mississippi. Peter S. Duponceau had not only complimented him on his linguistic work but had quoted at length from one of his lectures in the book on American Indian languages (*Mémoire sur le système grammatical des langues de quelques nations indiennes de l'Amérique du Nord*) which had won Duponceau a prize in France.[35]

For a long time Schoolcraft had seen the need for collecting and organizing information about the Indians on a wide scale. The Algic Society which he founded (1832), while philanthropic in its major aims, also included in its purpose the collection of statistical, linguistic, and ethnographic information on the Indians of the Great Lakes area. In 1842 he became one of the founders of the American Ethnological Society. That same year he made an extensive trip abroad and read a paper at the meetings of the British Association for the Advancement of Science. By the time he returned from Europe he had not only left the frontier behind; the broad range of his past experience and personal contacts enabled him to focus increasingly upon problems that concerned the American Indians at large. He made a trip through West Virginia, Ohio, and southern Michigan, which revitalized an old interest in archeology, a subject on which he published several papers. One of these, on the Grave Creek Mound, appeared in the first volume of the *Transactions of the American Ethnological Society* in 1845. The subject suggested to him such questions as: "What are the facts connected with the position of this gigantic structure? Its dimensions, its contents, and the era and purpose of its construction? Who erected it? What is the language and purport of the recently found inscription? Who were

---

[34] Thompson, *op. cit.*, p. 298.
[35] See Osborn and Osborn, *op. cit.*, pp. 404, 411-12.

the mound-builders? Was the continent known to Europeans before
the era of Columbus? What race of Red Men first entered the Mississippi valleys? Whence came they? Whither went they? Do their descendants remain? What are the leading facts of the mound period of
our history?[36] He was thinking about some of these problems because
this was the year he was engaged by the State of New York to make a
survey of the Six Nations which took him into the mound area of western New York state. Public interest in the mound problem was keen
at this time, so that when he published his book, which appeared the
same year Squier and Davis were completing their survey of the
mounds of the Middle West, Schoolcraft included some material on
"antiquities" in his volume.[37]

Having heard of the bequest of Smithson which was awaiting government action, Schoolcraft drew up a "Plan for the investigation of
American ethnology . . . " which he presented to the regents of the
newly organized institution in 1846. Although the Indians remain in the
foreground, the outline he submitted actually included mankind as a
whole, and it was broadly anthropological in concept. Among other
things he suggested a national museum. Although this plan was not
acted on at the time, after Schoolcraft's death it was reprinted in the
Report of the Smithsonian Institution for 1885.[38] This memorandum
was shortly followed by the memorialization of Congress by Schoolcraft
and others to collect and publish available information on the Indians
of the United States. It led to the project to which Schoolcraft devoted
ten years of his life.

In 1847 by Congressional action, backed by an appropriation, the
Secretary of War was authorized to have this work done. Schoolcraft
was given an appointment in the Office of Indian Affairs and commis-

---

[36] "Observations Respecting the Grave Creek Mound, in western Virginia; the antique inscription discovered in its excavation; and the connected
evidences of the occupancy of the Mississippi valley during the mound
period, and prior to the discovery of America by Columbus," pp. 371-372.
The "inscribed" tablet, later discredited, which excited Schoolcraft and others
at the time, is indicative of the kind of evidence which aroused such a keen
interest in the identity of the mound builders. See Cyrus Thomas, "Report
on the Mound Explorations of the Bureau of American Ethnology," *Twelfth
Annual Report of the Bureau of Ethnology*, Washington, 1894, "Inscribed Tablets," pp. 632 ff.
[37] *Notes on the Iroquois: or, contributions to the statistics, aboriginal
history, antiquities and general ethnology of western New York* (New York,
1846). (A popular account appeared the next year.)
[38] "Plan for the investigation of American ethnology, to include the
facts derived from other parts of the globe, and the eventual formation of a
Museum of Antiquities and the peculiar fabrics of nations; and also the
collection of a library, of the philology of the world, manuscript and printed.
Submitted to the Board of Regents of the Smithsonian Institution, at their
first meeting, at Washington, in September, 1846," pp. 907-914.

sioned to "collect and digest such statistics and materials as may illustrate the history, the present conditions, and future prospects of the Indian tribes of the United States." There is little doubt that, if it were to be done at all, Schoolcraft was the best prepared person to undertake this herculean assignment. One of his first steps was to draw up a questionnaire of 348 items, which was circulated under government auspices to Indian agents, missionaries, and others who, it was thought, might supply information.[38a] From 1851 to 1857 the six elephantine folio volumes, running to 600 pages each of *Historical and Statistical Information Respecting the History, Condition, and Prospects of the Indian Tribes of the United States, Collected and Prepared under the Direction of the Bureau of Indian Affairs . . . . Illustrated by S. Eastman, Captain, U. S. A.* successively appeared.[39] Though physically so monumental, they have never been considered a great scholarly monument. There was much harsh criticism at the time they were published, as well as later, ranging from comments on the author's style to the arrangement and organization of the data; an index did not appear until 1954.[40] Perhaps a reappraisal, focused upon Schoolcraft's ideas viewed in historical context, needs to be made. For despite the encyclopedic content, Schoolcraft seized every opportunity to express his personal views on the widest variety of topics. However we may evaluate them today, they were the views of a man who, if judged by his firsthand contacts with Indians and collection of data in the field, by his wide ranging interests in the subject matter of linguistics, ethnography, and archeology, and by the efforts he made to grapple with the significance of the available data in historical terms, was a unique figure in the preacademic period of American anthropology.

In 1842, the same year that the American Ethnological Society was founded, Lewis Henry Morgan (1818-1881), a young attorney in Aurora,

---

[38a] Further details concerning this circular are given by J. N. B. Hewitt in his preface to the manuscript of Edward Thompson Denig (1812-1862?), which he edited ("Indian Tribes of the Upper Missouri," *Forty-Sixth Annual Report of the Bureau of American Ethnology*, Washington, 1930, pp. 375-628). The manuscript was written about 1854. Denig was a trader who had married an Assiniboin woman and lived among the prairie tribes for more than two decades. It "consists of brief and greatly condensed replies" to the questions propounded in the Schoolcraft circular and deals with half a dozen tribes of the upper Missouri, although most of it concerns the Assiniboin.

[39] For bibliographical information on various editions and changes in title, see Osborn and Osborn, *op. cit.*

[40] See e.g. *North American Review* 77:245-62, 1853; *Historical Magazine* (1865) quoted in Osborn and Osborn, *op. cit.*, pp. 419-20; D. G. Brinton, *Myths of the New World* (Philadelphia, 1905). (Third Edition, 1896), p. 56 (this author is consistently anti-Schoolcraft); R. H. Pearce, *op. cit.*, p. 124. An index to the six volumes, compiled by Frances S. Nichols, appeared as *Bulletin 152 of the Bureau of American Ethnology*, 1954.

New York, having some leisure because of depression in business, joined a literary club. This was his first step towards world fame as an anthropologist. For the club soon was transformed into a fraternity, "The Order of the Iroquois." In a retrospective account, written in 1859, Morgan says: "As we hoped at that time to found a permanent order, with a charitable as well as a literary basis, we connected with it the idea of protecting, so far as it lay in our power, the remainder of the Iroquois living in this State; and particularly the band of Senecas at Tonawanda who then and since the year 1838 had been beset and hunted by the Ogden Land Company, to despoil them of their remaining lands. We visited the Indians at Onondaga and at Tonawanda, and at Buffalo, attending their councils from time to time, and making ourselves familiar with their conditions and wants; but more particularly we engaged with ardor, in the work of studying out the structure and principles of the ancient League by which they had been united for so many centuries. We wished to model our organization upon this and to reproduce it with as much fidelity as the nature and objects of our order would permit. This desire, on our part, led to the first discovery of the real structure and principles of the League of the Iroquois, which up to that time were entirely unknown, except in a most general sense."[41]

This initial contact with the Iroquois, followed in subsequent years by increasing personal intimacy and rapidly expanding knowledge, led directly to the publication in 1851 of Morgan's classical ethnographic monograph, *The League of the Ho-dé-no-sau-nee or Iroquois.* Morgan's friend Major Powell characterized his book as "the first scientific account of an Indian tribe ever given to the world;"[42] and A. A. Goldenweiser, who spent some time with them in the twentieth century, referred to it (1922) as "still the best general treatise on the Iroquois."[43] Morgan devoted particular attention to the Seneca and was assisted by Ely S. Parker, a fullblooded member of the tribe and an educated man, to

---

[41] Quoted by Leslie A. White from Morgan's Journal. ("How Morgan came to write *Systems of Consanguinity and Affinity,*" Papers of the Michigan Academy of Science, Arts and Letters 42:261, 1957.) Charles Talbot Porter, an associate of Morgan's in these activities, provides an account which is to be found in the appendix to Herbert M. Lloyd's edition of *The League* (New York, 1901). [This edition, long out of print, was again made available by the *Human Relations Area Files* in its *Behavior Science Reprints* (1954).] For fundamental biographic data on Morgan, see J. W. Powell, "Sketch of Lewis H. Morgan," *Popular Science Monthly* 18:114-21, 1880; W. H. Holmes, "Biographical Memoir of Lewis Henry Morgan, 1818-1881," National Academy of Sciences, *Biographical Memoirs* 6, 1909; Bernhard J. Stern, *Lewis H. Morgan, Social Evolutionist* (Chicago, 1931).
[42] Powell, *op. cit.,* p. 115.
[43] *Early Civilization* (New York, 1922), p. 418.

whom he pays special tribute in his Preface. Having published the
League, Morgan turned to business and "Indian affairs were laid entirely aside," he says,[44] until 1857. It was during these very years, it
may be recalled, that Schoolcraft's encyclopedic work on the Indians of
the United States was appearing, but he did not live to see the publication of Morgan's great seminal volume, *Systems of Consanguinity and
Affinity of the Human Family* (1871).

Taking up his Indian studies again in 1857, Morgan devoted himself particularly to a closer examination of "the laws of descent and
consanguinity of the Iroquois," which he now began to perceive in a
new perspective. He prepared a paper on "Laws of Descent of the
Iroquois" for the Montreal meeting of the American Association for the
Advancement of Science to which he had just been elected and within
which he founded the Anthropological Section.[45] The following year,
while at Marquette on Lake Superior, he discovered that Schoolcraft's
people, the Ojibwa, while differing in language, descent, and other
respects from the Iroquois, nevertheless had what he came to call the
"classificatory system" of relationship. From this time on Morgan began
to pursue this system among other North American Indian groups,
collecting some material himself and securing additional information by
correspondence. By 1859, he was requesting a member of the House of
Representatives in Washington for the use of his franking privilege in
order to distribute schedules he already had drawn up.[46] Finding that
the classificatory system was not only widespread among North American Indians, but occurred among the Tamil of southern India, "it now
became doubly desirable" he says, "to extend the field of inquiry, not
only so as [to] include the whole of India; but also Mongolia, Tibetan
[sic], Siberia, China, Siam, Japan, Australia, the Islands of the Pacific,
Africa and South America, as well as to finish the inquiry among the
North American Indians."[47]

This was the first time that the relevance of the systematic collection of comparative data on a world-wide scale had been clearly envisaged and brought to bear upon a problem in the field of ethnology.
Among other things, Morgan thought that the question of the Asiatic
origin of the Indians might be solved because he held the opinion that
systems of kinship were more stable than language.[48] Despite the end-

---

[44] White, *op. cit.,* p. 262.
[45] Stern, *op. cit.,* pp. 60-61.
[46] See Carter A. Woods, "Some Further Notes on Lewis Henry Morgan,"
AA 47:462-464, 1945.
[47] White, *op. cit.,* p. 267.
[48] See Woods, *op. cit.,* p. 463. In his letter to Congressman Edwin B.
Morgan (1859), he had said: "Albert Gallatin worked about ten years on this

less discussion of the derivation of the aboriginal population of the New World that had gone on in the past, this question was far from being settled at the time Morgan began his comparative inquiries on an extended scale. Schoolcraft had reintroduced the question of Jewish origins in his *Indian Tribes;* and Leslie A. White points out that in 1891, Daniel G. Brinton, in *The American Race*, "held that the American Indian came from Europe."[49] Through his friend Joseph Henry, Morgan arranged for the world-wide distribution of his schedules to diplomatic and consular agents of the United States under the auspices of the Smithsonian Institution. Both Henry, as Secretary of the Smithsonian, and Lewis Cass, Secretary of State at this time, wrote endorsing letters to these schedules, arranged in a pamphlet, which was entitled "Circular in Reference to the Degree of Relationship among Different Nations."[50]

Morgan's compilation and interpretation of the material collected, which Murdock has characterized as "perhaps the most original and brilliant single achievement in the history of Anthropology,"[51] was published as Volume 17 in *Smithsonian Contributions to Knowledge* (1871). Even before this volume had been printed, the receipt of the pamphlet itself stirred up fresh investigations. In the Pacific, Reverend Lorimer Fison sent Morgan data on Fijian and Tongan kinship systems in 1869; and the book on the Australians which Fison and Howitt later published was dedicated to Morgan who wrote an Introduction.[52]

A couple of years after the *Systems* had been published, Morgan met a young businessman, Swiss by birth, who lived in Illinois, and whose subsequent thinking and career he profoundly influenced. This was Adolph Francis Alphonse Bandelier (1840-1914) who, becoming a professional anthropologist during the last three decades of his life, did pioneer work in the Southwest and was active in archeological, ethnological, and historical investigations in Mexico, Peru, and Bolivia.[53] His novel, *The Delight Makers* (1890), is said by Kroeber to be "a more comprehensive and coherent view of native Pueblo life than any scientific volume on the southwest."[54]

·question using language as the instrument; but failed for the reason that languages change."

[49] White, *op. cit.*, p. 263 note.

[50] It is to be found in *Smithsonian Miscellaneous Collections* 2:1-33, 1862.

[51] George Peter Murdock, *Social Structure* (New York: Macmillan, 1949), p. 91.

[52] Lorimer Fison and A. W. Howitt, *Kamilaroi and Kurnai* (Sydney, 1880).

[53] For a sketch of his life see Leslie A. White, *Pioneers in American Anthropology. The Bandelier-Morgan Letters, 1873-1883.* 2 vols. (Albuquerque: University of New Mexico Press, 1940).

[54] Elsie Clews Parsons, *American Indian Life* (1922), p. 13.

At the time Morgan first met him, Bandelier was devoting all his spare time to the study of the Spanish sources dealing with the conquest and other documents that provided information on the Indian cultures of Middle America. Morgan had been thinking about these cultures, too, and this was the basis of an active correspondence over the next ten years. Led by his study of the data he had collected on kinship systems to plunge into historical speculations about the sequence of various forms of human social organization and institutions, Morgan had pretty well made up his mind before he published *Ancient Society* (1877) about the stages reached by American Indians. He was certain that a state of *civitas*, founded upon territory and property, could never have been reached in the New World. So any reports about the existence of monarchies or aristocracies were suspect. When applied in particular to the Aztecs, Morgan's deductions, in the light of the facts already reported, were not only novel but highly controversial.

Prescott's two volumes, the *Conquest of Mexico* and the *Conquest of Peru*, had been American best sellers in the eighteen-forties, and H. H. Bancroft in his *Native Races* (1874-1875) had only recently concluded from his examination of the early chroniclers and the work of other historians that "the Nahuas, the Mayas and the subordinate and lesser civilizations surrounding these [were] but little lower than the contemporaneous civilizations of Europe and Asia, and not nearly so low as we have hitherto been led to suppose."[55] Other scholars in pursuing their studies of the American Indians had included the Middle American area in their investigations long before this. In 1845 Gallatin had published his *Notes on the Semi-civilized Nations of Mexico, Yucatan, and Central America*, and the Astor Library had been collecting Indian grammars from Spanish America. Even before Prescott had published his *Conquest of Mexico* (1843), John Lloyd Stephens and Frederick Catherwood had penetrated the jungles of Yucatan and published *Incidents of Travel in Central America, Chiapas, and Yucatan* (1841), with its magnificent illustrations. Learned societies, too, had become interested in Spanish America: the American Philosophical Society, the New York Historical Society, and the American Antiquarian Society. These organizations had corresponding members in Spanish American countries. Within twenty years after the American Ethnological Society had been founded, over a dozen Latin Americans had been invited to membership.[56] By Morgan's time scholarly interest in the American

[55] *Native Races,* II, 805.
[56] For detailed information, see Harry Bernstein, "Anthropology and Early Inter-American Relations," *Trans. New York Academy of Sciences,* Sec. II, Vol. 10, 1947, pp. 2-17.

Indian from a linguistic, archeological, and ethnological point of view had far transcended United States boundaries, and the public, through Prescott, Stephens, and Bancroft, had acquired an image of Aztec and Maya culture.

Morgan, therefore, took a very radical stand when, on the basis of his own evolutionary hypothesis, supported by the scholarly erudition of Bandelier, he stoutly maintained that the Indians of Mexico had not evolved, any more than Indians elsewhere, beyond a democratic "gentile" organization; the Aztecs *could not* have had a monarchial form of government.[57] In a notorious review of Bancroft in 1876, entitled "Montezuma's Dinner,"[58] Morgan attacked both early observers and later historians. He accused the former of the "grossest perversion of obvious facts"; they were biased by European concepts and terminology; subsequent writers had perpetuated or embellished their errors; it was necessary, he thought, to reinterpret the data anew.

We are now in a better position to see how far Morgan projected his own image of the Iroquois upon the Mexican cultures of the preconquest period and how far he rendered a service at the time in tempering somewhat the picture of oriental magnificence and uniqueness that had been presented by stressing the comparability of the elaborated cultures of Middle America and the Andes with those elsewhere in the New World.[59]

When Morgan's inclusive evolutionary exposition of human development appeared, a chapter on the Aztec confederacy was included. *Ancient Society* fitted the intellectual temper of the Darwinian era, imbued as it was with the twin notions of evolution and progress. Translated into several European languages as well as into Chinese and Japanese, it became known throughout the world, but subsequently fell under radical criticism along with other treatments of human cultural development in evolutionary terms.

---

[57] See White, *op. cit.* (1940): "It is more than likely, I believe, that it was because Morgan did not find any evidence of the descriptive system among the American Indians that he concluded that they had not emerged from barbarism, had not attained to civilization. Added to this was the absence of iron-working and the alphabet in America. It is probable that these are the reasons for Morgan's assumption (which became a firmly seated conviction) that no American Indian group had outgrown the democratic gentile organization." (1:51.)

[58] *North American Review*, 122:265-308, 1876. Bancroft answered him as well as other critics. See Chapter 1 in his *Essays and Miscellany*. Bandelier modified his views about the early Spanish chroniclers in later years. See White, *op. cit.* (1940), 1:24-25.

[59] Cf. Roland B. Dixon on this point, "Some Aspects of the Scientific Work of Lewis Henry Morgan." In *The Morgan Centennial Celebration* at Wells College, Aurora, N. Y., *Researches and Trans. of the N. Y. State Archeological Association*, Vol. 1, No. 3, Rochester, 1919, p. 19.

It may be significant in considering the preacademic history of anthropology in the United States, that whereas Schoolcraft was elected to the American Philosophical Society, Morgan was elected to the National Academy of Sciences (1875) and was the first anthropologist to serve as President of the American Association for the Advancement of Science (1880). However we may appraise his work, Morgan's aims, like E. B. Tylor's, were scientific. His achievements and status gave him a professional standing although he never was affiliated with any government bureau or university.[60] From 1862 on, having given up his law practice, he devoted himself to his chosen field. In contrast with Schoolcraft, whose even broader range of intellectual interests and activities suggests a link with the great amateurs of the late eighteenth century, Morgan was deeply stamped by the intellectual climate of the nineteenth century.[61] He was as far removed from the frontier as were the New York Iroquois whom he studied; his Seneca friend and informant, Ely Parker, was an educated man. While Schoolcraft glimpsed horizons in anthropology beyond the study of the American Indian, his career culminated in a compendium of concrete information about them. Morgan, starting with empirical observations on a single group of Indians, went on to study kinship on a world-wide scale and elaborated a theory of human cultural development as a whole. When the Archaeological Institute of America was founded in 1879, Morgan was asked to prepare a plan for archeological exploration and research in the American field.[62] Judged both in terms of his achievements and the vital influence he exerted in his own time and beyond it, Morgan's historical position in relation to an evolving science of man is outstanding.

By the time Morgan died the Bureau of American Ethnology had been established in the Smithsonian Institution under the direction of one of his greatest admirers, John Wesley Powell.[63] The latter had supplied Morgan with Hopi kinship schedules years before, had corresponded with him, and had visited him in Rochester. Although familiar with the writings of Comte, Buckle, Mill, Darwin, and Spencer, Powell was especially influenced by Morgan's *Ancient Society*. Having great

---

[60] Stern, *op. cit.*, pp. 192-193, says: "All contemporary anthropologists wrote to him for counsel, sent him papers for criticism or made trips to Rochester to consult him."

[61] White has drawn some parallels between Morgan and Darwin. See "Morgan's Attitude toward Religion and Science," AA 46:230, note, 1944.

[62] Morgan had a long-standing interest in archeology and had published several papers. See Leslie A. White, "Lewis H. Morgan's Journal of a Trip to Southwestern Colorado and New Mexico, June 21 to August 7, 1878," *American Antiquity* 8:1-26, 1942.

[63] William Culp Darrah, in his biography of Powell (*Powell of the Colorado*, Princeton, 1957), devotes Chap. 16 to the Bureau of American Ethnology.

faith in man's capacity for progress, he added to Morgan's stages of Savagery, Barbarism, and Civilization a still higher level of human achievement—Enlightenment—which he thought would be realized in the future.[64] Powell's general views fitted the intellectual temper of the time. The Civil War had been surmounted, rapid economic changes were occurring, and Darwin's theory suggested a fresh interpretation of the idea of development beyond the purely biological realm. "The enlightened American reading public," says Hofstadter, "which became fascinated with evolutionary speculation soon after the Civil War, gave a handsome reception to philosophies and political theories built in part upon Darwinism or associated with it. Herbert Spencer, who of all men made the most ambitious attempt to systematize the implications of evolution in fields other than biology itself, was far more popular in the United States than he was in his native country."[65] Spencer's *Study of Sociology* was serialized in the *Popular Science Monthly* in 1872-73, the peak of his popularity being reached when he visited this country in 1882.

Powell, significantly enough, did not become a disciple of Spencer or a Social Darwinist. His position may have been influenced by his friend Lester F. Ward, whose *Dynamic Sociology*, published in 1883, became a landmark in American sociology. In the latter's hands, "sociology became a special discipline dealing with a novel and unique level of organization" since Ward made "a sharp distinction between physical, or animal, purposeless evolution and mental, human evolution decisively modified by purposive action."[66] Ward had been in the field with Powell in 1875, where he had studied prairie grasses in Utah. Knowing of his sociological interests, and considering Ward a genius, Powell found a position for him in the Geological Survey as a paleobotanist.[67] Here Ward was able to finish his famous book, for which Powell found a publisher. Powell, like Ward, saw a break in the evolutionary process and conceptualized cultural evolution as a phenomenon distinct from biological evolution. He said: "The laws of biotic evolution do not apply to mankind. There are men in the world so overwhelmed with the grandeur and truth of biotic evolution that they actually believe that man is but a two-legged beast whose progress in the world is governed by the same laws as the progress of the serpent or the wolf; and so science is put to shame . . . . That which makes man more than beast is culture. Culture is human evolution—not the devel-

---

[64] For Powell's general intellectual position, see Darrah, *op. cit.*, Chap. 22.
[65] Richard Hofstadter, *Social Darwinism in American Thought* (Revised Edition, Boston: Beacon Press, 1955), pp. 4-5.
[66] Hofstadter, *ibid.*, p. 68.
[67] Darrah, *op. cit.*, p. 280.

opment of man as an animal, but the evolution of the human attributes
of man. Culture is the product of human endeavor." Mitra, in introducing this quotation says: "it is remarkable how much Powell was preparing the way for freeing American anthropology from the shackles of
ultraevolutionism."[68]

Powell, of course, had been in close touch with the anthropological
activities of the Smithsonian Institution ever since Joseph Henry had
urged him to collect information on Indian languages and customs when
he was planning his exploration of the Colorado River more than a
decade before the Bureau of American Ethnology was organized. When
a display of Indian handicrafts, costumes, weapons, and archeological
remains was being prepared by the Smithsonian for the Centennial
Exposition in 1876, Powell contributed objects illustrating the handicrafts of the Utes and Paiutes he had collected in 1873-74.[69] In 1878
he attended the meetings of the American Association for the Advancement of Science and was elected vice-president of the anthropology
section, which at that time had had independent recognition for only
five years. F. W. Putnam was there, as a matter of course; so was
Bandelier; and Powell met W J McGee, who was interested in geological investigations.

When Powell became head of the Bureau in 1879, he proclaimed
that its purpose was "to organize anthropologic research in America."
He seems to have had in mind a Science of Man which could be pursued and exemplified through the empirical study of the American
Indians because its primary frame of reference was temporal and evolutionary. He developed his own conceptual scheme and, to some
extent, his own terminology. Taking human functional activities as his
point of departure and making use of a generalizing approach he identified five basic categories of social activity: industries, institutions,
expressions, instructions and esthetics.[70] A favorite word he used for
human society was demotic, i.e., the organized, customary, conventional activities of people. Aside from staff members of the Bureau, few
others accepted and made use of his categories and terminology. The
term "acculturation" which emerged in his discussion of similarities and
differences in culture referred to the fact that while some cultural

---

[68] Mitra, op. cit., p. 129.
[69] Darrah, op. cit., p. 260. Julian H. Steward, writing in 1939 ("Notes on
Hillers' Photographs of the Paiute and Ute Indians taken on the Powell Expedition of 1873," Smithsonian Miscellaneous Collections, Vol. 98, No. 18),
says: "Powell's extraordinary fine collection of Ute and Paiute specimens in
the United States National Museum is largely unknown to the scientific
world." (p. 2.)
[70] The outlines of Powell's schema can be found on page 99 of this
book.

similarities may be autogenous (independently originated), others may
be syngenous (commonly originated) due to the possibility of learning
by imitation. Although the term has become so familiar since the
middle thirties of this century, Powell used it very infrequently himself.
Mathews' *Dictionary of Americanisms* gives as a primary citation his
use of it in 1880.[71]

Powell's influence cannot be measured solely in terms of his personal contributions or the impact of his ideas but above all by his rare
capacities as an organizer and promoter. One wonders what the history
of American anthropology in the late nineteenth century would have
been like if the Bureau as he conceived and directed it had never
come into existence. Operating on a small budget, he did not depend
on staff members alone to pursue the research program he envisaged.
He engaged others to do special jobs. Publication could be assured
through the series of *Annual Reports* and *Bulletins* he initiated and,
between 1881 and 1894, *Contributions to North American Ethnology.*
In an obituary notice, A. F. Chamberlain wrote: "To have made possible the publication of the results of the labors of Yarrow, Holden, Royce,
Mallery, Dorsey, Gatschet, Cushing, Smith, Henshaw, Matthews,
Holmes, Thomas, Dall, MacCauley, Boas, Hoffman, Mooney, Mindeleff,
Murdock, Bourke, Turner, Fowke, Pilling, Fewkes, Hewitt, McGee
was an achievement of which one might be proud."[72] And, although it
was not published until after his death, the groundwork for the *Handbook of the American Indians North of Mexico*[73] (reissued commer-
cially in 1959 after it was long out of print) was laid under Powell's
direction. In 1885 he prophesied that it would be "one of the most
important contributions to the accurate study of Indian history ever
made."

In addition to organizing the Bureau of American Ethnology in
1879, Powell did double duty after 1881 when he accepted the directorship of the Geological Survey. And, outside these official duties, he was
the primary founder of the Anthropological Society of Washington and
later helped to organize the American Anthropological Association
.which grew out of it. He was also an active member of the American
Folklore Society, a founder of the Archaeological Institute of America,
and an incorporator of the Washington Academy of Sciences. In 1888

[71] Consult the following: "On Activital Similarities," *Third Annual Report
of the Bureau of Ethnology,* 1881-82; "From Barbarism to Civilization," *AA*
1:97 ff., 1888. The 1880 usage is found in Powell's *"Introduction to the Study
of Indian Languages,"* Second Edition, p. 46. *See also* pp. 787-88 of this book.
[72] *Journal of American Folk-Lore* 15:202 ff., 1902.
[73] *Bulletin 30 of the Bureau of American Ethnology,* ed. by Frederick
Webb Hodge, Part 1, 1907; Part 2, 1910 (Washington, D. C.).

he was elected president of the American Association for the Advancement of Science, the same honor which had been bestowed on his friend Morgan eight years before.

PHYSICAL ANTHROPOLOGY

It has been pointed out that the more comprehensive perspective on man opened up by the discovery of the New World inevitably focused attention upon the question of the origins of the Indians. When Biblical authority was appealed to, this question necessarily involved the problem of the origin of other races and of mankind as a whole. At first, the separate creation of races was too unorthodox to be seriously entertained, so that various migration theories which brought the Indians to America were advanced. Since only impressionistic observations of the physical characteristics of the American population were available for a long period, and these seemed quite uniform, linguistic and ethnographic facts were given equal and sometimes even more weight in speculations about origins. Physical characteristics were by no means considered to be independent variables; moral, psychological, or intellectual qualities were associated with them, and linguistic and cultural facts were introduced into the classification of racial subgroupings. The scientific hallmark of physical anthropology—measurements made directly upon the bodies of living subjects or upon the bones of the dead with specially designed instruments[1]—is essentially a nineteenth century development. In fact, physical anthropology as a science is usually dated from 1859 when the Société d'Anthropologie de Paris, under the leadership of Paul Broca (1824-1880) and his collaborators, was founded.[2] Thus, while linguistic and ethnographic data

---

[1] See Lucile E. Hoyme, "Physical Anthropology and its Instruments," *Southwestern J. of Anthropology* 9:408-430, 1953.

[2] Aleš Hrdlička, *Physical Anthropology: Its Scope and Aims; Its History and Present Status in the United States* (Philadelphia: Wistar Institute, 1919), pp. 10-11. It is of historical interest to note that in France at this period the term anthropology was used in its original and inclusive sense. Addressing the Society in 1862 Broca said: "We are not gathered here solely for the purpose of studying the actual state of human races . . . . We further propose, via the multiple channels of anatomy, physiology, history, archeology, linguistics, and finally paleontology, to find out what have been the origins, the filiations, the migrations, the mixtures of the numerous and diverse groups that compose the human species, in historical times, and during the ages that preceded the most remote memories of humanity." Paul Rivet, who quotes this passage (Letter to the Editor, *Diogenes* 13: 112-113, Spring, 1956), also quotes an equally comprehensive statement by Armand de Quatrefages (1856), who was the first official professor of anthropology in France.

were collected on the American frontier and "antiquities" were later dug up, reliable information on the physical traits of living Indians, or the measurement of skulls and other skeletal remains, was delayed. Nevertheless, long before precise information of this order could be made the empirical basis of physical anthropology, racial classifications had been made, speculations about the factors that produced these subdivisions of the human species had begun, and the question of differential psychological or characterological attributes of racial groups had provoked heated controversy. All these problems are reflected in the preacademic history of physical anthropology in the United States.

When Linnaeus (1735) included a human species in his over-all classification of living things, he differentiated at the same time varieties of *Homo sapiens*. The latter were mutable forms, in contrast with the immutable species that has been fashioned in the beginning by the Creator. Following Linnaeus, Blumenbach (1776) added a fifth variety of man, Malayan, to the four already distinguished, thus establishing his well-known system of five races, associated with the major geographical regions of the world, and differing in skin color. Learned men in America, as elsewhere, were acquainted with this classification, as well as others, although not all of them considered such attempts a matter of vital importance. For some, the determining factors that were responsible for the differentiation of varieties of the immutable species that was man presented a problem of greater interest than formal classification. It appeared that the answer was to be sought in external or environmental influences, climate, diet, or even social habits. To Blumenbach and Buffon, for example, a process of degeneration from the species-type as originally created seemed to be involved. Attention already has been called to the debate precipitated in Jefferson's time by Buffon with regard to the deleterious effect of the environment of the New World upon both its animal and human fauna. In America, Samuel Stanhope Smith, who stressed species unity as a necessary premise for a rational approach to the study of man, expressed a common attitude of the eighteenth century when, referring to the various racial classifications that had been advanced, he wrote: "The conclusion to be drawn from all this variety of opinion is, perhaps, that it is impossible to draw the line precisely between the various races of men, or even to enumerate them with certainty; and that it is itself a useless labor to attempt it."[3] At the same time, there were naturalists like Maupertuis, Prichard, and William Wells, who rejected the environmentalist explanation of race.[3a] Questions already were arising that

[3] *An Essay on the Causes of the Variety of Complexion and Figure in the Human Species* (New Brunswick, 1810), p. 240 n.
[3a] Prichard's original position was expressed in the first edition of his *Researches*.

only future advances in biology could answer. Greene points out that "the period before 1815 was remarkable not only for the interest displayed in the problems of race formation but also for the variety of theoretical approaches adopted in the attempt to solve it."[4]

While speculations about the ultimate source of the native population of America continued, one generalization about the racial traits of the Indians became so firmly entrenched in the eighteenth century that even later anthropometric work failed to shake it. Just as it was thought at first that the languages of the Indians must possess some distinctive characteristic, like polysynthesis, and that some underlying unity in their culture must exist because they were derived from the Lost Tribes of Israel, so the idea arose that in their physical characteristics they varied scarcely at all. The Eskimo of the Arctic were an exception, but everywhere else, from one end of the hemisphere to the other, there was racial unity. Stewart and Newman have traced this idea back to a statement of Antonio de Ulloa in 1772 which, in various forms, was continually repeated thereafter. ("Upon seeing an Indian from any region, one can say that one has seen all of them so far as color and general physical characteristics are concerned.")[5] Even after physical anthropology developed an anthropometric base, the idea of the homogeneity of the Indian type not only persisted, but the notion of variability was disparaged. This persistence is rooted in the fact that Samuel G. Morton (1799-1851), who has been labeled the father of American physical anthropology, maintained that with the exception of the "Polar tribes," the American population, including the mound builders, was of one race.

Morton's conclusion was based not simply on the impressions of casual observers but on measurements and observations on a sample of skulls from various regions of America that he began to collect in 1830 as part of his total series. His *Crania Americana* (1839), finely illustrated with lithographs, is classical because he systematically took ten measurements on each skull, six of them "from precisely the same landmarks and in the same way as they are taken today." Besides this, Morton dealt with the subject of artificial deformation of the head and "gave comparisons of skull capacity in series of skulls representing the

---

[4] John C. Greene, "Some Early Speculation on the Origin of Human Races," *AA* 56:39, 1954. *See also* for this period Earl W. Count, "The evolution of the race idea in Modern Western culture during the period of the pre-Darwinian nineteenth century," *Trans. New York Academy of Sciences,* Ser. 2, Vol. 8, pp. 139-165; and *This is Race* (New York, 1950).

[5] T. D. Stewart and Marshall T. Newman, "An Historical Resume of the Concept of Differences in Indian Types," *AA* 53:19-36, 1951. This statement in its original form ran: "Visto un Indio de qualquier region, se puede decir que se han visto todos en quanto al color y contextura."

five human races of Blumenbach's classification." He also provided an
excellent comparative review of what was known about the races of
man in the light of contemporary knowledge.[6] Morton's work immediately became authoritative; to the second volume of Schoolcraft's
Indian Tribes (1852), he contributed a section on the "Physical Type
of the American Indians."

It must not be thought, however, that when Morton is said to have
emphasized the racial unity of the American Indians he was thinking of
physical characteristics alone. The fact is that his sub-classifications are
confusing because he used mixed criteria. For he did not separate observed biological variables from cultural and linguistic facts or psychological and moral qualities. When he divided the American population into
two great families, Toltecan and American, and the latter into branches,
linguistic and cultural variables were brought into the picture. The
Toltecan family was distinguished by the fact that it "bears evidence of
centuries of demi-civilization."[7]   Moreover, speaking of the American
family, which "embraces all the barbarous nations of the new world"
except the Eskimo, Morton says that their intellectual faculties "appear
to be of a decidedly inferior cast when compared with those of the
Caucasian or Mongolian races."[8] In other words, psychological and
moral qualities are associated with racial characteristics; the "structure"
of the Indian mind as represented, at least, by the American family,
"appears to be different from that of the white man";[9] and contact with
Europeans and missionary efforts have had little effect. These Indians
"turn with avulsion from the restraints of civilized life."[10]

Stewart and Newman call attention to the fact that within a few
years of Morton's death "Daniel Wilson reported that Canadian crania
did not conform to Morton's standard type," that about the same time
Anders Retzius, the father of the cranial index, "divided the Indians
into dolichocephalic and brachycephalic groups," and that in 1866 J.
Aitken Meigs added a mesocephalic group.[11] At the present time, these
authors write: "Anthropologists are considering no longer simply the
problem of the unity or plurality of the Indian, but rather his variability
and its significance. The change in emphasis is an indication of prog-

---

[6] A. Hrdlička, *op. cit.*, pp. 34, 36.
[7] Samuel G. Morton, *Crania Americana; or, a Comparative view of the
Skulls of various Aboriginal Nations of North and South America; to which
is prefixed an Essay on the Varieties of the Human Species.* Illustrated by
78 plates and a colored map. (Philadelphia, 1839), p. 63.
[8] *Ibid.*, p. 81.
[9] *Ibid.*, p. 82.
[10] *Ibid.*, p. 63.
[11] Stewart and Newman, *op. cit.*, p. 22.

ress [for] interpretations of the physical variability of the American Indian have lagged behind description and classification."[12]

Morton's historical position is of importance in another respect. In his work the sometimes neglected relations between the beginnings of physical anthropology and phrenology is clearly exposed to view. Hoyme has pointed out that "in reconstructing the family tree of their science, physical anthropologists are likely to pass over phrenology quickly and put most emphasis on more sober sciences such as anatomy. Yet phrenology is as truly an ancestor of physical anthropology as astrology is of astronomy, or alchemy of chemistry. Indeed, phrenology has probably had much more influence on the development of physical anthropology than one may realize. Although Blumenbach and Camper and Bell had already pointed out race differences in the crania they observed, the phrenologists were the first to try to express these differences in terms of measurements. The landmarks from which they measured, as Topinard noted (1885), are almost the same as those used today by physical anthropology, although their names have been changed. The instruments which they used have left descendants in modern laboratories. Not least, the possible applications of the pseudoscience—in addition to stimulating popular interest—undoubtedly were an incentive to the scientific testing of its claims and to the assembling of cranial collections for study."[13] John C, Warren (1778-1856), whose *Account of the Crania of some of the Aborigines of the United States* is said by Hrdlička to be "the first publication in this field on the continent,"[14] had studied medicine at the University of Edinburgh, where phrenology was given academic recognition. Morton had studied at the same institution, but Warren became more closely associated with phrenology than Morton. After Warren became professor of anatomy at Harvard he engaged Schoolcraft to obtain American Indian crania for him, and he secured a collection of about five hundred crania assembled by the Boston Phrenological Society for Harvard, where it is to be found in the Warren Anatomical Museum.

---

[12] Stewart and Newman, *op. cit.*, p. 33.

[13] Hoyme, *op. cit.*, p. 412. Cf. John D. Davies, *Phrenology: fad and science; 19th-century American crusade* (New Haven, 1955), pp. 143 ff. Hrdlička, *op. cit.*, p. 10, says: "Even the teachings of Gall, however erroneous in application, have aided its [physical anthropology] growth, for they stimulated research into the variations of the head, skull, and brain, gave rise to various craniological collections, and were the main incentive to Morton's ultimate and remarkable work, the 'Crania Americana.'" *See also* Hrdlička, "Contributions to the History of Physical Anthropology in the United States of America with special reference to Philadelphia," *Proceed. Amer. Philosophical Society* 87:61-64, 1943.

[14] Hrdlička, *op. cit.*, p. 31.

Morton, while studying at Edinburgh in 1825, came under the influence of George Combe (1788-1858), who later became the world's
outstanding phrenologist after the death of John G. Spurzheim. Hoyme
points out that it was only five years later that Morton began his collection of skulls for use in his anatomy classes at the University of
Pennsylvania; "whether or not he also used them for phrenological
studies is unknown."[15] At all events, in his introductory letter to his
Crania Americana, Morton refers to himself as a "learner" in phrenology,
and says he is "free to acknowledge that there is a singular harmony
between the mental character of the Indian, and his cranial developments as explained by phrenology." Combe, a highly successful lecturer
in the United States, visited Morton when the latter was writing his
book and showed him "the method pursued by the phrenologists in
estimating the dimensions of the coronal region and anterior lobe of the
skull."[16] As a result, Combe contributed a phrenological essay to Morton's book. Morton, although not wholly committed, thought some combination of physical anthropology and phrenology would throw light
upon the nature and mentality of the Indian.

Since the fundamental premise of phrenology was that the brain
is the organ of the mind and that different parts of the brain have
different functions which can be directly interpreted through observations and measurements of the shape of the skull, there was an inherent
connection assumed to be present between anatomical traits and mental
functioning. Consequently, the attempt on the part of the phrenologists
to probe the mentality of the American Indian on the basis of empirical
observations represents a pioneer effort in the field of individual and
racial psychology.[17] Physical anthropology and psychology did not come
into such close rapport again until constitutional studies in the twentieth
century revived interest in the relation between the outward form of
the body and behavior.

George Combe, in his essay entitled "Phrenological Remarks on the
Relations between the Natural Talents and Dispositions of Nations, and

---

[15] Hoyme, *op. cit.*, p. 415.
[16] The words are those of Combe quoted by Hoyme, *op. cit.*, p. 415.
[17] Merle Curti, *The Growth of American Thought* (New York, 1943),
pp. 341-342, points out that: "Before the popularization and oversimplification of phrenology by dollar-minded quacks brought discredit, the doctrine
seemed to exemplify the new scientific spirit of the times. Repudiating the
traditional mental philosophy of the highly academic and metaphysical type
which dominated American colleges and intellectual life generally, phrenology taught, in the words of Combe, that 'the mind, as it exists by itself, can
never be an object of philosophical investigation.' For mind, to the phrenologist, was not independent of matter. 'The operations of the mind are the
mind itself.' These operations were said to be rooted in the complex and multiple organs making up the brain and the nervous system . . . ."

the Development of their Brains," says that: "No object can be presented to the philosophic mind more replete with interest than an inquiry into the causes of the differences of *national character*."[18] (Italics ours.) But the phrenologist, he says, is not satisfied with commonly held theories based on the assumption "that the capacities of the human mind have been, in all ages, the same; and that the diversity of phenomena exhibited by our species, is the result merely of the different circumstances in which men are placed."[19] He says that "those who contend that institutions came first, and that character follows as their effect, are bound to assign a cause for the institutions themselves. If they do not spring from the native mind, and are not forced on the people by conquest, it is difficult to see whence they can originate." Combe maintains that the phrenologist "has observed that a particular size and form of brain is the invariable concomitant of particular dispositions and talents, and that this fact holds good in the case of nations as well as of individuals." Consequently, "a knowledge of the size of the brain, and the proportions of its different parts, in the different varieties of the human race, will be the key to a correct appreciation of the differences in their natural endowments, on which external circumstances act only as modifying influences." Morton's book, therefore, provides an "authentic record in which the philosopher may read the native aptitudes, dispositions and mental force of these families of mankind."[20] Phrenological observations and measurements provide an index to "national character."

Whereas Schoolcraft, who himself was sympathetic to phrenology,[21] saw in myths and tales a possible route for exploring "savage mentality," those who followed a strict phrenological method thought they could arrive at psychological knowledge about the Indian by analyzing his "bumps." Lydia Maria Child, author of *Hobomok* (1824), a novel in which a white girl marries a noble savage, published a phrenological analysis of fifteen Indians in her *Letters from New York* (1843).[22] She found them greatly inferior to whites. In his *Travels in the Great Western Prairies* (1841), Thomas Farnham analyzed an Indian trapper he met who had been educated at Dartmouth. He found his civilized qualities were low but Benevolence, Ideality,

---

[18] In Morton's *Crania Americana, op. cit.*, p. 269.

[19] Combe, *ibid.*, p. 270, is here quoting Dugald Stewart, one of the famous Edinburgh group which included David Hume, Adam Smith, and Adam Ferguson. See Gladys Bryson, *op. cit.*

[20] Combe, *ibid.*, pp. 274-75. A somewhat fuller discussion of the same points may be found in Combe's book, *A System of Phrenology* (Boston, 1835), pp. 561 ff. ("On the coincidence between the natural talents and dispositions of nations and the development of their brains.")

[21] *Personal Memoirs, op. cit.*, pp. 14-15.

[22] pp. 247-257.

Wonder, Secretiveness, Destructiveness, Combativeness, Self-Esteem, and Hope were markedly developed.[23] Dr. John Wilson, surgeon of the ship *Beagle* which bore Darwin around the world, worked out a phrenological interpretation of the natives of Tierra del Fuego.[24] When I. A. Lapham published his pioneer study of the Wisconsin mounds in 1855, he included a phrenological analysis of a skull, prepared with the help of an unnamed "phrenological friend" in order "to give the reader more particular information respecting the supposed characteristics of this interesting relic of an extinct people." Commenting on the chart, he says: "Whether these figures can be relied upon as indicating the character and disposition of the individual to whom the skull belonged, may be doubted; though it will be perceived that their indications correspond with the general character of the aborigines in the large cautiousness, individuality, etc., and the deficient constructiveness, calculations, etc."[24a]

As Davies points out, one of the reasons why all phrenological societies assembled collections of crania was that "skulls of foreign races, especially uncivilized tribes. . .would reflect their collective personalities; Gall had maintained that it is to the disposition of savages and barbarians that one must go to study the natural dispositions of the civilized nations." "Both Spurzheim and Combe," he says, "had as one of their objects in coming to this country the study of the psychology of the Indian. The verdict was that the Indian not only was mentally inferior, like the Negro, but also, because of the peculiar organization of his mental organs, was intractable and untameable."[25]

Morton is also historically significant because he helped to further the great debate between the monogenists and polygenists that developed around the middle of the nineteenth century. This debate raged hotly in America because it brought to the fore the problem of innately determined mental characteristics and the "natural" inferiority of cer-

---

[23] See R. G. Thwaites, *Early Western Travels* (New York, 1904), vol. 28, p. 175. All of these terms were given a defined meaning in phrenological writing and appraised on a scale which took account of negative as well as positive forms of expression. "Combativeness," e.g., "obviously adapts man to a world in which danger and difficulty abound." On the positive side it is expressed as "courage to meet danger and overcome difficulties"; negatively it involves "love of contention and [a] tendency to provoke and assault." "Secretiveness," on the positive side, is "simply the propensity to conceal and is an ingredient in prudence," the restraint of emotions and ideas until they are submitted to judgment. "Cunning, deceit, duplicity and lying" are "abuses" of secretiveness. See Combe in Morton, *op. cit.*, p. 284.
[24] Davies, *op. cit.*, p. 143.
[24a] I. A. Lapham, "Antiquities of Wisconsin," *Smithsonian Contributions to Knowledge,* Vol. 7, Washington, 1855, pp. 81-82.
[25] Davies, *op. cit.*, pp. 144-146.

tain races, a question that bore directly upon the slavery of Negroes. It is interesting to note that the pluralists often granted the Indians savage virtues like bravery and courage, which they denied to the Negro.[26] Morton departed from the view maintained in the late eighteenth and early nineteenth century by men like Blumenbach, Cuvier, Lawrence, and Prichard, who thought the races of man were modifications of a single species. Although he was aware that his viewpoint challenged the accepted interpretation of the Scriptures, Morton attempted to demonstrate that there was racial plurality as far back as the evidence took him, thus setting the stage for the polygenists.[27] He concluded that the Indians were "the true autochthones; the primeval inhabitants of this vast continent."[28] And, in another place he says: "The American race is essentially separate and peculiar, whether we regard it in its physical, moral, or its intellectual relations. To us there are no direct or obvious links between the people of the old world and the new; for even admitting the seeming analogies to which we have alluded, these are so few in number, and evidently so casual, as not to invalidate the main position. . . ."[29]

The polygenists became the hereditarians of their time whereas the monogenists represented the environmentalist position. As the debate went on, especially in the hands of J. C. Nott (1804-1873), a student of Morton's and a southern physician, the polygenist stand was interpreted by some as progressive and as a "scientific" defense of the institution of slavery because it was demonstrable that the Negroes

---

[26] See Edward Lurie, "Louis Agassiz and the Races of Man," *Isis* 45:228, note 7, 1954. Reprinted separately as *Publications in the Humanities*, No. 12, Massachusetts Institute of Technology, Cambridge, 1955.

[27] In his "Memoir of the Life and Scientific Labors of Samuel George Morton," published in J. C. Nott and George R. Gliddon's *Types of Mankind* (Philadelphia, 1854), Henry S. Patterson documents fully, with quotations from letters as well as printed sources, the development of Morton's position. "The unity and common origin of mankind have, until recently," Patterson writes, "been considered undisputed points of doctrine. They seem to have been regarded as propositions not scientifically established, so much as taken for granted, and let alone. All men were held to be descended from the single pair mentioned in Genesis; every tribe was thought to be historically traceable to the regions about Mesopotamia; and ordinary physical influences were believed sufficient to explain the remarkable diversities of color, etc. These opinions were thought to be the teachings of Scripture not impugned by science, and were therefore almost universally acquiesced in. By Blumenbach, Prichard, and others, the unity is assumed as an axiom not disputed . . . . Morton was educated in youth to regard this doctrine as a scriptural verity, and he found it accepted as the first proposition in the existing Ethnology. As such he received it implicitly, and only abandoned it when compelled by the force of an irresistible conviction." (xliii and xlv)

[28] *Ibid.*, xlix.

[29] *Ibid.*, xlviii.

were "naturally" an inferior race. In 1844 Nott published *Two Lectures on the Natural History of the Caucasian and Negro Races,* which initiated a series of publications on polygenesis in which he relied heavily on the authority of Morton and Louis Agassiz. Known later for his anti-evolutionist views, at this earlier period Agassiz, a renowned biologist, became closely associated with the polygenists.[30] *Types of Mankind,* written by Nott in collaboration with George R. Gliddon and dedicated to Morton, first appeared in 1854 and had run through ten editions by 1871.[31] It will be unnecessary to discuss further details of the monogenist-polygenist controversy here except to note that Nott was responsible for supervising the publication of the American Edition of Count Arthur de Gobineau's notorious book *Essay on the Inequality of Human Races* (1856). Although Hrdlička characterizes the work of Nott and Gliddon as belonging to the category of "popular science" which did not advance "physical anthropology in this country to any great extent," [32] he says that the discussions of the monogenists and polygenists in general were "of much importance and assistance."[33]

From a descriptive point of view the horizon of physical anthropology in the United States had been broadened in 1848 by the publication of *The Races of Man and their Geographical Distribution* by Charles Pickering. This was Volume 9 of the *United States Exploring (Wilkes) Expedition* (1838-42). While some crania had been collected by this expedition, the book contained a map of the world showing the distribution of races and a series of plates, including pictures of natives of the Hawaiian Islands, Fiji, and Australia. *The Natural History of the Human Species* by Charles Hamilton was published a few years later (1851). Meanwhile, the rising interest in archeology stimulated the recovery of skeletal remains as well as tools, utensils, and other objects from the past. Before the conclusion of the Civil War the Smithsonian Institution, in the same pamphlet which was designed to promote inquiries into languages and customs of the living Indians (1863),[34] was encouraging the collection of crania and the systematic

---

[30] See Lurie, *op. cit.*

[31] Gliddon was the first American consular agent in Egypt and was interested in Egyptian archeology. He secured the collection of crania for Morton which was the basis of the latter's book, *Crania Aegyptica* (1844). Gliddon lectured in the United States. For his connection with John L. Stephens and E. G. Squier, see Victor W. von Hagen, *Maya Explorer* (1947), p. 44.

[32] Hrdlička, *op. cit.*, p. 154.

[33] *Ibid.*, p. 10.

[34] George Gibbs, "Instructions for Research relative to the Ethnology and Philology of America," *Smithsonian Miscellaneous Collections* 160, Washington, 1863. A section entitled "Crania" is prefaced by the statement that "among the first of the desiderata of the Smithsonian Institution, is a full series of the skulls of American Indians."

observation of the physical characteristics of the living. In a section headed "Physical Constitution," while nothing is said about the use of anthropometric instruments, the reader is advised that: "It is essential to notice the general stature of the people, the form of their bodies generally, and the proportions of their limbs; the form of the skull and the facial angle. . . . have these anything which distinguishes them from other people? What are the color and texture of their skin and hair? What beard have they? What is the color of their eyes? . . . . It is highly desirable, also, that photographs should be taken of individuals of each tribe."[35]

A year after the end of the Civil War, an event took place by which the foundation was laid for the subsequent development of physical anthropology, archeology, and cultural anthropology in direct association with an institution of higher learning. This event was the establishment, through a considerable bequest, of the Peabody Museum of American Archaeology and Ethnology at Harvard. A curatorship and a professorship were provided by the bequest. Both positions were assumed by Jeffries Wyman (1814-1874) who, at the time of his death, was said to be "indisputably the leading anthropologist of America."[36] Among other things Wyman is famous because he was the first to give a scientific description of the gorilla and because, almost immediately, he accepted the Darwinian theory of evolution.[37] When Wyman began his curatorship of the Peabody Museum in 1866, "the collection consisted of crania and bones of North American Indians, a few casts of crania of other races, several kinds of stone implements, and a few articles of pottery—in all, about fifty specimens."[38] In the same year, the Army Medical Museum was established in Washington.

In the latter half of the nineteenth century collections of skeletal material rapidly expanded and much of it was described. On the other hand, systematic observations on living Indians lagged far behind. In a monograph entitled *Physical Anthropology*, published in 1919, Hrdlička republished the article included in this volume in a considerably expanded form and to it he added a detailed account of the history of

---

[35] *Ibid.*, p. 8.
[36] A. S. Packard, "Memoir of Jeffries Wyman, 1814-1874," *Biogr. Mem. National Academy of Science*, Vol. 2:75-126.
[37] A. Hunter Dupree, "Jeffries Wyman's Views on Evolution," *Isis* 44: 243-246, 1953. T. D. Stewart, dealing with the immediate impact of Darwin's theory (1859-1871) on the handful of physical anthropologists in the United States, finds relatively little to report as compared with England and France. ("The Effect of Darwin's Theory of Evolution on Physical Anthropology" in *Evolution and Anthropology: A Centennial Appraisal*, the Anthropological Society of Washington, Washington, 1959, pp. 20-21.)
[38] Hrdlička, *op. cit.*, p. 46.

physical anthropology down to the date of writing. It will be unnecessary to cover the same ground here. But there are related topics, not
dealt with by him, such as paintings and photographs of Indians, which,
although not an integral part of the development of physical anthropology as a science, supplement anthropometric records. At the same
time they are valuable from an ethnographic point of view.

So far as paintings and drawings are concerned, while we do have
the pioneer work of Jacques Le Moyne de Morgues and John White
in the sixteenth century and the engravings of Théodore de Bry, "we
have no record of a large-scale Indian head or bust having been drawn
or painted by any white artist in America before the second quarter of
the eighteenth century."[39] Even so, we do not have any physical
measurements on the living until more than a century after this. However the work of the early painters of the American Indians may be
appraised in terms of esthetic values, or with respect to their realism
as portraits, as images of living Indians of the past, these pictorial
records are all that remain to us. "The success achieved by some of
the portraitists who drew and painted the Upper Missouri tribes,"
writes John C. Ewers, who showed his informants reproductions, "is
vouched for in the testimony of elderly, conservative, full-blooded
Indians obtained by the writer within the last decade." "These bits of
Indian testimony," he says, "indicate better than any theoretical judgments of mine the degree of success attained by the most gifted 'face
painters' in depicting Indians in the days before the camera. These
artists were not satisfied with documenting generalized Indian facial
types. They were drawing and painting recognizable likenesses of real
people."[40]

When daguerreotypy (1839) and later photography became available as techniques, they were used to picture Indians on the western
frontier. J. H. Fitzgibbon opened a daguerreotype gallery in St. Louis
in 1847 and is said to have had on display not only frontier scenes and
the pictures of prominent personages but the likenesses of Indian
chiefs.[41] John Mix Stanley, renowned for a series of paintings of American Indians which were destroyed in the Smithsonian fire of 1865, accompanied a party surveying for a northern railroad route in 1853 and

[39] John C. Ewers, "An Anthropologist looks at early pictures of North
American Indians," *N. Y. Historical Society Quarterly* 33:227, 1949. *See also*
Frank Weitenkampf, "How Indians were pictured in earlier days," *N. Y.
Historical Society Quarterly* 33:213-222, 1949; and "Early Pictures of North
American Indians: a Question of Ethnology," *Bull. N. Y. Pub. Lib.* 53:591-
614, 1949.
[40] *Ibid.*, p. 234.
[41] Robert Taft, *Photography and the American Scene. A Social History,
1839-1889* (New York: Macmillan, 1942), p. 249.

daguerreotyped Indians at Fort Union and Fort Benton.[42] After the Civil War exploring expeditions and other parties usually carried photographers.[43] Beginning with his second descent of the Colorado River in 1871, John K. Hillers became J. W. Powell's photographer. Julian H. Steward has published the pictures taken of Paiute and Ute Indians in 1873. "Few explorers in the U.S.," he says, "have had a comparable opportunity to study and photograph Indians so nearly in their aboriginal state."[44] Although selected primarily for their ethnographic value, they have physical anthropological interest too, although there are no set portraits. F. V. Hayden, who was interested in Indian ethnology, promoted photography when he was in charge of the U.S. Geological Survey of the Territories. William H. Jackson, an important figure in the history of American photography, was associated with the Hayden Surveys in the seventies. At South Pass in 1870 Jackson obtained photographs of the famous Shoshone chief Washakie and his village.[45] In 1877 Hayden published a "Descriptive Catalogue of Photographs of North American Indians" compiled by Jackson.[46] A thousand negatives were reported to be in the collection, representing twenty-five tribes. The subjects of the photographs taken in connection with the Surveys were systematically posed; front and profile views were taken when possible. Also when possible, a few anthropometric measurements were taken: stature, and the circumference of both head and chest. But there were difficulties involved in systematically photographing and measuring living subjects. "Usually it is only when an Indian is subjected to confinement that those measurements of his person which are suitable for anthropological purposes can be secured. In most cases, the Indian will not allow his person to be handled at all, or submit to any inconvenience whatever."[47] Thus, while photographers accompanied western surveys, and simple measurements such as those mentioned were put on record, so far as I can discover, government expeditions were not provided with experts capable of making systematic anthropometric observations.

---

[42] *Ibid.*, pp. 261-262. These daguerreotypes have not been found.

[43] Photographs of a Pawnee camp and Chief Peter La Cherre, taken by John Corbutt in 1866, are to be found in Taft, *op. cit.*, pp. 281-282.

[44] Julian H. Steward, "Notes on Hillers' Photographs of the Paiute and the Ute Indians taken on the Powell Expedition of 1873," *Smithsonian Miscellaneous Collections* Vol. 98, No. 18, 1939, p. 1. Cf. Taft, *op. cit.*, p. 288.

[45] See Taft, *op. cit.*, p. 299 and, for information on Jackson, p. 291.

[46] Department of the Interior, United States Geological Survey of the Territories, *Miscellaneous Publications* No. 9, Washington, 1877. A large proportion of the collection came from William Blackmore, an Englishman who maintained a private museum. There are also some photographs taken in Washington when delegations of Indians visited the capital.

[47] *Ibid.*, Hayden's Prefatory Note IV.

At the time of the Civil War measurements on northern white recruits were made and, according to Hrdlička, these "represent the first efforts of note on this continent in anthropology of the living,"[48] even though the data were not secured under ideal conditions or by experts. In the seventies Henry P. Bowditch (1840-1911), a professor of physiology at Harvard, instituted his well-known investigations on the growth of children. Anthropometric data on living Indians appears to have begun in 1865 with the Seneca Iroquois as subjects when Dr. George F. Buckley, a physician, measured Indians of military age located on reservations in the neighborhood of Buffalo, New York. Far from having any integral connection with previous studies of Indians, this project (only reported in detail by Marshall T. Newman in 1957)[49] was part of an anthropometric survey undertaken by the Sanitary Commission, a forerunner of the Public Health Service. Buckley was chief examiner of the Commission and his report appears in a study by Benjamin A. Gould (1869) intended to "present measurements for clothing size tariffs; physical and educational performance data; and enlistment, desertion, and mortality figures for Union Army troops." Newman says it is not clear "why, when the Civil War was over and mass troop recruiting was ended," Dr. Buckley measured the Iroquois.[50] While not satisfactory in all respects, these measurements "remain to this day the largest and most complete physical survey of a once powerful Eastern Indian group" because the Indians of this region of North America "were exterminated, absorbed, or driven west before physical anthropological studies came into being."[51]

F. W. Putnam (1839-1915), although primarily known for his work in archeology, is said by Hrdlička to have been "one of the best friends and promoters physical anthropology has had in this country."[52] He succeeded Wyman as curator of the Peabody Museum in 1875 and became Peabody Professor of Archeology at Harvard in 1886. Besides building up collections in the Museum, when he became associated with the World's Columbian Exposition at Chicago in 1891 he initiated a program which included anthropometric measurements on the living Indian of North America. This program was chiefly carried out by Franz Boas (1891-1894) who, under the auspices of a committee of the British Association for the Advancement of Science (consisting of E. B.

[48] Hrdlička, op. cit., p. 67.
[49] Marshall T. Newman, "The Physique of the Seneca Indians of Western New York State," Journal of the Washington Academy of Sciences, 47: 357-362, 1957.
[50] Ibid., p. 357.
[51] Ibid., pp. 358-357.
[52] Hrdlička, op. cit., p. 49.

Taylor, G. M. Dawson, Sir J. H. Lefroy, Daniel Wilson, R. G. Hali-
burton, and G. W. Bloxam), organized in the early eighties, already
had been investigating the physical characteristics, languages, and cultures of the Indians of the Northwest Coast. In 1888 Boas read a paper
on "Indian Skulls from British Columbia" before the New York Academy of Sciences; and the "First General Report on the Indians of British
Columbia," which includes more than a dozen pages of anthropometric material, appeared the following year. It was succeeded at intervals by others.[53] Under the auspices of the same committee A. F.
Chamberlain, the associate of Boas at Clark and who had participated
in the measurements of Worcester school children, made a study of the
Kootenay Indians in 1891 which included measurements and somatological observations.[54] In 1895 Boas published "Zür Anthropologie der
Nord Amerikanischen Indianer," a partial report on the program Putnam had set up in connection with the Exposition. Boas tabulates
mean statures and cephalic indices from Indians all over the country.
Although the number of measurements and indices reported is limited,
comparable data over such a wide geographical range had never been
available before.[55]

Thus, by the end of the nineteenth century, a fair sampling of
the physical characteristics of the living Indians of the United States
and certain regions of Canada was emerging, in addition to the skeletal
and cranial material that had been collected in museums. Although, as
Hrdlička points out, the Bureau of American Ethnology did not concern itself directly with physical anthropology, under its auspices the
collection of skeletal material was encouraged. Subsequent to the completion of a National Museum building in 1881, the "normal somatological material" which had been housed in the Army Medical Mu-

---

[53] See bibliography of Franz Boas in A. L. Kroeber, Ruth Benedict,
et al., "Franz Boas 1858-1942," Memoir, AAA, No. 61, AA 45 (1943) No. 3,
Part 2.

[54] Hrdlička, op. cit., p. 88, where references to Chamberlain's contributions to physical anthropology will be found. Livingston Farrand was
another associate of Boas who measured Indians in British Columbia. Ibid.,
p. 105. In the Northeast, under the direction of Boas, Labrador Eskimo were
measured by Leslie A. Lee and J. D. Sornberger in 1891-92 (unpublished).
Previously (1880) Virchow had reported authropometric data on a few Eskimo from this area and Boas himself measured some Labrador Eskimo. See
T. Dale Stewart, "Anthropometric Observations on the Eskimos and Indians of Labrador," Anthropological Series, Field Museum of Natural History,
Vol. 31, No. 1, Chicago, 1939.

[55] Published in the Verh. d. Berlin Ges. f. Anthrop., Ethn. u. Urg.
27:366-411, 1895. It is not stated precisely where and by whom the measurements were taken. Frederick Starr measured Cherokee Indians in connection
with the Exposition project, but the results were not published. See bibliography in W. H. Gilbert, Jr., "The Eastern Cherokees," Bulletin 133 of the

seum was transferred to the National Museum in 1898-99.[56] Instruction
in physical anthropology at Harvard began about the same time.[57] In
1903 a Division of Physical Anthropology was established in the National Museum under the curatorship of Hrdlička.[58] But an *American
Journal of Physical Anthropology* was yet to come (1918), as well as a
Society of Physical Anthropologists (1930).

ARCHEOLOGY

The investigation of American "antiquities" presented inherent
difficulties which were of a different order from those involved in the
recording of linguistic and ethnographic data, or even the measurement of skulls. Once crania were obtained, they could be described
and measured at leisure. If their geographical provenience were known,
generalizations could be made about the similarities and differences
observed in series of crania without reference to their archeological
context. Word lists could be written down in the field and so could
information about the customs of living people. And, in the case of
material objects like tools and utensils, notes could be made on the
observed use of them whether they were collected or not. However,
the excavation of objects from the ground, the description of mounds
and earthworks, or the remains of ruined cities obscured by verdant
jungle growth was another matter. The exposure, description, and
classification of material remains of this sort presented complicated
problems, such as the relation of various classes of excavated objects
to each other and to associated skeletal remains *in situ*, the interpretation of superimposed layers of material, the dating of these, and the
determination of the temporal relations of assemblages of objects found
at different sites to each other. All these problems required the
development of systematic procedures and techniques of excavation
before it was possible to make any reliable generalizations or reach any
valid historical conclusions.

Bureau of American Ethnology, 1943. Later Starr reported on 2,847 individuals,
representing twenty-three tribal groups in southern Mexico. See "The Physical
Characters of the Indians of Southern Mexico," Vol. 4, *Decennial Pub.,* University of Chicago, 1902, pp. 53-109.

[56] Hrdlička, *op. cit.,* p. 71. This author lists publications of the Smithsonian from 1851 to 1902 "relating more or less directly to physical anthropology" (pp. 72-75).

[57] *Ibid.,* p. 81.

[58] In 1904 Hrdlička issued a pamphlet entitled "Directions for collecting Information and Specimens for Physical Anthropology" (Part R of *Bull.
of the United States National Museum,* No. 39).

Besides this, the beginnings of interest in American antiquities predated any very useful information that could be derived from geology and paleontology. In early nineteenth century America these disciplines, which later became so closely associated with archeology, were in their infancy, too. While Schoolcraft qualified as a geologist and mineralogist and had a keen interest in archeology, he did not make any pioneer contributions in this field. It was, in fact, Thomas Jefferson who not only dug what he called a "barrow"; he reported his procedure in detail so that he can be credited with "the first published report of an archeological excavation in the east,"[1] as well as the anticipation of some of the rudiments of modern archeological field methods. For it must not be forgotten that, in contrast to the early work done in linguistics and physical anthropology, even Americans of the early nineteenth century could not turn to learned men in Europe for help in developing archeological techniques or in interpreting their data. In 1840, says Daniel, "apart from a group of intellectuals in Denmark and Sweden," prehistoric archeology "hardly existed";[2] and the "three-age system" that emerged from the thinking of these early Scandinavian archeologists and which provided the framework of European prehistory for so long a period thereafter, never proved applicable in the New World.[3]

Nevertheless, the old question concerning the origin and identity of the native population of America was revivified and reformulated when more and more American antiquities were brought to notice. In North America it was the "mounds" that stimulated interest and, in Middle America, the ruins of temples and cities in the jungle. The speculation that arose had its paradoxical aspect. Despite the fact that considerable information about the living Indians had accumulated, initially, the keen interest taken in the antiquities of the New World was not founded on a hope that these remains would illuminate the

---

[1] John Otis Brew, "A Selected Bibliography of American Indian Archeology east of the Rocky Mountains," Papers of the Excavators' Club, Vol. 2, No. 1, Cambridge, 1943, p. 88. Jefferson's account, from his Notes on the State of Virginia, has been reprinted in Robert F. Heizer, The Archaeologist at Work. A Source Book in Archaeological Method and Interpretation (New York: Harper, 1959).
[2] Glyn E. Daniel, A Hundred Years of Archeology (London: Duckworth, 1950), p. 54.
[3] Charles Rau, "The Archaeological Collection of the United States National Museum in charge of the Smithsonian Institution," Smithsonian Contributions to Knowledge (Vol. 22, No. 4, Washington, 1876, p. 7) notes that in North America the distinction between chipped stone implements and ground stone implements "cannot be respectively referred to certain epochs in the development of the aborigines of the country, and hence the here adopted separation of North American stone articles into a chipped and a ground series has no chronological significance whatever, but simply refers to the modes of manufacture."

prehistoric past of the Indians. Instead, American archeology became
a fascinating subject in the public mind because it was based on the
myth of a vanished race. It was thought that peoples superior to and
distinct from the contemporary living Indians may have occupied this
continent prior to them. If so, they must have been some superior
"grade" of Indians or have had some close connection with the past
civilizations of the Old World. For the white pioneers held the contemporary Indians in low esteem; they were essentially savages.
William Robertson had even minimized the cultural achievements of
the historical Indians discovered by the Spanish in Mexico and Peru,
and later, it will be recalled, Morgan was unwilling to accredit them
with a truly civilized stage of existence in his evolutionary scheme.

Then, too, in the background of American thought lay Volney's
Ruins: or a Survey of the Revolution of Empires, originally published
in France in 1791. Volney had visited America a few years later and
his book, translated in part by Jefferson and Joel Barlow, had been a
best seller in 1795 and appeared in cheap editions for a century thereafter. It provided a stimulus to romantic reflections on man's past, the
rise and fall of ancient peoples and their cultures. Elsewhere in the
world there had been the decline of civilizations and the persistence
of ruins; perhaps the same was true here.[3a] Thus, instead of leading
to an integration of archeological material with the established facts
about the Indians of the historical period, the investigation of American
antiquities led to a controversy between those who thought the mounds
and earthworks were constructed by some mysterious predecessors of
the Indians and those who attributed them to aboriginal Indian groups
of some kind. A resolution was not achieved until near the close of the
nineteenth century, so that an attack upon the genuine problems inherent in the prehistory of the New World peoples was greatly delayed.

It will be unnecessary to review the early speculations here,[4] but
by the late eighteenth century the question, Who were the Mound

---

[3a] See Rose Macaulay, *Pleasure of Ruins* (London: Weidenfeld and
Nicolson, 1953) for a fascinating and well-documented survey of the expression of a romantic attitude towards ruins in European culture in the
period before sober archeological investigations had gotten under way.
[4] These are discussed by Samuel F. Haven ("Archaeology of the United
States, or Sketches, Historical and Bibliographical, of the Progress of Information and Opinion respecting Vestiges of Antiquity in the United States,"
Smithsonian Contributions to Knowledge, Vol. 8, Washington, 1856); Cyrus
Thomas ("Report on the Mound Explorations of the Bureau of American
Ethnology," *Twelfth Annual Report of the Bureau of Ethnology*, Washington,
1894); and more briefly by Henry C. Shetrone (*The Mound-Builders*, New
York: Appleton, 1930). A review of the literature on the mound builders is
also to be found in Justin Winsor, *op. cit.*, pp. 369-412 ("The Progress of
Opinion Respecting the Origin and Antiquity of Man in America").

Builders?, was being raised by learned men. President Ezra Stiles, of Yale, who regarded the Indians as "Canaanites of the expulsion of Joshua," asked Franklin for his opinion. The latter suggested that the earthworks might have been erected by De Soto in defense against the Indians, a view at first supported by Noah Webster, who later changed his opinion.[5] B. S. Barton, who was interested in American antiquities as well as Indian languages, thought that the mounds might have been built by the descendants of Danish immigrants—probably "Toltecs"—and that they might have had a religious rather than a military function.[6] William Bartram, whose *Travels* became world famous, saw and described mounds and earthworks in the course of his botanizing expeditions through the southern states. Since the living Indians of the region could give him no information he concluded that these structures must have been built by a different people, whom he did not specifically identify. Bartram's observations were of such high quality that Squier made use of them in his *Ancient Monuments* (1848), as did Swanton in the twentieth century in order to show a connection between these structures and the historic tribes.[7] Jefferson maintained a balanced view of the problem. In a letter of 1787 he said: "It is too early to form theories on those antiquities, we must wait with patience till more facts are collected. I wish our philosophical societies would collect exact descriptions of the several monuments as yet known and insert them, naked, in their transactions."[7a]

Even before the beginning of the nineteenth century there were a few reliable descriptions of earthworks in the Ohio valley. In 1788, for instance, General Rufus Putnam, who served in the Revolution

---

[5] See G. Herbert Smith, "Noah Webster, the Archeologist," *AA* 33:620-624, 1931.

[6] Benjamin Smith Barton, *Observations on Some Parts of Natural History* (London, 1787), p. 65. See also "Papers relating to certain American Antiquities," *Trans. Amer. Philosophical Society*, Vol. 4, 1796.

[7] John R. Swanton, "The Interpretation of Aboriginal Mounds by Means of Creek Indian Customs," *Annual Report of the Smithsonian Institution, 1927*, Washington, 1928. Through a curious concatenation of circumstances, a manuscription of Bartram's, written in 1789 in reply to a series of questions sent him by B. S. Barton, came into the hands of S. G. Morton more than half a century later. Since it contained extremely valuable material on the southern mounds, not included in his *Travels*, Morton sent the manuscript to Squier, and it was later published in Vol. III of the *Transactions* of the AES (1853), for which Squier wrote a prefatory note. But since most of this edition was destroyed in a fire it did not become generally known until its republication in 1909. For further information see *The Travels of William Bartram*, edited with commentary and an annotated index by Francis Harper (New Haven: Yale University Press, 1958), p. 423.

[7a] Quoted in Brooke Hindle, *The Pursuit of Science in Revolutionary America* (Chapel Hill: University of North Carolina Press, 1956), p. 324.

under Washington, prepared a map of the Marietta works for the Ohio Company. "This document," says Shetrone, "may be regarded as the genesis of the science of archeology in the United States."[8] As the westward movement across the Alleghenies accelerated, interest in the "mound builders" increased because, in the Old Northwest and, indeed, throughout the whole of the Mississippi valley, more and more such remains were discovered. Settlers became familiar with them because growing population centers, like Marietta and Circleville, were often built where the remains of what was thought to be a vanished people were found.

The existence of the mounds and earthworks of the eastern Mississippi valley was well known to the public by 1800 and had various repercussions on the minds of Americans of the early nineteenth century. It is said that as a young man, Joseph Smith, who grew up in the mound area of western New York, "used to entertain his family and friends with accounts of what the mound builders looked like and what they did."[9] The inspiration of the epical story contained in the Book of Mormon (1830) has been connected by some scholars outside the church with the current folk-anthropology concerning the origin of the mound builders.

In more serious vein, opposing views of the identity of the mound builders continued to be advanced during the first decade of the nineteenth century.[10] In 1812, the American Antiquarian Society, an organization largely responsible for promoting a more scientific approach to the mound problem,[11] was founded. Reviewing the situation four decades later (1856), Samuel F. Haven, its distinguished librarian and

---

[8] Shetrone, op. cit., p. 13; cf. p. 10, Figure 2, where the map is reproduced. An early painting (1832) of the Marietta group is likewise illustrated (Figure 1).

[9] See Edward Hoagland Brown, "Harvard and the Ohio Mounds," The New England Quarterly 22:212, 1949; Fawn Brodie, No Man Knows My History: The Life of Joseph Smith (New York, 1945); Van Wyck Brooks, The Times of Melville and Whitman (New York, 1947), p. 91. Charles A. Shook, Cumorah Revisited (Cincinnati, 1910), pp. 25-47, discusses the possibility that Joseph Smith saw an unpublished romance of Solomon Spaulding which provided the framework for the Book of Mormon. Spaulding, originally a preacher, went into business at Conneaut, Ohio. While living there, he began to write romances based upon the mounds.

[10] See Haven, op. cit., and Thomas, op. cit., with reference in particular to Rev. Thaddeus M. Harris and Rt. Rev. James Madison, first Protestant Episcopal Bishop of Virginia and at one time president of William and Mary College.

[11] Wissler, op. cit., p. 195, says that this organization "at once set a high standard in research. It financed two major projects [i.e., those of C. Atwater, and I. A. Lapham who was the pioneer investigator of the Wisconsin mounds] and otherwise encouraged archeological research." See also Mitra, pp. 199-200, who errs in attributing the initials J. C. to Lapham.

one of the few who, from the very first, maintained a judicious viewpoint,[12] wrote: "The need of such a measure had become apparent; objects of archeological interest were known to exist in great numbers; but in the crude and defective state of information respecting them, no inferences worthy the name of scientific deductions could be derived from the features they presented. Not only accurate delineations and trustworthy descriptions, but aggregation and classification, were wanting to a development of their real nature and probable origin. . . . Vestiges of human forms of unnatural dimensions, were supposed to have been discovered. The valley of the Mississippi was like a wonder-book, full of marvels and mysteries, and productive of vague and dreamy lucubrations. While men of education were reviving one or another of the many theories of colonization from the old world, at some dim and distant period, faintly indicated by history or tradition, another class convinced themselves that giants and pigmies had, in turn or together, inhabited that region."[13]

––––––––––

[12] Winsor, *op. cit.*, p. 400, says: "The steady and circumspect habit of Haven's mind was conspicuous in his treatment of the mounds. It is to him that the later advocates of the identity of their builders with the race of the red Indian's look as the first sensibly to affect public opinion in the matter. He argued against their being a more advanced race (p. 154) and in his *Report of the American Antiquarian Society* in 1877 (p. 37) he held that it might yet be proved that the mound builders and red Indians were one in race, as J. H. McCulloh had already suggested." The latter's book, *Researches, philosophical and antiquarian, concerning the Aboriginal History of America*, had been published in 1829. See Mitra, *op. cit.*, pp. 104-105. What is particularly interesting in the passage Haven wrote in 1856 (p. 154) is the fact that even at this date he draws comparisons between the structures of the Mississippi valley and those of Middle and South America. "There are no ruins of temples or other structures of stone, wrought by the hammer or the chisel," he says, "such as abound in Central America. There are no traces of roads and bridges to connect territorial divisions, or facilitate the commerce of an organized state, such as are found in Peru. There are no distinct evidences of arts and manufactures employing separate classes of population, or conducted as regular branches of industry. There are no proofs of the practice of reducing metals from their ores, and melting and casting them for use and ornament — none of a knowledge of chemistry or astronomy . . . . In a word, tokens of civil institutions, of mechanical employments, and the cultivation of science and literature however humbly such as appear among the remains of Mexican and Peruvian civilization, have no positive counterpart in the regions of which we are speaking. Whatever may have been the kind or degree of social advancement attained to by the ancient dwellers in the valleys of the Ohio and Mississippi, those domestic arts and habits of luxury which attend the division of labor and the accumulation of private wealth, had not been sufficiently developed to leave any symbols behind them."
[13] Haven, *op. cit.*, p. 32. No one has yet written an account of the impact of the discovery of mound-builder remains on American culture considered as a whole. It would provide an interesting chapter in the history of folk-anthropology in the United States.

The conceptualization of the problem presented by the antiquities of the Mississippi valley in the early nineteenth century is nowhere more clearly epitomized than in Caleb Atwater's *Description of the Antiquities discovered in the State of Ohio and other Western States* (1820).[11] Atwater (1778-1867) was born in Circleville, Ohio, where he later served as postmaster. The town takes its name from the fact that, when it was laid out, concentric circles of aboriginal earthworks were closely followed by the outlying streets.[15] Atwater's work was supported by Isaiah Thomas, the benefactor and first president of the American Antiquarian Society and, on the descriptive side, it is one of the foundation stones of American archeology. Mitra calls him the "first true archeologist."[16] Yet, in historical perspective the fact should not be overlooked that the three-fold classification of antiquities adopted by Atwater embodies a priori the theory that the mound builders are a separate race. Recognizing that Europeans already have left remains, these constitute one of his categories. While he is afraid that this class of antiquities "may excite a smile," he "begs leave" to include what we would now class as historical archeology. As for the "Antiquities of Indians of the present race," he says they "are neither numerous nor very interesting." In other words, the rude stone axes, pestles, knives, arrowheads, etc., found by the settlers in their ploughed fields are "so exactly similar to those found in all the Atlantic States, that a description of them is deemed quite useless." The really important body of material, then, the "most highly interesting class of antiquities," are those which "owe their origin to a people far more civilized than our Indians, but far less so than Europeans." Atwater did not hesitate to attribute the mounds and earthworks to an Asiatic people, "Hindoos and southern Tartars"; after arriving in North America they moved south to Mexico and Peru. He had read Alexander von Humboldt's description of the Mexican "pyramid of Cholula" which was interpreted as a higher stage in the development of the type of tumuli found in the Middle West.[17] Thus, the study of the mounds opened up broad archeological horizons by stimulating the immediate search for comparative materials and inspiring sweeping hypotheses before the North American material itself was fully known in detail.

---

[14] Vol. 1 of the *Transactions and Collections of the American Antiquarian Society*, 1820.
[15] Shetrone, *op. cit.*, p. 251, reproduces a map of 1836.
[16] Mitra, *op. cit.*, p. 99. Shetrone, *op. cit.*, p. 22, refers to Atwater's work as "the earliest systematic examination of mounds and earth works" and says that "considering the almost total lack of precedent" his contribution "was a most creditable one."
[17] Atwater, *op. cit.*, pp. 111-121; pp. 213 ff. and p. 250.

Atwater's work marked the beginning of a series of surveys, the most classical being that of E. G. Squier, a newspaper editor of Chillicothe, Ohio, and a physician, E. H. Davis, of the same town. Between 1845 and 1847 they opened over two hundred mounds, explored about one hundred earthworks, and gathered a collection of specimens from a wider area than had hitherto been reported. Although their classification did not prove altogether satisfactory to later investigators, their approach to the problem marked a radical change from that of Atwater. In a summary report read before the American Ethnological Society, of which he was a member, Squier says: "At the outset all preconceived notions were abandoned, and the work of research commenced, as if no speculations had been indulged in, nor anything before been known, respecting the singular remains of antiquity scattered so profusely around us. It was concluded that, either the field should be entirely abandoned to the poet and the romancer, or, if these monuments were capable of reflecting any certain light upon the grand archeological questions connected with the primitive history of the American continent, the origin, migration, and early state of the American race, that then they should be carefully and minutely, and above all, systematically investigated." There have been "too few well-authenticated facts," he says, and "their absence has been poorly supplied by speculations"; "it seems strange that hitherto, while every other branch of research has enlisted active and enlightened minds in its elucidation, the archeological field has been left comparatively unoccupied."[18]

The massive *Ancient Monuments of the Mississippi Valley* appeared in 1848 as Volume 1 of *Smithsonian Contributions to Knowledge,* although the American Ethnological Society originally had planned to publish it before it had grown to such huge proportions. It was the harbinger of other publications on the mounds which appeared under government auspices, particularly after the Bureau of American Ethnology was inaugurated.[19]

Squier and Davis did not draw many general conclusions from their investigations but, significantly, they ventured to suggest some connections between the mound culture and that of the peoples of Mexico, Central America, and Peru.[20] Later Squier himself went to

[18] "Aboriginal Monuments of the Mississippi Valley," *Trans. of the Amer. Ethnological Society,* Vol. II, 1848, p. 134.
[19] Since, at this earlier date, there was no national museum, the specimens collected by Squier and Davis, after being offered to the New York Historical Society, finally were purchased in 1864 by William Blackmore for his private museum in Salisbury, England. Edward Hoagland Brown, *op. cit.,* p. 210.
[20] In the appendix to Squier's "Aboriginal Monuments of the State of New York" (1849), which appeared in Vol. 2 of *Smithsonian Contributions*

Middle America and then South America to continue archeological work and other activities. But before this, in his *Aboriginal Monuments of the State of New York* (1849), he directly linked some of the mounds of that region with the historical Iroquois. This was an extremely radical interpretation at the time. Yet it coincided with the views of men like Haven, McCulloh, Drake, and Schoolcraft,[21] who were inclined to ascribe the mounds to North American Indians, even without linking them with specific tribes. Schoolcraft said that "there is little to sustain a belief that these ancient works are due to tribes of more fixed and exalted traits of civilization, far less to a people of an expatriated type of civilization, of either an ASIATIC or EUROPEAN origin, as several popular writers very vaguely, and with little severity of investigation, imagined . . . . There is nothing, indeed, in the magnitude and structure of our western mounds which a semi-hunter and semi-agricultural population, like that which may be ascribed to the ancestors of Indian predecessors of the existing race, could not have executed." Consequently, "aboriginal archeology has fallen under a spirit of misapprehension and predisposition to exaggeration. The antiquities of the United States are the antiquities of barbarism, and not of civilization."[22]

Although Schoolcraft's views, and those of a few others, anticipated the resolution of the problem, and Squier and Davis initiated more careful and systematic field work than had been done before, not until long after the Civil War did the modern period in mound archeology really begin. But public interest was, perhaps, at its height prior to the middle of the last century. One evidence of this is the moving-panorama which Dr. Montroville Wilson Dickeson (1810-1882) exhibited in various cities from 1837 to 1844. Dickeson, who had excavated in the mound area and is referred to by Squier and Davis, presented his collection of objects to the Academy of Natural Sciences in Philadelphia. As his panorama unrolled, the observer saw the burial of De Soto, the effects of the great tornado of 1844, and scenes of the mounds and earthworks of the Middle West in their excavated and unexcavated state. Among the mound groups delineated were those

---

to *Knowledge*, a great deal of comparative material from Middle America and South America on defense structures, sepulchral mounds, sacred enclosures, and temples is assembled.

[21] See C. Thomas, *op. cit.*, p. 600, who says that the conclusions of McCulloh "based, as they were, on the comparatively slender data then obtainable, are remarkable, not only for the clearness with which they are stated and the distinctness with which they are defined, but as being more in accordance with all the facts ascertained than perhaps those of any contemporary."

[22] Schoolcraft, *Indian Tribes*, Vol. 1, p. 66, and Introductory Documents, XIII.

at Marietta, Circleville, Portsmouth, Bon Hom Island, Baluxie, Lake
Concordia, Caddo Parish, and the Chamberlin and Ferguson Groups.[23]

The Smithsonian Institution, ever alert to the need for collecting
material, included "Instructions for Archaeological Investigations in the
United States" in its *Annual Report* for 1861.[23a] The only true "antiquities of America" were conceived somewhat as Atwater had defined
them, that is, remains "of the races which had already passed away
before the discovery of the continent by Europeans, or whose extinc-
tion may be considered as coeval with that event." Special interest is
expressed in "specimens frequently disinterred in the Mexican States
belonging to the era of Aztec or Toltecan civilization." Besides the
widening of the geographical horizon indicated, it is quite clear in these
"Instructions" that progress in European archeology, in the phase of
development Daniel calls its Birth, was already beginning to influence
the conceptualization of problems and techniques in American archeology. It is noted, for example, that in dealing with antiquities of the kind
under discussion, objects may be "found under conditions which connect archaeology with geology." Specific reference is made to the Danish
collections, and it is suggested that "a similar investigation in America
may take us back to a very remote period in aboriginal history." A new
note was being struck here. In respect to techniques of excavation
reference is made to the necessity of establishing the "true relations of
these objects" *in situ,* and problems of dating and stratification are
broached. It is suggested that "in the case of the shell banks, the largest
trees, where any exist, should, if practicable, be cut down and the
annual rings counted," and the depth of the "superincumbent deposit
of earth should be measured and its character noted . . . whether it
has been stratified by the action of water," and so on. These, and other
suggestions, even though designed for amateurs, anticipate the procedures of a much later period.

---

[23] See J. Alden Mason, "Grand Moving Diorama, a Special Feature,"
Pennsylvania Archeologist 12:14-16, 1942. The panorama referred to was
acquired about 1899 by the University Museum, Philadelphia. It is now in
the possession of the St. Louis Art Museum. Mason quotes one of the hand-
bills used to advertise it: "MONUMENTAL GRANDEUR OF THE MIS-
SISSIPPI VALLEY, with scientific lectures on AMERICAN AERCHIOL-
OGY," going on to proclaim that "THIS GORGEOUS PANORAMA with
all the ABORIGINAL MONUMENTS of a large extent of country once
roamed by the RED MAN, was painted by the EMINENT ARTIST I. J.
EGAN, ESQ., and covers 15,000 feet of Canvass . . . ." Actually, the figure
is about 2,500 square feet. In regard to the admission charge, Mason points
out that in the days "when even a skilled workman received no more than
a dollar a day, twenty-five cents admission to a panorama was equivalent
to an orchestra seat to the grand opera today."
[23a] See *Sixteenth Annual Report of the Smithsonian Institution, 1861,*
Washington, 1862, pp. 392-396. George Gibbs was the author.

In its *Report* of 1862, the Smithsonian Institution reprinted a paper on "North American Archaeology" by Lord Avebury (Sir John Lubbock), which had been published in England previously in the *Natural History Review*. The author relied chiefly upon the classical volume of Squier and Davis, the later work of Squier on the New York mound area, Lapham's *Antiquities of Wisconsin* and Haven's *Archaeology of the United States*. Reference is also made to Atwater and Schoolcraft's *History, Conditions and Prospects*. This summary brought American archaeology to the attention of scholars throughout the world because it was included in Lord Avebury's famous book, *Pre-historic Times*. This volume, first published in 1865, reached its seventh edition in the early twentieth century. It was in this book that the author adopted the Danish three-age system; while, at the same time, following French scholars, he divided the Stone Age into two periods, introducing the English terms "paleolithic" and "neolithic."[23b] The interest of the American public in archeology must have been refreshed, too, by the inclusion of many objects from the mound area in the archeological collection assembled by the Smithsonian Institution for display as part of the United States Government representation at the Centennial Exposition in Philadelphia (1876). Among other specimens a series of beautifully carved stone pipes, such as those described by Squier and Davis years before, could be seen at first hand.[24]

A new era in American archeology began in the 1880's when the Peabody Museum of Harvard became active in mound excavation almost simultaneously with the broad program that was instituted under the auspices of the newly founded Bureau of American Ethnology. F. W. Putnam, always an energetic organizer and promoter, had become permanent secretary of the American Association for the Advancement of Science in 1873 and published an article on Illinois and Indiana mounds the same year.[25] After he became curator of the Peabody Museum, he was likewise a prime mover in the organization of the Archaeological Institute of America (1879), which ever since has given recognition to American archeology. In the early eighties Putnam initiated a program of archeological investigation which concentrated on the Turner Group of Mounds, representative of the Hopewell culture. Also, with the help of Alice C. Fletcher, pioneer musi-

---

[23b] John Lubbock, *Pre-historic Times, as illustrated by Ancient Remains, and the Manners and Customs of Modern Savages* (London: Williams and Norgate, 1865), pp. 2-3.

[24] Charles Rau, *op. cit.*, p. 7.

[25] "Description of an ancient fortification on the Wabash river, 1872." (*Boston Soc. Nat. History; Proc.* 15:28-35.) For early archeological contributions of Putnam, see bibliography in *Putnam Anniversary Volume*, 1909.

cologist and ethnographer of the Omaha, Putnam raised funds for the purchase of the Serpent Mound, the title to which was transferred to the Ohio State Archaeological and Historical Society in 1900.[26]

The archeological program of the Bureau of American Ethnology, once initiated, embraced wide geographical horizons. In the *Fourth Annual Report* (1882-83), Major Powell points out that originally the program of the Bureau "did not embrace any plan for archaeological investigations in the eastern portions of the United States, and in particular did not contemplate researches relating to the mounds; but Congress having directed that such work should be added to the functions of the Bureau, a limited amount of work was accomplished in this field during the past year." This work was immediately expanded by the creation of a Division of Mound Exploration. Cyrus Thomas was engaged to take charge of it. Powell's insight into the problem is indicated by his passing observation that it had been apparent to him for some years past "that a few, at least, of the important mounds of the valley of the Mississippi, had been constructed and used subsequent to the occupation of this continent by Europeans, and that some, at least, of the mound builders were therefore none other than known Indian tribes."[27] The program of the Bureau was further extended in 1882 when James Stevenson was directed to explore "that class of ancient remains in Arizona and New Mexico commonly known as 'cave and cliff dwellings.' "[28] His initial investigations were in the Cañon de Chelly. And, in 1889, a systematic exploration of the archeology of the Atlantic slope was initiated under the direction of Gerard Fowke, who had been associated previously with Thomas in the mound program.[28a] It was under the auspices of the Bureau of American Ethnology, in short, that, through a series of widely gauged programs, the empirical foundations of archeology in the United States were established on a broad geographical scale.

---

[26] For the essential facts about Putnam, see the obituary by Charles Peabody (*Journal of American Folk-Lore* 27:302-306, 1915), and E. H. Brown, *op. cit.*

[27] Report of Director, *Fourth Annual Report of the Bureau of Ethnology*, 1882-83, Washington, 1886, pp. xxix-xxx, "Mound Exploration." In the Director's Report to the *Twelfth Annual Report of the Bureau of Ethnology*, p. xl, Powell says that certain archeologists, by petition, asked Congress to enlarge the scope of the Bureau. Powell's biographer (Darrah, *op. cit.*, p. 261) says that: "George Crookham had acquainted him with the mound builders of Ohio. Wes as a child had dug his fingers into the earthworks at Chillicothe and Jackson, and treasured the flints and artifacts he found there . . . . [As a boy, he] collected specimens in the prehistoric earthworks at Delavan a few miles from the farm."

[28] *Fourth Annual Report of the Bureau of Ethnology, op. cit.*, p. xxxiv.

[28a] Gerard Fowke, "Archeological Investigations in James and Potomac Valleys," *Bulletin 23 of the Bureau of Ethnology*, Washington, 1894.

After a decade of research Cyrus Thomas published his accumulated evidence on the mounds in the *Twelfth Report* of the Bureau
(1890-91). He had phrased his problem differently from his predecessors by asking: Were the mounds built by the Indians? And he
insisted that "the questions relating to prehistoric America are not to
be answered by the study of its ancient monuments alone, but also
by the study of the languages, customs, arts, beliefs, traditions, and
folklore of the aborigines."[29] Briefly stated, the conclusions of Thomas,
carefully documented and argued, were that the ancestors of the historic Indians were responsible for building the mounds and earthworks
and that, while some of these monuments might be of considerable
antiquity, a few had been built subsequent to the discovery of America.

The myth of a vanished race that had plagued the interpretation
of the mound cultures of the Middle West and which Thomas helped
to resolve had likewise biased the interpretation of archeological remains in other areas of North America. In concluding his report Thomas
refers to the fact that there is no longer any question "that the ruined
pueblos of New Mexico and Arizona are attributable to the ancestors
of the sedentary tribes of those sections" and that it is "now conceded
that the cave and cliff dwellings and other remains of that region are
attributable to the ancestors of the present Pueblo tribes."[30]

The same question had arisen with respect to archeological
remains in Mexico and Central America, areas for which very little reliable information was available during the early period of mound exploration, although those who were investigating the latter remains sometimes referred to Middle American material. Thus the discovery of
cities and temples of what later became identified as the culture of
the Maya at a period when the mound problem had not been resolved,
yet at a time when public interest in "ruins" was extremely keen, was
a great archeological revelation. It was obvious, at once, that archi-
tecturally and esthetically, these structures were of a different order
than anything found within the borders of the United States. In 1841,
when *Incidents of Travel in Central America, Chiapas, and Yucatan*
by John Lloyd Stephens (1805-1852), illustrated by the superb drawings of Frederick Catherwood (1799-1854), was published, 20,000
copies were sold within three months.[31] Antedating Prescott's *Conquest*

[29] Cyrus Thomas, "Report on the Mound Explorations of the Bureau of
American Ethnology," Washington, 1894, pp. 20-21.
[30] *Ibid.*, p. 730.
[31] Victor Wolfgang von Hagen, *Maya Explorer. John Lloyd Stephens
and the Lost Cities of Central America and Yucatan* (Norman: University
of Oklahoma Press, 1947), p. 197. In 1843 it was followed by *Incidents of
Travel in Yucatan*, which reported on a second exploratory expedition.

of Mexico and the book of Squier and Davis on the mounds of the Middle West, it was a lively account of 3,000 miles of travel and contained the description of eight ruined cities.

Both Stephens and Catherwood, independently, had previously visited Near Eastern countries, including Egypt. In 1837, Stephens had published *Incidents of Travel in Egypt, Arabia Petraea, and the Holy Land*, which had been most successful. John R. Bartlett (1805-1886), an intimate friend of Stephens, and a founder of the American Ethnological Society, said he stimulated Stephens' interest in this new field of archeological exploration by showing him a copy of J. F. de Waldeck's illuminated folio volume, *Voyage Pittoresque et Archéologique*, which had been published in Paris in 1838.[32] Bartlett, a bookseller at the time, became corresponding secretary of the American Ethnological Society and also served as secretary of the New York Historical Society,[33] which, like the American Antiquarian Society and the American Philosophical Society, had corresponding members in Latin America. Von Hagen says that "America's literary air was suddenly becoming vibrant with Hispanic-American themes."[34]

Up to this time it had been Europeans rather than Americans who had been interested in the remains of older cultures in Middle America. But their speculations had served to perpetuate the theory that Egyptians, Jews, or other peoples of the Old World were responsible for any remains that fell into a "civilized" category.[35] Americans were familiar with Alexander von Humboldt's writings; after his explorations in South America and a year in Mexico (1803), he was enthusiastically received on a visit to the United States when he called on Jefferson before returning to Europe. While Humboldt saw no Maya ruins and had never visited Egypt, he had carefully distinguished the structure

---

[32] Von Hagen, *op. cit.*, pp. 72-73. For Further information on Waldeck (1766-1875), see Victor W. von Hagen, "Waldeck," *Natural History Magazine* 55 (1946); and Howard F. Cline, "The Apochryphal Early Career of Waldeck," *Acta Americana* 4 (1947).

[33] For a brief biographical note on Bartlett, see von Hagen, *Maya Explorer*, pp. 70-71. In Vol. II of the *Trans. of the Amer. Ethnological Society* (1843), pp. 1-151, Bartlett published "The Progress of Ethnology, an account of recent Archeological, Philological, and Geographical Researches in various parts of the Globe, tending to elucidate the Physical History of Man."

[34] *Ibid.*, p. 190.

[35] H. E. D. Pollock, "Sources and Methods in the Study of Maya Architecture," *The Maya and Their Neighbors* (New York: Appleton-Century, 1940) reviews the work of early observers. For a more popular account, see C. W. Ceram, *The March of Archeology* (New York: Knopf, 1958). Edward King, Viscount Kingsborough, published his nine-volume *Antiquities of Mexico* between 1830 and 1848.

of the Egyptian pyramids from those of the temple substructures he
saw in Mexico.[36]

The significance of the contributions of Stephens and Catherwood
lies not only in the fact, as Satterthwaite has said, that they "made the
first scientific circuit of the Maya archeological area,"[37] and that
Stephens gave straightforward descriptions, supplemented by the trustworthy drawings of Catherwood—the first of their kind. In addition to
this, "Stephens' sound opinion . . . as to the indigenous origin of the
ruins and their lack of tremendous age was of great importance at a
time when there was so much loose thought on the subject."[38] Stephens
had been to Egypt and explicitly stressed the fact that the sculpture
of the Maya was different from that of any other people of the world
and that their architecture, too, was distinct from that of the classical
world of Europe or the Orient. Unlike some writers who succeeded
him, Stephens, instead of using the term "pyramid," refers to "mounds,"
"terraces," or "pyramidal structures."[39] Summarizing his opinion on the
indigenous nature of the ruins he had seen, Stephens writes: "we have
a conclusion far more interesting and wonderful than that of connecting
the builders of these cities with the Egyptians or any other people. It
is the spectacle of a people skilled in architecture, sculpture, and drawing, and, beyond doubt, other more perishable arts, and possessing the
cultivation and refinement attendant upon these, not derived from the
Old World but, originating and growing up here without models or
masters, having a distinct, separate, and independent existence; like
the plants and fruits of the soil, indigenous."[40] According to Tozzer,
the work of El Padre del Mayismo—as Stephens has been called—

---

[36] See the comments of Pal Kelemen, *Battlefield of the Gods. Aspects
of Mexican History, Art and Exploration*, with an Introduction by Professor
Alfred M. Tozzer (London: Allen and Unwin, 1937), p. 173. "It is unfortunate," the author adds, "that even at the beginning of the twentieth century the reconstruction of pre-Columbian buildings should have been influenced by the chimera of similarity to the buildings of Egypt." Cf. Samuel
F. Haven, "Note on Alexander von Humboldt and His Services to American
Archeology," *Proceed. Amer. Antiquarian Society* 70:91-100, 1878. Von Hagen,
The Aztec: Man and Tribe, New American Library, 1958, p. 205, considers
von Humbolt's *Vues des Cordillères et Monuments des Peuples Indigènes
de l'Amérique* (Paris, 1810) "a landmark in American archeology," which
"deserves to be reconsidered. His attitude toward archeological remains as
fragments of history laid the solid base of American scholarship."
[37] Linton Satterthwaite, Jr., "Some Central Peten Maya Architectural
Traits at Piedras Negras," in Ramos Cesar Lizardi (ed.) *Los Mayas Antiguos*
(Mexico, 1941), p. 183.
[38] Pollock, *op. cit.*, p. 185.
[39] Keleman, *op. cit.*, pp. 72-73.
[40] Stephens and Catherwood, *Incidents* 2:442, 1841. Gallatin, who had
visited Stephens and Catherwood in New York after their first trip, published
his *Notes on the Semi-Civilized Nations of Mexico, Yucatan, and Central*

although more than a century old, "has probably fired more people with a desire to learn something about the Maya culture than any ten modern archeologists."[41]

Many years elapsed, however, before American archeologists became active contributors to archeological work in Hispanic America. It was A. P. Maudslay, an Englishman, who, beginning in 1881, is said to have laid the scientific foundation of Central American archeology. But before the end of the nineteenth century, W. H. Holmes, M. H. Saville, A. F. Bandelier, and G. B. Gordon, among others, had begun to publish the results of their observations under the auspices of such institutions as the Field Museum in Chicago, the Bureau of American Ethnology, and the Peabody Museum at Harvard.

It was not to be expected that American archeologists would become active in European archeology. But through a series of articles published from time to time in the *Annual Reports* of the Smithsonian Institution it was possible for them to keep informed about European developments.[41a] It was during the period between 1851 and 1867, according to Daniel, that the findings of Boucher de Perthes were accepted, that Darwin's *Origin of Species* appeared and that the tripartite system was applied in France to man's prehistory.[42] In America, *Types of Mankind* (1854), by Nott and Gliddon, was published during this same period. In a chapter entitled "Geology and Paleontology, in connection with Human Origins," the finds of Boucher are

America in 1845 (*Trans. of the Amer. Ethnological Society*, Vol. 1, pp. 1-352). In a section entitled "Conjectures on the Origin of American Civilization," which is ethnologically rather than archeologically oriented, Gallatin argues for independent development. He wants to know why it was, if this culture was derived from the Old World, it was based on maize, and why there was no alphabet, the art of working iron, wheel-barrows, "and at least the seeds of rice, millet, wheat, or of some other grain cultivated in the countries whence they came." He adds the pertinent remark that "in order to form a correct opinion, it is necessary to take into consideration, not only what the Mexicans knew. but also that which they did not know." (p. 187.)

[41] Introduction to Kelemen, *op. cit.*, p. 9.

[41a] In a note to a whole section on *Archaeology* published in the General Appendix to the *Smithsonian Report* for 1861, Joseph Henry writes (p. 345): "The article entitled 'General Views on Archaeology' by A. Morlot of Switzerland, of which a translation was given in the last *Smithsonian Report*, has tended so much to awaken a new interest in the study of the remains of the ancient inhabitants of this continent that we have been induced to insert a number of other articles on the same subject in the present report." These included "The Lacustrine Cities of Switzerland: Discovery of a Lost Population," "The Fauna of Middle Europe during the Stone Age," "Report upon the Antiquarian and Ethnological Collections of the Cantonal Museum at Lausanne." It was in this same volume that "Instructions for Archeological Investigations in the United States," by George Gibbs, appeared.

[42] Glyn E. Daniel, *op. cit.*, pp. 120-121.

discussed and some of them illustrated along with other European material. The question of man's antiquity in the New World is raised, the Lagoa Santa finds are referred to, and so is "Dr. Dowler's sub-cypress Indian, who dwelt on the site of New Orleans 57,600 years ago."[43] But in his review of North American archeology already referred to, Lord Avebury (1865) concluded that "on the whole, though the idea is certainly much less improbable than it was some years ago, there does not as yet appear to be any satisfactory proof that man co-existed in America with the Mammoth and Mastodon."[43a] In 1872, however, a prolonged debate was initiated by Charles C. Abbott's claim that there were paleolithic implements present in glacial deposits near Trenton, New Jersey. Abbott's claims were not substantiated;[44] and only after the discoveries at Folsom in the nineteen-twenties did the question of paleo-Indian remains in America come to rest upon a solid foundation. When Cyrus Thomas wrote his *Introduction to the Study of North American Archeology* in the last decade of the nineteenth century (1898), he said: "we put aside glacial or paleolithic man of America as yet wanting the credentials which entitle him to a place in scientific circles."[45] With this exclusion, his book reflects what had been accomplished in American archeology up to that time. His survey of the continent is organized into three broad geographical regions—Arctic, Atlantic, and Pacific—and, in the last area, he covers the Southwest as well as Mexico and Central America.

With the repudiation of the myth of long-vanished and mysterious peoples, and the rejection of the idea that man in America had an antiquity comparable to that of man in the Old World, with similar stages of prehistoric development, the ground was cleared by nineteenth century anthropologists for twentieth century developments. Beyond describing and classifying material, the task still remained of ordering archeological and physical anthropological data on a time scale with greater precision. It was now possible to integrate the past history of the aboriginal peoples of this continent with the study of historic tribes and cultures. The way was likewise cleared for such an integration by the reaction in ethnological thinking against the use of

---

[43] Nott and Gliddon, *op. cit.*, p. 350. This is one of the finds later rejected by Hrdlička (p. 15) when he published his systematic review, "Skeletal remains suggesting or attributed to Early Man in North America," *Bulletin 33 of the Bureau of American Ethnology*, Washington, 1907.
[43a] Lubbock (Lord Avebury), *op. cit.*, p. 236.
[44] See Dorothy Cross, *Archeology of New Jersey*, Vol. 1, pub. by the Archeological Society of New Jersey and the New Jersey State Museum, Trenton, 1941, p. 1; "The Effect of the Abbott Farm on Eastern Chronology," *Proceed. Amer. Philosophical Society*, 86:315-319, 1943.
[45] p. 4.

simple unilinear-stage formulae as sound models for the historical interpretation of ethnographic data. It was also recognized that biological, linguistic, and cultural data must initially be treated as independent variables. Everywhere more critical and less speculative attitudes were adopted as professionalism emerged and the academic period in American anthropology began.

Twentieth century anthropologists soon learned that there was no smooth, broad road to their goals. In all areas of the subject there was still a great deal of spade work to be done. In addition, anthropology began to expand beyond its old borders with the extension of interest outside the traditional study of the American Indian, the rise of sub-specialties and new problems, and the increase in professionally trained specialists. The aborigines of the New World were no longer an exotic novelty and a touchstone to broad anthropological problems. American anthropologists were beginning to invade Africa and the islands of the South Seas; they could be found studying European communities. A cycle was being completed. The academic descendants of those early scholarly students of man in the New World who had pursued their interest as an avocation were now oriented in true anthropological fashion to both pre-historic man and contemporary man throughout the world, and were intent upon increasing the fund of reliable knowledge about him.

FOUR

Anthropology in Philadelphia
1967

THE Philadelphia Anthropological Society has been unique, perhaps, insofar as it has never been exclusively an organization of professional anthropologists. Nor has it had any formal affiliations with educational institutions in this area (although it has never spurned their facilities). The Society has remained independent, highly flexible and fluctuating in personnel, while at the same time it has constantly reflected in microcosm what has been currently happening in anthropology at large. What it has done all along is to provide an open forum for the serious discussion of all phases of anthropology for those interested in attending its meetings. It has never attempted to popularize its lectures, or to attract the general public.

The Society did not start with a bang. It had a humble beginning and it remained small in numbers for many years. Documents for the earliest period are sadly lacking, so that we do not know all we should like to know about those years. We do know that prior to World War I a few men interested in anthropological problems met, more or less regularly, with Frank G. Speck in a downtown restaurant (some have called it a saloon!) for dinner. So we must honor Speck as our founder (J. A. Mason, 1950a).[1] Fortunately we have a list of speakers from 1914 on. In that year, William Chur-

[1] Referring to Speck as the founder of the Society, Mason goes on to say: "Probably no one now remembers, or ever remembered, when it actually began, for it commenced with an informal group meeting for dinner at Ostendorffs', a Philadelphia restaurant that has long since disappeared, where Frank could indulge his liking for oyster stew." Mrs. Speck tells me that the group sometimes met at their home. The year selected for the celebration of the anniversary was determined by Speck's recollection of the year when the dinners at Ostendorffs' began. Speck served in the more formal capacity of President of the Society from 1920 to 1922. (See J. A. Mason, 1950c, where some of these facts are more briefly stated.)

chill, well known at the time as a student of Polynesian linguistics and ethnology, is listed; and for 1915 we find the name of Ralph Linton, who took his master's degree at the University of Pennsylvania.

By the time I attended my first meeting in 1916, the established meeting place had been shifted to the University campus. I made my way upstairs to a small room on the third floor of Houston Hall. I was almost overwhelmed by the aura of dignity I encountered. There were scarcely a dozen people present. They were all men of scholarly mien. When I tiptoed to a seat they were quietly awaiting the arrival of the speaker. The latter, when he appeared, wore a beard and was tightly buttoned up in a long frock coat. He was a great scholar—W. Max Müller, the Egyptologist. His topic was "Experiences of a Linguist in North Africa." This is the first and last time I have ever seen a frock coat at any sort of anthropological meeting. Beards have sprouted again, but I fancy frock coats have disappeared forever.

There were no women present at this meeting because their presence was taboo. In fact, there was a hot debate soon afterwards before the rules were finally changed and women could become members. It was only then that Miss H. Newell Wardle, a founder of the American Anthropological Association, and at that time connected with the Academy of Natural Sciences, could be invited to join the Philadelphia Anthropological Society. There was certainly a cultural lag here, but the pattern was a repetition of events that had previously occurred in anthropological circles. In Washington, in the eighties of the last century, a group of women under the leadership of Alice Fletcher organized the Women's Anthropological Society of Washington, presumably as a reaction to exclusion from male discussion in that city (Lurie, 1966).[2] These women must have been terribly serious-minded and self-conscious, because they even banned refreshments on principle. An Anthropolocial Society meeting was not to be confused with a pink tea! However,

[2] Among the exhibits prepared by the Smithsonian Institution, when the annual meetings of the American Anthropological Association were held in Washington (1958) was one devoted to the Woman's Anthropological Society of Washington. This organization, founded in 1885, included civic activities which may be viewed as an early example of applied anthropology.

this group merged with the Anthropological Society of Washington in 1899, when 49 women were elected members of the men's organization at one fell swoop. Perhaps it was highly symbolic when, in Philadelphia, our first woman speaker (1920) was Elsie Clews Parsons. Her thesis in *The Old Fashioned Woman* (1913), it may be recalled, was to show, on the basis of comparative ethnographic data, how women in our society were thwarted by archaic attitudes. On the occasion of this meeting we had to move to College Hall because no women were allowed above the first floor of Houston Hall at night.

At a later period we held dinner meetings in the old Lido Restaurant on Woodland Avenue. It was here, I believe, that Lévy-Bruhl was our speaker, one of a series of foreign scholars who addressed us. These include Sir Peter Buck, J. H. Driberg, Daryll Forde, Julius Lips, C. G. Seligmann, D. H. Westermann, Sir Solly Zuckerman, and others. As for American colleagues, so many have spoken to us that I shall mention none. If I did so it would be a roll call of most of the distinguished anthropologists in the United States during the past generation. I will only say that we never have been able to pay honoraria. Yet we seem to have been eminently successful in prevailing upon the good will of our friends over many years.

Perhaps I should add that we have likewise had a number of speakers from fields other than anthropology. From psychology, for example, I recall W. Köhler and Ray Carpenter. The latter talked to us and showed us his movies long before most anthropologists had shown any interest in infrahuman primate behavior. Our presidents, too, have sometimes been drawn from other disciplines. Our oldest living past president, W. W. Hyde, is Professor Emeritus of Classics and Ancient History, now in his ninth decade of life.[3] J. W. Harshberger, Professor of Botany at the time and chairman of the department, was the author of a pioneer monograph, *Maize*, published in 1893. From Sumerology we have had Samuel Kramer; from business, Percy C. Madeira, Jr.; and from sociology, my old friend, the late James W. Woodard of Temple University.

Without deliberation, or set policy, the Philadelphia Anthropological Society throughout its history appears to have embraced the

[3] Professor Hyde is recently deceased.

inclusive conception of anthropology—in membership, officers, and speakers—which has characterized American anthropology as a whole. During the period 1914 to 1937, we heard about European archaeology and American archaeology; we listened to Orientalists and some Africanists; we heard cross-cousin marriage discussed and the devil worshippers of Kurdistan described; we were told about the pygmies of Dutch New Guinea and we were given accounts of Tungus and of African folk tales; we learned about racial studies in Polynesia and the heredity of body build. In 1921 Waterman gave us an account of the discovery of Ishi,[4] and in 1932 we had a talk on "Personality and Primitive Culture" by Kroeber.

I ask you now to follow me back into the more distant past, in order that the Philadelphia Anthropological Society may be seen in wider historical perspective as one of the many activities of anthropological interest that have had Philadelphia as their locale. But, just as we have no fully rounded account of the earliest years of our Society, because no one took the trouble to collect the information, in the same way, on a longer historical scale, we have no fully rounded account of what now would be recognized as matters of anthropological interest in the history of Philadelphia. References have been made today to fragments of this story, particularly to the role of members of the American Philosophical Society at a very early date. Here I wish to recall some facts which have aroused my personal interest, as I hope they may arouse yours.

Recently I ran across a reference to an Eskimo collection, presented to the venerable Library Company of Philadelphia in 1754. Was this the first ethnological collection exhibited here? And why did it turn up in Philadelphia? The answer is relatively simple if it is recalled that Philadelphians in the eighteenth century combined all sorts of intellectual interests with a spirit of enterprise. In 1753 a number of Philadelphia gentlemen, including Benjamin Franklin, fitted out a vessel to be sent in search of the Northwest Passage as well as possible lucrative trade on the coast of Labrador. The ship never accomplished its geographical aims, nor did it bring back the

---

[4] The full story of Ishi has now been beautifully expounded and fully documented by Theodora Kroeber (1961).

Golden Fleece, but it did reach Davis Strait. A collection of Eskimo garments and artifacts was made, which, "when presented to the Library as a gift from the 'North-West Company,' became one of the most popular exhibits in its growing museum." [5]

This example is indicative of the historical circumstances under which exotic objects from distant parts of the world originally were brought to the attention of the public in urban centers in the days before professional anthropologists existed. Another way in which such material was assembled and sometimes carefully studied was through the activities of private collectors. Pierre Eugene Du Simitière (1736–1784) was one such man in Philadelphia who perhaps deserves more attention than he has received. He was a miniature painter and a passionate collector of everything from documents to natural history. He opened his collection to public gaze on Arch Street in 1782. Among other things he was interested in Indian "antiquities." But he did more than collect and exhibit. If you will consult the notebooks he left, you will find the kind of exact descriptions of objects and their provenience which foreshadow a part of our anthropological tradition. He records, for example, that stone hatchets of various sizes and forms came from a certain field in New Jersey a little west of Trenton Ferry; that a "maneto-face mask of an Indian conjurer," has a "border of bear skin round the forehead and a tuft of feathers in the center," and that it was sent to him by George Clinton. Du Simitière, moreover, appears to have sensed that he was pioneering, since in 1770, apropos of his "Indian Antiquities" he says: ". . . it is a new subject and not touched upon by authors" (Potts, 1889, p. 349; Huth, 1945; Levey, 1951; Pennsyl-

[5] "In the thirties the efforts of Benjamin Franklin and the patronage of James Logan had assisted a group of Philadelphia tradesmen and a few gentlemen associates to the formation of the Library company, upon which the Proprietors conferred a plot of land and a charter in 1742. The acquisitions of this organization during its first two decades of existence reflect the primary desire of its middle-class members for serious books and volumes of instruction on a variety of subjects" (Bridenbaugh, 1942, p. 86). At the same time the Library Company paralleled "its collections of Books with a cabinet containing scientific apparatus and natural curiosities, to which the Eskimo collection . . . constituted a considerable addition." A cabinet of fossils was also accumulated, and a collection of medals considered to be of great value in the study of Roman history (*ibid.*, p. 353).

vania Historical Records Survey, 1940).[6] The date is long prior to
the meeting of the American Philosophical Society in 1797, over
which Thomas Jefferson presided and at which "a plan for collecting information respecting the antiquities of North America" was
first considered.[7]

Charles Willson Peale (1741–1827) was another painter-collector.
In his younger days he had mastered the saddler's trade, taught
himself painting, fought in the Revolution, and served briefly in the
Pennsylvania Assembly. Later he became a member of the American Philosophical Society. He was renowned for his portraits of
eminent contemporaries. Meriwether Lewis and William Clark, the
leaders of the most famous exploratory expedition in American history, were among those who sat for him.[8] The new knowledge
acquired by their expedition—geographical, mineralogical, botani-
cal, zoological—included information on the native Indian population of the vast unknown country west of the Mississippi. It first
became available in print in Biddle's *History* (1814), which De
Voto characterizes as "the first reliable account of whatever length,
of the Western tribes." He goes on to say: "It put a valuable bulk of
knowledge at the disposal of anyone who had interest in or use for
knowledge relating to the Indians of the West. So it has always been
a prime source for anthropologists and historians" (De Voto, 1953,
p. lii). Inquiry along ethnological lines was explicitly incorporated
and set forth in Jefferson's overall instructions to Lewis (Jackson,

[6] Bridenbaugh (1942, p. 354) says: "a most careful and systematically projected scheme for an 'American Museum' was evolved by the humble miniature
painter, antiquary and naturalist Pierre Du Simitière, who had devoted his
entire life to the assembling of materials and specimens for a natural and civil
history of America. . . . Without benefit of great wealth, the persistent
curiosity of this Swiss craftsman brought together much the same sort of
collection as that which Sir Hans Sloane made the foundation of the British
Museum. It was most unfortunate that at the time of his death in 1784 the
General Assembly of Pennsylvania considered it 'not expedient or consistent
with the state of the treasury' for the state to purchase and preserve his collections, refusal of which had been granted it by his will."

[7] Reference is to the Standing Committee on Antiquities of the American
Philosophical Society noted by Freeman in this volume. For further information see Chinard (1943).

[8] These portraits, in the collections of Independence National Historical
Park in downtown Philadelphia, are photographically reproduced in Jackson
(1962).

1962, No. 47, p. 62).[9] Besides this, a list of more than one hundred specific topics was drawn up, which provided a comprehensive outline to be followed in the collection of demographic facts and ethnographic data. Several eminent Philadelphians, personally known to Jefferson as fellow members of the American Philosophical Society, were confidentially informed about the expedition in its earliest planning stage. Since it was impractical to send specialists on the expedition, Lewis was sent to consult with them as men learned beyond the boundary of their own specialty. It was these men who were specifically asked to contribute to the topical questionnaire on the Indians with which the explorers were later provided. Dr. Benjamin Rush (1745?–1813), who had long before (1774) published his pioneer *Enquiry into the Natural History of Medicine Among the Indians in North-America and a Comparative View of their Diseases and Remedies with those of Civilized Nations*, was an important contributor,[10] Dr. Caspar Wistar (1761–1818) [11] and Dr. Benjamin Smith Barton (1766–1815), probably less so.[12] This ques-

[9] For categorical reference to the kind of information to be sought on the Indian population, see Jackson (1962, p. 62).

[10] Jefferson solicited the aid of Rush, a professor of medicine at the University of Pennsylvania and a leading American physician, in February 1803 (see Jackson, 1962, No. 13). In addition to contributing some suggested inquiries "relative to the natural history of the Indians," the questions were arranged under three headings: Physical History and Medicine, Morals, and Religion. Under Morals, in addition to other questions, we find: "Is Suicide common among them?—ever from love?" Under Religion he asked: "How do they dispose of their dead, and with what ceremonies do they inter them?" Rush already had devoted some thought to these matters, since he had given some questions to Alexander McGillivray (Chief of the Creeks) in 1790, and to Timothy Pickering in 1791 when the latter visited the Seneca (*ibid.*, p. 51n). See also pp. 157-60 and note for Clark's more elaborate list of questions (1804), based on Rush, with possible additions from Wistar and Barton.

[11] The questions suggested by Wistar have not survived, but the material may have been incorporated in Clark's later list (Jackson, 1962, No. 71 and note). Jefferson wrote to Wistar in much the same vein as he had written to Rush (*ibid.*, No. 12).

[12] Barton was a physician who was a lecturer at the University of Pennsylvania and who was interested in natural history as well as Indian ethnography and linguistics. For information on his linguistic work see Greene (1960). Jefferson's confidential letter to Barton in February 1803 (Jackson, 1962, No. 11) informs him about the proposed expedition under the leadership of Lewis and then goes on to say: "In order to draw his attention at once to the objects most desirable, I must ask the favor of you to prepare for him a note on the

tionnaire approach, initiated by Jefferson, set a precedent followed for a long time thereafter in the collection of data on the American aborigines.

Peale's interest in the collection and exhibition of objects in the field of natural history (including Indian "relics") culminated in his American Museum, the first natural history museum in America.[13] Begun in 1784 and at first quartered in an extension which Peale added to his home on Lombard Street, it gained national status a decade later when it was moved, or more literally paraded, into the new building the Philosophical Society had erected near Independence Hall. Here, in the early years of the nineteenth century, in addition to being able to see the famous mounted skeleton of a mastodon, more than a thousand stuffed birds, specimens of minerals, and a large number of portraits painted by Peale and his three sons, visitors were uniquely privileged to see a collection of objects from Indian tribes of the far West collected by Lewis and Clark. For Lewis shipped specimens of all kinds to Jefferson—minerals,

---

lines of botany, zoology, or of Indian history which you think most worthy of inquiry and observation. He will be with you in Philadelphia in two or three weeks, and will wait on you, and receive thankfully on paper, and any verbal communication which you may be so good as to make him." In a letter to Jefferson sent from Philadelphia in May, Lewis says that he has seen all three men mentioned above. He notes that Rush already had submitted queries and that "Drs. Barton and Wistar have each promised to contribute in like manner anything which may suggest itself to them as being of any importance in furthering the objects of this expedition" (*ibid.*, No. 40). Later Barton prepared inquiries on the customs and languages of the Indians for the expedition of Thomas Nuttall in 1810–1811, but Jackson (p. 161n) is doubtful whether Barton actually contributed any questions to Lewis and Clark. When Thwaites published his edition of the *Journals* of the expedition in 1904–1905, he included in the appendix to Vol. 7 (1904, pp. 283–87), a section titled, "Ethnological Information Desired." This was the first time that the detailed questionnaire prepared for use on the expedition had been printed in full. Although the manuscript which survives is in the handwriting of Clark, the editor of these volumes considered it to be a "transcript of instructions from Jefferson" (Hallowell, 1960, p. 17n; for additional information on the Lewis and Clark expedition in anthropological perspective see pp. 37–38). Consult the same essay for the later use of the notes and queries approach by Lewis Cass and the Smithsonian Institution.

[13] See Simpson (1942, p. 262) who says it was "probably the first of American public natural history museums, to be definitely founded and organized as such."

animal skins, plants, seeds, and examples of Indian handicrafts, weapons, and utensils—and most of these were passed on to Peale for exhibition in his museum.[14] A contemporary observer in the 1820s says that on entering the "Long Room," there could be seen in a corner case "a wax figure of Col. Lewis or Clark, I do not remember which, in a complete Indian costume. The case of the Indians and their dresses and implements were very attractive" (Colton, 1909, p. 230).

The figure referred to undoubtedly was Lewis. In a letter which Peale wrote to Jefferson in January 1808, he says: "A few weeks past I completed a wax figure of Captn. Lewis and placed it in the Museum, my object in this work is to give a lesson to the Indians who may visit the Museum, and also to shew my sentiments respecting wars. The Figure being dressed in an Indian Dress presented to Captn. Lewis by *Comeahwait*, Chief of the Shoshone Nation [and brother of Sacagawea], who was suspicious that Captn. Lewis ment to lead him into an ambuscade with his Enemies. The figure has its right hand on its breast and the left holds the *Calmut* which was given me by Captn. Lewis. In a Tablet I give the Story in a few words, and then add: 'This mantle, composed of 140 Ermine skins was put on Captn. Lewis by *Comehwait*, their Chief. Lewis is supposed to say, Brother, I accept your dress—It is the object of my heart to promote amongst you, our Neighbours, Peace and good will—that you may bury the Hatchet deep in the ground never to be takea up again—and that henceforward you may smoke the *Calmut* of Peace and live in perpetual harmony, not only with each

[14] See, e.g., Jackson (1962, No. 171, 1805). In this letter Jefferson, referring to the articles being sent on to Peale, says that he was keeping some specimens for "an Indian Hall I am forming at Monticello, e.g., horns, dressed skins, utensils, etc." This letter also refers to a live magpie and a Columbian Ground Squirrel ("a burrowing squirrel of the prairies," not yet classified at the time) which he is shipping to Peale. In Jackson, Nos. 173 and 177, Peale acknowledges the receipt in good condition of these live animals. Before he moved his Museum, it may be added, Peale kept a sort of menagerie in the yard and stables of his home. In November 1809, writing to his son Rembrandt informing him of Lewis' unexpected death, Peale refers to a consignment of specimens from Lewis himself which had just been received without any accompanying letter (*ibid.*, No. 302). He says these consisted of a collection of "Indian dresses, pipes, arrows, an Indian pot entire, skins of beavers etc., others etc. with some minerals, etc." Since Peale recorded accessions, an entry of December 1809 (*ibid.*, No. 306) provides a detailed inventory of this shipment.

other, but with the white man, your Brothers, who will teach you many useful Arts. Possessed of every comfort in life, what cause ought to involve us in War?'" (Jackson, 1962, No. 281). Peale adds a few homilies in regard to working for amicable relations, and then says: "Such I believe to be the sentiments of our friend Lewis, and which he endeavored to instill in the minds of the various savages he met with in his long and hazardous Tour. I am pleased when ever I can give an object which affords a moral sentiment to the Visitors of the Museum." The general tone of this pseudo address attributed to Lewis is not very far removed from the actual speech which President Jefferson had made to an Osage delegation in Washington a few years before. Referring to the change in sovereignty that had taken place, he said: "Never more will you have occasion to change your fathers. We are all now of one family, born in the same land, and bound to live as brothers; and the strangers from beyond the great water are gone from among us. The Great Spirit has given you strength, and has given us strength; not that we might hurt one another, but to do each other all the good in our power. Our dwellings indeed are very far apart; but not too far to carry on commerce and useful intercourse. You have furs and peltries which we want, and we have clothes and other useful things which you want. Let us employ ourselves then in mutually accomadating each other" (*ibid*, No. 127).[15]

Insofar as his ethnological collections are concerned, I believe that it is correct to say that Peale's attitude toward them is clearly distinguishable from that exhibited by Du Simitière toward similar material. There seems to be no evidence of even a glimmering of a genuine scientific approach on Peale's part. Peale's collections were eventually dispersed, as Du Simitière's had been, when in the latter case the General Assembly of Pennsylvania refused to purchase and preserve them. What remained of the Lewis and Clark collection ultimately reached the Peabody Museum in Cambridge.[16]

[15] Compare Jefferson's speech to the Osage delegation in Washington (Jackson, 1962, No. 127) and the actual speech of Lewis to the Oto (*ibid.*, No. 129).

[16] Willoughby (1905, p. 634) says that a great deal of the Peale collection passed to the Boston Museum which "in its earlier days was as noted for its cases of wax figures, its ethnological and natural history collections and historical objects as for its theatre." In 1899, however, its collections were dispersed "as gifts among the Museums of Boston and vicinity." The Peabody

Peale is also to be remembered for his portraits of Indians. Joseph Brant (Thayendanegea) was portrayed in 1797 wearing native costume with armband and gorget. Later the Seneca chief Red Jacket, opponent of Christian missions among the Iroquois, sat for both Peale [17] and another Philadelphia painter, John Neagle (1796–1865).[18] The latter painted several portraits of Western Indians when they stopped in Philadelphia en route to Washington. Indeed, some of the best portraits of Indians we have were painted in Philadelphia. Particularly noteworthy are those of the two Lenape Indians who came to Philadelphia to be cheated by John Penn in the notorious "Walking Treaty" of 1735. These were the work of Gustav Hessalius (1682–1755). John Ewers (1949, p. 228) says that they "are the first successful Indian portraits made in North America." [19] Since there was, of course, no photography in those days, to say nothing of anthropometry, and since the artists portrayed their subjects in native costume, these works of art are at the same time documents of prime anthropological value.[20]

As I have pointed out elsewhere, the historical roots of American anthropology were nourished in the "backwash of the frontier," the currents and eddies generated by the contacts between the early settlers and the Indian (Hallowell, 1959, p. 469). After the initial

---

Museum of Harvard received the ethnological collection, including the objects probably collected by Lewis and Clark. One of the most famous surviving objects in the Peabody Museum is a painted Mandan buffalo robe. For a description see Willoughby (p. 638) and a photograph. This robe appears in the invoice of articles forwarded from Fort Mandan to Jefferson in 1805. It is described as "1 Buffalow robe painted by a Mandan man representing a battle which was faught 8 years since, by the Sioux and Ricaras against the Mandans, Minitarras and Ahwahharways" (Jackson, 1962, pp. 235–36). In the same invoice reference is made to "1 earthen pot, such as the Mandans manufacture, and use for culinary purposes." Wedel illustrates two fragmentary Mandan pots which are now to be found in the University Museum (1957, p. 97 and Plate 38). There seems to be little doubt that they came from the Lewis and Clark expedition.

[17] These portraits by Peale are on view in Independence National Historical Park, Philadelphia.

[18] To be found in the Historical Society of Pennsylvania, Philadelphia.

[19] The Hessalius portraits of Tishcohan and Lapowinsa belong to the Historical Society of Pennsylvania.

[20] In 1958 the University Museum assembled an exhibition of paintings of North American Indians, which included the portraits mentioned above.

turmoil of contact had relaxed, the American aborigines aroused an increasing interest on the part of various kinds of learned men, most of whom were under the intellectual spell of the Enlightenment. Various manifestations of this ramified interest in the American Indians constitutes a distinctive part of American culture history. Among other things, it is directly linked with the later development of professional specialization. The men who initially concerned themselves with problems concerning the Indians were anthropologists without portfolios.[21] In its earliest phase American anthropology cannot be dissociated from the studies devoted to the languages, cultures, and physical characteristics of the American Indians by these men, most of whom were associated with the American Philosophical Society. This interest in Indians continued and greatly expanded in the nineteenth century. And it penetrated far beyond the scholarly realm. American dramatists, novelists, and poets became absorbed for a time in the Indian as a subject. In Philadelphia, *Metamora*, or *The Last of the Wampanoags*, was played every year except two for a quarter of a century by Edwin Forrest, the famous Philadelphia actor. In 1828 he had advertised for a play in which "the hero, or principal character, shall be an aboriginal of this country." This play became tremendously popular. It was in Forrest's repertoire for almost forty years. More Americans are said to have seen it in the nineteenth century than attended performances of *Tobacco Road* in the twentieth.[22]

One of the old problems which continued to attract attention

[21] In this respect a comparable situation existed in the earliest stages of other disciplines in America, even though in some cases their content had been more exactly defined. Writing about science in general in the days of the early republic, Dupree (1957, p. 7) says: "Science was not separate from philosophy, the arts, or literature in either organization or personnel. Within the framework of natural philosophy and natural history, the particular fields of physics and chemistry, botany, zoology, and mineralogy were clear, but nobody imagined that a man should devote his whole time to one of them. Indeed, almost none of the members [of the American Philosophical Society or the American Academy of Arts and Sciences] were even professional scientists. Many were doctors, lawyers, or clergymen, making their living and spending much of their time in ways unconnected with science." In fact, the term *scientist* was not coined until 1840, when William Whewell deliberately introduced it "to describe a cultivator of science in general" (Bell, p. 8).

[22] It was played even after Forrest's death, and a radio version was broadcast in 1939. For further information see Clark (1943).

throughout the last century was the question of Indian origins. In approach and treatment there is a radical antithesis soon to be observed between older writers on this subject and the way the problem is handled after increasing data have accumulated and disciplinary specialization has begun to emerge. William Penn, Quaker founder of Pennsylvania, was among those in a long line of thinkers who believed that the aborigines of this country were descendants of the Lost Tribes of Israel.[23] More than a century later Elias Boudinot (1740–1821), a prominent Philadelphian of his time, expressed similar views. Boudinot had served as president of the Continental Congress. He was a friend of George Washington, who appointed him Director of the Philadelphia Mint. Later he became a trustee of Princeton College. In 1816 he published a book titled *A Star in the West; or, a Humble Attempt to Discover the Long Lost Ten Tribes of Israel, Preparatory to Their Return to Their Beloved City, Jerusalem.* Boudinot's scholarship was in the tradition of the many speculative writers who preceded him. Among other things he converted the Indian war whoop into "Y-O-He-Wah," a corruption of "Jehovah." And he said that the Choctaw Indians intermixed the word "Ha-le-leu-yah" into their lamentations for the dead.[24]

As the nineteenth century wore on speculations of this kind declined, and in Philadelphia there were increasing opportunities for anyone interested to see actual specimens of Indian workmanship, both ethnological and archaeological, as well as some skeletal material. Names now long familiar to all anthropologists begin to crop up. The Academy of Natural Sciences assumed prominence. Flowering from small beginnings in 1812, a large hall was built in 1826 and exhibits and lectures soon became available to the public. Closely associated with the Academy were pioneers in American physical anthropology. Of particular eminence was Samuel G.

[23] For references to the history of this tradition of speculation see Hallowell (1960, pp. 4–6) and Wauchope (1962, Chapter 4 and Bibliography, pp. 142–43).

[24] For further comments on Boudinot, particularly with reference to the speculation of Richard Brothers in England, see Hungerford (1941, pp. 84–85). "The one found in the American Indians the fulfillment of Biblical prophecy; the other found that fulfillment in the English" (described by Brothers as descendants of the Lost Tribes). "Yet so fine a line distinguishes success from failure in scholarship that whereas Richard Brothers, Boudinot's English compeer, was confined to a mad house, Boudinot served as a trustee of Princeton College."

Morton (1799–1851), with whose *Crania Americana* (1839) physical anthropology in the United States may be said to have begun. His famous collection of crania, judged to be the largest in the world at the time, was purchased from his executors after his death and presented to the Academy of Natural Sciences. Other men associated with this institution whose contributions to physical anthropology are a matter of record were: J. Aitken Meigs (1829–1879), author of an early detailed article (1861) on 48 cranial measurements and determinations that should be taken on the skull; Joseph Leidy (1823–1891), and Harrison Allen (1841–1897). Meigs was made a Foreign Associate Member of the Anthropological Society of Paris in 1860, and an Honorary Fellow of the Anthropological Society of London in 1863.[25]

Archaeological and ethnological collections were also acquired by the Academy; the Haldeman collection of New World material, which included specimens from Middle and South America, the superb archaeological material from the Southern United States excavated by Clarence B. Moore, and the Vaux collection of archaeological material from Europe (Mitra, 1933, pp. 185–86). When the Academy celebrated its 125th Anniversary in 1937, the major feature was an international symposium on early man. It was organized by Edgar B. Howard, who had studied anthropology and geology at the University of Pennsylvania.[26] This conference was attended by scholars from all over the world. V. Gordon Childe, Kaj Birket-Smith, and Dorothy A. E. Garrod received honorary degrees of Doctor of Science from the University of Pennsylvania at this time at a special convocation held in the auditorium of its Museum. This celebration actually marked the heyday of the Academy's anthropological interests.

In the field of medicine, the assembly of skeletal material and prep-

[25] For the bibliographies of these men and biographical details, see Hrdlička (1919). See Brinton (1897) for a review of Allen's work. For the position of Morton and other Philadelphians in the polygenist-monogenist controversy, see Stanton (1960).

[26] He received his Master's degree in the Department of Anthropology and his doctorate in the Department of Geology (1935). For additional information see the *Obituary* by J. Alden Mason (1942b). Thirty-six papers presented at the symposium were collected and published in March 1937, edited by George Grant MacCurdy (MacCurdy 1937).

arations of anatomical interest, without the concentration upon crania which typified physical anthropology at an early stage, had attracted the attention of physicians even earlier. In Philadelphia, this interest was pursued by Dr. Caspar Wistar (1761–1818), who belonged to an earlier generation than Morton. It culminated in a more fully ramified biological context, including comparative anatomy and physical anthropology, with the foundation of the Wistar Institute of Anatomy and Biology seventy years ago.

Caspar Wistar, having secured his medical degree from the University of Pennsylvania in 1782, continued his studies abroad. Inspired by the example of John Hunter (1728–1793), whose collection became the nucleus of the world-famous Hunterian Museum in London, Wistar began to assemble his own anatomical collection. Returning to the United States, he became professor of anatomy at his alma mater in 1808. Wistar was one of the Philadelphia physicians consulted by Jefferson when the Lewis and Clark expedition was being planned, and in 1815 he became Jefferson's successor as President of the American Philosophical Society. His collection was presented by his widow to the University. It was fostered and augmented by Dr. William E. Horner, who had long been his assistant and colleague, and later by Dr. Joseph Leidy. When Provost William Pepper, also a physician, promoted the foundation of the Wistar Institute, incorporated in 1892, the University of Pennsylvania contributed the Wistar-Horner anatomical collection and the land for a building.[27] Dr. Pepper was the first President of the Institute, and Dr. Harrison Allen, a pioneer physical anthropologist, became its first Director. The latter completed his pioneer work on Hawaiian skulls just before his death in 1897.

In this century the Institute became enriched by additional collections, including osteological material that had been housed in the University Museum until 1915; it became famous for its collection of the brains of distinguished men and the work done in comparative anatomy by Henry H. Donaldson (1857–1938), whose book on the *Growth of the Brain* (1897) was a pioneer work. Among other

[27] For information on Dr. Caspar Wistar and the foundation of the Institute, see *Proceedings* (1900, pp. 153–54). For additional information on the Institute, H. H. Donaldson, Ralph Linton, and Ernest W. Hawkes, see Hrdlička, pp. 110–11).

material, an important series of Eskimo crania and other skeletal material had been acquired, which was studied by both Ralph Linton and Ernest W. Hawkes. The latter, who was the first to receive his Doctor's degree (1915) after a Department of Anthropology had been organized here, made observations and measurements on this collection the subject of his dissertation. Besides this, the Wistar Institute became the publisher of the *American Journal of Physical Anthropology*, founded by Hrdlička in 1918, many years before the American Association of Physical Anthropologists was itself organized.

In addition to being the locale of expanding anthropological collections of many different kinds during the last century, Philadelphians also had the opportunity of seeing special visiting exhibits. George Catlin brought his Indian Gallery here before he took it to Europe in 1839. It comprised almost 500 paintings of Indians and Indian life, besides specimens of clothing and handicrafts. As Ewers says: "No one had brought the Wild West to civilization in pictorial form for everyone to see before" (Ewers, 1956, p. 502). The *Philadelphia Saturday Courier* (1838) said: "There is not in our land, nor in any part of Europe . . . anything of the kind more extraordinary or more interesting" (McCracken, p. 188). Catlin was no stranger to Philadelphia. Pennsylvania-born, and raised in the Wyoming Valley, he moved to Philadelphia in order to devote his full time to painting after briefly practicing law for a few years. In 1824 he was elected an academician of the Pennsylvania Academy of Fine Arts, which included among its members Charles Willson Peale. It was in this same year, too, that Catlin had his first glimpse of Western Indians, a delegation en route to Washington having stopped for a few days in Philadelphia. Of this event, which imbued him with the inspiration for his life's work, he later wrote:

My mind was continually reaching for some branch or enterprise of the art, on which to devote a whole life-time of enthusiasm; when a delegation of some ten or fifteen noble and dignified looking Indians, from the wilds of the 'Far West,' suddenly arrived in the city for a few days, arrayed in all their classic beauty—with shield and helmet,—with tunic and manteau,—tinted and tassled off, exactly for the painter's pallette! In silent and stoic dignity, these lords of the forest strutted about the city for a few days, wrapped in their pictured robes, with

142

their brows plumed with the quills of the war-eagle, attracting the attention of all who beheld them. After this they took their leave for Washington City, and I was left to reflect and regret, which I did long and deeply, until I came to the following deductions and conclusions. . . . Man, in the simplicity and loftiness of his nature, unrestrained and un-fettered by the disguises of art, is surely the most beautiful model for the painter,—and the country from which he hails is unquestionably the best study or school of the arts in the world; such I am sure, from the models I have seen, is the wilderness of North America. And the history and customs of such a people, preserved by pictorial illustrations, are themes worthy the life-time of one man, and nothing short of the loss of my life shall prevent me from visiting their country, and becom-ing their historian. . . . I set out on my arduous and perilous undertaking with the determination of reaching, ultimately, every tribe of Indians on the Continent of North America, and of bringing home faithful portraits of their principal personages, both men and women, from each tribe, views of their villages, games, etc. and full notes on their character and history. I designed, also, to procure their costumes, and a complete collection of their manufactures and weapons, and to perpetuate them in a *Gallery unique*, for the use and instruction of future ages (Catlin, 1841, Vol. 1, pp. 2–3).

Since Catlin was familiar with Peale's Museum, it seems likely that the plan of Peale's exhibition rooms was an important element in his determination to present his Indian paintings, along with relevant ethnographic collections, in the form of the unique gallery to which he refers.

As in other parts of the country, the mysterious Mound Builders aroused tremendous popular interest here in the early decades of the last century.[28] One Philadelphian who became actively interested in excavation was Dr. Montroville Wilson Dickerson (1810–1882), who spent several years traveling and digging in the Mississippi Valley. As a consequence, Dr. Dickerson designed a panorama which was exhibited together with his collection around the middle of the century in Philadelphia and elsewhere. The panorama was advertised as covering more than 15,000 square feet of canvas, al-though in reality we now know that it only covered about 2,500 square feet, because Dr. Mason measured it. As the panorama un-rolled, the spectator saw the burial of De Soto, the effects of the

[28] See Hallowell (1960, pp. 74–85) for further information and references.

great tornado of 1844, and scenes of the mounds and earthworks of the Middle West in their excavated and unexcavated state. Among the mound groups delineated were those at Marietta, Circleville, Portsmouth, Bon Hom Island, Baluxie, and Lake Concordia. This panorama was acquired by the University Museum in 1899. It was last shown in 1941, at a meeting of the Eastern States Archaeological Federation.[29]

One of the great events of nineteenth-century Philadelphia was the Centennial Exposition in 1876. At this time the Indian Bureau of the Department of the Interior and the Smithsonian Institution collected material for a joint display of the ethnology and archaeology of the United States (Ewers, 1959).[30] At this exposition, objects from the mounds already made famous by Squier and Davis in their *Ancient Monuments of the Mississippi Valley* (1848) could be seen at first hand. Frank Hamilton Cushing (1857–1900), then a young man of nineteen, might be said to have been a living part of the ethnological exhibits. He edified the public by his remarkable talent for imitating Indian handicrafts of all kinds. For he had mastered the art of stone chipping, pottery and basket making, weaving and skin-dressing. It was not until after this that Major Powell gave him a job at the Bureau of American Ethnology, which led to his sojourn in the Southwest, where he lived as an adopted Zuñi from 1879–1884 (Cushing, 1920). Returning to Philadelphia in the mid-nineties, Cushing had his portrait, in Zuñi costume painted by the great Thomas Eakins in his studio on Chestnut Street. Cushing is seen wearing a buckskin suit with many necklaces of turquoise and a turquoise in his large earring. Hanging on the wall behind him are a

---

[29] For additional information see Mason, 1942a. The Dickerson archaeological collections were exhibited in Philadelphia in 1867 and again at the Centennial Exposition a decade later. After this they were transferred to Memorial Hall in Fairmount Park, where they remained until 1885, "Soon thereafter," Mason says, "they were acquired by the Department of Archaelogy and Paleontology of the University of Pennsylvania, which later became the University Museum." The diorama was exhibited by the Art Museum of St. Louis in 1949 and later acquired by that museum. See also McDermott (1958, pp. 170–72).

[30] A special appropriation for this display was obtained, and collecting was mainly confined to "those parts of the United States which were not already properly represented" since, after the Exposition closed, the specimens were to be transferred to the Smithsonian.

number of Zuñi objects. A piece of turreted pottery stands on a slab
above a fire at the lower right. Cushing proved that he had not lost
his talent for handicrafts by making a pair of moccasins for the
artist.[31] Cushing's classic paper on copper working appeared later
(1894), and the stunning wooden sculptures and other objects of
the Key Marco culture he excavated are among the prize exhibits of
the University Museum.

Beginning with the eighties, we enter a new era. We see the
establishment of archaeological collections at the University of
Pennsylvania, along with a concomitant program of research. And
we see the emergence of Daniel G. Brinton (1837–1899) as a leader
in the promotion of anthropology as an academic discipline, conceived in essentially the same inclusive terms in which we view the
subject today.

The archaeological collections marked the beginning of what
later became the University Museum, which celebrated its 75th anniversary in 1962.[32] I need not go into a history of the Museum in
any detail here, since Percy C. Madeira Jr., has written one (1964).
Suffice it to say that, beginning with a small collection of objects
donated to the University in the eighties, Provost William Pepper
(1843–1898) established a museum of archaeology and paleontology
in the old library building soon after its completion in 1889. The
collection remained there until the University Museum building was
completed a decade later. Stewart Culin (1858–1929), of later game
fame, was director of this collection during this period. Concur-

[31] This portrait is to be found in the Thomas Gilcrease Institute of American
History and Art, Tulsa, Oklahoma. A photograph is included in Porter (1959,
Plate 47).

[32] On this occasion J. Eric S. Thompson (Faculty Board of Archaeology,
Cambridge University) gave the Convocation Address and was awarded an
Honorary Degree (J. E. S. Thompson, 1962). In an article describing "The Department of Archaeology" (1892b) seventy years before (1892) Brinton refers to
an American section, an Assyrian section, an Egyptian section, etc. "By the 1st
of April 1891," he says (p. 378) "there were nearly 10,000 entries in the American department of the Museum, representing about 30,000 objects, besides
material which was still on hand, but at that date not entered in the catalogue."
The United States, he says, is represented by objects from thirty-six states
and six territories and, outside this area, there are specimens from Canada, the
West Indies, New Zealand, Samoa, Fiji, the New Hebrides, the Solomon
Islands, Torres Straits, and Australia. Several boxes of remains of the Swiss
Lake Dwellers were also included in the collection at this time.

rently, Pepper founded an archaeological association, the purpose of which was to provide funds, independently of the University, for the promotion of archaeological research and publication. Mrs. Phoebe Hearst, whose later patronage of anthropology at the University of California is familiar, was an active member for a time of the archaeological association organized and led by Dr. Pepper.

About the same time Provost Pepper, hearing about a projected expedition to southern Iraq, worked out an arrangement which led to excavations at Nippur under the auspices of the University. Beginning in 1888, thousands of cuneiform tablets from the Temple Library were recovered in a series of pioneer expeditions. In 1891, Dr. Pepper created the Department of Archaeology and Paleontology, which he directed after his resignation as Provost in 1894. He likewise promoted the erection of the building which became the present University Museum. It has been called "the last creation of Dr. Pepper's genius," but he did not live to enter it. As a consequence of his far-flung archaeological interests, Pepper also served a term as President of the Pennsylvania branch of the Archaeological Institute of America, which had been founded in 1879 (*Proceedings,* 1900, pp. 159–63). This organization, from the start, gave recognition to American as well as Old World archaeology. F. W. Putnam was active in its formation, and Lewis H. Morgan was asked to prepare a plan of research in the American field (White, 1942, pp. 1–2). Thus Dr. Pepper, although not an archaeologist himself, was actively in touch for a decade with current developments everywhere in this field, and devoted himself in particular to the promotion of research under University auspices. It was he who, learning of the archaeological work already done by Max Uhle, secured his services for the famous dig at the Temple of Pachacamac in Peru (1895–1896). This was the scene, says Mason, "of the first scientific archaeological work in Peru" (J. A. Mason, 1957, p. 100).[33] Cushing's

[33] For additional information on Uhle see Rowe (1954). The latter says (p. 1) that "when Uhle started work, American Archaeology was wholly without depth. A good deal of digging and collecting had been done and local styles were fairly well known in some areas, but American antiquities were all simply 'pre-Columbian.' It was Uhle who first applied modern principles of stratigraphy and seriation to American materials and sorted them out into a chronological sequence. This is only part of his achievement, but it is probably the part that will be longest remembered." For the more explicit circumstances under which Uhle was brought to Philadelphia and those which later lured

excavations in Florida were also promoted by Pepper during this period, in support of which the aid of Mrs. Hearst was obtained.[34]

Daniel G. Brinton, only a few years older than William Pepper was also a physician by training, receiving his M.D. from Jefferson Medical College in 1861. But the years he spent in private practice were few.[35] He was a man with the widest intellectual interests, and a prolific writer besides. Among other things, he published on the poetry of Whitman and Browning as well as in the medical field. In anthropology he dealt with somatological, archaeological, ethnographical, and linguistic data. He ranged far beyond the American Indian, although he is best known, perhaps, for work in this area, particularly in linguistics and mythology.[36] Brinton was very active in the American Philosophical Society, as John Freeman points out in these proceedings, and in 1884 he was made Professor of Ethnology and Archaeology in the Academy of Natural Sciences. Two years later he became Professor of American Linguistics and Archaeology at the University of Pennsylvania, a position which, while a signal honor, carried no pecuniary rewards for the incumbent.

---

him to the University of California, see pp. 4, 6. It appears that it was Pepper's death in 1898 which was the major factor which led Uhle to accept an offer from California. Mrs. Phoebe Hearst, who became his patron there, was a close friend of Pepper and shared the latter's interest in archaeology, as we have indicated.

[34] These excavations were sometimes referred to as the Pepper-Hearst Expedition. It should be noted that under the provostship of William Pepper (1881–1894), the University underwent a phenomenal expansion and achieved a national recognition. The faculty was trebled, attendance increased from 800 to almost 3,000, more than a dozen new departments were created, and there was a large increase in endowments. See, e.g., Thorpe's biography of Pepper (1904, p. 458).

[35] In 1862, returning from a year's study abroad, he joined the Medical Corps of the Union army, and was not discharged until 1865. In 1867 he became assistant editor of the *Medical and Surgical Reporter;* in 1874 he was made editor, and held this position until 1887. His published writings include 23 books and more than 200 articles.

[36] Stewart Culin prepared a bibliography for the memorial meeting held under the auspices of the American Philosophical Society (*Proceedings*, 1900, pp. 42–67); a selected bibliography, broadly relevant to physical anthropology, is to be found in Hrdlička (1919, pp. 63–64); and in his obituary notice Chamberlain lists publications "dealing more or less directly with Folk-Lore, Mythology, and allied topics."

By this time Brinton's work in American linguistics was internationally known. Besides many articles, he had initiated his unique *Library of Aboriginal American Literature* (1882), each volume of which comprised "a work composed in a native tongue by a native," with notes, glosses and other sections designed to make the text intelligible to the student.[37] In 1886, he was the first American to receive the medal of the Société Américaine de France for his "numerous and learned works on American Ethnology." While never a field archaeologist, Brinton was nevertheless erudite in this area also. In 1883 the article "American Archaeology" in the American Supplement to the *Encyclopaedia Britannica* was written by him, and both hemispheres were covered in a 116-page article on "Prehistoric Archeology" which Brinton contributed to the *Iconographic Encyclopaedia* in 1886. In the field of American archaeology Brinton was among the first (1866) to argue, on the basis of documentary evidence, that the Mound Builders were Indians, related to historic tribes, and not an alien or mysterious people. This article long antedated the "modern" period in mound archaeology, which culminated in the report of Cyrus Thomas in 1894 (Brinton, 1881).[38]

At the University, Brinton taught courses which were limited to graduate students. In content they included, among other things: methods of archaeological exploration, the characteristics of the remains of different archaeological provinces in North and South America, the structure of American Indian languages and the characteristics of different linguistic stocks, the relations of archaeology to ethnography, and the evolution of religion.

Despite the fact that in formal terms his offerings were never labeled anthropology, there is ample evidence to show that Dr. Brinton looked upon himself as an anthropologist in the inclusive sense in which that term was already being used in the United States, and that his contemporaries were aware of this fact and placed him in this category. In 1891, for example, Otis T. Mason in a review of Brinton's book *Races and Peoples*, took particular notice of the

[37] At the suggestion of the bibliographer J. C. Pilling, Brinton prepared a list of his publications in the field of American linguistics. This was privately printed and circulated in 1898 under the title *A Record of Study in Aboriginal American Languages*. There are 15 general articles and books listed; 14 items deal with languages north of Mexico, 31 with the Indian languages of Mexico and Central America, and 16 with those of the West Indies and South America.
[38] For the Mound Builders as a problem, see Hallowell (1960, pp. 75–81).

author's appointment to the faculty of the University and said: "If
we are not mistaken this is the first attempt by an institution of higher
learning in our country to found a professorship of anthropology"
(O. T. Mason, 1891). Brinton's identification as an anthropologist
becomes even more apparent when we turn to the phrasing of the
addresses of speakers at the Memorial Meeting held in January 1900,
six months after his death.

Provost Charles Custis Harrison, who presided at this meeting,
although referring to Brinton's chair by title, goes on to say that his
"devotion to what he himself called 'the new science of anthropology' was most interesting. He had the utmost confidence, not only
in the importance of the science itself as a science, but also in its
practical value as an applied science in politics, education and legisla-
tion. He was not in any way a mere 'collector' or 'observer' in the
familiar sense of these words." (*Proceedings*, 1900, pp. 216–17). On
the same occasion, F. W. Putnam (1839–1915), a contemporary of
Brinton, whose activies as a promoter in the general field of anthropology had ranged far and wide, was present. At the time he was
Professor of American Archaeology and Ethnology at Harvard, and
like Brinton he had been the recipient of the degree of Doctor of
Science from the University of Pennsylvania during the previous
decade. At the Memorial Meeting he represented the American Association for the Advancement of Science, which he had served as
Permanent Secretary for twenty-five years, and as President in 1898.
In the course of his remarks, he said that a fitting memorial to
Brinton on the part of the University would be the establishment,
not of a chair of archaeology as the Provost had suggested, but
rather of a professorship of anthropology. He went on to say that
this would give "further aid and encouragement to that branch of
American science which he loved so well and worked so earnestly
to advance," and that it would likewise "meet with the hearty approval and coöperation of all workers in anthropology throughout
the country" (*ibid.*, p. 239).

What I wish to emphasize particularly is the fact that in this
country Brinton was the pioneer in teaching anthropology [39] (De

[39] In 1906 the greater part of one issue of the *American Anthropologist* (n.s.,
Vol. 8, No. 3) was devoted to "Recent Progress in American Anthropology. A
Review of the Activities of Institutions and Individuals from 1902 to 1906."
In the section devoted to the University of Pennsylvania (pp. 479–83) it is

Laguna, 1960, p. 102), that the nomenclature suggested in his article of 1892 prevailed,[40] and that he was first and last an active promoter of anthropology as an autonomous academic discipline, including a program of gruaduate work leading to the doctorate. In the Prefatory Note to a pamphlet privately printed and circulated in 1892 and bearing the title *Anthropology, as a Science and as a Branch of University Education in the U.S.*, Brinton says: "the rightful claims of this science will be recognized only when it is organized as a department by itself, with a competent corps of professors and docents, with well-appointed laboratories and museums, and with fellowships for deserving students." On June 2 of the same year he wrote to Provost William Pepper making "some suggestions for establishing instruction in the science of anthropology in the University, to form a constituent part of the branches eligible for the degree of Ph.D." He reviewed the precedents for such instruction both in faculty and personnel and in research materials which, he believed, would make possible the implementation of his proposal.[41]

---

stated (p. 482) that "when in 1886 Dr. Brinton was appointed to the chair of American Archaeology and Linguistics at the University of Pennsylvania, that institution took the initial step in a movement which, taken up soon afterward by Harvard, has led to the introduction of anthropology as a distinct branch of learning into all the principal universities in the United States. In founding a chair of American Archaeology and Ethnology [sic], Pennsylvania was not only the first of American universities to recognize the claim of these special branches of investigation, but was the first to introduce the study of anthropology as a distinct science. It is well known that Dr. Brinton's comprehensive exposition of his subject embraced the whole science of anthropology, and his lectures foreshadowed the later development of instruction in anthropology in America. Although first in this movement, the University of Pennsylvania did not subsequently make so rapid progress in this particular direction as some of the other American universities. In recent years, however, there has been renewed activity in this respect."

[40] This article, an abstract of an address delivered before the Anthropological Society of Washington in April, was published in the *American Anthropologist* in July 1892 and is reprinted in DeLaguna (1960). The terminology and content of the subject had been under considerable discussion by this time, and J. W. Powell, who had developed a special terminology of his own, commented on Brinton's paper. It is interesting, as DeLaguna says (p. 99), "that Brinton's taxonomy has won out in the long run, despite Powell's great prestige as director of the Bureau of Ethnology."

[41] Here I am indebted to Professor Leonidas Dodson, Archivist of the University of Pennsylvania, since I have not seen the letter cited referred to elsewhere.

His suggestion, however, did not lead to any action at the time. But it was in the same year that Brinton was invited to examine the first person to receive a Ph.D. in Anthropology at an American university. The candidate was Alexander Francis Chamberlain (1865–1914) at Clark University (Chamberlain, 1900, pp. 219, 220). While there was no anthropology department there, it will be recalled that G. Stanley Hall brought Franz Boas to Clark in 1889 where he taught for three years. But since no department was organized, the program so boldly initiated did not flourish.[42]

After his death, Brinton's library passed to the University Museum, where it is still housed. On May 13, 1937, the centenary of his birth was celebrated at the Delaware County Institute of Science in Media, Pennsylvania. Brinton had been an active member of the Institute when he made his home in Media in his later years. Delegates from many learned societies attended, and they were addressed by Edwin C. Conklin and Clark Wissler (J. A. Mason, 1938). In 1942 the Philadelphia Anthropological Society initiated a series of monographs dedicated to Brinton's memory. These publications were largely made possible through contributions from his heirs.

Although Brinton had initiated the teaching of anthropology at the University, his major influence was exerted more widely through his writings and activities elsewhere,[43] since no organized academic program was developed under his direction. And following his death there was no one of equal anthropological distinction available on the local scene. Stewart Culin, who remained in Philadelphia until 1903, when he joined the staff of the Brooklyn Museum, offered some courses in the University Museum between 1900 and 1902. However, the first undergraduate courses *listed* as anthropology, were given by George Byron Gordon (1870–1927), who became Curator of Anthropology in 1904, and later Director of the Museum. It was not until Frank G. Speck arrived in 1907 that a more fully rounded program began to emerge, including the intro-

[42] George A. Dorsey, who received his Ph.D. from Harvard University in 1894, was the first to acquire a doctorate from a university in the United States in which there was a formally organized department of anthropology.

[43] He was, for example, President of the World's Fair Congress of Anthropology held in conjunction with the Columbia Exposition in Chicago, 1893, making the opening address. See DeLaguna (1960, pp. 423–34). In 1894 Brinton served as President of the AAAS, a distinction he shared with three other nineteenth-century anthropologists: Morgan, Powell, and Putnam.

duction of graduate instruction leading to a doctorate, thus bringing to delayed fruition Brinton's recommendations of 1892.[44]

Frank G. Speck had studied at Columbia University under Franz Boas, but in 1908 was awarded the first Ph.D. in Anthropology at Pennsylvania. His thesis, "The Ethnology of the Yuchi Indians," was published as the initial volume in the newly established Anthropological Publications of the University of Pennsylvania Museum (1909). Speck organized the Department of Anthropology in 1910, and for several years thereafter courses continued to be given within the Museum walls, as they had previously. The lecture hall used for larger classes was the Widener Auditorium, which was remodeled in 1961 into the offices now occupied by the Anthropology Department. I am sometimes surprised to find myself sitting in the balcony of this old lecture hall. For that is where my office is. It was from the floor of this same lecture hall that as an undergraduate I first heard Frank Speck address his class in Anthropology I, although I was not enrolled in it. At that time I had not the faintest notion that I should ever become an anthropologist. Nor did I anticipate the fact that Frank and I would become intimate friends, that he would be my mentor in anthropology, and that we would become so closely associated in the department for many years.

I trust that the odd bits of historical information that I have patched together suggest some kind of underlying continuity, or even cumulative trends, in the history of anthropology in Phila-

[44] J. Alden Mason (1950a), who was graduated from the University of Pennsylvania in 1907, has provided some recollections of this period: "Well I remember the supplementary sheet in the catalogue of 1903–4 in my freshman year. Among other 'Special Announcements' it stated that beginning in 1904–5, elective courses would be given in anthropology. There were two one-semester courses that first year; 701, General Anthropology, and 702, American Archeology and Ethnology. In 1905–6, General Anthropology was enlarged to a full year course, and 703, Ethnology of Europe, replaced it as a one-semester course." Mason pursued graduate work there after 1907, taking some courses with Speck after the latter arrived on the scene. "The year 1909–10 was a productive one at Pennsylvania for anthropologists," Mason goes on to say. "Both Frank G. Speck and Edward Sapir taught full time, with G. B. Gordon teaching part time. I again held a scholarship, a full-time one this year and profited greatly. At the end of that year Sapir went to head the Anthropology Department of the Geological Survey of Canada and I went to California for more graduate work [with Kroeber], not to return to Pennsylvania until 1926."

delphia. I believe that further research in depth, including the correspondence of important figures, would reveal connecting links and
developmental sequences more clearly. But this remains for the future. Anthropology at large has not yet developed an acute historical consciousness. As I see it, the history of anthropology in Philadelphia is only a small segment of a larger whole. I hope I have said
enough, however, to indicate that anthropological activities here,
when viewed in historical perspective, have been an integral part of
a wider flow of events elsewhere and have influenced them as well.
Awareness of past events should lead to a more rational appraisal of
contemporary aims and achievements, as well as a sounder evaluation of our future goals and the best means to achieve them.

REFERENCES

Bell, Whitfield J., Jr. (1955). *Early American Science: Needs and
Opportunities for Study.* Williamsburg, Va., Institute of Early American History and Culture.

Biddle, Nicholas (1814). *History of the expedition under the command
of Captains Lewis and Clark, to the sources of the Missouri, thence
across the Rocky Mountains and down the River Columbia to the
Pacific Ocean. Performed during the years 1804-5-6. By order of the
government of the United States.* Prepared for the press by Paul
Allen. 2 vol. Philadelphia, Bradford and Inkeep.

Boudinot, Elias (1816). *A star in the West; or, a Humble Attempt to
Discover the Long Lost Ten Tribes of Israel, Preparatory to the
Return to their Beloved City, Jerusalem.* Trenton, N.J., D. Fenton, S.
Hutchinson, and J. Dunham.

Bridenbaugh, Carl and Jessica (1942). *Rebels and Gentlemen. Philadelphia in the Age of Franklin.* New York, Reynal and Hitchcock (Reissued as a paperback, 1962).

Brinton, Daniel G. (1866). "The Mound-builders of the Mississippi
Valley," *Historical Magazine,* 11, pp. 33–37.

———(1881). "The Probable Nationality of the Mound-builders,"
American Antiquarian, 4, pp. 9–18.

———(1883). "American Archaeology," *Encyclopaedia Britannica,*
American Supplement, 1, pp. 278–86.

———(1886). "Prehistoric Archaeology," *Iconographic Encyclopaedia,*
2, p. 16

————(1892a). *Anthropology, as a Science and as a Branch of University Education in the United States.* Privately printed.

————(1892b). "The Department of Archaeology," in *Benjamin Franklin and the University of Pennsylvania.*, ed. by Francis Newton Thrope. Washington, D.C., Bureau of Education, 1893.

————(1892c). "The Nomenclature and Teaching of Anthropology," *American Anthropologist* 5, pp. 263–71. (Reprinted in De Laguna).

————(1895). "The Aims of Anthropology," American Association for the Advancement of Science, 44, *Proceedings*, pp. 1–17.

————(1897). "Dr. Allen's Contributions to Anthropology," American Academy of Natural Sciences of Philadelphia, 46, *Proceedings*, pp. 522–29.

Brinton, Daniel G. (1898). *A Record of Study in American Aboriginal Languages.* Media, Pa., privately printed.

Catlin, George (1841). *Letters and Notes on the Manners, Customs, and Conditions of the North American Indians.* 2 vol. London, published by the author at Egyptian Hall, Piccadilly.

Chamberlain, Alexander F. (1900). "In Memoriam: Daniel Garrison Brinton," *Journal of American Folklore*, 12, pp. 215–25.

Chinard, Gilbert (1943). "Jefferson and the American Philosophical Society," American Philosophical Society, 87, *Proceedings*, pp. 263–76.

Clark, Barrett H. (ed.) (1943). *Favorite American Plays of the Nineteenth Century.* Princeton, Princeton University Press.

Colton, Harold S. (1909). "Peale's Museum," *Popular Science Monthly*, 75, pp. 221–38.

Cushing, Frank Hamilton (1894). "Primitive Copper Working; An Experimental Study," *American Anthropologist*, 7, pp. 93–117.

————(1896). "Preliminary Report on the Exploration of Ancient Key Dwellers' Remains on the Gulf Coast of Florida," American Philosophical Society, 35, *Proceedings*, pp. 329–432.

————(1920). *Zuni Breadstuff.* Indian Notes and Monographs 8, New York, Museum of the American Indian, Heye Foundation.

De Laguna, Frederica (ed.) (1960). *Selected Papers from the American Anthropologist, 1888–1920.* New York, Harper and Row.

De Voto, Bernard (1953). *The Journals of Lewis and Clark.* Boston, Houghton Mifflin.

Dupree, A. Hunter (1957). *Science in the Federal Government.* Cambridge, Belnap Press of Harvard University.

Ewers, John C. (1949). "An Anthropologist Looks at Early Pictures of North American Indians," *New York Historical Society Quarterly*, 33, pp. 222–35.

———(1956). "George Catlin, Painter of Indians and the West," *Annual Report of the Smithsonian Institution for 1955*. Washington, pp. 483–506.

———(1959). "A Century of American Indian Exhibits in the Smithsonian Institution," *Annual Report of the Smithsonian Institution for 1958*. pp. 513–52.

Greene, John C. (1960). "Early Scientific Interest in the American Indian: Comparative Linguistics," American Philosophical Society, *Proceedings*, 104, pp. 511–17.

Hallowell, A. Irving (1957). "The Backwash of the Frontier: The Impact of the Indian on American Culture," *Annual Report of the Smithsonian Institution for 1958*, pp. 447–72. Washington, 1959. (This article is reprinted from *The Frontier in Perspective*, ed. by Walker D. Wyman and Clifton B. Kroeber. Madison, University of Wisconson Press, 1957. The Smithsonian reprinting contains 8 plates not in the original.)

———(1960). "The Beginnings of Anthropology in America," in Frederica De Laguna (ed.), *Selected Papers from the American Anthropologist, 1888–1920*, New York, Harper and Row, pp. 1–90.

Hrdlička, Ales (1919). *Physical Anthropology: Its Scope and Aims; Its History and Present Status in the United States*. Philadelphia, Wistar Institute of Anatomy and Biology.

Hungerford, E. B. (1941). *Shores of Darkness*. New York, Columbia University Press.

Huth, Hans (1945). "Pierre Eugene DuSimitière and the Beginnings of the American Historical Museum," *Pennsylvania Magazine of History*, 69, pp. 315–25.

Jackson, Donald (ed.) (1962). *Letters of the Lewis and Clark Expedition with Related Documents 1783–1854*. Urbana, University of Illinois Press.

Kroeber, Theodora (1961). *Ishi in Two Worlds: A Biography of the Last Wild Indian in North America*. Berkeley and Los Angeles, University of California Press.

Levey, Martin (1951). "The First American Museum of Natural History," *Isis*, 42, pp. 10–12.

Lurie, Nancy Oestreich (1966). "Women in Early American Anthropology," in June Helm (ed.), *Pioneers of American Anthropology* (Seattle, University of Washington Press), pp. 31–81.

McCracken, Harold (1959). *George Catlin and the Old Frontier*. New York, Dial Press.

MacCurdy, George Grant (ed.) (1937). *Early Man, as Depicted by*

Leading Authorities at the International Symposium, the Academy of Natural Sciences, Philadelphia, March 1937. Philadelphia, Lippincott.

McDermott, John Francis (1958). *The Lost Panoramas of the Mississippi.* Chicago, University of Chicago Press, pp. 170–72.

McHenry, Margaret (1946). *Thomas Eakins who Painted.* Privately printed.

Madeira, Percy (1964). *Man in Search of Man.* Philadelphia, University of Pennsylvania.

Mason, J. Alden (1938). "Brinton Anniversary," *Journal of American Folklore* 51, pp. 106–7.

———(1942a). "Grand Moving Diorama, a Special Feature," *The Pennsylvania Archaeologist* 12 (1942), No. 1, pp. 14–16. [Reprinted in *Minnesota History*, 23 (1942), pp. 352–54.]

———(1942b). "Obituary of Edgar B. Howard," *American Antiquity*, 9, pp. 230–34.

———(1950a). "Frank Gouldsmith Speck, 1881–1950," Philadelphia Anthropological Society, *Bulletin*, 3, No. 4. (Obituary notice.)

———(1950b). "The Beginnings of Anthropology at the University of Pennsylvania," Philadelphia Anthropological Society, *Bulletin*, No. 3.

———(1950c). "Frank Gouldsmith Speck, 1881–1950." *University Museum Bulletin* 15, No. 1, pp. 3–5. With photograph of Speck. This number contains Frank G. Speck, "Concerning Iconology and the Masking Complex in Eastern North America," p. 6–57.

———(1957). *The Ancient Civilizations of Peru.* Penguin Books.

Mason, Otis T. (1891). "Review of D. G. Brinton's 'Races and Peoples,'" *American Anthropologist*, 4, pp. 68–88.

Mitra, Panchanan (1933). *A History of American Anthropology.* University of Calcutta.

The Noble Savage, The American Indian in Art, with an introduction by Robert C. Smith. (Exhibition at the University Museum, 1958).

Pennsylvania Historical Records Survey (1940). Descriptive Catalogue of the DuSimitière Papers in the Library Company of Philadelphia.

Porter, Fairfield (1959). *Thomas Eakins.* New York, George Braziller, 1959 (Great American Artists series).

Potts, William J. (1889). "DuSimitière, Artist, Antiquary, and Naturalist, Projector of the First American Museum with some Extracts from his Notebook," *Pennsylvania Magazine of History*, 13, pp. 341–75.

"Recent Progress in American Anthropology. A Review of the Activities of Institutions and Individuals from 1902–1906. Presented to the Fifteenth International Congress of Americanists, Quebec. 1906," *American Anthropologists*, 1906, N.S. 8, No. 3, pp. 441–558.

Proceedings, American Philosophical Society. (1900). Memorial Volume 1.

Rowe, John Howland (1954). "Max Uhle, 1856–1944. A Memoir of the Father of Peruvian Archaeology," *University of California Publications in American Archaeology and Ethnography*, 46, No. 1, pp. 1–134, plates 1–14. Berkeley and Los Angeles.

Simpson, George G. (1942). "The First Natural History Museum in America," *Science*, 96, pp. 261–63.

Stanton, William (1960). *The Leopard's Spots. Scientific Attitudes toward Race in America, 1815–1859*. Chicago, University of Chicago Press.

Thomas, Cyrus (1894). "Report on the Mound Explorations of the Bureau of American Ethnology," Bureau of American Ethnology, 12th Annual Report, 1890–91, pp. 27–730.

Thompson, J. Eric S. (1962). "Convocation Address," *Expedition*, 4, No. 3, pp. 14–16.

Thorpe, Francis Newton (1904). *William Pepper*. Philadelphia, Lippincott.

Thwaites, Reuben Gold, ed. (1904–5) *Original Journals of the Lewis and Clark Expedition, 1804–1806, printed from the original manuscript in the library of the American Philosophical Society and by direction of its committee on historical documents, together with manuscript material of Lewis and Clark from other sources . . . now for the first time published in full and exactly as written*. 8 vols. (New York, Dodd, Mead and Co.)

Wauchope, Robert (1962). *Lost Tribes and Sunken Continents. Myth and Method in the Study of American Indians*. Chicago, University of Chicago Press.

Wedel, Waldo R. (1957). "Observations on Some Nineteenth Century Pottery Vessels from the Upper Missouri," *Anthropological Papers* No. 51, Bulletin 164, Bureau of American Ethnology, Washington.

White, Leslie A. (ed.) (1942). "Lewis H. Morgan's Journal of a Trip to Southwestern Colorado and New Mexico, June 21 to August 7, 1878," *American Antiquity*, 8, pp. 1–26.

Willoughby, Charles C. (1905). "A Few Ethnological Specimens Collected by Lewis and Clarke," *American Anthropologist*, 7, pp. 633–41.

III | PSYCHOLOGY AND CULTURE

INTRODUCTION

Anthony F. C. Wallace

For Hallowell, the central issue in the interdisciplinary domain of psychology-and-culture was the problem of *perception*. Whether he was considering the culture of a specific people, like the Ojibwa, or the cultures of early man as a group, always pivotal in his approach was a certain conception of the individual actor. Man, for him, was always a being confronted with a world without and a world within, seeing this dual reality always through a cognitive screen provided by a combination of unique life experience and standardized cultural meanings. His very choice of the Rorschach inkblots—a test of perception—as his principal tool in psychological research bespeaks the fundamental role of perceptual processes in his conception of man. And this image of man as perceiver informed his teaching as well as his research. I well remember, as a graduate student of his, sitting in the seminar room, being reminded week after week that, as a philosopher has said, the fact that things are as they are does not explain why they look as they look. A favorite demonstration was the constellation Ursa Major. After noting that the Ojibwa and also the members of the class, reared in a Western European tradition, agreed in perceiving certain northerly stars as a great bear, he then presented material on cultures in which these stars were perceived as elements of other concepts. He recounted, with a chuckle, the bewildered reaction of a naive student who could not accept this and who insisted, "But it *does* look like a bear!"

In pursuing this issue, Hallowell was proceeding along a line of inquiry that was classical in both anthropology and psychology. Franz Boas, who had instructed both Hallowell and Hallowell's teacher at the University of Pennsylvania, Frank Speck,

Anthony F. C. Wallace is professor of anthropology at the University of Pennsylvania.

had made the problem of perception central to his anthropology too. In his German university years, Boas had been trained in the newly developing field of psychophysics. Here he had learned to study how the characteristics of the observer determined his perception of physical phenomena. Boas had gone on to generalize this Kantian view of epistemology to include a concern with the way the historically constituted "genius of a people" determines their perception of their geography, of the cultural repertoire presented to them for acceptance by their neighbors, and even of themselves. Thus, in his work on the cultural determinants of perception Hallowell was carrying forward the investigation of one of the great problems not only of psychology and anthropology, but of epistemology and the philosophy of science.

The first of the two psychological papers reprinted in this collection provides a very careful review of the intermingling of ethnological and psychological research in the early days of our discipline, long before the rather self-conscious emergence of "culture and personality" as a special subfield, created in response to the impact of psychoanalytic theories. What is noteworthy in Hallowell's review is the importance many of the early psychologists accorded to cross-cultural information. It was crucial to them, in their assault upon the remains of sensationalist and associationist doctrines, to demonstrate the importance of culturally derived schemata in human perception and learning. And, conversely, early anthropologists were eager to teach their psychological and medical colleagues that thinking and perceiving are always to some extent social acts, thus always to some extent shaped by culture.

The second paper represents, from the standpoint of this discussion, one of the logical goals of Hallowell's thinking— the recognition that a perceptional act, the recognition of self, was critically important in human evolution. For with this achievement man became capable of that degree of autonomous moral awareness, of normative regulation of his own conduct, which distinguishes him among the animals. It is interesting, however, that in the review of human evolution he gives so little attention to the structuralist tradition. Lévi-

Strauss and Chomsky are not mentioned, of course (most of their work remained to be published at the time Hallowell was writing this piece). He does discuss Jung, who can be viewed as an early structuralist (his "archetypes" anticipate the later writings of linguistics and anthropologists on "wired-in" structures of the human mind). But Hallowell was more interested in *varying* perceptions and cognitions as products of varying cultural environments than in *constancies* on mental structures as products of constant human nature. Thus in addressing, in this last paper, the question of the nature of man, he insists on viewing human nature as a process rather than as a set of givens.

FIVE

Psychology and Anthropology

1954

I. Introduction

IF THE RELATIONS between anthropology and psychology[1] are considered merely abstractly or without awareness of historical circumstances, any appraisal of the present situation or their future relations will lack clarity and depth. Although there have been discussions, particularly in the past three decades, of the more general, as well as certain specific, aspects of these relations, and research in

[1] For the purpose of this chapter *psychology* is defined in the broadest terms; so is *anthropology*. In effect, the nature and range of psychology coincides with the conception of this discipline as set forth in *The Place of Psychology in an Ideal University,* Cambridge: Harvard University Press, 1947, p. 2; the Report of the University Commission to Advise on the Future of Psychology at Harvard, Alan Gregg, chairman, C. I. Barnard, D. W. Bronk, L. Carmichael, J. Dollard, T. M. French, E. R. Hilgard, W. S. Hunter, E. L. Thorndike, L. L. Thurstone, J. C. Whitehorn, R. M. Yerkes:

"Psychology is actually what psychologists do and teach: defined briefly, it is the science of human and animal behavior, both individual and social. To expand this definition, psychology is the systematic study, by any and all applicable and fruitful methods, of organisms in relation to their behavior, environmental relations, and experience. Its purpose is to discover facts, principles, and generalizations which shall increase man's knowledge, understanding, predictive insight, directive wisdom and control of the natural phenomena of behavior and experience, and of himself and the social groups and institutions in which and through which he functions. Psychologists seek to provide a basic science of human thinking, character, skill, learning, motives, conduct, etc. which will serve all the sciences of man (e.g., anthropology, sociology, economics, government, education, medicine, etc.) in much the same way and to the same extent that biology now serves the agricultural and medical sciences."

some areas of common interest has taken place,[2] no one has yet writ-

[2] See Alfred C. Haddon, *History of Anthropology*, 1st edition, New York: Putnam, 1910; 2nd edition, London: Watts and Company, 1934; T. K. Penniman, *A Hundred Years of Anthropology*, New York: Macmillan, 1936; Robert H. Lowie, *The History of Ethnological Theory*, New York: Farrar and Rinehardt, 1937; Wilhelm Mühlmann, *Methodik der Völkerkunde*, Stuttgart: Enke, 1938.

More than a quarter of a century ago A. A. Goldenweiser, writing a chapter on "Cultural Anthropology" that appeared in H. E. Barnes, *The History and Prospects of the Social Sciences* (1925), made the interesting observation that:

"In reviewing the work of Rivers and the American anthropologists I took occasion to note a revival of interest in psychological problems which arose in the course of cultural studies. The American students, in particular, were keenly conscious of the necessity of a psychological technique to supplement the objective studies of the historian of culture. But to recognize this necessity was one thing, to supply the technique another. The attempts in this direction first of all produced a crop of theoretical discussions dealing with the general relations of psychology and sociology, discussions which bring to mind the old controversy over the folk-soul between Wundt on the one hand and Steinthal and Lazarus on the other, as well as the prolonged disquisitions among sociologists over the content and nature of sociology."

The references Goldenweiser gives are as follows: Robert H. Lowie, "Psychology and Sociology," *American Journal of Sociology*, Vol. 21, 1915, pp. 217–229; W. H. R. Rivers, "Sociology and Psychology," *Sociological Review*, Vol. 9, 1916, pp. 1–13; A. L. Kroeber, "The Possibility of a Social Psychology," *American Journal of Sociology*, Vol. 23, 1918, pp. 633–651; A. M. Hocart, "Ethnology and Psychology," *Folk Lore*, Vol. 75, 1915, pp. 115–138; R. R. Marett, *Psychology and Folk Lore*.

Goldenweiser himself had by this time published "Psychology and Culture," *Publications of the American Sociological Society*, Vol. 19, 1925, pp. 15–24 and, in 1927, the chapter he contributed to *The Social Sciences and Their Interrelations*, W. F. Ogburn and A. A. Goldenweiser, eds., was entitled "Anthropology and Psychology." Both of these were later reprinted in the volume of his selected papers, *History, Psychology, and Culture*, New York: Knopf, 1933. No reference was made by Goldenweiser to the significant article published in 1924 by Marcel Mauss, "Rapports réels et pratiques de la psychologie et de la sociologie," *Journal de Psychologie Normale et Pathologique*, nor to the Presidential Address of C. G. Seligman, "Anthropology and Psychology: A Study of Some Points of Contact," *Journal of the Royal Anthropological Institute*, Vol. 54, 1924.

In present-day perspective, what is significant about all of the citations made by Goldenweiser is that they antedate the subsequent literature of the personality and culture movement, so that not one of them, including Goldenweiser's own articles, appears in Haring's bibliography, *Personal Character and Cultural Milieu: A Collection of Readings*, compiled by Douglas G. Haring, revised ed., Syracuse University Press, 1948. Of the additional items to which I have called attention Seligman is given, but Mauss is not. Although Goldenweiser contributed a chapter entitled "Some Contributions of Psychoanalysis to the Interpretation of Social Facts" to *Contemporary Social Theory*, edited by H. E. Barnes, Howard Becker, and Frances B. Becker, he is concerned with various psychoanalytic writers and their critics rather than with the research, already begun, in the personality and culture area.

In 1939 Gillin published a review article, with bibliography, of the literature dealing with "Personality in Preliterate Societies," *American Sociological*

ten a detailed history of all the varied influences and counterinfluences exerted at successive periods in the development and expansion of these disciplines. Nevertheless, it seems desirable to survey briefly some of the relevant facts even if our historical résumé must be sketchy and incomplete.

The most outstanding impression received when this over-all viewpoint is adopted is that there have been many more significant connections than are ordinarily supposed, at least from the anthropological side, even if these have not always led to cooperative research; some have even provoked negative reactions. Anthropologists generally have been far from insensitive to psychology. Thus, while no exception need be taken to Kluckhohn's statement that "the dominant currents in American anthropology prior to, roughly, 1920 were descriptive and historical," and "awareness of *psychiatry* in other than the most diffuse sense that there was such a thing as 'mental disease' was almost completely lacking," it is misleading to say that "the prevalent trend of American anthropology was *anti-psychological*" (italics mine).[3] If psychology is given its broadest connotation and anthropology considered in all its historical aspects, it is apparent, on the contrary, that from its beginnings, both abroad and in America, anthropology has been almost continuously influenced by psychology, but not always with respect to the same problems. Writing in England Haddon seems to have been aware of this. His *History* contains a brief chapter entitled "Comparative Psychology" in the first edition (1910), and an expanded chapter "Individual and Ethnic Psychology" in the revised edition (1934). Referring to this country he says, "In the United States of America, thanks to the influence of Boas, psychology has been well recognized by students as an essential factor in ethnology."[4] It may likewise be noted in passing that the founder of the Bureau of American Ethnol-

---

Review, Vol. 4, pp. 681–702; and in 1944 Kluckhohn systematically analyzed the concrete contributions which reflected "The Influence of Psychiatry on Anthropology in America during the Past One Hundred Years," *One Hundred Years of American Psychiatry*, edited by J. K. Hall, G. Zilboorg, and H. A. Bunker, New York: Columbia University Press. For additional guidance to the personality and culture literature see Haring, *op. cit.*; *Personality in Nature, Society, and Culture*, Clyde Kluckhohn and Henry A. Murray, eds., 2nd edition, 1953, New York: Knopf; and A. Irving Hallowell, "Culture, Personality, and Society" in *Anthropology Today*, A. L. Kroeber, ed., Chicago: University of Chicago Press, 1953.

[3] Kluckhohn, 1944, *op. cit.*

[4] Haddon, *op. cit.*, p. 68. This statement only occurs in the revised edition.

ogy, J. W. Powell, in an article on "Anthropology" published in the
Universal Cyclopaedia (1900), discussed the subject under the headings: Somatology, Psychology, Ethnology.⁵

It is only if psychology is defined very narrowly, or the influence
of closely related specialties like psychiatry or psychoanalysis is considered, or when the traditional interests of specialized groups of
anthropologists, such as linguists or archeologists, are referred to,
that a complete absence of interest or influence before 1920 can be
alleged. For nearly a century, many outstanding anthropologists
have been interested in various psychological problems; and it has
always been quite generally recognized that such problems were intimately connected with some of the large, central, and perennial
questions that anthropologists sought to answer. Besides his concern
with Elementargedanken and Völkergedanken, Bastian, for example,
was interested in abnormal psychology; he reported firsthand observations on possession in a psychological journal.⁶ Among other things,
Waitz posed the question of national character: "The question has
been frequently asked," he says, "in what consists the national character of a people? The preceding investigation has shown that it depends on so many conditions that an exact analysis is extremely difficult. That it is not the race alone which determines it, is proved by
there being different nationalities within the same race. It is therefore probable . . . that the mental peculiarities of peoples are generally more flexible and changeable than the physical characters of the
race, and are transmitted with a less degree of constancy."⁷ Andrew

⁵ The special interest of this article does not lie in its concrete content, but
in the fact that Powell wrote it and that he refers to psychology as "an integral
part of anthropology." He finds it necessary to distinguish two basic schools of
psychological thought: one that claims psychology as a natural science, and a
"second school, which is earlier in history, and still the larger," which assumes
the existence of a "spiritual soul" and has intimate connections with philosophy.

⁶ P. W. A. Bastian, "Ueber psychische Beobachtungen Naturvölkern," Publications of Die Gesellschaft für Experimental-Psychologie zu Berlin, Leipzig,
1890, Vol. 2, pp. 6–9. T. K. Oesterreich, Possession: Demoniacal and Other
Among Primitive Races, in Antiquity, the Middle Ages, and Modern Times,
New York: Richard R. Smith, 1930, p. 378 says: "The extraordinary importance
accruing to the phenomena of possession amongst primitive races has hitherto
been insufficiently appreciated by ethnology. One single ethnologist, Adolf
Bastian, whose numerous works have not attracted the attention they deserved
owing to their abstruse literary form, was fully alive to it. In his works we
meet possession at every turn, and their unsupported testimony would be adequate to demonstrate its significance in the savage world."

⁷ Theodore Waitz, Introduction to Anthropology, London, 1863, edited by
J. Frederick Collingwood with numerous additions by the author, from the
first volume of Anthropologie der Naturvölker.

Lang was interested in parapsychology, and declared that "anthropology must remain incomplete while it neglects this field, whether among wild or civilized men."[8] Frazer explicitly articulated his concern with mental as well as cultural evolution.[9]

Whatever the professional preoccupations of anthropologists have been, one inescapable problem has always directed their attention to psychology: some basic assumptions always had to be made about the psychological nature of man and human behavior. These assumptions had either to be derived from "common sense" or some attention paid to the data and conclusions of psychology as a recognized discipline, irrespective of the latter's stage of development or the specialized preoccupations of the psychologists of any particular period. For instance, the question of racial differences in "mentality," especially intellectual superiority or inferiority, involved a problem central to all anthropological research. Could a basic "psychic unity" of mankind be assumed, or was it necessary to consider the possibility that there were innate racial barriers to "culture progress" or even to the acquisition of "higher" cultural forms by the "lower" races in a process of "diffusion"? Boas, writing in 1910, said that "the ultimate aim of Waitz's great work is the inquiry into the question whether there are any fundamental differences between the mental make-up of mankind the world over, racially as well as socially."[10] But in Waitz's time, and for a long period thereafter, it was not possible to approach this question by means of psychological tests of any kind. Yet the assumption of psychic unity became traditional, nonetheless.

Furthermore, as more and more data were accumulated and characteristic problems defined, it is not surprising that the attitudes of anthropologists toward psychological concepts and formulations

[8] Quoted by Haddon, op. cit., p. 61, with reference to The Making of Religion, 1898. In his Cock Lane and Common Sense (1894) Lang had first called attention to "savage spiritualism," which he said "wonderfully resembles, even in minute details, that of modern mediums and séances. . . ." A few contemporary anthropologists have manifested interest in parapsychology. See, e.g., Victor Barnouw, "Siberian Shamanism and Western Spiritualism," Journal of the American Society for Psychical Research, Vol. 36, 1942, pp. 140–168; and "Paranormal Phenomena and Culture," ibid., Vol. 40, 1946, pp. 2–21. Margaret Mead has served as a member of the Board of Trustees of the American Society for Psychical Research and, in March 1953, John R. Swanton in a communication directed to "Fellow Anthropologists," drew attention to this field.

[9] James G. Frazer, "Scope and Method of Mental and Anthropological Science," Science Progress, Vol. 16, 1922.

[10] Franz Boas, "Psychological Problems in Anthropology," American Journal of Psychology, Vol. 21, 1910, pp. 371–384.

should increasingly reflect their own mastery of data, special interests, and conclusions. The negative reaction to intelligence tests as a reliable means of determining innate mental differences attributable to race was not only an indication of a continuing interest in the question of the psychic unity of man; it was a determined effort to demonstrate the direct relevance of the data and concepts of physical and cultural anthropology to a basic psychological problem. The instinct doctrines formulated by McDougall and others became another pertinent focus of anthropological knowledge and appraisal. Thus anthropologists have not hesitated to make independent judgments of what psychologists have had to offer them.

It has now become increasingly apparent, moreover, that psychological problems which were not of special interest to contemporary psychologists, or not even recognized by anthropologists themselves, have nevertheless been inherent in certain data and concepts of anthropology. Tylor's classical definition of culture, for example, asserts that culture is acquired. This simple statement actually embodies a host of psychological problems of no particular interest to the psychologist of Tylor's day. Again, anthropologists have been able to make use of the fact that culture is transmitted in human societies from one generation to another, without exploring the actual psychological processes and consequences involved in it. Similarly, while the empirical facts of diffusion were so ardently studied in detail, the psychological problems inherent in the transmission of culture traits and complexes from one group of people to another were not dealt with at all. The recent interest in personality and culture is by no means a completely unique phenomena: it only represents a more explicit articulation of the kind of psychological problem that is inherent in anthropological data. For the point of departure is the old and well established anthropological dictum that culture is acquired by the individual and that empirically, one culture may vary greatly from another in pattern and content. So the question is raised: What psychological significance have these facts with reference to the differential psychological structuring and behavior of one group of people as compared with another?

Since both psychology and anthropology have grown up as autonomous and rapidly developing disciplines, it was not to be expected that at any particular time the major problems and interests of one would be found immediately useful to the other. In the first place, there has been no established and unchanging body of data, concepts, principles, and laws characterizing psychology as a unified science at any one period. What we have is not only a developing but a rapidly expanding discipline, or congeries of disciplines. Reviewing the preceding five decades of psychology in 1940, Bruner and Allport[11] noted thirty-seven types of psychological interest and distinguished and characterized the shifting foci of these interests from decade to decade. All this is mirrored in the twenty divisions of the American Psychological Association as it exists today.

Although Kroeber has remarked[12] that "psychology is apparently less developed than anthropology," on the contrary, the diverse and expanding interests of anthropology in recent decades parallels the history of psychology. Anthropology is not a tightly knit and unified discipline either,[13] nor is it concerned with problems that have been traditionally defined to the exclusion of others any more than is psychology. The demonstrable fact is that the expanding interests of both disciplines, while formally approaching the study of man from quite different points of view, are more and more focusing on certain common problems and overlapping fields of interest.

What has been happening in psychology is inadvertently specified in a review of the second edition of Boring's *History of Experimental Psychology* (1950).[14] The reviewer says that psychologists "will ask but one question about it: Does it now really go beyond the development of structural psychology; beyond sensation, perception, and the classical treatment of the higher mental processes; beyond that somewhat limited group of men who arrogated to themselves the name of experimental psychologists and, by implication, relegated the student of learning, the mental tester, the social psychologist, and others to the fields only partially within the realm of science? There is no simple answer to the question." Perhaps not. But is it not significant historically that the reviewer also stresses the fact that to the author "psychology's greatest names are Darwin and Freud, Helmholtz and James" and that "Boring is no longer concerned with whether one can properly call these men 'experimental psychologists' or even 'psychologists.'" Besides this, it is precisely

[11] Jerome S. Bruner and Gordon W. Allport, "Fifty Years of Change in American Psychology," *Psychological Bulletin*, Vol. 37, 1940.
[12] A. L. Kroeber, *The Nature of Culture*, copyright 1952 by the University of Chicago, Introduction to section entitled "Psychologically Slanted," p. 299.
[13] See the Wenner-Gren Symposium volumes, *Anthropology Today* (1952) and *An Appraisal of Anthropology Today* (1953).
[14] Charles W. Bray in *Science*, Nov. 3, 1950.

in such areas of psychological investigation as learning, mental testing, and social psychology, that the recent interests of the anthropologist have been found to overlap those of the psychologist.

At earlier periods, however, a comparable situation existed. If we
go back to the first half of the nineteenth century, we find that, in
certain instances, anthropologists and psychologists were not so
sharply distinguished as subsequently and that it was a well recognized fact that they had some common interests. In the second half
of the century, under the impact of the theory of biological evolution in the post-Darwinian period, new areas of this kind emerged. In
the *Descent of Man* (1871) and the *Expression of the Emotions in
Man and Animals* (1872) Darwin himself insisted on psychological as
well as biological continuities between man and other animals so
that these books precipitated even more violent reactions than his
earlier *Origin of Species*. Romanes coined the term "comparative
psychology" and began to write about mental evolution and the evolution of intelligence. (*Mental Evolution in Animals*, 1883.) Once imbued with the evolutionary idea, both psychologists and anthropologists envisaged wider and wider areas that seemed to demand integral treatment in a common frame of reference. If evolution was to
be accepted as a process that transcended the biological realm, it
did not stop with the emergence of man. There was a further question of vital importance. Had not mental as well as cultural evolution
taken place in the course of man's long career upon this earth? Sir
James G. Frazer, who is so often cited in anthropological literature
as a typical example of late nineteenth-century evolutionary thinking as applied to human *cultural* development, may, at the same
time, be cited as an example of an anthropologist who defined his
own basic orientation with reference to a psychological problem,
that is, the question of *mental* evolution. Frazer held that not only
ethnographic data, but the ontogenetic development of the child and
the study of patients in mental hospitals could contribute to this
problem. The key to his position is to be found in his acceptance of
the theory of recapitulation.[15] "It is a reasonable inference," he says,
"that, just as the development of their bodies in the womb repro-

[15] See A. Irving Hallowell, "The Child, The Savage, and Human Experience," *Proceedings of the Sixth Institute on the Exceptional Child*, Langhorne,
Pa.: The Woods Schools, 1939, pp. 8–34; reprinted in Haring, *op. cit.*, for a
critical appraisal of the recapitulation theory in psychology and psychoanalysis.

duces to some extent the corporeal evolution of their remote ancestors out of lower forms of animal life, so the development of their
minds from the first dawn of consciousness in the embryo to the full
light of reason in adult life reproduces to some extent the mental
evolution of their ancestors in ages far beyond the range of history.
This inference is confirmed by the analogy which is often traced between the thought and conduct of children and the conduct of savages; for there are strong grounds for holding that savage modes of
thinking and acting closely resemble those of the rude forefathers of
the civilized races. Thus a careful study of the growth of intelligence
and of the moral sense in children promises to throw much light on
the intellectual and moral evolution of the race."[16]

Since Frazer took the position that "the first broad and sharp
division" in the general science of man "is between the study of
man's body and the study of his mind," he expressed a preference
for "the more general name of mental anthropology" for the division
of the subject in which he himself worked, rather than the term "social anthropology." Taken at its face value there was no attempt
here to exclude psychological questions on any *a priori* grounds
from anthropological consideration but rather categorically to embrace them. What Frazer firmly believed was that anthropology
had a specific psychological contribution to make to the study of
the human mind. To him the province "of mental or social anthropology" was "the study of the mental and social conditions of the
various races of mankind, especially of the more primitive races compared to the more advanced, with a view to trace the general evolution of human thought, particularly in its earlier stages. This comparative study of the mind of man is thus analogous to the comparative study of his body which is undertaken by anatomy and physiology."

While it may seem strange to us now to characterize Frazer as
a psychologically oriented anthropologist, nevertheless, I believe
that it was the particular kind of psychological interest which Frazer
represented that explains why Freud turned to him and the use he
made of Frazer's work. For Freud, too, was concerned with mental
evolution as a generic human problem, as well as with psychological
development in the individual. And he, too, embraced the concept
of recapitulation and attempted to relate the neurotic and the sav-

[16] James G. Frazer, *op. cit.*, p. 586.

age. Curiously enough, Frazer was antipathetic to psychoanalysis and never read Freud.[17]

The psychological counterpart to the broad-gauged evolutionary approach articulated by Frazer has been variously labelled "comparative," "genetic," or "developmental" psychology.[18] While some psychologists of an older generation, like Hall and Baldwin, adopted the theory of recapitulation and made it an integral part of their thinking, as did Frazer and Freud, this working hypothesis is not a necessary assumption of developmental psychology.[19] Nevertheless, the central importance that was once given to it as well as the fact that, as an auxiliary hypothesis, the inheritance of acquired characters was often invoked as the means whereby the experience of past generations of individuals was assimilated to the biological heritage of succeeding generations, seem to have dampened interest in the genuine problems that exist in this area,[20] for biologists came to re-

[17] B. Malinowski, *A Scientific Theory of Culture and Other Essays*, Chapel Hill: University of North Carolina Press, 1944, p. 182, says that Frazer not only rejected "psychoanalysis and all that it meant. He could never be persuaded to read anything by Freud or his school, in spite of the fact that Freud's anthropological contributions are based on Frazer."

[18] Heinz Werner, *Comparative Psychology of Mental Development*, New York: Harpers, 1940, p. 3, points out that "the concept 'developmental psychology' is perfectly clear if this term is understood to mean a science concerned with the development of mental life and determined by a specific method, i.e., the observation of psychological phenomena from the standpoint of development." On the other hand, "there are certain investigators who, when they use the term 'developmental psychology,' refer solely to the problems of *ontogenesis*. The mental development of the individual is, however, but one theme in genetic psychology. Related to the developmental psychology of the individual is the developmental study of larger social unities, a field of interest intimately linked with anthropology and best known by the name of *ethnopsychology*. The question of the development of the human mentality, if not arbitrarily limited, must lead further to an investigation of the relation of man to animal and, in consequence, to an *animal psychology* oriented according to developmental theory."

[19] *Ibid.*, p. 26.

[20] Wayne Dennis, discussing "Developmental Theories" in *Current Trends in Psychological Theory*, Pittsburgh: University of Pittsburgh Press, 1951, points out that "it would not be inaccurate to say that developmental psychology began with a theory—the theory of recapitulation. Child psychology, the most productive segment of developmental psychology, began shortly after the promulgation of the theory of evolution when all scientific minds were inflamed by this great conceptual achievement." But after the movement had arrived at the "concise hypothesis" that "ontogeny recapitulates phylogeny, . . ." its decline was imminent. The evolutionary viewpoint had seemed to open up wide unconquered scientific vistas to child psychology. But on closer approach these beckoning plains proved to be inhabited only by unsubstantial figures and retreating will-o'-the-wisps. There was not a testable hypothesis in the entire landscape."

ject both the recapitulation theory and the notion that acquired characters could be inherited. Contemporary anthropologists, along with their rejection of unilineal cultural evolution have shied away from developmental psychology. When applied to ethnic groups it immediately recalls the kind of unpalatable formulation of "primitive mentality" expounded by Lévy-Bruhl. The fact remains, however, that developmental psychology is a prime example of the emergence in the post-Darwinian period of a problem area common to anthropology and psychology that poses questions that have by no means been solved.[21]

The relations of anthropologists and psychologists, therefore, should be thought of in terms of the changing and expanding interests of both disciplines, of special areas of inquiry, and concrete problems. Are we now entering a period in which there are potentialities present for new and more systematically organized relations that can be directed toward significant research? Are there bodies of data, concepts, and principles in both disciplines that will enable us to unify our approach to the study of man and human behavior?

II. Historical Retrospect

In any historical review of the pioneers of nineteenth-century anthropology the work of two influential figures, Theodor Waitz (1821–1864) and Adolph Bastian (1826–1905) is never omitted. Both of these men had achieved scholarly maturity in the pre-Darwinian period. The first volume of Waitz's *Anthropologie der Naturvölker* had appeared several months before the *Origin of Species* and Bastian's three-volume work *Der Mensch in der Geschichte* was published in 1860. It is likewise well known that both men were psychologically oriented. What has not always been sufficiently stressed, however, is the more concrete fact that they were influenced by a prominent and original figure in early nineteenth-century psychology. Both Waitz and Bastian were Herbartians.[22]

Since Herbart (1776–1841) "represented a departure from the dominant associationist school, inasmuch as he conceived of the mind throughout in terms of dynamic forces rather than of passive

21 See the remarks of Brewster Smith in this volume.
22 See Paul Honigsheim, "The Philosophical Background of European Anthropology," *American Anthropologist*, Vol. 44, 1942, p. 380.

mechanisms,"[23] these pioneer anthropologists may be said to have followed a progressive trend of their time. Waitz, in fact, had published books on psychology a decade before the first volume of his *Naturvölker* appeared.[24] And Ribot, in his book on German psychology (1885) remarks upon what is to us a paradox today. He says that the psychological titles of some of Bastian's early books are deceptive. They are much more *anthropological* than psychological![25] On the other hand, Lowie says that Waitz's *Naturvölker* "is largely a treatise on primitive mentality" and, as contrasted with Klemm, "the depth of his psychological insight" is noteworthy.[26] While it is ordinarily pointed out that both Waitz and Bastian espoused the notion of the psychic unity of man, Lowie does not refer to Herbart's influence on them. This might be of little interest, were it not for the fact that Lazarus and Steinthal, who first promoted *Völkerpsychologie*, were likewise Herbartians.[27] Quite aside from any evaluation of their achievement, it was from Herbart that they adopted what was at that time a novel idea: "that psychology remains incomplete as long as it considers man only as an isolated individual."[28] Consequently, when Lowie directs our attention to the fact that "decades

[23] J. C. Flugel, *A Hundred Years of Psychology, 1833–1933*, New York: Macmillan, 1933, p. 23. This author finds in Herbart's psychological system certain faint resemblances to Freud. Thomas Ribot, *German Psychology Today*, New York: Scribners, 1886, p. 24, points out that "the first efforts toward a scientific psychology in Germany are due to Herbart. They constitute a transition from the pure speculation of Fichte and Hegel to the unmetaphysical psychology."

[24] Ribot, *op. cit.*, refers to his distinguished place in German psychology.

[25] *Ibid.*, p. 67. One example cited is *Beitrage zur vergleichenden Psychologie. Die Seele und ihre Erscheinungsformen in der Ethnographie*, Berlin, 1868.

[26] Lowie, 1937, p. 16.

[27] Ribot, *op. cit.*, pp. 60 ff.; Fay B. Karpf, in *American Social Psychology: Its Origins, Development, and European Background*, New York: McGraw-Hill, 1932, pp. 42 ff., discusses this movement in relation to Herbart. "Ethnic" rather than "folk" psychology is the preferable English rendering. (See Howard Becker in this volume.)

[28] Ribot, *op. cit.*, devotes a chapter to the "School of Herbart and the Ethnographic Psychology." He says (p. 51): "At first sight it seems strange enough that so concrete a form of psychology should attach itself to the school of Herbart; but, in fact, the disciples have only developed some of their master's views. This point deserves attention, for one would hardly suppose that the founder of the mathematical psychology would have attached great importance to such investigations. He maintains, however, that psychology remains incomplete as long as it considers man only as an isolated individual. He was convinced that society was a living and organic whole, ruled by psychological laws that are peculiar to it." Explicit references to the sources of these statements in Herbart's work are given.

before Rivers [Bastian] argued that a science of mental life must take cognizance of ethnographic data, because the 'individual's thinking is made possible only by his functioning in a social group,' "[29] the psychological source of Bastian's view is obscured if his link with Herbart is not made explicit.

The full implication and expansion of Herbart's germinal idea belongs to the history of social psychology. In the immediately subsequent period psychologists concentrated more and more upon the study of "mind" in the laboratory, rather than in "society,"[30] and

[29] Lowie, 1937, p. 36; see Mühlman, *op. cit.*, for a more extended discussion of Bastian's sociopsychological interests.

[30] It is particularly interesting, therefore, to note that Ribot, *op. cit.*, in the chapter devoted to a discussion of Lazarus and Steinthal, Waitz, and, briefly, Bastian, refers to the famous passage in Hume in which this eighteenth-century philosopher says:

"Would you know the sentiments, inclinations and course of life of the Greeks and Romans? Study well the temper and actions of the French and English. . . . Mankind are so much the same in all times and places that history informs us of nothing new or strange in this particular. Its chief use is ever to discover the constant and universal principles in human nature. . . ."

Ribot (p. 52) then goes on to say:

"In our day we think differently: We believe that this abstract study, amounting to some general characteristics, gives a knowledge of man but not of men: We believe that all who share our common humanity were not cast in a common mould, and we are curious about the smallest of these differences. Hence a new conception in psychology.

"As long as naturalists confined themselves to a pure description of races and species considered as permanent; as long as historians, indifferent to the variations of the human soul in the lapse of ages, spread upon all their recitals the same uniform and monotonous varnish; an abstract psychology, like that of Spinoza and Condillac, seemed the only psychology possible. Nothing else was thought of, and when a very refined and subtle spirit was subjected to minute analysis, it was said of this psychology: It has given us to know man.

"But when the idea of evolution was introduced into the sciences of life and into historical study, stirring and reviewing the whole, psychology felt the impulse. The question was raised: Is this abstract study of man sufficient? Does it give more than broad traits and general conditions; to be simple and exact, does it not need completion? The lower forms of humanity have exhibited particular modes of feeling and action, and the history of civilized peoples has shown variations in sentiment, in social ideals, in moral or religious conceptions, and in the languages that express them. Psychology has profited by it. It occupies, in fact, in the structure of human knowledge a very exact place between biology below and history above."

Ribot here indicates, in principle, his appreciation of the need for a wider frame of reference in the study of human psychology, one which includes cultural variables, in the contemporary sense. But the particular orientation and methodology of Lazarus and Steinthal was not adequate for this task and "orthodox" psychology maintained its basic biological orientation for a long time to come.

anthropologists became more and more concerned with the broad sweep of human history, interpreted in terms of unilinear series of cultural events. Psychology began to attain its independence; the experimental laboratory became the symbol of its scientific status; Wundt was the officiating priest. The problems centered around psycho-physics, visual and auditory sensations, reaction time, and so on. Attention was centered upon responses that could be empirically established as *common* to all subjects, individual differences not being considered significant. It was on the basis of observations of this nature that a science of psychology was to be built up, so that Boring in the first edition of his *History of Experimental Psychology* could define it as "the psychology of the generalized, human, normal, adult mind as revealed in the psychological laboratory."[31]

It was to men belonging to this tradition in psychology that Haddon turned when he organized the Torres Straits Expedition (1898). W. H. R. Rivers had studied in Germany and had begun lecturing at Cambridge on the physiology of the sense organs in 1893. He planned one of the earliest systematic courses in experimental psychology anywhere in the world and the first in England. In 1897 Rivers was appointed Lecturer in Experimental Psychology and the Physiology of the Special Senses.[32] Three others on this expedition famous in anthropological history were C. S. Myers and William McDougall, students of Rivers, who later attained eminence in psychology, and C. G. Seligman, a young physician, who subsequently became a distinguished figure in anthropology. Although the latter's chief contribution to the work of the expedition was made as a medical man, Meyer Fortes says that Seligman "was deeply interested in the ethnological and psychological investigations as well, and took a share in them . . . and saw at first hand the importance of studying the psychology of primitive peoples." Twenty years later, stimulated by his experience as a staff member of the shell-shock hospital at Maghull during World War I and his association there

[31] E. G. Boring, *A History of Experimental Psychology*, New York: Century, 1929, p. viii.

[32] Rivers contributed a chapter on "Vision" to the outstanding *Textbook of Physiology* edited by Sir Edward S. Schafer (1900). Along with James Sully, A. F. Shand, Wm. McDougall, and others, he was a founder of the British Psychological Society in 1901. C. S. Myers became secretary in 1904 and Rivers served as one of the editors between 1904 and 1912. As early as 1910 a paper on "The Psychology of Freud and his School" was read before the Society by Bernard Hart. For further details see Beatrice Edgell, "The British Psychological Society," *British Journal of Psychology*, Vol. 37, 1947, pp. 113–132.

with Bernard Hart, Seligman, together with his wife, Brenda Z. Seligman, became vitally interested in the general relations of psychology to anthropology, in particular the bearing of psychoanalytic theories upon ethnological work. Fortes says that "he was dissatisfied with the concepts and methods of experimental psychology. Now he had an opportunity of experimenting with psycho-therapeutic methods based on new theories, especially those of psychoanalysis, which appealed strongly to his scientific sense. On taking up his anthropological work again after the war, Seligman turned these experiences to fertile use."[33]

The kind of work Myers and McDougall did on the expedition to the Torres Straits typified the psychological interests of the time. Writing a posthumous account of Rivers' work Myers later (1923) said: "Rivers interested himself especially in investigating the vision of the natives—their visual acuity, their color vision, their color nomenclature, and their susceptibility to certain visual geometric illusions. He continued to carry out psychological work of the same comparative ethnological character, after his return from the Torres Straits, in Scotland . . . during a visit to Egypt in the winter of 1900,

[33] Obituary notice in *Man*, Vol. 61 (1941), pp. 2, 4. Among the most important bibliographical items of the Seligmans that have a psychological interest are the following: C. G. Seligman, "Anthropology and Psychology: A Study of Some Points of Contact," *Journal of the Royal Anthropological Institute*, Vol. 54, 1924, pp. 13–46; "Anthropological Perspective and Psychological Theory," *ibid.*, Vol. 62, 1932, pp. 193–228; "Temperament, Conflict, and Psychosis in a Stone-Age Population," *British Journal of Medical Psychology*, Vol. 9, 1929, pp. 189–190. Brenda Z. Seligman, "The Incest Barrier," *British Journal of Psychology*, Vol. 22, 1932; "Incest and Descent," *Journal of the Royal Anthropological Institute*, Vol. 59, 1929; "The Part of the Unconscious in Social Heritage," in E. E. Evans-Prichard, ed., *Essays in Honor of C. G. Seligman*, London, 1934, pp. 307–317.

In the Introduction that Seligman wrote to J. S. Lincoln's *The Dream in Primitive Cultures*, London: The Cresset Press, 1935, he urged contemporary anthropologists to make themselves aware of psychological theory and asked: "How can a profitable give and take relationship between psychology and anthropology best be established at the present time? This is a problem," he goes on, "to which the writer of the Introduction has given much thought in recent years. Brought up in the main in the Tylorian (comparative) School of anthropology, having thereafter gained some knowledge of and made use of the Historical School of Rivers, and of late years watched the development of the functional method, the writer has become convinced that the most fruitful development—perhaps indeed the only process that can bring social anthropology to its rightful status as a branch of science and at the same time give it the full weight in human affairs to which it is entitled—is the increased elucidation in the field and integration into anthropology of psychological knowledge."

and from 1901–1902 in his expedition to the Todas of Southern India."[34]

What is of particular interest, now that we can view Rivers' work in the light of later developments, is the highly compartmentalized nature of his psychological interests, on the one hand, and his ethnological pursuits, on the other.[35] This lack of integration continued throughout his career, despite the fact that he no doubt aimed, as Lowie says, "to ally ethnology with psychology";[36] that he was influenced by Freudian theory in his later years,[37] and that, before becoming so thoroughly committed to the diffusionist theories of Elliot Smith and Perry, he raised some basic points in social psychology. When, for example, he asks in his 1916 essay on "Sociology and Psychology":[38] "How can you explain the workings of the human mind without a knowledge of the social setting which must have played so great a part in determining the sentiments and opinions of mankind?" he strikes a note that is far removed from his earlier specialized research in physiological psychology. This trend in his thinking is also exemplified when he dissents from Westermarck's view that it is more or less obvious that the blood feud can be explained everywhere by revenge by observing that so simple an answer leaves us about where we started. Rivers is of the opinion that

[34] Charles S. Myers, "The Influence of the late W. H. R. Rivers," in W. H. R. Rivers, *Psychology and Politics*, New York: Harcourt, 1923, pp. 158 ff.

[35] Elliot Smith recognized this. In the Preface to *Psychology and Ethnology*, New York: Harcourt, 1926, p. xiv, he says: "When Dr. Rivers embarked upon his first independent expedition [to the Todas] he worked both at psychology and at the investigation of religion and sociology. But the two lines of work were kept more or less distinct the one from the other. The psychological research was essentially physiological in nature and had no close or direct bearing on the other branch of his study the results of which were published in the volume *The Todas* (1906)."

[36] Lowie, 1937, p. 172.

[37] See *Instinct and the Unconscious*, 1922.

[38] In the *Sociological Review*, Vol. 9. Two years previously Rivers had expressed the opinion (*Kinship and Social Organization*, p. 3) that "the ultimate aim of all studies of mankind, whether historical or scientific, is to reach an explanation in terms of psychology, in terms of the ideas, beliefs, sentiments, and instinctive tendencies by which the conduct of man, both individual and collective, is determined." Rivers explains (1916) that by psychology he refers to the "science which deals with mental phenomena, conscious and unconscious." For psychologists, he says, he knows he begs the question by using the term "mental." What he wants to avoid, however, is "confusing mental processes with the social processes I regard as the subject matter of sociology." In particular, he is opposed to McDougall's broad definition of psychology in terms of behavior.

there are special questions for inquiry here: "Is revenge a universal human characteristic? Is it an emotion which has the same characteristics and the same content among all peoples, or does it vary with the physical and social environment? . . . An answer to one or more of these questions is suggested by some of the cases cited by Professor Westermarck, but he does not consider them from these points of view."[39] But such remarks of Rivers are often in the nature of *aperçus*. Although he touched upon vital issues,[40] he never initiated any serious research into questions of this kind.

Rejecting the approach of the classical evolutionists after his expedition to Melanesia, Rivers devoted more and more attention to the diffusionist theory sponsored by G. Elliot Smith and W. J. Perry. Personally, I have never been able to discover in his work any appreciation of the kinds of problems that later became the center of personality and culture studies, despite the knowledge he acquired of psychoanalytic theory. Nevertheless, the work in physiological psychology Rivers did in the Torres Straits, Egypt, and in India, provided substantial evidence for the first time that supported the hypothesis of psychic unity, considered at the psychophysical level. G. Murphy notes that Rivers' statement that "pure sense acuity is much the same in all races, has not been overthrown by subsequent research."[41]

Besides this, Rivers held the conviction that training "in the experimental methods of the psychological laboratory" was the "best training" for the field anthropologist, quite apart from special preparation for the investigation of psychological problems, as such. Rivers expressed this conviction to Sir F. C. Bartlett as a young man when the latter first went to Cambridge "somewhat undecided about a future career, but rather hoping to take up field work in anthropology." Many years later (1937) when Bartlett had become a distinguished psychologist he said that he was "sure that Rivers was

[39] "Sociology and Psychology," *op. cit.*

[40] Referring to the fact that "those explanations of custom which derive our economic scheme from human competitiveness, modern war from human combativeness, and all the rest of the ready explanations that we meet in every magazine and modern volume, have for the anthropologist a hollow ring." Ruth Benedict (*Patterns of Culture*, 1934, p. 214) points out that "Rivers was one of the first to phrase the issue vigorously. He pointed out that instead of trying to understand the blood feud from vengeance, it was necessary rather to understand vengeance from the institution of the blood feud."

[41] Gardner Murphy, *Historical Introduction to Modern Psychology*, revised edition, New York: Harcourt, Brace, 1950, pp. 359–360.

right" and goes on to express the personal opinion "that every anthropology student who hopes to make original contributions to his subject ought, at some period of his training—preferably in the later stages—to spend six months or a year in the psychology laboratory," although he believes that his course should not be "identical with that of the student who is to devote his life to research and teaching in experimental psychology."[42]

While Bartlett followed a career in psychology rather than anthropology, he never lost interest in the latter subject.[43] Furthermore, it seems reasonable to infer that the sociopsychological point of view that he developed as a psychologist was related to his anthropological interests, and in particular to his association with Rivers. In his *Psychology and Primitive Culture* (1923) he was asking:[44] "Are we, in our search for explanations, always to go back to the individual as he may be pictured to exist outside of any particular social group? Shall we endeavour to find an origin for all forms of social behaviour at some presocial stage? At first sight it may seem as if we are bound to do this, if our study is legitimately to be called psychological. For psychology is generally regarded as dealing essentially with the individual." Referring to Tylor and more particularly Frazer, he says that the researches of the latter "yield constant attempts to account for the absolute origin of rites and ceremonies in terms of individual experiences, the individual not being considered specifically as a member of any social group. . . ." This method, Bartlett goes on to say, has been considered mistaken by other investigators. But "looking upon it as distinctly psychological, they propose to banish psychology from the study of primitive culture." Making references to Kroeber's statement in his review of Freud's *Totem and Taboo* (1920) that despite Frazer's "acumen his efforts are prevailingly a dilettantish playing; but in the last analysis they are psychological, and as history only a pleasing fabrication"; and that "Ethnology like every other branch of science, is work, and not a game in which lucky guesses score"; Bartlett remarks that, "there is no good reason for regarding either Sir James Frazer's work, or psychology, as a game of

[42] F. C. Bartlett, "Psychological Methods and Anthropological Problems," *Africa*, Vol. 10, 1937, pp. 401–420.

[43] His name appears in the *International Directory of Anthropologists*, 3rd ed., Washington, D.C., 1950.

[44] Bartlett, 1923, pp. 8–11. Quoted by permission of the Cambridge University Press.

lucky guesses. But there is equally no good reason for regarding Frazer's type of explanation as the only type which can be called psychological. . . ." The psychologist is "not forced to consider only very remote antecedents, and with the curious exception of his studies in the realm of primitive culture, he never has agreed to do so. . . . In general, our problem is to account for a response made by an individual to a given set of circumstances *of which the group itself may always be one*. . . . The individual who is considered in psychological theory, in fact, is never an individual pure and simple. The statements made about him always have reference to a particular set of conditions. The individual with whom we deal may be the individual-in-the-laboratory, or the individual-in-his-everyday-working-environment, or—and in social psychology this is always the case—the individual-in-a-given-social-group."

This sociopsychological point of view links Bartlett and Rivers, although the latter never fully developed his ideas. Moreover, Bartlett says that the lectures on which his *Psychology and Primitive Culture* were based were undertaken "mainly on the advice" of Rivers; their subject matter was "many times discussed . . . with him" and, since Rivers had died before they were published, the author in paying tribute to Rivers says that he owes "more to him for his friendship and interest than I can adequately express."[45]

Radcliffe-Brown likewise studied psychology under Rivers. He says ". . . I was for three years his pupil in psychology, and was his first pupil in social anthropology in the year 1904. Rivers was from first to last primarily a psychologist, and was an inspiring teacher in psychology."[46] Radcliffe-Brown's profound interest in problems of social organization and his later contributions to this specialized field have obscured the fact that his first book, *The Andaman Islanders*, had a psychological focus. While not published until 1922 it was completed by 1914, and although the author expresses some dissatisfaction with Chapters 5 and 6 ("Interpretation of Andamanese Customs and Beliefs"), nevertheless it is these particular chapters he considers to be of special methodological importance. And they are the chapters in which the psychological focus is exemplified. "We

45 *Ibid.*, Preface, p. viii.
46 R. R. Radcliffe-Brown, "The Present Position of Anthropological Studies," Presidential Address, Sec. H, British Association for the Advancement of Science, 1930, p. 146. Reprinted in *Structure and Function in Primitive Society*, Glencoe: Free Press, 1953.

have to explain," he says,[47] "why it is that the Andamanese *think and
act* in certain ways. The explanation of each single custom is provided by showing what is its relation to the other customs of the
Andamanese *and to their general system of ideas and sentiments*"
(italics ours). Chapter 5 deals with the psychological significance of
ceremonies with special reference to their role in the collective expression and transmission of systems of "sentiments"; Chapter 6 with
the part that myths and legends play "in the mental life of the
Andaman Islander." Far from being "merely the products of a somewhat childish fancy" they "are the means by which the Andamanese
express and systematize their fundamental notions of life and nature
and the sentiments attaching to these notions."[48]

Radcliffe-Brown states five working hypotheses, all of which involve the concept of "sentiment." The first one is that "a society depends for its existence on the presence in the minds of its members
of a certain system of sentiments, by which the conduct of the individual is regulated in conformity with the needs of society."[49]
Consequently, in the case of the Andamanese, he is concerned with
the demonstration that "the social function of the ceremonial customs of the Andaman Islanders is to maintain and to transmit from
one generation to another the emotional dispositions on which the
society (as it is constituted) depends for its existence."[50] It is made
abundantly clear that the manner in which human beings are psychologically structured lies at the core of the persistence and functioning of a socio-cultural system. Besides this, although it may be
postulated that there is "a general substratum that is the same in all
human societies,"[51] the psychological organization of the individuals
of one society as compared with another vary concomitantly with
cultural differences: "a system of sentiments or motives will clearly
be different in different cultures, just as the system of moral rules is
different in societies of different types." Sentiments, moreover (as

[47] *The Andaman Islanders: A Study in Social Anthropology*, Cambridge University Press, 1922, p. 230.
[48] *Ibid.*, p. 330.
[49] *Ibid.*, pp. 233–234.
[50] In "Religion and Society," a lecture delivered in 1945 and printed in
Structure and Function, Radcliffe-Brown reiterates this hypothesis. He says:
"Thirty-seven years ago (1908) in a fellowship thesis on the Andaman Islanders
(which did not appear in print until 1922) I formulated briefly a general theory
of the social function of rites and ceremonies. It is the same theory that underlies the remarks I shall offer on this occasion."
[51] *Ibid.*, pp. 401 ff.

stated in hypothesis 3), "are not innate but are developed in the individual by the action of society upon him."[52]

Radcliffe-Brown's definition of sentiment—"an organized system of emotional tendencies centred about some object"—is that of A. F. Shand and William McDougall, although this is not explicitly stated.[53] Although the concept of sentiment is much too restricted a psychological construct for dealing with the complexities and varying patterns of affective and motivational phenomena that manifest themselves in the human personality, the broad psychological assumptions implied in Radcliffe-Brown's hypotheses are essentially the same as those which have appeared in personality and culture studies. In the latter it is likewise assumed that (a) however they may be construed or labelled, there are psychological constants that define the dynamics of a human level of adjustment everywhere; (b) any particular socio-cultural system is dependent for its persistence and functioning upon the characteristic psychological structuralization of its constituent members; (c) this psychological organization is acquired through social interaction and learning on the part of the individual; (d) it differs from one society to another; and (e) various institutions function with reference to the maintenance and expression of the affective and motivational structures of individuals. The major difference is one of research interest. Radcliffe-Brown is

[52] *Ibid.*, p. 234.

[53] *Ibid.*, footnote p. 234. McDougall integrated Shand's notion of sentiment with his own doctrine of instincts and contended that a theory of sentiments should be the foundation of a social psychology. (*Introduction to Social Psychology*, Boston: Luce, 1910.) He says (p. 122), "To such an organized system of emotional tendencies centred about some object, Mr. Shand proposes to apply the name 'sentiment'." E. Westermarck in his *Origin and Development of the Moral Ideas*, London: Macmillan, 1906, Vol. 1, p. 110, also used sentiment in the sense proposed by Shand. In his Huxley Memorial Lecture for 1932 ("Anthropological Perspective and Psychological Theory," *Journal of the Royal Anthropological Institute*, Vol. 62, 1932, pp. 193–228), C. G. Seligman said: "It is a remarkable fact that the concepts which have been laboriously achieved by the students of conscious behaviour seem to have been of little avail hitherto in anthropology. An examination of the writings of British anthropologists who attempt psychological explanation or analysis (Radcliffe-Brown, Malinowski, Brenda Z. Seligman) seems to show that the only concept derived from the psychology of conscious behaviour that has been of any service is that of the 'sentiment.' Is this to be attributed to the negligence of anthropologists, or rather to the fact that the psychological problems arising in anthropology lie for the most part not in the sphere of cognition—to which most attention has been paid in the psychology of consciousness—but in the sphere of motive and emotion, which is not intelligible without taking into account the findings of Freud, Jung, and a number of psychopathologists?"

interested in the function of concrete rites and ceremonies with reference to relatively abstract systems of sentiments. Culture and personality studies are concerned with discovering the actual psychological organization and dynamics of the human personality as it
functions in different socio-cultural contexts, as well as the concrete
factors in the life history of the individuals which are responsible
for varying patterns of psychological structuring.

Although William McDougall, like Rivers, had been a member
of the expedition to Torres Straits,[54] and later spent some time in
Borneo, which led him to collaborate with Charles Hose on an anthropological book,[55] it is somewhat paradoxical that these field experiences led to no subsequent contacts of a fruitful nature with
anthropology. Even though McDougall was well aware of the fact
that nineteenth-century psychology had proved of little use to the
social sciences, and pointed out in his *Introduction to Social Psychology* (1908)[56] that a "very important advance of psychology
toward usefulness is due to the increasing recognition that the adult
human mind is the product of the moulding influence exerted by the
social environment, and of the fact that the strictly individual mind,
with which alone the older introspective and descriptive psychology
concerned itself, is an abstraction merely and has no real existence,"
nevertheless, his brand of social psychology provoked negative rather
than positive reactions among anthropologists. Ogburn and Goldenweiser (1927)[57] remark that McDougall's instinct psychology did
exert an early wave of psychological influence upon the social sciences generally, but that it was a "blind trail."

Before the end of the nineteenth century interest in what soon
became known as "differential psychology" had begun to crystallize.
This development represented a departure from the central problems
of the experimental psychologists of this time as well as from the associationist tradition which was concerned with the general principles whereby "ideas" became associated, with no allowance for individual variations. Questions began to be raised about group differ-

[54] In his intellectual autobiography McDougall (*A History of Psychology in
Autobiography,* C. Murchison, ed., 1930, p. 201) says: ". . . I was already interested in such topics as totemism, exogamy, and primitive religion, having read
Tylor, Lang, Frazer, and other authorities in the field."
[55] *The Pagan Tribes of Borneo,* 2 vols., London: Macmillan, 1912. Mc-
Dougall left for Borneo after having spent only five months in Torres Straits.
[56] P. 16.
[57] Ogburn and Goldenweiser, *The Social Sciences,* p. 4.

ences of various kinds, as well as differences among individuals. James McKeen Cattell (1860–1944) after his sojourn at Wundt's laboratory, had become interested in the measurement of individual differences. The term "mental test," referring to measures of ability at the sensory and motor level rather than intelligence, was first employed by him in 1890. What is of particular interest here is that Kroeber studied psychology under Cattell before he studied anthropology under Boas and that psychology was accepted as a minor for his doctorate.[58] Furthermore, two other anthropologists, Livingston Farrand and Clark Wissler, worked with Cattel in his early days at Columbia and published monographs[59] which Roback characterizes as a "harbinger of the avalanche of tests with which we were to be deluged a half-century later."[60] The subsequent application of intelligence tests in the exploration of racial differences in mentality has been critically reviewed by Klineberg, Nadel, and more recently by Anastasi and Foley.[61]

Meanwhile, William Stern (1871–1938) in Germany, had proposed the name "differential psychology" for a branch of the subject that would study "differences among individuals as well as among racial and cultural groups, occupational and social levels, and the two sexes" in a book first published in 1900.[62] Stern likewise founded an institute and a journal for applied psychology. In the latter there was published in 1912 a guide for the investigation of certain psychological problems among primitive peoples.[63] The anthropologist Richard Thurnwald wrote an introduction. The following year, the same journal published the results of Thurnwald's own field obser-

[58] A. L. Kroeber, *The Nature of Culture,* University of Chicago Press, 1952, p. 300.

[59] J. M. Cattell and L. Farrand, "Physical and Mental Measurements of the Students of Columbia University," *Psychology Review,* Vol. 3, 1896; Clark Wissler, "The Correlation of Mental and Physical Tests," *Psychological Monographs,* 1901, 3, No. 16, pp. 62 ff.

[60] A. A. Roback, *History of American Psychology,* New York: Library Publishers, 1952.

[61] Otto Klineberg, *Race Differences,* New York: Harper, 1935; Anne Anastasi and John P. Foley, Jr., *Differential Psychology: Individual and Group Differences in Behavior,* New York: Macmillan, 1949; S. F. Nadel, "The Application of Intelligence Tests in the Anthropological Field," in F. C. Bartlett, ed., *The Study of Society, Methods and Problems,* New York: Macmillan, 1939.

[62] Anastasi and Foley, *op. cit.,* p. 13.

[63] *Vorschläge zur psychologischen Untersuchung primitiver Menschen gesammelt und herausgegeben vom Institut für angewandte Psychologie.* Beihefte zur Zeitschrift für angewandte Psychologie und psychologische Sammelforschung, 5, Teil I, Leipzig, 1912.

vations made in 1906–1909, *Ethno-psychologische Studien an Süd-seevölkern auf dem Bismarck-Archipel und den Salomo-Inseln.*[64] In the earlier publication Thurnwald had maintained that the whole study of ethnology centers around the comprehension of the psychological peculiarities of non-European peoples. It is by this means he says that we really get to know them. Before he undertook his 1906 expedition Thurnwald had turned to Carl Stumpf (1848–1936) who consulted other psychologists. The result was an assembly of questions from a broad area of psychological interest which were to be tested for their utility in ethno-psychological research. This pioneer work on the part of Thurnwald did not, of course, include the use of standard intelligence tests, as later developed, or personality tests. But it did include a collection of drawings and verbal associations to selected vocabularies. Later (1925) Thurnwald founded the *Zeitschrift für Völkerpsychologie und Soziologie,* a journal which, in Lowie's words, "gave full scope to his interests, at once wide and deep, in economics, sociology, jurisprudence, and psychology" and made him "one of the foremost liaison officers of the social sciences."[65]

By the time anthropology had begun to assume the characteristics of an organized discipline in the United States, Wundt (1832–1921 was already a world-renowned figure. The effort he had made to establish psychology as an independent unified scientific discipline based upon experimental laboratory methods had borne fruit. Besides this, Wundt was unique among the psychologists of his period for his vision and unusual breadth of interests. His famous *Völkerpsychologie* was a product of the last twenty years of his life. Wundt, says Murphy,[66] "tries to bring together experimental psychology, child psychology, animal psychology, folk psychology; nothing that was psychology was foreign to him. He poured his energies into examination of nearly every corner of mental life." It

[64] *Ibid.,* 6, Leipzig, 1913. See also Thurnwald's later publication "Psychologie des primitiven Menschen" in Gustav Kafka, *Handbuch der vergleichenden Psychologie,* Vol. 1, Munchen, 1922, pp. 147–320.

[65] Lowie, *op. cit.,* p. 242. The following articles represent Thurnwald's point of view: "Probleme der Völkerpsychologie und Soziologie," *Zeitschrift für Völkerpsychologie und Soziologie,* Vol. 1, 1925, pp. 1–20; "Zum gegenwärtigen Stande der Völkerpsychologie," *Kölner Vierteljahrshefte für Soziologie,* IV, Jahrgang, neue Folge, 1925, pp. 32–43. See also F. H. C. Van Loon and R. Thurnwald, "Un questionnaire psycho-physico-morophologique pour l'étude de la psychologie des races," *Revue Anthropologique,* Vol. 40, 1930, pp. 262–277.

[66] Murphy, *op. cit.,* p. 159.

is of historical significance that he believed that cultural and historical data were relevant material for the psychologist. In consequence, he envisaged problems that centered upon the inter-relations
among the historic process, the individual, and varying cultural
forms and contents. Rejecting such terms as *Gemeinpsychologie*
and *Sozialpsychologie* he chose *Völkerpsychologie* as the term he
thought best suited to characterize this area of psychological interest
as Lazarus and Steinthal had already done. While it is quite true that
Wundt's folk psychology in terms of central focus and problems is
not equivalent to what later became known as social psychology
in America—it has been said that it represented an "heroic attempt
to save philosophy of history for science"[67]—nevertheless, the
kind of problems posed by Wundt, rather than his attempted solution
of them, are genuine. It is worth noting that in Kroeber's article
(1918) on "The Possibility of a Social Psychology"[68] he took as his
point of departure H. K. Haeberlin's article on Wundt.[69] Commenting upon his own article in 1951 he says:

Of course, my "social psychology" of the time was something very different from the social psychology of today, which psychologists and sociologists have jointly reared as a discipline that deals with out-groups, minorities, stereotypes, adjustments, attitudes, leadership, propaganda, public opinion, and other interpersonal relations within a society, without
reference to cultural content or forms except so far as a cultural content
may be needed to define a sociopsychological situation.

What I was dreaming of, as a distant possibility, was a true processual
science causally explaining the pageant of the history of culture. I do not
see in 1951 that we are appreciably nearer such a science than we were in
1918. I still think that the processes through which cultural forms can be
explained causally must be largely or essentially psychological in nature.
In late years I have several times discussed "cultural psychology," though
as an inevitable psychological reflection or quality which all cultures must
bear rather than as their basic process or cause. I do not think that in and
by themselves the interpersonal or social relations of men in groups will
ever explain the specific features of specific cultures—certainly not their
ideologies, knowledge, skills, art, or understanding. Modern social psychologists do not even pose the problem. They are not interested in the

[67] Fay B. Karpf, *op. cit.*, p. 61, in the course of an extended discussion of
Wundt, pp. 51–65.
[68] *American Journal of Sociology*, Vol. 23, pp. 633–651; reprinted in ab-
breviated form in *The Nature of Culture*, copyright 1952 by the University of
Chicago.
[69] "Foundations of Wundt's Folk Psychology," *Psychology Review*, Vol. 23,
1916.

interrelation of cultural facts; just as I, in 1918, for all my talking about
social psychology, was interested in culture and very little in social interrelations. In fact, next to culture, I was then and am now much more interested in the qualities and motivations of individuals than in what human
beings do to one another in groups. The present paper must have puzzled
both sociologists and psychologists at the time and since. I am doubly appreciative of their forbearance.[70]

According to Kroeber's conception of "cultural psychology" one
of its tasks would be to proceed to the characterization of cultures empirically "without any set plan, merely noting those psychological traits which obtrude themselves in each culture, with
special alertness toward such as seem to cohere into a consistent

[70] *The Nature of Culture*, p. 52. It should be borne in mind that in the 1918
article Kroeber stated that he conceived the "business" of the psychologist to be
"the determination of the manifestations and processes of consciousness as consciousness." It was at this same period, too, that his "Eighteen Professions"
(*American Anthropologist*, 17, 1915, pp. 283–288) and "The Superorganic"
(*Ibid.*, 19, 1917, pp. 163–213), stirred up considerable dissent in regard to their
psychological implications on the part of the three contemporary anthropologists
who were most interested in psychology. It is not without significance, perhaps,
that all of them were trained by Boas. Goldenweiser, in his chapter on "Cultural
Anthropology" (in H. E. Barnes, *History and Prospects of the Social Sciences,*
1925) writes: "Kroeber's theoretical broadside was met by Sapir, Haeberlin,
and me, who, while endorsing Kroeber's main contention as to cultural autonomy,
took exception to his inadequate appreciation of the role of the individual in
history, his over-confident assumption of historical determinism, as well as his
theoretically inadmissible identification of psychology with biology." Haeberlin
("Anti-Professions," *American Anthropologist*, vol. 17, 1915, p. 759) had previously remarked that "as soon as Dr. Kroeber will have become conscious of the
dogmatism of his biological psychology, all other obstacles towards an understanding must fall like a house of cards. He will recognize the impossibility of
building a cloister-wall about history, he will no longer look askance on the psychologically inclined anthropologist as a hybrid form of two distinct crafts,
psychology will no longer be a bugaboo—in short, there will be complete unison
of the 'professions' and the 'anti-professions'." Nevertheless, Kroeber has continued to emphasize the sharp distinctions, as he conceives them, between the
tasks of the psychologist and the anthropologist. In his *Anthropology* (New York:
Harcourt, 1948) p. 572, while he points out that "modern psychologists recognize that the total picture of any natural or spontaneous human situation always
contains a cultural ingredient," and that a " 'pure' unconditioned mind" is an
abstraction, he says that "the business of psychologists, however, is to try to hold
this cultural factor constant in a given situation, to account for or to equalize it,
and then proceed to their own specific problems of investigating the mind *as if*
it were 'pure,' of investigating the psychic aspects of the behavior of individual
human beings, and after that man in general." Kroeber makes no reference,
however, to any particular psychologists, or schools of psychological thought,
nor to how psychologists themselves have conceived their central problem,
either at present or in the past.

larger orientation."[71] Such an approach seems reminiscent in some respects of Wundt's idea, namely, a psychological history of man culturally viewed. At the end of his article[72] Haeberlin says: "What an intrinsic association of psychology and history can attain is well exemplified by numerous passages in Wundt's work on folk-psychology, when we abstract from all his theoretical foundations. There we find psychological interpretations of historical phenomena executed with a brilliancy characteristic of Wundt's genius. Such interpretations of Wundt's will mark the monumental significance of his work long after folk-psychology as such will have been recognized as [an] 'Unding' "!

At the end of his chapter on "Cultural Psychology" Kroeber raises the question "whether the findings of a systematically developed cultural psychology will be expressed in the terms and concepts of individual psychology, or whether a new set of concepts will have to be added to these. . . ." This is precisely the problem that Wundt faced and it is the general consensus of opinion that despite his concepts of "apperception" and "creative synthesis" he did not altogether escape the individualistic bias that prevailed.[73] On the other hand, Wundt did see the need for bringing the functioning of the "higher" mental processes in man into connection with the facts of culture even if psychologists were not prepared to handle these phenomena in the laboratory. He made an heroic effort to relate cultural data to psychological data at a time when the major emphasis in psychology was still individualistic, physiological, and biological. In the opinion of G. Stanley Hall his "doctrine of apperception . . . took psychology forever beyond the old associationism which had ceased to be fruitful"; he "established the independence of psychology from physiology" and "he materially advanced every branch of mental science and extended its influence over the whole domain of folklore, mores, language, and primitive religion."[74]

In any event, it would seem to be of some historical significance that it was Hall, a student of Wundt's, who was a key figure in the early promotion in the United States of anthropology and child psy-

[71] *Anthropology*, p. 621; cf. the previously unpublished paper "Culture, Events, and Individuals" (1946) in *The Nature of Culture*, pp. 104–109.

[72] Haeberlin, 1916, *op. cit.*

[73] Karpf, *op. cit.*, p. 53.

[74] Preface to American edition of Sigmund Freud, *A General Introduction to Psychoanalysis*, New York: Garden City Publishing Company, 1938, p. 6.

chology, as well as psychoanalysis.[75] He appears to have reflected his mentor's views regarding the importance of anthropology and ethnic psychology in relation to the study of the growth and development of the human mind when, after becoming President of Clark University in 1888, he invited Franz Boas there in connection with the program he envisaged for the development of genetic psychology. Boas stayed only a few years, but A. F. Chamberlain (1865–1914), the first student to receive a doctorate under Boas, remained. In addition to the anthropological field work he carried on among the Kutenai and the Mississauga Ojibwa, Chamberlain continued to function in the child psychology program at Clark. Roback, with no mention of his anthropological connection, refers to the fact that "in the early days of Clark, pedagogy and child psychology flourished under men like W. H. Burnham and A. F. Chamberlain."[76] His two books, *Child and Childhood in Folk-Thought* (1896) and *The Child: A Study in the Evolution of Man* (1900), received more attention from psychologists than anthropologists.[77]

In 1909 it was Hall who invited Freud, Jung, Jones, and other psychoanalysts, along with psychiatrists, psychologists, and biologists, to deliver lectures at the celebration of the twentieth anniversary of the opening of Clark University. On this occasion the subject of Boas' lecture was "Psychological Problems in Anthropology."[78] The purpose of it was "to point out a direction in which anthropological data may be used to good advantage by the psychologist." It is interesting to remark his concept of the scope of anthropology and the relation of anthropological data to psychological problems which Boas expresses in his opening paragraph.

> The science of anthropology deals with the biological and mental manifestations of human life as they appear in different races and in different societies. The phenomena with which we are dealing are therefore, from one point of view, historical. We are endeavoring to elucidate the events which have led to the formation of human types, past and present,

[75] For Hall's "firsts" see Roback, *op. cit.*, pp. 154–155.

[76] Roback, *op. cit.*, p. 160.

[77] Chamberlain edited the *Journal of American Folklore* for almost a decade (1900–1908) and contributed for a considerable period a section to the *American Anthropologist* devoted to systematic abstracts of periodical literature.

[78] *American Journal of Psychology*, Vol. 21, 1910, pp. 371–384, embodied in *The Mind of Primitive Man*, 1st edition, New York: Macmillan, 1911. This volume of the *American Journal of Psychology* also contains lectures given by Freud, Jung, etc. on the same occasion.

and which have determined the course of cultural development of any given group of men. From another point of view the same phenomena are the objects of biological and psychological investigations. We are endeavoring to ascertain what are the laws of hereditary and of environmental variability of the human body. . . . We are also trying to determine the psychological laws which control the mind of man everywhere, and that may differ in various racial and social groups. Insofar as our inquiries relate to the last-named subject, their problems are problems of psychology, though based upon anthropological material.

So far as Boas' connection with Wundt is concerned, we know that, besides being familiar with his work, he brought Wundt to the attention of his students in his early years of teaching at Columbia. Writing thirty years later Benedict[79] reported that to Boas one of the central problems of anthropology "was the relation between the objective world and man's subjective world as it had taken form in different cultures."

Kroeber has pointed out that Boas "seems to have been wholly uninfluenced by Cattell, in spite of their long and close association on *Science* and at Columbia. He spent much time in his seminars, for several years, on Wundt; but it was the *Völkerpsychologie*, not the experimental psychology which Wundt helped found or organize, that occupied him."[80] Two early students of Boas took a special interest in Wundt. H. K. Haeberlin published the authoritative article already mentioned; A. A. Goldenweiser frequently referred to Wundt in his writings and, in addition, published an obituary notice in *The Freeman* (1921) upon the occasion of Wundt's death.[81]

Goldenweiser maintained (1922) that Wundt represented a psychological position greatly in advance of that reflected in the work of such English evolutionists as Spencer, Tylor, or Frazer, who were still deeply immersed in the individualistic, rational, and empirical tradition of the associationistic school. Wundt, says Goldenweiser, "discarded the crude rationalism of Spencer and Tylor. To him early man was not an aboriginal thinker facing nature as a set of problems or questions to which animism or magic could provide an answer or

[79] "Franz Boas, 1858–1942," A. L. Kroeber, Ruth Benedict, Murray B. Emereau, et al., *American Anthropologist*, Vol. 45, no. 3, Part II, 1943.

[80] *Ibid.*

[81] The major references to W. Wundt's theories are *Early Civilization*, 1922, reprinted in *History, Psychology and Culture*, 1933; "Psychological Postulates of Wundt's Folk-Psychology," a section of "Anthropology and Psychology," in the *Social Sciences and Their Interrelations*, edited by Ogburn and Goldenweiser, 1927, also reprinted in *History, Psychology and Culture*, pp. 77–80.

solution. Wundt saw clearly that man's reactions to the world—and especially his earliest reactions—were least of all rational and deliberate; rather were they spontaneous and emotional. The associationism of Frazer also collapsed before Wundt's doctrine of apperception, in which the atomistic and analytical view of mind was supplemented by an approach in which its integrative and creative functions were emphasized. Again, Wundt realized that the psychological foundations of civilization cannot be sought in the isolated individual, but that the group always actively cooperated in the production of attitudes and ideas. With great erudition and an originality that has often been underestimated, Wundt examined from this general standpoint the phenomena of language, art, religion, and mythology, social organization and law. Without espousing the doctrine of a separate folk-soul—a doctrine sponsored, e.g., by such German philologist-philosophers as Steinthal and Lazarus—Wundt insisted that civilization was impossible without the interrelated experiences of individuals in communication. Without laying himself open to the accusation of over-emphasizing the social—the principal weakness of the Durkheim school—Wundt joined the ranks of most modern sociologists and ethnologists in stressing the social and cultural setting."[82] Some of these same points were, of course, those made by Lévy-Bruhl who, in his earliest and most famous book (1910) directly challenged the psychological assumptions of the English evolutionists.[83] And Malinowski, despite his generally laudatory attitude towards Frazer, is fully aware of the deficiences of the kind of psychological interpretations for which Frazer was famous.[84]

In 1927, and even later, Goldenweiser expressed the view that

[82] *History, Psychology, and Culture,* copyright by Alfred A. Knopf, Inc., pp. 189–190.

[83] *Les fonctions mentales dans les sociétés inférieures;* English translation, *How Natives Think,* London: Allen and Unwin, 1926, Introduction.

[84] Malinowski, *A Scientific Theory of Culture and Other Essays,* Chapel Hill: University of North Carolina Press, 1944, p. 188.

"Frazer was essentially addicted to psychological interpretations of human belief and practice. His theory of magic, as the result of association of ideas; his three consecutive hypotheses about the origins of totemism in terms of belief in 'external soul,' 'magical inducement of fertility,' and in 'animal incarnation,' are essentially conceived in terms of individual psychology. Those who know his treatment of taboo, of the various aspects of totemism, of the development of magic, religion, and science, well realize that, throughout, Frazer in his explicit theories is little aware of the problems of social psychology. He is as already mentioned, fundamentally hostile to psychoanalysis, while behaviorism never enters his universe of discourse."

Wundt still had psychological meat for the contemporary anthropologist and other social scientists.[85] In particular, he calls attention
to the value of Wundt's conception of the "mutation of motives" and
the "heterogeny of ends," as applied in the study of the dynamics of
culture.[86] Nadel (1951) finds the latter idea useful, if (as he says) we
disregard the special evolutionary implications which Wundt gave it.
For Nadel, "it corrects the slight presumption of adequacy which
goes with the word 'integration' and it also emphasizes the fluidity
and the dynamic character of this integration of purposes, which is
constantly 'becoming' and never final."[87]

From 1900 onward, says Flugel, "we find psychology embarking
on the process of specialization incidental to the growth of new
schools, each school having its own peculiar methods and outlook
and even to a considerable extent its own peculiar jargon, so that
the total picture becomes one of increasingly violent and bewildering
activity; eventually, indeed, there are 'psychologies' rather than
'psychology' and students begin to complain that what is taught in
one center bears little resemblance to that which they have learned
in another. It is the period of psychoanalysis, behaviorism, and
Gestalt, of mental tests and the psychology of individual differences,
of 'factors,' of reflexology, and of the application of psychological
methods and concepts to the hither-to quite foreign fields of industry and commerce."[88]

Setting aside the influence derived from psychoanalytic psychology and psychiatry for the moment, we may ask: What were the influences of behavioristic psychology and Gestalt psychology on
anthropology? A closer scrutiny of the facts than it is possible to
give here would, I believe, show that the influence of behaviorism

[85] And Malinowski, *Scientific Theory,* p. 25, refers to the volumes of Wundt's
Völkerpsychologie as among the anthropological works which "command our
respect and admiration."

[86] Goldenweiser, *History, Psychology, and Culture,* copyright by Alfred A.
Knopf, Inc., pp. 79–80.

"This contribution of Wundt's to the dynamics of cultural life went over
the heads of the evolutionists, the diffusionists shut their doors . . . against it,
and even the critical anthropologists who should have known better, were too
busy disposing of their predecessors to do it justice. It is to be hoped that the
superior discernment embodied in Wundt's concept will not be wasted on social
thinkers during the present period of mutation of motives and purposes in the
entire field of the sciences of society."

[87] S. F. Nadel, *The Foundations of Social Anthropology,* Glencoe: Free Press,
1951, p. 386.

[88] Flugel, *op. cit.*

far surpasses that of any other school of psychological thought. Nor is it difficult to understand why. As pointed out by Bruner and Allport, the period 1908–1918 was the one characterized by behaviorism and objectivistic methods and aims. This is also the period when anthropology in America was getting well under way. By this time anthropologists knew so much about cultural variability and were so fascinated by the questions raised that any psychology that was primarily concerned with generic innate traits of man appeared to have no reference to the vital problems of the anthropologist. Thus Lowie, writing in 1917, asserted that "culture is, indeed, the sole and exclusive subject matter of ethnology, as consciousness is the subject matter of psychology," and went on to say that "the science of psychology, even in its most modern ramifications of abnormal psychology and the study of individual variations, does not grapple with *acquired* traits nor with the influence of *society* on individual thought, feeling, and inclination. It deals on principle exclusively with *innate* traits of the individual."[89] In 1940 Klineberg, referring to this statement of Lowie's, says that it has "now a somewhat antiquated flavor."[90] However, if the characterization of psychology expressed by Boring is recalled, and consideration is given to the fact that mental tests were being focused upon the discovery of "native" intelligence and that, in early child psychology, "natural" and "universal" stages in ontogenetic development were stressed, often colored by the recapitulation theory under Hall's influence, and it is not forgotten that it was the behaviorists who greatly stimulated the study of learning and that personality and social psychology had, as

[89] R. H. Lowie, *Culture and Ethnology*, New York: Douglas C. McMurtrie, 1917, pp. 5, 16. Clark Wissler in his address to the AAAS, as Chairman of Section H, 1915 ("Psychological and Historical Interpretations for Culture," *Science*, Vol. 43, 1916, pp. 193–201) expressed a similar viewpoint. "Psychologists give their attention to innate phenomena," he said, "especially man's psycho-physical equipment. If we extend the meaning of the term behavior so as to include consciousness, we may say that psychologists are concerned with the behavior of man as an individual." Wissler goes on to say that while "it may be that there is a problem in the comparative behavior of the individuals comprising ethnic groups . . . it is a psychological one and must be solved by the use of psychological data. Anthropologists give it little concern because they see in differences of individual behavior no significant cultural correlates." Known cultural phenomena since the paleolithic "necessitate no change in man's innate equipment nor in his innate behavior. So, on the whole, anthropology is quite indifferent to the problem of comparative behavior because it is concerned with the objective aspects of what is learned in life."

[90] Otto Klineberg, *Social Psychology*, New York: Holt, 1940, p. 5.

yet, no scientific respectability, Lowie's impression of the central interest of psychology in America in the second decade of this century can be easily appreciated.

Behaviorism had an appeal for the anthropologists because it, too, was opposed to the prevailing doctrine of instincts (substituting for them more specific physiological needs or drives), innate mental differences, or innate anything. Watson practically guaranteed to make a specialist in any of the professions or arts out of a healthy infant "regardless of his talents, peculiarities, tendencies, abilities, . . . or race of his ancestors."[91] This extreme environmentalist doctrine fitted in very well with the idea that culture was acquired, and that individuals with different cultural backgrounds acquired different sets of habits. The behaviorists promoted the study of learning but, says Asch,[92] "adopted a particular account of the learning process founded in the old doctrine of association and elaborated in the investigations of conditioned responses. Dominant in this concept were the role of *trial* and *error*, and the operations of *reward* and *punishment*. This formulation of the learning process was based primarily on the interpretation of the problem-solving activities of infra-human organisms but was given a general application and extended to the human level." Soon the term "conditioning," one of the verbal earmarks of the behaviorist, became almost as familiar in anthropological as in psychological literature, even though the purely technical psychological meaning of it and the theory behind it remained unexamined. Wissler remarked in 1923 that ". . . anthropologists are, in the broad sense, behaviorists, and so stand shoulder to shoulder with those psychologists to whom the same term applies. . . ."[93] And

[91] J. B. Watson, *Behaviorism*, New York: Norton, 1925, p. 82. Referring to the psychological scene in the years following 1910 Boring (*History of Experimental Psychology*, p. 494, first edition) says:
"Some conservatives were Wundtians, some radicals were functionalists, more psychologists were agnostics. Then Watson touched a match to the mass, there was an explosion, and behaviorism was left. Watson founded behaviorism because everything was all ready for the founding. Otherwise, he could not have done it. He was philosophically inept, and behaviorism came into existence without a constitution. Ever since, the behaviorists have been trying to formulate a satisfactory epistemological constitution and thus to explain themselves."
[92] Solomon E. Asch, *Social Psychology*, copyright 1953 by Prentice-Hall, Inc., New York, p. 12.
[93] Clark Wissler, *Man and Culture*, New York: Crowell, 1923, p. 251. At the same time the hypothesis Wissler developed to account for a "universal pattern" of culture is a theory involving psychobiological determinism. He postulates an innate cultural drive since he says (pp. 264–265) "that the pattern for

Nadel (1951) says: "A few sociologists and anthropologists have fully accepted the tenets of behaviourism; many more make concessions to it. If the use of the term 'conditioning' is any evidence, almost the whole of modern anthropology has gone behaviourist. But mostly this and similar verbal concessions are only just that—whether they result from lip service or eclecticism. In either case the essence of behaviourism has been misunderstood: it offers a challenge, not an expedient." "Certainly, behaviouristic psychology in its early and extreme form was as naive as it was ambitious," says Nadel, ". . . moreover, most behaviourists would claim that they have outgrown the crudeness and assurance of this early approach." But according to him, "some anthropologists . . . still subscribe to it. The textbook on anthropology by Chapple and Coon (1942) is an example. G. P. Murdock's article on 'The Common Denominators of Culture' at least savours of 'primitive' behaviourism."[94]

In Nadel's opinion "the earlier claims of behaviorists to be all-embracing are only slightly toned down" even in the later system of Hull to which specific reference is made. Hull was not only an important figure as one of the few theoreticians that America has produced, but because at Yale he directly influenced such anthropologists as Murdock, Gillin, Ford, and Whiting. As compared with other anthropologists who may have used the vocabulary of behaviorism or been influenced by general behavioristic concepts, this group is fully aware of the postulates and implications of Hull's system in all their ramifications.

Although it would be difficult to prove it, part of the early resistance to psychoanalytical psychology and the study of personality in culture, was probably due to the entrenchment by that time of behaviourism as the sort of psychology that was objective and scientific, as compared with psychoanalysis which again raised the ghost of the innate dynamic tendencies in man in a new form and seemed to have a subjective aura about it.

Malinowski's final and systematic exposition of his views is an

---

culture is just as deeply buried in the germ plasm of man as the bee pattern in the bee" so that "a human being comes into the world with a set, or bias, to socialization, according to a definite pattern, . . . by reason of which a man is a human being and not a termite, a bee, nor even a monkey. The human pattern, therefore, is a part, if not the whole, of man's inborn behavior . . . man builds cultures because he cannot help it, there is a *drive* in his protoplasm that carries him forward even against his will."

[94] Nadel, *op. cit.*, pp. 57, 59.

outstanding example of a considered approach to culture in behavioristic terms. It is more important to recognize this fact than to fall
back upon his own self-labelling and call him a "functionalist." For
Malinowski is quite explicit about his psychological position. He says
that "the approval of psychoanalysis does not in any way detract
from the great importance which behaviorism promises to acquire
as the basic psychology for the study of social and cultural processes
[italics ours]. By behaviorism I mean the newer developments of
stimulus and response psychology as elaborated by Professor C. Hull
at Yale, Thorndike at Columbia, or H. S. Liddell at Cornell. The
value of behaviorism is due, first and foremost, to the fact that its
methods are identical as regards limitations and advantages with
those of anthropological field work. In dealing with people of a different culture, it is always dangerous to use the short-circuiting of
'empathy,' which usually amounts to guessing as to what the other
person might have thought or felt. The fundamental principle of the
field worker, as well as of the behaviorist, is that ideas, emotions, and
convictions never continue to lead a cryptic, hidden existence within
the unexplorable depths of the mind, conscious or unconscious. All
sound, that is experimental, psychology can deal only with observations of overt behavior, although it may be useful to relate such observations to the shorthand of introspective interpretation."[95]

The implications of this behavioristic approach, shared by anthropologists other than Malinowski, have been sharply generalized
by Asch.[96] "Culture becomes in this view a superstructure of habits
and tendencies, 'a vast conditioning apparatus' geared to the gratification of primary needs. The prime movers of action are the biological
needs; these provide the energy for all other psychological processes.
All modifications of behavior, in particular social motives and practices, take place in relation to the gratification of primary needs.
. . . We find here also the bold claim that the fact of society, the
course of history, the growth of thought have introduced no new
ends, that for all man's achievements his ends remain the same as
those of infra-human organisms. He differs from these solely in the
possession of a superstructure of an elaborate set of tools, material
and psychological. Human activities are either consummations of
primary needs or means to their consummation. If we find in society

[95] Malinowski, *op. cit.*, Chapel Hill: University of North Carolina Press, 1944,
p. 23; for Nadel's comments on Malinowski's position see *Foundations*, p. 378.
[96] Asch, *op. cit.*, copyright 1953 by Prentice-Hall, Inc., New York, p. 14.

what appear at first sight to be other needs or ends, say for companionship, or knowledge, we must trace them to their instrumental
value for primary needs. There can be nothing new in the way of
purpose and aspiration. The crux of the doctrine is to deny this possibility; there can only be more circuitous ways of satisfying primary
needs. As one noted anthropologist [Malinowski] has stated: 'By
human nature, therefore, we mean the biological determinism which
imposes on every civilization and on all individuals in it the carrying
out of such bodily functions as breathing, sleep, rest, nutrition, excretion, and reproduction'."[97]

It may be noted in passing that the reductionistic implications of
such a behavioristic approach to culture have their parallel in
Freud's treatment of culture in *Civilization and Its Discontents.*
Furthermore, it is just this reductionism, and its implications for
personality theory as well, that represents one of the central points
of difference between Jung and Freud and which led to the break
between them. In a broad and fundamental sense, Freud, as well as
many psychiatrists, are within the behaviorist tradition of psychological thinking.

The use of such concepts as "configuration" and "pattern," as
applied to a culture, do not actually indicate any direct or profound
influence of Gestalt psychology upon anthropology. They are even
more superficial indications of genuine influence than is the frequent
occurrence of the term "conditioning" in anthropological literature
a clue to what a systematic behavioristic approach means. Kroeber,
for instance, introduces his chapter on "Patterns" by observing that
they "are those arrangements or systems of internal relationship
which give to any culture its coherence or plan, and keep it from
being a mere accumulation of random bits. They are, therefore, of
primary importance. However, the concepts embraced under the
term 'pattern' are still a bit fluid; the ideas involved have not yet
crystallized into sharp meanings. It will therefore be necessary to
consider in order several kinds of patterns."[98] No references are
made to *Gestalt* psychology in this chapter, but in a section of the
previous one, entitled "Content and Form; Ethos and Eidos; Values,"
attention is called to the elementary point that "a system or configuration is always, in its nature, more than the mere sum of its parts;
there is also the relation of the parts, their total interconnections,

[97] The quotation is from Malinowski, *op. cit.,* p. 75.
[98] Kroeber, *Anthropology,* New York: Harcourt, 1949, p. 311.

which add up to something additionally significant. This is well recognized in 'Gestalt' or configurational psychology. The 'form' of culture may therefore be regarded as the pattern of interrelations of the contents that constitute it."[99]

Honigmann, in his summarization of the literature on "the configuration approach," makes no reference to Gestalt psychology, but stresses the fact that such pioneers as Sapir and Benedict "followed the leads of German historical philosophers like Dilthey and Spengler, who had already approached conceptualization of similar phenomena in their *Weltanschauung* and *Zeitgeist* studies."[100] Sapir had employed the term "spirit" or "genius" in his famous article "Culture, Genuine or Spurious" (1924).[101] In her earliest articles on "Psychological Types" (1930)[102] and "Configurations of Culture in North America" (1932)[103] Benedict made no reference to Gestalt psychology. In her *Patterns of Culture* (1934) she gives explicit credit to Dilthey and Spengler for recognizing "the importance of integration and configuration" *in cultures*,[104] giving only passing mention to Gestalt psychology.[105] Boas, in his introduction to her book, calls attention to the fact that the author "calls the genius of culture its configuration." Long before this, however, Boas himself had been interested in the same question. For in writing the obituary of H. K. Haeberlin (1919)[106] in which he emphasizes the "keen psychological interest of the latter" Boas observes that ". . . the wider concept of culture as dominating all the phases of tribal life occupied his attention. . . . With remarkable clearness of vision . . . he grasped the psy-

[99] *Ibid.*, p. 293.

[100] John J. Honigmann, "Culture and Ethos of Kaska Society," New Haven: *Yale University Publications in Anthropology*, No. 40, 1949, p. 10. Goldenweiser discussing the influence of Wilhelm Dilthey expresses the opinion that "of modern movements, *Gestalt* psychology and configurationism in anthropology without articulating directly with Dilthey are obviously related to him in intellectual orientation. . . ." ("The Relation of the Natural Sciences to the Social Sciences" in *Contemporary Social Theory*, edited by H. E. Barnes, Howard and Frances B. Becker, New York: Appleton-Century, 1940, p. 93, footnote.)

[101] *American Journal of Sociology*, Vol. 29, 1924, pp. 401–429.

[102] *Proceedings of the 23rd International Congress of Americanists*, New York: 1930, pp. 572–581.

[103] *American Anthropologist*, Vol. 34, 1932, pp. 1–27.

[104] *Patterns of Culture*, Penguin edition, p. 47.

[105] She observes (*ibid.*) that while psychologists of this school have worked "chiefly in those fields where evidence can be experimentally arrived at in the laboratory . . . its implications reach far beyond the simple demonstrations which are associated with its work."

[106] *American Anthropologist*, Vol. 21, 1919, pp. 71–74.

chological basis of culture as a unit." From Haeberlin's "Idea of Fertilization in the Culture of the Pueblo Indians.[107] Boas quotes the statement "that culture is not comprehensible as a summation of diffused elements is proved by the re-interpretation of heterogeneous traits according to a uniform scheme of interrelated ideas. The problem of the cultural setting of the Pueblos is therefore a psychological one."

What Benedict really brought into focus initially, therefore, was the question of how we are to conceptualize and study the "wholeness" of cultures, in contrast with an analytic approach that made primary use of such concepts as culture "traits" and "complexes."[108] She is dissatisfied with functionalism. She says, "Malinowski, somewhat disappointingly, does not go on to the examination of these cultural wholes, but is content to conclude his assignment with pointing out in each context that each trait functions in the total cultural complex, a conclusion which seems increasingly the beginning of inquiry rather than its peroration. For it is a position that leads directly to the necessity of investigating in what sort of a whole these traits are functioning and what reference they bear to the total culture. In how far do the traits achieve an organic interrelation? Are the *Leitmotivs* in the world by which they may be integrated many or few? These questions the functionalists do not ask." It is in this article, too, that Benedict says that her prime characterizations of psychological types in the Southwest have referred to the ethos of these people and that "cultural configurations stand to the understanding of group behavior in the relation that personality types stand to the understanding of individual behavior."[109]

The question of culture-wholes is thus related to the concept of "ethos" and this connection is brought out both by Honigman and

[107] *American Anthropological Association, Memoir,* 3, 1916.

[108] Cf. John Gillin, "The Configuration Problem in Culture," *American Sociological Review,* Vol. 1, 1936, pp. 373–386, and Clyde Kluckhohn, "Patterning as Exemplified in Navaho Culture" in *Language, Culture, and Personality: Essays in Memory of Edward Sapir,* L. Spier, et. al., eds., Menasha, Wisconsin: Banta, 1941. More recently John Gillin and George Nicholson ("The Security Functions of Cultural Systems," *Social Forces,* Vol. 30, 1951, pp. 179–84) have offered a mathematical model for dealing with the security functions of cultures considered as wholes. The concept of ethos is introduced with reference to an index that "would be a measure of the quality of the way in which a culture defines threats."

[109] Benedict, *Configurations,* pp. 2, 23. There is a reference in this article to William Stern's book on the human personality (1919).

Kroeber. The further step which Benedict took was to translate the "patterns" or "configurations" of the cultures of peoples into psychological terms. Whiting and Child epitomize the problem upon which Benedict focused attention in *Patterns of Culture* by saying that she "shows that many of the major aspects of a culture fit into a pattern or configuration which may be described in terms of motivational orientation or personality type. This basic orientation is held to have an important selective effect in the adoption, development, and modification of all sorts of specific aspects of the culture. The basic orientation, of course, Benedict believes to be culturally rather than biologically transmitted; in this book she is not concerned with the effect of culture on personality but with the selective effect on culture which this orientation has, once it has been established."[110] While this approach did not involve the use of Gestalt psychology in any technical sense, it represents a noteworthy parallelism, in principle, between the rejection of an older "elementaristic" approach on the part of the Gestalt psychologists and a similar movement away from an analytic approach to culture on the part of some anthropologists. Asch has called attention to this analogy,[111] and concludes that "as a result elementarism in anthropology gave way to the more fruitful assumption that the unit of investigation is the society." Nadel, who has acknowledged a debt to Gestalt psychology,[112] discusses a whole series of problems inherent in any approach to cultures or societies as wholes ranging through ethos and eidos to culture and personality. In his opinion "the theory of culture patterns has a mixed ancestry. It subscribes to the tenet of Gestalt psychology that the 'whole is more than its parts'; it draws on such popular conceptions as the 'spirit of the times' or the 'genius' of a people or civilization; it also harks back to Nietzsche's early philosophy and the German 'verstehend Psychologie'; and it claims some kinship with the theories of personality."[113]

Even if it be acknowledged that there is a significant analogy between the anthropologists' interest in cultures conceived as integral functioning wholes and the Gestalt idea, we may ask: What is the direct relevance of Gestalt psychology to anthropological re-

[110] John W. M. Whiting and Irvin L. Child, *Child Training and Personality: A Cross-Cultural Study*, New Haven: Yale University Press, 1953, p. 2.
[111] Asch, *op. cit.*, copyright 1953 by Prentice-Hall, Inc., New York, p. 61.
[112] Nadel. *op. cit.*, Preface, p. vi.
[113] *Ibid.*

search, and what does the record show? To what extent have anthropologists actually made use of the principles, methods, and concepts of Gestalt psychology in their work? What is the relevance,
for instance, of the principles of this school to those areas of anthropological research where, instead of the primary concern being with
patterns of culture or ethos, attention is focused upon the differential
behavior of human beings as members of different socio-cultural
systems? The manner in which the individual responds to the meaningful aspects of the world in which he has to live and act, his
perceptions and his motivations, in short, the "psychological field"
constituted for him by his membership in a group, certainly suggests
the relevance of the kind of approach that Gestalt psychologists
have developed. Nevertheless, compared to the influence exerted by
behaviorism, Gestalt psychology seems to have had only the most
superficial effects upon anthropological research. This is particularly
noteworthy since two of the founders of the movement have themselves manifested an interest in the use of ethnographic data. Wertheimer's discussion of number concepts in the thinking of primitive
peoples, although originally published in 1912,[114] does not appear to
have interested anthropologists, at least in the United States. And
while Köhler's *Mentality of Apes* is universally known, his "Psychological Remarks on Some Questions of Anthropology" (1937)[115] has
gone practically unnoticed. It is in this article that Köhler sagely
observes that "though some anthropologists do not like to admit it,
psychological principles play an important role in the interpretation
of anthropological facts. Theoretical difficulties may, therefore, arise
quite as easily from inadequate psychological notions as from the
strange ways of primitive mentality." And toward the close of the
article he observes that although "hardly a word has been said about
primitive religion, none about primitive art, again none about social
life with all its institutions and ramifications, I am convinced that in
these fields, too, psychology can be of more help now than, say,
thirty or even twenty years ago. But for such help other principles
besides those of the present essay will have to be introduced."

There are several reasons why anthropologists have not been immediately attracted to Gestalt psychology. In the first place, the rele-

114 Max Wertheimer, "Über das Denken der Naturvölker: Zahlen und Zahl-
gehelde," *Zeitschr. f. Psychologie,* 60, 1912. Translation in Willis D. Ellis, *A
Source Book of Gestalt Psychology,* New York: Harcourt, 1938.
115 *American Journal of Psychology,* Vol. 50, 1937, pp. 271–288.

vance of this approach can only become significant for the anthropologist who is interested in behavior and not simply in culture *per
se* or even cultural configurations abstracted from human behavior.
Besides this, both Wertheimer and Köhler are particularly interested
in cognitive processes at the level of psychodynamics, and not in
culture and personality. Furthermore, since the general point of
view of Gestalt psychology is antithetical to the radical environ-
mentalism that characterized behaviorism in its early stage, any dogmatic form of cultural determinism is incongruous with the Gestalt
approach. In the article referred to, Köhler, for example, explicitly
rejects the assumption that "the individual is no more than an empty
container for the products of group mentality," the same point which
was raised by Sapir, Goldenweiser, and Haeberlin in their criticism
of Kroeber and which is even more pertinent with reference to the
"culturology" of Leslie White.[116] Finally, while the approach of
Gestalt psychology is particularly relevant to the study of the complex relations existing between the organization of the psychological
and social fields of the individuals of one society as compared with
another, which may also, in part, be considered functions of differential cultural factors, a relativistic viewpoint is not maintained.[117]
For instance, it is Köhler's position that while magical beliefs may
differ from one society to another, and while the individual derives
his beliefs from his group membership, nevertheless, "to some extent magic exists in practically every society . . . [and] at least
some of its major premises are not peculiar to a few specific tribes
but are the common property of all mankind below a certain high
level of sophistication. From this common stock, which general developmental psychology is entitled to study and to explain, different

[116] As, for example, when White writes ("The Individual and the Cultural
Process" in *American Association for the Advancement of Science, Centennial
Volume*, 1950, pp. 74–81) that the individual is "merely an organization of
cultural forces and elements that have impinged upon him from the outside and
which find their overt expression through him. So conceived, the individual is
but the expression of a suprabiological cultural tradition in somatic form," or
that "relative to the culture process the individual is neither creator nor determinant; he is merely a catalyst and a vehicle of expression." Perhaps the most
extreme epitomization of this position is White's statement ("The Locus of
Mathematical Reality: An Anthropological Footnote," *Philosophy of Science*,
Vol. 14, 1947, p. 296) that after all, possibly "the most effective way to study
culture scientifically is to proceed *as if* the human race did not exist."

[117] See, e.g., Chapter 13 in Asch, *op. cit.*, "The Fact of Culture and the
Problem of Relativism."

societies, with their different environments and histories, have in fact devised different varieties of actual practices. I do not believe that we can fully understand the origin of such varieties before we know on what ground magic in general grows." With the increasing interest that is developing in constancies and cultural universals, the point of view of Gestalt psychology in regard to such problems may prove more relevant to anthropology in the future than it has in the past.[118]

Personally, I have found Koffka's concept of a "behavioral" as differentiated from a "geographic" or objective environment of particular usefulness in defining the organism-environment relations at the human level.[119] From a psychological standpoint the environment of man is always a culturally constituted behavioral environment. Gestalt psychologists have also stressed self-perception as an essential constituent of the structuralization of the psychological and social fields of the human being during a period when behaviorists and other academic psychologists avoided any discussion of the self. In "The Self and Its Behavioral Environment" I have discussed the relevance of cultural variability in the self-image and self-con-

[118] Donald N. Michael ("A Cross-Cultural Investigation of Closure," *Journal of Abnormal and Social Psychology*, 48 (1953), pp. 225–230), for example, wishing to determine whether closure may be considered "a general law of innate perceptual organization" or whether "differences in cultural conditioning" influence the perception of closure, set up an experiment in which he tested the responses of Navajo and white subjects with respect to the detection of "small openings in tachistoscopically presented circular stimuli." Despite the well known fact that the Navajo are motivated to non-closure in the execution of certain ornamental designs by the values of their culture, no significant differences in the perception of closure were found in the two groups of experimental subjects.

[119] For a more extended discussion, see "The Self and Its Behavioral Environment" in *Explorations*, Feb. 1954 (Toronto, Canada). Without systematic qualification, or further analysis, the term "environment" has long proved ambiguous and unsatisfactory. The distinction made by Koffka is followed by other Gestalt psychologists, although they may use a different terminology. Lewin contrasts "objective environment" or "foreign hull" of the life space and "psychological" environment; David Krech and Richard S. Crutchfield (*Theory and Problems of Social Psychology*, New York: McGraw-Hill Book Company, Inc., copyright 1948, p. 38) write: "The real environment of a person is that environment which would be described by an objective observer; the psychological environment is that which would be described by the experiencing person himself. . . . The very same physical environment can result in radically different psychological environments for two different persons." The same statement may be generalized for what I have called "the culturally constituted behavioral environment" of different *groups* of mankind.

cepts of different peoples in relation to basic orientations that appear
to be primary functions of all cultures, once it is recognized that self-
awareness is a product of the socialization process and a primary
constituent of a human personality structure essential for the functioning of any human society.

Asch, approaching social psychology systematically from a Gestalt point of view, makes a further point. He insists that other
psychological schools of thought, no matter whether they have taken
the form of environmental or instinct doctrines, have failed to clarify
"the invariant or the mutable characteristics of men. . . . Traditional instinct and habit psychologies have little of relevance to say
about the specific properties of human orientation; they give the
appearance of having solved the problems of social life when they
have simply bypassed them. In particular, they do not face seriously
the problems of order in individual and social action when they describe men as a sum of instincts and habits. A psychology of drives
and habits can hardly find a conceptual place for the psychological
structures most characteristic of man—for the reality of a self, of
kinship relations, or a sense of values. It results in the description of
an individual who is not capable of novelty, who is not a genuinely
social being but is only a more complicated form of a pre-social, pre-
human individual. It is a crude fallacy to assume that no changes occur in the social field other than the detailed modifications in the
sequence and arrangement of elementary functions. We must keep
open the view that many distinctive psychological operations take
form only within a social field and that the changes they produce
alter individuals at their center."[120]

If we now consider the twentieth century development in American anthropology that has been most familiarly labelled as the study
of personality and culture, we are struck by a very interesting historical fact. Whereas other psychological influences upon anthropology all can be derived from psychology in the somewhat narrow
academic sense, in this case the source lay entirely outside this tradition. The interest that led to investigations in the personality and
culture area, in short, represents but a single aspect of the tremendous influence which psychoanalytic theories have had upon the
whole intellectual climate of our time, especially those disciplines
concerned with human behavior, including, of course, academic

[120] Asch, *op. cit.*, copyright 1953 by Prentice-Hall, Inc., New York, pp. 76, 78.

psychology itself.[121] These theories were novel and they were radical; they challenged fundamental and highly cherished assumptions about the nature of man; it was inevitable that they should arouse antagonism and be subjected to the sharpest criticism. But quite aside from any technical detail, a few significant general facts may be noted here which have a direct bearing upon the reaction of anthropologists to them.[122]

In the first place, it is interesting to note that these new theories grew out of psychotherapy with individual patients and that the actual life experiences of the patient became a focal point of attention. This kind of empirical material, quite aside from any interpretation of it in relation to the psychodynamics of individual adjustment, was a far cry from the kind of information the cultural anthropologist was accustomed to collect. His aim was to obtain data that would permit valid descriptive generalizations about the cultural attributes of human populations considered in their group aspects, rather than about the component individuals of such populations considered as functioning personalities. This is what led Sapir to observe that: "It is what all the individuals of a society have in common which is supposed to constitute the true subject matter of cultural anthropology and sociology. If the testimony of an individual is set down as such, as often happens in our anthropological mono-

[121] Appraising the situation from the standpoint of psychoanalysis, Heinz Hartmann, Ernst Kris, and Rudolph M. Loewenstein ("Some Psychoanalytic Comments on 'Culture and Personality'" in *Psychoanalysis and Culture: Essays in Honor of Géza Róheim*, New York: International Universities Press, 1951, pp. 3–4) write: "The juxtaposition of culture and personality designates a vast area of research, rich in promise and stimulation. Investigators working in this area tend to point with pride to their attempts at interdisciplinary cooperation. Their views, however, differ frequently and in essential points, and one may well gain the impression that we are faced with a transitory period, in which affairs are unsettled and results tentative." The authors go on to say that the point of departure for their comments is the fact "that many psychological propositions used by workers in the field are derived from psychoanalysis. During the present phase of historical development the scientific access to problems of human conflict, and hence of personality, initiated by Freud, is exercising influence on the social sciences which previously had relied on common-sense psychology [sic]. . . . No other branch of the social sciences has taken this call for new data more seriously than Anthropology. A wealth of material assembled during the best part of a generation is witness to the fruitfulness of the contact."
[122] Since Kluckhohn, *op. cit.*, has so ably surveyed the anthropological literature which reflects this influence in its earliest stages, the reader is referred to his article for documentation of the work of such pioneers as Sapir, Benedict, and Mead, as well as others.

graphs, it is not because of an interest in the individual himself as a matured and single organization of ideas but in his assumed typicality for the community as a whole."[123] Although P. W. Schmidt, as early as 1906, had called attention to the need for more information about individuals in non-literate cultures,[124] and Radin had published the "Personal Reminiscences of a Winnebago Indian" in 1913,[125] the personal document approach in anthropology[126] was greatly stimulated and the qualitative aspects of the material collected assumed more clinical overtones once its psychological significance became apparent. This emphasis was promoted, for instance, by Edward Sapir, who familiarized himself with psychoanalytic theory at an early date.[127] Kluckhohn remarks that "although his own published contributions to this field are relatively slight, the influence of Edward Sapir in the direction of arousing interest in all kinds of personal documents is enormous."[128] Goldenweiser (1940) discussing recent trends in anthropology chooses "The Individual" as one of his three major headings and remarks that "among the anthropologists of the new functionalism with their disciples and followers, and among several of the younger members of the Boas school, the search for the individual has become something of an obsession."[129]

In the second place, the individuals from whom the psychoanalysts derived their basic data were those whose life adjustments were

[123] Edward Sapir, "Cultural Anthropology and Psychiatry," *Journal of Abnormal and Social Psychology*, Vol. 27, 1932, pp. 229–242.

[124] P. W. Schmidt, "Die Moderne Ethnologie," *Anthropos*, Vol. 1, 1906, pp. 592–644.

[125] Paul Radin, *Journal of American Folklore*, Vol. 26, 1913, pp. 293–318.

[126] See Clyde Kluckhohn, "The Personal Document in Anthropological Science" in Louis Gottschalk, Clyde Kluckhohn, and Robert Angell in *The Use of Personal Documents in History, Anthropology, and Sociology*, New York: Social Science Research Council, Bulletin 53, 1945, pp. 79–173; and A. L. Kroeber, "The Use of Autobiographical Evidence" in *The Nature of Culture*.

[127] His reviews of Freud's *Delusion and Dream*, and Oskar Pfister's *The Psychoanalytic Method* appeared in *The Dial*, the same year (1917) that he took issue with Kroeber in the *American Anthropologist* ("Do We Need a Superorganic?"). Kroeber (*The Nature of Culture*, copyright 1952 by the University of Chicago, p. 300) has reported the fact that he practiced psychoanalysis in San Francisco (1920–1923) but found that this experience gave him no insights that helped him understand culture better. Any negativism towards "culture-personality," he says is the "result of disillusionment rather than of prejudgment."

[128] Kluckhohn, *The Personal Document*, p. 88.

[129] "Leading Contributions of Anthropology to Social Theory," *Contemporary Social Theory*, Barnes, Becker, and Becker, eds., p. 480.

disturbed in one way or another. Thus the orientation of the analyst was, to begin with, directed towards the "abnormal," rather than the "normal." This orientation likewise was in contrast to the approach of the anthropologist. But this very orientation itself appears to have attracted the attention of anthropologists because it raised a question relevant to the known diversity in culturally constituted norms and value systems. Wide variation in social organization, economic life, art forms, and morals was a familiar fact. Might not psychopathological phenomena, at the level of individual behavior, be considered in a relativistic frame of reference? A number of articles began to appear that dealt with this general subject, including some case material. In the same year (1934) that Benedict's *Patterns of Culture* was published, her article "Anthropology and the Abnormal" appeared.[130] About the same time John M. Cooper published an article entitled "Mental Disease Situations in Certain Cultures: A New Field of Research."[131] Hallowell likewise discussed this subject[132] and Kroeber contributed a chapter to a book on *The Problem of Mental Disorder*.[133] These all followed the seminal article "Cultural Anthropology and Psychiatry" by Edward Sapir that had appeared in 1932.

The most significant aspect, however, of psychoanalytic theory that directly influenced anthropologists was the novel structural concepts of the human personality it offered. Not only was the personality conceived as a functioning whole; psychoanalytic theories dealt with the genesis, motivational patterns, and dynamics of personality. Neither academic psychologists nor orthodox psychiatrists had developed anything comparable. As Gillin has pointed out "the word 'personality' is not mentioned in the index, published in 1928, of the first forty volumes of the *American Anthropologist*. . . . The index of the publications of the Bureau of American Ethnology is also barren of the word, as is also that of Lowie's *The History of Ethnological Theory*. . . ."[134] And Kroeber remarks that "as late as 1915 the very word 'personality' still carried overtones chiefly of

[130] *Journal of General Psychology*, Vol. 10, 1934, pp. 59–80.

[131] *Journal of Abnormal and Social Psychology*, Vol. 29, 1934–1935, pp. 10–17. See also "The Cree Witiko Psychosis," *Primitive Man*, Vol. 6, 1933, pp. 20–24.

[132] A. I. Hallowell, "Culture and Mental Disorder," *Journal of Abnormal and Social Psychology*, Vol. 29, 1934–1935, pp. 1–9.

[133] Edited by Madison Bentley, New York: 1934.

[134] Gillin. *op. cit.*, 1939. p. 681.

piquancy, unpredictability, intellectual daring: a man's personality was much like a woman's 'it'."[135] Anthropologists had not only by-passed the individual, normal or abnormal; concentration upon abstracted culture "traits" and "complexes" and references to individuals as "carriers" of culture even implied some basic dichotomy between man and culture. A vital issue was obscured. How was it possible for societies with all the widely different patterns of culture with which the anthropologist was becoming more and more familiar to function as integral units, if there were not some intimate connection between the psychological structure of their component individuals and the systems of culture they exhibited? Did not the very existence of a *human* social order raise the question of personality organization? Such questions could scarcely be attacked until some working hypothesis about the nature of the human personality as a structural whole had been developed. The older theories of the nature of the human mind were not adequate.

While anthropologists reacted negatively to Freud's own interpretations of the psychological significance of certain cultural phenomena, as exemplified in *Totem and Taboo*,[136] it soon dawned upon them that there were implications in his theory that he himself did not clearly envisage. The positive point which struck fire was the hypothesis that early childhood training and experiences were of paramount importance with relation to the kind of personality structure developed by the individual; that parents or others who were responsible for child training were surrogates of the larger cultural whole, and that the same socialization process that anthropologists had always assumed to be necessary for the transmission of culture from generation to generation was, at the same time, the process in which the personality of the individual was structured. Here again, the cross-cultural data suggested that customary modes of child training and the relations of parents and children were variable features in human societies. *Group* differences in child training might correlate with a typical personality structure on the one hand and a characteristic culture pattern on the other. And since psychoanalytic theory emphasized the crucial importance of certain kinds of infant experience, such as bowel training and weaning, it was possible to obtain information about such facts through field investigation.

[135] *The Nature of Culture*, copyright 1952 by the University of Chicago, p. 116.

[136] See, e.g., Kroeber, *op. cit.*, for the reviews he wrote in 1920 and in 1939.

Besides this, psychoanalytic theory presented anthropologists, as well as psychologists, with a novel concept of human nature. In anthropology the "psychic unity" of man had become a vague concept and it had been approached chiefly with questions of racial differences in mind. It had no reference to any constructs that could be directly related to the dynamics of the personality structure of man. By documenting the role of unconscious, biologically rooted impulses in man's conduct, and the necessity for some compromise with the demands imposed by an organized, culturally constituted mode of social existence, psychoanalytic theory had transcultural implications. Ubiquitous psychological mechanisms such as conflict, repression, sublimation, rationalization, etc., were said to be generic to the adjustment of all human beings, whatever the culture patterns of their society. Sapir grasped the importance of this contribution of psychoanalytic theory at once. In 1921 he expressed the opinion that "the really valuable contribution of the Freudian school seems to me to lie in the domain of pure psychology. Nearly everything that is specific in Freudian theory, such as the 'Oedipus-complex' as a normative image or the definite interpretation of certain symbols or the distinctively sexual nature of certain infantile reactions, may well prove to be either ill-founded or seen in distorted perspective, but there can be little doubt of the immense service that Dr. Freud has rendered psychology in his revelation of typical psychic mechanisms. . . . Psychology will not willingly let go of these and still other Freudian concepts, but will build upon them, gradually coming to see them in their wider significance."[137] Sapir proved entirely correct in this judgment. For as Hilgard points out (1949): "The mechanisms of adjustment were the features of Freudian theory that we earliest domesticated within American academic psychology. They now have a respectable place in our textbooks, regardless of the theoretical biases of our text-book writers."[138] It can be assumed, I think, that they have become an integral part of anthropological thinking about human behavior as well.

The history of culture and personality studies in anthropology, consists largely of the way in which psychoanalytic concepts, constructs, and theories have been accepted in whole or in part,

[137] In a review of Rivers, *Instinct and the Unconscious*, reprinted in *Selected Writings of Edward Sapir*, edited by D. Mandelbaum, Berkeley: University of California Press, 1949.

[138] Ernest R. Hilgard, "Human Motives and the Concept of the Self," *The American Psychologist*, Vol. 4, 1949, p. 374 (Presidential Address, American Psychological Association, 1949).

modified or combined with learning theory, and related to cultural or sociological material. What is particularly impressive is that Freud rather than Jung, Rank, Adler, or other analysts has proved to be the most influential figure, although Kluckhohn draws attention to the fact that Radin, in the late twenties, predicted that Jung would have a greater influence than the others.[139] In his recent discussion of *Jung's Psychology and Its Social Meaning*, Progoff stresses the fact that "In the United States, Radin's work stands out as the major exception to current academic anthropological views and the general lack of appreciation for Jung's concepts."[140] On the other hand, Radin appears to entertain critical reservations of the most fundamental

[139] Kluckhohn's reference is to "History of Ethnological Theories," *American Anthropologist*, 31, 1929, pp. 26–30, where Radin says: "It is the application of the psycho-analytical theories of Jung that is most likely to have the most profound influence upon ethnology. This is, after all, to be expected, if for no other reason than that Jung's attitude, in addition to containing entirely new concepts introduced by him, represents in a manner, the synthesis of current theories of psycho-analysis." Cf. *Social Anthropology*, New York, 1932, p. 16. In a journal promoted by Radin in the 1920's in which the "functional, dynamic, and human side of primitive culture" was to be particularly stressed, along with the psychological, the approach to Winnebago Myth Cycles employed was explicitly attributed to Jung. (*Primitive Culture. An International Journal Devoted to the Study of Social Anthropology*. Only a single issue, dated July 1926, appeared.) A four-fold chronological sequence was suggested which corresponds, says Radin, "to what I take to be the substance of Jung's theory. The Trickster period would then represent his undifferentiated, the Hare his imperfectly differentiated, the Red-Horn his well-differentiated, and the Twin his integrated libido" (pp. 12–13). Only the first cycle (the Trickster) was published in *Primitive Culture*. In a later publication which contains all four cycles (*Winnebago Hero Cycles: A Study in Aboriginal Literature*, Supplement to *International Journal of American Linguistics*, Vol. 14, No. 3, Memoir I, July 1948) Radin does not explicitly refer to the earlier publication of the Trickster Cycle in *Primitive Culture*. Nevertheless, he reiterates the fact that "these four cycles, within limits, lend themselves to a definite temporal sequence" (pp. 8–9) without, however, making their Jungian derivation so specific. It may be noted that Radin has contributed articles to *Eranos Jarhbuch*, a publication chiefly devoted to the application of various aspects of Jung's theories.

Kluckhohn likewise makes reference to William Morgan, an American psychiatrist influenced by Jung, who has published on the Navajo. But certainly no American anthropologist of eminence, except Radin, seems to have come under Jung's influence in any respect, although both Kroeber and Sapir reviewed his work at an early date, as well as that of Freud (Kroeber, "Analytical Psychology and Psychology of the Unconscious" in the *American Anthropologist*, 20 (1918); Sapir, "Psychological Types" in *The Freeman*, 8 (1923).

[140] Ira Progoff, *Jung's Psychology and Its Social Meaning*. An introductory statement of C. G. Jung's psychological theories and a first interpretation of their significance for the social science. (New York: The Julian Press, 1953, p. 274.)

nature. "If, for the early evolution of man's culture and thought," he says, anthropologists "cannot accept the findings and conclusions of Freud's psychoanalysis or Jung's complex psychology, they must at least do more than simply state their objections, however justified these appear. They owe it to their subject to attempt to utilize as many as possible of the suggestions Freud, Jung, and their followers have thrown out and the new lines of inquiry they have initiated, this, despite the fact that they may, as I personally do, disagree fundamentally with the viewpoint, the methods, and the conclusions of the latter."[141]

In England, Seligman applied Jung's psychology of types to both "savage" and "civilized" peoples in his Presidential Address to the Royal Anthropological Institute in 1924. Subsequently, John Layard, although not a professional anthropologist in the strictest sense of the term, but whose *Stone Men of Malekula*, 1942, reports the field work he did in the New Hebrides many years before, has made systematic use of Jungian psychology. His interpretations of the significance of the incest tabu, marriage sections in Australia and Ambrym, myths, ceremonies, and other cultural data in these terms lead to highly novel results.[142]

III. Current Developments and Future Trends

While the importance of psychoanalytic theory as the major stimulus which promoted the most striking and novel psychological inquiries and hypotheses developed by twentieth century anthropology should not be minimized, I venture to say that this specific impetus already has passed its peak. So far as the future relations of

[141] Paul Radin, *Winnebago Hero Cycles, op. cit.*

[142] See in particular "The Incest Taboo and the Virgin Archetype," *Eranos-Jahrbuch*, 12 (1945), pp. 254–307 (this volume was a *Festgabe* for Jung on the occasion of his 70th birthday); "Primitive Kinship as Mirrored in the Psychological Structure of Modern Man," *British Journal of Medical Psychology*, Vol. 20 (1944–1946), pp. 118–134; "The Making of Man in Malekula," *Eranos-Jahrbuch*, 16 (1949), pp. 209–283; "Der Mythos der Totenfahrt auf Malekula," *ibid.* (1937); "Maze Dances and the Ritual of the Labyrinth in Malekula," *Folk-Lore*, 47 (1936). Layard is likewise the author of *The Lady of the Hare* (London: Faber and Faber, 1944). This is a study of the healing power of dreams, in which the author presents a detailed documentary account of an analysis of a woman which he made in which the hare is a central image; the latter part of the book is a comparative study of the mythology of the hare on a world-wide basis.

anthropology and psychology are concerned in the development of a science of social man the ground is already prepared for what may prove to be further influences emanating from psychology rather than from psychoanalytic psychiatry. Furthermore, it seems likely that such influences will turn out to be much more positive and fructifying than those exerted at any period in the past for several reasons. First, anthropologists are rapidly developing a better psychological perspective relative to their own data; secondly, certain lines of specialized inquiry in psychology are more directly related to the interests of anthropologists than ever before; and, in the third place, psychologists are becoming more acutely aware of the data of anthropology and their relation to their own inquiries. There are a number of focal areas in which developments are now taking place which are of direct concern to anthropologists.

1. Personality Theory and Personality Tests. Personality theory is now being rapidly assimilated into general psychology. In a recent chapter dealing with this area of inquiry MacKinnon and Maslow conclude their historical review as follows:[143]

> The field of personality is extraordinarily rich in fascinating hunches, hypotheses, and theories. These have come in greatest number and with greatest richness from psychiatrists and clinicians, who, however, have not been noted as a group for experimental emphasis or methodological sophistication. Fortunately, there are mounting signs of an integration of personality theory into the general theory of psychology. To the extent that a true rapprochement is achieved, psychology will increasingly focus its attention upon the more dynamic and more molar aspects of behavior, and in turn, the various and often conflicting theories of personality development, structure, and function will be subjected to the test of rigorous scientific investigation which alone can yield the facts required for their ultimate rejection, modification, or validation.

Anthropologists who are interested in personality and culture will have to keep abreast of such developments in psychology and it may be that psychiatry will be vitally influenced by anthropology and psychology rather than the reverse. It has been said already that "psychiatry rests upon three main disciplines, medicine, psychology,

[143] Donald W. MacKinnon and A. H. Maslow, "Personality," Chapter 13, Harry Helson, ed., in *Theoretical Foundations of Psychology*, New York: Van Nostrand, 1951. See also, Donald W. MacKinnon, "Fact and Fancy in Personality Research" in *The American Psychologist*, Vol. 8, 1953, pp. 138–146, and Robert Leeper, "Current Trends in Theories of Personality" in *Current Trends in Psychological Theory*, Pittsburgh: U. of Pittsburgh Press, 1951.

and social anthropology. In this framework psychology is conceived of as dealing broadly with behavior, but more particularly with psychodynamics. Psychodynamics is mainly now a clinical and speculative subject. The challenge to psychology is to help put it on a scientific basis. There is little evidence that the job can be done alone by psychiatry."[144] A specific example which may be indicative of a general trend is the position taken by Whiting and Child in their recent study of child training and personality. Their investigation is "oriented toward testing generalized hypotheses applicable to any case" rather than "toward seeking concrete understanding of specific cases. . . . Most studies which have been concerned with general hypotheses about culture and personality," they write, "have tended to express those hypotheses in terms of the concepts of psychoanalytic theory. Here we differ sharply from our predecessors. We have preferred to use, to a much greater extent, concepts drawn from the general behavior theory that has been developed by academic and experimental psychologists."[145]

A somewhat analogous situation is emerging in the case of personality tests. Those of the projective type, of which the Rorschach and the Thematic Apperceptive Test are representative and most widely used, came out of the clinic rather than the psychological laboratory. Herman Rorschach was a Swiss psychiatrist; Henry A. Murray, the inventor of the TAT has a psychiatric as well as a psychological background. Both tests have been used by psychiatrists and clinical psychologists, but it is psychologists who are now undertaking the task of appraising their validity and reliability in a rigorous fashion. American anthropologists first began to use the Rorschach test in their studies of personality and culture in the late 1930's and, somewhat later, the TAT.[146] Much of the work done so

[144] Paul E. Huston, "Some Observations on the Orientation of Clinical Psychology," *The American Psychologist*, Vol. 8, 1953, p. 196. See likewise *Psychiatry and Medical Education*, Report of the 1951 Conference held at Cornell University, Ithaca, N.Y., June 21–27, 1951, Organized and Conducted by the American Psychiatric Association and the Association of American Medical Colleges, Washington: American Psychiatric Association, 1952, Chapter 5, "Human Ecology and Personality in the Training of Physicians."

[145] Whiting and Child, *op. cit.*, pp. 5 and 13.

[146] See A. Irving Hallowell, "The Rorschach Technique in the Study of Personality and Culture," *American Anthropologist*, Vol. 47, 1945, pp. 195–210, and Jules Henry and Melford E. Spiro, "Psychological Techniques: Projective Tests in Field Work" in A. L. Kroeber, ed., *Anthropology Today, An Encyclopedic Inventory*, Chicago: University of Chicago Press, 1953.

far has been of a pioneer nature, carried on during a period when even clinical psychologists made less use of the Rorschach than today. Elsewhere[147] I have discussed this technique in relation to personality and culture studies, as well as to certain broad theoretical issues that concern the nature and condition of human perception, based upon an overall appraisal of the protocols we now have from hundreds of individuals with varying cultural backgrounds in different parts of the world. In the conclusion to this paper, I have stressed the following points: (a) the importance of adequate training for those who propose to use the test; (b) the necessity for carefully evaluating its possibilities, as well as its limitations, in relation to the aims of a systematically designed study; (c) the presentation of the results obtained in accordance with the same requirements demanded of those who use the Rorschach in clinical practice; (d) and that such results be subjected to the same standards of evaluation. In order that such standards be met a closer cooperation will be necessary with psychologists who are using the test as well as with those who are appraising it. At the same time, the results obtained from the use of the Rorschach by anthropologists should be greatly enhanced.

2. **Learning Theory.** Learning theory is one of the most highly specialized areas of recent psychological research, especially in the United States. Developments in this field cannot be neglected in the future by the psychologically oriented anthropologist who is interested in a science of social man. Learning theory is as relevant to a deeper understanding of the nature of culture viewed in terms of the remarkable persistence of characteristic patterns in time and the processes of culture change and acculturation, as it is to an understanding of the psychological aspects of the socialization process and the acquisition of a personality structure by the individual. Nevertheless, within psychoanalytic theory there is very little attention paid to learning. What has been stressed, on the contrary, is a succession of developmental stages closely correlated with maturational processes. However firm the evidence for any such stages may turn out to be,[148] a ubiquitous succession of this sort does not help us

147 A. Irving Hallowell, "The Rorschach Test in Personality and Culture Studies" in Bruno Klopfer, ed., *Further Contributions to the Rorschach Technique*, Vol. II, *Applications*. (In press.)
148 In cooperation with members of the Gesell Institute of Child Development, Margaret Mead and Frances Cooke Macgregor (*Growth and Culture. A*

to understand how differential personality characteristics, which have group as well as idiosyncratic dimensions, are acquired, or the psychological consequences of what is learned in one society as compared with another. Consequently, Murdock[149] has called for an integration, at the level of theory, of contributions from psychoanalysis and psychiatry relating to personality development, of contributions from behavioristic psychology to learning theory, combined with the contributions of sociology and cultural anthropology. And, at the beginning of their exposition of "A Dynamic Theory of Personality" Mower and Kluckhohn explicitly state that they have drawn upon "three relatively independent lines of scientific development: psychoanalysis, social anthropology, and the psychology of learning."[150] Personality theory and learning theory cannot be divorced from each other in a developing science of social man because the persistent attributes of a socio-cultural system are dependent upon psychological processes. The very existence of a culture is dependent upon the fact that certain aspects of it become an integral part of the functioning individual. Tolman has remarked that "psychology is in large part a study of the internalization of society and of culture within the individual human actor,"[151] and Newcomb speaks of the individual as having "somehow got society inside himself. Its ways of doing things become his own."[152] If this were not so no one could live his culture nor could he hand it on. A science of social man demands reliable knowledge of the learning process; the recognition of the bare fact that learning occurs or *ad hoc* references to this

---

Photographic Study of Balinese Childhood, Based upon Photographs by Gregory Bateson, Analyzed in Gesell Categories, New York: G. P. Putnam Sons, 1951) have attacked this problem and presented results which show certain broad similarities as well as significant differences in developmental patterns.

[149] George P. Murdock, "The Science of Human Learning, Society, Culture, and Personality," *Scientific Monthly*, Vol. 69, 1949, pp. 377–381.

[150] O. H. Mower and Clyde Kluckhohn, "Dynamic Theory of Personality" in *Personality and the Behavior Disorders*, edited by J. McV. Hunt, New York: Ronald Press, 1944, Vol. 1, pp. 69–135. The learning theory used is of the S-R type. It is stated (p. 79) that "the great unifying principle in the version of learning theory that is here espoused is the proposition that all behavior is *motivated* and that all learning involves reward."

[151] E. C. Tolman in Talcott Parsons and Edward A. Shils, eds., *Toward A General Theory of Action*, Cambridge: Harvard University Press, 1951, p. 359.

[152] Theodore M. Newcomb, *Social Psychology*, New York: Dryden, 1950, p. 6. See likewise Melford E. Spiro, "Culture and Personality: The Natural History of a False Dichotomy," *Psychiatry*, Vol. 14, 1951, pp. 19–46, and Talcott Parsons, "The Superego and the Theory of Social Systems," *ibid.*, Vol. 15, 1952, pp. 15–25.

process in connection with certain problems can only lead to the oversimplification or distortion of vital questions.

Many years ago (1927) A. A. Goldenweiser made some observations on the "Psychological Postulates of Evolution" during the course of which he attempted to draw an analogy between the process of cultural change and the learning process. His hypothesis was that since cultural change involves the overcoming of the inertia of past habits there is a period of delay during which cumulative pressures build up ("or psychologically, summation of stimuli") followed by the overcoming of resistance so that "the change comes— with a spurt." He then goes on to say that "we know from the study of the learning process that it is not gradual but jerky. So also with culture, for, from one angle, culture is learning and the psychology also is the same. The delay comes from inertia due to pre-existing habits, only that in the case of culture the inertia of the individual is greatly reinforced by institutional inertia. This lengthens the delay and adds to the explosive character of the change when it does come."[153] Surely, a little knowledge is a dangerous thing. While learning theory is relevant to the empirical facts of culture change, the analogical approach of Goldenweiser is misleading and irrelevant.

Although the need for reliable knowledge about the learning process is generally recognized, nevertheless the fact remains, as Newman says, that "there is no single theory of learning. Perhaps there cannot be." At the same time there is no lack of learning *theories* and these theories reflect, as in a mirror, various psychological orientations. "Ask a psychologist," continues Newman, "what is his view of learning and you will discover his scientific credo, his beliefs and prejudices, his love of empirical fact, of deductive elegance, of operational rigor, of didactic power."[154] The uses of learning theory already made by some anthropologists reflect this very fact. So far, the

[153] Goldenweiser, "Anthropology and Psychology," reprinted in *History, Psychology and Culture,* copyright by Alfred A. Knopf, Inc. p. 74.

[154] Edwin B. Newman, "Learning" in *Theoretical Foundations of Psychology,* New York: Van Nostrand, 1951, p. 390. For other surveys and discussions of learning theory see, in particular, Ernest R. Hilgard, *Theories of Learning,* New York: Appleton-Century, 1948; James J. Gibson, "The Implications of Learning Theory for Social Psychology" in M. J. G. Miller, ed., *Experiments in Social Process: A Symposium on Social Psychology,* New York: McGraw-Hill, 1950; and for current trends in "perceptual learning" theory, Harry F. Harlow, "Learning Theories," Wayne Dennis, Robert Leeper, et al., in *Current Trends in Psychological Theory,* Pittsburgh: University of Pittsburgh Press, 1951.

behavioristic theory of Hull has furnished the major model.[155] Gillin
has made use of it in his text, *The Ways of Men*. John Whiting uses
this model of learning theory systematically in his analysis of the
acquisition of Kwoma culture by the child, and Beatrice Whiting in
her analysis of patterns of social control.[156] Miller and Dollard's book,
Social Learning and Imitation, representing the same point of view,
contains a chapter on "Copying in the Diffusion of Culture." "Copying can become an acquired drive," they write, "providing copying
behavior has become rewarded. Conditions of social contact offer the
best opportunity for rapid copying, since they bring the learner into
contact with the model and critic who can rapidly elicit the correct
response. The prestige of the model is the crucial matter in mobi-
lizing the copying drive and setting in motion the attempt to match
responses. Copying is rarely exact, owing to various circumstances,
chief among them the pressure put on the incoming habit by the pre-
existing matrix of the receiving culture."[157] Gillin[158] and Hallowell[159] have made use of the Miller-Dollard paradigm of learning
in relation to acculturation, Horton[160] in his cross-cultural study of
alcoholism, and Holmberg[161] in his analysis of the effects of the
frustration of the hunger drive among the Siriono. Spiro, on the

[155] The reason particular anthropologists have turned to S-R learning theory
seems to have been largely circumstantial. For, in fact, both Tolman and Lewin
were concerned with social learning and applied their theories in this area, but
up to the present time they have not exercised any discernible influence on
anthropologists.

[156] John W. M. Whiting, *Becoming a Kwoma: Teaching and Learning in a
New Guinea Tribe*, New Haven: Yale University Press, 1941; Beatrice B. Whit-
ing, "Paiute Sorcery," *Viking Fund Publications in Anthropology*, No. 15, New
York: Wenner-Gren Foundation, 1950.

[157] Neal E. Miller and John Dollard, *Social Learning and Imitation*, New
Haven: Yale University Press, 1941. In their preface the authors state their obligation to "Prof. George P. Murdock for aid in preparing the chapter on diffusion and for a most helpful reading of the manuscript as a whole. Prof. B.
Malinowski gave us a single, but significant, interview in the diffusion problem."

[158] John Gillin, "Parallel Cultures and the Inhibitions to Acculturation in a
Guatemalan Community," *Social Forces*, March, 1945; "Acquired Drives in
Culture Contact," *American Anthropologist*, Vol. 44, 1942, pp. 545–554.

[159] A. Irving Hallowell, "Sociopsychological Aspects of Acculturation" in
The Science of Man in the World Crisis, Ralph Linton, ed., New York: Columbia University Press, 1945.

[160] Donald Horton, "The Functions of Alcohol in Primitive Societies: A
Cross-Cultural Study," *Quarterly Journal of Studies on Alcohol*, Vol. 4, 1943,
pp. 199–320.

[161] Allan R. Holmberg, *Nomads of the Long Bow. The Siriono of Eastern
Bolivia*, Smithsonian Institution, Institute of Social Anthropology, Pub. No. 10,
Washington: United States Government Printing Office, 1950.

other hand, turning to learning theories for assistance in explaining
the process by which the Ifaluk acquire a belief in malevolent ghosts,
expresses the opinion that "social scientists may have been too hasty
in accepting the experimental laws of learning because some cultural
phenomena, at least, cannot be explained by current learning
theories."[162] And in Gibson's opinion the experimentally founded
theories, such as Hull's, "do *not* fit the facts of social learning in one
important respect. As now formulated, they do not account for the
astonishing prevalence of moral behavior among human adults." The
need for a theory of *social* learning is, therefore, acute and Gibson
warns that, "If the social psychologist does not formulate a theory
of learning, the cultural anthropologist will have to do so—and
also the psychiatrist, the clinician, the educator, and the student of
child development."[163]

One anthropologist, Gregory Bateson,[164] has made an important
contribution to learning theory. Harry F. Harlow, an exponent of
perceptual learning theory writes: "After we had published a formulation of our theory we found that it had in principle already been
proposed by the anthropologist Bateson, who had described the
phenomenon as 'deutero-learning' and had italicized the words which
we believed most descriptive of the theory, the animal *learns to
learn*. Our contribution has been to provide extensive, rigidly controlled experimental data in support of such a theoretical formulation. Bateson wrote: 'We need some systematic framework or classification which shall show how each of these habits is related to the
others, and such a classification might provide us with something
approaching the chart we lack.' Our own researches, we believe,
provide or have begun to provide this 'systematic framework.' Bate-

[162] Melford E. Spiro, "Ghosts: An Anthropological Inquiry into Learning
and Perception," *Journal of Abnormal and Social Psychology*, Vol. 48, 1953,
pp. 376–382.

[163] Gibson, *op. cit.*, pp. 151 and 152. As examples of collaborative efforts he
cites Mowrer and Kluckhohn, Miller and Dollard, and the report of a committee
of the National Society for the Study of Education, 1942. For an appraisal of
learning theory with special reference to the concept of culture used by Miller
and Dollard, see Omar K. Moore and Donald J. Lewis, "Learning Theory and
Culture," *Psychological Review*, Vol. 59, 1952, pp. 380–388. Moore is a sociologist, Lewis a psychologist.

[164] Gregory Bateson, "Social Planning and the Concept of Deutero-learning"
in *Science, Philosophy and Religion*, Second Symposium, New York: Conference on Science, Philosophy and Religion, 1942, pp. 81–97. Reprinted in
abridged form in T. H. Newcomb and E. L. Hartley, eds., *Readings in Social
Psychology*, New York: Holt, 1947, pp. 121–128.

son in his paper discusses the anthropological implications of such a theory. We have indicated its possible role in personality formation in a theoretical paper."[165] Mutual influences of this sort indicate, in principle, the possible benefits for a developing science of social man that can be derived from the coordination of knowledge in psychology and anthropology in a single problem area.

3. **Social Psychology.** The tardy development of a theoretically mature and experimentally oriented social psychology has handicapped the relations between anthropology and psychology in the past. "The rapid growth and transformation of social psychology," says Brewster Smith, "has come only in the recent postwar years."[166] Just as in the case of learning theory, there is no united front in social psychology. But it is perhaps significant that social psychologies written from a Gestalt point of view have commanded more and more attention. Krech and Crutchfield have argued recently, moreover, that general psychology *is* social psychology:

. . . not only do the same fundamental principles apply to both social and non-social behavior, but the general psychologist as well as the social psychologist is literally forced to study the behavior of man as a social being. Whether we are studying the behavior of man in a laboratory, in the clinic, or in a crowd, whether we are studying his perception of colored papers, his performance on an intelligence test, or his decision about participating in a lynching, we are studying the behavior of a man as influenced by his past and present interpersonal relationships reaching into each of his psychological activities no matter how simple or apparently remote. As a consequence every man lives in a social world, and no psychologist, whatever his interests, does or can study the behavior of an asocial man.[167]

Whatever the reaction to such a statement on the part of psychologists may be, it is thoroughly intelligible, and even acceptable, to many anthropologists. It is the kind of position that could become a common meeting ground. At the same time it is a far cry from the

---

[165] Harry F. Harlow, "Levels of Integration Along the Phylogenetic Scale. Learning Aspect" in *Social Psychology at the Crossroads*, edited by J. H. Rohrer and M. Sherif, New York: Harper and Brothers, 1951, pp. 138–139, and "The Formation of Learning Sets" *Psychological Review*, Vol. 56, 1949, pp. 51–65. For comments on Harlow and with references to culture see also O. Hobart Mowrer, *Learning Theory and Personality Dynamics*, New York: Ronald Press, 1950, pp. 332 ff.

[166] M. Brewster Smith, Review, "Some Recent Texts in Social Psychology," *Psychological Bulletin*, Vol. 50, 1953, p. 150.

[167] By permission from *Theory and Problems of Social Psychology*, by David Krech and Richard S. Crutchfield, copyright 1948, McGraw-Hill Book Company, Inc., pp. 7–8.

position which Kroeber, Lowie, and Wissler identified as characteristic of psychologists. But it is close to that of Bartlett, whom Krech
regards as a pioneer[168] and, farther back, we cannot but recall the
implications of the position taken by the Herbartians—Waitz and
Bastian. They, too, would probably have accepted this fundamental
frame of reference, as would Rivers, Seligman, or Boas.

The major implication of this psychological orientation in contrast to that of the traditional experimental psychologist, is that
whereas the latter, as Krech points out, "has always assumed, usually
implicitly, that in studying perception, for example, he was studying a process independent of the social background, affiliations,
prejudices, and values of the receiver,"—and that "among the variables which the perception psychologist, or the learning psychologist included in this theoretical model of the perceiver and learner
there was no room for social values and mores," the former assumes
that "every basic psychological process of man—his perception,
learning, remembering, wanting, feeling, etc.—must be understood
within the social context of the perceiver, the learner, the remem-
berer, the wanting man."[169] Although Krech does not explicitly say
so, it is obvious that the cross-cultural data of the anthropologist
are directly relevant to the investigation of such processes. Not only
the personality structure but the complex relations that exist between such processes as those mentioned and the psychological field
of behavior as structured by the cultural variables that characterize
different socio-cultural systems, suggest special problems for inquiry.

A number of psychologists have become interested in "social
perception," and the relation of perception and personality.[170] "How-

[168] David Krech, "Psychological Theory and Social Psychology" in Harry
Nelson, ed., *Theoretical Foundations of Psychology*, New York: Van Nostrand,
1951, p. 666. Referring to Bartlett's *Remembering* (1932) Krech says: "Here, for
the first time, was the principle generalized that while there appeared to be
universal laws of memory and perception, the nature of these processes and
the specific errors in memory and perception which people made could not be
understood except in terms of the cultural backgrounds and socially determined
interests and mores of the subjects."
[169] Krech, *ibid.*, p. 665.
[170] See J. S. Bruner and Leo Postman, "An Approach to Social Perception"
in *Current Trends in Social Psychology*, Pittsburgh: University of Pittsburgh
Press, 1948; Robert R. Blake and Glenn V. Ramsey, eds., *Perception: An Approach to Personality*, New York: Ronald Press, 1951. Wayne Dennis has a
chapter in this volume dealing with "Cultural and Developmental Factors in
Perception."

222 Psychology and Culture

ever varied the terminology," writes Gibson, "a central conviction is shared by these students of social perception: they are sure that the doctrine of the passive perceiver who simply mirrors the world is a myth and is now disposed of for good. What a man perceives, they say, depends on his personality and his culture. Men of different cultures perceive quite different worlds. There are, in short, folkways of perception." But Gibson advises caution in drawing any categorical conclusion without qualification. He goes on to say that "an enthusiasm for social psychology and a sense of the urgency of its problems is something that I share. But I cannot agree with the social perceptionists that the kind of problems they study are the prototype of all problems in perception. I would be willing to agree with them that all perception is in a certain sense socialized perception if they were willing to agree in turn that all perception is just as truly psychophysical perception."[171] However this issue may be resolved, it is of vital interest from an anthropological[172] as well as a psychological point of view and its solution is of fundamental importance to a science of social man.

4. **Human Nature.** Asch, in the first chapter of his *Social Psychology*, reaffirms the notion that "it is the goal of psychology to furnish a comprehensive doctrine of man, one that will provide a tested foundation for the social sciences." At the basis of these disciplines, he says, "there must be a *comprehensive conception of human nature*"[173] (italics ours). Almost twenty years before this volume appeared Paul Radin at the very end of his book *The Method and Theory of Ethnology*, expressed the view that the study of cultural anthropology ultimately led to the same central problem, but he was inclined to look to psychoanalysis for illumination. "Before concluding," he wrote, "let me refer briefly and superficially to what is perhaps the core of all investigations of culture: can we ever arrive at any satisfactory knowledge of what constitutes human nature? To say with Boas and so many ethnologists and sociologists that the culture picture hides this knowledge from us forever is a counsel of

[171] James J. Gibson, "Theories of Perception" in *Current Trends in Psychological Theory*, Pittsburgh: University of Pittsburgh Press, 1951, pp. 94–95, and *The Perception of the Visual World*, Boston: Houghton Mifflin, 1950.

[172] See, for example, Verne F. Ray, "Techniques and Problems in the Study of Human Color Perception," *Southwestern Journal of Anthropology*, Vol. 8, 1952, pp. 251–259; A. Irving Hallowell, "Cultural Factors in the Structuralization of Perception" in *Social Psychology at the Crossroads*.

[173] Asch, *op. cit.*, copyright 1953 by Prentice-Hall, Inc., New York, p. 5.

despair. Some significant light can surely be obtained, even if today the technique for this type of investigation has not as yet been perfected. Here again I feel that a psychoanalyst like Jung is on the correct trail."[174] More recently, Kroeber (1948) construing "human nature" as the "original" or "the general nature of man" views it as "a pretty vague and uncharacterized thing," perhaps a limiting factor in cultural development, but certainly not related causally to the manifold forms that culture assumes. He records his impression that, "psychologists have become very unwilling to discuss the inherent psychic nature of man. It is definitely unfashionable to do so. When the subject is faced at all, it is usually only to explain human nature away as fast as possible, and to pass on to less uneasy and more specific topics. Human nature is going the way the human 'mind' has gone. Instead, psychologists for the last few decades have increasingly dealt with the concept of personality."[175]

Although the term human nature has assumed a variety of meanings and so has become a weasel word, there are signs that the concept is far from moribund and that it may yet be given a more specific meaningful content which will prove to be of heuristic value in a science of social man. It is not likely, of course, that separately either psychologists or anthropologists will be able to formulate "a comprehensive conception of human nature." Besides, psychoanalytic theory is of great importance here. Roheim introduces his chapter on "The Unity of Mankind" with the quotation from Kroeber cited above and takes modern cultural anthropologists to task because of their negative attitude towards such unity.[176] Recently, however, there appears to be a developing interest in this topic on the anthropological side as represented, for example, in such publications as those of Bidney, Spiro, and Washburn.[177] Kluckhohn's

[174] Paul Radin, The Method and Theory of Ethnology, New York: McGraw-Hill, 1933, p. 267.

[175] A. L. Kroeber, Anthropology, New York: Harcourt, 1948, p. 619.

[176] Geza Roheim, Psychoanalysis and Anthropology: Culture, Personality, and the Unconscious, New York: International Universities Press, 1950. "The culturalist school will have nothing to do with a basic unity of mankind," he says (p. 489) and, "modern or 'cultural' anthropology tacitly negates the basic unity of mankind as well as the separateness of the individual—it sees only nations" (p. 491).

[177] David Bidney, "Human Nature and the Cultural Process," American Anthropologist, Vol. 49, 1947, pp. 375–399; Melford E. Spiro, "Human Nature in Its Psychological Dimensions," ibid. (in press); S. L. Washburn, "Evolution and Human Nature," ibid. (in press).

discussion of "Universal Categories of Culture" is focused in the same direction,[178] and Redfield has made some pertinent observations. Among other things he says: "In this territory we find ourselves characterizing human nature as a recognized and respectable subject matter of our science, and it is no surprise that certain branches of psychology and sociology have anticipated us. What is creditable to anthropology is that we learn from them. What is creditable to them is that they often modify their views under our influence. But conjointly this area of investigation is now opened. . . ."[179]

On the phylogenetic side, man's psychological distinctiveness from other primates, rather than any capacities or characteristics he may share with them now needs to be as closely examined and discriminated as does his morphological and physiological distinction from them.[180] Kenneth Oakley has observed that despite the fact that man "has been described as the reasoning animal, the religious animal, the talking animal, the tool-making animal, and so on, we are still in need of a working definition of man."[181] Any such definition, any answer to the query, What is man? involves the question, What is human nature? and in particular, the psychological distinctiveness of man. It is significant that LeGros Clark has expressed the opinion that "probably the differentiation of man from ape will ultimately have to rest on a *functional* rather than on an anatomical basis, the criterion of humanity being the ability to speak and to make tools"[182]

[178] Clyde Kluckhohn, "Universal Categories of Culture" in *Anthropology Today*.

[179] Robert Redfield in his discussion of "Culture, Personality and Society," the paper contributed by A. I. Hallowell to *Anthropology Today* in *An Appraisal of Anthropology Today*, edited by Sol Tax, Loren C. Eiseley, Irving Rouse, Carl F. Vogelin, Chicago: University of Chicago Press, 1953, p. 127. For a set of working assumptions regarding the nature of man used in applied social science see Alexander H. Leighton, *The Government of Men*, Princeton: Princeton University Press, 1945, Part II and Appendix; and *Human Relations in a Changing World: Observations on the Use of the Social Sciences* by the same author, New York: Dutton, 1949.

[180] See in particular, T. C. Schneirla, "Levels in the Psychological Capacities of Animals" in *Philosophy for the Future*, edited by Roy W. Sellars, V. J. McGill, Marvin Farber, New York: Macmillan, 1949; and Henry W. Nissen, "Phylogenetic Comparisons" in S. S. Stevens, ed., *Handbook of Experimental Psychology*, 1951.

[181] Kenneth Oakley, "A Definition of Man," *Science News*, 20, Penguin Books, 1951.

[182] W. E. LeGros Clark, *History of the Primates: An Introduction to the Study of Fossil Man*, 2nd ed., London: Handbook, British Museum, Department of Geology, 1950, p. 73.

(italics ours). But what underlies man's capacities, not only for speaking and tool-making, but the creation of manifold *varieties* of speech forms and technologies, world-views, value systems, and other forms of culture? What enables him to maintain them, elaborate them, change them and to readjust himself to influences derived from alien culture patterns?

It can hardly be maintained that man's peculiar and unique psychological characteristics are fully understood, despite the increasing depth and breadth of our knowledge derived from comparative psychology. It was only two decades ago that, writing as a mammalogist, G. S. Miller insisted that human sexuality was, for the most part, equivalent with primate sexuality.[183] Ford and Beach, combining data from psychology and cultural anthropology, give us a quite different and more reliable picture of human sexual behavior in phylogenetic perspective.[184] Hilgard, discussing learning theories, has pointed out that sometimes psychologists have given the impression that "there are no differences, except quantitative ones, between the learning of lower animals and primates, including man." He goes on to say, however, that "while this position is more often implied than asserted, it is strange that the opposite view is not more often made explicit—that at the human level there have emerged capacities for retaining, reorganizing, and foreseeing experiences which are not approached by the lower animals, including the other primates. No one has seriously proposed that animals can develop a set of ideals which regulate conduct around long-range plans, or that they can invent a mathematics to help them keep track of their experiences. Because a trained dog shows some manifestations of shame, or a chimpanzee some signs of cooperation, or a rat a dawning concept

[183] G. S. Miller, Jr., "The Primate Basis of Human Sexual Behavior," *Quarterly Review of Biology*, Vol. 6, 1931, pp. 379–410.

"The main characteristics of human sexual behavior, contrary to a widely prevalent belief, are not peculiar to man," the author says. There are only two human "specializations" which "have had any significance in directing the general course of cultural development." The first is "a stronger tendency than most other primates to form continuing sexual partnerships" (this was prior to Carpenter's observations on the monogamous gibbon). The second is "that in man alone of all mammals is the male known to be able to force his sexual will on an unconsenting or unconscious female, a peculiarity that seems to arise from human ingenuity combined with the human pelvic adjustments to the upright posture."

[184] Clellan S. Ford and Frank A. Beach, *Patterns of Sexual Behavior*, New York: Harper and Hoeber, 1951.

of triangularity, it does not follow that these lower organisms, clever as they are, have all the richness of human mental activity."[185]

Harlow, on the basis of animal experimentation, concludes that "the ability of the human animal to form and utilize multiple perceptual learning sets probably differentiates him from other animals to as great a degree as does the ability to utilize spoken language. Even monkeys and chimpanzees show very limited ability to form effective sets to differentiate tiny, detailed stimuli, or tiny, detailed variations between stimuli, in contrast to the human being whose incredible skill along these lines enables him to read the *Scientific American*, *Time*, the *Reader's Digest*, the *Daily Worker*, and the *Chicago Tribune*."[186] Harlow does not point out that still other capacities of man enabled him to *invent* systems of writing, the alphabet, and the mechanical means that brought the printed page into existence and that the capacities represented in these inventions and discoveries did not occur among the people of a single culture, or race, nor in an integrated series of learning situations. Whatever may differentiate human learning abilities from those of other animals, such abilities must be assumed to be part of our human nature as are man's capacities, under the necessary motivational conditions, for transcending what he has learned through the reorganization of his knowledge and experience.[187] This would hardly be possible were

[185] Ernest R. Hilgard, *Theories of Learning*, New York: Appleton-Century, 1948, pp. 329–330.

[186] Harry F. Harlow, "Learning Theories" in *Current Trends in Psychological Theory*, 1951, p. 82.

[187] Although H. G. Barnett (*Innovation: The Basis of Cultural Change*, New York: McGraw-Hill, 1953) does not explicitly phrase the question with reference to human nature, nevertheless, the fundamental position he assumes and the fact that he has attempted to formulate "a general theory of the nature of innovation" strikes a new note in anthropological inquiry which is also bound to be of interest to sociologists and psychologists. "Students of the history of cultural growth," he says, "have been forced to answer the question of human inventiveness in their efforts to interpret the meaning of multiple occurrences of the same phenomena in different ethnic groups" (p. 18). But back of all interpretations (not only diffusionist or evolutionary, but the more intermediary position of American ethnologists) there lies the tendency to accept "one of two antithetical propositions relative to human inventiveness" (p. 17): human beings are believed to be either fundamentally creative or uncreative. One of the major difficulties that has stood in the way of resolving this antithesis has been conceptual. An understanding of the sources of cultural change at the grass roots level has been blocked by definitions of invention that "place the emphasis, not upon change itself, but upon estimates of its significance. They rate individual variation in terms of its degree, in terms of attitudes toward it, or in terms of its cultural consequences . . . a vast amount of such variation is ignored

it not for a unique but ubiquitous feature of man's psychological structuralization. This is the emergence of a dominant integrative center of the human personality and the development of ego-centered processes which permit self-objectification and likewise a basic orientation in a self-other dimension. A world of objects other than self, as well as the self as an object, necessarily emerge in the socialization process, although they have a varied cultural content given them.[188] Another unique facet of the psychological structure of man that distinguishes him from any other animal is the superego which, as Parsons says, "must be understood in terms of the relation between personality and the total common culture, by virtue of which a stable system of social interaction on the human level becomes possible." Ego-centered processes are modified by the internalization of attitudes and values derived from the cultural system in which the individual is socialized. The distinctive psychological structuralization of men, the novel qualitative features that characterize the psychodynamics of a human level of adjustment, combined with the generic capabilities of man that are rooted in the phylogenetic status of our species, lie at the very core of our human nature.

Viewed functionally and historically, it appears to be the indeterminate aspect of man's nature that makes him unique, the inherent potentialities of which, under the necessary motivational conditions, may lead to new and varied forms of social, cultural, and psychological adjustment. These potentialities can only be fully appreciated if, instead of looking backward from our present point of temporal vantage and contemporary knowledge, we select an earlier

---

because it does not fall within the arbitrarily established range of novelty. It is passed over if it does not elicit comment, or if it is not repeated or imitated, or if it otherwise is without lasting effects. The problem of change is thus shunted into the problem of measuring it." Barnett then goes on to point out that in actual fact "nothing is more common or certain than individual variability in concept or reaction." This is the source of variations that are labelled innovations because they acquire social significance. "Their fate is something apart from their origins . . . change as such is a universal phenomenon. Human beings have an infinite capacity for responding divergently. . . ." (p. 19.) If this proposition is acceptable, its significance for a science of social man cannot be overrated.

[188] Asch, op. cit., Chapter 10, "The Ego," and A. Irving Hallowell, "Personality Structure and the Evolution of Man," American Anthropologist, Vol. 52, 1950, pp. 159–173; and "The Self and Its Behavioral Environment" in Explorations, Feb., 1954.

point in time and, looking forward imaginatively, compare what we know now about the culture history of man with what could only have been speculation then. Human behavior *is* relative to traditional culture patterns and historic circumstances but, at the same time, it is relative to unrealized potentialities that inhere in man's human nature and which permit the emergence of novelty in his mode of life. One of the great weaknesses of theories of cultural evolution which have stressed a series of inevitable stages in linear succession, as well as of diffusionist theories and doctrines of geographic or cultural determinism, has been an inadequate conception of the distinctive psychological nature of man.

Perhaps it is characteristic of man to be always different yet always the same. Perhaps this is what anthropologists have sensed without formulating it, since in moving from one people to another the field worker always has assumed that there were both psychological and cultural constants to be expected: identifiable emotions such as sorrow or hate, self-awareness and reflective thought, a scheme of moral values, a world view, tools, etc. Perhaps Pascal went to the heart of the matter when he said that the "nature of man is his whole nature." Eighteenth-century philosophers looked for what was common to man everywhere and identified what they found with the "natural" in contrast with customs that were local and provincial and consequently not related to human nature. On the other hand, anthropologists were, at first, more concerned with cultural differences than with cultural universals and they have been inclined to overstress cultural relativism. But cultural diversities and common denominators of culture[189] are part of the total human picture; both categories of phenomena must be related to the whole nature of man. Experimental psychologists once sought mainly for constancies, for responses that could be directly related to man's innate biological equipment and which could be taken as representative of the functioning of the human mind under the controlled conditions observed. They ignored the study of man as a social being and the varieties in his culturally constituted mode of life. But can human nature be exclusively identified with what is biologically innate and invariant, when man, the culture-building animal, is constantly reinterpreting his experience, reconstituting his world view, inventing

[189] George P. Murdock, "The Common Denominators of Cultures" in R. Linton, ed., *The Science of Man in the World Crisis*, New York: Columbia University Press, 1945.

new technologies, and adjusting his behavior accordingly? Philosophers once stressed the rational capacity of man; psychoanalysts
have demonstrated the depth of man's irrationality. But cannot potentialities for rational behavior be a part of man's nature at the
same time that unconscious impulses may limit his rationality? Neither rationality nor irrationality taken alone expresses the whole nature of man. Long before the days of psychoanalysis Nietzsche seemed
to have sensed the issue: "Man in contrast to the animals," he said,
"has developed a profusion of contradictory impulses and qualities.
Thanks to this synthesis within his character he could become the
master of the world!" A scientific approach to the question of human
nature demands further knowledge of all the attributes that underlie
the manifold adjustments of a creature that exhibits so complex a
mode of living as man.

SIX

Personality, Culture, and Society
in Behavioral Evolution

1963

INTRODUCTION

One of the most significant contemporary areas of discussion concerning the study of man centers on his social nature, varying modes of cultural adaptations, and their psychological consequences. Although in certain respects this is an old problem, conceptualization and analysis have been rapidly reaching a new level of sophistication. Particularly noteworthy is the convergence of interest manifested by representatives of disciplines which,· in the recent past, made their own abstractions, pursued their own special problems, and often ignored, or paid little attention to, relevant data and theories in other fields. In the historical perspective of a little over a century, it would appear that a cycle is being completed. In the nineteenth century, psychology and anthropology were in their early stages. Boundaries were less sharply drawn; ideas were advanced and problems stated that transcended the more specialized concerns that later characterized both of these disciplines. At that time J. F. Herbart (1776–1841) is said to have "represented a departure from the

From *Psychology: A Study of a Science*, by Sigmund Koch. Copyright 1963 by McGraw-Hill, Inc. Used with permission of McGraw-Hill Book Company.

* Originally prepared for this volume, sections of the manuscript were contributed to the Darwin centennial celebration (University of Chicago, November 24–28, 1959), and were published in *Evolution after Darwin* [224]. Since then, the manuscript has been revised and a new introduction and conclusion included.

dominant associationist school, inasmuch as he conceived of the mind throughout in terms of dynamic forces rather than of passive mechanisms" [63, p. 23][1] and he maintained that "psychology remains incomplete as long as it considers man only as an isolated individual." In fact, "he was convinced that society was a living and organic whole, ruled by psychological laws that are peculiar to it [189, p. 51].

Both Theodore Waitz (1821–1864) and Adolph Bastian (1826–1905), who are numbered among the pioneers of anthropology, were influenced by Herbart. Waitz had published books on psychology a decade before his *Anthropologie der Naturvölker* (1859) appeared. It was soon translated into English. In this book he was concerned with differences in human mentality and the question of national character. He did not believe that national differences could be explained on the basis of race because there are different nationalities within the same race. "It is therefore probable," he said, "that the mental peculiarities of peoples are generally more flexible and changeable than the physical characters of the race, and are transmitted with a less degree of constancy [235, p. 381].[2] Bastian, a tireless world traveler, a voluminous writer, and director of the Berlin Ethnological Museum, argued that a science of mental life must take cognizance of ethnographic data because "the individual's thinking is made possible only by his functioning in a social group [152, p. 36].[3] Lazarus and Steinthal, both Herbartians, were the first to promote *Völkerpsychologie* and it was they who founded the *Zeitschrift für Völkerpsychologie und Sprachwissenschaft*. [See 189, pp. 60 ff.; 123, pp. 42 ff.]

At a later period, Wundt (1832–1921), the founder of experimental psychology, rounded out his life's work with his massive 10-volume *Völkerpsychologie,* in which he attempted to link the study of the individual mind with such historical social products as language, custom, and myth in a comprehensive system, following his principle of "creative synthesis." Allport says:

> The most significant thing about Wundt is his insistence that the study of all higher mental processes falls in the province of *Völkerpsychologie*. He did not believe that individual psychology, especially as pursued in the psychological laboratory, could account for men's thought. Thinking is heavily conditioned by language, by custom, and by myth, which to him were the three primary problem areas of *Völkerpsychologie*. Wundt would have felt at home in modern-day discussions of "social perception" [5, p. 36].

[1] Flugel finds in Herbart's psychological system faint resemblances to Freud. For further information on the relations of Freud and Herbart, see [119, vol. 1, pp. 371 ff.].

[2] For the influence of Herbart on Waitz and Bastian, see [103, p. 380].

[3] For a more extended discussion of Bastian's sociopsychological interests, see [161].

But by the time Wundt had begun to publish the first part of his *Völker-psychologie* (1900), both anthropology and psychology had developed specialized and highly characteristic areas of inquiry.

The new specialization is exemplified by the roles which William McDougall, C. S. Myers, and W. H. R. Rivers played on the Torres Straits expedition (1898), which had been organized by the Cambridge anthropologist A. C. Haddon, and which was characterized by Allport as "a landmark in the collaboration of social scientists" [5, p. 35]. Rivers, for example, had been lecturing on the physiology of the sense organs at Cambridge since 1893 and was responsible for planning the first systematic course in experimental psychology to be given in England. His work in psychophysiology in Torres Straits led him to the conclusion that pure sensory acuity is much the same in all races. Rivers likewise developed the genealogical method, which later became of classical importance in the investigation of the social structures of nonliterate peoples. Looking back, we note that at this period his psychological work and his pioneer work in social anthropology remained unintegrated. By 1916, however, Rivers was asking: "How can you explain the workings of the human mind without a knowledge of the social setting which must have played so great a part in determining the sentiments and opinions of mankind?" [190, p. 2]. But though Rivers touched upon many vital issues, he never initiated serious research along sociopsychological lines [75].

In the early part of this century, it would have been difficult for anyone to have predicted the later convergence of interest which focused upon the social, cultural, and psychological dimensions of man as a social being. Yet if we consider the interests of individuals rather than the manifest programs of disciplines, there are discernible beginnings.

American anthropologists, under the influence of Franz Boas, opposed early instinct doctrines in psychology, the racial interpretation of intelligence tests, and the generic concept of a primitive mind inferior to that of civilized man. Boas, nevertheless, recognized the relevance of psychology at a time when the major interests in physical anthropology, archeology, and cultural anthropology were chiefly descriptive and historical. He held Galton in high esteem and, in his seminars early in this century, discussed Wundt's *Völkerpsychologie*. According to Lowie [153, p. 1011], Wundt was also read "to some extent" by his students (Kroeber, Goldenweiser, Lowie, Haeberlin, Sapir, Reichard). Besides this, Boas delivered a lecture on "Psychological Problems in Anthropology" [18] at the celebration of the twentieth anniversary of Clark University (1909), the historic occasion when G. Stanley Hall invited Freud, Jung, Ferenczi, and Jones, to participate. Lowie says, moreover, that Boas "unremittingly preached the necessity of seeing the native from within" [153, p. 1009], and Benedict has remarked that to him one of the central questions of anthropology was "the relation between the objective world and man's subjective world as it had taken form in different cultures" [15, p. 27].

Perhaps it was no accident that the pioneers in the study of culture and personality—Sapir, Benedict, and Mead—were trained in anthropology by Boas and that early students like Goldenweiser, Haeberlin, Radin, and Lowie were psychologically knowledgeable.[4] At an early date too, Sapir, Goldenweiser, Radin, and Kroeber familiarized themselves with psychoanalytic theory.[5] Kroeber has reported that he practiced psychoanalysis in San Francisco from 1920 to 1923. He says, however, that this experience gave him no insights that helped him "to understand culture any better" [133, p. 300; see also p. 299] and it was the clarification of culture which Kroeber considered "the most significant accomplishment of anthropology in the first half of the twentieth century" [132, p. 87]. Indeed, he showed no enthusiam for the culture and personality studies that emerged later and wrote a negatively toned review (1920) of Freud's *Totem and Taboo* which reflected the general anthropological attitude of the time.[6] Eventually, however, it was an early phase of psychoanalytic theory that inspired culture and personality studies.

Perhaps I have said enough, however sketchily, to indicate ·that— although psychological problems lurked in the background of anthropological thinking, and some anthropologists reacted strongly to psychological theories—no positive focus emerged to link anthropological and psychological concepts and theories during the period when both disciplines were developing their characteristic abstractions, concepts, and specializations. Since the concept of culture has always implied inherent behavioral plasticity and emphasized socially acquired traits as

[4] Haeberlin published an article on Wundt in the *Psychological Review* (1916), and Goldenweiser, besides making frequent references to Wundt in his writings, published an obituary notice in *The Freeman* (1921). For more explicit details, see [75, pp. 184, 188–189]. For other references to articles written in the twenties by Goldenweiser and Lowie representing their interest in the relations of psychology to the social sciences, see [75, p. 161]. Writing in England, Haddon observes that "in the United States of America, thanks to the influence of Boas, psychology has been well recognized by students as an essential factor in ethnology" [71, p. 68].

[5] For references to Sapir's book reviews, see [75, p. 204], for Goldenweiser's articles [75, p. 161]. In 1929, Radin expressed the opinion that "it is the application of the psychoanalytic theories of Jung that is most likely to have the most profound influence upon ethnology" [see 75, p. 208]—a prediction that has not been fulfilled.

[6] Kroeber's original review of *Totem and Taboo*, which appeared in the *American Anthropologist*, was succeeded by a later one in the *American Journal of Sociology* (1939). Both are reprinted in his collected papers [133]. He closes the 1939 review by saying that if he may speak for ethnologists, the latter "though remaining unconverted, have met Freud, recognize the encounter as memorable, and herewith salute him."

opposed to innate characters, anthropologists were inclined to react
negatively to psychological concepts or theories which stressed innate behavioral determinants. This has been true with respect to all varieties of
instinct doctrines. It was also an immediate barrier to the acceptance of
certain aspects of orthodox psychoanalytic theory in its early stages. The
same attitude emerged in the critical appraisal of intelligence tests as
direct indexes to innate factors, particularly when such tests were used to
measure the capacities of people with a cultural background different
from our own. For the same reason, most anthropologists have been
skeptical of anything that savors of racial or constitutional psychology.
As a matter of fact, there were anthropologists of an older generation
who held the position explicitly stated by Lowie in 1917:

. . . [Since] culture is, indeed, the sole and exclusive subject matter of
ethnology, as consciousness is the subject matter of psychology, the science
of psychology, even in its most modern ramifications of abnormal psychology,
and the study of individual variations, does not grapple with *acquired* traits
nor with the influence of *society* on individual thought, feeling and inclination. It deals on principle exclusively with *innate* traits of the individual [149,
pp. 5, 16].[7]

Brewster Smith has also observed, "what runs through an otherwise
heterogeneous history [of psychology] is a pervading focus on the individual" [217, p. 33]. It can thus be appreciated why it was difficult to
bridge the gap between anthropology and psychology in any very positive
fashion until recently.

As a matter of historical fact, it was not until the emergence of social
psychology in its contemporary form that there was a shift in emphasis
within psychology itself. Asch says:

The idea of such a discipline [involved the] culmination of a series of
great changes in thinking about nature and society [and] in part a reaction
against the narrowness of a general psychology which found no place in its
scheme for some of the most essential properties of men. The scientific psychology from which it sprang restricted its observations to the relations between an individual and an environment that strictly excluded other persons;
it was not concerned with relations between persons or between persons and
groups. The movement toward a social psychology represented an insistence

[7] Wissler [250], in his address as chairman of Section H, AAAS, in 1915 expressed a similar viewpoint. "Psychologists," he said, "give their attention to innate
phenomena, especially man's psychophysical equipment. If we extend the meaning
of the term behavior so as to include consciousness, we may say that psychologists
are concerned with the behavior of man as an individual." Both Wissler and Lowie
served as chairmen of the Division of Anthropology and Psychology of the National
Research Council. Wissler pursued his graduate work at Columbia under J. McKeen
Cattell and had a Ph.D. in psychology (1901). He took some courses with Boas
during his last year of graduate studies.

that these major and neglected parts of human psychology be taken seriously. It stood for the belief that no psychology can be complete that fails to look directly at man as a social being [7, p. 364].

At the same time, twentieth-century anthropologists were preoccupied with their own abstractions and conceptualizations. As they became more and more immersed in the study of culture, its analysis, functioning, and variant forms, they receded farther and farther from any direct concern with the actual behavior of individuals.[8] In contrast with traditional academic psychologists, psychoanalysts, and psychiatrists (whose emphasis was on the concrete behavior of the ever-present individual in the laboratory or on the couch or in the clinic or hospital), the abstractions of anthropologists led them into the realm of the description and comparison of the different cultural attributes of human societies.

It was a departure from traditional anthropology when some anthropologists in the twenties and thirties began to devote attention to the relations between cultural differences and the life history and personality organization of individuals in nonliterate societies. In its early days, as Singer says, "the field of culture and personality theory and research was considered an American heresy in anthropology." He adds, "Today it is no longer a heresy, and in a few more years it will no longer be distinctively American" [216, p. 9]. This movement arose from an appreciation of psychoanalytic personality theory, with its emphasis upon the vital importance of childhood experiences on the life history of the individual. However, these experiences were viewed by anthropologists in the setting of the entire culture in which the child was raised rather than in the narrower one of the family circle.[9] Instead of highlighting the customs, values, and institutions of a society and subordinating the individuals as psychologically undifferentiated *bearers* of a culture, they considered human beings as differentiated personalities for whom the culture specified patterns and values of social behavior and whose personality structure it molded in a characteristic way. Academic psy-

---

[8] The logical extreme of this line of thinking is represented by Leslie White's "culturology." "Culture thus becomes a continuum of extrasomatic elements," he says. "It moves in accordance with its own principles, its own laws; it is a thing *sui generis*" [248, p. 374]. "Relative to the culture process the individual is neither creator nor determinant; he is merely a catalyst and a vehicle of expression" [249, p. 80]. At the other pole, Radin, who published "The Autobiography of an American Indian" in 1920 [181], was a pioneer in the personal-document approach in anthropology [75, p. 204].

[9] See Rapaport [183, p. 102] for a discussion of the "Psychosocial Point of View" in psychoanalytic theory. He points out that although "the social determination of behavior is not alien to classic psychoanalytic theory, [at first] these social conceptions were not generalized into an explicit psychoanalytic social psychology" [see also 138].

chology was also soon drawn upon by a number of investigators to supply the model for a learning theory useful in studying the acquisition of culture in the socialization process.[10]

We are only now beginning to see the wider implications of this new movement. It has, in fact, sharply refocused attention upon the old problem of the social nature of man.[11] Concrete studies of the social relations of individuals in particular societies have been the basis for new hypotheses. These have considered the relations of culture to the psychodynamics of the individual as an integral part of organized systems of social action, and they have added new dimensions to the study of the social nature of man as he was more abstractly conceived in the past. The psychological aspects of the problem are being more explicitly formulated than ever before; in addition, they have been reinforced by the revitalization of social psychology following World War II. Brewster Smith has observed that the culture and personality movement "was thus an attempt to join together what should never have been held asunder in the first place" [217, p. 56]. And, more recently, Bert Kaplan has expressed the opinion that this field "stands at the crossroads of many of the most important problems of both individual and societal functioning" [122, p. 1]. In his *Epilogue*, he goes so far as to say that "the one prediction I feel most secure in making is that the [culture and personality] field as a whole will gradually encompass more and more of the central issues of man's existence and his efforts at control and transformation and will become, finally, the vital center of a future science of man."

For anthropology there have also been latent and very complex psychological problems inherent in the concept of culture itself as it was defined by Tylor in his *Primitive Culture* (1871): "Culture, or civilization . . . is that complex whole which includes knowledge, belief, art, law, morals, custom, and any other capabilities and habits acquired by man as a member of society" [cf. 135]. This classic definition was focused on the products of behavioral interaction in society, not on behavior itself. From that time on, anthropologists took it for granted that cultures are transmitted from generation to generation—without examining the

---

[10] E.g., Mowrer and Kluckhohn [160]. They explicitly state at the beginning of their exposition of a "Dynamic Theory of Personality" that they have drawn upon "three relatively independent lines of scientific development: psychoanalysis, social anthropology, and the psychology of learning." The learning theory used is of the S-R type.

[11] Allport writes: "Our intellectual ancestors, for all their fumbling, were asking precisely the same question we are asking today. How does one generation, they wanted to know, impose its culture and its thought-forms upon the next? What happens to the mental life of the individual when he enters into association with others? And long before social psychology became a science political philosophers sought an answer to the question, *What is the social nature of man?*" [5, p. 3].

process. Similarly, the diffusion of culture and the impact of the culture of one people on another (acculturation) were studied without an analysis of the psychological processes involved [12]. Broadly stated, what culture and personality studies did was to focus attention on the integral aspects of the primary process in human social adaptation by connecting the established facts of cultural variability and patterning with the psychological processes necessary for the need satisfaction and socialization of the child, the personal adjustment of the adult, and the maintenance of a sociocultural system. The special problems implicit in this whole area of inquiry, the methods employed in the investigation of them, and the results so far reported call for no comment here, since they have been widely discussed elsewhere [216, 74, 75, 101, 122, 235a].

If culture and personality studies have had any wider significance than their value as case studies, it lies in the fact that by directing attention to the conditions under which primary processes in human adjustment occur, they raised further questions of general anthropological and psychological interest. Mainly, these investigations have been concerned with specific differences in personality structure and functioning which can be shown to be related to cultural differences. But implicit in these data are indications that universal dynamic processes are involved —processes which are related to the psychobiological nature of modern man as a species. There are implications of capacities which must be related to generic psychological attributes of Homo sapiens that have deep roots in the evolutionary process. All human individuals, through learning, become psychologically structured for participation in discrete sociocultural systems. On the other hand, the hominids, considered psychobiologically as an evolving group of primates, became the "creators" of culture in the generic sense.

In conventional terminology, the psychological dimension of evolution has long been phrased as the evolution of "mind." But this terminology reflects the mentalistic concepts of an older period of psychology in which "mind," "intelligence," and "reason" were key terms. The fact that the psychological organization of the human being is just as much a function of his membership in an organized social group as it is a function of his inherited organic equipment was overlooked. John Dewey [51] emphasized this point prior to the initiation of culture and personality studies and before social psychology had assumed its present form. He said in 1917, "What we call 'mind' means essentially the working of certain beliefs and desires, and these in the concrete—in the only sense in which mind may be said to *exist*—are functions of associated behavior varying with the structure and operation of social groups." Thus, instead of being viewed as "an antecedent and ready-made thing," mind "represents a reorganization of original activities through their operation in a given environment. It is a formation, not a datum, a product and a cause only after it has been produced."[12]

One of the seminal contributions of the psychoanalysts—daily faced with people needing help in readjusting to their life situations—was hypothesizing a model of personality organization which was conceptualized in "structural" terms. Whether we accept their particular model or not, it has proved useful in clinical practice. It has also been helpful in analyzing the dynamics of human behavior in sociocultural contexts of all sorts. In phylogenetic perspective, the psychoanalytic model of personality structure suggests that one of the things we must account for in human evolution is a generic type of personality organization which did not exist at the earliest hominid level, not simply a "human mind" in the abstract. In the psychoanalytic model, the "rationality" of the human mind is counterbalanced by an irrationality linked with biologically rooted forces which are intelligible in an evolutionary perspective. In adopting the genetic point of view, psychoanalysts have shown concern for the universal process in the ontogenetic experiences of mankind which, in Freud's thinking in particular, were closely related to phylogenetic developments. In consequence, evolution has always assumed a prominent position in the structure of psychoanalytic theory [183, pp. 60, 69].

In principle, of course, anthropologists, like academic psychologists and psychoanalysts, have always been oriented to man as a whole. Consequently, explicit or implicit assumptions have been made about the nature of man. For a long period, anthropologists have assumed a psychic unity in man (i.e., Homo sapiens), although this has remained a vague concept. It has been one of the assumptions underlying the idea that all cultural and linguistic data are inherently comparable; it underlies the notion that all races and peoples have the same capacity for cultural development and are equally capable of readjustment through culture change. Although Kroeber [131, p. 619] some years ago recorded his impression that "psychologists have become very unwilling to discuss the inherent psychic nature of man,"[13] Asch asserts that "it is the goal of psychology to furnish a comprehensive doctrine of man, one that will

---

[12] Allport observes: "What was formerly ascribed to the mind of the *Volk* [i.e., ethnic psychology] is now largely subsumed under the current concept of *culture*. 'Personality in culture' promises to be a far more productive concept than 'the mind of the group' has been" [5, p. 37].

[13] He thinks that while the psychic unity of man "cannot be considered to be either a proved fact or an axiomatic principle . . . it is so overwhelmingly borne out by the run of total experience that the anthropologist or the sociologist feels warranted in assuming the principle of essential psychic unity as at least a sufficient approximation to truth, and to employ it as a working hypothesis, or at any rate as a convenient symbol" [131, p. 573].

provide a tested foundation for the social sciences." At the basis of these disciplines, he says, "there must be a comprehensive conception of human nature" [6, p. 5].[14] Long before this, Radin had asked:

Can we ever arrive at any satisfactory knowledge of what constitutes human nature? To say with Boas and so many ethnologists and sociologists that the culture picture hides this knowledge from us forever is a counsel of despair. Some significant light can surely be obtained, even if today the technique for this type of investigation has not as yet been perfected. Here again, I feel that a psychoanalyst like Jung is on the correct trail [182, p. 267].

Anthropologists have by no means given up in despair. Spiro has discussed psychic unity and human nature in terms of the distinctive characteristics of a human personality structure generic to man.[15] However, discussion about human nature and the psychic unity of man has not confronted the problem in evolutionary terms, despite the fact that both anthropology and psychology assume that modern man is a product of biological evolution. The attributes of man's psychic unity, or his human nature, have remained ambiguous. This is largely because the question of whether such attributes are not themselves the end product of earlier stages of hominid evolution has not been satisfactorily answered. Furthermore, there are other vital questions which cannot be dissociated from the nature of human nature or the psychic unity of man when an evolutionary frame of reference is adopted. For instance, it was not so long ago that the late E. A. Hooton pointed out that considerable "difficulties have been encountered in formulating a scientific definition of man" [104, p. 1]. Does this term apply primarily to Homo sapiens as ordinarily used in the social and psychological sciences; if not, what other extinct genera or species of the hominids are to be included? Are our criteria morphological, or are they behavioral as well?

The recent discovery of new fossil material now requires us to make distinctions in our terminology which are in accord with the paleontological facts. Of the new material, the remains of the Australopithecines are of paramount importance. Their over-all dental morphology conforms to that found in more advanced hominids. And, although their cranial capacity is lower than that of the more advanced hominids, they had achieved bipedal locomotion. Consequently these primates, associated with Villafranchian fauna of Lower Pleistocene date, are now placed

[14] Discussing behaviorism, Asch finds Malinowski's conception of human nature inadequate [6, p. 14]. Malinowski had written: "By human nature we mean the biological determinism which imposes on every civilization and on all individuals in it the carrying out of such bodily functions as breathing, sleep, rest, nutrition, excretion, and reproduction" [155, p. 75].

[15] For a summary of changing opinions in anthropological thinking about human nature, see [216, pp. 16–22].

among the Hominidae. Structurally and behaviorally they represent an earlier level of hominid development than the Pithecanthropus group, once considered to represent the earliest-known hominid type [105, 144, 145, 147, 242]. We now know that the earliest hominids were small-brained and newly bipedal. Large brains did not announce the advent of hominid evolution, as Sir G. Elliot Smith argued in 1912 and as Sir Arthur Keith did later with reference to Piltdown. "Recent finds of fossil men and other primates," writes Straus, "indicate that it is the brain that was the evolutionary laggard in man's phylogeny; indeed, the studies of Tilly Edinger of the phylogeny of the horse brain suggest that this may well be a general rule in mammalian evolution" [222, p. 370]. Darwin himself remarked, "We must bear in mind the comparative insignificance for classification of the great development of the brain in man" [quoted by Le Gros Clark, 145, p. 192].

In the light of this new knowledge, it is now apparent that the familiar terms "man" and "human" are colloquial terms. They are *not* equivalent to the zoological term *Hominidae* or to the adjectival form *hominid*. The australopithecines were early hominids, but they were not "human" in the sense that we are human. We represent the terminal product of hominid development. It is difficult now to make use of the colloquial term "man" in discussing evolution [144, pp. 6–9]. Our temporal predecessors in the zoological family Hominidae were not all "men" in the usual lay meaning of the term. This indicates a broadening of our knowledge, as well as the reality of the evolutionary process itself. In current zoological classification, the subfamily *Homininae*—as distinguished from the subfamilies *Oreopithecinae* and *Australopithecinae* —serves to differentiate later from earlier groups of hominids. And the term *euhominid* is coming into use to designate "men"—both living and extinct—belonging to the most evolved group of the family Hominidae, the Homininae [see 108, pp. 137, 351, and Glossary; 91]. Most specialists in the taxonomy and phylogeny of the primates are convinced that the australopithecines stand much nearer to the contemporary ancestors of man than any other group of primates.

Contemporary attention has been directed toward a more integral approach to the investigation of personality, society, and culture as observed in Homo sapiens, without reference to the fact that these interdependent variables occur in a species with a complex evolutionary history. Thus the question arises: Can a thorough comprehension of the nature of Homo sapiens be achieved without the perspective which an evolutionary frame of reference provides? Phylogenetically, we have to consider the gross morphological features which led to the initial hominid radiation and subsequent changes, such as the expansion of the brain, which imply important behavioral and psychological consequences. Ontogenetically, we have to consider the question of neoteny and the social and psychological consequences of an extended period of dependency and the lengthening of the life span. Socioculturally, we have to consider the social structures observed in living nonhominid primates in relation to the evolution of social organization in the hominids which eventuated in the cultural mode of adaptation familiar to us in Homo sapiens. The properties of nonlinguistic systems of communication and their relations to the attribute of speech in Homo sapiens are also relevant. Viewed ecologically, hominid adaptation—as compared with that of most other primates—is terrestrial; this involves questions concerning a change in food habits, the development of technology, and the localization of social groups and their interrelations (territorialism).

Since culture, in the generic sense, has been said by anthropologists to be the crucial attribute that differentiates man from other primates, we must inquire whether all aspects of culture as observed in Homo sapiens came into being together at an early hominid stage. Did the australopithecines manufacture tools, speak, pray, exercise property rights, draw, paint, and recognize moral values? Is there any relation between the expansion of the brain and cultural adaptation? Are "half-brained" hominids as capable of cultural adaptation as those with an expanded cortex? Is speech a necessary condition for the earliest phases of cultural adaptation? And is there any relation between toolmaking, as contrasted with tool using, and speech? Do nonhominid primates show any traces of what has been called "culture" in Homo sapiens? And what of psychological structure? What kind of psychological capacities and mechanisms underlie a cultural mode of adjustment? And what is the relation between the development of systems of social action in the primates and the emergence of cultural systems characterized by a normative orientation?

In this paper I have attempted to give the broad outlines of a *conjunctive* approach to human evolution. The organic, psychological, social, and cultural dimensions of the evolutionary process are taken into account as they are related to underlying conditions that are necessary and sufficient for a human level of existence. I have also devoted some attention to earlier opinions to bring into sharper focus the problems that need reconsideration in the light of contemporary knowledge. "Behavioral evolution" is, perhaps, the term which best defines the framework of a conjunctive approach. "Evolution" implies connected and continuing processes of change and development in behavior as well as structure. Biologists too are taking an increasing interest in behavioral evolution [191]. Some years ago, Nissen remarked that "one of the weakest links in the sciences dealing with evolution, the one most needed to strengthen its facts and theoretical framework is that dealing with behavior" [169, p.

106]. It is in behavioral perspective that we can best conceptualize the major categories of variables to be examined to determine the evolutionary status of Homo sapiens. Whether we consider hominid evolution ecologically, socially, psychologically, or linguistically, behavior is the unifying center to which we must return at each adaptive level. As we proceed to higher levels, we must consider new integrations of determinants brought about by potentialities for behavioral adaptations that did not previously exist, for example, the consequences of bipedal locomotion, the adoption of new food habits, the use and manufacture of tools, the expansion of the brain, the effects of a new level of pyschological integration in the later hominids, and the role of speech in the symbolic mediation and social relations. In the evolutionary process, differential behavior patterns provide major clues to significant variables. Modern man represents a late stage in a complex chain of evolutionary events. His "human" nature and the varieties of psychological and cultural adjustments that we observe in culture and personality studies imply capacities that must be related to generic properties of Homo sapiens which have a long evolutionary history of their own.

Any attack on problems of behavioral evolution, of course, has inherent methodological difficulties. A direct observational approach at all stages is not possible. For the past, we can only make inferences and deductions from nonbehavioral data. But we can observe and compare the behavior of different species of living primates—with full appreciation of the fact that they represent their own specialized modes of adaptation. In the case of the hominids, archeological data provide us with both material products and the consequences of social interaction as it is expressed in traditional usage (where the manufacture of tools can be established). But the archeologist is not concerned with the problem of behavioral evolution. His attention is chiefly directed to the forms, distributions, and temporal relations of objects; from this, the early cultures of the euhominids can be inferred. Questions of behavioral evolution, on the other hand, force us to look behind the tool and ask questions which neither the archeologist nor the physical anthropologist can answer by a direct appeal to his data. Tools as products of behavior raise questions of another order. To account for a toolmaking tradition or the lack of one, we have to consider the psychobiological capacities which are a necessary condition of toolmaking; intervening variables have to be inferred. Such problems must be faced sooner or later; indeed, behavioral criteria frequently have been invoked in dealing with questions of human evolution, but there has not been sufficient discussion of the psychological implications. Inevitably there will be different interpretations of the facts of behavioral evolution, but the areas of dispute will be narrowed with the accumulation of new data.

THE PSYCHOCULTURAL DIMENSION OF EVOLUTION

Darwinism helped to define and shape the problems of modern psychology as it did those of anthropology. An evolution of "mind" within the natural world of living organisms was envisaged. Now a bridge could be built to span the deep and mysterious chasm that separated man from other animals which, according to Descartian tradition, must forever remain unbridged. Darwin himself explicitly set processes of reasoning, long considered an exclusively human possession, in an evolutionary perspective and advanced an evolutionary interpretation of the facial and postural changes of man when expressing emotion [46, 47].[16] He argued that mental differences in the animal series present gradations that are quantitative rather than qualitative in nature.

To A. R. Wallace, on the other hand, the evolution of the brain represented a sharp mutational development in man that permitted adaptive capacities far beyond those necessary for survival on a primitive level of human existence. He had had more intimate contacts with primitive peoples than Darwin, and was immensely impressed with their abilities. The position he took was a challenge to Darwin's theory of natural selection. "Natural Selection," Wallace wrote, "could only have endowed the savage with a brain a little superior to that of an ape, whereas he actually possesses one but very little inferior to that of the average members of our learned societies" [quoted in 56, p. 63]. Eiseley points out that, in 1864, Wallace "set forth the idea that with the rise of man, natural selection was ceasing to act upon the body and was coming to act almost solely upon the human intelligence. Man, he contended, was old and had attained the upright posture long before the final changes in the skull and brain which characterize our living species. Other animals had continued to change and modify under evolutionary pressure; in man, by contrast, all but mental evolution has largely ceased" [56; cf. 57, p. 306].

Although Darwin was later accused of gross anthropomorphism by some of his critics, he stimulated scholars to think and write about mental evolution. On the other hand, Wallace's views were discounted because, in the end, he fell back upon a theological explanation. Romanes, a disciple of Darwin, coined the term "comparative psychology,"[17] and it was not long before a phylogenetic dimension had been added to the program of scientific psychology.

[16] [Cf. 236.] Margaret Mead relates Darwin's work to the developing interest in "the non-verbal aspects of human communication—the new science of kinesics."

[17] His *Animal Intelligence* [193], published in 1883, "is the first comparative psychology that was ever written, and its author used this term believing that comparative psychology would come to rank alongside of comparative anatomy in importance" [20, p. 473].

In its early stages, comparative psychology had little interest for anthropologists. Psychologists, in reaction against anecdotalism, demanded more rigorously controlled observations; lower mammals, such as the rat, and insects, became preferred laboratory subjects. Observational results, even though highly reliable, did not throw much light on the phylogenetic roots of human psychology. It was only when laboratory studies of infrahuman primates, like the chimpanzee, initiated by Yerkes, Köhler, and Schultz, developed to a high point that they engaged anthropological interest [252, pp. 289–301]. Henry Nissen's [165] pioneer field observations of the chimpanzee were published in 1931; the studies of C. R. Carpenter [25, 26, 27, 28] on New and Old World monkeys and the gibbon followed shortly. A new body of information on nonhominid primates began to accumulate. We now have reliable data on a few samples of the ecology and organization of primate societies [for bibliography to 1957, see 31] supplementing behavioral observations made under laboratory conditions. At the present time, experimental research on nonhominid primates is also expanding [e.g., 82, p. 273]. While hitherto both kinds of studies were made by psychologists, a few anthropologists (e.g., Imanishi, Washburn, and De Vore) have now begun to study nonhominid primates in the field.

Also under the stimulus of Darwin's ideas as applied to man historians, economists, sociologists, linguists, cultural anthropologists, and others began to apply evolutionary ideas to human institutions on a wide scale. Language, religion, art, marriage and the family, law, and economic organization were studied comparatively to discover whether orderly development sequences could be established. These efforts, however, were chiefly confined to developments in a single species of the Hominidae—Homo sapiens. Fossil material and archeological remains were scanty at the time, and field studies of nonhominid primates living in their native state were nonexistent. Besides, the evolutionary hypothesis was closely linked with the older idea of progress as it was applied by social scientists and humanists. This reinforced the reconstruction of series of unilinear stages which more or less paralleled the concept of orthogenesis in biology. In this form, theories of social and cultural evolution persisted into the early years of this century.

Since it was assumed that processes of evolution were not confined to the organic sphere alone, a corollary psychological question arose in conjunction with the attempts to establish the stages of cultural evolution in man's long struggle from savagery to civilization. Could it not be shown that in the cultures of present-day nonliterate peoples there was mirrored a reflection of primitive mind? J. G. Frazer, who adhered to the recapitulation theory, was among those who explicitly linked this problem with the generic question of mental evolution. He thought that ethnographic data were relevant, as were studies of the ontogenetic development of the child and of patients in mental hospitals. He said that "this comparative study of the mind of man is thus analogous to the comparative study of his body which is undertaken by anatomy and physiology" [65, p. 586].[18] But when unilinear stages of cultural evolution were rejected by most twentieth-century anthropologists, the notion of "primitive mind" as applied to nonliterate peoples collapsed with them. The conclusion was drawn that culture change and development in Homo sapiens is not primarily linked with an evolution in mentality. Outside of anthropology, the more inclusive concept of genetically determined mental evolution—in so far as it was based on the theory of recapitulation in its original extreme form—became generally defunct with the rejection of this theory by biologists [48, chap. 1; 75, pp. 167–170; 76, chap. 2].

Wayne Dennis has written—

. . . it would not be inaccurate to say that developmental psychology began with a theory—the theory of recapitulation. Child psychology, the most productive segment of developmental psychology, began shortly after the promulgation of the theory of evolution when all scientific minds were inflamed by this great conceptual achievement [50, p. 2].

But after the movement had arrived at the "concise hypothesis" that "ontogeny recapitulates phylogeny," its decline was imminent. "The evolutionary viewpoint had seemed to open up wide unconquered vistas to child psychology. On closer approach, these beckoning plains proved to be inhabited only by insubstantial figures and retreating will-o'-the-wisps. There was not a testable hypothesis in the entire landscape." While some psychologists of an older generation—men like G. Stanley Hall and J. M. Baldwin—had adopted the theory of recapitulation and made it an integral part of their thinking, as did Frazer and Freud, this working hypothesis is not a necessary assumption of "developmental psychology." Heinz Werner [244, p. 3] points out that the concept—

. . . is perfectly clear if this term is understood to mean a science concerned with the development of mental life and determined by a specific method [i.e., the observation of psychologists, when they employ this term, refers only to ontogenesis] . . . . The mental development of the individual is, however, but one theme in genetic psychology. [Related to it] is the developmental study of larger social unities, a field of interest intimately linked with anthropology and best known by the name of *ethnopsychology*. The question of the development of the human mentality, if not arbitrarily limited, must lead further to an investigation of the relation of man to animal and, in consequence, to an *animal psychology* oriented according to developmental theory [244, p. 3].

[18] In this paper Frazer expresses a preference for "the more general name of mental anthropology," rather than "social anthropology" for the division of the subject in which he worked.

Thus the psychological dimension of evolution, which to Darwin was an integral part of the total evolutionary process and of vital significance for our comprehension of man's place in nature, fell into abeyance.

It is true that animal psychologists continued to investigate some problems comparatively; but special areas of investigation, such as learning behavior in rats, emerged into the foreground, while a primary focus on evolutionary questions as such receded. Schneirla, in a review of trends in comparative psychology, emphasizes the fact that "most American animal psychologists at present seem to be *really* non-evolutionary minded, in the sense that they show no special zeal to find how man differs mentally from lower animals and vice versa, but rather focus strenuously on general problems without much attention to phyletic lines" [204, p. 563].

In anthropology, the rejection of nineteenth-century unilinear theories of cultural evolution, along with the notion of a demonstable level of primitive mentality in Homo sapiens, meant that evolution, once so inclusively conceived, was effectively reduced to investigations in the area of physical anthropology. Physical anthropologists, moreover, concerned themselves chiefly with morphological problems, not behavior. Only recently has a shift in interest become apparent. J. S. Weiner, reader in physical anthropology at Oxford, in an appraisal of the field, writes:

> There is one large baffling topic on which our evolutionary insight still remains very meagre—the emergence of the peculiar attributes of human intelligence, temperament, and social organization. Wide as the morphological gap is between men and apes, we know there are distant ancestral links between them. How far is this apparent also in the working of the brain, and in behavior? . . . It remains an unfortunate fact that of all aspects of physical anthropology this one, which carries so much promise to the sociologist and social psychologist no less than to the human biologist, should at the present time be the most neglected of all fields of study [243, pp. 34–35].[19]

At the same time, the fact that so many twentieth-century anthropologists were preoccupied with culture led to a somewhat paradoxical situation. While continuing to give lip service to organic evolution, they held a crucial evolutionary issue in abeyance. Culture was taken for

[19] Cf. the investigations of ethologists, reviewed by Hinde [95]. Lashley in his introduction to the classical papers of the ethologists, *Instinctive Behavior* [200], notes on p. ix: "They have traced patterns of instinctive activity among related species and have shown that behavior may be as clear an index of phylogenetic relationship as are physical structures." In contrast with American psychologists, these zoologists have focused their attention upon instinctive rather than learned behavior, and their observations have been made in the field rather than the laboratory. The chief animal groups studied so far have been invertebrates and lower vertebrates [see also 228, 229].

granted and stressed as the unique possession of Homo sapiens and of earlier types of hominines, dating far back to the Pleistocene. The chief evidence was the association of tools with these early euhominids. In the 1920s, Kroeber's paper on "Sub-human Cultural Beginnings" [129] was practically unique. So far as Homo sapiens was concerned, it was assumed that all living races possessed equally the necessary psychological capacities for acquiring culture. Culture, as an attribute of all human societies, was abstracted and studied as such. Culture "traits," "complexes," and "patterns" became key terms. This preoccupation with culture led to a *re*-creation of the old gap between man and the other primates—the gap which, it had been thought, the adoption of an evolutionary frame of reference would bridge. The repeated emphasis given to speech and culture as *unique* characteristics of man sidestepped the essence of the evolutionary problem.[20] Distinctive characteristics of the most highly evolved primate were asserted without any reference to the prior capabilities, conditions, or events in the evolutionary process that made these distinctive characteristics possible. For unless culture and speech be conceived as sudden and radical emergents, they must be rooted in behavioral processes which cannot be considered apart from behavioral evolution any more than the distinctive structural characteristics of man can be considered apart from morphological evolution. Unless the nature of such linkages is established, one must ask how far the emphasis on distinctive attributes of man has advanced understanding of his evolutionary position in the animal series beyond the descriptive epithets of an earlier day. One thinks of such characterizations of man as the rational animal, the toolmaking animal, the cooking animal, the laughing animal, the animal who makes pictures, or *animal symbolicus*. All these characterizations stress man's differences from other living creatures. Like the criteria of culture and speech, they emphasize discontinuity rather than the continuity inherent in the evolutionary process.

A statement made by Carpenter a few years ago clearly articulates an opposition to any such sharp descriptive dichotomization between man and other primates. He said he found untenable a number of assumptions that seemed acceptable to many of his colleagues. One of these was that "the phenomena known as 'mind,' language, society, culture and 'values' exist exclusively on the level of human evolution" [30, p.

[20] The emphasis on uniqueness has an analogy in earlier discussions of man's biological status. "The opposition to Darwin's thesis of the evolutionary origin of man," Le Gros Clark points out, "naturally led his critics to search for anatomical characters in which the human body could be said to be 'unique,' thus providing arguments for removing man in any system of classification as far as possible from other mammals (especially the apes). In some cases, indeed, these arguments were pushed to an extreme of absurdity, which today we are apt to find rather astonishing" [145, p. 186]. Reference is made to the wrangle over "hippocampus minor."

93]. And Hebb and Thompson say that "exposure to a group of adult chimpanzees gives one the overwhelming conviction that one is dealing with an essentially human set of attitudes and motivations" [90, p. 543]. Thus, while cultural anthropologists have continued to render formal homage to the idea of evolution, its significance has not been actively pursued. The statements of Carpenter and Hebb and Thompson should remind us that there remain crucial evolutionary questions which transcend the old problem of unilinear stages of cultural development in Homo sapiens and the morphological problems dealt with by physical anthropologists.

Some years ago Le Gros Clark, referring to the question of the zoological classification of the australopithecines, said:

> Taxonomic difficulties of this sort, of course, are bound to arise as discoveries are made of fossils of a seemingly transitional type, and with the increasing perfection of the fossil record, probably the differentiation of man from ape will ultimately have to rest on a functional rather than an anatomic basis, the criterion of humanity being the ability to speak and make tools [143, p. 73].

We must ask, then, what special capacities and conditions underlie the phenomena of speaking and toolmaking. Effective use of such criteria is hardly possible without considering what these capacities and conditions may be. For, as Nissen observes, "To say that man differs from the other primates in his capacity for tool-making and language is not very useful until we have identified the mechanisms and processes which produce these complex end results" [169, p. 102]. We cannot depend on the evidence from human paleontology and archeology alone. In so far as speech is concerned, it is now known that reliable inferences cannot be made from brain anatomy [188, p. 92]. Furthermore, it seems doubtful that speech as observed in Homo sapiens possesses properties as a system of communication which can be treated as a phenomenal unity in phylogenetic perspective. The question is: How far can speech actually be projected into the past? Do we not have to know more than we now know about the properties of nonlinguistic systems of communication at subhuman levels in order to understand the position of speech in behavioral evolution?

Critchley notes that Sir Arthur Keith "believed that the faculty of speech could be traced back as far as Neanderthal man, but no further," although his anatomical evidence was not very convincing [42, p. 304]. On the other hand, L. S. Palmer, "basing his opinion upon the anatomical characteristics of the mandible," argues that perhaps the australopithecines could speak. The kind of evidence advanced in both instances seems even more indirect than older inferences from the details of endocranial casts, regarding which F. Weidenreich once said that this sort of evidence is no more reliable than any other form of phrenology. However, it is of some interest to note that whereas in the past speech was often given great historical depth, in recent years it is being argued by some [e.g., J. B. S. Haldane, 72, and R. J. Pumphrey, 180] that it is a very, *very* recent development. What may prove to be a more positive approach to the anatomical basis of the evolution of speech has been followed by Du Bruhl [53], who has considered the anatomical changes in the oral anatomy brought about by erect posture. Reviewing this author's book, H. L. Shapiro says:

> Standing erect, he shows, shortened the length of the oral cavity, increased its angulation with the neurocranium, moved forward the foramen magnum and along with it, the position of the throat. These adaptive modifications, resulting from postural changes, have limited the space between chin and throat and have led to a drastic alteration in the laryngo-velar relations. As an accidental by-product of these anatomical arrangements, expelled air has been given access to the oral cavity where the formation of distinctive and varied sounds becomes possible through tongue movements established in feeding habits. Invoking "opportunism" and the "selective premium" of established neural mechanisms put to the new use of speech, Du Bruhl offers a concept that envisages the possibility that speech could have evolved at a very early stage of hominid evolution [214].

In Schneirla's [204, p. 582] opinion, an adequate comparative study of group communicative behavior "is long overdue, particularly to clarify the relationships of concepts such as 'sign,' 'signal,' and 'symbol,' as well as the criteria of 'language,' all of which appear to suffer from a heavy load of speculation and a minimum of systematic research" [cf. 41; 24, p. 156 ff]. Perhaps expanding research in the area of "paralanguage" in man, as defined by Trager [231], may provide some new leads.

Hockett has recently pointed out that—

> . . . part of the problem of differentiating Man from the other animals is the problem of describing how human language differs from any kind of communicative behavior carried on by non-human or pre-human species. Until we have done this, we cannot know how much it means to assert that only Man has the power of speech [97, p. 570].

He has approached the problem by identifying seven "key properties" of the speech of Homo sapiens and comparing them with the available data on nonhuman systems of communication. Hockett discovered that there was considerable overlapping in the properties selected, although they did "not recur, as a whole set, in any known non-human communicative system" [97, p. 574]. This suggests that the combination of properties that characterize speech, those "design-features" which "seem to be of

crucial importance in making it possible for language to do what it does"
[98, p. 32], did not arise full blown. It is argued that this assemblage of
properties, as related to man's lineage, "could not have emerged in just
any temporal sequence. Some of them either unquestionably or with high
likelihood imply the prior existence of some of the others" [97, p. 581].
Consequently, Hockett is led to suggest a tentative evolutionary reconstruction.

In a later article (1960) which is illustrated by many clearly designed
charts and tables, Hockett says:

Although the comparative method of linguistics, as has been shown,
throws no light on the origin of language, the investigation may be furthered
by a comparative method modeled on that of the zoologist. The frame of
reference must be such that all languages look alike when viewed through it,
but such that within it human language as a whole can be compared with
the communicative systems of other animals, especially the other hominoids,
man's closest living relatives, the gibbons and great apes. The useful items
for this sort of comparison cannot be things such as the word for "sky";
languages have such words, but gibbon calls do not involve words at all. Nor
can they be even the signal for "danger," which gibbons do have. Rather,
they must be the basic features of design that can be present or absent in any
communicative system, whether it be a communicative system of humans,
of animals or of machines [99, p. 89].

In his earliest paper, the author identified seven design features. In this
article he discusses thirteen.

It is probably safe to assume that nine of the thirteen features were already present in the vocal-auditory communication of the protohominids—
just the nine that are securely attested for the gibbons and humans of today.
That is, there were a dozen or so distinct calls, each the appropriate vocal
response (or vocal part of the whole response) to a recurrent and biologically
important type of situation: the discovery of food, the detection of a
predator, sexual interest, need for maternal care, and so on. The problem
of the origin of speech, then, is that of trying to determine how such a system could have developed the four additional properties of displacement,
productivity and full-blown traditional transmission. Of course, the full story
involves a great deal more than communicative behavior alone. The development must be visualized as occurring in the context of the evolution of the
primate horde into the primitive society of food-gatherers and hunters, an
integral part, but a part, of the total evolution of behavior [99, p. 92]

One of the key properties of a human system of communication is
"cultural transmission,"[21] a property absent in the communication sys-

---

[21] Hockett [98, p. 36] says: "A behavior pattern is transmitted culturally if it is
not only learned but taught, and if the teaching behavior, whatever it may be, is
also learned rather than genetically transmitted" [97, pp. 579–580].

tems of primates and other animals. This factor becomes highly significant chronologically and, I think, has wider implications than those developed by Hockett. He suggests, in effect, that although learning and the social transmission of habits, or what he calls a "thin sort" of culture, may have existed at a very early stage in the development of the higher primates, the associated system of communication that prevailed may have operated without "cultural transmission" [97, p. 36]. In other words, what I prefer to call a "protocultural" stage may have been chronologically prior to speech but not, of course, to some other system of communication. The evolutionary significance of this chronology as adapted to communication lies in the fact that the conditions which permitted a protocultural stage to develop were, at the same time, among the necessary prerequisites of a communication system characterized by the total assemblage of properties considered by Hockett.

This kind of evolutionary inquiry is, of course, a far cry from earlier approaches, particularly those which began by concentrating on the problem of "primitive" languages spoken by Homo sapiens. These proved as fruitless as attempts to discover evidence of "primitive mind" in our species. These failures, however, may have helped to expose genuine evolutionary problems more clearly. Hockett's approach permits us to have a fresh look at speech in greater evolutionary depth. And by direct observation, we know that whereas some of the great apes have been able to acquire a "thin sort" of human culture when closely associated with members of our species, they do not have the capacity to acquire and use our distinctive form of linguistic communication, even when systematically motivated [e.g., 88, chap. 8]. There seems little reason to doubt that psychological capacities of crucial importance lay back of the ultimate emergence among the hominids of a characteristic system of communication. While this system shared some design features with that of nonhominid primates, capacities that transcended those of other primates permitted the development and integration of novel features. These, in turn, resulted in the functional potentialities of speech as we know it in Homo sapiens.

Man has long been defined as the "toolmaker." Yet if tools are taken as an index of a human status, considerable preliminary analysis is required to make this criterion useful. Oakley [170, 171, 172, 173] has been more precise than previous writers in his *Man, the Tool Maker* [170]. Nevertheless, an English biologist, Pumphrey, has remarked that "'Subman, the Implement Maker' would have been a more accurate if less impressive title at least for the first half of his book." Pumphrey sees "no valid reason for assigning intellect to a maker of implements. . . . The web of a garden-spider and the nest of a chaffinch are highly fabricated implements," whereas genuine tools, which he thinks cannot be assigned to early members of the Hominidae, "were made in order to make something else with them" [180, pp. 27–28]. Even if we define the tool concept in terms of some very general adaptive function, without further analysis it is not very useful for making distinctions in an evolutionary frame of reference. Bartholomew and Birdsell say, "In contrast to all other mammals, the larger arboreal primates are, in a sense, tool-users in their locomotion [since,] as they move through the maze of the tree tops, their use of branches anticipates the use of tools in that they routinely employ levers and angular movements" [8, pp. 482–483], which is a very broad interpretation of tool using. These authors draw the conclusion, moreover, that "protohominids were dependent on the use of tools for survival."

There is ample evidence that both biologists and psychologists have had their own difficulties in dealing with the question: What constitutes tool-using? [e.g., 166; 227, pp. 109, 332]. And because the phenomenon of "tool using" is not confined to the primates alone, it is necessary to understand the varying factors that underlie what has been called "tool using" in other animals, to interpret properly the phenomenon of tool using in the behavioral evolution of the primates and the differential factors that made tool*making* possible as a unique development within the hominids.

In psychological experiments with infrahominid primates, "instrumentation," as it is usually called, includes piling boxes to secure food, the manipulation of sticks to achieve a similar goal, or pole vaulting. Interestingly, high proficiency in instrumentation under laboratory conditions appears to be a function of previous experience in related situations. Harlow, referring to Köhler's earlier construct of "insight learning," says, "Insightful behavior on instrumentation problems apparently occurs only in animals that have had previous opportunity for experience in related situations" [81, p. 217]. However, it is individual learning rather than social learning that is involved in "tool using" of this order. Sultan's success in "making" a tool was a unique individual achievement. Nissen says, "The nearest thing to the manufacture of tools in the ordinary sense seen in primates is the observation reported by Köhler of a chimpanzee fitting together two short sticks in order to make a long one. This observation has not been repeated" [166, p. 562].

While there would seem to be no question of the capacity of some primates to use tools as a means of achieving a desired goal when sufficiently motivated, this potentiality is only one of the prerequisites for a more highly developed stage of tool using. However, it seems quite likely that, under natural conditions, some rudimentary habits of tool using in the narrower rather than the broadest sense may have been individually learned and socially transmitted in nonhominid or early hominid groups. If so, this would exemplify what I have called a "proto-cultural" stage [77]. Nevertheless, the conditions operative at such a stage in primate groups are not in themselves sufficient to account for the still more advanced level of *toolmaking*. If the latter is invoked as a functional criterion for human status, we need to do more than differentiate between tool using and toolmaking. We must ask whether toolmaking presupposes a higher order of psychological structuralization and functioning than tool using; whether it implies a social system different from that of nonhominid primates, or a different system of communication.[22]

Toolmaking as observed in Homo sapiens is a skilled act—learned in a social context where speech exists and usually performed with reference to a purposeful use at some *future* time. Many years ago, Kroeber noted the chimpanzee's inability "outside of posed problems to manufacture tools or lay them aside for the future" [129, p. 336]. And Linton noted the anticipatory dimension of the human toolmaking situation. "This indicates," he said, "a distinct type of psychology, the realization of operation [sic] in the time stream, which no other animal shows. I think this is the point, actually, where the human mind emerges, even more than in the capacity for reorganization of experience we call 'thinking' " [225, p. 266]. Straus observes, "Man is peculiar in the extent to which he lives in the three dimensions of time. It is this peculiarity that gives use to his remarkable degree of foresight or anticipation which is perhaps best expressed in tool-making, to use this term in its broadest sense" [221, p. 133]. Therefore, when interpreting the archeological evidence, do we not have to make up our minds whether toolmaking necessitates a sense of self-orientation in time—and possibly institutionalized property rights which assure continued control over the tool?

·When we have direct evidence of the persistence of characteristic techniques of manufacture and tool styles, as well as evidence of innovation or invention (i.e., a toolmaking tradition), we have indexes to a human level of cultural adaptation. But this involves far more than tool-

[22] [See 24.] In 1937, Grace A. de Laguna [49] argued that "it is scarcely credible, even aside from the more theoretical psychological considerations, that the art of chipping stone implements could have been developed by men who had not yet learned to speak." In a later unpublished manuscript, de Laguna has expressed her thought by saying: *"Homo faber is Homo cogitans."* Compare Révész [188, pp. 92–93], who equates *Homo faber* with *Homo loquens.* Compare Vallois, who points out that toolmaking, "un phénomène essentiel de l'hominisation culturelle," undoubtedly was preceded by an earlier stage of utilization . . . "qui n'impliquait encore qu'une hominisation à ses débuts. Les processus qui ont permis la fabrication doivent au contraire correspondre à une cérébralisation déjà avancée ainsi que, peut-être, à un certain usage de la parole. Une telle fabrication suppose en effet l'apparition de nouveaux centres corticaux et de nouvelles connexions sensitivo-motrices. Elle suppose l'idée d'une transmission des techniques d'un individu à un autre" [232, p. 211].

making per se or mere social transmission. Heinz Hartmann, in discussing the "reality principle" in human adaptation, points out that it—

. . . implies something essentially new, namely the familiar *function of anticipating* the future, orienting our actions according to it and correctly relating means and ends to each other. It is an ego function and, surely, an adaptation process of the highest significance. We may assume that ego development enters this process as an independent variable, though naturally the ego function involved may secondarily yield pleasure" [87, pp. 42–43].

If toolmaking is interpreted as an early indication of the reality principle, involving ego functions among other things, a psychological dimension could then be added to our conceptualization of the personality structure of early hominids which would be correlative with the point made by Linton [225, p. 266] and Straus [221, p. 133].

The more perplexing evolutionary problems arise in cases where the material evidence is ambiguous. The problem is particularly difficult where the early hominids responsible for the archeological remains had a smaller cranial capacity than later hominids of the Middle Pleistocene and after. At first, the general opinion prevailed that the bipedal australopithecines of Villafranchian age were not toolmakers, although Dart maintained that, in addition to their hominoid anatomical characters, "they were human in employing skeletal parts to subserve the function of implements in the business of obtaining and preparing . . . food, in getting and dividing it" [44, p. 335]. With the Leakeys' recent discovery of *Zinjanthropus boisei*, however, dated as upper Villafranchian and classified as a new genus of the Australopithecinae [141, 142; cf. 239], the fact of toolmaking in one genus of this group is now established. For, in this case, the discovery is unique in that the hominid remains were excavated from a living site, where they were associated with pebble tools of Oldowan type, along with the broken bones of small animals which had apparently been eaten. Consequently, as Howell says, "the new australopithecine from Olduvai Gorge represents the oldest fully authenticated toolmaker so far known" [106; see also 105].

These new empirical facts serve to sharpen an old question: What is the relation between brain size and the psychological capacities for cultural adaptation as we know it in Homo sapiens? Although no final answer can be given at present, Le Gros Clark, writing prior to the discovery referred to above, has reminded us that the range of variability in the cranial capacity of modern man is very wide (900 cc.–2,300 cc.) and that "while the cranial capacity of fossil hominids can give information on the brain volume, it provides no information on the complexity of organization of the nervous tissue of which it was composed" [147, p. 312; cf. 175]. Oakley raises the question, is it possible that

. . . systematic tool-making arose, not gradually as most nineteenth-century evolutionists led us to imagine, but suddenly and spread rapidly? . . . The earliest tools and weapons would have been improvisations with whatever lay ready to hand. Although the hominids must have begun as occasional tool-users, ultimately they were only able to survive in the face of rigorous natural selection by developing a system of communication among themselves which enabled cultural tradition to take the place of heredity. At this point systematic tool-making replaced casual tool-using, and it may be that this change-over took place in the australopithecine stage. It would not be surprising, in view of the close correlation between culture and cerebral development, if there had been at this stage intense selection in favour of larger brains, with the result that the transition from the small-brained Australopithecus to the larger-brained Pithecanthropus took place in a comparatively short space of time [174, p. 207].

Washburn has indicated that there may be chronological questions that will have to be considered, that is, the sequential development of tool using, toolmaking, speech, and a fully developed cultural mode of adaptation. It may be, he says, that—

tool use requires much less brain than does speech and might have started as soon as the hands were freed from locomotor functions. Oral traditions essential for complicated human society probably were not possible with less than 700 or 800 cc. of brain, and there is no likelihood that elaborate traditions of tool making are possible at lesser capacities, although simple pebble tools might well be [240, p. 432; p. 428, table].

This brief discussion of speech and tools as behavioral criteria of a human status has, I hope, indicated some of the preliminary problems met with in applying them. The evolutionary problem becomes even more complicated if, to begin with, we attempt to operate with the concept of culture as the criterion of a human status—that "complex whole" of Tylor's classic definition which, he said, is acquired by individuals as members of society. How can we apply such an abstract generic concept, derived from empirical observations of a very concrete nature, in any meaningful analysis of the developmental aspects of human evolution and adaptation?

Wissler tried to solve the problem by assuming the phenomenal unity of what he called a "universal pattern" of culture.[23] His solution was reductionistic. He projected this pattern—including speech—full-fledged from the properties he conceived the "germ plasm" to possess. "The pattern for culture is just as deeply buried in the germ plasm of man as the bee pattern in the bee," he said. "The human pattern . . . is a part, if not the whole, of man's inborn behavior. . . . Man builds cultures be-

[23] Referred to by Kroeber as "that seed lightly tossed out by Wissler that has never germinated" [134, p. 198].

cause he cannot help it, there is a *drive* in his protoplasm that carries him forward even against his will" [251, pp. 264–265]. Wissler, however, did not specify any particular genus or species of the Hominidae. He did not say whether the same universal pattern for culture was embedded alike in the genes of Pithecanthropus and Homo, and, at the time he wrote, the problem presented by the australopithecines had not yet arisen. While it is doubtful that any simple biologistic approach to the evolutionary roots of culture can be any more fruitful than preformationistic theories in biology, at the same time it must be recognized that Wissler was grappling with a genuine problem. It seemed clear to him that, despite the plasticity of the behavior of Homo sapiens and the varying traits, complexes, and patterns of different cultures, there were constant and recurrent categories of culture that transcended any particular mode of cultural adaptation.

Thirty years later Kluckhohn, discussing the question of universal categories of culture, pointed out that, although in the earlier history of anthropology there were those who recognized universal categories for a decade or more before Wissler and for an even longer period subsequently—

The attention of anthropologists throughout the world appears to have been directed overwhelmingly to the distinctiveness of each culture and to the differences in human custom as opposed to the similarities. The latter, where recognized, were explained historically rather than in terms of the common nature of man and certain invariant properties in the human situation [127, p. 511].

The point I wish to stress here is that there are inescapable psychological as well as evolutionary questions raised by "cultural universals," once such phenomena are in any way thought to be related to the nature of man and the human situation. Even if we do not accept Wissler's "universal pattern" concept as such or his reductive explanation, he was correct in viewing universals in phylogenetic perspective. Jung's theory of archetypes is focused upon the same problem of universals, couched in psychocultural terms. His remark that man is probably "born with a specifically human mode of (general) behavior and not with that of a hippopotamus or with none at all" [120, p. 436] sounds much like Wissler. Jung's aim in exploring what he has called the "collective" unconscious, as distinguished from the repressed unconscious of Freudian thinking, has been to develop a hypothesis to explain recurrent and presumably generic psychic phenomena which manifest themselves in art, myths, dreams, psychoses, and other ways. *Archetypes* are psychic propensities or dispositions which are part of a human psychobiological heritage seen both in a historical and phylogenetic perspective. How, when, where, and in what particular form archetypes are concretely manifested depends upon many variables [121, pp. 292–294; see also 117]. Jung's reference to Wundt's rejection of Bastian's *Elementarge-danken* as part of a common psychological heritage of man savors of the same attitude that we find expressed by anthropologists concerned more with cultural differences than cultural universals [120, p. 377].

Quite aside from the specific hypotheses of either Wissler or Jung, the fact remains that cultural universals do not find a ready explanation in cultural-historical terms. Furthermore, it seems probable that a closer examination would indicate that some of them, at least, point directly to the functioning of basic features of a human personality structure that would appear to be a necessary condition for the existence of many aspects of cultural adaptation. For instance, categories of Wissler's "universal pattern" were subsequently elaborated by Murdock, who itemized a long list of what he called "common denominators" of culture which occur "in every culture known to history or ethnography" [163, p. 124]. Among the many items he lists is "eschatology." It is a particularly interesting item when its underlying psychological implications are considered. For concepts concerned with a future life, in order to become functionally significant, require a concept of self as being in some sense indestructible and persistent in future time. Consequently, a capacity for self-awareness and self-identification must be assumed as psychological universals. Furthermore, since this future existence of the self requires a locale, a level of personality organization is indicated which not only implies ego functioning but a capacity for symbolizing self in space, as well as in time [cf. 76, p. 100]. In phylogenetic terms, the evolutionary status of Homo sapiens implies common psychological potentialities. These would appear to be as necessary for the functioning of notions of eschatology as for the manufacture of tools and other forms of cultural adaptation.

In the light of our present anatomical and archeological evidence, we oversimplify the problem of human evolution if we do not press beyond such general categorical correspondences as *man-speech* and *tools-culture*. Without qualification and further analysis, we cannot associate every aspect of the kind of cultural adaptation we find in Homo sapiens with all members of the Hominidae any more than we can attribute to them a common "human nature." This latter concept always has proved difficult [see 17, 134]. Sometimes it has been given a purely biological content. Among anthropologists, it often has received a rela-tivistic connotation, despite lip service to the "psychic unity of mankind" [218, p. 21]. Spiro has given the concept a more precise meaning by asserting that "the structure and functioning of human personality constitutes man's universal human nature, psychologically viewed. Its universality is not only descriptively true; it is analytically true, as well.

In the absence of human personality there could be no human culture"
[218, p. 29]. In phyletic perspective human nature is, then, the consequence of an evolutionary process. However conceptualized, it cannot be
attributed to the earliest hominids in any meaningful sense. In a psychological frame of reference, a human personality structure did not arise as
a sudden mutation in the evolution of the hominids any more than a
saltatory constellation of anatomical traits suddenly gave rise to man.[24]
Howells said a number of years ago:

> Heretofore we have been given to talking about "the appearance of
> man"—the tyranny of terminology—as if he had suddenly been promoted
> from colonel to brigadier general, and had a date of rank. It is now evident
> that the first hominids were small-brained, newly bipedal, proto-Australopith
> hominoids, and that what we have always meant by "man" represents later
> forms of this group with secondary adaptations in the direction of large
> brains and modified skeletons of the same form [107].

Analogically, it is equally doubtful whether we should any longer
talk in terms of the "appearance of culture," as if culture, along with
"man," had suddenly leaped into existence. Moreover, if the ancestral
hominids were at all like the australopithecines, it seems unlikely that
they could have had a system of communication that was fully the
equivalent of human speech.[25] There is no positive evidence, it might also
be noted, that they had fire [176]. Further discoveries and analysis, no
doubt, will illuminate the nature of their toolmaking, particularly with
respect to the degree of tool differentiation and standardization of
technique and form which prevailed. In the light of our present knowledge, we can attribute neither a fully developed cultural mode of adaptation nor a human personality structure to all the Hominidae.

Thus, instead of assuming that culture possessed a phenomenal unity
from the start and trying to identify its existence in the past, it seems

[24] See Washburn's important paper [237], also Heberer's article [91]. Heberer
writes: "Wir dürfen wohl sagen, dass, wie bereits Nehring (1895) vermutete und
heute vielfältig werden kann . . . der Mensch 'zuerst mit den unteren Ex-
tremitäten Mensch geworden' ist. Die Erwerbung des Bipedalismus schuf die
Vorbedingung für die definitive Hominisation durch Cerebralization. Ein prono-
grades Wesen konnte keinen humanen Status erreichen, ebensowenig wie dies
einem Brachiator möglich war" [91, p. 537]. And "Die Hominisation begann mit
dem Eisetzen des evolutiven Trends, der zur Erwerbung des Bipedalism und zur
Reduktion des Gebisses mit fortschreitendem Ersatz der Zähne durch die Hände
(Instrumentalhilfen) führte. Mit diesen Erwerbungen wurde die kritische Phase
erreicht, in der sich die Ubergang vom subhumanen zur humanen Zustand volbezog"
[cf. 145, p. 196].
[25] Oakley [172] does not think it necessary to assume that the earliest hominid
tool users, or even toolmakers possessed speech. He likewise believes that a system
of gestural communication preceded speech [171].

more fruitful to consider certain aspects of behavioral evolution that are noncultural in nature, but which are among the indispensable conditions that made cultural adaptation possible in the later phases of the evolution of the hominids. The most important of these conditions are sociopsychological in nature. Our empirical data are derived from observation on subhominid primates in their natural habitat or under laboratory conditions, for deductions from comparative behavior are as methodologically legitimate as those from comparative anatomy. Nissen points out:

It might well be that if we had a record of behavior as complete as the fossil record of structures, this would yield as convincing a body of evidence for evolution as does the latter. As a matter of fact, a study of the behaviors of living species alone—together with the paleontological evidence regarding the order in which these forms appeared—provides in itself a substantial basis for postulating a process of evolution [169, p. 99].

THE DIMENSION OF SOCIAL STRUCTURE

Social systems are not unique to Homo sapiens. And, even at this highly evolved level, social structure is now frequently differentiated analytically from culture or personality organization. Eggan, for example, has expressed the opinion that "the distinction between society and culture, far from complicating the procedures of analysis and comparison, has actually facilitated them." He goes on to say that "social structure and culture patterns may vary independently of one another, but both have their locus in the behavior of individuals in social groups" [55, p. 746].[26]

In approaching the sociopsychological dimension of primate evolution, a distinction of the same order is useful. Life in structured social groups is characteristic of primates and long antedated anything that can be called a "cultural mode of adaptation" among the more advanced hominids. Social structure can thus be treated as an independent variable. While at the highest level of primate behavioral evolution there are no organized societies without culture (or the reverse), at lower levels there were societies without culture. In phylogenetic perspective, a necessary locus and an indispensable condition for a cultural system is an organized system of social action. It likewise seems reasonable to assume that systems of social action at lower primate levels require some system of communication for their operation. To characterize such a system as

[26] [Cf. 74, p. 600]. Parsons [177] has added an organic reference point in this exposition of his general theory of action to the other categorical abstractions previously distinguished, i.e., personality or psychological system, social system, and cultural system.

"language" is ambiguous and even misleading without further analysis of the design features of the system. Then, too, consideration of the sensory mode of communication is required [72, 90, 204, p. 582; 213, chap. 9]. Among primates, both visual and acoustic modes appear to be extremely important. Schultz speaks of the intricate "silent vocabulary" of the non-hominid primate.

Crouching down, presenting buttocks, extending hands in pronation, exposing teeth partly or fully, raising eyebrows, protruding lips, shaking branches, pounding chest, dancing in one place, walking backwards, etc.— all are actions full of definite meaning. . . . The long lists of different postures, gestures and facial movements characteristic of monkeys and apes have not yet been compiled, but any careful observer realizes that they represent an intricate and voluminous "silent vocabulary" of great aid in social intercourse. In the perfectly adapted arboreal life of monkeys and apes the limited variety of sounds, together with the great variety of meaningful gestures and facial expressions, is fully adequate for all social life within such close contact as permits seeing and hearing these detailed means of communication [211].[27]

So far as the utterance of sounds is concerned, Schultz says they "are the essence of primate life . . . ; the simian primates are by far the noisiest of all mammals." In species that have been closely investigated, like the howling monkeys of Panama and the lar gibbon, differentiated vocalizations have been shown to have functional significance in the social coordination of the individuals belonging to a group [22, chap. 8; 29, p. 242]. According to Schultz:

The primatologist regards language not as something radically new and exclusively human, but rather as the result of a quantitative perfection of the highly specialized development of man's central nervous control of the anatomical speech apparatus in the larynx, tongue and lips, the latter being as good in an ape as in man. . . . As soon as the early hominids had ventured into open spaces, had begun to use and even make tools and had cooperated in hunting, the total variety of all means of expression needed additions which could come only from an increase in sounds, since the comparatively little changed anatomy had already been fully used for all possible gestures, etc. . . . Gestures have always persisted in human evolution, but they have become overshadowed by an infinitely greater variety of sounds in increasing numbers of combinations [211, p. 62].

Oakley and others have suggested that early hominids may have depended primarily on gestures, "mainly of mouth and hands, accompanied by cries and grunts to attract attention," and that speech may

[27] Carpenter [29, p. 242] says: "Each known genus of primate has a repertoire of gestures which are employed consistently and which stimulate consistent reactions." Examples are given.

have been a comparatively late development [171, p. 75]. If so, a mode of communication, infrahominid in origin, would have persisted into the protocultural phase of hominid evolution. Unfortunately, this interpretation must remain speculative. Yet it may be that, when the neurological basis of speech is clarified, we may be in a better position to make chronological deductions [53; 219, p. 8]. It is difficult to imagine, however, how a fully developed cultural mode of adaptation could operate without speech. If one of the necessary conditions for the functioning of a typically human system of communication is a speech community, an organized social system is as necessary for human language as it is for a cultural mode of adaptation. This condition was present even at the nonhominid level. So what we can discern in primate evolution is a behavioral plateau which provided the necessary context but, at first, not all the sufficient conditions for speech and culture.

It will be unnecessary here to consider the structure and functioning of infrahuman primate societies in detail. But a few general comments and interpretations may be ventured, despite the limitations of our present knowledge, for our samples of reliable observations on primate societies in their natural state are woefully small, particularly for prosimian groups.[28] Besides this, it is not yet possible to consider nonhominid primate societies systematically in the larger perspective of mammalian societies [22, p. 221]. There are terminological difficulties also. Descriptive terms like "family," "polygamy," "harem," "clan," and even "culture" and "acculturation"—familiar enough when employed with reference to Homo sapiens—sometimes have been applied to primates at the infrahominid level. Since no systematic terminology has been developed, these labels must be used with caution, especially when evolutionary questions are at issue.

Variations in type of mateship, of course, have suggested the closest human analogies. Since lar gibbons, for example, live in groups which consist of one male and one female and their young, we have a close analogy to the "nuclear family" in man [164], which likewise represents a monogamous type of mateship. Some biological writers have applied the term "family" exclusively to this kind of primate social unit, despite the fact that in anthropological writing the connotation of the term "family" is never limited to the nuclear family. The gibbon type of mateship, in which the sexual drive of the male is low, would seem to be a limiting case in the range of social units found among the more evolved primates, and without evolutionary implications. In Homo sapiens we

[28] [For bibliography to 1957, see 31.] Imanishi's 1960 paper [116] is the first full length review in English of the work that has been done on *Macaca fuscata* at the Japan Monkey Center, although a brief review was previously published by Frisch [68].

find two types of polygamous mateships, polygyny and polyandry, and
social structures based on these are ordinarily called "families." Relatively
rare in man in an institutionalized form, polyandrous mateships appear
to be absent in infrahuman primates. On the other hand, polygynous
mateships are common in both monkeys and apes. Among the chimpanzee and gorilla, this type of mateship seems to furnish the basis of independent social groups. Among some monkeys (for instance, the baboon),
"harems" occur as subgroups within larger "troops" or "bands." Monogamous mateships, on the other hand, do not occur in groups of larger
size because females in heat mate with more than one male. Past attempts to establish any regular evolutionary sequence of mateship within
Homo sapiens have failed. So have attempts to link any *particular* type of
mateship in the infrahuman primates with early man, as Westermarck
tried to do in the belief that there was evidence to show that the gorilla
was monogamous. He urged that this "fact" was of significance in the
study of sexual relationships and marriage in man.

Westermarck, however, was on the right track and must be evaluated
in historical perspective. Hart points out:

What had really happened to evolutionary theory between 1859 and
1891 was that, while Huxley had spent his life labouring on the genetic
front to get his contemporaries to accept "the unitary view of organic nature" and to reject the old dualistic view which saw man on one level, the
rest of the animal world on another with an impassable gap eternally fixed
between, the pass had been betrayed by Spencer and his followers, who, by
assuming that society was one thing and biology another, had merely substituted a new dualism for the older one, and had opened up as big a gap
between man and the rest of nature as had been there in pre-Darwinian
days. The extraordinary thing is not that this should have happened, but
that nobody seems to have been aware of what was happening until Westermarck pointed it out [84, p. 108].

In his *History of Human Marriage,* Westermarck said:

If we want to find the origin of marriage, we have to strike into another path . . . which is open to him alone who regards organic nature as
one continued chain, the last link of which is man. For we can no more
stop within the limits of our own species, when trying to find the root of our
physical and social life, than we can understand the condition of the human
race without taking into consideration that of the lower animals" [245, p. 9].

Etkin [60] argues for a monogamous protohominid social structure but
on quite different grounds than did Westermarck at the turn of the
century.

Perhaps it might be better to recognize that, since there are only a
limited number of possibilities in mateships, it is not surprising to find

them recurring at both the nonhominid and hominid levels of evolutionary development in the primates and in social units of varying size and composition. Whatever form they take, all these mateships serve the same reproductive ends. Their importance lies in this constancy in biological function rather than in any direct relation that can be shown to the evolution of group organization. They all lie close to biologically rooted central tendencies and continuities in behavioral evolution which link Homo sapiens to his precursors. What we find as the common social core of all but the lowest primate groups, despite their variation, is the continuous association of adults of both sexes with their offspring during the portion of the latter's life cycle that covers the period from birth to the threshold of maturity. This core pattern of associated individuals, when considered with reference to their interrelated roles, is linked with the fact that basic functions are involved—the procreation, protection, and nurture of offspring—born singly, relatively helpless at birth, and dependent for a considerable period thereafter. Variations in mateship or size of the group may occur without affecting these functions. Besides this, the sex needs of adults and the food needs of all members of the group can be taken care of. The role of the female in relation to her young does not seem to vary widely nor does the behavior of infants and juveniles. The protective role of the male in relation to infants and juveniles is similar in gibbon and howler, even though the young of the group in the latter case are not all his own offspring and the actual zoological relationship between these two species is remote. Among monkeys and apes, the adult males never provide food for juveniles or females. After weaning, the juveniles always forage for themselves. Whether we call nonhominid primate groups "families," "clans," "troops," or "bands," their basic social composition can be expressed by the same general formula:[29]

$$x \text{ males} + x \text{ females} + x \text{ infants} + x \text{ juveniles}$$

Whatever the mating types or size of early hominid groups may have been, their social composition must have conformed to this fundamental

[29] Imanishi [116, p. 397] has recommended *oikia* "as a technical term designating the minimum unit of social life found in any species of animal, regardless of the composition of that unit." In nonhominid primates then, "the clan in howling monkeys, the family in gibbons, the small nesting party or sleeping group in redtail monkeys, and the harem in chacma baboons, would each be describable as an *oikia*." Larger groups would be aggregates of *oikiae*. Washburn [238, p. 405], however, doubts the usefulness of this term. Imanishi also holds the opinion that "a band in which promiscuity prevails cannot be called a 'family' even though the two males in it [as in Nissen's reference to a chimpanzee group in 1931] are a father and his mature son. In other words, we may legitimately consider it a family only if we can establish the absence of incest between this mature son and his mother."

pattern. This generic type of social structure, associated with territorialism, must have persisted throughout the extremely long period during which major morphological changes occurred in the species of the primate order, including those which ultimately differentiated the Hominidae from the Pongidae and later hominids from earlier ones. Underlying it physiologically was the type of ovarian cycle characteristic of practically all the primates. In contrast with some mammalian species in which females have only one oestrus period a year, primate females, along with those of a limited number of other mammalian species, are characterized by the recurrence of successive oestrus cycles in the course of a year. The primates belong to this group of permanent polyoestrus species [22, p. 147]. While breeding has been said to be continuous rather than seasonal in the primates, recent observations of the Japanese macaque have reopened this question. It is of great importance in establishing reliable facts about reproduction in nonhominid primate species, and because the answer to this question is relevant to the importance of the sexual bond as a primary factor in primate social organization [for further details see 116]. In the course of primate evolution, however, as Beach [9, 11, 64] has pointed out, some emancipation from strictly hormonal control of sexual behavior occurred, and this further distinguished the higher primates from other mammalian species. Cortical control came to play an increasing role in sexual behavior, and this tendency reached its culmination in hominid evolution with the remarkable expansion of the brain. Thus, the way lay open for the development in human societies of a normative orientation toward sexual behavior.

The evolutionary significance of the social organization of primate groups cannot be fully appreciated, however, without considering behavior patterns other than those directly connected with reproduction. The structuralization of these infrahuman societies is by no means a simple function of differential roles determined by sex and age. Of central importance is the structuralization of interindividual patterns of behavior by an order of social ranking in the group, a dominance gradient. Males are quite generally dominant over females, and the females associated with them may outrank other females. While it appears that in different species the "slope" of the dominance gradient varies considerably, some kind of rank order occurs. The importance of this in the operation of the social structure lies in the fact that it serves to reduce aggression between males, it determines priorities to mates and food, it influences the spatial disposition of individuals within the group, affects the socialization of group habits, and may determine the relations of groups adjacent to one another.

The ranking position of individuals, nevertheless, is not fully determined once and for all; an individual's role in the dominance hierarchy may change. Psychological factors such as individual experience in inter-individual relations and social learning become involved in its functioning and affect the motivation of behavior, as Carpenter [27, pp. 256–257] has indicated. Individuals become socially adjusted from birth through the mediation of learning processes. "Descriptions of mother-infant relations in monkeys and chimpanzee leave no doubt as to the importance of learning in the filial responses of immature primates. The infant learns to obey gestures and vocal communications given by the mother and derives considerable advantage from her tuition and guidance," Beach says [10, p. 426].[30] Indeed, modern research is showing that the primates are by no means unique among gregarious animals with respect to the importance of social learning and a dominance gradient. J. P. Scott asserts:

In animals which are capable of learning, social behavior becomes differentiated on the basis of mutual adaptation and habit formation as well as on the basis of biological differences. As shown by Ginsburg and Allee (1942) the formation of a dominance order is at least in part related to the psychological principles of learning. Once such a relationship is formed and firmly established by habit, it may be extremely difficult to upset it by altering biological factors, as shown by Beeman and Allee (1945). . . . Experiments which modify the social environment have tended to bring out the general principles of socialization. Any highly social animal that has been studied so far has behavioral mechanisms whereby, early in development, an individual forms positive social relationships with its own kind and usually with particular individuals of its kind [212, pp. 217, 218].

With respect to the socialization factor in behavioral evolution, Collias.points out: "In both insect and vertebrate societies, maintenance of cooperative relations depends to a large extent on socialization of the young. Among vertebrates, this trend reaches its climax in the primates" [38, p. 1087]. It seems reasonable to assume, therefore, that the intimate relation between learning and social structure, so fundamental to the functioning and elaboration of cultural adaptation, was well established in the nonhominid primates prior to the anatomical changes that led to both erect posture and the expansion of the brain.

Furthermore, by direct observation of both monkeys and apes, we know that learned habits may be socially transmitted, even in the absence of speech. The most striking cases have been reported by observers who have been studying *Macaca fuscata* at the Japanese Monkey Center dur-

[30] See also [203, p. 104 ff.] in regard to ontogenetic factors influencing group organization. Cf. Schiller [201], who believed there is evidence that primates have distinctive *manipulative* patterns of activity available that are not derived from experience.

ing the past decade. These "Japanese apes" have been lured from their forest habitat into open feeding places, where, among other things, they have been offered new foods. Systematic observation has shown that newly acquired food habits, such as eating candies, became quite socialized. Imanishi points out, moreover, that young macaques acquire the candy-eating habit more quickly than adults and that some mothers learned to eat candies from their offspring, rather than the other way round [115, p. 51]. It has likewise been observed that the spread of a new food habit may be directly related to the dominance gradient which is a central feature of their social structure. Adult females of high rank were observed to imitate the wheat eating of a dominant male very quickly and the habit was passed on to their offspring. Females of lower rank, in a more peripheral position in the group, only later acquired the habit from their offspring, who, in turn, had picked it up through association with their playmates. The rate of transmission was extremely rapid in this case, the entire process occurring within two days [68, p. 589]. In another instance, a young female initiated the habit of washing sweet potatoes before eating them. This habit, having been transmitted to her playmates as well as to her mother, was slowly transmitted to a number of groups during the next three years. The same class of phenomenon in the anthropoid apes is illustrated by nest building among chimpanzees [169, p. 106] and the transmission of the technique of working the drinking fountain at Orange Park, which chimpanzees learned from each other [252, p. 52].

The social transmission of culture has sometimes been stressed as one of its chief earmarks. But to my mind, it is only one of the necessary conditions of cultural adaptation rather than a distinguishing characteristic. It only confounds the conceptualization and the investigation of hominid evolution if the term "culture" is applied without qualification to the phenomena of social transmission of simple habits in infrahuman species. J. P. Scott writes:

The more the capacities for learning and for variable organization of behavior are present, the more it is possible for an animal to learn from its parents and pass the information along to the next generation. As we accumulate greater knowledge of natural animal behavior, we find more and more evidence that many animals possess the rudiments of this new ability, which we can call cultural inheritance. The migration trails of mountain sheep and the learned fears of wild birds are two of many examples . . . At the present time all our evidence indicates that cultural inheritance exists only in quite simple form in animals other than man, but future research may show that it is more common and complex than we now suspect [213, p. 237].

Social transmission is more usefully conceived as a prerequisite of culture and an earmark of a protocultural behavioral plateau. Concepts of culture that lay primary emphasis on shared and socially transmitted behavior without qualification do not enable us to make a necessary distinction of degree between different levels of behavioral evolution. Voegelin has made the acute observation that, while there is a general agreement that all culture involves learned behavior, "additional conditions are generally invoked before learned behavior is granted the status of culture," and that "if ever the converse statement were made (*that all learned behavior is culture*), it would necessarily imply that infrahuman animals have culture" [233, p. 370]. Harlow clearly discriminates between infrahominids and Homo sapiens when he says, "In a limited sense, however, any animal living in a group and capable of facile learning must develop a *semblance of a culture,* since it must have learned to be influenced in its behavior by the ways of its fellows." At the same time, he points out that "no animal other than man has a *true culture* in the sense of an organized body of knowledge passed down from generation to generation" [79, p. 127; italics mine]. The facts that some animals besides the primates may learn from each other, that in primate groups there seems to be good evidence that social learning and socially transmitted habits do occur, and that some chimpanzees in social interaction with members of our species have acquired "culture traits" do not indicate that a full-fledged level of cultural adaptation has been reached in these species.[31] Other capacities and conditions are required before this higher level can be realized. Indeed, neither learning nor the socialization and transmission of learned habits seems to have reached an optimum level of functioning in any nonhominid species. While it is true that a variety of gregarious animals possess the *rudiments* of an ability to be influenced by the behavior of other individuals of their species, the part which this ability plays in their total life history, their social relations, and their ecological adjustments needs more precise analysis. Phylogenetically, it is *only* in the primates that capacities and conditions arose which led to the transcendance of more than a protocultural stage.

[31] Yerkes thought the characterization of chimpanzee as "cultureless" to be "a seriously misleading statement, if not demonstrably false." He says that "the elements or makings of cultural exhibits are present" but that "they are relatively unimpressive because unstable, fragmentary, variable, and seldom integrated into functionally important wholes. Probably they should be described as intimations or primitive stages in patterns of behavior which have as yet acquired few functional relations" [252, p. 52]. Nissen [169, pp. 105–106], referring to nest building in chimpanzees, writes: "There is pretty good evidence . . . that this nest-building is not instinctive, as in birds, but is, rather, transmitted by imitation or tuition from one generation to the next; it is, therefore, one of the very few items of behavior seen in these animals which may be classified as cultural" [cf. 167, p. 426].

What appears to be of significance in the framework of behavioral evolution is that some primates are distinguished from other animals by a higher capacity for *observational* learning. Munn concludes that "it is only in monkeys and apes that anything clearly approximating such observational learning can be demonstrated and even at this level the problems solved by imitation are relatively simple" [162, pp. 129–130. Instances of spontaneous imitation on the part of Viki (the chimpanzee) were operating a spray gun, and prying off the lids of cans with a screw driver, 89].

If we use the term "culture" to refer to different levels of behavioral evolution, our vocabulary fails to discriminate the quantitative and qualitative differences between cultural adaptation in the hominines and the more rudimentary "cultural" manifestations found in infrahuman animals—to say nothing of possible differences between primates and non-primates. Dobzhansky, in a brief discussion on the "Rudiments of Cultural Transmission among Animals," singles out one essential difference between what I have characterized as protocultural and cultural levels of adaptation, although he does not analyze specific cases in detail, and his chief citations refer to birds[32] rather than to primates.

In animals the individuals of one generation transmit to those of the next what they themselves learned from their parents—not more and not less. Every generation learns the same thing which its parents have learned. In only very few instances the evidence is conclusive that the learned behavior can be modified or added to and that the modifications and additions are transmitted to subsequent generations [52, pp. 340–341].

Simple conditioning and possibly observational learning account for these facts. The greater capacity for observational learning in primates also accounts for the socialization of nest-building habits among chimpanzees and the spread of the habit of washing sweet potatoes observed in the macaque group referred to. But so long as social transmission was dependent on capacities of this sort, the kind of acquired habits transmitted or any innovations which could become significant in the adaptation of the group were severely limited. Intervening factors, probably of a neurological order, were required before either the number or the kind of innovations possible at this level could be transcended and become effective through new mechanisms of socialization. As Bidney has said, "The identification of culture with the social heritage is, to my mind, not only a misnomer but also a serious error, since it implies that the essential feature of culture is the fact of communication and transmission,

[32] See Hochbaum [96] for a discussion of tradition in birds. The use of the term "tradition" by ornithologists clearly differentiates the existence of socially transmitted habits from the phenomenon of culture in human adaptation.

whereas I maintain that the essential feature is the combination of invention and acquisition through habituation and conditioning" [17, p. 27].[33]

Moreover, learning and the transmission of acquired behavior patterns could not acquire paramount importance until they could function in social structures of a higher order and wider geographical range than those represented among the infrahominid primates. At this level, social structures were highly provincial systems of social action because of their association with discrete territories. The phenomenon of territoriality, according to Carpenter, "reduces stress, conflict, pugnacity, and non-adaptive energy expenditure" [32, p. 245] in each group by isolating it from other groups; at the same time, it sets up a barrier to the integration of groups and the development of social structures of a wider range and more complex order [30, p. 98]. In the case of the Japanese macaques, for example, groups are almost totally isolated from each other in their natural state. It is said that "even where several groups live in contiguous territories, the inter-group relations are practically non-existent. Encounters between distinct groups are extremely rare, and even when they occur both groups keep at a safe distance from each other" [68, p. 591]. Offspring do not associate with parents after sexual maturity has been reached. They leave their primary group and form new groups. Individuals of two or more generations are not continuously associated in the same group during their lifetime. Consequently, continuity in learned habits is strictly limited. There is no way for experience to become cumulative, either spatially or temporally, beyond the narrowest range. Thus, in order for a cultural level of adaptation to be reached, structures of a wider range were required as a necessary social setting. This further step was contingent upon the development and functioning of psychological capacities that transcended those which had been sufficient for narrow-range social structures. In short, the social integration of larger groups, distributed more widely, and characterized by a greater diversity in role required a transformation in psychological structure.

We do not know what objective factors underlay the increase in the size and range of early hominid groups. Change to a carnivorous diet and hunting have been suggested. Washburn says:

Whether early man scavenged from the kills of the big carnivores, followed herds looking for a chance to kill, drove game, or followed a wounded

[33] Cf. the remarks of Kroeber [131, p. 253] on the use of the term "social heredity." Bidney distinguishes between "culture in general" and human or "anthropo-culture," which is peculiar to man. For him, "all animals which are capable of learning and teaching one another by precept or example are capable of acquiring culture." He maintains that "this implies an evolutionary approach to the concept of culture which recognizes degrees of culture from the sub-human to the human level" [17, pp. 125, 127].

animal, his range of operations must have been greatly increased over that of arboreal apes. The world view of the early human carnivore must have been very different from that of his vegetarian cousins. The interests of the latter could be satisfied in a small area, and the other animals were of little moment, except for the few which threatened attack. But the desire for meat leads animals to know a wider range and to learn the habits of many animals. Human territorial habits and psychology are fundamentally different from those of apes and monkeys [240, p. 434].

THE BIOLOGICAL DIMENSION: NEOTENY AND BRAIN ENLARGEMENT

A concomitant condition for the maximization of the sociopsychological importance of learning appears to have been the extension of the period during which the young become socialized. In the late nineteenth century, John Fiske, an ardent follower of Spencer and Darwin, linked such an extension of the learning period in man directly with evolution through what he called the "prolongation of infancy." In this fact alone, he thought he had discovered the essential key to man's distinction from other animals and the explanation of human psychological, familial, and cultural development. Fiske was impressed both with A. R. Wallace's account of the behavior of an infant orang raised by hand after its captured mother died[34] and by Wallace's suggestion that "natural selection, in working toward the genesis of man, began to follow a new path and make psychical changes instead of physical changes" [62, p. 28]. Fiske developed the thesis that the human being was born "in a very undeveloped condition, with the larger part of his faculties in potentiality rather than in actuality" [62, p. 9]. The period of helplessness is the period of "plasticity. . . . The creature's career is no longer exclusively determined by heredity . . . it becomes educable . . . it is no longer necessary for each generation to be exactly like that which has preceded" [62, p. 2]. Thus, "man's progressiveness and the length of his infancy are but two sides of the same fact"; "it is babyhood that has made man what he is." Infrahuman primates approached the point where "variation in intelligence" came to be "supremely important, so as to be seized by natural selection in preference to variations in physical constitution." But in a remote period, "our half-human forefathers reached and passed this critical point, and forthwith their varied struggles began age after age to result in the preservation of bigger and better

[34] Fiske [62, p. 26] says it occurred to him immediately that "if there is any one thing in which the human race is signally distinguished from other mammals, it is in the enormous duration of their infancy"; a point he did not recollect ever seeing any naturalist so much as allude to. But Fiske was not quite as original as he thought [e.g., 148].

brains, while the rest of their bodies changed but little. . . . Zoologically the distance is small between man and the chimpanzee; psychologically it has become so great as to be immeasurable" [62, p. 11].

We can see from these passages that Fiske anticipated a number of points frequently emphasized later in cultural anthropology and in evolutionary biology. But the theory he develops, while emphasizing the important role of learning in human experience and the potentialities of man for cultural development, does not account for the biological foundations of the extended period of dependency. He likewise makes "bigger and better brains" chronologically subsequent to the distinctive human condition that fired his imagination. Nor could he have anticipated the fact that later knowledge of the social organization of the nonhominid primates would fail to support his conviction that the prolongation of infancy "must have tended gradually to strengthen the relations of the children to the mother, and eventually to both parents, and thus give rise to the permanent organization of the family." For in Fiske's view, when this step was accomplished, "the Creation of Man had been achieved" [62, pp. 12–13].

While Fiske's theory, although once so widely known, is seldom referred to today, the fact should not be overlooked that the relations between the factors dealt with by him have not yet been satisfactorily resolved. Even now it is sometimes forgotten that an extended period of dependency and opportunities for social learning in man do not explain the genesis of cultural adaptation, even though these conditions may be of primary categorical importance in understanding the adjustment processes that relate an individual to his culture. While we now know more about the phylogenetic basis of what Fiske called the "prolongation of infancy," its precise psychological significance is a matter of dispute.

From comparative anatomy the fact seems well established that the larger apes, and particularly the gorilla, develop adult characteristics much earlier than does Homo sapiens. The latter has been called a "fetalized" animal by Bolk [19]; that is, certain features that are characteristic of the fetal stages of apes persist in human adults. It is an example of a well-known evolutionary process which, generically, is usually referred to as "neoteny": fetal and/or juvenile features of an ancestral form persisting in the adult stage of descendants [33, 34, 48]. In man, the rate of development of some characteristics has been retarded. On the other hand, De Beer says:

> The reproductive glands have probably not varied their rate of development, for the human ovary reaches its full size at the age of about five, and this is about the time of sexual maturity of the apes and presumably of man's ancestors. The human body is, however, not ready for the reproductive glands to function until several years later. The retardation is due to the

action of hormones which play an important part in regulating the speed of development. . . . At the same time, of course, in other directions, the evolution of man has involved progressive changes of vast importance, some of which, however, might not have been possible (e.g., the development of the brain), had it not been for certain features of neoteny (e.g., the delay in the closing of the sutures of the skull) [48, pp. 75–76].

It is the combination of various characters, considered with reference to their rate of ontogenetic development, that is peculiar to man.[35]

While such anatomical facts are well established, the psychological inferences drawn from them have varied in emphasis. Roheim maintains that the temporal disharmony between the development of what he calls the "Soma" and the "Germa" is the crucial point. Human sexuality becomes precocious because it develops at about the same rate as in other higher primates, but in our species full bodily growth is delayed. The consequence is that unconscious psychological mechanisms have come into play to repress, project, or transform sexual impulses before the individual is mature enough in other respects to engage in actual sexual activities. The Oedipus complex is universal not because it is derived from past events that have become inherited,[36] but because it "is a direct derivative of our partly premature, partly conservative (prolonged or retarded) rate of growing up" [192, p. 424].[37] "Our sexual ethics are based on juvenalization" [192, p. 413]. (Perhaps it should be added that in *both* man and the anthropoids sexual organs reach maturity earlier than full body growth, but in man the time difference is greater.) Montagu, on the other hand, sees in neoteny an evolutionary step whose major psychological significance is related to man's potentialities for learning. He says:

[35] Schultz [208, p. 53]. And see his 1956 publication for an authoritative comparative treatment of the details of growth and development in various primate species. Schultz concludes that it is erroneous to emphasize retardation exclusively in man's ontogenetic development, since "ontogenetic specializations can consist of accelerations as well as retardations in man as well as in all other primates" [209, p. 959].

[36] Roheim [192, p. 424] says, "This ultra-Lamarckian point of view is untenable," i.e., Freud's primal-horde theory.

[37] Roheim says: "It is a curious fact that while man's delayed infancy is universally admitted hardly anybody uses this fact in the sense that I do. The usual statement is that the delayed infancy makes it possible to condition human beings and that it is why psychology depends on conditioning, i.e., on culture. What culture depends on is then of course the kind of question no well behaved anthropologist should ask, because looking for origins is 'outmoded,' in fact it is nineteenth century, a truly terrible thing, a word loaded with the worst possible kind of *mana*. Quite apart, however, from this aspect of the question, how is it that nobody recognizes that in this one fact we have one of the most important keys to the understanding of human nature?" [192, p. 409]

The shift from the status of ape to the status of human being was the result of neotenous mutations which produced a retention of the growth trends of the juvenile brain and its potentialities for learning into the adolescent and adult phases of development. It is clear that the nature of these potentialities for learning must also have undergone intrinsic change, for no amount of extension of the chimpanzee's capacity for learning would yield a human mind [159, p. 90; cf. 158, p. 22].

Besides this, account must be taken of the biological fact that in primate evolution the life span of individuals was progressively lengthened while the onset of puberty and the beginning of fertility was more and more chronologically delayed. Culminating in man, the outcome was that the interval between generations became greater. This fact needs to be considered with reference to the association of individuals in larger social groups and in relation to the need for the development of the kind of psychological structure that would permit the coordination of the behavior of individuals of both sexes and widely differing ages over a longer time period, in order that interindividual relations in these more complex social systems might be successfully integrated.

While it is impossible to sustain the view that fetalization is completely responsible for all of modern man's distinctive psychocultural characteristics,[38] perhaps we may follow Sir Julian Huxley's view that while—

. . . it will not account for all the special characters we possess, notably the special enlargement of the association areas of our cortex, and the full adaptation of our feet and legs to bipedal terrestrial existence, it has certainly helped us to escape from anthropoid specialization. It is this possibility of escaping from the blind alleys of specialization into a new period of 'plasticity and adaptive radiation which makes the idea of paedomorphosis [fetalization, neoteny] so attractive in evolutionary theory. Both its possibilities and its limitations deserve the most careful exploration [111, p. 20].

If so, important steps in sociopsychological evolution beyond the non-hominid or early hominid level may have been contingent upon the situational effects produced by biological factors. These factors prolonged dependency of the young, delayed reproduction, and increased the life span in an already advanced hominid. At the same time, psychological functions were being greatly enhanced through the enlargement of certain areas of the brain.[39]

[38] The unkindest cut of all has come from Cuenot [43], who has said that man "can be considered a gorilla fetus whose development and growth have been greatly retarded."
[39] Bernhard Rensch, who has been investigating the effects of increased body size on the relative size of the brain and its parts, and on higher psychological

With respect to this particular development, there may well have been a critical transition period. However, an arbitrary Rubicon of 750 cc. [125][40] between the higher apes and the australopithecines on the one hand, and the early Homininae and recent man on the other, while perhaps of some crude taxonomic value, does not in itself permit significant behavioral inferences. "It is quality of brain rather than quantity, absolute or relative, that is all important," as Straus says [225].

Today we know considerably more than we did a generation ago about the functioning of various parts of the cortex as well as other parts of the brain. And new insights and hypotheses with evolutionary reference are coming to the fore. Washburn, referring to the diagram in Penfield and Rasmussen [178] showing the way the body is represented on the cortex, points out that there is unequal representation but that "the areas which are largest are the ones of greatest functional importance." Thus, "when the brain increased in size, the area for hand increased vastly more than that for foot," a fact which "supports the idea that the increase in the size of the brain occurred after the use of tools, and that selection for more skillful tool-using resulted in changes in the proportions of the hand and of the parts of the brain controlling the hand." The areas concerned with speech are also large and so are the frontal lobes which have been said to be connected, in part, with foresight and planning.

Our brains are not just enlarged, but the increase in size is directly related to tool use, speech, and to increased memory and planning. The general pattern of the human brain is very similar to that of ape or monkey. Its uniqueness lies in its larger size and in the particular areas which are enlarged. From the immediate point of view, this human brain makes culture possible. But from the long-term evolutionary point of view, it is culture which creates the human brain [238, pp. 27–29].

---

functions, has advanced the hypothesis [184, pp. 197–198]: "In man's line of descent we may at least consider the increase of the cortex, the relative increase of 'progressive,' i.e., more complicated, cortex-regions, the absolute increase of the number of neurons and of dendritic ramifications, as . . . selectively advantageous factors. Thus the trend towards the human level of brain organization may be regarded as inevitable. Another important factor here is the prolongation of the juvenile phase found in many large animals. This could only occur where multiple births, and therefore intrauterinal selection for rapidity of development, had been eliminated. But once this had taken place, the prolongation of the juvenile phase was favored by selection because thereby the period of learning, that is to say the period of gaining experience and of exploration by play, is also extended. Thus the evolution of man, too, was inevitable" [cf. 185, 186].

[40] See comments by Schultz [208, pp. 49–50]. The Hayeses, however, suggest "the possibility that most of the fourfold increase in cranial capacity from anthropoid to man took place after the appearance of culture and language, and therefore after primate behavior had become essentially human" [89, p. 116].

In recent years, too, as a consequence of rapid advances in neuro-anatomy and physiology, there has been a revival of interest in, and many discussions of, the brain mechanisms which underlie the phe-nomena of awareness, consciousness, attention, memory, and the func-tional integration of experience [e.g., 2, 136, 178, 179, 234].[41] So far as integrative functions are concerned, the present weight of evidence appears to focus upon the influence exercised by the masses of nerve cells in the upper part of the brain stem upon the more recently evolved cortical areas. An older notion that the cortex itself was of prime signifi-cance because it was somehow the "seat of consciousness" no longer seems to make complete neurological sense. Although no unanimity of opinion has been reached, hypotheses should emerge in time which will lead to further clarification of the relations between neurological evolution, psychological functioning, and cultural adaptation. Of central impor-tance in this complex web of relationships is the distinctive psychological focus of consciousness in Homo sapiens—the capacity for self-objectifica-tion which is so intimately linked with the normative orientation of all human societies.

SOCIOPSYCHOLOGICAL EVOLUTION AND NORMATIVE ORIENTATION

Although we can never check developmental stages in the enlargement of the brain by direct observation of behavior, we do know what the be-havioral outcome was in the most highly evolved hominid. Here, along with a greater diversification in the forms of social structure in Homo sapiens, we are confronted with a radical change in their underlying dynamics. At this more advanced stage, a normative orientation becomes

[41] Penfield and Rasmussen write: "It is apparent that there are important con-nections which conduct both ways between areas of cortex and specific nuclei of the diencephalon, and that in the process of encephalization a varying degree of autonomy has been handed over to the large cortical projections. It does not neces-sarily follow, however, that all function, either new or old, has been handed over in this way nor that correlation between the activities of the different cortical areas is necessarily carried out in the cortex rather than in the diencephalon. . . . Popu-lar tradition, which seems to be largely shared by scientific men, has taken it for granted that the cortex is a sort of essential organ for the purposes of thinking and consciousness, and that final integration of neural mechanisms takes place in it. Perhaps this is only natural since there has been an extraordinary enlargement of the cortex in the human brain, and, at the same time, man seems to be endowed with intellectual functions of a new order." However, "the whole anterior frontal area, on one or both sides, may be removed without loss of consciousness. During the amputation the individual may continue to talk, unaware of the fact that he is being deprived of that area which most distinguishes his brain from that of the chimpanzee" [178, pp. 204, 205–206, 226].

an inherent aspect of the functioning of all sociocultural systems, since traditionally recognized standards and values are characteristic of them. Techniques are appraised as good or bad; so are the manufactured objects themselves. Property rights are regulated according to recognized standards. Knowledge and beliefs are judged true or false. Art forms and linguistic expression are brought within the sphere of normative orientation. Conduct is evaluated in relation to ethical values. All cultures are infused with appraisals that involve cognitive, appreciative, and moral values [230, pp. 344–346; 128, pp. 388–433].[42]

It has been said by a biologist that the foundation of any kind of social order is dependent upon role differentiation.[43] The general principle underlying social organization at any level is that role behavior on the part of individuals is, within limits, predictable in a wide variety of situations.[44] This is what makes it possible to establish empirically characteristic patterns of behavior interaction whether in invertebrates, vertebrates, or primates, despite the fact that the relative importance of innate versus learned determinants may vary widely at different levels. Normative orientation in man implements regularities in social systems at a more complex psychological level of development through role differentiation that is mediated by socialized values and goals. While some contemporary biologists, like Darwin a century ago in his *Descent of Man*, have given particular emphasis to the moral sense of man,[45] this aspect of social adjustment is but one facet of man's normative orientation. If all the ramifications of the normative orientation of human societies are taken into account, we have a major clue to the kind of psychological transformation that must have occurred in hominid evo-

[42] A value orientation, whether "held by individuals or in the abstract-typical form, by groups," and varying from explicit to implicit, is defined by Kluckhohn et al. as "a generalized and organized conception, influencing behavior, of nature, of man's place in it, of man's relation to man, and of the desirable and non-desirable as they may relate to man-environment and interhuman relations" [128, p. 411].

[43] Jennings, assuming a phylogenetic perspective and speaking of infrahuman animals, said: "Only if the individuals play different functional roles is there social organization" [118, p. 105].

[44] Cf. the discussion of "role expectations" in Sarbin [198, p. 226 ff.]. "Persons occupy positions or statuses in interactional situations. Psychologically considered, positions are cognitive systems of role expectations, products of learning. Role expectations are bidimensional; for every role expectation of other there is a reciprocal role expectation of self. The organized actions of the person, directed towards fulfilling these role expectations, comprise the role" [198, p. 225].

[45] Dobzhansky says, "It is man's moral sense which makes him truly human" [52, p. 376]; cf. 52a, pp. 340 req. And Simpson, asserting that "man is a moral animal," says: "It requires no demonstration that a demand for ethical standards is deeply ingrained in human psychology. Like so many human characteristics, indeed most of them, this trait is both innate and learned. Its basic mechanism is evidently part of our biological inheritance" [215, p. 294]. See also Waddington [234a].

lution to make this level of adaptation possible, and some measure of its depth and significance for an understanding of the dynamics of human systems of social action.

In their analysis of the functional prerequisites of a human society, Aberle and his associates [1] introduce the concept of an "actor," with cognitive, affective, and goal-directed orientation, but they do not discuss the psychological prerequisites of this actor. While this is irrelevant in their frame of reference, in phylogenetic perspective the capacities of the actor are crucial. For the functioning of a system of action as a normatively oriented social order requires a capacity for self-objectification, identification with one's own conduct over time, and appraisal of one's own conduct and that of others in a common framework of socially recognized and sanctioned standards of behavior.[46] Without a psychological level of organization that permits the exercise of these and other functions, moral responsibility for conduct could not exist, nor could any social structure function at the level of normative orientation. Learning remains important, of course, but it functions at a higher level of sociopsychological integration. The relations between needs, motivation, goals, and learning become more complex. The analysis of Aberle and his associates inevitably includes the "normative regulation of means," the "regulation of affective expression," and the "effective control of disruptive forms of behavior." Value systems have an ordering function in social interaction; they promote the broad behavioral expectancies which are of the essence of role differentiation in a *sociocultural* system.

Man, for example, has departed very radically from his primate forerunners in ecological development through the invention and use of technological devices of all kinds and in economic organization. A normative orientation in these spheres of activity is epitomized by the standards applied to the distribution of goods and services and to the ownership of property. One of the universal functions of all systems of property rights, which are among the common denominators of culture, is to orient individuals in human societies toward a complex set of basic values inherent in their day-to-day operation. This kind of value orientation is just as crucial in relation to the motivation and interpersonal relations of individuals as are the values associated with sexual behavior. Property rights are not only an integral part of the economic organization of any human system of social action; they likewise implement the functioning of the social order in relation to the resources of the physical environment through normative means. Discussion of "property" among

[46] Consequently, it is thoroughly intelligible why role theorists, more than any other group, as Sarbin points out, "have developed and used the conception of the self as an intervening variable" [198, p. 238].

infrahuman animals have centered around such phenomena as food sharing, the defense of the nest, prey, territorial domain, and so forth. The
question is: In what sense are such phenomena comparable with the
socially recognized and sanctioned rights in valuable objects that characterize property in human societies? In the latter the basis of ownership
is the correlative obligations others have to allow me to exercise *my*
property rights. A owns B against C, where C represents all other individuals. It is an oversimplification to omit C and simply say A owns B
[see 76, chap. 12]. Among infrahuman animals, we meet with entirely
different conditions. All we observe is the utilization, or possession (in the
sense of physical custody or use), of certain objects which bear some
relation to the biological needs of the organism or group of organisms.
We cannot properly speak of rights, obligations, and privileges in societies
where there is no normative orientation. We can only refer to such abstractions when a cultural system as well as a system of social action
exists. "Use values" may exist at a protocultural stage in the primates,
but they function in social systems with different properties.

Another example of normative orientation in human societies is
the well-known phenomenon of incest avoidance. With its associated
manifestations of shame, guilt, and anxiety, it long presented a puzzling
sociopsychological problem because the underlying psychological structure
was not thoroughly understood.[47] Such patterns of avoidance, with both
constant and variable features, do not and could not operate at a nonhominid level where genealogical relations between individuals are not
known, where socially sanctioned value systems are not present, and
where the phenomena of self-identification and moral responsibility for
conduct does not exist. Kroeber has pointed out that "the incest taboo is
the complement of kin recognition." Abstraction, in turn, "involves ability
to symbolize, in other words, speech" [130, p. 206]. Consequently, incest
taboos could not arise among primates incapable of self-other orientation in a web of differentiated moral relationships. In social interaction,
the individual could not be held responsible for differentiated responses to
kin until the latter were explicitly classified through linguistic or other
means. Although precisely the same genealogical relationships existed at
a lower level of primate social organization, they could not be consciously identified and utilized as a basis of differential social interaction
until the individual "actors" participating in the system developed a
personality structure that permitted self-objectification and the use of
symbolic means in playing sanctioned roles within a common framework
of values.

Further ramifications of the basic significance of normative orienta-

[47] Lowie, e.g., in his *Primitive Society* [150], expressed the view that incest taboos
have an instinctive basis. Later he changed his mind [151, p. 67].

tion and its psychological correlate of self-awareness in the evolution of a fully developed mode of cultural adaptation cannot be considered here. But the question can be raised as to whether the capacity for self-objectification was common to all the Hominidae from the beginning. Perhaps we might venture to say that, although some of the psychological *anlagen* were present at a protocultural stage, a capacity for self-objectification and role differentiation functioning in intimate relations with socially sanctioned value systems were sociopsychological developments that only became established in typical form long after the initial steps in hominid anatomical differentiation had taken place. One of the reasons for this, as we shall see, is that these developments were contingent upon a system of communication that was not only socially transmitted but, through symbolic mediation, gave unique and characteristic scope to the novel psychological capacities that had been developing through the expansion of the hominid brain.

EGO AND SELF-OBJECTIFICATION

While it has been widely recognized that self-awareness is a characteristic phenomenon in Homo sapiens,[48] the psychological structure that underlies it has been seriously studied only since the rise of a more general interest in personality structure, mainly under the impact of psychoanalytic theories. The evolutionary aspects of the problem have been scarcely touched.[49] Indeed, there have been "many psychologists

[48] For example, Bidney at the outset of his *Theoretical Anthropology* [17, p. 3] writes: "Man is a self-reflecting animal in that he alone has the ability to objectify himself, to stand apart from himself, as it were, and to consider the kind of being he is and what it is that he wants to do and to become. Other animals may be conscious of their affects and the objects they perceive; man alone is capable of reflection, of self-consciousness, of thinking of himself as an object." The psychologist David Katz, writing more than twenty years ago, likewise stressed what he called "objectivization" as a human differential [124, p. 253]. More recently, Rollo May has given particular emphasis to human self-awareness. "We can never see man whole," he says, "except as we see him, including ourselves, as the mammal who has a distinctive capacity for awareness of himself and his world. Herein lie the roots of man's capacity to reason and deal in symbols and abstract meaning. And herein lies also the basis for a sound view of human freedom" [157, p. 313; cf. 156, pp. 84–85]. Other comparable opinions could be cited, e.g., Dobzhansky [52a, pp. 337 ff.].

[49] Stanley Cobb, in discussing the papers contributed to the symposium *Brain Mechanisms and Consciousness* [2], says: "Although some of the authors seem to confuse the concepts of 'mind' and 'consciousness,' Fessard seems to agree with me that 'consciousness' is but one attribute of 'mind.' I would say [it is] *that part which has to do with awareness of self and of environment.* It varies in degree from moment to moment in man and from fish to man in phylogeny. It may be that invertebrates and even plants have rudimentary forms of awareness of self" [37, p. 202]. It is difficult, however, to follow Cobb through to this point! Sir Julian

of the modern period," as Asch says, "who have spoken of the individual organism as of a congeries of capacities and tendencies without a self-character" [6, p. 276]. It has been pointed out, moreover, that "between 1910 and 1940, most psychologists preferred not to mention 'ego' or 'self' in their writings" [199, chap. 20]. The publication of G. W. Allport's article in 1943 [4] initiated a renewed interest in ego and self on the part of social psychologists in particular. Nowadays, "ego" and "self" are familiar terms, although the connotation given them is not standardized. However, no one uses the ego concept in any substantive sense but rather as a psychological construct useful in conceptualizing a subsystem of the total personality, objectively approached, with reference to its development, structure, and functioning. If we wish to be rigorous, it is best to speak of a group of ego processes or functions, although this is sometimes awkward. Ego functions have a wide range; they are intimately connected with such cognitive processes as attention, perception, thinking, and judgment, because ego processes are involved in determining adjustments to the outer world in the interests of inner needs, particularly in a situation where choice or decision, and hence delay or postponement of action, is required [cf. 223, p. 4].[50]

On the other hand, the concept of self carries a reflexive connotation: "I" can think of "me." I can discriminate myself from other objects perceptually; I can conceive of myself as an object; I can develop attitudes toward myself. Thus the self is a phenomenal datum, whereas the ego is a construct. "The self can be observed and described; the ego is deduced and postulated. The ego may be conceived in quasi-physiological terms as a sub-system of the organism" [154, p. 234; cf. 6, chap. 10; 223]. Furthermore, the self does not mirror the ego—the subject's capacity for self-objectification does not imply his objective knowledge of the psychodynamics of his total personality.

Huxley has suggested that since *"mind* and *mental* have various undesirable connotations, it is best to drop them and to speak of awareness. Psychology in the customary sense can then be regarded as part of the general study of awareness and its evolution." This would include "the way in which new possibilities of awareness are in fact realized, and also of the limitations on their realization . . . . There are two evolutionary prerequisites for a high organization of awareness involving the incorporation of individual experience by learning: (1) a long youth period . . . ; (2) homothermy, permitting greater uniformity and continuity of awareness. Prerequisites for the further organization of the awareness-system, to enable it to incorporate experiences from other individuals and from past generations. are (1) social life, (2) the capacity to organize awareness in the form of concepts, (3) true speech. These have permitted the evolution of the unique type of awareness-system found in man" [113, pp. 558–559; cf. 110].

   [50] Hartmann [86] distinguishes ego, a psychic subsystem of the total personality, with functions distinguishable from the id and superego, from self, one's own person.

Considered in evolutionary perspective, the ego may be said to be the major "psychological organ" that structurally differentiates the most highly evolved members of the Hominidae from subhominid primates and probably other hominids of lower evolutionary rank. It lies at the core of a human personality structure as we know it in Homo sapiens. Hall and Lindzey, for example, point out that "among the theorists who, in some way, make prominent use of the ego or self concept are Adler, Allport, Angyal, Cattell, Freud, Goldstein, Jung, Murphy, Murray, and Sullivan" [73, p. 545; cf. 218, pp. 27–28]. It permits adaptation at a new behavioral level. Since, in ontogenetic development, the beginnings of ego processes can be identified in the first half year of life well before the acquisition of speech, we can say that, while ego development occurs in a context of social interaction, in its initial stages it is not contingent upon the prior existence of either speech or culture. The underlying capacities for ego functioning must have deeper psychobiological roots.[51] This is the area in which the evolutionary problem lies. Rapaport, discussing the general, or psychological, theory of psychoanalysis with reference to the drive-object conception of reality, writes:

While the instincts of animals on lower evolutionary levels appear to be directly and more or less rigidly coordinated to specific external stimuli, the instincts of animals on higher evolutionary levels appear to be less rigidly coordinated to such specific stimuli. This difference may be characterized as a progressive internalization of the regulation of behavior [which is] considered coterminous with the establishment of the ego [183, p. 98].

Heinz Hartmann has been a pioneer in the development of psychoanalytic ego psychology. He says that we must not overlook important relations between animal instinct and human ego functions. His point is that "many functions, which are taken care of by instincts" in the lower animals "are in man functions of the ego." But, he says, we should not identify the nature and role of instincts in animals with "drives" in man. "The id, too, does not appear to be a simple extension of the instincts of lower animals. While the ego develops in the direction of an ever closer adjustment to reality, clinic experience shows the drives, the id-tendencies, to be far more estranged from reality than the so-called animal instincts generally are" [85, p. 379 ff.]. With reference to ontogenesis, Hartmann has been responsible for stressing an early "undifferentiated phase," in contrast with the notion that the id is chronologically older than the ego, and the concept of a "conflict-free ego sphere" [86]. In the early undifferentiated stage of ontogenetic development, there are no ego functions and no differentiation of self from the world outside. With respect

[51] While there is a considerable literature on the body-image phenomenon, the relations between body image, ego, and self-concepts are still under discussion [61].

to phylogenetic development, Hartmann says that while psychoanalysts do "attribute a sort of ego to animals" [87, p. 48; no species indicated]—

. . . we cannot speak, in regard to the animal, of that kind of separation into ego and id which exists in the human adult. The very fact that the concept of instincts as it pertains to the lower animals is much more comprehensive than the concept of instinctual drives as it pertains to man prevents such a separation. It is possible, and even probable, that it is just this sharper differentiation of the ego and the id—the more precise division of labor between them—in human adults which on the one hand makes for a superior, more flexible relation to the outside world and, on the other, increases the alienation of the id from reality [cf. 85].

Discussing Hartmann's conception of reality, Rapaport says:

In animals of lower evolutionary levels the instincts are the guarantees of reality adaptedness; man's drives have lost much of this role, and thus inborn adaptedness is with him more a potentiality than an actuality; processes of adaptation outweigh inborn adaptedness. This potentiality for internalized regulation of behavior actualizes in the course of the development of the ego, which thus becomes man's organ of adaptation . . . Hartmann goes even further and conceives of the reality to which man adapts as one created by him and his predecessors [183, p. 100].

Related to Hartmann's views are those of H. E. Erikson. "Man is potentially preadapted . . . to a whole evolving series of such environments [which] are not 'objective,' but rather social environments which meet his maturation and development half-way" [183, p. 100].

These views are of central importance in a conjunctive approach to human evolution. They reinforce other evidence which indicates that the general evolutionary trend is one in which the role of central cortical functions, acting as intervening variables, becomes increasingly important. Ego processes and functions in Homo sapiens would appear to represent the culmination of this trend in the primates, laying the foundation, among other things, for the more psychologically complex "inner world" of man. At the same time, the potentialities for relative autonomy from the external environment, in the purely "objective" sense, can be appreciated as an inherent part of later hominid evolution and the role which culturally constituted "behavioral" environments came to play in man's psychosocial adaptation.

Since, in contrast to the more peremptory determinants of behavior, ego processes refer to those aspects of behavior which are delayable, bring about delay, or are themselves products of delay [59, p. 5], evidence for the phylogenetic roots of the ego may be sought in the functional equivalents of ego processes and functions at lower primate levels.

Although Nissen does not make the inference himself, I think that the examples he gives in support of his assertion that the higher anthropoids are "guided by a delicately balanced system of values," may be taken as evidence of the functioning of rudimentary ego processes:

The larger and stronger male chimpanzee deferring to his female companion in the division of food, even after the female is pregnant and no longer suitable as a sex partner—the animal "punishing" the misbehavior of his cagemate and in position to inflict serious injury, but contenting himself with merely nipping him painfully—the chimpanzee refusing to expose himself to the frustration of occasional failure in a difficult problem, although he could get a desirable tidbit 50 per cent of the time by merely continuing to make a simple and easy response—these are but a few of many instances of a finely adjusted hierarchy of values. Like man, the chimpanzee has many values only indirectly related to primary needs, as for food, sex, and knowledge [169, p. 108].

It need not be inferred, I think, that the values referred to by Nissen were socially sanctioned, or that the chimpanzee is capable of consciously relating or appraising his own conduct with reference to socially acquired values. These values of the chimpanzee do not represent fully articulated values in the human sense. We are still at a protocultural level of sociopsychological functioning where no normative orientation exists.

However, the intervening variables that appear to be determinative in these situations exemplify the behavioral outcome of the shift from physiological to cortical controls which laid the foundation that enabled the Pongidae and, no doubt, their protohominind relatives, to develop a new level of psychobiological adaptation. I cannot escape the impression, either, that the behavior of the chimpanzees at Orange Park exemplifies the integration of attention, perceiving, thinking, purposiveness, and the postponement of action, in a rudimentary form, which are among the ego processes and functions attributed to Homo sapiens. Seeing visitors arriving, they ran quickly to the drinking fountain and, after filling their mouths with water, quietly waited for the closer approach of the visitors before discharging it at them. Hebb and Thompson, who report this observation [90, p. 539], do not refer to ego processes or function but use the episode to illustrate the chimpanzees' capacity for what is called "syntactic behavior," which they consider crucial in phylogenesis. In involves an "increasing independence of the conceptual activity from the present sensory environment, and an increasing capacity for entertaining diverse conceptual processes at the same time." Among other things it "eventually makes speech possible." "At the lowest level, it is the capacity for delayed response or a simple expectancy; at the highest level, for 'building' not only a series of words but also of sentences, whose meaning only becomes clear with later words or sentences." To my mind, Hebb's concept of syntactic behavior falls along the psychological dimension in phylogenesis where we must look for the rudimentary phases of ego processes and functions.[52] At the same time, I do not think that behavioral evidence such as that cited, which appears to indicate the functioning of rudimentary ego processes, allows us to make the further inference that this behavior involves self-objectification.

The capacity for self-objectification represents a level of psychological integration that requires the operation of additional factors. On the one hand, self-objectification is rooted in a prior development of rudimentary ego functions; on the other, the representation and articulation of a sense of self-awareness is contingent upon the capacity for the symbolic projection of experience in socially meaningful terms, i.e., in a mode that is intelligible interindividually. There must be a functional integration of intrinsic representative processes with some extrinsically expressible means of symbolization. An extrinsic mode is necessary in order to mediate socially transmitted and commonly shared meanings in a system of social action. There must become available to an individual some means whereby inwardly as well as outwardly directed reference to his own experience and that of others, and to objects and events in his world that are other than self, can find common ground. Outward behavior can be perceived and imitated through observational learning in nonhominid primates. Emotional experiences can become contagious. But what is privately sensed, imaged, conceptualized, or thought cannot be imitated or responded to without an overt sign extrinsic to the experience itself. Working the drinking fountain at Orange Park or nest building in the chimpanzee can be socialized without the mediation of any form of extrinsic representation. There is no evidence to suggest that either the chimpanzee or any other nonhominid has developed a traditional means whereby it is possible for an individual to represent himself and other objects and events to himself as well as to others. Consequently, even though capacities for ego-centered processes may exist, they can attain only a limited functional range.

In phylogenetic perspective there is evidence that intrinsic symbolic processes (i.e., central processes that function as substitutes for or representatives of sensory cues or events that are not present in the immediate perceptual field) occur not only in subhominid primates but in some lower species. But even in the higher apes the functioning of these representative processes appears to be limited, as is a capacity for ego processes. But it is difficult to know precisely what these limits are. Schneirla, making reference to Crawford's experiment [40] on the cooperative solving of problems by chimpanzees, says that these animals

---

[52] Hebb and Thompson make a most illuminating comment: "It is probably a common experience to all who have worked at the Yerkes Laboratories to feel that the bare bones of human personality, the raw essentials, are being laid open before his eyes. At the same time, it is hard to convey this to others, and to support it with behavioral evidence" [90, p. 544].

. . . were able to learn a gestural form of communication and use it symbolically. [They were enabled] to summon one another by means of self-initiated gestures such as gentle taps on the shoulder. These were truly symbolic, and not merely signals to action. The chimpanzee who tapped was presenting, in anticipation of its social effect, a special cue which had come to symbolize, i.e., to stand for meaningfully, the expected social result. The symbolic, anticipative, and directive nature of this gestural cue was indicated by the fact that, when shoulder taps were insufficient, or slow in producing co-operation, the active animal would turn to pulling alone, or might act forcibly and directly to get the second animal involved in pulling. Although it is not known how far and in what ways such gestural devices may be involved in chimpanzee group communication under natural conditions, their use is probably very limited [205, pp. 64–65].[53]

Interpreted in this way, the gestures referred to may be considered a rudimentary and highly limited mode of displacement or extrinsic symbolization. The function of these gestures was, of course, imposed by the nature and circumstances of the experiment. In this framework, conditions were not favorable for the perpetuation of these gestures through social learning and transmission in a wider group.

A unique observation illustrates the presence of intrinsic symbolic processes in chimpanzees, tantalizing because of their incommunicability. It is reported that Viki sometimes played with what appeared to be an imaginary pull-toy which she towed around on an imaginary string [88, chap. 11]. Viki, of course, could not deliberately communicate the content of her experience to ape or man, even if she had so desired. She could only act out her fantasy. Mrs. Hayes could only observe what she saw and guess what the probable image was that motivated Viki's behavior. Viki did not have the capacity to abstract, objectify, and transform the content of her intrinsic symbolic processes into a symbolic form extrinsic to the experience itself. For the same reason, we can be certain that she could not think about herself as an object playing with her pull-toy. Because there was no system of extrinsic symbolization available as a means of communication, the world that Viki and Mrs. Hayes could share was very limited psychologically. It may be that one of the major reasons chimpanzees cannot be taught to speak is that they are not capable of manipulating second-order abstractions of the type necessary for

[53] In a later publication, Schneirla notes that "a child's attainment of sentences marks a new advance from the stage of unitary verbal symbols, and contrasts sharply with a monkey's inability to master symbolic relationships beyond the simplest abstractions. In a far wider sense, man's capacity for repatterning verbal symbols serially, or for attaining such symbols at all, is qualitatively far above the functional order represented by the gestural symbolic processes to which the chimpanzee seems developmentally limited, although not altogether dissimilar in its ontogenetic basis" [207, p. 102]. I am not concerned here with the introduction of symbolic cues into laboratory investigations by the experimenter [80, p. 493 ff.].

extrinsic symbolization even though lower levels of abstraction are possible for them.

The earliest unequivocal proof of the capacity of Homo sapiens for extrinsic symbolization in a visual mode is found in the cave art of the Upper Paleolithic. Here we find the graphic representation of such animals as mammoth, rhinoceros, bison, wild horse, reindeer, etc., which could not have been present in the perceptual field of the artist when the drawings were made. The location of them in most of the caves excludes this possibility.[54] The number of human, or human-like figures, is small in proportion to the hundreds of animal drawings. So far as the figures of wild animals are concerned, we can only infer that the men of this period had highly accurate and vivid memory images of the contemporary fauna (intrinsic symbolization). At the same time, their capacity to abstract essential features of their images and represent them in a material medium is demonstrated. When the animals themselves were not present, the drawings of them in a naturalistic style could convey to other men what was "in" the artist's "mind." While the iconic type of symbolization employed required some abstraction, there is a relatively close correspondence in form between the object seen, the memory image, and the graphic symbolization.

But there also seems to be evidence in the cave art of a related human capacity, that is, the ability to project graphically synthetic images of fabulous creatures, animal-like or human-like, which were not objects of ordinary perceptual experience. These belong, rather, to the world of creative imagination. The beast with two horns at Lascaux is the prime example of the representation of a fantastic animal.[55] Many examples of ambiguous human figures—synthesizing both

[54] In one cave I visited I remember crawling along a low gallery on my knees, with candle in hand, for a considerable distance before reaching the end of it. Discouraged at not finding any drawings, I turned over on my back for a rest. There above me were several drawings of wild horses. And Laming says: "At Arcy-sur-Cure the engravings are discovered only after a painful crawl of about 80 yards over slippery clay and sharp-pointed calcite. Such remote recesses, difficult of access and laborious of approach, are almost as numerous as the painted and engraved caves themselves. The placing of all these figures in remote parts of dark caverns seems to bear witness to a pursuit of the arduous, the magical, and the sacred" [139, p. 158].

[55] Breuil writes: "By its massive body and thick legs, it resembles a bovine animal or a Rhinoceros; the very short tail is more indicative of the latter; the flanks are marked with a series of O-shaped oval splashes; the neck and ears are ridiculously small for the body; the head with a square muzzle, is like that of a Feline; two long stiff straight shafts, each ending in a tuft, are like no known animal horns, unless, as Miss Bate suggested, those of the Pantholops of Thibet . . . . This is not the only example of a composite unreal animal in Quaternary art, but it is the most spectacular" [23, p. 118 and Fig. 89]. The drawing measures about 5 ft. 6 in.

human and animal characteristics—are known. It is these figures which have proved the most difficult to interpret in the whole repertoire of cave art, since in style they do not fit the realistic tradition of the animal art.[56] The older view that these semihuman figures were the representation of actual human beings wearing masks or the skins of animals has been steadily losing ground. In the cave of Trois Frères, the figure originally called a "sorcerer" by Breuil and Bégouën is now thought by them to be the representation of the "Spirit controlling the multiplication of game and hunting expeditions" [23, pp. 176–177]; in other words, it is a god or a personage of an other-than-human class.[57] If the humanly ambiguous figures are thought of as belonging to such a class, I believe that it may be argued that we have evidence suggesting that a system of beliefs is reflected in the art. If such be the case, this category of figures is equivalent to the personages that appear in the myths of living primitive peoples. In this case, the cave art would offer evidence of a level of imaginative functioning and conceptual creativity that transcended a purely naturalistic reproduction of what was perceived. It could be interpreted as revealing capacities in early representatives of Homo sapiens that are psychologically equivalent to capacities of living peoples studied in their full cultural context, where the details of world view and religious beliefs have been recorded.[58]

The symbolism embodied in speech is in a different mode, since sound clusters are given a meaning-content that is unrelated to the form or qualities of the objects or events represented. Nevertheless, it seems to me that we must assume that the same basic capacities for extrinsic

[56] For illustrations of 250 examples of these figures and a systematic classification and analysis of them, see [195].

[57] Laming is of the opinion that "the imaginary animals and the semi-human figures are . . . incompatible with the theory of sympathetic magic" which has been applied to the animal art. Considered as a whole, she also finds untenable "the theory that they represent hunting masks or have some connection with ritual hunting dances." "Why should the sorcerers, who were probably the artists of the tribe, depict themselves on the walls of the sanctuary wearing their masks?" she asks. It seems more likely that these drawings "represent mythical beings who were perhaps connected in some way with the history of the ancestors of the group" [139, pp. 191–192].

[58] Cf. the discussion of "persons" of an other-than-human class among Ojibwa [78]. Persons of this category are reified beings in the behavioral world of the Ojibwa and are equivalent to characters in their myths. Among them these narratives are true stories. Since metamorphosis is possible, a hard and fast line cannot even be drawn between the outward appearance of *human* persons and animals. Persons of the other-than-human class in particular, appear in myths and dreams in animal form. If the Ojibwa had an art similar to that of the Upper Paleolithic peoples and we had no other evidence, it can be imagined how difficult it would be to interpret the graphic representations they had made of persons of an other-than-human class.

symbolization are involved. Art forms are as indicative of these capacities as are speech forms. Among other things, graphic art in all its manifestations requires abstraction, or it could not function as a means of representation. In any case, it is hard to believe that the people of the Upper Paleolithic did not possess a vocal system of representation (although we have no direct evidence of speech) as well as a fully developed mode of cultural adaptation equivalent to that of the nonliterate peoples of historic times. Viki and other chimpanzees, if considered as representative of an advanced level of infrahominid behavior, manifest as little capacity for graphic symbolization of an extrinsic type as for vocal symbolization [see the colored reproductions of Viki's paintings in *Life*, Dec. 3, 1951]. By the time we reach the Upper Paleolithic, the infrahominids have been left far behind on the ladder of behavioral evolution.

Systems of extrinsic symbolization necessitate the use of material media which can function as vehicles for the communication of meanings. Abstraction and conceptualization are required since objects or events are introduced into the perceptual field as *symbols*, not in their concrete reality. Thus systems of extrinsic symbolization involve the operation of the representative principle on a more complex level than do processes of intrinsic symbolization. In the case of Homo sapiens, extrinsic symbolic systems, functioning through vocal, graphic, plastic, gestural, or other media, make it possible for groups of human beings to share a common world of meanings and values. A cultural mode of adaptation is unthinkable without systems of extrinsic symbolization.

From a phylogenetic point of view, the capacity for individual and social adaptation through the *integral* functioning of intrinsic symbolic processes and extrinsic symbolic systems enabled an evolving hominid to enlarge and transform his world. The immediate, local, time-and-space-bound world of other primates, who lack the capacity for dealing effectively with objects and events outside the field of direct perception, could be transcended. Speech, through the use of personal pronouns, personal names, and kinship terms made it possible for an individual to symbolize, and thus objectify, himself in systems of social action. Self-related activities, both in the past and future, could be brought into the present and reflected upon.[59] What emerged was a personality structure in which ego processes and functions had become salient at a high level of integration—self-awareness. The inner world of private experience and the outer world of public experience became intricately

[59] Cf. Révész, who writes, "Without the verbal formulation of subjective experience and ethical standards, self-consciousness is incomplete and self-knowledge and self-control equally so. To be conscious of one's own self, to examine one's own endeavors, motives, resolves, and actions, necessarily presupposes language" [188, p. 104].

meshed through symbolic mediation. In the human societies, the self-image became, in part, a culturally constituted variable; self-orientation became integrated with other basic orientations toward the world that enabled the individual to think, feel, and act in a culturally constituted behavioral environment [76, chap. 4]. As a result of self-objectification, human societies could function through the commonly shared value orientations of self-conscious individuals, in contrast with the societies of nonhominid and probably early hominid primates, where ego-centered processes remained undeveloped or rudimentary. In fact, when viewed from the standpoint of this peculiarity of man, culture may be said to be an elaborated and socially transmitted system of meanings and values which, in an animal capable of self-awareness, implements a type of adaptation which makes the role of the human being intelligible to himself, both with reference to an articulated universe and to his fellow men.

The central importance of ego processes and self-awareness that we find distinctive in Homo sapiens can be viewed from another angle. Since self-objectification involves self-appraisal in relation to sanctioned moral conduct, we can see the social as well as the individual adaptive value of unconscious psychological processes such as repression, rationalization, and other defense mechanisms. Culturally constituted moral values impose a characteristic psychological burden, since it is not always easy, at the level of self-awareness, to reconcile idiosyncratic needs with the demands imposed by the normative orientation of the self. For animals without the capacity for self-objectification, no such situation can arise. Freedman and Roe write:

Only in man is there simultaneously such a rigidity of social channeling and such a degree of potential plasticity and flexibility for the individual. Incompatible aims and choices which are desirable but mutually exclusive are inevitable conditions of human development. This discrepancy between possibility and restriction, stimulation and interdiction, range and construction, underlies that quantitatively unique characteristic of the human being: conflict [66, p. 461].

In Homo sapiens, unconscious mechanisms may be viewed as an adaptive means that permits some measure of compromise between conflicting forces. They relieve the individual of part of the burden not only forced upon him by the requirements of a morally responsible existence but by the fact that the normative orientation of any human social order permeates all aspects of living. A human level of existence requires an evolutionary price; man as a species has survived, despite proneness to conflict, anxiety, and psychopathology [cf. 66, p. 422]. Freud's interpretation is to be found in his *Civilization and Its Discontents:* "The price of progress in civilization is paid for in forfeiting hap-

piness through the heightening of the sense of guilt" [67, p. 123]. There
seems to be little question that one of the crucial areas of individual
adjustment turns upon the sensitivity of the self to feelings of anxiety and
guilt.

Psychoanalysts, in particular, have come more and more to recognize that psychological maladjustment centers around the structural
core of the human personality. David Beres, for example, writes: "There
is then in man this unique structure, the ego, which in its full function
allows for the expression of those qualities which distinguish the human
from the animal and which, in their malfunction, give to his behavior
and thought the characteristically human forms of mental illness" [16,
pp. 170, 231].

Leopold Bellak has recently reviewed the shift in focus that has
occurred in psychoanalytic thinking:

The novelty in psychoanalysis was originally its introduction of the unconscious in the sense of the unconsciousness of feelings, the unawareness
of previously experienced events, the covert nature of motivations, and the
hidden meaning of dreams and symptoms. Slowly attention focused on the
forces responsible for this unconsciousness, notably repression [13, pp. 25–26].

A new era, however, "dedicated to the analysis not only of the unconscious but of the ego and its defences," was initiated with Anna
Freud's book *The Ego and the Mechanisms of Defense* (1936). So
that now "the pendulum has swung nearly full cycle, in that there is
so much talk about ego psychology today that the forces of the unconscious are possibly already somewhat in disregard" [13, pp. 25–26; cf.
220, p. 146].

Franz Alexander, commenting on the same shift of interest, says,

Mental disease represents a failure of the ego to secure gratification for
subjective needs in a harmonious and reality-adjusted manner and a breakdown of the defenses by which it tries to neutralize impulses which it cannot harmonize with its internal standards and external reality. . . . The
highest form of integrative function requires conscious deliberation. Everything which is excluded from consciousness is beyond the reach of the ego's
highest integrative functions. . . . Psychoanalytic therapy aims at the extension of the ego's integrative scope over repressed tendencies by making
them conscious [3, p. 78 ff.].[60]

Thus, in the terminology I have been using here, psychological
functioning at a level of self-awareness is as important for rational
personal adjustment as it is for the functioning of sociocultural systems.
Furthermore, as Schneirla points out, it is an error stemming from an

[60] Cf. Hartmann's remarks on the synthetic or organizing functions of the ego
[85, pp. 383–384].

inadequate comprehension of the complex nature of a human level of existence to assume "that man's 'higher psychological processes' constitute a single agency or unity which is capable of being sloughed off" even under extreme provocation. On the contrary—

. . . socialized man even under stress of extreme organic need or persistent frustration does not regress to the "brute level." Rather, he shifts to some eccentric and distorted variation of his ordinary personality, which varies from his prevalent socialized make-up according to the degree of integrity and organization attained by that adjustment system [202, p. 273].

This is why we find variations in the symptomatology and incidence of mental disorders in man when we consider them in relation to differences in cultural modes of adaptation. These phenomena often have been given a purely relativistic emphasis. But increasing evidence suggests that they probably can be ordered to psychodynamic principles and etiological factors that operate universally [14, 226]. Direct comparison, moreover, between the psychopathology of the "civilized" individual mind and the "primitive" mind savors more than ever of a pseudoevolutionary problem.

CONCLUSIONS

What we observe in the behavior of Homo sapiens is the evolutionary culmination and unique integration of structures and functions which had developed over a span of millions of years in the long and complex history of the primates. The human nature of Homo sapiens cannot be fully grasped outside this framework. The cultural level of adaptation which has been said to be the characteristic feature of a human level of existence requires a developmental conceptualization which includes prerequisite conditions of a noncultural order and a discrimination of organic, social, and psychological variables operating in the past. I have used the construct "protoculture" as a means of identifying the necessary, but not sufficient, conditions which appear to be the evolutionary prerequisites of the fully developed phase of cultural adaptation as represented in Homo sapiens.

On the assumption that the hominid line of evolutionary radiation initially involved the genetic establishment of the structural changes which led to a bipedal upright posture and a terrestrial mode of adaptation, two stages of protocultural development which preceded cultural adaptation may be tentatively postulated. The first stage can be associated with the prehominids, and evidence for it is derived from observations on living groups of nonhominids. In the chronology of behavioral evolution, this protocultural stage may be conceived as having great temporal depth; at the same time, its most distinguishing features may be thought of as continuous with the earliest level of hominid morphological differentiation. In its sociological and psychological dimensions, it links the prehominids with the *early* hominids, and also provides some of the necessary conditions for *later* hominid cultural adaptation.

The second stage of protocultural development can be conceptually associated with the earliest hominids *prior* to the genetic establishment of an expanded cortex in the more evolved members of this group, the subfamily Homininae. This differentiation of two levels of protocultural development, based as it is on structural changes which have behavioral implications, is not intended to be precise. But it enables us to distinguish behavioral continuities and differences in relation to known structural changes and ecological relations and it provides us with a somewhat more differentiated chronological sequence than would a simple dichotomous distinction between infrahominid and hominid levels. The second protocultural stage, in short, is a construct which enables us to distinguish an intermediate phase of behavioral evolution. In this phase, certain features of an earlier protocultural stage persisted, but were modified by the structural changes which adapted the early hominids to a new ecological niche. In turn, this second protocultural stage was transformed; with the expansion of the brain, a new level of behavioral evolution, characterized by a fully developed mode of cultural adaptation, came into being.

The most important feature of the earliest protocultural stage (exemplified by nonhominid primates) was the existence of social structures or systems of social action. These structures were based on role differentiation, which partially depend upon the socialization of individuals mediated by observational learning, some tutelage perhaps, and unlearned systems of sign communication, both gestural and vocal. The latter embodied some design features which were later incorporated in the more elaborated system of linguistic communication that we find associated with the later level of cultural adaptation. There was social transmission of some group habits at the earlier level; perhaps there was occasional tool using of the simplest kind. In other words, it was a form of social organization which, in so far as it was a system of social action in which learning was related to social structure and to the transmission of social habits, exemplifies some of the basic conditions which are required for cultural adaptation. Particularly striking, in the light of present knowledge, is the lack of any evidence that there were any socially transmitted forms of communication in nonhominid societies, even though some of the design features of the languages characteristic of Homo sapiens were already present.[61]

---

[61] Carpenter says: "The limitations of capacities for communication, especially for symbol communication, seem to stop non-human primate social development at the level of limited contemporary social groupings, to preclude the development of tribal kinship and to make it impossible for them to have any except the *anlagen* of cultural traditions" [29, p. 242].

So far as learned behavior is concerned, its importance in relation to culture has been both exaggerated and oversimplified. As Nissen said, "Experience will not make a man out of a monkey" [169, p. 105]. Learning in the form of simple conditioning is found far down the animal scale.[62] Cultural adaptation cannot be equated with learned and socially transmitted behavior, although it is one of the necessary conditions underlying it. Equally important in behavioral evolution is how much is learned and what is learned, relative to the psychological capacities and total life adjustments of the animal.[63]

In anthropological writing prior to the culture and personality movement, the vital connection between learning, social organization, and culture remained vague; the gap had not been bridged between abstracted culture patterns and the behavior of specific individuals through such concepts as socialization or enculturation, personality structure, status, and role. The fact had been overlooked that a culture can be perpetuated only through the characteristic psychological structuralization of individuals in an organized system of social action. At a protocultural stage, what was learned differed both quantitatively and qualitatively from what was observed at a later stage in behavioral evolution. Particularly significant in primate evolution is the fact that learning became linked with social structure and the transmission of habits through a socialization process at the subhominid level. Here learning already played a part in the life history of the individual and the functioning of the social order that closely parallels at many points the part it continued to play in human *sociocultural* systems. Nor has there been sufficient

[62] Harlow argues that "there is no evidence that any sharp break ever appeared in the evolutionary development of the learning process" [83, p. 288]. At the same time, "it is quite clear that evolution has resulted in the development of animals of progressively greater potentialities for learning and for solving problems of increasing complexity" [83, p. 269].

[63] Hilgard is not content with the implicit, if not always explicit, generalization from comparative studies that "there are no differences, except quantitative ones, between the learning of lower mammals and man." At the human level, he says, "There have emerged capacities for retraining, reorganizing, and foreseeing experiences which are not approached by the lower animals, including the other primates. No one has seriously proposed that animals can develop a set of ideals that regulate conduct around long-range plans, or that they can invent a mathematics to help them keep track of their enterprises. . . . Language in man is perhaps the clearest of the emergents which carries with it a forward surge in what may be learned. It seems plausible enough that other advances in the ability to learn must have come about as the nervous system evolved through successive stages below man. . . . There are probably a number of different kinds of learning which have emerged at different evolutionary periods, with the more highly evolved organisms using several of them. It is quite probable that these different kinds of learning follow different laws, and it is foolhardy to allow our desire for parsimony to cause us to overlook persisting differences" [94, p. 461].

stress on the fact that at the earliest protocultural level, characterized ecologically by arboreal adaptation and territoriality, arboreal trails had to be learned [32, p. 241].

Considered in evolutionary perspective, a cultural mode of adaptation required an environmental setting in which ecological relations provided a foundation for later developments, in addition to sociopsychological prerequisites and the functioning of some system of communication. Consequently, a second protocultural stage which distinguished the hominid line of evolution from that of the pongids was initiated concomitantly with the structural changes. Arboreal adaptation may have played a part in the earlier evolution of the primates, and this may have included the development of distinctive psychological capacities and behavioral patterns. But it is difficult, if not impossible, to imagine an arboreal domain as the ecological matrix of cultural adaptation as observed in Homo sapiens. If we take a long-range view of ecological adaptation in the primates (excluding cases in which terrestrial adaptation has been achieved by such Old World monkeys as the baboons, who retained their pronograde mode of locomotion), we can reconstruct a successive series of arboreal adaptations. The series begins high in the tropical treetops where lower primate forms occupy a niche, leads downward to lower arboreal habitats, and ultimately arrives at a terrestrial niche occupied by the hominids. Le Gros Clark says:

[In the primates] each successive grade has developed a new ecological domain, leaving behind representatives of antecedent grades (more or less modified for their local habitat of course) in occupation of the particular arboreal environment for which they had already become adapted. It may be said, indeed, that the trees of African and Asiatic forests still retain in rough outline a stratified population of Primates which represents the successive grades of the evolutionary tree of this order. [The] smallest and more primitive types (tree-shrews), by confining their activities mainly to the more attenuated branches of the treetops, lead a secluded life within the protection of foliage and have thus become effectively segregated from the larger types [146, pp. 320–321].

Le Gros Clark does not specifically make the point, but it seems to me that the hominids, in developing upright posture and orthograde locomotion, have taken an almost predictable step in the series of ecological readaptations which characterize primate evolution. The new ecological domain of the early hominids subsequently became the theater of the cultural adaptation of the more advanced hominids (Homininae).

Terrestrial living provided the ecological framework of these later developments. When the necessary psychological capacities, accumulated experience, and technological traditions had been developed, the hominids were able to accelerate the behavioral differences between themselves and other primates, achieving greater independence of their environment through increasing knowledge of its inanimate resources and its fauna and flora and through a succession of discoveries and inventions. Even if capacities for *tool using* were present in arboreal primates, how could the properties of stone have been discovered, exploited, and developed into the lithic industries of a *toolmaking* tradition by creatures who spent little or no time on the ground? How could the domestication of animals and the cultivation of plants come about? How could fire become of importance in the life of primates confined to an arboreal niche? Terrestrial living was one of the necessary prerequisites for cultural adaptation. It provided the opportunity for discovering new food resources. Ultimately it made possible the shift, through a possible scavenging stage, to hunting large mammals, cooking meat, and the omnivorous diet of the Homininae. Eiseley has pointed out that, so far as organic inheritance is conceived, the hominid gut is not that of a true meat eater. Nevertheless, euhominids did become carnivorous and thus underwent, according to Eiseley, "a transition in food habits which is unique on the planet" [56]. Details regarding this transition during the second protocultural phase may, in time, be filled in by evidence from archeological research. So far, there is no positive evidence that fire was used in the earliest stage of terrestrial adaptation.[64] Since fire could be brought completely under control only by fire-making implements, or tools, it may well be that they were only developed along with other tools employed in hunting and cutting meat. (I refer to the most rudimentary of tools. Even very simple cutting tools could have made it possible to supplement a vegetarian diet with the meat of small animals.)

It can be assumed, I think, that territoriality persisted into the second protocultural stage. A question arises as to whether there was any change in the size of organized social groups. Oakley's estimated size for the range of australopithecine groups is 10 to 200 individuals. Washburn and DeVore point out that "this corresponds almost exactly to the range in size observed in baboons. Since both are plains-living, primarily vegetarian forms," they say, "the comparison is of particular interest" [241]. Sahlins has estimated the size of human hunting groups to range between 20 and 50 [197]. Present data suggests that the size of localized groups may not have increased during the earliest phases of a cultural mode of adaptation. Their composition, however, undoubtedly did change to include individuals of several generations, as psychological restructuralization provided the foundation for modes of social control

[64] Oakley thinks: "It is probable that the earliest paleolithic fire-users were not *fire-makers*, but collected this precious commodity from natural conflagrations, and conserved it." There is evidence that fire was used earlier in Asia and Europe than Africa. "The oldest acceptable indications of the use of fire by man in Europe and Western Asia are associated with Acheulian hand-axe culture" [176].

that were based on superego functioning as well as external social sanctions.

We assume that hominid differentiation involved selection for immaturity, as indicated by the fact that maturation was slower, dependency of the young longer, and menarche later, so that longevity increased and the generation span became greater than at the subhominid level. If this is correct, there must have been a feedback into the system of social organization which affected the length of the period of socialization and the social transmission of new habits.

We can also assume that the new ecological domain to which the early hominids were becoming adapted provided increased opportunity to exercise behavioral potentialities already present. Motor functions like grasping hands were freed for new uses, and the discriminatory function of binocular stereoscopic vision facilitated new developments in tactile skills, manual dexterity, and probably visual imagery. It would appear that toolmaking arose in this period if the later australopithecines may be taken as representative; according to Washburn, this development may have had a feedback effect upon the expansion of the brain. Washburn and Avis have expressed the opinion that tool using may require "much less brain than does speech and might have started as soon as the hands were freed from locomotive functions" [240, p. 432]. Since the cortex had not yet undergone expansion, cranial capacity may have only ranged from 450 to 600 cc (australopithecines) and communication may well have remained at the nonhominid stage, thus maintaining another link with the earlier protocultural period.

In a new ecological setting, with greatly expanded possibilities for life adjustment provided by bipedal locomotion and some minor changes in social structure and food habits, the early hominids might have continued their existence at this level of adaptation indefinitely if another organic change had not occurred. This was the rapid expansion of the brain. Through the addition of neurons and their intricate systems of cerebral organization, the brain became the neurophysiological basis of the mode of behavioral adaptation that has been called "cultural" in Homo sapiens and antecedent types of Homininae. Psychological restructuralization occurred; it became manifest through the generic type of personality structure observable in Homo sapiens, it released novel potentialities whose feedback into the already existing systems of social action transformed them psychodynamically through the now possible normative orientation. For example, while parents and their offspring previously had been associated in systems of social action, the development of incest taboos radically affected their relations psychologically. It likewise affected the roles of other individuals brought within the categories of kinship. Mediated by the development of extrinsic forms of symbolization which appeared in speech and in the arts, cultural adaptation may be viewed as the culmination of social evolution in the primates to which new dimensions were added. This development could not have occurred, however, without the distinctive combination of prerequisite conditions already found in the protocultural phases of behavioral evolution.

There was a quantitative maximization of social learning, reinforced by teaching; this led to qualitatively distinctive consequences because of the role which learning came to play in the formation of a human personality structure and the functioning of the higher mental processes. Cognitive processes were raised to a new level of functioning by means of culturally constituted symbolic forms; these now could be manipulated creatively through reflective thought, imagination, and novel forms of expression. Cultural modes of adaptation—or certain aspects of them— could also be thought about, objectified, analyzed, judged, and even remodeled to some degree by hominids who had achieved a capacity for self-awareness and had become objects to themselves in a world of other objects. In the behavioral evolution of the primates, the great novelty was not simply the development of a cultural mode of adaptation. It was the psychological restructuralization that made this new mode of existence possible and also provided the potentialities for cultural readjustment and change. The psychological basis of culture lies not only in a capacity for highly complex forms of learning, but in a capacity for transcending what is learned—a potentiality for innovation, creativity, reorganization, and change.[65]

In time, men even initiated systematic rational inquiries into the nature of the inanimate world, the world of living things, and man himself—despite the fact that this knowledge conflicted at many points with the traditional world view of their culture. In modern times, scientific investigations have demonstrated this extraordinary capacity of our species to the highest degree. We now feel far removed from the infrahominid level of societal organization or the level of thought and action possible for the earliest hominids. Yet our mode of existence, elaborate as it may be, is linked with theirs in the same sense that all higher forms of organic life are linked with antecedent forms through the evolutionary process. In fact, most of the categories of variables which appear again and again in the studies of contemporary man can be projected into the far-distant past. For a comprehensive understanding of the evolutionary roots of human behavior, a conjunctive approach is just as relevant as it is for a study of contemporary man. Too radical ab-

[65] Cf. Henry, who points out that "because his mechanism for determining personal relations lacks specificity," man's unique evolutionary path is set for him "by his constant tendency to alter his modes of social adaptation. Put somewhat in value terms, man tries constantly to make a better society, i.e., one in which he can feel more comfortable. When he makes a 'mistake,' he tries to change. This is one way in which he evolves" [92, pp. 221–222].

stractions of the morphological, sociological, ecological, or psychological variables considered above leads to fragmentary knowledge in either case.

In either framework, too, man's social nature emerges as a paramount fact which cannot be ignored. The higher primates, like the later hominids, were gregarious animals. But this must not be taken as a banal descriptive fact. Their social existence took the form of discretely organized systems of social action, even though these were more restricted in numbers and differentiation of roles than ours. Behavioral evolution must be thought of as the concomitant evolution of continuously present and changing social relations, structured in systems of social action—not as the evolution of the behavioral attributes of isolated individuals. Consequently the genetic changes which took place in the primates, as in other animals, present problems in population genetics, the population units in this case being the social groups referred to. Thus, organic, ecological, social, and psychological variables all need to be considered in relation to each other at all levels of behavioral evolution.[66]

In Homo sapiens, personality, society, and culture have been conceptually differentiated for special types of analysis and investigation. At the same time, their interdependence is now well recognized. They cannot be postulated as independent variables either in the study of modern man or in human behavioral evolution. Considered phylogenetically, we gain some insight into the temporal depth of their intimate connections, as well as their relation to organic and ecological variables. Besides this, the significance of these integral connections is brought into focus both with respect to the sociopsychological nature of modern man as a product of evolution and the primary adaptive processes inherent in the achievement of the sociocultural systems which have become characteristic of his mode of life.

REFERENCES

1. Aberle, D. F., Cohen, A. K., Davis, A. K., Levy, M. J., Jr., & Sutton, F. X. The functional prerequisites of a society. *Ethics,* 1950, **60,** 100–111.
2. Adrian, E. D., Bremer, F., Delafresnaye, J. F., & Jasper, H. H. (Eds.) *Brain mechanisms and consciousness.* Springfield, Ill.: Charles C Thomas, 1954.
3. Alexander, F. The evolution and present trends of psychoanalysis.

[66]Cf. the thesis expounded by Dobzhansky that "man has both a nature and a 'history,'" and that "human evolution cannot be understood as a purely biological process, nor can it be adequately described as a history of culture. It is the interaction of biology and culture. There exists a feedback between biological and cultural processes" [52a, p. 18].

Acta Psychol., 1950, **7,** 126–133. Reprinted in H. Brand (Ed.), *The study of personality: a book of readings.* New York: Wiley, 1954.

4. Allport, G. W. The ego in contemporary psychology. *Psychol. Rev.,* 1943, **50,** 451–478.

5. Allport, G. W. The historical background of modern social psychology. In G. Lindzey (Ed.), *Handbook of social psychology.* Vol. 1. Reading, Mass.: Addison-Wesley, 1954.

6. Asch, S. E. *Social psychology.* Englewood Cliffs, N.J.: Prentice-Hall, 1952.

7. Asch, S. E. A perspective on social psychology. In S. Koch (Ed.), *Psychology: a study of a science.* Vol. 3. New York: McGraw-Hill, 1959. Pp. 363–383.

8. Bartholomew, G. A., Jr., & Birdsell, J. B. Ecology and the protohominids. *Amer. Anthrop.,* 1953, **55,** 481–498.

9. Beach, F. A. Evolutionary changes in the physiological control of mating behavior in mammals. *Psychol. Rev.,* 1947, **54,** 297–315.

10. Beach, F. A. Instinctive behavior: reproductive activities. In S. S. Stevens (Ed.), *Handbook of experimental psychology.* New York: Wiley, 1951.

11. Beach, F. A. Evolutionary aspects of psychoendocrinology. In Anne Roe & G. G. Simpson (Eds.), *Behavior and evolution.* New Haven, Conn.: Yale Univer. Press, 1958.

12. Beals, R. Acculturation. In A. L. Kroeber (Ed.), *Anthropology today: an encyclopedic inventory.* Chicago: Univer. Chicago Press, 1953.

13. Bellak, L. Psychoanalytic theory of personality. In J. L. McCary (Ed.), *Psychology of personality: six modern approaches.* New York: Logos Press, 1956.

14. Benedict, P. K., & Jacks, I. Mental illness in primitive societies. *Psychiatry,* 1954, **17,** 377–389.

15. Benedict, Ruth. Franz Boas as an ethnologist. In Franz Boas, 1858–1942. Mem. 61, *Amer. Anthrop. Ass.,* 1943, **45,** No. 3, Part 2.

16. Beres, D. Ego deviation and the concept of schizophrenia. In *The psychoanalytic study of the child.* Vol. 11. New York: International Universities Press, 1956. Pp. 164–235.

17. Bidney, D. *Theoretical anthropology.* New York: Columbia Univer. Press, 1953.

18. Boas, F. Psychological problems in anthropology. *Amer. J. Psychol.,* 1910, **21,** 371–384.

19. Bolk, L. *Das Problem der Menschwerdung.* Jena: Fischer, 1926.

20. Boring, E. G. *A history of experimental psychology.* New York: Appleton-Century-Crofts, 1950.

21. Bourlière, F. Classification et caractéristiques des principaux types de groupements sociaux chez les vertébrés sauvages. In P. Grassé (Ed.), *Structure et physiologie des sociétés animales.* Paris: Centre National de la Recherche Scientifique, 1952. Pp. 71–79.

22. Bourlière, F. *The natural history of mammals.* (2nd ed.) New York: Knopf, 1956.

23. Breuil, H. *Four hundred centuries of cave art.* Montignac, Dor-

dogne: Centre d'Études et de Documentation Prehistoriques, 1952.
24. Brown, R. W. *Words and things*. Glencoe, Ill.: Free Press, 1958.
25. Carpenter, C. R. A field study of the behavior and social relations of the howling monkeys. *Comp. Psychol. Monogr.*, 1934, **10.**
26. Carpenter, C. R. A field study in Siam of the behavior and social relations of the gibbon (Hylobates lar.). *Comp. Psychol. Monogr.*, 1940, **16.**
27. Carpenter, C. R. Characteristics of social behavior in non-human primates. *Trans. N.Y. Acad. Sci.*, 1942, **4,** (Ser. II), 248–258.
28. Carpenter, C. R. Concepts and problems of primate sociometry. *Sociometry*, 1945, **8,** 55–61.
29. Carpenter, C. R. Social behavior of non-human primates. In P. Grassé (Ed.), *Structure et physiologie des sociétés animales.* Vol. 34. Paris: Centre National de la Recherche Scientifique, 1952. Pp. 227–245.
30. Carpenter, C. R. Tentative generalizations on grouping behavior of non-human primates. *Hum. Biol.*, 1954, **26,** 269–276. Reprinted in J. A. Gavan (Ed.), *The non-human primates and human evolution.* Detroit, Mich.: Wayne State Univer. Press, 1955.
31. Carpenter, C. R. Soziologie und Verhalten freilebender nichtmenschlicher Primaten. In *Handbuch der Zoologie*. Bd. 8, Lief. 18. Berlin: Walter de Gruyter, 1958. Pp. 1–32.
32. Carpenter, C. R. Territoriality: a review of concepts and problems. In Anne Roe & G. G. Simpson (Eds.), *Behavior and evolution.* New Haven, Conn.: Yale Univer. Press, 1958.
33. Carter, G. S. *Animal evolution*. London: Sidgwick & Jackson, 1951.
34. Carter, G. S. The theory of evolution and the evolution of man. In A. L. Kroeber (Ed.), *Anthropology today.* Chicago: Univer. Chicago Press, 1953.
35. Chance, M. R. A. What makes monkeys sociable. *The New Scientist,* March, 1959.
36. Chance, M. R. A., & Mead, A. D. Social behavior and primate evolution. *Sympos. Soc. exp. Biol.*, 1953, **7,** 395–439.
37. Cobb, S. Awareness, attention, and physiology of the brain stem. In P. H. Hoch & J. Zubin (Eds.), *Experiments in psychopathology.* New York: Grune & Stratton, 1957.
38. Collias, N. E. Social life and the individual among vertebrate animals. *Ann. N.Y. Acad. Sci.*, 1950, **50,** 1074–1092.
39. Count, E. W. The biological basis of human sociality. *Amer. Anthrop.*, 1958, **60,** 1049–1085.
40. Crawford, M. P. The cooperative solving of problems by young chimpanzees. *Comp. Psychol. Monogr.*, 1937, **14,** No. 2.
41. Critchley, M. Animal communication. *Trans. Hunterian Soc. London,* 1958, **16,** 90–111.
42. Critchley, M. The evolution of man's capacity for language. In S. Tax (Ed.), *The evolution of man.* Vol. 2. *Evolution after Darwin.* Chicago: Univer. Chicago Press, 1960.
43. Cuenot, L. L'homme ce Neotenique. *Bull. Acad. roy. Belgique* (Brussels), 1945, **31.**

44. Dart, R. A. Cultural status of the South African man-apes. *Annu. Rep., Smithsonian Instn.* (*1955*). Pp. 317–338.
45. Dart, R. A. *Adventures with the missing link.* New York: Harper, 1959.
46. Darwin, C. *The descent of man.* London: Murray, 1871.
47. Darwin, C. *The expression of the emotions in man and animals.* New York: Appleton-Century-Crofts, 1873. (A new edition with a preface by Margaret Mead was published by the Philosophical Library, New York, 1956.)
48. De Beer, G. R. *Embryos and ancestors.* New York: Oxford, 1951.
49. De Laguna, Grace A. *Speech: its function and development.* New Haven, Conn.: Yale Univer. Press, 1927.
50. Dennis, W. Developmental theories. In *Current trends in psychological theory.* Pittsburgh, Pa.: Univer. Pittsburgh Press, 1951.
51. Dewey, J. The need for a social psychology. *Psychol. Rev.*, 1917, **24**, 266–277.
52. Dobzhansky, Th. *Evolution, genetics, and man.* New York: Wiley, 1955.
52a. Dobzhansky, Th. *Mankind Evolving. The Evolution of the Human Species.* New Haven, Conn.: Yale Univer. Press, 1962.
53. Du Bruhl, E. L. *Evolution of the speech apparatus.* Springfield, Ill.: Charles C Thomas, 1958.
54. Edinger, Tilly. Objets et resultats de la paleoneurologie. *Ann. Paleontol.*, 1956, **42**, 97–116.
55. Eggan, F. Social anthropology and the method of controlled comparison. *Amer. Anthrop.*, 1954, **56**, 743–763.
56. Eiseley, Loren C. Fossil man and human evolution. In W. L. Thomas, Jr. (Ed.), *Yearbook of anthropology, 1955.* New York: Wenner-Gren Foundation for Anthropological Research, 1955.
57. Eiseley, Loren C. *Darwin's century: evolution and the men who discovered it.* New York: Doubleday, 1958.
58. Erikson, E. H. *Childhood and society.* New York: Norton, 1950.
59. Erikson, E. H. Identity and the life cycle. Selected papers. With a historical introduction by D. Rapaport. *Psychol. Issues Monogr.*, 1959, No. 1. Published by International Universities Press, New York.
60. Etkin, W. Social behavior and the evolution of man's mental faculties. *Amer. Naturalist*, 1954, **88**, 129–142.
61. Fisher, S., & Cleveland, S. E. *Body image and personality.* New York: Van Nostrand, 1958.
62. Fiske, J. *The meaning of infancy.* Boston: Houghton Mifflin, 1909. (Reprinting of "The meaning of infancy" from *Excursions of an evolutionist,* 1884, and "The part played by infancy in the evolution of man" from *A century of science, and other essays,* 1899.)
63. Flugel, J. C. *A hundred years of psychology, 1833–1933.* New York: Macmillan, 1933.
64. Ford, C. S., & Beach, F. A. *Patterns of sexual behavior.* New York: Harper, 1951.

65. Frazer, J. G. Scope and method of mental and anthropological science. *Sci. Progress,* 1922, **16**, 580–594.
66. Freedman, L. Z., & Roe, Anne. Evolution and human behavior. In Anne Roe & G. G. Simpson (Eds.), *Behavior and evolution.* New Haven, Conn.: Yale Univer. Press, 1958.
67. Freud, S. *Civilization and its discontents.* London: J. Cape, 1930.
68. Frisch, J. E. Research on primate behavior in Japan. *Amer. Anthrop.,* 1959, **61**, 584–596.
69. Fuller, J. L., & Scott, J. P. Heredity and learning ability in infrahuman animals. *Eugenics Quart.,* 1954, **1**, 28–43.
70. Greenberg, J. H. Language and evolutionary theory. In Essays in linguistics. *Viking Fund Publ. Anthrop.,* 1957, No. 24. (Published by Wenner-Gren Foundation for Anthropological Research, New York.)
71. Haddon, A. C. *History of anthropology.* (Rev. ed.) London: Watts, 1934.
72. Haldane, J. B. S. Animal communication and the origin of human language. *Sci. Progr.,* 1955, **40**, 385–401.
73. Hall, C. S., & Lindzey, G. *Theories of personality.* New York: Wiley, 1957.
74. Hallowell, A. I. Culture, personality, and society. In A. L. Kroeber (Ed.), *Anthropology today.* Chicago: Univer. Chicago Press, 1953.
75. Hallowell, A. I. Psychology and anthropology. In J. Gillin (Ed.), *For a science of social man.* New York: Macmillan, 1954.
76. Hallowell, A. I. *Culture and experience.* Philadelphia: Univer. Pa. Press, 1955.
77. Hallowell, A. I. The structural and functional dimensions of a human existence. *Quart. Rev. Biol.,* 1956, **31**, 88–101.
78. Hallowell, A. I. Ojibwa metaphysics of being and the perception of persons. In R. Tagiuri & L. Petrullo (Eds.), *Person perception and interpersonal behavior.* Stanford, Calif.: Stanford Univer. Press, 1958.
79. Harlow, H. F. Levels of integration along the phylogenetic scale: learning aspect. In J. H. Rohrer & M. Sherif (Eds.), *Social psychology at the crossroads.* New York: Harper, 1951.
80. Harlow, H. F. Thinking. In H. Helson (Ed.), *Theoretical foundations of psychology.* New York: Van Nostrand, 1951.
81. Harlow, H. F. Primate learning. In C. P. Stone (Ed.), *Comparative psychology.* (3rd ed.) Englewood Cliffs, N.J.: Prentice-Hall, 1952.
82. Harlow, H. F. Current and future advances in physiological and comparative psychology. *Amer. Psychologist,* 1956, **11**, 273–277.
83. Harlow, H. F. The evolution of learning. In Anne Roe & G. G. Simpson (Eds.), *Behavior and evolution.* New Haven, Conn.: Yale Univer. Press, 1958.
84. Hart, C. M. H. Social evolution and modern anthropology. In H. A. Innes (Ed.), *Essays in political economy in honour of E. J. Urwick.* Toronto: Univer. Toronto Press, 1938.
85. Hartmann, H. Psychoanalytic theory of instinctual drives. *Psychoanal. Quart.,* 1948, **17**, 368–388.

86. Hartmann, H. Comments on the psychoanalytic theory of the ego. In *The psychoanalytic study of the child.* Vol. 5. New York: International Universities Press, 1950.

87. Hartmann, H. Ego psychology and the problem of adaptation. D. Rapaport (Trans.). *J. Amer. Psychoanal. Ass. Monogr.,* 1958, No. 1. (Published by International Universities Press, New York.)

88. Hayes, Cathy. *The ape in our house.* New York: Harper, 1951.

89. Hayes, K. J., & Hayes, Catherine. The cultural capacity of chimpanzee. In J. A. Gavan (Ed.), *The non-human primates and human evolution.* Detroit, Mich.: Wayne State Univer. Press, 1955.

90. Hebb, D. O., & Thompson, W. N. The social significance of animal studies. In G. Lindzey (Ed.), *Handbook of social psychology.* Vol. 1. Reading, Mass.: Addison-Wesley, 1954.

91. Heberer, G. von. Die Fossilgeschichte der Hominoidea. In H. Hofer, A. H. Schultz, & D. Starck (Eds.), *Primatologia.* Vol. 1. New York: Karger, 1956. Pp. 379–560.

92. Henry, J. Culture, personality, and evolution. *Amer. Anthrop.,* 1959, **61,** 221–226.

93. Herrick, C. J. *The evolution of human nature.* Austin, Tex.: Univer. Tex. Press, 1956.

94. Hilgard, E. R. *Theories of learning.* (2nd ed.) New York: Appleton-Century-Crofts, 1956.

95. Hinde, R. A. Some recent trends in ethology. In S. Koch (Ed.), *Psychology: a study of a science.* Vol. 2. New York: McGraw-Hill, 1959.

96. Hochbaum, H. A. *Travels and traditions of waterfowl.* Minneapolis, Minn.: Univer. Minn. Press, 1955.

97. Hockett, C. F. *A course in modern linguistics.* New York: Macmillan, 1958.

98. Hockett, C. F. Animal "languages" and human language. In J. N. Spuhler (Ed.), *The evolution of man's capacity for culture.* Detroit, Mich.: Wayne State Univer. Press, 1959.

99. Hockett, C. F. The origin of speech. *Scient. Amer.,* 1960, **203,** 89–96.

100. Hofer, H., Schultz, A. H., & Starck, D. (Eds.) *Primatologia: Handbuch der Primatenkunde.* Vol. 1. New York: Karger, 1956.

101. Honigmann, J. J. *Culture and personality.* New York: Harper, 1954.

102. Honigmann, J. J. Psychocultural studies. In B. J. Siegel (Ed.), *Biennial review of anthropology—1959.* Stanford, Calif.: Stanford Univer. Press, 1959.

103. Honigsheim, P. The philosophical background of European anthropology. *Amer. Anthrop.,* 1942, **44,** 376–387.

104. Hooton, E. The importance of primate studies in anthropology. In J. A. Gavan (Ed.), *The non-human primates and human evolution.* Detroit, Mich.: Wayne State Univer. Press, 1955.

105. Howell, F. C. The Villafranchian and human origins. *Science,* 1959, **130,** 831–844.

106. Howell, F. C. Commentary on Leakey's "The newest link in human evolution." *Current Anthrop.,* 1960, **1,** 76–77.

107. Howells, W. W. Origin of the human stock: concluding remarks of the

Chairman. *Cold Spring Harbor Symp. quant. Biol.*, 1950, **15**, 79–86

108. Howells, W. W. *Mankind in the making.* New York: Doubleday, 1959.

109. Huxley, J. *Man stands alone.* New York: Harper, 1941.

110. Huxley, J. *Evolution in action.* New York: Harper, 1953.

111. Huxley, J. The evolutionary process. In J. Huxley, A. C. Hardy, & E. B. Ford (Eds.), *Evolution as a process.* London: G. Allen, 1954.

112. Huxley, J. Evolution, cultural and biological. In W. L. Thomas, Jr. (Ed.), *Yearbook of anthropology—1955.* New York: Wenner-Gren Foundation for Anthropological Research, 1955.

113. Huxley, J. Psychology in evolutionary perspective. *Amer. Psychologist,* 1956, **11**, 558–559.

114. Imanishi, K. Social behavior in Japanese monkeys, *Macaca fuscata. Psychologia,* 1957, **1**, 47–54. (In English)

115. Imanishi, K. Identification: a process of enculturation in the subhuman society of *Macaca fuscata. Primates,* 1959, **1**, 1–29. (English summary)

116. Imanishi, K. Social organization of subhuman primates in their natural habitat. *Current Anthrop.,* 1960, **1**, 393–407. (Comments by Bourlière, Carpenter, Chance, Emlem, Schultz, Washburn, De Vore, Zuckerman.)

117. Jacobi, Jolande. *Complex archetype symbol in the psychology of C. G. Jung.* R. Manheim (Trans.). New York: Pantheon Books (Bollingen Ser. 57), 1959.

118. Jennings, H. S. The transition from the individual to the social level. In *Biological symposia,* Vol. 8. R. Redfield (Ed.), *Levels of integration in biological and social systems.* Lancaster, Pa.: Cattell Press, 1942.

119. Jones, E. *The life and work of Sigmund Freud.* New York: Basic Books, 1953–57. 3 vols.

120. Jung, C. G. The spirit of psychology. In J. Campbell & Olga Frock-Kapteyn (Eds.), *Spirit and nature* (papers from the Eranos yearbooks, Ser. 1). New York: Pantheon Books (Bollingen Ser. 30, 1), 1954.

121. Jung, C. G. Commentary on the Tibetan book of the dead. In Violet S. de Laszlo (Ed.), *Psyche and symbol: a selection of the writings of C. G. Jung.* New York: Doubleday (Anchor Books), 1958.

122. Kaplan, B. Introduction and Epilogue. In B. Kaplan (Ed.), *Studying personality cross-culturally.* Evanston, Ill.: Row, Peterson, 1961.

123. Karpf, Fay B. *American social psychology: its origins, development, and European background.* New York: McGraw-Hill, 1932.

124. Katz, D. *Animals and men: studies in comparative psychology.* New York: Longmans, 1937.

125. Keith, A. *A new theory of human evolution.* London: Watts, 1948.

126. Kluckhohn, C. The personal document in anthropological science. In The use of personal documents in history, anthropology, and sociology. *Soc. Sci. Res. Counc. Bull,* 1945, No. 53.

127. Kluckhohn, C. Universal categories of culture. In A. L. Kroeber (Ed.), *Anthropology today.* Chicago: Univer. Chicago Press, 1953.

128. Kluckhohn, C., et al. Values and value-orientations in the theory of action. In T. Parsons & E. A. Shils (Eds.), *Toward a general theory of action.* Cambridge, Mass.: Harvard Univer. Press, 1951. Pp. 388–433.

129. Kroeber, A. L. Sub-human cultural beginnings. *Quart. Rev. Biol.*, 1928, **3**, 325–342.
130. Kroeber, A. L. The societies of primitive man. In *Biological symposia,* Vol. 8. R. Redfield (Ed.), *Levels of integration in biological and social systems.* Lancaster, Pa.: Cattell Press, 1942.
131. Kroeber, A. L. *Anthropology.* New York: Harcourt, Brace, 1948.
132. Kroeber, A. L. Anthropology. *Scient. Amer.*, 1950, **183**, 87–94.
133. Kroeber, A. L. *The nature of culture.* Chicago: Univer. Chicago Press, 1952.
134. Kroeber, A. L. On human nature. *S.W. J. Anthrop.*, 1955, **11**, 195–204.
135. Kroeber, A. L., & Kluckhohn, C. Culture: a critical review of concepts and definitions. *Papers Peabody Mus. Amer. Archeol. & Ethnol.*, 1952, **47**, No. 1. (Published by Harvard University Press, Cambridge, Mass.)
136. Kubie, L. S. Some implications for psychoanalysis of modern concepts of the organization of the brain. *Psychoanal. Quart.*, 1953, **22**, 21–68.
137. La Barre, W. *The human animal.* Chicago: Univer. Chicago Press, 1954.
138. La Barre, W. Influence of Freud on anthropology. *Amer. Imago*, 1958, **15**, 275–328.
139. Laming, Annette. *Lascaux paintings and engravings.* Baltimore, Md.: Penguin, 1959.
140. Lashley, K. S. Persistent problems in the evolution of mind. *Quart. Rev. Biol.*, 1949, **24**, 28–42.
141. Leakey, L. S. B. A new fossil skull from Olduvai. *Nature*, 1959, **184**, 491–493.
142. Leakey, L. S. B. The newest link in human evolution: the discovery by L. S. B. Leakey of *Zinjanthropus boisei. Current Anthrop.*, 1960, **1**, 76.
143. Le Gros Clark, W. E. *History of the primates: an introduction to the study of fossil man.* London: British Museum, 1950.
144. Le Gros Clark, W. E. *The fossil evidence for human evolution: an introduction to the study of paleoanthropology.* Chicago: Univer. Chicago Press, 1955.
145. Le Gros Clark, W. E. The study of man's descent. In S. A. Barnett (Ed.), *A century of Darwin.* Cambridge, Mass.: Harvard Univer. Press, 1958.
146. Le Gros Clark, W. E. *The antecedents of man: an introduction to the evolution of the primates.* Chicago: Quadrangle Books, 1960.
147. Le Gros Clark, W. E. The crucial evidence for human evolution. *Amer. Scient.*, 1959, **49**, 229–313.
148. Lovejoy, A. O. The length of human infancy in eighteenth century thought. *J. Phil.*, 1922, **19**, 381–385.
149. Lowie, R. H. *Culture and ethnology.* New York: McMurtrie, 1917.
150. Lowie, R. H. *Primitive society.* New York: Liveright, 1920.
151. Lowie, R. H. *The family as a social unit* (Papers of the Michigan Academy of Science, Arts, and Letters). Ann Arbor, Mich.: Univer. Mich. Press, 1933.
152. Lowie, R. H. *The history of ethnological theory.* New York: Holt-Rinehart-Winston, 1937.

153. Lowie, R. H. Reminiscences of anthropological currents in America half a century ago. *Amer. Anthrop.*, 1956, **58**, 995–1016.
154. MacLeod, R. B. The place of phenomenological analysis in social psychological theory. In J. H. Rohrer & M. Sherif (Eds.), *Social psychology at the crossroads*. New York: Harper, 1951.
155. Malinowski, B. *A scientific theory of culture and other essays*. Chapel Hill, N.C.: Univer. N.C. Press, 1944.
156. May, R. *Man's search for himself*. New York: Norton, 1953.
157. May, R. The historical meaning of psychology as a science and profession. *Trans. N. Y. Acad. Sci.*, 1955, **17** (Ser. 2), 312–314.
158. Montagu, M. F. A. Time, morphology, and neoteny in the evolution of man. *Amer. Anthrop.*, 1955, **57**, 13–27. Reprinted in *Anthropology and human nature*. New York: Porter Sargent, 1957.
159. Montagu, M. F. A. Neoteny and the evolution of the human mind. *Explorations*, 1956, No. 6, 85–90. Reprinted in *Anthropology and human nature*. New York: Porter Sargent, 1957.
160. Mowrer, O. H., & Kluckhohn, C. Dynamic theory of personality. In J. McV. Hunt (Ed.), *Personality and the behavior disorders*. Vol. 1. New York: Ronald, 1941. Pp. 69–135.
161. Mühlmann, W. *Methodik der Völkerkunde*. Stuttgart: Enke, 1938.
162. Munn, N. L. *The evolution and growth of human behavior*. Boston: Houghton Mifflin, 1955.
163. Murdock, G. P. The common denominator of cultures. In R. Linton (Ed.), *The science of man in the world crisis*. New York: Columbia Univer. Press, 1945.
164. Murdock, G. P. *Social structure*. New York: Macmillan, 1949.
165. Nissen, H. W. A field study of the chimpanzee: observations of chimpanzee behavior and environment in Western French Guinea. *Comp. Psychol. Monogr.*, 1931, No. 1.
166. Nissen, H. W. Primate psychology. In P. L. Harriman (Ed.), *Encyclopedia of psychology*. New York: Citadel Press, 1946.
167. Nissen, H. W. Phylogenetic comparison. In S. S. Stevens (Ed.), *Handbook of experimental psychology*. New York: Wiley, 1951.
168. Nissen, H. W. Social behavior in primates. In C. P. Stone (Ed.), *Comparative psychology*. Englewood Cliffs, N.J.: Prentice-Hall, 1951.
169. Nissen, H. W. Problems of mental evolution in the primates. In J. A. Gavan (Ed.), *The non-human primates and human evolution*. Detroit, Mich.: Wayne State Univer. Press, 1955.
170. Oakley, K. P. *Man the tool-maker*. London: British Museum, 1950.
171. Oakley, K. P. A definition of man. *Sci. News*, 1951, No. 20, 69–81.
172. Oakley, K. P. Skill as a human possession. In C. J. Singer et al. (Eds.), *History of technology*. Vol. 1. New York: Oxford, 1954.
173. Oakley, K. P. The earliest tool-makers. *Antiquity*, 1956, **30**, 4–8.
174. Oakley, K. P. Tools makyth man. *Antiquity*, 1957, **31**, 199–209. Reprinted in *Annual Report, Smithsonian Institution* (1958). Pp. 431–445.

175. Oakley, K. P. Tools or brains. Which came first? *Archeol. Newsltr.* (London), 1958, **6**, 48.

176. Oakley, K. P. On man's use of fire, with comments on tool-making and hunting. In S. L. Washburn (Ed.), *Social life of early man*. Viking Fund Publications in Anthropology, No. 31. New York: Wenner-Gren Foundation for Anthropological Research, 1961.

177. Parsons, T. An approach to psychological theory in terms of the theory of action. In S. Koch (Ed.), *Psychology: a study of a science*. Vol. 3. New York: McGraw-Hill, 1959.

178. Penfield, W., & Rasmussen, T. *The cerebral cortex of man*. New York: Macmillan, 1950.

179. Penfield, W., & Roberts, L. *Speech and brain-mechanisms*. Princeton, N. J.: Princeton Univer. Press, 1959.

180. Pumphrey, R. J. *The origin of language*. Liverpool: Liverpool Univer. Press, 1951. Reprinted in *Acta Psychol.*, 1953, **9**, 219–239.

181. Radin, P. The autobiography of an American Indian. *Univer. Calif. Publ. Archeol. & Ethnol.*, 1920, **16**, 381–473. A somewhat revised edition appeared in 1926 as *Crashing thunder*.

182. Radin, P. *The method and theory of ethnology*. New York: McGraw-Hill, 1933.

183. Rapaport, D. The structure of psychoanalytic theory: a systematizing attempt. In S. Koch (Ed.), *Psychology: a study of a science*. Vol. 3. New York: McGraw-Hill, 1959. Pp. 55–183.

184. Rensch, B. The relation between the evolution of central nervous functions and the body size of animals. In J. Huxley, A. C. Hardy, & E. B. Ford (Eds.), *Evolution as a process*. London: G. Allen, 1954.

185. Rensch, B. Increase of learning capability with increase of brain size. *Amer. Naturalist*, 1956, **90**, 81–95.

186. Rensch, B. *Homo sapiens vom tier zum halbgott*. Göttingen: Vandenhoeck & Ruprecht, 1959.

187. Révész, G. Is there an animal language? *Hibbert J.*, 1953–54, **70**, 141–143.

188. Révész, G. *The origins and prehistory of language*. New York: Longmans, 1956.

189. Ribot, T. *German psychology today*. New York: Scribner, 1886.

190. Rivers, W. H. R. Sociology and psychology. *Sociol. Rev.*, 1916, **9**, 1–13.

191. Roe, Anne, & Simpson, G. G. (Eds.) *Behavior and evolution*. New Haven, Conn.: Yale Univer. Press, 1958.

192. Roheim, G. *Psychoanalysis and anthropology*. New York: International Universities Press, 1950.

193. Romanes, G. J. *Animal intelligence*. New York: Appleton-Century-Crofts, 1883.

194. Romanes, G. J. *Mental evolution in man*. New York: Appleton-Century-Crofts, 1888.

195. Saccasyn-Della Santa, E. *Les figures humaines du paléolithique supérieur Eurasiatique*. Antwerp: De Sekkel, 1947.

196. Sahlins, M. D. The social life of monkeys, apes, and primitive man. In

J. H. Spuhler (Ed.), *The evolution of man's capacity for culture.*
Detroit, Mich.: Wayne State Univer. Press, 1959.

197. Sahlins, M. D. The origin of society. *Scient. Amer.,* 1960, **203,** 76–86.

198. Sarbin, T. R. Role theory. In G. Lindzey (Ed.), *Handbook of social psychology.* Vol. 1. Reading, Mass.: Addison-Wesley, 1954.

199. Sargent, S. S. *Social psychology.* New York: Ronald, 1950.

200. Schiller, Claire H. (Ed.) *Instinctive behavior.* New York: International Universities Press, 1957. (Introduction by K. S. Lashley.)

201. Schiller, P. H. Innate motor action as a basis of learning: manipulative patterns in the chimpanzee. In Claire H. Schiller (Ed.), *Instinctive behavior.* New York: International Universities Press, 1957.

202. Schneirla. T. C. Levels in the psychological capacity of animals. In R. W. Sellars, V. S. McGill, & M. Farber (Eds.), *Philosophy for the future.* New York: Macmillan, 1949.

203. Schneirla, T. C. The "levels" concept in the study of social organization of animals. In J. H. Rohrer & M. Sherif (Eds.), *Social psychology at the crossroads.* New York: Harper, 1951.

204. Schneirla, T. C. A consideration of some conceptual trends in comparative psychology. *Psychol. Bull.,* 1952, **49,** 559–597.

205. Schneirla, T. C. The concept of levels in the study of social phenomena. In M. Sherif & G. W. Sherif (Eds.), *Groups in harmony and tension.* New York: Harper, 1953.

206. Schneirla, T. C. Interrelationships of the "innate" and the "acquired" in instinctive behavior. In *L'instinct dans le comportement des animaux et de l'homme* (Foundation Singer-Polignac). Paris: Masson, 1956.

207. Schneirla, T. C. The concept of development in comparative psychology. In D. B. Harris (Ed.), *The concept of development.* Minneapolis, Minn.: Univer. Minn. Press, 1957.

208. Schultz, A. H. Primatology in its relation to anthropology. In W. L. Thomas, Jr. (Ed.), *Yearbook of anthropology, 1955,* New York: Wenner-Gren Foundation for Anthropological Research, 1955.

209. Schultz, A. H. Postembryonic age changes. In H. Hofer, A. H. Schultz, & D. Starck (Eds.), *Primatologia.* Vol. I. Basel: Karger, 1956. Pp. 887–964.

210. Schultz, A. H. Past and present views of man's specialization. *Irish J. med. Sci.,* 1957, 341–356.

211. Schultz, A. H. Some factors influencing the social life of primates in general and of early man in particular. In S. L. Washburn (Ed.), *Social life of early man,* Viking Fund Publications in Anthropology, No. 31. New York: Wenner-Gren Foundation for Anthropological Research, 1961.

212. Scott, J. P. The analysis of social organization in animals. *Ecology,* 1956, **37,** 213–221.

213. Scott, J. P. *Animal behavior.* Chicago: Univer. Chicago Press, 1958.

214. Shapiro, H. L. Review of Du Bruhl's "evolution of the speech apparatus." *Man,* 1960, No. 199.

215. Simpson, G. G. *The meaning of evolution.* New Haven, Conn.: Yale Univer. Press, 1950.

216. Singer, M. A survey of culture and personality theory and research. In B. Kaplan (Ed.), *Studying personality cross-culturally.* Evanston, Ill.: Row, Peterson, 1961.
217. Smith, M. B. Anthropology and psychology. In J. Gillin (Ed.), *For a science of social man.* New York: Macmillan, 1954.
218. Spiro, M. E. Human nature in its psychological dimensions. *Amer. Anthrop.,* 1954, **56,** 19–30.
219. Spuhler, J. N. Somatic paths to culture. In J. N. Spuhler (Ed.), *The evolution of man's capacity for culture.* Detroit, Mich.: Wayne State Univer. Press, 1959.
220. Stierlin, H. Contrasting attitudes toward the psychoses in Europe and in the United States. *Psychiatry,* 1958, **21,** 141–147.
221. Straus, W. L. Closing remarks. In J. A. Gavan (Ed.), *The nonhuman primates and human evolution.* Detroit, Mich.: Wayne State Univer. Press, 1955.
222. Straus, W. L. The Great Piltdown hoax. *Annu. Rep. Smithsonian Inst.,* 1954.
223. Symonds, P. M. *The ego and the self.* New York: Appleton-Century-Crofts, 1951.
224. Tax, S. (Ed.) *The evolution of man.* Vol. 2. *Evolution after Darwin.* Chicago: Univer. Chicago Press, 1960.
225. Tax, S., Eiseley, Loren C., Rouse, I., & Voegelin, C. F. (Eds.) *An appraisal of anthropology today.* Chicago: Univer. Chicago Press, 1953.
226. Teicher, M. I. Three cases of psychoses among the Eskimo. *J. ment. Sci.,* 1954, **100,** 527–535.
227. Thrope, W. H. *Learning and instinct in animals.* London: Methuen, 1956.
228. Tinbergen, N. *Social behavior in animals.* New York: Wiley, 1953.
229. Tinbergen, N. Behavior, systematics, and natural selection. In S. Tax (Ed.), *The evolution of life.* Vol. 1. *Evolution after Darwin.* Chicago: Univer. Chicago Press. 1960.
230. Tolman, E. C. A psychological model. In T. Parsons & E. A. Shils (Eds.), *Toward a general theory of action.* Cambridge, Mass.: Harvard Univer. Press, 1951, Pp. 279–361.
231. Trager, G. L. Para-language: a first approximation. *Stud. Linguistics,* 1958, **13,** 1–12.
232. Vallois, H. Le problème de l'hominisation. In *Les processus de l'hominisation.* Paris: Centre National de la Recherche Scientifique, 1958.
233. Voegelin, C. F. Culture, language, and the human organism. *S.W. J. Anthrop.,* 1951, **7,** 357–373.
234. Von Bonin, G. *Essay on the cerebral cortex.* Springfield, Ill.: Charles C Thomas, 1950.
234a. Waddington, C. H. *The Ethical Animal.* New York: Athenuem, 1961.
235. Waitz, T. *Introduction to anthropology.* London: Longman, Roberts & Green, 1863. Edited with numerous additions by the author from J. F. Collingwood, *Anthropologie der Naturvölker.* Vol 1.
235a. Wallace, A. F. C. *Culture and Personality.* New York: Random, 1961.

236. Walters, R. H. Historical background of comparative psychology. In C. P. Stone (Ed.), *Comparative psychology.* (3rd ed.) Englewood Cliffs, N.J.: Prentice-Hall, 1951. Pp. 9–29.
237. Washburn, S. L. The analysis of primate evolution with particular reference to the origin of man. *Cold Spring Harbor Symp. quant. Biol.,* 1950, **15**, 67–78.
238. Washburn, S. L. Speculations on the interrelations of the history of tools and biological evolution. In J. N. Spuhler (Ed.), *The evolution of man's capacity for culture.* Detroit, Mich.: Wayne State Univer. Press, 1959.
239. Washburn, S. L. Tools and human evolution. *Scient. Amer.,* 1960, **203**, 63–75.
240. Washburn, S. L., & Avis, Virginia. Evolution of human behavior. In Anne Roe & G. G. Simpson (Eds.), *Behavior and evolution.* New Haven, Conn.: Yale Univer. Press, 1958.
241. Washburn, S. L., & DeVore, I. Social behavior of baboons and early man. Viking Fund Publications in Anthropology, No. 31. New York: Wenner-Gren Foundation for Anthropological Research, 1961.
242. Washburn, S. L., & Howell, F. C. Human evolution and culture. In S. Tax (Ed.), *The evolution of man.* Vol. 2. *Evolution after Darwin.* Chicago: Univer. Chicago Press, 1960.
243. Weiner, J. S. Physical anthropology: an appraisal. *Amer. Scientist,* 1957, **45**, 79–87. Reprinted in *Evolution and anthropology: a centennial appraisal.* Washington.: Anthropological Society of Washington, 1959.
244. Werner, H. *Comparative psychology of mental development.* New York: Harper, 1940.
245. Westermarck, E. *History of human marriage.* New York: St. Martin's Press, Inc., 1903.
246. White, L. A. The origin and nature of speech. In W. S. Knickerbocker (Ed.), *Twentieth century English.* New York: Philosophical Library, 1940.
247. White, L. A. On the use of tools by primates. *J. comp. Psychol.,* 1942, **34**, 369–374.
248. White, L. A. Ethnological theory. In R. W. Sellars, V. J. McGill, & M. Farber (Eds.), *Philosophy for the future.* New York: Macmillan, 1949.
249. White, L. A. The individual and the culture process. *Centennial.* Washington: American Association for the Advancement of Science, 1950.
250. Wissler, C. Psychological and historical interpretations of culture. *Science,* 1916, **43**, 193–201.
251. Wissler, C. *Man and culture.* New York: Crowell, 1923.
252. Yerkes, R. M. *Chimpanzees: a laboratory colony.* New Haven, Conn.: Yale Univer. Press, 1943.
253. Zukerman, S. L'hominisation de la famille et des groupes sociaux. In *Les processus de l'hominisation.* Paris: Centre National de la Recherche Scientifique, 1958.

IV | OJIBWA ECOLOGY AND
SOCIAL ORGANIZATION

INTRODUCTION

Fred Eggan

A. I. Hallowell early became interested in both ecology and social organization, and together they encompass an important segment of his contributions to anthropology. As he notes in his autobiographical account (section I, above), it was his early contacts with Frank Speck that led to his interest in the hunting territories of the Northern Algonkian Indians; but his contributions to the study of social organizations were largely his own.

The two papers that follow, "Cross-Cousin Marriage in the Lake Winnipeg Area" and "Northern Ojibwa Ecological Adaptation and Social Organization," reflect Hallowell's continuing interest in the Northern Ojibwa whom he had intensively studied in the 1930s. The first-mentioned paper is a remarkable contribution and ranks as one of the genuine classics of American anthropology. Hallowell's early field and library researches, in which he discovered correspondences between kinship terminologies and possible marriage practices, led him to ask: "Was Cross-Cousin Marriage Practiced by the North-Central Algonkian?"[1] This idea received no support from the Algonkian experts of the late 1920s, but it soon turned out that W. D. Strong had found cross-cousin marriage in operation among the Naskapi of northern Labrador, and Hallowell made plans to go into the field to see whether the practice could be found among the North-Central groups.

Hallowell selected the Northern Ojibwa and Cree of the Lake Winnipeg region for his initial studies and almost immediately found cross-cousin marriage in full operation among the conservative groups. He notes that he went into the field both "functionally" and "problem oriented"—all he had to do was

Fred Eggan is professor emeritus of anthropology at the University of Chicago.

313

ask the right questions. But he did much more. With census data and genealogies he worked out the fundamental principles of the social system, noting that the marriage of cross cousins "can not be viewed as an independent custom or unit trait, but rather as an integral part of the operation of the social system as a whole."

Hallowell also studied the more acculturated bands of both Ojibwa and Cree, where the marriage practices and kinship terminologies were at variance with those of the conservative groups, and proposed a hypothesis to explain the modifications in terms of acculturative processes and differences in local conditions. The virtues of this hypothesis are many. As I have said elsewhere:

> It puts the social structure of the region in perspective and makes it possible to formulate problems in sociocultural dynamics more adequately than otherwise. It also orders a great deal of apparently random social and cultural behavior with economy and finesse. And it has the further virtue of being testable by additional field work and by further historical research. [2]

With this paper Hallowell started us off in new and more profitable directions.

In the meantime Hallowell continued his interest in ecological problems. Frank Speck had begun his pioneer researches among the Montagnais and Naskapi as early as 1908, and his papers on land use and ownership began to appear in 1915. Speck assumed that the family hunting territories that he was mapping were aboriginal, and his students and associates initially followed his lead; but gradually their studies led to a greater concern for the ecological adjustments of winter life and to a consideration of the migratory or sedentary characteristics of the game animals on which the Northern Woodland populations depended. John M. Cooper provides a summary of the new perspectives:

> It looks as if land tenure among hunting peoples is delicately responsive to ecology, especially to the fauna exploited as the staple food supply. It looks likewise as if such tenure can and does adapt and change readily and simply in accordance with changing local ecological conditions. [3]

In the late 1930s Hallowell had begun an investigation of
variation in the size of Algonkian hunting territories, a copy
of which he sent me in 1941, noting that he intended to analyze
his Ojibwa data in more detail when he had more time. This
expanded manuscript was finally published after the war as
"The Size of Algonkian Hunting Territories: A Function of Ecological Adjustment"[4] and is an important step in Hallowell's
conceptualization of ecological problems. Here he is relatively
unconcerned with the problem of the aboriginal character of
the family hunting territory system and concentrates on the
specific conditions that control the variables of size and composition of the winter hunting groups, the size of the hunting
tracts, and the rules for their transfer. He concludes that investigations based on sound ecological hypotheses would lead
to "an explanation of the actual factors that control the size
of the Algonkian hunting grounds as well as the basic dynamics
of the hunting territory system as a whole."[5]

Hallowell's own interests had shifted to other problems,
however, and he became more concerned with the necessary
and sufficient conditions that make human existence possible.
Here he develops the conception of the *behavioral* environment,
as exemplified in the personality structure and world view of
the Ojibwa and as represented in the papers in section V. But
later he returned to the relation between ecological adaptation
and social organization as part of a general survey of Northern
Ojibwa life. In the second paper of this section, Hallowell surveys the seasons and their characteristic social groupings and
reviews the hunting territory system in terms of ecological
adjustments and historical events. Here the social organization is viewed not only in terms of the local situation but also
in terms of a common world view and system of values. Kinship terms, for example, are not only guides to interpersonal
relationships but also a means by which "the normative orientation of the self in a traditional system of socially sanctioned
roles and values was achieved." In the relationship between
grandparents and grandchildren contacts with other-than-
human persons were important, thus relating Ojibwa social
structure to the cosmology. Hallowell concludes that "the
basic social sanctions involved in the maintenance of the social

structure are dependent, among other things, upon culturally
constituted beliefs, values, personal experience, and the personality organization of Ojibwa individuals."

With this statement Hallowell brings together many of the
basic concepts he had developed with regard to society, culture, and the individual, and his papers in this volume and elsewhere show how they are related in the life experiences of the
Northern Ojibwa. In his autobiographical account he tells how
he was led to the attempt to see the Ojibwa world as the Ojibwa
saw it, and how this led to the concept of a behavioral environment as "an environment culturally constituted in such a way
that it structures the major psychological field in which individuals act, forming their basic cognitive orientation." This
enlarged conception of the environment has played a major
role in his contributions to human evolution. As he says, "Man
is an animal who has been able to survive by making cultural
adaptations in which his own imaginative interpretations of
the world have been fed back into his personal adjustment to
it."

NOTES
    1. *Proceedings of the Twenty-third Congress of Americanists*
(New York, 1928), pp. 519–44.
    2. F. Eggan, "Social Anthropology: Methods and Results,"
in *Social Anthropology of North American Tribes*, enlarged ed.,
ed. F. Eggan (Chicago: University of Chicago Press, 1955),
p. 533.
    3. J. M. Cooper, "The Culture of the Northeastern Indian
Hunters: A Reconstructive Interpretation," in *Man in Northeastern North America*, ed. F. Johnson. Papers of the R. S.
Peabody Foundation for Archeology, vol. 3, 1946, p. 284.
    4. *American Anthropologist* 51 (1949): 35–45.
    5. Ibid., p. 44.

Cross-Cousin Marriage
in the Lake Winnipeg Area
1937

In a paper read at the International Congress of Americanists in 1928,[1] I pointed out that Ojibwa, Ottawa, and Algonkin kinship terms recorded in early documents reflected cross-cousin marriage so positively, that it seemed reasonable to infer that this form of mating had formerly been practised. Up until that time no ethnologist had reported this custom from any Algonkian people,[2] although two statements by early nineteenth-century observers (H. Y. Hind and Duncan Cameron) apparently referred to the practice of cross-cousin marriage by some of the Saulteaux-Ojibwa bands between Lake Nipigon and Lake Winnipeg.[3]

I attributed the contemporary absence of the custom to the transformation of native marriage institutions under white influences, and pointed to evidence which showed that the contemporary relationship terms of several bands in the linguistic groups under discussion were variants of an older pattern which harmonized with cross-cousin marriage. As a correlative and better documented instance of modern changes in Algonkian relationship terms under changing conditions, I referred to my study of the St. Francis Abenaki kinship system.[4]

Shortly after the Congress I met William Duncan Strong. He had just returned from northern Labrador and told me of his discovery that cross-cousin marriage was practised by the Barren Ground Band of the Naskapi and that this custom was clearly reflected by their kinship system.[5]

With Strong's data as a basis I undertook a comparative study of Cree-Montagnais-Naskapi terms, using both pub-

317

lished sources and two manuscripts of the seventeenth century. It was possible to show that throughout this linguistic group there were not only consistent lexical indications of cross-cousin marriage, but a striking equivalence between the terms used and those employed by the Ojibwa-Ottawa-Algonkin.[6] In the meantime Speck had secured positive evidence regarding the practice of cross-cousin marriage by the Mistassini band of Montagnais and to a certain extent at Lake St. John.[7]

Wishing to pursue the possible distribution of the custom to the west, I was fortunate enough to receive a grant-in-aid from the Social Science Research Council in support of field work in the environs of Lake Winnipeg. Just before leaving Philadelphia in June, 1930, I received a publication by J. C. Boileau Grant, on the somatology of several Cree and Saulteaux bands in the region I planned to visit.[8] He had made his observations in the summer of 1927. One of the bands measured, a group I was later to visit, made their summer headquarters at Island Lake, 115 miles east of northern Lake Winnipeg. In some prefatory remarks under the caption 'marriage' Grant wrote, '*though for the most part it is the custom of these Indians to marry their cousins*, they nevertheless adhere to the tradition of not marrying into their own totem.' Not being an ethnologist, Grant did not realize the significance of his statement in regard to cousin-marriage, nor did he explain that cross-cousins were meant.

Although I was not aware of it at the time, E. S. Curtis in his summary account of the Western Woods Cree, published in 1928, had already referred to their practice of cross-cousin marriage and its connection with their kinship structure.[9] Consequently, Curtis must be credited with the earliest published reference to cross-cousin marriage as a going concern among a contemporary Algonkian people. And, in the summer of 1927 when on the Upper Albany River, J. M. Cooper met an Anglican minister, himself a Saskatchewan Cree, who told him, quite unsolicited, that cross-cousin marriage was permitted in this Algonkian group.[10]

Thus while encouraged by the observations of Strong, Speck,

and Grant, I did not know of these other independent reports of cross-cousin marriage among the western Cree when I started my own field inquiries in the Lake Winnipeg region.

During the course of the summer I visited three bands of Swampy Cree (Grand Rapids,[11] Norway House, Cross Lake) and two groups of Saulteaux-Ojibwa (Island Lake, Berens River). In the summers of 1931 and 1932 short visits were made to the Saulteaux bands at Wanipigow River and Poplar River. Since that time I have made a more detailed study of the social organization and general ethnography of the three bands on the Berens River. Other investigators such as D. Jenness,[12] Regina Flannery,[13] J. M. Cooper,[14] T. Michelson,[15] and Ruth Landes[16] have also reported the occurrence of cross-cousin marriage elsewhere among Cree, Ojibwa and Montagnais speaking peoples.

The positive generalizations which can be made from the data already secured in the Lake Winnipeg area are the following:

1. The kinship pattern of all of the bands visited and of those about which I have information is of the 'bifurcate collateral' type,[17] the generation principle is paramount and since there are no specific terms for relatives by marriage, the characteristic equations that occur are the following:

(*a*) mother-in-law = father's sister = mother's brother's wife.

(*b*) father-in-law = mother's brother = father's sister's husband.

(*c*) son-in-law = cross nephew = husband of parallel niece.

(*d*) daughter-in-law = cross niece = wife of parallel nephew.

(*e*) woman's sister-in-law = woman's female cross-cousin.

(*f*) man's brother-in-law = man's male cross-cousin.

(*g*) sibling-in-law of opposite sex = cross-cousin of opposite sex.

(*h*) The term for 'sweetheart' is identical with the last mentioned term or a derivative of it.

2. Inquiry revealed that the mating of cross-cousins was

RELATIONSHIP OF ISLAND LAKE WIVES TO HUSBANDS

MARRIAGES (numbers to left, husbands; to right; wives) (1)	FIRST CROSS-COUSINS				SECOND CROSS-COUSINS								Number of Relationships
	mother's brother's daughter	father's sister's daughter	mother's half brother's daughter	father's half sister's daughter	mother's mother's brother's daughter's daughter	mother's mother's sister's son's daughter	mother's father's brother's son's daughter	mother's father's sister's daughter's daughter	father's father's brother's daughter's daughter	father's father's sister's son's daughter	father's mother's brother's son's daughter	father's mother's sister's daughter's daughter	
GENERATION III													
14\7	X												1
6\13		X											1
21\28	X												1
16\10	X												1
19\27	X												1
17\30	X												1
GENERATION IV													
39\{132, 133, 134}	X	X						X			X		4
44\36	X	X			X						X		4
45\37		X								X			2
46\38		X								X			2
32\40	X										X		2
22\29	X										X		2
33\41	X										X		2
34\42	X										X		2
53\50		X								X			2
48\51	X										X		2
49\52	X										X		2
GENERATION V													
147\144	X									X	X		3
137\152				X						X			2
157\114	X	X			X			X		X	X		6
169\124		X	X		X			X			X		5
98\94	X			X	X					X	X		5
91\84	X			X	X					X	X		5
93\86		X								X			2
107\101	X										X		2
95\118	X	X						X			X		4
81\88	X										X		2
83\90							X			X			2
110\104									X	X			2
87\80					X	X	X		X	X			5
92\85									X	X			2
Totals	20	10	1	3	6	1	2	4	3	13	16	0	79

(1) These are the numbers that appear on genealogical charts in the possession of the author, which may later be published.

recognized as a traditional form of marriage, that a certain proportion of married individuals now living were of this relationship, and that unions of this sort were still contracted.

When I asked an English-speaking Indian (Alfred Settie) at Norway House whether it was possible to marry *ki·tim*, he replied, 'You bet your life. That's what they all do here!' The United Church Missionary, Rev. S. D. Gaudin, who speaks Cree fluently and at that time had been in missionary work forty years, said that sixty per cent of the Indians of this band were married to their cousins.[18] He added that the percentage was higher farther to the north but that nowadays, at Norway House, since parents no longer arranged matches for their children, the custom was dying out. Rev. S. D. Gaudin began his missionary work among the Cree of the Nelson House Band in 1891, where he remained fifteen years. Native customs were in full swing when he went there, and he said that the degree of inbreeding was much higher than it is now or in the Norway House band.

In addition to securing kinship terms, sample genealogies and other information in the Cree and Saulteaux bands personally visited, data obtained from Indians belonging to other groups, or whose parents or relatives belonged to these bands, is sufficient to include, tentatively, the following bands in our generalizations:

Cree: Norway House, Cross Lake, Grand Rapids, Nelson House, Split Lake, Oxford House, Gods' Lake.[19]

Saulteaux: All of the bands bordering on eastern Lake Winnipeg from Poplar River on the north to Wanipigow River on the south, and in the interior those at Little Grand Rapids,[20] Pekangikum, Sandy Lake, Deer Lake and Island Lake.[21]

3. What are the fundamental principles of cross-cousin marriage among these Cree and Saulteaux peoples? How does it work? In the first place, their kinship pattern defines the social status of individuals in such a way that only persons of the same generation are potential mates.[22] Secondly, in one's own generation, there is a dual classification of relatives of the

opposite sex: (a) full (or half) siblings, parallel cousins of the first degree and more remote cousins, or other individuals who fall into the terminological category of 'siblings'; (b) cross-cousins of the first degree, siblings-in-law of opposite sex, second 'cross-cousins,' and other related persons who fall into the terminological category of 'cross-cousin of opposite sex.'

Since kinship terms are widely extended in usage, individuals actually *unrelated* by blood may fall into either of these two groups. If two unrelated men, for instance, marry sisters they will adopt the term 'brother' for each other, while unrelated women who marry brothers will call each other 'sister.' In the case of the Saulteaux, who have a sib organization, a man visiting a strange camp will call all of the girls of his approximate age group 'cousin,' except those belonging to his own sib, those whom he can classify as 'sisters,' through some known blood connection, or those whom he can 'place' through the terminology he knows that his parents apply to their parents.

In a community with a kinship pattern of this sort it is inevitable that persons who call each other 'cousin' should marry, not through the compulsion of precept, but because of the prohibition of sibling marriage.[23] But the actual *degree* of blood relationship that exists between the members of these unions may vary from zero to that between first cousins. The marriage of cross-cousins in this latter, narrow sense cannot be viewed as an independent custom or unit trait, but rather as an integral part of the operation of the social system as a whole.

If such a social system, ideally conceived, is thought of as operating in face-to-face groups, where everyone addresses everyone else by a kinship term and no one marries outside the group, then *all* marriages would occur between individuals who previously called each other by a 'cousin' term. Furthermore, if the population in which such a marital situation operated were not replenished by new family lines, through the marriage of outsiders into it or the migration to it of new family units, the original family lines would inevitably become more and more highly linked. While this is, of course, a theoretical, rather than a realistic, picture of conditions either today or in the past among the Lake Winnipeg bands, it nevertheless has been very closely approached in some instances.   For the areal density of population has always been low in this area and there is every reason to believe that marriages in the past have been intra-group (or intra-local) rather than inter-group (inter-local) affairs.[24]

In view of these general conditions the collection of genealogical data is the only possible means of obtaining any precise notion of the extent of inbreeding or information in respect to the presence or absence of actual blood relationship, between married persons.   At Island Lake I was lucky enough to secure as informant, a man (Richard Munias) who not only spoke English but who happened to be a member of the Sturgeon sib, whose family had intermarried with a family of the Sucker sib over a number of generations.   In his father's generation, for example, six marriages between first cross-cousins had occurred.   These were the total number possible between the children of two brothers and a sister.   In the genealogical material obtained, which included 188 individuals all told (chiefly lineal and collateral relatives of my informant) the number of married individuals in four generations is 152. Of these, 64 persons (31 men and 33 women) married first or second cousins (thirty marriages being monogamous and one polygamous), all but four of these marriages being between relatives of the former class.   Among these, there are twice as many cases (20) in which a man is married to his mother's brother's daughter, as those (10) in which he is married to his father's sister's daughter.   It is a striking fact that a number of the wives are not only related to their spouses as *double* first cousins, but that *all* of the individuals of generations IV and V (see Table) who are related to their spouses as first cousins are related to them as second cousins, too.   My informant's wife, for instance (No. 114) in addition to being his double cross-cousin of the first degree (mother's brother's daughter *and* father's sister's daughter) is related to him as second cousin in four other ways (mother's mother's brother's daughter's daughter, mother's father's sister's daughter's daughter, father's father's sister's son's daughter, father's

mother's brother's son's daughter). All of the women, moreover, who are related to their husbands *only* as second cousins
are related to them in more than one way.

In this connection, Radcliffe-Brown's differentiation of
Australian kinship systems into Type I (Kariera) and Type II
(Arunta) comes to mind.[25] 'The Kariera kinship system,' he
says, 'is based on and implies the existence of the form of
marriage known as cross-cousin marriage' (p. 15). 'A man
may only marry a woman to whom he applies the same term
of relationship that he does to his own mother's brother's
daughter. If it is possible for him to marry the daughter of an
actual brother of his own mother he normally does so, but of
course this only happens in a limited number of instances'
(p. 17). 'The Aranda system (Type II) divides the female
relatives whom a man may marry in the Kariera system into
two parts, from one of which he must now choose his wife
while those of the other are forbidden to him' (p. 21). This
system 'also requires a special marriage rule, by which a man
marries his mother's mother's brother's daughter's daughter or
some relative who is classified with her and denoted by the
same term of relationship' (p. 20).

Putting matters in another way we may say that Type II is
a system in which the marriage of *first* cross-cousins has been
suppressed and the marriage of second or more remote cross-
cousins encouraged. But both types are actually based upon
cross-cousin marriage, unless we think of the latter in the
narrowest terms.[26] In the Island Lake genealogy the four
marriages of second cousins would be typical examples of those
which occur in kinship systems of Type II in Australia. But
sociologically among the Saulteaux they are undifferentiated
from those of first cousins. In one sense the biological basis
of any such differentiation is more apparent than real. In a
population where marriages of first cross-cousins occur with
any frequency, and particularly where these marriages are un-
restricted (i.e., of the bilateral type) as in the case of both the
Saulteaux and the Kariera, the inbreeding that results progressively reduces the number of ancestors of the individuals
of succeeding generations.[27] Consequently, as I have already

pointed out, individuals become related as *both* first and second cousins. If more information were available about the ascendants of Generation III (Table) the same thing would probably be true for them. In Australia, where the density of population is low and comparable to that of the Lake Winnipeg groups and where there are likewise economic similarities [28] it seems to me that among the Kariera and other bands with Type I marriage comparable inbreeding must occur. A proportion of marriages must at the same time be those of first and second cross cousins, while others are unions of second cousins (Type II). Viewed from this standpoint Type II represents a cross-cousin marriage system of a restricted kind but based upon the same principles as Type I. It limits the degree of possible inbreeding.[29]

In the social system of the Island Lake Saulteaux and other groups of the Lake Winnipeg region then, marriages between the children of full brothers and sisters occur (i.e., cross-cousin marriage in the narrowest sense) and in addition there are marriages of second cross-cousins, who are the children of parallel cousins (i.e., *terminological* brothers and sisters).

How far the magnitude of inbreeding in the Island Lake genealogy cited is a fair sample of inbreeding in the band as a whole, which numbered a little over 700 at the time, I do not know. I was able to spend only a few days there and have never returned since.

My genealogical study of the Berens River Bands, which have the same kinship organization and social customs as the Island Lake Saulteaux, supports the general observations stated above and makes it possible to make a further point, although my analysis of the relationships of the individuals involved in about 200 marriages is not yet completed. This analysis, when finished, will give the relative incidence of first and second cross-cousin marriages during several generations for the entire native population of the river as well as data on other kinds of blood relationship among married individuals or the absence of it and the social classification of these from the native viewpoint.

In one case, for instance, a man married his mother's co-

wife's brother's daughter.   Now a co-wife is terminologically
equated with mother's sister and therefore the co-wife's
brother's daughter is in turn classified with a cross-cousin.
Biologically the individuals involved in this marriage were not
related at all.   But since the parents of these individuals used
'brother' and 'sister' terms for each other, the marriage is a
cross-cousin marriage from the native standpoint and likewise
falls into this category if the objective criterion be a marriage
of the children of siblings (in the extended sense) of the
opposite sex.

   Of considerable frequency is another type of cross-cousin
marriage in which the individuals may not be either related
by blood, nor the children of terminological brothers and
sisters.   Such cases are those in which a man may marry his
brother's wife's sister, or a woman her brother's wife's brother
(or equivalent marriages of siblings-in-law).   On account of
the fact that the term for 'siblings-in-law of opposite sex'
(*ni·nαm*) is the same as that for a cross-cousin, such marriages,
from the native standpoint, fall into the same class as the
cross-cousin marriages described above.   I may add that the
reason these marriages occur quite frequently is because on the
Berens River and elsewhere in this region it is considered desirable for the brothers of one family to marry a series of sisters
in another.   At Poplar River there is one such instance in
which six brothers married six sisters, the two families being
unrelated when the *original* marriage took place, which is not,
of course, to be classified as a cross-cousin marriage.   But
when unrelated individuals marry there is a special term
(*ndindawa*) adopted between their parents that binds the latter
together in much the same fashion *as if* they were related as
siblings and siblings-in-law to each other.   It is obvious, too,
that a social system that permits or encourages cross-cousin
marriage will also involve the marriages of a series of siblings
of one family with a series of siblings in another family, even
aside from cases such as those referred to above.   Consequently it may be assumed, I think, that regardless of blood
relationship or the terminology employed by parents, such
marriages are actually an integral part of the social system

considered as a whole.   Marriages of fraternities and sororities are also mentioned in the mythology.

From the standpoint of native culture, therefore, it is impossible to define cross-cousin marriage (1) in terms of *one* specific biological relationship (i.e., first cousins), or (2) a more inclusive degree of biological relationship (i.e., second or more remote cousins) or (3) even with exclusive reference to the use of 'sibling' terms by the parents of individuals to the union. The actual formula is very simple. All marriages between persons who are *ni·nam* (the Saulteaux term) to each other are cross-cousin marriages in terms of the social system in actual operation and in the thought of the Indians themselves.[30]

While in the past, as I have suggested above, a large proportion of marriages must have been cross-cousin marriages in the widest sense, this is not to be understood as equivalent to the assertion that *all* marriages fell into this category. I have many marriages in my Berens River genealogies of several generations ago that according to the characterization of the Indians themselves were not between *ni·namak*. A good many of these, I may say, seem to have been inter-group (local or band) marriages.

Without genealogically supported evidence of the incidence of various classes of marriage between blood kin, and without an understanding of how cross-cousin marriage works in terms of the social system considered as a whole, intertribal comparisons cannot mean very much. Nor do I see how historical problems can be intelligently formulated. Cross-cousin marriage among the Lake Winnipeg Cree and Saulteaux is certainly something different from cross-cousin marriage among the Miwok and other California groups, or from that occurring on the Northwest coast, or elsewhere.[32] To discuss it as a 'culture trait' divorced from the social context of which it is a part and in terms of which it is integrated with other traits in different ways among different peoples, can only lead to superficial and inept comparisons, if it does not involve an actual distortion of fact.

4. If the fundamental principles of the kinship system and

marital practices of the Algonkian bands of the Lake Winnipeg area, as outlined above, are correct, then certain problems of cultural dynamics can be more adequately formulated with reference to this type of aboriginal social organization as a datum line.

As already pointed out, my personal contacts have been principally with the Indians living in the bush country on the eastern shore of Lake Winnipeg and inland,[32] where an aboriginal social organization of the type described remains essentially intact.[33] On the western side of the Lake the penetration of the country by roads and railroads, and the suitability of its soil for farming,[34] have led to incursions by white settlers and, in the course of time to more radical transformations in the economic life, the religious beliefs, and the social organization of Indians whose native languages and culture were originally identical with those across the Lake. Moreover, in earlier times, as well as now, some visiting back and forth occurred. The history of the Midewiwin shows how close the connections were only a few decades ago [35] and there is blood relationship through intermarriage and the migration of families. Members of the Moose sib, for example, at the mouth of the Berens River are descendants in the male line of an ancestor born on the west side of Lake Winnipeg, some of whose lineal and collateral descendants still live there. Several men of the Berens River band were also born across the Lake.

Under these general conditions I think we may assume that any differences in kinship terminologies, kinship patterns, or marital practices that the Indians west of Lake Winnipeg exhibit, are the result of modern local conditions or, putting it another way, variants under specific circumstances of the master pattern of social organization once common to all the Indians of this region.

While I have not investigated this problem in detail, a single instance that came to my attention will illustrate its importance. At Fisher River today there are domiciled [36] most of the remnants of the Saulteaux that formerly constituted the St. Peters band.[37] In 1907 they surrendered their lands and were moved from their old reserve on the Red River, near Selkirk. The old St. Peters Indians were among the first to come in contact with the white settlers on the Red River and as early as 1875 the Deputy Superintendent of Indian affairs characterized them as 'the best settled and most progressive of all the Bands which have been a party to Treaty No. 1.' [38] There is said to be a very high percentage of white blood in the Saulteaux division of the Fisher River Band today,[39] many of these Indians are farmers and consequently lead a more sedentary life than the hunters and fishermen of the eastern side of the Lake and they may still be considered as 'progressive' when compared with most of the bands of the area.

In this group, according to my informant,[40] first cousins of neither type marry and blood relationship *in itself* is considered a bar to marriage. So far as the usage of kinship terms is concerned, what seems to have happened is this: the old terms neither have been outmoded nor become recrystallized into a distinctively new pattern of usage. Their application simply has become more fluid through synonymous usages that do not occur in the bands which have retained the aboriginal social system. Thus Anglicized synonyms for 'my mother' (*nimama*) and 'my father' (*nipapa*) have come into vogue,[41] descriptive terms occur for 'father's brother,' 'father's sister,' and 'mother's sister,' the term for 'mother's brother' (= father-in-law) may be likewise used for 'father's brother' and the term for 'father's brother' (= stepfather) for 'mother's brother,'[42] but the term for 'mother-in-law,' on the other hand, has become restricted and no longer is equivalent to 'father's sister.' In the first descending generation from Ego the term for cross-nephew (= son-in-law) or cross-niece (= daughter-in-law) may be used for parallel nephew and niece respectively, and in one's own generation the distinction between parallel and cross-cousin is no longer rigidly maintained, the tendency being to group these together as against full brothers and sisters. *Ni·nam* can therefore be used for cousins in the English sense as well as for sibling-in-law of the opposite sex. Only the diminutive of this term conveys the sense of 'sweetheart.' Evidence of such a radical change in kinship pattern and marital practice, controlled as it is by specific data on the aboriginal social systems of related Saulteaux groups of the same region, suggests a broader problem.

5. If, as now seems more likely than a few years ago, it can be assumed that the fundamental social organization of the Algonkian peoples north of the Great Lakes and the St. Lawrence River was once essentially similar to that in the Lake Winnipeg area, then the problem of contemporary variants in northern Algonkian kinship systems and marital practices may profitably be attacked in terms of this hypothesis. Only recently Fred Eggan [43] has admirably and conclusively demonstrated that the confusing and hitherto sometimes irreconcilable data on the kinship system of the Indians of the Gulf States can be understood as variants, under different conditions of acculturation, of the Crow pattern that underlies them. It seems to me that northern Algonkian kinship systems are likewise intelligible as variants of a basic pattern that has undergone modification as the result of acculturative processes and differences in local conditions.

NOTES

1. Was Cross-cousin Marriage Practiced by the North-Central Algonkian? Proceedings, Twenty-third International Congress of Americanists, N. Y., 1928, 519–544.

2. R. H. Lowie, Primitive Society, 1920, 27, wrote, 'While relatively rare in America, this usage is reported from the northern coast of British Columbia, from central California and Nicaragua; and the fact that in South America Chibcha women have a single word for husband and father's sister's son suggests that they too, frequently mated with cross-cousins.'

3. Hallowell, *op. cit.*, 522.

4. Recent Changes in the Kinship Terminology of the St. Francis Abenaki. Proceedings, ICA 22 (Rome), 1928, vol. 2, 97–145.

5. See W. D. Strong, Cross-cousin Marriage and the Culture of the Northeastern Algonkian. American Anthropologist 31: 277–288 (1929).

6. A. I. Hallowell, Kinship Terms and Cross-cousin Marriage of the Montagnais-Naskapi and the Cree. AA 34: 171–199 (1932).

7. F. G. Speck, Mistassini Notes, Indian Notes (Museum of the American Indian, Heye Foundation), vol. 7, no. 4 (1930), 421–424.

8. J. C. Boileau Grant, Anthropometry of the Cree and Saulteaux Indians in Northeastern Manitoba. Bull. 59, Canada Dept. of Mines, Ottawa, 1929.

9. E. S. Curtis, The North American Indians, 18: 70–71 and 156.

10. Personal communication, Dr. Cooper, Feb., 1937.

11. Mouth of the Saskatchewan River.

12. The Ojibwa Indians of Parry Sound, their Social and Religious Life. Bull. 78, Canada Dept. of Mines, 1935, 98.

13. Found in 1933, 1935 among Eastmain and Rupert House Montagnais. MS. field notes.

14. Definitely established in 1932 among Ft. George Montagnais, in 1933 among Albany Cree, in 1934 among Neoskweskaw (formerly Nitcikun) Montagnais. As regards Moose Factory Cree and Rupert House Montagnais, Dr. Cooper writes me (Feb. 14, 1937), 'I have statements (1932, 1933, 1934) from one or more informants from each of these groups that permissive or preferential cross-cousin marriage obtained but other informants were hazy or in certain cases denied its occurrence.' In all these instances the information refers to first cross-cousins.

15. First hand information from Great Whale River and Albany River, where bilateral cross-cousin marriage occurs, and from Moose Factory and Attawapiscat, where the typical marriage is between a man and his father's sister's daughter. At Weenusk, the kinship system favors cross-cousin marriage but 'both types apparently are forbidden' (Personal information—Feb. 12, 1937).

16. Ojibwa Sociology, Columbia University Contributions to Anthropology, N. Y., 1937. Chapters II and IV (in press).

17. See R. H. Lowie, Relationship Terms, Ency. Brit. 14 ed. 1929. 19: 85. It should be noted, however, that in the kinship terminology 'father's brother' = 'step father' so that while formally the pattern is bifurcate collateral, psychologically and sociologically it is equivalent to the bifurcate merging pattern, as an example of which Lowie cites the Ojibwa proper.

18. At first he said 75%, but I am inclined to think that even 60% is too high. I mention his estimate rather as an indication of the common occurrence of the custom than as an accurate measure of its magnitude. Genealogical data are the necessary basis for any quantitative statements of incidence.

19. Dr. Michelson offers corroboration from another source in his letter, op. cit., 'From a physical anthropologist I know it [cross-cousin marriage] occurs at Oxford House and God's Lake.'

20. Berens River.

21. The latter are on the borderline between Cree and Ojibwa (Saulteaux) speaking peoples.

22. There are cases where this formal impediment has been overcome but it is unnecessary to consider them here.

23. This rule is supported by the fear that its infringement will result in sickness.

24. My Berens River genealogies offer definite evidence on this point.

25. A. R. Radcliffe-Brown, The Social Organization of Australian Tribes, Oceania, Monograph No. 1, 1931.

26. When Tylor first called attention to the marriage of cross-cousins (On a Method of Investigating the Development of Institutions. JAI (1889), 18: 245–269), he spoke only of *first cousins*, and in other definitions given since and discussions of the subject it is not always clear how far the writer has taken the occurrence of the marriage of second cousins or individuals terminologically classified as cross-cousins into account. In Notes and Queries on Anthropology (5th ed. 1929), 56, the implication of the definition given there ('Cousins of which the mother of one is sister to the father of the other are called *cross-cousins*') suggests a highly restricted usage.

27. In an unpublished ms. I have dealt with the magnitude of inbreeding in the Island Lake genealogy as measured by Raymond Pearl's Coefficients of Inbreeding and Relationship.

28. See Radcliffe-Brown, op. cit., p. 35, for data on Kariera.

29. Inquiry among the Plains Cree and Plains Ojibwa (Saulteaux) in the summer of 1931 leads me to infer that marriages of first cross-cousins are infrequent, but that marriages of second cross-cousins have a fairly high incidence

in some groups. Father Moulin, who, at the time, had been at the Hobbema Reserve (Alta.) for twenty-eight years, stated that the marriage of first cousins was extremely rare among these Cree. On the other hand, the tendency for the grandchildren of a brother and sister to marry was so pronounced that it necessitated that he obtain special dispensation in about 50% of the marriages he performed. He believed that these marriages were usually those of second cross-cousins. He also thought that formerly, when the bands were smaller and the Indians separated during the hunting season, the marriage of first cousins must have occurred. Besides there must have been inbreeding, since all the Indians here are descendents of a few families. I have no information to show that this suppression of first-cousin marriages, however, has affected the fundamental principle of the kinship system of the Plains Cree and Ojibwa, which is essentially that of their Woodland relatives. But it would be interesting to know whether this restriction, if it could be genealogically substantiated, is a result of their association with the peoples of Plains culture, where cousin marriages are tabu, or is explicable in some other fashion, such as the influence of the missionaries.

30. As I worked out the blood connections between certain individuals in my genealogies it often happened that I was able to point to distant relationships that these individuals themselves were only partially aware of. They had not made precise blood connection a matter of reflection.

31. Perhaps this is one of the reasons why the various theories, advanced from time to time as 'historical' explanations of cross-cousin marriage *per se*, have only seemed plausible with respect to specific conditions. As Paul Kirchhoff has pointed out (Verwandtschaftsbezeichnungen und Verwandtenheirat, Zeitschrift für Ethnologie, Band 64, 1932, 64), all these explanations work either on the basis of pre-suppositions seldom realized, or they explain too little. But I do not find any evidence in the case of these Algonkian peoples, that would support his general principle that marriage with cross-cousins evolved from older forms of kin marriage, particularly those between individuals of different generations.

32. Except for a brief visit to the Cree of Grand Rapids (mouth of the Saskatchewan) in 1930 and to the Saulteaux of Jack Head in 1936.

33. With exceptions that need not be considered here.

34. The basin of Lake Winnipeg lies along the western contact zone between the rocks of the Pre-Cambrian Shield and the Paleozoic limestones so that the terrain east of it is of fundamentally different geological origin than that to the west of it.

35. See A. I. Hallowell, The Passing of the Midewiwin in the Lake Winnipeg Region. AA 38: 32–51 (1936).

36. Along with some Cree, originally from Norway House.

37. This band was a party to Treaty No. 1 (1871).

38. See Annual Report, Canadian Department of Indian Affairs, 1875, 38.

39. More than half was reported to be mixed bloods in the Report of 1875, *op. cit.*

40. The grandson of Red Eagle who signed the Treaty of 1871, who in turn was the son of the famous Pegwis who previously negotiated with Lord Selkirk.

41. A development that has likewise occurred in a number of bands on the Eastern side of the Lake.

42. Both of which usages are contrary to a bifurcate collateral pattern.

43. Historical Changes in the Choctaw Kinship System. AA 39: 34–52 (1937).

EIGHT

Northern Ojibwa Ecological Adaptation and Social Organization

1976

The traditional manner of life characteristic of the Berens River Ojibwa is permeated with linguistic, social, and cultural features that correlate with the ecological adaptation they have made to the climate and topography of the Canadian Shield. Although this physical environment should be considered a limiting rather than a determining factor, its basic influence has remained relatively constant despite acculturation. Native terms in their lunar calendar and for seasons of the year reflect awareness of recurrent natural changes and serve to orient activities in an annual cycle. Temperatures, for example, range from -20° F in winter to +72° F or more in the hottest part of the summer. Linguistic terminology punctuates the consequence of these changes in temperature as it affects their terrain—the arrival and departure of migrant birds, the habits of fur-bearing animals, and the people's economic activities.

Summer, in Ojibwa terminology, covers our months of June, July, and August, corresponding precisely to the period when temperatures are the highest. And Freezing over Moon (November) in their lunar calendar signifies the advent of winter. Even before this, snow—averaging perhaps 50 to 100 inches during the winter—may begin to cover the forests. Midwinter Moon (February) is approximately correlative with the lowest temperatures. Although the snow may begin to melt in April, called Goose Moon because these migrant birds are first seen about this time, it does not disappear entirely until early May. In this month the ice breaks up; it is the Moon of the Loons, and several months of open water follow. The appearance of leaves on the deciduous trees is referred to by the "moon name" for June, which heralds the coming of the summer season.

Correlated with these changes in their physical environment we find not only changes in Ojibwa occupations but seasonal movement of the population. These movements have roots in the distant past and in aboriginal culture. Because of them, the Ojibwa have been characterized, until very recently, by the fact that they occupied no fixed settlements all the year round. Schoolcraft drew attention to this as early as 1834. On this account the size, composition, organization, and functioning of Ojibwa social groups must be conceptualized in relation to seasonal movements of population. And their sociocultural system must be thought of as functioning primarily in terms of relatively small, face-to-face localized groups correlated with these seasonal movements and the economic activities associated with this basic ecological adaptation. The face-to-face group that was the effective unit of social and economic organization at all seasons was the extended family.

The late fall, winter, and early spring was the season for hunting and trapping. During this period the characteristic localized unit of population was what I shall call the *winter hunting group.* When the ice broke up, members of such groups moved their camps to traditional places where fishing was good. Here members of one hunting group, relatively isolated during the winter months, joined members of other hunting groups. These new concentrations of population during open water were larger and somewhat different in composition from the winter hunting groups. I shall call them *summer fishing settlements.* The population movements of the Ojibwa involved, then, a maximum dispersal of small localized population units during the season of hunting and trapping and relatively larger concentrations of population during the season of open water when fishing became a major activity. Except in the most acculturated band at the mouth of the Berens River, this was still the basic pattern during the period of my observation.

WINTER HUNTING GROUPS

From field data collected from the two least acculturated bands of the river, Pekangikum and Little Grand Rapids, I found that the population split up into thirty-two winter hunting groups. The average number of individuals per group was sixteen, and the ratio of hunters to nonhunters was one to three.

Typically, the winter hunting group was an extended family. It was composed of at least two married couples and their children united by kinship bonds between parents and children or between siblings. In half of such groups one or more married sons were associated with their fathers. That this is a typical pattern is shown by the fact that in cases where this association was not found, there were no married sons. In such instances, one or more sons-in-law were members of the group. Cases where *both* sons and sons-in-law were present were infrequent.

Another variant of the basic pattern of the association of sons with their fathers in the winter hunting group is illustrated by the cases of association of married brothers in such a group after the death of their father. This association of closely related males in the winter hunting group is an expression of the patricentered emphasis which is characteristic of all the northern Algonkians, a feature of their aboriginal culture. Since hunting is a male occupation, closely related males of an extended family were inevitably brought into close association in hunting and trapping activities. And, functionally, sons-in-laws could easily play the same role in the winter hunting groups as sons.

Among the Ojibwa, however, like other northern Algonkians, there is another feature that characterizes the functioning of winter hunting groups, although its historical roots involve a moot question. This is the association of each group with a delimited tract of land. For the Indians of the whole river these averaged 93 square miles in area, with a range from 13 to 212 square miles. This association has been labeled a *hunting territory system*, since members of the same winter hunting group return to the same territory year after year. Rights to these tracts are recognized and trespass resented. Their approximate boundaries could easily be traced by the Indians themselves. I recorded them on large-scale maps.

No rigid principles of inheritance governed the transmission of these hunting territories, for they were not needed. The rights recognized were focused upon usufruct, not on the possession of the land itself. The size of a tract was dependent upon the number of active hunters, the abundance of game, and the topography. Geographical area was of secondary importance. Any rule of primogeniture would have been impractical, and the territory of a man with half a dozen sons could scarcely have been split into economically equal parts at his death. What happened was that men who had hunted together in an established tract went on hunting there for many years. There was no pressure on them to change, since other groups of hunters occupied localities elsewhere. It was inevitable, then, that a son would continue to hunt in the same territory after his father's death, just as he had hunted there before it and perhaps had learned to hunt there as a boy. On the other hand, a man who had hunted with his father-in-law might continue to do so after the latter's death, although not inevitably. Since a winter hunting group never comprised a single nuclear family, the association of partners followed kinship lines. And, in this patricentered culture, this led in most cases to the association for long periods of men of the same paternal lineage, with particular hunting tracts identified with this pattern of relationship.

What needs emphasis is the fact that, considered from a primarily economic point of view, the association of related men and their families in winter hunting groups does not necessarily involve the recognition of established rights to a specific hunting territory. Indeed, a seasonal return to the same hunting tract assumes considerable stability in the population occupying a given region. Yet the Northern Ojibwa, as I have pointed out, are known to have undergone great geographical expansion. In the past, winter hunting groups similar in size and composition to those found later moved into new regions. Evidence for this is found in the genealogies I collected, combined with information about the specific location of the hunting areas of a few identifiable individuals of past generations. Thus, although winter hunting groups and the hunting territory system have sometimes been considered interdependent variables, and for this reason the aboriginality of the latter has been asserted, this inevitable association is unnecessary. If we consider winter hunting groups and the hunting territory system as independent variables, the historical question takes another form. This question concerns the possible changing relationships between basic ecological adaptation, changing economic realities, and social organization at successive historical periods. Considered in these terms some older patterns could persist while at the same time innovations could occur. There is no reason to doubt, for example, that the characteristic kinship structure of the Northern Ojibwa, the socioeconomic role of the extended family, and the association of male kin in hunting activities persisted through both earlier and later phases of the fur trade. What has been suggested is that the hunting territory system of the northeren Algonkians in general, as observed in operation in the twentieth century, can be attributed to the impact of the fur trade.

Some evidence for this has been produced in regions other than the one under discussion here. What has been stressed is the accentuation on recognized boundaries and on the property rights of the active hunters of the winter hunting group to the exchange value, in trade goods, of the fur caught in their own traps. Certainly it is true that the proceeds from the fur catch are not shared as directly among the members of the winter hunting group as is the meat of large game animals like the caribou or moose. With the initiation of the fur trade each hunter had his own personal account with the traders and was responsible for his own "debt." Recognized rights to the tract where a man's traps were laid assumed a different economic importance, because of the exchange value of the fur caught, as compared with animals hunted and consumed as food. What probably happened in the

Berens River region, and perhaps elsewhere, is that preceding the full crystallization of the hunting territory system there was a period during which less exclusive rights to hunting tracts prevailed. There were hunting areas, which although they might be returned to, had less clearly defined boundaries than at a later period, or there may have been considerable wandering about from one winter to another. I suspect that historically these variations must have been characteristic of the period of Ojibwa expansion when the Berens River Ojibwa, among others, were occupying new regions. At the same time, there is no surviving tradition among these people of any allotment system by "chiefs" or leading men. Such men would not have had sufficient power for this.

It seems likely then that the institutionalization of a full-fledged hunting territory system, integrated with the seasonal dispersion of winter hunting groups, developed after the Ojibwa population was established in the Berens River region. This would be a nineteenth century development for the most part, during the period of closer and closer contact with the Hudson Bay Company and increasing dependence on trade goods. Nevertheless, the changes that occurred did not affect the basic seasonal habits of the Ojibwa in relation to their physical environment, nor did it affect the framework of their socio-cultural system considered as a whole.

Summer Fishing Settlements

As compared with the 32 winter hunting groups of the inland bands of the Berens River, during the summer the same population was concentrated in five fishing settlements. Members of the Lake Pekang-ikum band were to be found in three of these, one on the lake of the same name, the others located at Poplar Narrows on the river and at Duck Lake. People of the Little Grand Rapids band were to be found in two settlements, one at Pauingessi, but in much larger numbers near the rapids.

There was no superordinate community organization in these summer fishing settlements. Ostensibly they were simply aggregates of the members of the winter hunting groups who camped near each other at traditional spots during the season of open water. Numerically, this was the time of year when the largest number of Indians were to be found together, and opportunities for social interaction on a wider scale occurred. Married daughters who were isolated from their parents all winter on their husbands' hunting territories might spend the summer encamped with their parents. It was at these summer encampments that the Midéwıwin was formerly held, and, at the time of my observations, *Wabano* ceremonies, dances, and occasionally conjuring performances.

In the summer of 1932, for example, the largest settlement of members of the Pekangikum band, with a population of 122, was to be found on the lake of the same name where the reservation is situated. The Poplar Narrows settlement was a little over half as large, and the Duck Lake settlement of 50 persons was the smallest. Despite the absence of any overall community organization of the summer settlements, the organization they did possess is clearly discernible at the subsettlement level. The population was not scattered at random but nucleated locally, as casual observation indicated and mapping of the location of the dwellings, along with the collection of census data, determined with greater precision. Little groups of birchbark dwellings or canvas tents, but practically no log cabins, were found in clusters, spatially distinct from other clusters of dwellings—often a considerable distance away. One of these dwelling clusters occupied a small island offshore at a distance of perhaps two miles, and the trail through the bush to another, from where I was camped, was at least a mile. The pattern of dwelling clusters for the settlement as a whole could not be seen, however, from any one point of observation. There were five of these dwelling clusters at Lake Pekangikum, while at Poplar Narrows there were two and at Duck Lake one. Farther down the river at Grand Rapids there were ten of them, although they were less clearly distinguishable in space. These dwelling clusters of the upriver bands ranged from 10 to 50 persons, the average being 26. In the Lake Pekangikum settlement this figure was 24, and at Grand Rapids it was 20 persons. What is primarily significant, however, is that in social composition these dwelling clusters represented the localization during the summer months of extended families. At Pekangikum, for example, 61 percent of married sons with living fathers were associated with this parent in the same dwelling cluster; 52 percent of married daughters were associated with their fathers in a similar way. And on the island mentioned the dwelling cluster consisted of a fraternity of three brothers and their families. Thus, in sociological terms, the dwelling clusters were equivalent with the winter hunting groups. There was cooperation in economic tasks and food sharing within the groups. The fact that a large proportion of the individual dwellings of the clusters were occupied by nuclear families, averaging 5.5 persons in the Pekangikum settlements and slightly fewer at Little Grand Rapids, is of subordinate importance when the functioning of the inhabitants of the dwelling cluster as members of extended families is taken into account.

In this respect there is actual continuity with the past. The members of a dwelling cluster at an earlier period would, in most cases, have occupied a multiple-family type of dwelling, the *cåbandawan*. In this older type of dwelling, there was more than one entrance and more than one hearth within. An extended family would have lived under one roof, but the women of the nuclear families composing it would be responsible for gathering their own wood and doing their own cooking. In one of the myths collected, a series of brothers married to series of sisters enlarge a *cåbandawan* to accommodate them all. Furthermore, the multiple-family dwelling in the past was as characteristic of winter as of summer living, although I do not mean to imply that there were no other types of dwellings, such as the teepee-shaped *pikogan*. Even at the time of which I speak, the log cabins that some of the inland Indians had constructed on their hunting territories actually functioned as multiple family dwellings, although this type of structure was not found in the summer settlements.

We must conclude, I think, that the inhabitants of the dwelling clusters in the summer, like the members of the winter hunting groups during the rest of the year, represent in microcosm the primary functioning units of the Northern Ojibwa sociocultural system. The summer fishing settlements described were macroassemblages of relatively contiguous and semilocalized extended family groups that functioned as independent units in summer, just as similar groups functioned in a similar way during the winter when, however, each group was completely isolated from others. Consequently, in groups encamped at favorable fishing places during the summer there was no need for any kind of formal organization beyond that which already existed. At both seasons, too, clan ties as well as kinship prompted intergroup linkages.

It was, then, the absence of any level of supergroup organization and leadership that confronted the Dominion government with problems when they included all the Indians of the Berens River in the treaty of 1875. I have tried to document here the forms in which this primary level of social organization characteristic of these Indians persisted until recent times, despite the creation of a "band" organization as a superstructure. In this respect, however, the Berens River Band, on the reservation at the mouth of the river, presented a contrasting picture reflecting the impact of acculturation at the level of social organization as well as in other ways. In this locality, there was a settlement occupied all year round. No dwelling clusters were discernable, and in winter the men who hunted usually left their families behind when they visited their hunting grounds. It was here, too, that the band chief in residence continuously played a more influential role than those of similar status inland.

KINSHIP PATTERN AND SOCIAL ORGANIZATION

At all seasons of the year, of course, the Indians of the semiautonomous units of population described actually were part of a larger whole. Ever since they became adherents to a treaty with the Dominion government, individuals have been identified with the various bands that were set up. But before this there was nothing comparable to the modern band organization, nor was there any tribal organization to which all the Ojibwa of the region belonged. Consequently, I have emphasized the relative functional autonomy of the localized groups as observed. These may be seen as a link with the past, and even during the period of my observation the inland Indians in particular were little affected by the band organization in their everyday life. The source of the unifying factors that bound Indians of the Berens River region together and transcended the localized groups at all seasons was a common linguistic and cultural heritage that had roots in the distant past. Among other things, this heritage included a common world view and a system of values that even at the the the time of my observations had not been completely dissipated. Many facets of it still affected their lives.

Among other things, since the use of their native language continued, kinship terms were still used in the traditional way to address and refer to other persons in daily life. They functioned as direct guides to interpersonal relations, since customary attitudes and patterns of social behavior, including sexual and marital relationships, were implied in their use. Consequently, kinship terms were not merely a device for discriminating the relationship of persons but were at the same time a way of achieving the normative orientation of the self in a traditional system of socially sanctioned roles and values. Kinship terms have a socially adaptive function as a signal system to discriminate customarily distinguishable social positions, statuses, and roles in human societies. In the sociocultural system of the Ojibwa they functioned as a means of promoting orderly social interaction, whether with reference to interpersonal relations in localized groups or with respect to the interaction of individuals belonging to different groups.

From childhood on, kinship terms oriented the behavior of the individual in a social world that embraced members of his extended family, persons primarily affiliated with other groups, and, as we shall see later, other-than-human persons (or spiritual beings) who appeared in dreams. The common linguistic and cultural heritage of these Indians provided the means of structuring their relations with each other wherever they were.

Besides a common kinship pattern and traditionally shared values, their cultural heritage included a clan system. Even though the clans were not as functionally important as was kinship in daily life, they did give emphasis to lineages, both real and fictitious, through the patrilineal affiliation of the individuals belonging to them. Furthermore, these clans were not localized. When moving about in summer, for instance, many individuals could find members of their own clan in almost all of the settlements. Since the membership of the eight clans represented in the total population varied from more than 250 individuals to fewer than a dozen, members of the largest clans, Sturgeon and Moose, were found in every settlement, while members of the Duck clan were to be met only at Little Grand Rapids. Nevertheless, representatives of seven clans were to be found in the two summer settlements of the Little Grand Rapids band in the middle of the river, while members of six clans were to be found in the three settlements of the Lake Pekangikum band, and the same number in the single settlement at the mouth of the river.

As might be expected, the traditional patterns of their social world and their seasonal movements led to intermarriage between Ojibwa of different localized groups and also between individuals belonging to the three bands on the river. My genealogical data, which includes a sample of approximately two hundred marriages, suggest that there was a period when intermarriage between the members of the different lineages who had migrated to the river in the late eighteenth and early nineteenth centuries tended to consolidate and expand the population of the new region into which they had moved. It also appears, however, that as time went on, there was increasing social interaction between members of the newly constituted Berens River bands and similarly organized groups outside this region. This was particularly true of the members of the band at the mouth of the river. Their location there provided a better opportunity for contacts over a wide geographical area than was possible for the Indians farther inland at the same period. But under contemporary conditions such contacts are possible for individuals of all bands. However, even at the time of my own

observations I recall hearing of a girl belonging to the Little Grand
Rapids Band who said she would never marry an Indian of her own
band.

If we consider the percentages of marriages men made with women
belonging to their own bands compared with those made with women of
other bands, my genealogies indicate that the former constitute a large
majority. Nevertheless, interband mariages occur in considerable
numbers over the generations recorded. The figure for men of the Lake
Pekangikum and Little Grand Rapids Bands respectively are 38 and 35
percent. The proportion of such marriages by men of the Berens River
Band was even higher. Besides this, the number of different bands from
which they obtained their wives was four times greater than that of the
men of the inland bands. If the latter married women outside their own
band, their mates came from other Berens River bands. Men from the
mouth of the river went much farther afield. Some of them married
women from bands on the western side of Lake Winnipeg or south of
the mouth of the Berens River. In fact, almost ten percent of them did
not marry Ojibwa women at all, but married Cree women from bands
north of Lake Winnipeg.

KINSHIP PATTERN AND BEHAVIOR

Since the Ojibwa kinship pattern is of a well-known type, it is
unnecessary to consider it formally here, or to present a list of native
terms. All that is required is an understanding of a few simple
principles that determine the general pattern of the system and
structure the basic social interaction of individuals.

In the first place, one of the chief features of this system which the
outsider must grasp is that there are no special terms for affinal
relatives—that is, mother- and father-in-law, son-in-law, daughter-
in-law, brother- or sister-in-law. All persons in the social world of the
Ojibwa are assimilated to classes of kin which, in our kinship system,
fall into the category of blood relatives. Among the Ojibwa, however,
any such genetic connections, although known, of course, are of
secondary importance in the connotation of kinship terms. Their use of
terms had a primary social function, uncorrelated with any precise
discrimination of genetic relationships except in the case of actual
parents. All terms except those used to designate Ego's own father and
mother are used for classes of kin in a widely extended sense. Thus,
from the standpoint of any Ego in Ojibwa society, *all* Ojibwa are kin of
some sort. They belonged to precisely the same classes of kin who are
represented as individuals in the winter hunting group, a dwelling

cluster, a summer settlement, or anywhere else. Possessing a common speech and common values, the Ojibwa structure social relations in a social system coterminous with the culturally constituted world of the Ojibwa as an ethnic group.

In the second place, a generation status is implied in the use of all terms. And as a consequence sexual relations or marriage between classes of relatives belonging to different kinship generations fall within the incest tabu. Besides this, and the existence of patrilineal clans, and an awareness that it is wrong to marry anyone of the same clan, it is the effective operation of the kinships system rather than any rule of clan exogamy considered independently that exerts the primary normative force in Ojibwa social relations. As a matter of record, there are extremely few violations of clan exogamy in my genealogies. However, in several cases of father–daughter incest known to me and in the case of a man who married his stepdaughter, the tabu against clan endogamy was also violated. On the other hand, the four cases of mother–son incest I heard about did not violate this tabu. The basic consequence of the operation of Ojibwa kinship system is to limit approved sex relations and marriage to individuals of two distinguishable classes of kin in the generation of every Ego.

In the third place, an understanding of the structuralization of social relations through the Ojibwa kinship system requires not only a necessary awareness of terminological distinctions but a knowledge of the contrasting attitudes and patterns of interpersonal behavior that correlate with different classes of kin. The central feature of Ojibwa social organization lies in the integral relationship between the two classes of kin that are formed in Ego's generation—siblings and nonsiblings—and the reciprocal distinction made by individuals of Ego's parents' generation between the *children* of classifactory siblings of their own sex and the offspring of siblings of opposite sex. An Ojibwa child not only must learn terminological distinction between siblings and nonsiblings of his own generation associated with contrasting roles; correlatively he must learn that the reciprocal roles he is requested to play toward the parents of these two classes of kin require contrasting patterns of behavior as well as terminological distinction. Once a child becomes aware of these differential modes of conduct and terminology and is able to act in accordance with them, his roles in the entire social system become crystallized.

A child soon learns, for example, not only that he has many siblings but that his father and mother likewise have many kin of the same class. He discovers through experience, moreover, that all the men whom his father calls "brother" play a role toward him which resembles very closely that of his own father, and they use the same kinship terms in direct address that they apply to their own children. Reciprocally, the term that the child is taught to use for the "brothers" of his father has a social connotation that is well conveyed by the English term "stepfather." Consequently, in his own generation Ego identifies the children of these men as siblings and uses brother and sister terms for them, as they do in addressing him.

It is also typical of the Ojibwa use of kinship terms that the *male* children of men who call each other "brother" perpetuate the use of this term for each other through successive generations. This patterning is reinforced by the patrilineal emphasis that is characteristic of Ojibwa culture and is expressed in behavior. It is consonant with the typical association of related males in the winter hunting groups as well as in the dwelling clusters of the summer settlements. Consequently, a child's relations with all the men called "brother" by his father, and whose children are siblings to him, are characterized by a special intimacy derived from experience as well as terminological usage. They form a distinct group among the male kin of the Ojibwa child.

At the same time, the wives of this group of men constitute a distinct class of women in relation to any Ego. For an Ojibwa child also discovers that a corresponding kinship pattern and comparable roles likewise apply to all the women who are "sisters" to his mother. Ego belongs to the same kinship class as the children of these women who are "stepmothers" to him. Furthermore, these women, as the term used for them suggests, belong to the kinship class in his parents' generation from which Ego's mother and all the wives of the men his father calls "brother" are drawn. Thus terminology, status in the kinship system, attitudes, and behavior are all integrated from the standpoint of the Objibwa child. I discover that in addition to my own parents, I have stepparents; that in addition to my own brothers and sisters I have many other siblings. All of these are my closest kin even though in the case of siblings not all of them belong to my own clan. For the existence of patrilineal clans leads to one differential feature between classifactory siblings related to Ego through the paternal line and those related through the maternal line. The children of women whom my mother calls "sister" may be married to men of a different clan, so that because of patrilineal descent their children may belong to a clan other than my own. On the other hand, the children of my father's "brothers" necessarily belong to my own clan for the same reason.

The mastery of a contrasting configuration of terms, attitudes, and behavior toward another category of kin is also required of the Ojibwa child. And in the case of this second pattern, too, there are integral connections between a class of kin in Ego's generation and the parents of any individuals belonging to this class. What the child learns is that the children of the women his father calls "sisters" and his mother calls "brothers" (their siblings of opposite sex, contrasted with those of the same sex as themselves) constitute a terminological class of *nonsiblings* in his own generation. But what is particularly important is to learn how to behave properly toward these kin. Broadly speaking, the patterns of behavior that must be adopted toward them are the reverse of those which are expected in the social interaction of Ego with persons who are siblings to him and the parents of this class of kin.

Instead of the intimacy with which Ego can approach his "step-fathers" and "stepmothers," it is necessary, for example, to maintain a pattern of social distance in relation to all the women his father calls "sister," and for whom he uses a distinct term. He must avoid women of this class as much as possible and speak to them directly only when absolutely necessary. And toward all the men his mother calls "brother" he must adopt an attitude that conveys respect; the freer kind of relationship that he has with his father or "stepfathers" is completely inappropriate. In the presence of kin who belong either to the class of "fathers' sisters" or "mothers' brothers," any reference to sexual matters, particularly of a bawdy nature, must be avoided. If this does occur, it is embarrassing to everyone. This once happened in my tent, full of men at the time, when a young fellow failed to notice that a man in the class of his "mother's brother" was there. The latter really wanted to laugh at what the young man said, but simply bent his head and looked at no one. The same pattern of verbal avoidance of sexual topics applies between men and between women of Ego's generation who are other than siblings to each other.

At the same time, this broad pattern of social avoidance, of which verbal references of a sexual nature are a part, is familiar to every Ojibwa child. But it has a different context. It is the pattern on which behavior toward all siblings of opposite sex has been molded. Kin in this relationship never participate together in common pastimes, games, or other activities. There are traditional games played by boys and others played by girls. In fact, the social solidarity that unites siblings of the same sex in many ways also punctuates the patterns of avoidance existing between those of opposite sex. Consequently, the "sisters" of Ego's father, or the "brothers" of his mother, although belonging to a different generation, exemplify in their relations with each other the

same avoidance pattern with which Ego is acquainted in social relations
with kin of the same class in his own generation. Thus, if Ego is male,
the avoidance of women of the "father's sisters" class, simply identifies
him further with the class of males in his parents' generation already
referred to, and his "sisters," in the same way, become identified in
their conduct with their mothers and "stepmother." It is in this way
that the avoidance patterns of successive generations are linked and
integrated into the total structure of Ojibwa society. In daily life
siblings of opposite sex are never seen alone in a canoe together or
walking together for even the shortest distance through the bush. In the
same way a man would never be seen under the same circumstance with
any woman in the category of "father's sisters," nor any woman with a
man in the kinship class of her mother's brothers.

What distinguishes the relations of *nonsiblings of opposite sex* in
Ego's generation, then, is that instead of a pattern of avoidance,
permissiveness is not only allowed but given particular emphasis. The
way this is accomplished is by the use of a kinship term used
reciprocally and solely by individuals in this kind of relationship. The
term *ninam* actually signals the possibility of sexual relations and
marriage. The English rendering "sweetheart" closely approximates its
Ojibwa connotation. Persons using this term between them are
permitted the greatest freedom in speech and are defined as potential
spouses. In the context of Ojibwa social life this freedom inevitably has
a sexual focus. In the absence of any kind of organized social or
economic activities in which unmarried boys and girls participate
together, and in the absence of any motivation that inhibits social
interaction, sex is the only common interest on which the relationship
of nonsiblings can be patterned.

The verbal aspects of this permissive behavior have been labeled a
"joking relationship," since the bawdiest kind of allusions are heard.
Such exchanges are almost compulsive whenever "sweethearts" meet,
regardless of age or marital status. Any occasion may be enlivened by
the laughter of everyone present, especially when the exchanges are
between men and women. Once I was trying to obtain some information on religious beliefs from a very old man whom I had never seen
before. His wife and my interpreter happened to be *ninamak* to each
other. The whole session was disrupted when these elderly folk,
grandparents to most of those present, began joking. When I made the
trip inland in 1932 with William Berens, we had scarcely beached our
canoe at Duck Lake before he had established a joking relationship
with a very old woman. He was two hundred miles from home, and his

last trip up the river had been forty years before. Yet because this woman was the sister of a man who fell into his nonsibling kin class, William Berens could establish a permissive relationship with her instantaneously. It was punctuated by a quick verbal exchange. "Which side of the wigwam do you sleep on ?" he asked. And when she told him, he said that he would be around that night. At another place we visited a middle-aged married woman said to him, "Can you still make your way through?" to which he replied, "The older you get the stiffer the horn." On another occasion I was included in the joking when an unmarried Indian and myself passed two young girls who were *ninamak* to him. It was they, not he, who started the fun.

Horseplay was also an aspect of the permissive pattern between "sweethearts." One informant told me that when he was a young boy his mother noticed him pushing his sister around playfully and half-wrestling with her one day. She reprimanded him immediately. "Quit that," his mother said, "she's not (your) *kinam*," thus emphasizing the difference between the behavior expected between nonsiblings of opposite sex as compared with siblings. Another man told me that in the middle of a cold winter night he arrived at the wigwam where his brother and other kin were sleeping. When he entered he threw himself down beside his brother's wife and snuggled up against her under the rabbit-skin blanket. Everyone woke up and there was uproarious laughter. Besides this, it was part of the fun to refer to the episode later in a boastful way, saying that he had been under the blankets with his "sweetheart." Once when I wished to take a picture of an old man, I sat him on a box and started to fix my tripod. He sat with his legs wide apart. Quick as a flash the wife of the man I was staying with—a middle-aged Christian woman and a pillar of the mission—started to laugh and made a gesture as if to unbutton the old man's fly. Everyone else laughed, too. He was (her) *kinam*.

Although it was not encouraged, men and women in this relationship might become lovers before either of them married. But since girls as a rule married at an early age, such cases were of little importance. What requires emphasis is that after marriage it was expected that the permissive pattern of behavior between *ninamak* would be limited to bawdy talk or the kind of horseplay mentioned. The fact that all the wives of one's classifactory brothers were one's *ninamak*, did not imply any sexual privileges. In fact, any hint of an affair with a married woman of this category was considered scandalous, although not as bad as sexual relationships with women of other kinship classes. It may also be pointed out that, by and large, individuals in the *ninamak* relationship were only infrequently found in the same winter hunting group or dwelling cluster. The siblings of Ego were the most typical members of these groups belonging to the same generation. But in the summer settlements, "sweethearts" were always to be found. They were constantly met at ceremonies, dances, and on other occasions.

The parents of Ego's *ninamak*, as I have said, belonged to the kinship class of "father's sisters" and "mother's brothers." After marriage with any specific *ninam*, of course, some particular man and woman in the category of Ego's parents' siblings of opposite sex became what in our conceptual scheme would be a father- and mother-in-law. Although this was a new relationship and a man was expected to help his "father-in-law" by hunting with him if needed, no changes in behavioral patterns were involved. The avoidance patterns already established between a man and any of his "father's sisters" continued, as did the respectful attitude toward their spouses. And, since there were no special terms for affinal relatives, no terminological changes were necessary. Consequently, the avoidance pattern between a woman and her daughter's husband can hardly be labeled a "mother-in-law tabu" comparable to what we find among other people, despite the fact that it shares some of the same characteristics. All we can say is that this pattern of avoidance among the Northern Ojibwa did not begin after marriage but was characteristic of other relationships as well.

One way to characterize the Ojibwa kinship system is to say that it was based on bilateral cross-cousin marriage. Empirically, however, this involved mating between actual first cousins, that is, the children of Ego's father's sisters or mother's brothers in the genetic sense. Probably not more than 25 percent of the marriages were between individuals as closely related as this. And, as I have indicated, the Ojibwa themselves did not think in these terms. Individuals were not motivated to choose first cousins as spouses. Consequently, although the marriage of actual cross cousins does occur, these cannot be regarded as *preferential* marriages. It seems better, then, to characterize the system in its own terms by saying that what it does is to identify a class of mates for Ego in every generation which *includes* first cousins as well as others more remotely related. So long as the extended incest tabus built into the system were maintained, the only spouses possible were individuals chosen within the class of potential mates defined.

Similar questions arise about the occurrence of other types of preferential marriages—the levirate, sororate, and sororal polygamy. If the levirate is defined as the preferential marriage of a widow with her deceased husband's actual brother, this kind of marriage occurred so infrequently that it cannot be said to be traditional or customary. On the other hand, the Ojibwa kinship system did promote the marriage of a widow to a man in the terminological class of brother to her deceased husband. The sororate offers a parallel case. I have no information indicating that it was a preferential type of marriage. However, I was once present when a man was discussing the possibility of a marriage between his son-in-law (a widower) and his daughter. The older sister of the latter had been the man's first wife. But I do not know whether this marriage took place.

With respect to sororal polygamy at an earlier period when plural marriages were permitted, there are some data in my genealogies. But the information is ambiguous. In six out of eight polygamous marriages the husbands did have actual sisters as wives. On the face of it this suggests preferential marriage. On the other hand, Cenawagwashang, who belonged to one of the most remote generations recorded and was one of the oldest members of the Moose clan inland, presents an interesting case. Although he was notorious because he had six wives, the largest number recalled for any man, none of them were actual sisters, although three belonged to the same clan. A contemporary belonging to the Sturgeon clan and well remembered as a prominent leader of the *Midēwīnin* had two wives. These women belonged to different clans. If sororal polygamy represented a preferential type of mating at one time, it might have been expected that these representative men of the old regime would have followed an established custom. But in these cases as well as in the other six the wives were *terminological* sisters, even though they belonged to different clans.

The terms "grandfather" and "grandmother" and the reciprocal term "grandchild" as used by the Ojibwa signaled behavioral correlates and connotations that in certain respects set these relationships apart from those already described. In daily life the social relations of children and grandparents are essentially permissive, resembling those of Ego to parents and stepparents in some respects. But there are some differences. In the degree of permissiveness, for instance, a point is reached where an old man may joke a little with his "granddaughter," even to the extent of making sexual allusions. No stepfather would go that far. At the same time, considered as a mode of address, grandparent terms are used in an extended sense to include all persons in the kinship generation older than parents. They always carry overtones of respect, associated with advanced age, experience, and presumed wisdom. Associated with the grandparent status, too, is a special role. Personal names were once bestowed upon all Ojibwa infants by persons of the grandparent class in a traditional ceremony that began to decline with the spread of christianity. These native names were sacred names and carried benefits for the child. They were derived from the contacts the namers, particularly a grandfather, had had in dream experiences with spiritual beings, or other-than-human persons. A further link between persons of this category and human beings of the grandparent class is the fact that, collectively, other-than-human persons were referred to as "our grandfathers." Besides this, the Ojibwa believed that they came into direct personal contact with other-than-human persons in their dreams. In this context the kinship terms grandfather and grandchildren were those used in direct address, and the dreamer benefited from experiences of this kind. Consequently, the relationship between grandparents and grandchildren leads us directly from a consideration of the interrelated roles of the Ojibwa social structure to their traditional world view. An understanding of their cognitive outlook is necessary for a comprehension of the functioning of their sociocultural system considered as a whole. The basic social sanctions involved in the maintenance of the social structure are dependent among other things, upon culturally constituted beliefs, values, personal experience, and the personality organization of Ojibwa individuals.

V | OJIBWA CULTURE AND
WORLD VIEW

INTRODUCTION

Melford E. Spiro

Each of the papers in this section may be viewed as an explication and application of a theoretical framework that Hallowell developed in his classic paper "The Self and Its Behavioral Environment" (see *Culture and Experience*, chap. 4). It is probably not inaccurate to claim that this paper laid the foundation for the "phenomenological" approach to the anthropological study of both culture and personality. In an intellectual era in which behaviorism was a dominant mode in the behavioral sciences, Hallowell had argued even earlier for the importance of personality as a mediating process between environmental stimuli and behavioral responses. But in this paper he went even further: he contended that in addition to analyzing personality from the perspective of the outside observer, it is important to view it from the perspective of the actor himself. While behavioristic psychology and much of social and cultural anthropology dismissed the "inner world" of social actors—the world of ideas, wishes, fantasies, cognitions, and so on—as illusory, or as not susceptible of scientific inquiry, or as irrelevant to their respective concerns, and while psychoanalytic psychology, although taking the inner world seriously, conceptualized its structure and functions from the perspective of the observer, Hallowell had begun to emphasize the importance of studying the inner world from the perspective of the social actors.

To denote this inner world, Hallowell proposed the term "self." The self is the perceiving and experiencing ego as it is known to the actor himself. It is that perceptual object which is alluded to by such terms as "I" and "me" and which is distinguished from a contrasting set of objects experienced as

Melford E. Spiro is professor of anthropology at the University of California, San Diego.

"other-than-self." The acquisition of a self and of self-awareness, Hallowell argued, is crucial for the operation of a human
social order because, to the degree that the latter order is a
moral order, social actors must assume responsibility for their
own conduct. This assumption therefore requires that they
monitor their behavior by reference to the appropriate cultural
norms and rules, and such monitoring procedures require
self-judgments and self-evaluations that are possible only
through self-awareness and by a consciousness of the continuity of the self across space and time.

After demonstrating the importance of the self-concept for
the functioning of sociocultural systems, Hallowell went on
to demonstrate how the self is in large measure culturally constituted, and (this being the case) how it is cross-culturally
variable. In rich detail, Hallowell showed that culture provides
those "basic orientations" that constitute some of the conditions for the "development, reinforcement, and effective functioning of self-awareness." These include a self-orientation,
object orientation, spatiotemporal orientation, motivational
orientation, and normative orientation.

Having demonstrated the importance of the phenomenological self, Hallowell went on to show that the environment
with which the self sustains its transactions is no less phe-
nomenologically conceived. Hence, in order to understand
human behavior it is not enough to attend to the objective environment described by physical geography, or even to the
behavioral environment described by ethological biology, or
even to the cultural environment described by conventional
anthropology. In addition, we must attend, so he argued, to
the environment as it is experienced by the actor himself; for
it is in terms of this environment that "he thinks, is motivated
to act, and satisfies his needs." Like the self, this phenome-
nologically conceived environment—so Hallowell argued in
masterly fashion and rich detail—is also culturally constituted
and therefore cross-culturally variable. Hence, to understand
social behavior in terms of the psychological field of social
actors it is necessary to understand how culturally constituted
selves interact with their culturally constituted behavioral environments.

It is to these themes that the papers in this section are addressed. If it is not apparent by now it will surely become apparent from the following papers that Hallowell was one of the
first anthropologists to address the current emic-etic distinction in ethnographic reporting. As these papers indicate, however, his emic approach differs from some contemporary emic
approaches in three ways. First, although Hallowell attends
to ethnosemantic analysis in constructing an emic view of
Ojibwa culture, ethnosemantic data make up only a small proportion of his data base. Second, he is concerned not with the
phenomenological meaning of culture per se but with its relationship to social behavior. Third, since he is as much interested in the self as he is in culture, he is concerned not only
with cognitive variables but with the total configuration of
variables—motivational and affective, as well as cognitive—
that affect the actors' encounters with their behavioral environment.

Like almost all of Hallowell's ethnographic work, these papers are instructive not only for Algonkian specialists but for
any scholar who is concerned with the meaning of human culture and the relationships it sustains to the behavior and personality of social actors. Thus, "Ojibwa Ontology, Behavior,
and World View," which Hallowell characterizes as an essay
in ethnometaphysics, develops in rich detail the relationships
among spatiotemporal orientations and notions of self, of person, and of person perception in relationship to the culturally
constituted behavioral environment of the Ojibwa. Raymond
Fogelson (pers. comm.) may well be right in claiming that this
is perhaps "the most important" of Hallowell's essays, the one
that will have "the largest and most continuing impact."

In characteristic fashion, in "Ojibwa World View and Disease"
Hallowell transcends the conventional boundaries of medical
anthropology, just as his work on property, for example, transcends the conventional boundaries of economic anthropology. To be sure, this article presents the usual ethnographic
data on illness, diagnosis, therapy, medical practioners, and
so on, but these medical data subserve a more general theoretical problem concerning the operation of sociocultural systems; namely, How do stateless societies—those without

centralized authority and formal legal sanctions—maintain
social order and social control?

   In "The Role of Dreams in Ojibwa Culture," Hallowell again
is not content, as is usually the case, to trace the relationships
between Ojibwa dreams and the dominant themes in Ojibwa
culture or social behavior. Rather, he uses the dream as a vehicle to explore the relationships between fantasy and reality,
sacred and profane, excess and restraint, as they relate to symbolization, psychobiological functioning, and individual and
group adaptation. In this essay Hallowell is able to show that
for the Ojibwa, at least, the unconscious world of the dream
is an important basis for their adaptation to the conscious
world of society and culture.

   In each of these essays, the rich ethnographic data not only
serve to support a theoretical argument but provide a three-
dimensional picture of living actors utilizing their culture to
cope with culturally specific and generically human existential
problems.

NINE

Ojibwa Ontology, Behavior, and World View

1960

> It is, I believe, a fact that future investigations will thoroughly confirm, that the Indian does not make the separation into personal as contrasted with impersonal, corporeal with impersonal, in our sense at all. What he seems to be interested in is the question of existence, of reality; and everything that is perceived by the sense, thought of, felt and dreamt of, exists.
>
> PAUL RADIN

Introduction

IT HAS BECOME increasingly apparent in recent years that the potential significance of the data collected by cultural anthropologists far transcends in interest the level of simple, objective, ethnographic description of the peoples they have studied. New perspectives have arisen; fresh interpretations of old data have been offered; investigation and analysis have been pointed in novel directions. The study of culture and personality, national character and the special attention now being paid to values are illustrations that come to mind.. Robert Redfield's concept of world view, "that outlook upon the universe that is characteristic of a people," which emphasizes a perspective that is not equivalent to the study of religion in the conventional sense, is a further example.

"World view" [he says] differs from culture, ethos, mode of thought, and national character. It is the picture the members of a society have of the properties and characters upon their stage of action. While "national character" refers to the way these people look to the outsider looking in on them, "world view" refers to the way the world looks to that people looking out. Of all that is connoted by "culture," "world view" attends

The courtesy of the Stanford University Press is acknowledged for permission to use portions of a paper by the author which appeared in *Person Perception*, ed. by R. Tagiuri and L. Petrullo.

especially to the way a man, in a particular society, sees himself in relation
to all else. It is the properties of existence as distinguished from and related
to the self. It is, in short, a man's idea of the universe. It is that organization of ideas which answers to a man the questions: Where am I? Among
what do I move? What are my relations to these things? . . . Self is the
axis of "world view." [1]

In an essay entitled "The Self and Its Behavioral Environment," I
have pointed out that self-identification and culturally constituted
notions of the nature of the self are essential to the operation of all
human societies and that a functional corollary is the cognitive orientation of the self to a world of objects other than self. Since the
nature of these objects is likewise culturally constituted, a unified
phenomenal field of thought, values, and action which is integral with
the kind of world view that characterizes a society is provided for its
members. The behavioral environment of the self thus becomes
structured in terms of a diversified world of objects other than self,
"discriminated, classified, and conceptualized with respect to attributes
which are culturally constituted and symbolically mediated through
language. Object orientation likewise provides the ground for an
intelligible interpretation of events in the behavioral environment on
the basis of traditional assumptions regarding the nature and attributes
of the objects involved and implicit or explicit dogmas regarding the
'causes' of events." [2] Human beings in whatever culture are provided
with cognitive orientation in a cosmos; there is "order" and "reason"
rather than chaos. There are basic premises and principles implied,
even if these do not happen to be consciously formulated and articulated
by the people themselves. We are confronted with the philosophical
implications of their thought, the nature of the world of being as they
conceive it. If we pursue the problem deeply enough we soon come
face to face with a relatively unexplored territory—ethno-metaphysics.
Can we penetrate this realm in other cultures? What kind of evidence
is at our disposal? The forms of speech as Benjamin Whorf and the
neo-Humboldtians have thought? [3] The manifest content of myth? Observed behavior and attitudes? And what order of reliability can our
inferences have? The problem is a complex and difficult one, but this
should not preclude its exploration.

In this paper I have assembled evidence, chiefly from my own field
work on a branch of the Northern Ojibwa, [4] which supports the infer-

ence that in the metaphysics of being found among these Indians, the action of persons provides the major key to their world view.

While in all cultures "persons" comprise one of the major classes of objects to which the self must become oriented, this category of being is by no means limited to *human* beings. In Western culture, as in others, "supernatural" beings are recognized as "persons," although belonging, at the same time, to an other than human category.[5] But in the social sciences and psychology, "persons" and human beings are categorically identified. This identification is inherent in the concept of "society" and "social relations." In Warren's *Dictionary of Psychology* "person" is defined as "a human organism regarded as having distinctive characteristics and social relations." The same identification is implicit in the conceptualization and investigation of social organization by anthropologists. Yet this obviously involves a radical abstraction if, from the standpoint of the people being studied, the concept of "person" is not, in fact, synonymous with human being but transcends it. The significance of the abstraction only becomes apparent when we stop to consider the perspective adopted. The study of social organization, defined as human relations of a certain kind, is perfectly intelligible as an objective approach to the study of this subject in any culture. But if, in the world view of a people, "persons" as a class include entities other than human beings, then our objective approach is not adequate for presenting an accurate description of "the way a man, in a particular society, sees himself in relation to all else." A different perspective is required for this purpose. It may be argued, in fact, that a thoroughgoing "objective" approach to the study of cultures cannot be achieved solely by projecting upon those cultures categorical abstractions derived from Western thought. For, in a broad sense, the latter are a reflection of *our* cultural subjectivity. A higher order of objectivity may be sought by adopting a perspective which includes an analysis of the outlook of the people themselves as a complementary procedure. It is in a world view perspective, too, that we can likewise obtain the best insight into how cultures function as wholes.

The significance of these differences in perspective may be illustrated in the case of the Ojibwa by the manner in which the kinship term "grandfather" is used. It is not only applied to human persons but to spiritual beings who are persons of a category other than human. In fact, when the collective plural "our grandfathers" is used, the reference is primarily to persons of this latter class. Thus if we study Ojibwa social organization in the usual manner, we take account of only one set of "grandfathers." When we study their religion we discover other "grandfathers." But if we adopt a world view perspective no dichotomization appears. In this perspective "grandfather" is a term applicable to certain "person objects," without any distinction between human persons and those of an other-than-human class. Furthermore, both sets of grandfathers can be said to be functionally as well as terminologically equivalent in certain respects. The other-than-human grandfathers are sources of power to human beings through the "blessings" they bestow, i.e., a sharing of their power which enhances the "power" of human beings. A child is always given a name by an old man, i.e., a terminological grandfather. It is a matter of indifference whether he is a blood relative or not. This name carries with it a special blessing because it has reference to a dream of the human grandfather in which he obtained power from one or more of the other-than-human grandfathers. In other words, the relation between a human child and a human grandfather is functionally patterned in the same way as the relation between human beings and grandfathers of an other-than-human class. And, just as the latter type of grandfather may impose personal taboos as a condition of a blessing, in the same way a human grandfather may impose a taboo on a "grandchild" he has named.

Another direct linguistic clue to the inclusiveness of the "person" category in Ojibwa thinking is the term *windīgo*. Baraga defines it in his *Dictionary* as "fabulous giant that lives on human flesh; a man that eats human flesh, cannibal." From the Ojibwa standpoint all *windīgowak* are conceptually unified as terrifying, anthropomorphic beings who, since they threaten one's very existence, must be killed. The central theme of a rich body of anecdotal material shows how this threat was met in particular instances. It ranges from cases in which it was necessary to kill the closest of kin because it was thought an individual was becoming a *windīgo*, through accounts of heroic fights between human beings and these fabulous giant monsters, to a first-hand report of a personal encounter with one of them.[6]

The more deeply we penetrate the world view of the Ojibwa the more apparent it is that "social relations" between human beings

(*änicinábek*) and other-than-human "persons" are of cardinal significance. These relations are correlative with their more comprehensive
categorization of "persons." Recognition must be given to the culturally
constituted meaning of "social" and "social relations" if we are to
understand the nature of the Ojibwa world and the living entities in it.[7]

Linguistic Categories and Cognitive Orientation

Any discussion of "persons" in the world view of the Ojibwa must
take cognizance of the well known fact that the grammatical structure
of the language of these people, like all their Algonkian relatives,
formally expresses a distinction between "animate" and "inanimate"
nouns. These particular labels, of course, were imposed upon Algonkian languages by Europeans;[8] it appeared to outsiders that the Algonkian differentiation of objects approximated the animate-inanimate
dichotomy of Western thought. Superficially this seems to be the case.
Yet a closer examination indicates that, as in the gender categories of
other languages, the distinction in some cases appears to be arbitrary,
if not extremely puzzling, from the standpoint of common sense or in
a naturalistic frame of reference. Thus substantives for some, but not
all—trees, sun-moon (*gízis*), thunder, stones, and objects of material
culture like kettle and pipe—are classified as "animate."

If we wish to understand the cognitive orientation of the Ojibwa,
there is an ethno-linguistic problem to be considered: What is the
meaning of animate in Ojibwa thinking? Are such generic properties
of objects as responsiveness to outer stimulation—sentience, mobility,
self-movement, or even reproduction—primary characteristics attributed to all objects of the animate class irrespective of their categories as physical objects in our thinking? Is there evidence to sub-
stantiate such properties of objects independent of their formal linguistic
classification? It must not be forgotten that no Ojibwa is consciously
aware of, or can abstractly articulate the animate-inanimate category
of his language, despite the fact that this dichotomy is implicit in his
speech. Consequently, the grammatical distinction as such does not
emerge as a subject for reflective thought or bear the kind of relation
to individual thinking that would be present if there were some formulated dogma about the generic properties of these two classes of objects.

Commenting on the analogous grammatical categories of the Central
Algonkian languages with reference to linguistic and nonlinguistic

orders of meaning, Greenberg writes: "Since all persons and animals
are in Class I (animate), we have at least one ethnoseme, but most of
the other meanings can be defined only by a linguiseme." In Greenberg's opinion, "unless the actual behavior of Algonquian speakers
shows some mode of conduct common to all these instances such that,
given this information, we could predict the membership of Class I,
we must resort to purely linguistic characterization."[9]

In the case of the Ojibwa, I believe that when evidence from beliefs,
attitudes, conduct, and linguistic characterization are all considered
together the psychological basis for their unified cognitive outlook can
be appreciated, even when there is a radical departure from the framework of our thinking. In certain instances, behavioral predictions can
be made. Behavior, however, is a function of a complex set of factors
—including actual experience. More important than the linguistic
classification of objects is the kind of vital functions attributed to them
in the belief system and the conditions under which these functions
are observed or tested in experience. This accounts, I think, for the
fact that what we view as material, inanimate objects—such as shells
and stones—are placed in an "animate" category along with "persons"
which have no physical existence in our world view. The shells, for
example, called *migis* on account of the manner in which they function
in the Midewiwin, could not be linguistically categorized as "inanimate." "Thunder," as we shall see, is not only reified as an
"animate" entity, but has the attributes of a "person" and may be
referred to as such. An "inanimate" categorization would be unthinkable from the Ojibwa point of view. When Greenberg refers to
"persons" as clearly members of the animate grammatical category he
is, by implication, identifying person and human being. Since in the
Ojibwa universe there are many kinds of reified person-objects which
are other than human but have the same ontological status, these, of
course, fall into the same ethnoseme as human beings and into the
"animate" linguistic class.

Since stones are grammatically animate, I once asked an old man:
Are *all* the stones we see about us here alive? He reflected a long while
and then replied, "No! But *some* are." This qualified answer made
a lasting impression on me. And it is thoroughly consistent with
other data that indicate that the Ojibwa are not animists in the sense
that they dogmatically attribute living souls to inanimate objects such

as stones. The hypothesis which suggests itself to me is that the allocation of stones to an animate grammatical category is part of a culturally constituted cognitive "set." It does not involve a consciously formulated theory about the nature of stones. It leaves a door open that our orientation on dogmatic grounds keeps shut tight. Whereas we should never expect a stone to manifest animate properties of any kind under any circumstances, the Ojibwa recognize, *a priori,* potentialities for animation in certain classes of objects under certain circumstances.[10] The Ojibwa do not perceive stones, in general, as animate, any more than we do. The crucial test is experience. Is there any personal testimony available? In answer to this question we can say that it is asserted by informants that stones have been seen to move, that some stones manifest other animate properties, and, as we shall see, Flint is represented as a living personage in their mythology.

The old man to whom I addressed the general question about the animate character of stones was the same informant who told me that during a Midewiwin ceremony, when his father was the leader of it, he had seen a "big round stone move." He said his father got up and walked around the path once or twice. Coming back to his place he began to sing. The stone began to move "following the trail of the old man around the tent, rolling over and over, I saw it happen several times and others saw it also."[11] The animate behavior of a stone under these circumstances was considered to be a demonstration of magic power on the part of the Midé. It was not a voluntary act initiated by the stone considered as a living entity. Associated with the Midewiwin in the past there were other types of large boulders with animate properties. My friend Chief Berens had one of these, but it no longer possessed these attributes. It had contours that suggested eyes and mouth. When Yellow Legs, Chief Berens's great-grandfather, was a leader of the Midewiwin he used to tap this stone with a new knife. It would then open its mouth, Yellow Legs would insert his fingers and take out a small leather sack with medicine in it. Mixing some of this medicine with water, he would pass the decoction around. A small sip was taken by those present.[12]

If, then, stones are not only grammatically animate, but, in particular cases, have been observed to manifest animate properties, such as movement in space and opening of a mouth, why should they not on occasion be conceived as possessing animate properties of a "higher" order? The actualization of this possibility is illustrated by the following anecdote:

A white trader, digging in his potato patch, unearthed a large stone similar to the one just referred to. He sent for John Duck, an Indian who was the leader of the *wábano*, a contemporary ceremony that is held in a structure something like that used for the Midewiwin. The trader called his attention to the stone, saying that it must belong to his pavilion. John Duck did not seem pleased at this. He bent down and spoke to the boulder in a low voice, inquiring whether it had ever been in his pavilion. According to John the stone replied in the negative.

It is obvious that John Duck spontaneously structured the situation in terms that are intelligible within the context of Ojibwa language and culture. Speaking to a stone dramatizes the depth of the categorical difference in cognitive orientation between the Ojibwa and ourselves. I regret that my field notes contain no information about the use of direct verbal address in the other cases mentioned. But it may well have taken place. In the anecdote describing John Duck's behavior, however, his use of speech as a mode of communication raises the animate status of the boulder to the level of social interaction common to human beings. Simply as a matter of observation we can say that the stone was treated *as if* it were a "person," not a "thing," without inferring that objects of this class are, for the Ojibwa, necessarily conceptualized as persons.

Further exploration might be made of the relations between Ojibwa thinking, observation, and behavior and their grammatical classification of objects but enough has been said, I hope, to indicate that not only animate properties but even "person" attributes may be projected upon objects which to us clearly belong to a physical inanimate category.

The "Persons" of Ojibwa Mythology

The Ojibwa distinguish two general types of traditional oral narratives: 1. "News or tidings" (*tăbătcamowin*), i.e., anecdotes, or stories, referring to events in the lives of human beings (*ănícinábek*). In content, narratives of this class range from everyday occurrences, through more exceptional experiences, to those which verge on the legendary. (The anecdotes already referred to, although informal, may be said to belong to this general class.) 2. Myths (*ätíso'kanak*),[13] i.e., sacred stories, which are not only traditional and formalized; their narration is seasonally restricted and is somewhat ritualized. The significant thing about these stories is that the characters in them are regarded as living entities who have existed from time immemorial. While there is genesis through birth and temporary or permanent form-shifting through transformation, there is no outright creation. Whether human or animal in form or name, the major characters in the myths behave like people, though many of their activities are depicted in a spatio-temporal framework of cosmic, rather than mundane, dimensions. There is "social interaction" among them and between them and *änicinábek*.

A striking fact furnishes a direct linguistic cue to the attitude of the Ojibwa towards these personages. When they use the term *ätíso'kanak,* they are not referring to what I have called a "body of narratives." The term refers to what we would call the characters in these stories; to the Ojibwa they are living "persons" of an other-than-human class. As William Jones said many years ago, "Myths are thought of as conscious beings, with powers of thought and action."[14] A synonym for this class of persons is "our grandfathers."

The *ätíso'kanak,* or "our grandfathers,"' are never "talked about" casually by the Ojibwa. But when the myths are narrated on long winter nights, the occasion is a kind of invocation: "Our grandfathers" like it and often come to listen to what is being said. In ancient times one of these entities (*Wisekedjak*) is reputed to have said to the others: "We'll try to make everything to suit the *änicinábek* as long as any of them exist, so that they will never forget us and will always talk about us."

It is clear, therefore, that to the Ojibwa, their "talk" about these entities, although expressed in formal narrative, is not about fictitious characters. On the contrary, what we call myth is accepted by them as a true account of events in the past lives of living "persons."[15] It is for this reason that narratives of this class are significant for an understanding of the manner in which their phenomenal field is culturally structured and cognitively apprehended. As David Bidney has pointed out, "The concept of 'myth' is relative to one's accepted beliefs and convictions, so that what is gospel truth for the believer is sheer 'myth' and 'fiction' for the non-believer or skeptic. . . . Myths and magical tales and practices are accepted precisely because pre-scientific folk do not consider them as merely 'myths' or 'magic', since once the distinction between myth and science is consciously accepted, the acquired critical insight precludes the belief in and acceptance of magic and myth."[16] When taken at their face value, myths provide a reliable source of prime value for making inferences about Ojibwa world outlook. They offer basic data about unarticulated, unformalized, and unanalyzed concepts regarding which informants cannot be expected to generalize. From this point of view, myths are broadly analogous to the concrete material of the texts on which the linguist depends for his derivation, by analysis and abstraction, of the grammatical categories and principles of a language.

In formal definitions of myth (e.g., *Concise Oxford Dictionary* and Warren's *Dictionary of Psychology*) the subject matter of such narrative often has been said to involve not only fictitious characters but "supernatural persons." This latter appellation, if applied to the Ojibwa characters, is completely misleading, if for no other reason than the fact that the concept of "supernatural" presupposes a concept of the "natural." The latter is not present in Ojibwa thought. It is unfortunate that the natural-supernatural dichotomy has been so persistently invoked by many anthropologists in describing the outlook of peoples in cultures other than our own. Linguists learned long ago that it was impossible to write grammars of the languages of nonliterate peoples by using as a framework Indo-European speech forms. Lovejoy has pointed out that "The sacred word 'nature' is probably the most equivocal in the vocabulary of the European peoples . . ."[17] and the natural-supernatural antithesis has had its own complex history in Western thought.[18]

To the Ojibwa, for example, *gîzis* (day luminary, the sun) is not a natural object in our sense at all. Not only does their conception differ; the sun is a "person" of the other-than-human class. But more important still is the absence of the notion of the ordered regularity in movement that is inherent in our scientific outlook. The Ojibwa entertain no reasonable certainty that, in accordance with natural law, the sun will "rise" day after day. In fact, *Tcakábec,* a mythical personage, once set a snare in the trail of the sun and caught it. Darkness continued until a mouse was sent by human beings to release the sun and provide daylight again. And in another story (not a myth) it is recounted how two old men at dawn vied with each other in influencing the sun's movements.

The first old man said to his companion: "It is about sunrise now and there is a clear sky. You tell the sun to rise at once." So the other old man said to the sun: "My grandfather, come up quickly." As soon as he had said this the sun came up into the sky like a shot. "Now you try something," he said to his companion. "See if you can send it down." So the other man said to the sun: "My grandfather, put your face down again." When he said this the sun went down again. "I have more power than you," he said to the other old man, "The sun never goes down once it comes up."

We may infer that, to the Ojibwa, any regularity in the movements of the sun is of the same order as the habitual activities of human beings. There are certain expectations, of course, but, on occasion, there may be temporary deviations in behavior "caused" by other persons. Above all, any concept of *impersonal* "natural" forces is totally foreign to Ojibwa thought.

Since their cognitive orientation is culturally constituted and thus given a psychological "set," we cannot assume that objects, like the sun, are perceived as natural objects in our sense. If this were so, the anecdote about the old men could not be accepted as an actual event involving a case of "social interaction" between human beings and an other-than-human person. Consequently, it would be an error to say that the Ojibwa "personify" natural objects. This would imply that, at some point, the sun was first perceived as an inanimate, material thing. There is, of course, no evidence for this. The same conclusion applies over the whole area of their cognitive orientation towards the objects of their world.

The Four Winds and Flint, for instance, are quintuplets. They were born of a mother (unnamed) who, while given human characteristics, lived in the very distant past. As will be more apparent later, this character, like others in the myths, may have anthropomorphic characteristics without being conceived as a human being. In the context she, like the others, is an *ätiso'kan*. The Winds were born first, then Flint "jumped out," tearing her to pieces. This, of course, is a direct allusion to his inanimate, stony properties. Later he was penalized for his hurried exit. He fought with *Misábos* (Great Hare) and pieces were chipped off his body and his size reduced. "Those pieces broken from your body may be of some use to human beings some day," *Misábos* said to him. "But you will not be any larger so long as the earth shall last. You'll never harm anyone again."

Against the background of this "historic" event, it would be strange indeed if flint were allocated to an inanimate grammatical category. There is a special term for each of the four winds that are differentiated, but no plural for "winds." They are all animate beings, whose "homes" define the four directions.

The conceptual reification of Flint, the Winds and the Sun as other-than-human persons exemplifies a world view in which a natural-supernatural dichotomy has no place. And the representation of these beings as characters in "true" stories reinforces their reality by means of a cultural device which at the same time depicts their vital roles in interaction with other persons as integral forces in the functioning of a unified cosmos.

Anthropomorphic Traits and Other-than-Human Persons

In action and motivations the characters in the myths are indistinguishable from human persons. In this respect, human and other-than-human persons may be set off, in life as well as in myth, from animate beings such as ordinary animals (*awésiak*, pl.) and objects belonging to the inanimate grammatical category. But, at the same time, it must be noted that "persons" of the other-than-human class do not always present a human appearance in the myths. Consequently, we may ask: What constant attributes do unify the concept of "person"? What is the essential meaningful core of the concept of person in Ojibwa thinking? It can be stated at once that anthropomorphic traits in outward appearance are not the crucial attributes.

It is true that some extremely prominent characters in the myths are given explicit human form. *Wisekedjak* and *Tcakábec* are examples. Besides this they have distinctive characteristics of their own. The former has an exceptionally long penis and the latter is very small in size, yet extremely powerful. There are no equivalent female figures. By comparison, Flint and the Winds have human attributes by implication; they were born of a "woman" as human beings are born; they speak, and so on. On the other hand, the High God of the Ojibwa, a very remote figure who does not appear in the mythology at all, but is spoken of as a "person," is not even given sexual characteristics. This is possible because there is no sex gender in Ojibwa speech.

Consequently an animate being of the person category may function in their thinking without having explicitly sexual or other anthropomorphic characteristics. Entities "seen" in dreams (*pawáganak*) are "persons"; whether they have anthropomorphic attributes or not is incidental. Other entities of the person category, whose anthropomorphic character is undefined or ambiguous, are what have been called the "masters" or "owners" of animals or plant species. Besides these, certain curing procedures and conjuring are said to have other-than-human personal entities as patrons.

If we now examine the cognitive orientation of the Ojibwa towards the Thunder Birds it will become apparent why anthropomorphism is not a constant feature of the Ojibwa concept of "person." These beings likewise demonstrate the autonomous nature of Ojibwa reification. For we find here a creative synthesis of objective "naturalistic" observation integrated with the subjectivity of dream experiences and traditional mythical narrative which, assuming the character of a living image, is neither the personification of a natural phenomenon nor an altogether animal-like or human-like being. Yet it is impossible to deny that, in the universe of the Ojibwa, Thunder Birds are "persons."

My Ojibwa friends, I discovered, were as puzzled by the white man's conception of thunder and lightning as natural phenomena as they were by the idea that the earth is round and not flat. I was pressed on more than one occasion to explain thunder and lightning, but I doubt whether my somewhat feeble efforts made much sense to them. Of one thing I am sure: My explanations left their own beliefs completely unshaken. This is not strange when we consider that, even in our naturalistic frame of reference, thunder and lightning as perceived do not exhibit the lifeless properties of inanimate objects. On the contrary, it has been said that thunder and lightning are among the natural phenomena which exhibit some of the properties of "person objects."[19] Underlying the Ojibwa view there may be a level of naïve perceptual experience that should be taken into account. But their actual construct departs from this level in a most explicit direction: Why is an avian image central in their conception of a being whose manifestations are thunder and lightning? Among the Ojibwa with whom I worked, the linguistic stem for bird is the same as that for Thunder Bird (*pinési*; pl. *pinésīwak*). Besides this, the avian characteristics of Thunder Birds are still more explicit. Conceptually they are grouped with the hawks, of which there are several natural species in their habitat.

What is particularly interesting is that the avian nature of the Thunder Birds does not rest solely on an arbitrary image. Phenomenally, thunder does exhibit "behavioral" characteristics that are analogous to avian phenomena in this region.[20] According to meteorological observations, the average number of days with thunder begins with one in April, increases to a total of five in midsummer (July) and then declines to one in October. And if a bird calendar is consulted, the facts show that species wintering in the south begin to appear in April and disappear for the most part not later than October, being, of course, a familiar sight during the summer months. The avian character of the Thunder Birds can be rationalized to some degree with reference to natural facts and their observation.

But the evidence for the existence of Thunder Birds does not rest only on the association of the occurrence of thunder with the migration of the summer birds projected into an avian image. When I visited the Ojibwa an Indian was living who, when a boy of twelve or so, saw *pinési* with his own eyes. During a severe thunderstorm he ran out of his tent and there on the rocks lay a strange bird. He ran back to call his parents, but when they arrived the bird had disappeared. He was sure it was a Thunder Bird, but his elders were skeptical because it is almost unheard of to see *pinési* in such a fashion. But the matter was clinched and the boy's account accepted when a man who had *dreamed* of *pinési* verified the boy's description. It will be apparent later why a dream experience was decisive. It should be added at this point, however, that many Indians say they have seen the nests of the Thunder Birds; these are usually described as collections of large stones in the form of shallow bowls located in high and inaccessible parts of the country.

If we now turn to the myths, we find that one of them deals in considerable detail with Thunder Birds. Ten unmarried brothers live together. The oldest is called *Mätcíkíwis*. A mysterious housekeeper cuts wood and builds a fire for them which they find burning when they return from a long day's hunt, but she never appears in person. One day the youngest brother discovers and marries her. *Mätcíkíwis* is jealous and kills her. She would have revived if her husband had not broken a taboo she imposed. It turns out, however, that she is

not actually a human being but a Thunder Bird and, thus, one of the
ätiso'kanak and immortal. She flies away to the land above this earth
inhabited by the Thunder Birds. Her husband, after many difficulties,
follows her there. He finds himself brother-in-law to beings who are
the "masters" of the duck hawks, sparrow hawks, and other species
of this category of birds he has known on earth. He cannot relish the
food eaten, since what the Thunder Birds call "beaver" are to him like
the frogs and snakes on this earth (a genuinely naturalistic touch since
the sparrow hawk, for example, feeds on batrachians and reptiles).
He goes hunting gigantic snakes with his male Thunder Bird relatives.
Snakes of this class also exist on this earth, and the Thunder Birds
are their inveterate enemies. (When there is lightning and thunder this
is the prey the Thunder Birds are after.) One day the great Thunder
Bird says to his son-in-law, "I know you are getting lonely; you must
want to see your people. I'll let you go back to earth now. You have
nine brothers at home and I have nine girls left. You can take them
with you as wives for your brothers. I'll be related to the people on
earth now and I'll be merciful towards them. I'll not hurt any of them
if I can possibly help it." So he tells his daughters to get ready. There
is a big dance that night and the next morning the whole party starts
off. When they come to the edge of Thunder Bird land the lad's wife
said to him, "Sit on my back. Hang on tight to my neck and keep
your eyes shut." Then the thunder crashes and the young man knows
that they are off through the air. Having reached this earth they make
their way to the brothers' camp. The Thunder Bird women, who have
become transformed into human form, are enthusiastically received.
There is another celebration and the nine brothers marry the nine
sisters of their youngest brother's wife.

This is the end of the myth but a few comments are necessary. It
is obvious that the Thunder Birds are conceived to act like human
beings. They hunt and talk and dance. But the analogy can be pressed
further. Their social organization and kinship terminology are precisely
the same as the Ojibwa. The marriage of a series of female siblings
(classificatory or otherwise) to a series of male siblings often occurs
among the Ojibwa themselves. This is, in fact, considered a kind of
ideal pattern. In one case that I know of six blood brothers were
married to a sorority of six sisters. There is a conceptual continuity,
therefore, between the social life of human beings and that of the

Thunder Birds which is independent of the avian form given to the latter. But we must infer from the myth that this avian form is not constant. Appearance cannot then be taken as a permanent and distinguishable trait of the Thunder Birds. They are capable of metamorphosis, hence, the human attributes with which they are endowed transcend a human outward form. Their conceptualization as "persons" is not associated with a permanent human form any more than it is associated with a birdlike form. And the fact that they belong to the category of ätíso'kanak is no barrier to their descending to earth and mating with human beings. I was told of a woman who claimed that North Wind was the father of one of her children. My informant said he did not believe this; nevertheless, he thought it would have been accepted as a possibility in the past.[21] We can only infer that in the universe of the Ojibwa the conception of "person" as a living, functioning social being is not only one which transcends the notion of person in the naturalistic sense; it likewise transcends a human appearance as a constant attribute of this category of being.

The relevance of such a concept to actual behavior may be illustrated by one simple anecdote. An informant told me that many years before he was sitting in a tent one summer afternoon during a storm, together with an old man and his wife. There was one clap of thunder after another. Suddenly the old man turned to his wife and asked, "Did you hear what was said?" "No," she replied, "I didn't catch it." My informant, an acculturated Indian, told me he did not at first know what the old man and his wife referred to. It was, of course, the thunder. The old man thought that one of the Thunder Birds had said something to him. He was reacting to this sound in the same way as he would respond to a human being, whose words he did not understand. The casualness of the remark and even the trivial character of the anecdote demonstrate the psychological depth of the "social relations" with other-than-human beings that becomes explicit in the behavior of the Ojibwa as a consequence of the cognitive "set" induced by their culture.

Metamorphosis as an Attribute of Persons

The conceptualization in myth and belief of Thunder Birds as animate beings who, while maintaining their identity, may change their outward appearance and exhibit either an avian or a human form exemplifies an attribute of "persons" which, although unarticulated abstractly, is basic in the cognitive orientation of the Ojibwa.

Metamorphosis occurs with considerable frequency in the myths where other-than-human persons change their form. *Wisekedjak,* whose primary characteristics are anthropomorphic, becomes transformed and flies with the geese in one story, assumes the form of a snake in another, and once turns himself into a stump. Men marry "animal" wives who are not "really" animals. And *Mikīnäk,* the Great Turtle, marries a human being. It is only by breaking a taboo that his wife discovers she is married to a being who is able to assume the form of a handsome young man.

The senselessness and ambiguities which may puzzle the outsider when reading these myths are resolved when it is understood that, to the Ojibwa, "persons" of this class are capable of metamorphosis by their very nature. Outward appearance is only an incidental attribute of being. And the names by which some of these entities are commonly known, even if they identify the character as an "animal," do not imply unchangeableness in form.

Stith Thompson has pointed out that the possibility of transformation is a "commonplace assumption in folk tales everywhere. Many of such motifs are frankly fictitious, but a large number represent persistent beliefs and living tradition."[22] The case of the Ojibwa is in the latter category. The world of myth is not categorically distinct from the world as experienced by human beings in everyday life. In the latter, as well as the former, no sharp lines can be drawn dividing living beings of the animate class because metamorphosis is possible. In outward manifestation neither animal nor human characteristics define categorical differences in the core of being. And, even aside from metamorphosis, we find that in everyday life interaction with nonhuman entities of the animate class are only intelligible on the assumption that they possess some of the attributes of "persons."

So far as animals are concerned, when bears were sought out in their dens in the spring they were addressed, asked to come out so that they could be killed, and an apology was offered to them.[23] The following encounter with a bear, related to me by a pagan Ojibwa named Birchstick, shows what happened in this case when an animal was treated as a person:

One spring when I was out hunting I went up a little creek where I knew suckers were spawning. Before I came to the rapids I saw fresh bear tracks. I walked along the edge of the creek and when I reached the rapids I saw a bear coming towards me, along the same trail I was following. I stepped behind a tree and when the animal was about thirty yards from me I fired. I missed and before I could reload the bear made straight for me. He seemed mad, so I never moved. I just waited there by the tree. As soon as he came close to me and rose up on his hind feet, I put the butt end of my gun against his heart and held him there. I remembered what my father used to tell me when I was a boy. He said that a bear always understands what you tell him. The bear began to bite the stock of the gun. He even put his paws upon it something like a man would do if he were going to shoot. Still holding him off as well as I could I said to the bear, "If you want to live, go away," and he let go the gun and walked off. I didn't bother the bear anymore.[24]

These instances suffice to demonstrate that, at the level of individual behavior, the interaction of the Ojibwa with certain kinds of plants and animals in everyday life is so structured culturally that individuals act as if they were dealing with "persons" who both understand what is being said to them and have volitional capacities as well. From the standpoint of perceptual experience if we only take account of autochthonous factors in Birchstick's encounter with the bear his behavior appears idiosyncratic and is not fully explained. On the other hand, if we invoke Ojibwa concepts of the nature of animate beings, his behavior becomes intelligible to us. We can understard the determining factors in his definition of the situation, and the functional relations between perception and conduct are meaningful. This Indian was not confronted with an animal with "objective" ursine properties, but rather with an animate being who had ursine attributes and *also* "person attributes." These, we may infer, were perceived as an integral whole. I am sure, however, that in narrating this episode to another Indian, he would not have referred to what his father had told him about bears. That was for my benefit!

Since bears, then, are assumed to possess "person attributes," it is not surprising to find that there is a very old, widespread, and persistent belief that sorcerers may become transformed into bears in order better to pursue their nefarious work.[25] Consequently some of the best documentation of the metamorphosis of human beings into animals comes from anecdotal material referring to cases of this sort. Even contemporary, acculturated Ojibwa have a term for this. They all know what a "bearwalk" is, and Dorson's recent collection of folk traditions, including those of the Indian populations of the Upper Peninsula of Michigan, bears the title *Bloodstoppers and Bearwalkers*. One of Dorson's informants gave him this account of what he had seen:

When I was a kid, 'bout seventeen, before they build the highway, there was just an old tote road from Bark River to Harris. There was three of us, one a couple years older, coming back from Bark River at nighttime. We saw a flash coming from behind us. The older fellow said, 'It's a bear-walk, let's get it. I'll stand on the other side of the road (it was just a wagon rut) and you stand on this side.' We stood there and waited. I saw it 'bout fifty feet away from us—close as your car is now. It looked like a bear, but every time he breathe your could see a fire gust. My chum he fall over in a faint. That brave feller on the other side, he faint. When the bear walk, all the ground wave, like when you walk on soft mud or on moss. He was goin' where he was goin'.[26]

It is clear from this example, and others that might be added, that the Indian and his companions did not perceive an ordinary bear. But in another anecdote given by Dorson, which is not told in the first person, it is said that an Indian "grabbed hold of the bear and it wasn't there—it was the old woman. She had buckskin bags all over her, tied on to her body, and she had a bearskin hide on."[27] I also have been told that the "bearwalk" is dressed up in a bearskin. All such statements, of course, imply a skeptical attitude towards meta-morphosis. They are rationalizations advanced by individuals who are attempting to reconcile Ojibwa beliefs and observation with the disbelief encountered in their relations with the whites.

An old-fashioned informant of mine told me how he had once fallen sick, and, although he took various kinds of medicine these did him no good. Because of this, and for other reasons, he believed he had been bewitched by a certain man. Then he noticed that a bear kept coming to his camp almost every night after dark. This is most unusual because wild animals do not ordinarily come anywhere near a human habitation. Once the bear would have entered his wigwam if he had not been warned in a dream. His anxiety increased because he knew, of course, that sorcerers often transformed themselves into bears. So when the bear appeared one night he got up, went outdoors, and shouted to the animal that he knew what it was trying to do. He threatened retaliation in kind if the bear ever returned. The animal ran off and never came back.

In this case there are psychological parallels to Birchstick's encounter with a bear: In both cases the bear is directly addressed as a person might be, and it is only through a knowledge of the cultural background that it is possible fully to understand the behavior of the individuals involved. In the present case, however, we can definitely say that the "animal" was perceived as a human being in the form of a bear; the Indian was threatening a human person with retaliation, not an animal.

A question that I have discussed in *Culture and Experience* in connection with another "bearwalk" anecdote, also arises in this case.[28] Briefly, the Ojibwa believe that a human being consists of a vital part, or *soul,* which, under certain circumstances may become detached from the body, so that it is not necessary to assume that the body part, in all cases, literally undergoes transformation into an animal form. The body of the sorcerer may remain in his wigwam while his soul journeys elsewhere and appears to another person in the form of an animal.

This interpretation is supported by an account which an informant gave me of a visit his deceased grandchild had paid him. One day he was traveling in a canoe across a lake. He had put up an improvised mast and used a blanket for a sail. A little bird alighted on the mast. This was a most unusual thing for a bird to do. He was convinced that it was not a bird but his dead grandchild. The child, of course, had left her body behind in a grave, nevertheless she visited him in animal form.

Thus, both living and dead human beings may assume the form of animals. So far as appearance is concerned, there is no hard and fast line that can be drawn between an animal form and a human form because metamorphosis is possible. In perceptual experience what looks like a bear may sometimes *be* an animal and, on other occasions, a human being. What persists and gives continuity to being is the vital part, or soul. Dorson goes to the heart of the matter when he stresses the fact that the whole socialization process in Ojibwa culture "impresses the young with the concepts of transformation and of 'power', malign or benevolent, human or demonic. These concepts underlie the entire Indian mythology, and make sensible the otherwise childish stories of culture heroes, animal husbands, friendly thunders, and malicious serpents. The bearwalk idea fits at once into this dream world— literally a dream world, for Ojibwa go to school in dreams."[29]

We must conclude, I believe, that the capacity for metamorphosis is one of the features which links human beings with the other-than-human persons in their behavioral environment. It is one of the generic properties manifested by beings of the person class. But is it a ubiquitous capacity of all members of this class equally? I do not think so. Metamorphosis to the Ojibwa mind is an earmark of "power." Within the category of persons there is a graduation of power. Other-than-human persons occupy the top rank in the power hierarchy of animate being. Human beings do not differ from them in kind, but in power. Hence, it is taken for granted that all the *ätíso'kanak* can assume a variety of forms. In the case of human beings, while the potentiality for metamorphosis exists and may even be experienced, any outward manifestation is inextricably associated with unusual power, for good or evil. And power of this degree can only be acquired by human beings through the help of other-than-human persons. Sorcerers can transform themselves only because they have acquired a high order of power from this source.

Powerful men, in the Ojibwa sense, are also those who can make inanimate objects behave as if they were animate. The *Midé* who made a stone roll over and over has been mentioned earlier. Other examples, such as the animation of a string of wooden beads, or animal skins, could be cited.[30] Such individuals also have been observed to transform one object into another, such as charcoal into bulle:s and ashes into gunpowder, or a handful of goose feathers into birds or insects.[31] In these manifestations, too, they are elevated to the same level of power as that displayed by other-than-human persons. We can, in fact, find comparable episodes in the myths.

The notion of animate being itself does not presume a capacity for manifesting the highest level of power any more than it implies person-attributes in every case. Power manifestations vary within the animate class of being as does the possession of person-attributes. A human being may possess little, if any, more power than a mole. No one would have been more surprised than Birchstick if the bear he faced had suddenly become human in form. On the other hand, the spiritual "masters" of the various species of animals are inherently powerful and, quite generally, they possess the power of metamorphosis. These entities, like the *ätíso'kanak*, are among the sources from which human beings may seek to enhance their own power. My Ojibwa friends

often cautioned me against judging by appearances. A poor forlorn
Indian dressed in rags might have great power; a smiling, amiable
woman, or a pleasant old man, might be a sorcerer.[32] You never can
tell until a situation arises in which their power for good or ill becomes
manifest. I have since concluded that the advice given me in a common sense fashion provides one of the major clues to a generalized
attitude towards the objects of their behavioral environment—particularly people. It makes them cautious and suspicious in interpersonal
relations of all kinds. The possibility of metamorphosis must be one
of the determining factors in this attitude; it is a concrete manifestation
of the deceptiveness of appearances. What looks like an animal, without
great power, may be a transformed person with evil intent. Even in
dream experiences, where a human being comes into direct contact
with other-than-human persons, it is possible to be deceived. Caution
is necessary in "social" relations with all classes of persons.

Dreams, Metamorphosis, and the Self

The Ojibwa are a dream-conscious people. For an understanding of
their cognitive orientation it is as necessary to appreciate their attitude
towards dreams as it is to understand their attitude towards the characters in the myths. For them, there is an inner connection which is
as integral to their outlook as it is foreign to ours.

The basic assumption which links the *ätíso'kanak* with dreams is
this: Self-related experience of the most personal and vital kind includes
what is seen, heard, and felt in dreams. Although there is no lack of
discrimination between the experiences of the self when awake and
when dreaming, both sets of experiences are equally self-related. Dream
experiences function integrally with other recalled memory images in
so far as these, too, enter the field of self-awareness. When we think auto-
biographically we only include events that happened to us when awake;
the Ojibwa include remembered events that have occurred in dreams.
And, far from being of subordinate importance, such experiences are
for them often of more vital importance than the events of daily waking
life. Why is this so? Because it is in dreams that the individual comes
into direct communication with the *ätíso'kanak,* the powerful "persons"
of the other-than-human class.

In the long winter evenings, as I have said, the *ätíso'kanak* are
talked about; the past events in their lives are recalled again and again

by *änícinábek*. When a conjuring performance occurs, the voices of some of the same beings are heard issuing from within the conjuring lodge. Here is actual perceptual experience of the "grandfathers" during a waking state. In dreams, the same other than-human persons are both "seen" and "heard." They address human beings as "grand-child." These "dream visitors" (i.e., *pawáganak*) interact with the dreamer much as human persons do. But, on account of the nature of these beings there are differences, too. It is in the context of this face-to-face personal interaction of the self with the "grandfathers" (i.e., synonymously *átíso'kanak, pawáganak*) that human beings receive important revelations that are the source of assistance to them in the daily round of life, and, besides this, of "blessings" that enable them to exercise exceptional powers of various kinds.

But dream experiences are not ordinarily recounted save under special circumstances. There is a taboo against this, just as there is a taboo against myth narration except in the proper seasonal context. The consequence is that we know relatively little about the manifest content of dreams. All our data come from acculturated Ojibwa. We do know enough to say, however, that the Ojibwa recognize quite as much as we do that dream experiences are often qualitatively different from our waking experiences. This fact, moreover, is turned to positive account. Since their dream visitors are other-than-human "persons" possessing great power, it is to be expected that the experiences of the self in interaction with them will differ from those with human beings in daily life. Besides this, another assumption must be taken into account: When a human being is asleep and dreaming his *òtcatcákwin* (vital part, soul), which is the core of the self, may become detached from the body (*mīyó*). Viewed by another human being, a person's body may be easily located and observed in space. But his vital part may be somewhere else. Thus, the self has greater mobility in space and even in time while sleeping. This is another illustration of the deceptiveness of appearances. The body of a sorcerer may be within sight in a wigwam, while "he" may be bearwalking. Yet the space in which the self is mobile is continuous with the earthly and cosmic space of waking life. A dream of one of my informants documents this specifically. After having a dream in which he met some (mythical) anthropomorphic beings (*mémengwécīwak*) who live in rocky escarpments and are famous for their medicine, he told me that he had later identified precisely the rocky place he had visited and entered in his dream. Thus the behavioral environment of the self is all of a piece. This is why experiences undergone when awake or asleep can be interpreted as experiences of self. Memory images, as recalled, become integrated with a sense of self-continuity in time and space.

Metamorphosis may be *experienced* by the self in dreams. One example will suffice to illustrate this. The dreamer in this case had been paddled out to an island by his father to undergo his puberty fast. For several nights he dreamed of an anthropomorphic figure. Finally, this being said, "Grandchild, I think you are strong enough now to go with me." Then the *pawágan* began dancing and as he danced he turned into what looked like a golden eagle. (This being must be understood as the "master" of this species.) Glancing down at his own body as he sat there on a rock, the boy noticed it was covered with feathers. The "eagle" spread its wings and flew off to the south. The boy then spread his wings and followed.

Here we find the instability of outward form in both human and other-than-human persons succinctly dramatized. Individuals of both categories undergo metamorphosis. In later life the boy will recall how he first saw the "master" of the golden eagles in his anthropomorphic guise, followed by his transformation into avian form; at the same time he will recall his own metamorphosis into a bird. But this experience, considered in context, does not imply that subsequently the boy can transform himself into a golden eagle at will. He might or might not be sufficiently "blessed." The dream itself does not inform us about this.

This example, besides showing how dream experiences may reinforce the belief in metamorphosis, illustrates an additional point: the *pawáganak*, whenever "seen," are always experienced as appearing in a specific form. They have a "bodily" aspect, whether human-like, animal-like, or ambiguous. But this is not their most persistent, enduring and vital attribute any more than in the case of human beings. We must conclude that all animate beings of the person class are unified conceptually in Ojibwa thinking because they have a similar structure—an inner vital part that is enduring and an outward form which can change. Vital personal attributes such as sentience, volition, memory, speech are not dependent upon outward appearance but upon the inner vital essence of being. If this be true, human beings and other-than-human persons are alike in another way. The human self does not die; it continues its existence in another place, after the body is buried in the grave. In this way *ánícinábek* are as immortal as *átíso'kanak*. This may be why we find human beings associated with the latter in the myths where it is sometimes difficult for an outsider to distinguish between them.

Thus the world of personal relations in which the Ojibwa live is a world in which vital social relations transcend those which are maintained with human beings. Their culturally constituted cognitive orientation prepares the individual for life in this world and for a life after death. The self-image that he acquires makes intelligible the nature of other selves. Speaking as an Ojibwa, one might say: all other "persons"—human or other than human—are structured the same as I am. There is a vital part which is enduring and an outward appearance that may be transformed under certain conditions. All other "persons," too, have such attributes as self-awareness and understanding. I can talk with them. Like myself, they have personal identity, autonomy, and volition. I cannot always predict exactly how they will act, although most of the time their behavior meets my expectations. In relation to myself, other "persons" vary in power. Many of them have more power than I have, but some have less. They may be friendly and help me when I need them but, at the same time, I have to be prepared for hostile acts, too. I must be cautious in my relations with other "persons" because appearances may be deceptive.

The Psychological Unity of the Ojibwa World

Although not formally abstracted and articulated philosophically, the nature of "persons" is the focal point of Ojibwa ontology and the key to the psychological unity and dynamics of their world outlook. This aspect of their metaphysics of being permeates the content of their cognitive processes: perceiving, remembering, imagining, conceiving, judging, and reasoning. Nor can the motivation of much of their conduct be thoroughly understood without taking into account the relation of their central values and goals to the awareness they have of the existence of other-than-human, as well as human, persons in their world. "Persons," in fact, are so inextricably associated with notions of causality that, in order to understand their appraisal of events and the kind of behavior demanded in situations as they define

them, we are confronted over and over again with the roles of
"persons" as *loci* of causal'ty in the dynamics of their universe. For
the Ojibwa make no cardinal use of any concept of impersonal forces
as major determinants of events. In the context of my exposition the
meaning of the term *manitu*, which has become so generally known,
may be considered as a synonym for a person of the other-than-human
class ("grandfather," *ätíso'kan, pawágan*). Among the Ojibwa I
worked with it is now quite generally confined to the God of Christianity, when combined with an augmentative prefix (*k'tci manītu*). There
is no evidence to suggest, however, that the term ever did connote an
impersonal, magical, or supernatural force.[33]

In an essay on the "Religion of the North American Indians"
published over forty years ago, Radin asserted "that from an examination of the data customarily relied upon as proof and from individual
data obtained, there is nothing to justify the postulation of a belief in
a universal force in North America. Magical power as an 'essence'
existing apart and separate from a definite spirit, is, we believe, an
unjustified assumption, an abstraction created by investigators."[34] This
opinion, at the time, was advanced in opposition to the one expressed
by those who, stimulated by the writings of R. R. Marett in particular,
interpreted the term *manitu* among the Algonkians (W. Jones), *orenda*
among the Iroquois (Hewitt) and *wakanda* among the Siouan peoples
(Fletcher) as having reference to a belief in a magical force of some
kind. But Radin pointed out that in his own field work among both
the Winnebago and the Ojibwa the terms in question "always referred
to definite spirits, not necessarily definite in shape. If at a vapor-bath
the steam is regarded as *wakanda* or *manitu,* it is because it is a spirit
transformed into steam for the time being; if an arrow is possessed of
specific virtues, it is because a spirit has either transformed himself–
into the arrow or because he is temporarily dwelling in it; and finally,
if tobacco is offered to a peculiarly-shaped object it is because either
this object belongs to a spirit, or a spirit is residing in it." *Manitu,* he
said, in addition to its substantive usage may have such connotations
as "sacred," "strange," "remarkable" or "powerful" without "having
the slightest suggestion of 'inherent power', but having the ordinary
sense of these adjectives."[35]

With respect to the Ojibwa conception of causality, all my own
observations suggest that a culturally constituted psychological set

operates which inevitably directs the reasoning of individuals towards an explanation of events in personalistic terms. *Who* did it, *who* is responsible, is always the crucial question to be answered. Personalistic explanation of past events is found in the myths. It was *Wisekedjak* who, through the exercise of his personal power, expanded the tiny bit of mud retrieved by Muskrat from the depths of the inundating waters of the great deluge into the inhabitable island-earth of Ojibwa cosmography. Personalistic explanation is central in theories of disease causation. Illness may be due to sorcery; the victim, in turn, may be "responsible" because he has offended the sorcerer—even unwittingly. Besides this, I may be responsible for my own illness, even without the intervention of a sorcerer. I may have committed some wrongful act in the past, which is the "cause" of my sickness. My child's illness, too, may be the consequence of my past transgressions or those of my wife.[36] The personalistic theory of causation even emerges today among acculturated Ojibwa. In 1940, when a severe forest fire broke out at the mouth of the Berens River, no Indian would believe that lightning or any impersonal or accidental determinants were involved. *Somebody* must have been responsible. The German spy theory soon became popular. "Evidence" began to accumulate; strangers had been seen in the bush, and so on. The personalistic type of explanation satisfies the Ojibwa because it is rooted in a basic metaphysical assumption; its terms are ultimate and incapable of further analysis within the framework of their cognitive orientation and experience.

Since the dynamics of events in the Ojibwa universe find their most ready explanation in a personalistic theory of causation, the qualitative aspects of interpersonal relations become affectively charged with a characteristic sensitivity.[37] The psychological importance of the range and depth of this sensitive area may be overlooked if the inclusiveness of the concept of "person" and "social relations" that is inherent in their outlook is not borne in mind. The reason for this becomes apparent when we consider the pragmatic relations between behavior, values, and the role of "persons" in their world view.

The central goal of life for the Ojibwa is expressed by the term *pimädäziwin*, life in the fullest sense, life in the sense of longevity, health and freedom from misfortune. This goal cannot be achieved without the effective help and cooperation of *both* human and other-than-human "persons," as well as by one's own personal efforts. The help of other-than-human "grandfathers" is particularly important for men. This is why all Ojibwa boys, in aboriginal days, were motivated to undergo the so-called "puberty fast" or "dreaming" experience. This was the means by which it was possible to enter into direct "social interaction" with "persons" of the other than-human class for the first time. It was the opportunity of a lifetime. Every special aptitude, all a man's subsequent successes and the explanation of many of his failures, hinged upon the help of the "guardian spirits" he obtained at this time, rather than upon his own native endowments or the help of his fellow *änícinábek*. If a boy received "blessings" during his puberty fast and, as a man, could call upon the help of other-than-human persons when he needed them he was well prepared for meeting the vicissitudes of life. Among other things, he could defend himself against the hostile actions of human persons which might threaten him and thus interfere with the achievement of *pīmädäzīwin*. The grand-father of one of my informants said to him: "you will have a long and good life if you dream well." The help of human beings, however, was also vital, especially the services of those who had acquired the kind of power which permitted them to exercise effective curative functions in cases of illness. At the same time there were moral responsibilities which had to be assumed by an individual if he strove for *pīmädäzīwin*. It was as essential to maintain approved standards of personal and social conduct as it was to obtain power from the "grandfathers" because, in the nature of things, one's own conduct, as well as that of other "persons," was always a potential threat to the achievement of *pīmädäzīwin*. Thus we find that the same values are implied throughout the entire range of "social interaction" that charac-terizes the Ojibwa world; the same standards which apply to mutual obligations between human beings are likewise implied in the reciprocal relations between human and other-than-human "persons." In his relations with "the grandfathers" the individual does not expect to receive a "blessing" for nothing. It is not a free gift; on his part there are obligations to be met. There is a principle of reciprocity implied. There is a general taboo imposed upon the human being which forbids him to recount his dream experiences in full detail, except under certain circumstances. Specific taboos may likewise be imposed upon the suppliant. If these taboos are violated he will lose his power; he can no longer count on the help of his "grandfathers."

The same principle of mutual obligations applies in other spheres of life. The Ojibwa are hunters and food gatherers. Since the various species of animals on which they depend for a living are believed to be under the control of "masters" or "owners" who belong to the category of other-than-human persons, the hunter must always be careful to treat the animals he kills for food or fur in the proper manner. It may be necessary, for example, to throw their bones in the water or to perform a ritual in the case of bears. Otherwise, he will offend the "masters" and be threatened with starvation because no animals will be made available to him. Cruelty to animals is likewise an offense that will provoke the same kind of retaliation. And, according to one anecdote, a man suffered illness because he tortured a fabulous *windīgo* after killing him. A moral distinction is drawn between the kind of conduct demanded by the primary necessities of securing a livelihood, or defending oneself against aggression, and unnecessary acts of cruelty. The moral values implied document the consistency of the principle of mutual obligations which is inherent in all interactions with "persons" throughout the Ojibwa world.

One of the prime values of Ojibwa culture is exemplified by the great stress laid upon sharing what one has with others. A balance, a sense of proportion must be maintained in all interpersonal relations and activities. Hoarding, or any manifestation of greed, is discountenanced. The central importance of this moral value in their world outlook is illustrated by the fact that other-than-human persons share their power with human beings. This is only a particular instance of the obligations which human beings feel towards one another. A man's catch of fish or meat is distributed among his kin. Human grandfathers share the power acquired in their dreams from other-than-human persons with their classificatory grandchildren. An informant whose wife had borrowed his pipe for the morning asked to borrow one of mine while we worked together. When my friend Chief Berens once fell ill he could not explain it. Then he recalled that he had overlooked one man when he had passed around a bottle of whiskey. He believed this man was offended and had bewitched him. Since there was no objective evidence of this, it illustrates the extreme sensitivity of an individual to the principle of sharing, operating through feelings of guilt. I was once told about the puberty fast of a boy who was not satisfied with his initial "blessing." He demanded that he dream of all the leaves of all the trees in the world so that absolutely nothing would be hidden from him. This was considered greedy and, while the *pawágan* who appeared in his dream granted his desire, the boy was told that "as soon as the leaves start to fall you'll get sick and when all the leaves drop to the ground that is the end of your life." And this is what happened.[38] "Overfasting" is as greedy as hoarding. It violates a basic moral value and is subject to a punitive sanction. The unity of the Ojibwa outlook is likewise apparent here.

The entire psychological field in which they live and act is not only unified through their conception of the nature and role of "persons" in their universe, but by the sanctioned moral values which guide the relations of "persons." It is within this web of "social relations" that the individual strives for *pīmādäzīwin*.

NOTES

[1] Redfield 1952, p. 30; cf. *African Worlds.*

[2] Hallowell 1955, p. 91. For a more extended discussion of the culturally constituted behavioral environment of man see *ibid.*, pp. 86-89 and note 33. The term "self" is not used as a synonym for ego in the psychoanalytic sense. See *ibid.*, p. 80.

[3] See Basilius 1952, Carroll in Whorf, 1956, Hoijer, 1954, Feuer, 1953.

[4] Hallowell 1955, chap. 5.

[5] Bruno de Jésus-Marie 1952, p. xvii: "The studies which make up this book fall into two main groups, of which the first deals with the theological Satan. Here the analysis of exegesis, of philosophy, of theology, treat of the devil under his aspect of a personal being whose history—his fall, his desire for vengeance—can be written as such." One of the most startling characteristics of the devil ". . . is his agelessness" (p. 4). He is immune to "injury, to pain, to sickness, to death . . . . Like God, and unlike man, he has no body. There are in him, then, no parts to be dismembered, no possibilities of corruption and decay, no threat of a separation of parts that will result in death. He is incorruptible, immune to the vagaries, the pains the limitations of the flesh, immortal" (p.5). "Angels have no bodies, yet they have appeared to men in physical form, have talked with them, journeyed the roads with them fulfilling all the pleasant tasks of companionship" (p. 6).

[6] Hallowell 1934b, pp. 7-9; 1936, pp. 1308-9; 1951, pp. 182-83; 1955, pp. 256-58.

[7] Kelsen 1943, chapter 2, discusses the "social" or "personalistic interpretation of nature" which he considers the nucleus of what has been called animism.

[8] In a prefatory note to *Ojibwa Texts,* Part I, Jones says (p. xiii) that " 'Being' or 'creature' would be a general rendering of the animate while 'thing' would express the inanimate." Cf. Schoolcraft's pioneer analysis of the animate and inanimate categories in Ojibwa speech, pp. 171-72.

[9] Greenberg 1954, pp. 15-16.

[10] I believe that Jenness grossly overgeneralizes when he says (p. 21): "To the Ojibwa ... all objects have life. ..." If this were true, their *inanimate* grammatical category would indeed be puzzling.

Within the more sophisticated framework of modern ᵗ.ological thought, the Ojibwa attitude is not altogether naïve. N. W. Pirie points out (pp. 184-85) that the words "life" and "living" have been borrowed by science from lay usage and are no longer serviceable. "Life is not a thing, a philosophical entity: it is an attitude of mind towards what is being observed."

[11] Field notes. From this same Indian I obtained a smoothly rounded pebble, about two inches long and one and a half inches broad, which his father had given him. He told me that I had better keep it enclosed in a tin box or it might "go." Another man, Ketegas, gave me an account of the circumstances under which he obtained a stone with animate properties and of great medicinal value. This stone was egg shaped. It had some dark amorphous markings on it which he interpreted as representing his three children and himself. "You may not think this stone is alive," he said, "but it is. I can make it move." (He did not demonstrate this to me.) He went on to say that on two occasions he had loaned the stone to sick people to keep during the night. Both times he found it in his pocket in the morning. Ketegas kept it in a little leather case he had made for it.

[12] Yellow Legs had obtained information about this remarkable stone in a dream. Its precise location was revealed to him. He sent two other Indians to get it. These men, following directions, found the stone on Birch Island, located in the middle of Lake Winnipeg, some thirty miles south of the mouth of the Berens River.

[13] Cognate forms are found in Chamberlain's compilation of Cree and Ojibwa "literary" terms.

[14] Jones, *Texts,* Part II, p. 574n.

[15] The attitude manifested is by no means peculiar to the Ojibwa. Almost half a century ago Swanton remarked that "one of the most widespread errors, and one of those most unfortunate for folk-lore and comparative mythology, is the off-hand classification of myth with fiction. ..." On the contrary, as he says, "It is safe to say that most of the myths found spread over considerable areas were regarded by the tribes among which they were collected as narratives of real occurrences."

[16] Bidney 1953, p. 166.

[17] Lovejoy and Boas 1935, p. 12; Lovejoy 1948, p. 69.

[18] See, e.g., Collingwood 1945, also the remarks in Randall 1944, pp. 355-56. With respect to the applicability of the natural-supernatural dichotomy to primitive cultures see Van Der Leeuw 1938, pp. 544-45; Kelsen 1943, p. 44; Bidney 1953, p. 166.

[19] Krech and Crutchfield 1948 write (p. 10): "clouds and storms and winds are excellent examples of objects in the psychological field that carry the perceived properties of mobility, capriciousness, causation, power of threat and reward."

[20] Cf. Hallowell 1934a.

[21] Actually, this was probably a rationalization of mother-son incest. But the woman never was punished by sickness, nor did she confess. Since the violation of the incest prohibition is reputed to be followed by dire consequences, the absence of both may have operated to support the possibility of her claim when considered in the context of the Ojibwa world view.

[22] Thompson 1946, p. 258.

²³ Hallowell 1926.

²⁴ Hallowell 1934a, p. 397.

²⁵ Sorcerers may assume the form of other animals as well. Peter Jones, a converted Ojibwa, who became famous as a preacher and author says that "they can turn themselves into bears, wolves, foxes, owls, bats, and snakes. . . . Several of our people have informed me that they have seen and heard witches in the shape of these animals, especially the bear and the fox. They say that when a witch in the shape of a bear is being chased all at once she will run around a tree or hill, so as to be lost sight of for a time by her pursuers, and then, instead of seeing a bear they behold an old woman walking quietly along or digging up roots, and looking as innocent as a lamb" (Jones 1861, pp. 145-46).

²⁶ Dorson 1952, p. 30.

²⁷ Ibid., p. 29. This rationalization dates back over a century. John Tanner, an Indianized white man who was captured as a boy in the late eighteenth century and lived with the Ottawa and Ojibwa many years, refers to it. So does Peter Jones.

²⁸ Hallowell 1955, pp. 176-77.

²⁹ Dorson 1952, p. 31.

³⁰ Hoffman 1891, pp. 205-6.

³¹ Unpublished field notes.

³² See Hallowell 1955, Chapter 15.

³³ Cf. Skinner 1915, p. 261. Cooper 1933 (p. 75) writes: "The Manitu was clearly personal in the minds of my informants, and not identified with impersonal supernatural force. In fact, nowhere among the Albany River Otchipwe, among the Eastern Cree, or among the Montagnais have I been able thus far to find the word Manitu used to denote such force in connection with the Supreme Being belief, with conjuring, or with any other phase of magico-religious culture. Manitu, so far as I can discover, always denotes a supernatural personal being. . . . The word Manitu is, my informants say, not used to denote magical or conjuring power among the coastal Cree, nor so I was told in 1927, among the Fort Hope Otchipwe of the upper Albany River."

³⁴ Radin 1914a, p. 350.

³⁵ Ibid., pp. 349-50.

³⁶ "Because a person does bad things, that is where sickness starts," is the way one of my informants phrased it. For a fuller discussion of the relations between unsanctioned sexual behavior and disease, see Hallowell 1955, pp. 294-95; 303-4. For case material, see Hallowell 1939.

³⁷ Cf. Hallowell 1955, p. 305.

³⁸ Radin 1927, p. 177, points out that "throughout the area inhabited by the woodland tribes of Canada and the United States, overfasting entails death." Jones, Texts, Part II, pp. 307-11, gives two cases of overfasting. In one of them the bones of the boy were later found by his father.

REFERENCES

African Worlds: Studies in the Cosmological Ideas and Social Values of African Peoples. 1954. Published for the International African Institute. London, Oxford University Press.

Baraga, R. R. Bishop. 1878. A Theoretical and Practical Grammar of the Otchipive Language. Montreal, Beauchemin and Valois.

Baraga, R. R. Bishop. 1880. A Dictionary of the Otchipive Language Explained in English. Montreal, Beauchemin and Valois.

Basilius, H. 1952. "Neo-Humboldtian Ethnolinguistics," Word, Vol. 8.

Bidney, David. 1953. Theoretical Anthropology. New York, Columbia University Press.

Bruno de Jésus-Marie, père, ed. 1952. Satan. New York, Sheed and Ward.

Chamberlain, A. F. 1906. "Cree and Ojibwa Literary Terms," Journal of American Folklore, 19:346-47.

Collingwood, R. G. 1945. The Idea of Nature. Oxford, Clarendon Press.

Cooper, John M. 1933. "The Northern Algonquian Supreme Being," Primitive Man, 6:41-112.

Dorson, Richard M. 1952. Bloodstoppers and Bearwalkers: Folk Traditions of the Upper Peninsula. Cambridge, Mass., Harvard University Press.

Feuer, Lewis S. 1953. "Sociological Aspects of the Relation between Language and Philosophy," Philosophy of Science, 20:85-100.

Fletcher, Alice C. 1910. "Wakonda," in Handbook of American Indians. Washington, D.C.: Bureau of American Ethnology, Bull. 30.

Greenberg, Joseph H. 1954. "Concerning Inferences from Linguistic to Non-linguistic Data," in Language in Culture, ed. by Harry Hoijer. (Chicago University "Comparative Studies in Cultures and Civilizations.") Chicago, University of Chicago Press.

Hallowell, A. Irving. 1926. "Bear Ceremonialism in the Northern Hemisphere," American Anthropologist, 28:1-175.

——— 1934a. "Some Empirical Aspects of Northern Saulteaux Religion," American Anthropologist, 36:389-404.

——— 1934b. "Culture and Mental Disorder," Journal of Abnormal and Social Psychology, 29:1-9.

——— 1936. "Psychic Stresses and Culture Patterns," American Journal of Psychiatry, 92:1291-1310.

——— 1939. "Sin, Sex and Sickness in Saulteaux Belief," British Journal of Medical Psychology, 18:191-97.

——— 1951. "Cultural Factors in the Structuralization of Perception," in John H. Rohver and Muzafer Sherif, Social Psychology at the Crossroads. New York, Harper.

——— 1955. Culture and Experience. Philadelphia, University of Penna. Press.

Hewitt, J. N. B. 1902. "Orenda and a Definition of Religion," American Anthropologist, 4:33-46.

Hoffman, W. J. 1891. The Mide'wiwin or "Grand Medicine Society" of the Ojibwa. Washington, D.C., Bureau of American Ethnology 7th Annual Report.

Hoijer, Harry, ed. 1954. Language in Culture. Memoir 79, American Anthropological Association.

Jenness, Diamond. 1935. The Ojibwa Indians of Parry Island, their social and religious life. Ottawa, Canada Department of Mines, National Museum of Canada Bull. 78, Anthropological Series 12.

Jones, Peter. 1861. History of the Ojibway Indians. London.

Jones, William. 1905. "The Algonkin Manitu," Journal of American Folklore, 18:183-90.

——— Ojibwa Texts. (Publications of the American Ethnological Society, Vol. 7, Parts I and II.) Leyden: 1917; New York: 1919.

Kelsen, Hans. 1943. Society and Nature: A Sociological Inquiry. Chicago, University of Chicago Press.

Krech, David, and Richard S. Crutchfield. 1948. Theory and Problems of Social Psychology. New York, McGraw-Hill.

Lovejoy, Arthur O. 1948. Essays in the History of Ideas. Baltimore, Johns Hopkins Press.

Lovejoy, Arthur O., and George Boas. 1935. Primitivism and Related Ideas in Antiquity. Baltimore, Johns Hopkins Press. Vol. I of A Documentary History of Primitivism and Related Ideas.

Pirie, N. W. 1937. "The Meaninglessness of the Terms 'Life' and 'Living,' " in Perspectives in Biochemistry, ed. by J. Needham and D. Green. New York, Macmillan.

Radin, Paul. 1914a. "Religion of the North American Indians," Journal of American Folklore, 27:335-73.

—— 1914b. Some Aspects of Puberty Fasting among the Ojibwa. Geological Survey of Canada, Department of Mines, Museum Bull. No. 2, Anthropological Series, No. 2, pp. 1-10.

—— 1927. Primitive Man as Philosopher. New York, D. Appleton & Co.

Randall, John Herman, Jr. 1944. "The Nature of Naturalism," in Naturalism and the Human Spirit, ed. by H. Krikorian. New York, Columbia University Press.

Redfield, Robert. 1952. "The Primitive World View," Proceedings of the American Philosophical Society, 96:30-36.

Schoolcraft, Henry R. 1834. Narrative of an Expedition through the Upper Mississippi to Itasca Lake, the Actual Source of the River .... New York, Harper.

Skinner, Alanson. 1915. "The Menomini Word 'Häwätûk,' " Journal of American Folklore, 28:258-61.

Swanton, John R. 1910. "Some practical aspects of the study of myths," Journal of American Folklore, 23:1-7.

Tanner, John. 1830. Narrative of the Captivity and Adventures of John Tanner, ed. by E. James.

Thompson, Stith. 1946. The Folktale. New York, Dryden Press.

Van Der Leeuw, G. 1938. Religion in Essence and Manifestation. London, Allen and Unwin.

Whorf, Benjamin Lee. 1956. Language Thought and Reality: Selected Writings of Benjamin L. Whorf, ed. with an introduction by J. B. Carroll; Foreword by Stuart Chase. New York, Wiley.

TEN

Ojibwa World View and Disease

1963

ALL CULTURES provide a cognitive orientation toward a world in which man is compelled to act. A culturally constituted world view is created, which, by means of beliefs, available knowledge and language, mediates personal adjustment to the world through such psychological processes as perceiving, recognizing, conceiving judging and reasoning (cf., 18). It is a blueprint for a meaningful interpretation of objects and events, which, intimately associated with a normative orientation, becomes the basis for reflection, decision and action. A psychological "field", or behavioral environment, is defined, and a foundation provided for a consensus with respect to goals and values (22). The motivations and satisfactions of individuals can be directed towards traditionally defined ends, while there is also scope for variation in the interpretation of the meaning of particular events, the choice of modes of action, and the achievement of individual goals consonant with the value system.

Since disease, in some form, is ubiquitous, it becomes, as Ackerknecht says, "one of the fundamental, vital problems which face every society, and every known society develops methods to deal with disease, and thus creates a medicine (3, p. 2; cf., 11, p. 772).[1]

[1] Marston Bates, (9, p. 158) has stressed the importance of changing disease patterns in human history and geography: "We have diseases that are apparently 'new' in modern times, diseases that have changed greatly in geographical pattern, and diseases that have disappeared—without deliberate interference from man, without benefit of science or medicine. In fact, the pattern of disease. as

Consequently, we find that the cognitive orientation of any culture provides a basis for an understanding of the occurrence of sickness, particularly in cases where fear and anxiety arise because there is a serious threat to life itself, as well as to health. An individual requires an answer to such questions as: Why am I sick? Why is my child sick? What can I do about it? The explanation of illness, as well as the therapeutic means for treating it, become culturally constituted variables in content, while, at a higher level of abstraction, they fall within the category of cultural universals.[2]

Explanation means what is intellectually satisfying, when considered within a frame of cognitive reference that is ultimate, because it is deeply embedded in a culturally constituted world view. Discussing the newly emerging cognitive orientation that arose in the centuries following the Renaissance, Basil Willey observed:

> an explanation "explains" best when it meets some need of our nature, some deep-seated demand for assurance. "Explanation" may perhaps be roughly defined as a restatement of something— event, theory, doctrine, etc.—in terms of the current interests and assumptions. It satisfies, as explanation, because it appeals to that particular set of assumptions, as superseding those of a past age or of a former state of mind. Thus, it is necessary, if an explanation is to seem satisfactory, that its terms should seem ultimate, incapable of further analysis. . . . All depends upon our presuppositions, which in turn depend upon our training, whereby we have come to regard (or to feel) one set of terms as ultimate, the other not. An explanation commands our assent with immediate authority, when it presupposes the "reality," the "truth," of what seems to us most real, most true. One cannot, therefore, define "explanation" absolutely; one can only say that it is a statement which satisfies the demands of a particular time or place [53, pp. 12-13].

we look back over history, seems constantly to have been changing. The relation between disease and mortality, the effect of disease on human populations, has thus never been a constant or easily calculable factor. When we try to figure out the role of disease in the history of human populations, we are thus on uncertain ground."

[2] For a general discussion of "Universal Categories of Culture," *see* Kluckhohn (28). Theories of disease and medicine are not referred to there.

The *rationality* of explanation, therefore, presents a nice problem when considered in cross-cultural perspective (4). When judged from the standpoint of the cognitive orientation of a particular culture, the explanation of, and the treatment for, disease may be seen to follow logically from traditional cultural premises.[3] On the other hand, from the standpoint of modern Western scientific medicine, the explanations of disease found in non-literate societies may appear absurd. We know, however, that the later stages of Western medicine were preceded by earlier stages, and that modern medicine is intimately connected with the development of Western science. Science depends upon more than rationality; it involves the systematic testing and retesting of hypotheses, and the aspiration towards expanding areas of objective inquiry and validation.[4] Consequently, the kind of explanation satisfying to scientifically oriented men in modern Western culture is of a different order than that found in primitive societies, insofar as medicine is an integral part of the unique scientific tradition of the West.

Nevertheless, the explanation and treatment of disease, even at our level of development, still remains relevant to the cognitive orientation of Man. Insofar as Western culture is characterized by a higher level of rationality, objectivity and the availability of tested knowledge than occurs in the cultures of primitive peoples, we know that these features are a consequence of radical changes in the history of Western culture, which led to the transcendence of

[3] This is what led Rivers to say that primitive medicine was "even more rational than ours, because its modes of diagnosis and treatment followed more directly from their ideas concerning the causation of disease" (45, p. 52). Rather points out that: "Ideas of the nature of disease, although they may seem to rest on a basis of pure experience (or) to arise independently of movements in other realms of thought, are in fact implicated in more fundamental intellectual patterns dominant in particular times and places" (42, p. 351).

[4] De Laguna has pointed out that, "supported by an unassailable faith in the universal order in which all facts have their place," science is a mode of thought with "a capacity for continuous self-transcendence" (13, p. 158). "It belongs to the very nature of science both continuously to transform and regenerate itself, and to expand", she says (13, p. 165). It is for these reasons, among others, that it is distinguishable from modes of thought found in other cultures, particularly those of primitive peoples.

an older world view. A much closer analysis of medicine in primitive culture will be required before we can decide whether or not the roots of such features exist in such societies, and how far irrational and non-objective features still persist in our own medical tradition.

In the past, with less detailed ethnographic knowledge available than we possess today, and, under the influence of nineteenth century unilinear theories of cultural evolution, non-literate societies were often grouped together in the most superficial way, and subjected to all kinds of generalizations. Ackerknecht has pointed out that some students decided that certain primitives had no medicine at all because their's did not fit our pattern; others concluded that their's was an "immature or degenerate variety of our medicine". On the other hand:

> "Primitive medicine was studied by putting aside consciously every magic and religious element and served even as a model of logical and causal thinking. There developed a myth of primitive 'empiricism'. A great handicap also was the clinging of medical historians to outmoded anthropological theories (Tylor, Spencer) and the permanent confusion with folk medicine." What was overlooked is the fact that "there is not one medicine but numerous and quite different medicines in the different parts of the world," past and present, and that "primitive medicine is not a queer collection of errors and superstitions, but a number of living unities in living cultural patterns, quite able to function through the centuries in spite of their fundamental differences from our pattern" [1, pp. 503-4].

Today, we still do not know the complete range or typology of systems of primitive medicine, particularly with respect to the basic cognitive orientation of the cultures in which they occur, and their functions as integral parts of socio-cultural systems.[5]

---

[5] In 1942, Ackerknecht presented sketches of the medicine of the Cheyennes, Dobuans and Thongas, and wrote: "It is an almost hopeless task to try to understand and evaluate the medicine of one primitive tribe while disregarding its cultural background or to explain the general phenomenon of primitive medicine by purely enumerating that in the medical field primitives use spells,

Furthermore, the historical fact should not be overlooked that, despite the ubiquity of various and changing forms of organic, functional and mental diseases, and without reliable knowledge of their etiology, the early hominids and later *Homo sapiens* not only evolved, but ultimately populated the earth. The development of a scientifically rooted medical tradition, such as that which has emerged only recently in Western culture, was not a necessary condition for human organic evolution, or Man's social and cultural adaptation. It is of interest, then, to anthropology and medicine alike, to discover how man came to terms with disease, both in his biological adaptation and in his many and varied modes of cultural adaptation.

One of the basic dimensions of further inquiries is emerging more clearly today: it has become increasingly evident that, in addition to the core of biological continuities that link modern man with his earlier hominid ancestors and primate forebears, there were, also, continuities in structured modes of social living. Not only the hominids, but the primate forerunners of the hominids, lived in organized social groups. At all stages of hominid development, illness must be conceptualized in a social setting, specifically in relation to the *cultural* mode of adaptation which arose in the course of hominid evolution, and which was built upon the foundation of earlier types of social structures. Once we give emphasis to the historical depth of Man's social nature, and his cultural mode of adaptation as a specialized form of social existence, which distinguishes him from other primates, I believe that the confrontation of man with disease can be seen in better perspective.

Instead of considering systems of primitive medicine chiefly with respect to their degree of effectiveness in curing the ills of the human *organism*, we might ask: What potential relations can we

---

prayer, blood-letting, drugs, medicine men, twins, toads, human fat and spittle, etc..... What counts are not the forms, but the place medicine occupies in the life of a tribe or people, the spirit which pervades its practice, the way in which it merges with other traits from different fields of experience" (1). Clements' monograph *Primitive Concepts of Disease* (12) is not altogether satisfactory.

see between Man's confrontation with sickness, the development
of systems of medicine, and the functioning of a cultural mode of
adaptation? For, once this mode of adaptation had become an integral part of the evolution of the hominids, socio-cultural systems
became the matrix of Man's survival. We cannot dissociate the persistence of hominid populations, viewed biologically, from the distinctive mode of adaptation which characterized them.

In the absence of reliable knowledge about the etiology of disease, early man could not have been prepared to cope with sickness
effectively, either conceptually or practically. Indeed, systems of
medicine that could actually enhance biological survival to any
significant degree do not seem to have evolved in any non-literate
group of which we have knowledge. On the other hand, even at a
fairly early period, the occurrence of sickness could have become
the focus of an interpretation that was integrally linked with the
maintenance of evolving systems of social action, and characterized
by a normative orientation and an evolving capacity for self-awareness (23). This possibility is based on the assumption that illness
easily generates fear and anxiety, particularly if it becomes a serious threat to life. And these emotions are not confined to the
afflicted individual alone. There is evidence, too, from psychoanalytic data, that sickness may be unconsciously experienced as
punishing (punishment fantasies and dreams). And, even in our
own culture, where a scientific medical tradition generally prevails, sickness may consciously give rise to feelings of guilt.[6] It is
difficult, in any case, to think of illness as a *rewarding* experience.

[6] Whiting and Child point out that "even in our society some degree of guilt
is a frequent reaction to one's getting sick. Even with our scientific knowledge
about the causes of many diseases, we are perfectly capable of making use of this
knowledge to justify (perhaps quite rationally) feelings of guilt about having
gotten sick. One person may blame his illness on his having imprudently over-
eaten the night before, another on a long drinking bout, and another on his
carelessness in exposing himself to contagion from his relatives or acquaintances.
In primitive societies self-blame is generally more conspicuous as a reaction to
illness, although it still shows a great deal of variation from one society to
another" (52, p. 228).

In the early phases of cultural adaptation, as well as later, the absence of any reliable knowledge of the nature of disease, of any conceptualization of "natural" or impersonal causes of events (in our sense), made an interpretation of sickness as a penalty for disapproved conduct plausible as an explanation. It could be integrated with the functioning of interpersonal relations of various kinds. Thus, insofar as primary moral values could be linked with the unpredictable and periodic occurrence of the illness of individuals, a workable psychological means was provided for reinforcing conformity with approved values, through the generation of fear, anxiety and guilt. While such an interpretation of sickness could not lead to any kind of treatment that promoted the survival of individuals—since available knowledge did not permit any systematic appraisal of biological and physical agencies—a disease sanction could become adaptive in relation to the maintenance and persistence of socio-cultural systems; in these systems, the appraisal of one's own conduct and that of others, in relation to commonly shared moral values, became one of the vital foci of social integration. The human individual was considered to be responsible for his conduct. His social relations with other persons were of paramount consideration in reflection and action.

Speculative as these remarks may be insofar as the actualities of human evolution are concerned, the empirical data available on primitive societies do indicate a fairly widespread use of illness as a social sanction; a systematic cross-cultural study of the subject would be highly desirable. A disease sanction can function in a wide variety of culture contexts, and in association with world views that differ considerably in content. Sickness can be interpreted as emanating from a variety of sources—gods and other supernatural entities, human beings (sorcerers) or the moral misconduct of the victim himself.

"Other-than-human persons" may become involved in illness, as well as human beings. The many sources to which it is possible to attribute illness, combined with its linkage with primary emotions,

is one of the great advantages of such a sanction in relation to
man's organized social existence. It may represent one of the oldest
types of sanctions in human socio-cultural development. Without
offering any speculation regarding its role in man's evolution,
Ackerknecht has referred to its characteristic occurrence in many
primitive societies—in contrast with our own—and emphasized, at
the same time, the distinctive *social role* that it plays. Disease is,
with us, he says:

> In the last analysis, a biological, individual, and non-moral prob-
> lem. No guilt is involved when we suffer from hereditary, infec-
> tious, or degenerative diseases. Even in venereal diseases, we
> strive to eliminate the moral aspect as it has proved to be a
> handicap in their eradication. If you get appendicitis or cancer,
> you will never think of associating this with your behavior to-
> ward your neighbor or mother-in-law or your ancestral spirits.
> We do not usually associate disease with whether or not our per-
> sonal relations are good, whether we keep certain religious or
> social rules or not. But this is exactly what the primitive does.
> Disease derived from sorcery, from taboo violation, from the
> anger of ancestral or other spirits is the expression of social ten-
> sions. A seemingly independent, biological problem is thus wo-
> ven into the whole socio-religious fabric in such a way that dis-
> ease and its healer play a tremendous social role, a role that, in
> our society, is assumed rather by judges, priests, soldiers, and
> policemen. In many primitive societies, disease becomes the most
> important social sanction. Primitive medicine contains a moral
> element which is almost absent in ours. 'Be peaceful, pay your
> debts, abstain from adultery, in order to protect yourself *and
> your family* from disease.' It thus becomes possible to treat dis-
> ease by pacifying offended persons. New light is here thrown on
> the marked interest of the primitive community in the diseased
> person and its participation in healing rites. This social role of
> disease may also partly explain the persistency of primitive medi-
> cine, quite apart from its intrinsic medical value. The purely
> curative effect of certain rites may be negligible, but they are
> upheld because they fulfill important social functions" [3, pp.
> 27-8; cf. 7].

The Ojibwa World View

The northern Ojibwa, the group of American Indians I have studied at first hand, and whose attitude toward disease I wish to discuss in the framework of their world view, are among the peoples whose central values are reinforced by the belief that sickness is a penalty for bad conduct (madjīijīwé bαzīwin).[7] Located east of Lake Winnipeg, along the Berens River, these Ojibwa retained their aboriginal system of beliefs to a considerable degree until recent years. During the decade I visited them (1930-1940), there was one band which had not become entirely Christianized.

The Ojibwa's relative conservatism was due partly to the fact that, unlike many other North American Indians, they remained nomadic hunters and fishermen, for the physical environment they inhabited was not fitted for agriculture, and the white population remained sparse. I shall not deal with the changing aspects of their culture here, but shall endeavor, rather, to present the substantive aspects of their outlook upon the world, as it was constituted for them, in terms of their aboriginal cognitive orientation.[8]

There are many inherent difficulties to be faced when an outsider attempts to synthesize data from many different sources and articulate the world view of a people. For *world view* "refers to the way the world looks to that people looking out". It involves a different perspective than the one assumed when we look at culture and behavior from the outside. "Of all that is connoted by 'culture'," Redfield says, " 'world view' attends especially to the way a man, in a particular society, sees himself in relation to all else" (43, p. 23). In seeking a people's world view, it is necessary, therefore, to avoid, as far as possible, the imposition of categories of

[7] *Phonetic key to Ojibwa terms:*

a, as in father	c, approximates *sh* in ship
ä, as in hat	j, approximates *z* in azure
ī, as in pique	dj, approximates *j* in judge
α, as *u* in but	tc, approximates *ch* in church

[8] For further detail on this, *see* Hallowell, 1955 (22), particularly, chap. 5, and, for the changes that have occurred in Ojibwa culture, part IV.

thought, classifications of phenomena, and terminology which is closely associated with modern scientific thought, or the traditional philosophy of Western culture. Otherwise, the actual cognitive orientation, and the inner logic of their world view may be distorted. While anthropologists are becoming increasingly aware of this problem, only a few years ago Kluckhohn had to point out that "in cultural anthropology we are still too close to the phase in linguistics when non-European languages were being forcibly recast into the categories of Latin grammar" (28, p. 508).

A case in point is the term "natural", which, paired with the term "supernatural," has had its own complex history in Western thought. Both terms involve categorical implications which cannot be casually applied to the cognitive orientation of primitive peoples. Many years ago, Lovejoy observed that the "word 'nature' is probably the most equivocal in the vocabulary of the European peoples" (37, p. 12; cf., 36, p. 69). More recently, Bidney has pointed out that "the dichotomy of the natural and the supernatural implies a scientific epistemology and critical, metaphysical sophistication which must not be assumed without reliable evidence" (10, p. 166).[9]

With respect to the Ojibwa, let me say at once that neither "natural" nor "supernatural" are terms appropriate for describing their world outlook. Instead of any fundamental dichotomy, there is, rather, a basic metaphysical unity in the ground of being. In *their* behavioral environment we cannot say, for example, that the sun is a "natural object". It would also involve a distortion of their thinking to say that the sun is a "personified" object. For this would imply that, at some point in the past, the sun was perceived as an inanimate material thing, and later given animate properties.

---

[9] With respect to the general applicability of the natural-supernatural dichotomy to primitive cultures, *see* Leeuw (34, pp. 544-545). Ackerknecht says: "Supernaturalistic', though often used by the best authorities, is quite obviously a misnomer for these primitive representations, as it presupposes the notion of the predictable natural which primitives characteristically do not have. This notion of natural is a much later invention" (7, p. 5 n.).

There is, of course, no evidence for this, and all speculation along such lines reflects simply a Western cultural bias, from which we must completely detach ourselves if we are to enter the culturally constituted worlds of other peoples.

Ojibwa speech gives us a direct clue to the fundamental difference between our own outlook upon a natural world of objects and their outlook. For example: the term *gīzis*. In the first place, it applies to both the sun and the moon, the latter being distinguishable by the prefix for "night". Secondly, *gīzis* is formally classified as *animate,* in a grammatical scheme which differentiates animate and inanimate objects. It is thus apparent that the Ojibwa classification does not altogether coincide with our "naturalistic" outlook.

It would be erroneous, however, to infer from this single example that the Ojibwa are "animists" in the classical sense—although one anthropologist has said that "to the Ojibwa . . . all objects have life" (26, p. 21). This can hardly be the case, in view of the existence of an *in*animate grammatical category in their language. A complex problem is involved here but, for the purposes of the present discussion it will be sufficient to note that while the Ojibwa recognize a category of *living things,* the classes of objects which fall into this category do not all fit our categorization, although most of them do. (As will be seen below, one particular class of animate, living beings—*persons*—is of paramount importance in the Ojibwa world view, although there, their conceptualization is characterized by an inclusiveness which transcends our familiar categorization.)

The concept of causation also requires a few comments. The context of events in the Ojibwa world, as represented in myths, traditional anecdotes and descriptions of illness and its treatment, all carry implications that have causal connotations, in the elementary sense that certain events are interpreted as having an influence on other events. Because of this presumed linkage, it is inferred that, for the Ojibwa, without the occurrence of some previous event, a subsequent one would not have taken place. The Ojibwa, however,

do not generalize abstractly about causation: references are concrete and particularistic. Consequently, we have to discover what
notion of causation is in fact implicit in their world view.

Needless to say, we do not find any notion of mechanical or impersonal modes of causation to be paramount. The Ojibwa do not
entertain any concept of a natural world, comparable to that which
has become characteristic of the view of modern Western culture.
This does not imply, however, that events in their phenomenal
world are haphazard or unpredictable. They are not. The Ojibwa
observe the regular movements of the sun, and these movements
are expected, from day to day. At the same time, these regularities
are, to them, comparable to the predictable habits of a *person,*
rather than the consequence of "natural" laws. And, just as the
habits of a person may be interrupted by some unexpected event,
or be influenced by other persons, so the regular movements of the
sun may undergo unexpected variations under certain circumstances. This viewpoint can be documented by two brief illustrations:

In the distant past, a mythical personage once set a snare in the
path which the sun regularly traveled. The sun was caught, and
could not move. Darkness continued until a mouse was sent by
human beings to release the sun and provide daylight again.

In another story (not a myth), it is recounted how two old men,
at dawn, vied with each other in influencing the sun's movements:

> The first old man said to his companion: "It is about sunrise
> now and there is a clear sky. You tell Sun to rise at once." So the
> other old man said to Sun: "My grandfather, come up quickly."
> As soon as he had said this, Sun came up into the sky like a shot.
> "Now you try something," he said to his companion. "See if you
> can send it down." So the other man said to Sun: "My grand-
> father, put your face down again." When he said this, Sun went
> down again. "I have more power than you," he said to his com-
> panion, "Sun never goes down once it comes up."

Both these examples give the flavor of the Ojibwa outlook, since they refer to events accepted as actual occurrences. They illustrate the predominant Ojibwa theory of causation. I have marshalled evidence elsewhere to show that the conceptualization of "persons" and their activities provide the fundamental clue to the dynamics of the Ojibwa phenomenal world.[10] Myth, anecdote and personal experience reflect a unified outlook. Various classes of events are connected in some way with the activities of "persons". In the Ojibwa universe, events may be said to be the consequence of the behavior of persons. The most ready explanation of events is a "personalistic" theory of causation. *Who* did it? or *Who* is responsible? is always the crucial question.

A personalistic explanation of past events is found in the Ojibwa myths. It was *Wisakedjàk* who, through the exercise of his personal power, expanded the tiny bit of mud retrieved by Muskrat from the waters of the Great Deluge, and expanded it into the island-earth of Ojibwa cosmography. Thunder is attributable to the Thunderbirds, characters in mythology, who dwell in a land located above the flat earth which is the Ojibwa habitat. I was once asked to expound the white man's explanation of thunder, but I could not make myself intelligible. A naturalistic frame of reference was much too foreign to their thought. One summer, when a severe forest fire broke out, no Indian would believe that lightning, or any other impersonal or accidental cause of fire, was involved. *Somebody* must have been responsible. Since World War II had begun, the German spy theory immediately became popular. "Evidence" began to accumulate; strangers had been seen in the bush, and so on.

The distinctive character of the personalistic theory of causation of the Ojibwa is grounded in an *inclusive* conceptualization of *persons*. Their conceptualization transcends the concept of persons familiar to us in psychology and the social sciences insofar as for us

[10] I have omitted any discussion of the Supreme Being of the Ojibwa, since this personage, while immanent in their phenomenal world, does not become an active presence in the lives of individuals and, so far as I was able to discover, plays no role in relation to disease (23).

persons and human beings usually are categorically identified.[11] Consequently, if we are to fully apprehend the Ojibwa world out-look, it is necessary to take cognizance of their categorization of *persons* rather than impose our concepts upon them. In this con-nection, it is of interest to note that, in the field of social psychol-ogy, Krech and Crutchfield have expounded a frame of reference in which they employ the concept of *person objects*. They ask: "In what essential respects are these person objects different from other objects in the psychological field?" Their answer is that "person objects" differ from others:

> and are especially important in determining behavior because they have, among other characteristics, the properties of *mo-bility, capriciousness, unpredictability;* because they are the perceived loci of a great deal of *causation;* because they are per-ceived to have *power* qualities—to provide rewards and threaten punishment; because they are perceived as *sensitive* and *recip-rocally reactive*" (30, p. 9).

These writers argue, moreover, that the qualities which give per-son objects their importance as stimuli are not unique to human beings. Animals, plants, and even inanimate objects may be per-ceived as exhibiting these qualities (cf., 29, p. 669).

Considered with reference to Krech and Crutchfield's discussion of the properties of person objects, the world view of the Ojibwa appears less exotic. All the qualities of person objects they mention can be documented for the *persons* of the Ojibwa universe. The latters' reciprocal sensitivity and power qualities are of particular importance, as, also, are their conceptualization as loci of causality.

Although it will be unnecessary to discuss all possible exceptions here, it should be said that the persons of the Ojibwa universe do not include animals and plants, as such. And one distinctive prop-erty of persons must be emphasized: the capacity for metamorpho-sis. Thus, both living and dead human beings, for example, may

---

[11] As, for example, by Warren, who defines *person* as "a human organism re-garded as having distinctive characteristics and social relations" (49).

assume the form of animals. So far as appearance is concerned, there is no hard and fast line that can be drawn between an animal form and a human form, because of this possibility for metamorphosis. In perceptual experience, what looks like a bear *may be* an animal, but, under some conditions, it is a human being. The outward appearance of persons is not stable. What persists, and gives continuity to being, is the vital part, or soul. Metamorphosis is one of the generic properties manifest by beings of the person class, but not manifest by all animate beings.

To the Ojibwa, then, human beings *(änishanábek)*, i.e., Ojibwa Indians, are only one class of persons. The other class of persons, I believe, it is preferable to characterize as "other-than-human beings", rather than supernatural beings, since their essential properties as persons are the same (24). While they do not differ from human beings in kind, other-than-human persons occupy the top rank in the power hierarchy of animate beings. Metamorphosis is more characteristic of them, than of human beings, because it is an earmark of power. This second class of persons includes the four Winds, Sun and Moon, Thunderbirds, the "owners" or "masters" of the various species of plants and animals, and the characters in myths *(ätisokának)*. Collectively, this class of persons is spoken of as "our grandfathers". This is why the two old men, in the anecdote cited above, addressed the Sun as they would any elderly human being—kinship terms do not indicate precise genealogical connections in either case. Their use of a kinship term does however indicate the essential unity and inclusiveness of beings of the *person* category.

Although I cannot go into all the evidence here, the class of "other-than-human persons" must be thought of as made up of living entities who are integrally related to human beings, in a "cosmic" society, and constantly interact with them. One typical mode of "social" interaction in it is in dreams, so that the term *pawáganak,* dream visitors, is essentially a synonym for "our grandfathers". Although there is no lack of discrimination between ex-

periences of a human person when he is awake and when he is
asleep, both sets of experiences, to the Ojibwa, are equally self-
related. That is to say, dream images function integrally with other
recalled memory images insofar as they, too, enter the field of self-
awareness. The power qualities of persons of the other-than-human
class are exploited by the Ojibwa in the puberty fast for boys,
where direct "social" contacts are sought in order to obtain some
of the power which the *pawáganak* are willing to share with human
beings. In this role, other-than-human persons are conventionally
referred to, in the anthropological literature, as "guardian spirits".
The moral aspect of this "face to face" contact is indicated by the
fact that "blessings" obtained impose an obligation upon the recipient, which may take the form of a personal tabu. Consequently,
from the Ojibwa point of view, "social interaction" with persons
of the other-than-human class is not metaphorical.

Another typical occasion upon which there is "social interaction" of this type is at conjuring ceremonies, where the voices of
other-than-human persons are heard issuing from the conjuring
tent, and repartee occurs between members of the audience and
these persons. It is also believed that when myths are narrated
(which occurs only on winter nights) "our grandfathers" are invoked, and come and listen to the stories. These stories, as is the
case in many other societies, are not fiction[12] to the Ojibwa. They
are true stories about "our grandfathers", who often appear in a

_____

[12] This attitude is not peculiar to the Ojibwa. More than half a century ago,
Swanton pointed out that "one of the most widespread errors, and one of those
most unfortunate for folk-lore and comparative mythology, is the off-hand classification of myth with fiction ..." On the contrary, he wrote: "it is safe to say
that most of the myths found spread over considerable areas were regarded by
the tribes among which they were collected as narratives of real occurrences"
(47). More recently, Bidney has observed: "The concept of 'myth' is relative to
one's accepted beliefs and convictions, so that what is gospel truth for the believer is sheer 'myth' and 'fiction' for the non-believer or skeptic. ... Myths and
magical tales and practices are accepted precisely because pre-scientific folk do
not consider them as merely 'myths' or 'magic', since once the distinction between myth and science is consciously accepted, the acquired critical insight
precludes the belief in and acceptance of magic and myth" (10, p. 166).

cosmic setting, as their main characters. Whether human or animal in form or name, they possess all the attributes of persons and behave like people.

Although it is convenient, and even necessary, to refer to myths as "narratives", the term for them in Ojibwa does not refer to this aspect at all, but to the characters. "Myths" are therefore living personal entities, equivalent to "our grandfathers" and *pawáganak*. If we equate them with fiction, we completely distort the Ojibwa attitude toward them. It is for this reason that I have taken myths "seriously", as one of the most reliable sources of information on the cognitive orientation of the Ojibwa. They offer basic data about unarticulated and unanalyzed concepts which have not been abstracted and consciously discussed.

The Ojibwa world then is populated with persons, human and other-than-human, who occupy it along with plants, animals and inanimate objects. Persons of both classes play differentiated roles and interact with each other.

Although the persons of the Ojibwa world may sometimes act unpredictably, the great cosmic society is unified, because in all areas of "social interaction", the same values prevail. For human beings, the central goal of life is expressed by the term *pimädazi-win*, life, in the fullest sense—life in the sense of longevity, health, and freedom from misfortune. This goal cannot be achieved without the help and cooperation of both human and other-than-human persons, in addition to one's own personal efforts. The help of "our grandfathers" is particularly important. This is why the puberty fast for boys was so important in aboriginal days: it was the opportunity of a lifetime. Every special aptitude—all a man's subsequent success, and the explanation of many of his failures, hinged upon the aid then of other-than-human persons. The acquisition of specialized curing power as well as defenses against the hostile power of others, mediated through disease, depended upon the assistance of persons of the other-than-human class.

Hunger, among the Northern Algonkian hunters, sometimes

has been called "the silent enemy". Looking at the world from an Ojibwa point of view, there was another "silent enemy"—disease—which caused far more anxiety. There were traditional means available (weapons, traps, knowledge of the habits of animals, and so forth) for a realistic solution to the food problem, but the Ojibwa were less well equipped to deal with sickness. While any detailed discussion of their *materia medica* would require separate treatment,[13] it may be noted that in their vocabulary *mɑckīkī* (usually translated "medicine"), actually included material substances employed for purposes other than the cure of illness. Both "hunting magic" and "love magic" *(materia magica)*, for example, were included within the *mɑckīkī* category.

Thus while there undoubtedly was a crude empiricism present, their culturally based cognitive orientation was not of a kind which could motivate the development of a medicine that was thoroughly pragmatic, not to say scientific. Objectively viewed, their culture provided them with better adaptive potentialities for an existence depending on hunting and fishing, however precarious at times, than it did for combating disease.

Illness as a Social Sanction

In the previous section, I have indicated why the basic structure

---

[13] Ritzenthaler, in his study of a band of Ojibwa (Chippewa) in northwestern Wisconsin, was struck by their "hyper-consciousness" regarding health (44, p. 176). While he concluded that the level of health in the community actually was substandard, so that the contemporary preoccupation with sickness did have a realistic basis, nevertheless he expresses the firm conviction, based on ethnographic data, that this concern with health, exemplified in an exaggerated form the same concern entertained by the Ojibwa in "pre-contact times" (44, p. 229). Comparative data on less acculturated groups support this conclusion (44, pp. 232-233). Ritzenthaler likewise essays the wider generalization that, considered "in terms of human behavior the attitude of a primitive people toward disease is more influential than the disease itself" (44, p. 246). For additional comments on Ojibwa anxiety about health, see Landes (32, p. 178). (For specific details on the use of plants in Ojibwa medicine, see Densmore [14]; on the use of the enema syringe, see Densmore [14, pp. 331-332] and Hallowell, 1935 [19].)

It may be noted that the Ojibwa, like other North American Indians, "probably knew nothing of measles, smallpox, malaria, yellow fever, or cholera, and many other infectious diseases before contact with the white man" (5).

of the world view of the Ojibwa must be conceptualized in terms of a "cosmic society" of "persons", both human and other-than-human. The dynamics of the Ojibwa universe involves the functioning of persons in highly differentiated roles and patterns of "social interaction", including the recognition of personal responsibility for conduct, rights and obligations between persons. This social web of interpersonal relations is distinctive, because, while analogous to the social orders of mankind, for the Ojibwa it includes other-than-human persons, with equivalent properties, who play a vital part in their daily lives and in the functioning of a greater social whole.[14] The question we now have to answer is how confrontation with various types of disease, as objective fact, is related to the phenomenology of the Ojibwa world, and the reinforcement of moral values in Ojibwa society.

First, it is necessary to distinguish between ailments like colds, headaches, disturbances of digestion and so forth, which are considered relatively inconsequential, and more serious cases of sickness. The latter are those which prove resistive to treatment and thus arouse anxiety. Sigerist points out that some differentiation "between minor, common and therefore obvious ailments that they can handle themselves, and serious sickness that is mysterious and cannot be cured unless it has been explained", and thus requires "the special knowledge and skill of the medicine man," is practically universal among primitive peoples (46, p. 126). Ackerknecht has also discussed this distinction. He emphasizes the fact that indispositions of the former category "are not important enough to

[14] Since completing this paper, I have become acquainted with Robin Horton's article on a definition of religion (25). He states: "In every situation commonly labelled religious we are dealing with action directed towards objects which are believed to respond in terms of certain categories—in our own culture those of purpose, intelligence and emotion—which are also the distinctive categories for the description of human action. The application of these categories leads us to say that such objects are 'personified'. The relationships between human beings and religious objects can be further defined as governed by certain ideas of patterning and obligation such as characterize relationships among human beings. In short, religion can be looked upon as an extension of the field of peoples' social relationships beyond the confines of purely human society" (25, p. 211).

theorize about," and that no real explanation may be offered. Consequently, "to call such attitudes 'naturalistic' or 'rational' seems to inject into the data, contents they actually do not have" (4, p. 478). My own observation of the Ojibwa confirms his position. Furthermore, ailments of this category do not enter the picture at all insofar as disease operates as a social sanction.

But when sickness becomes a threat to *pīmädazīwin,* when it arouses fear and anxiety, it becomes a matter of reflection and concern on the part of the patient, as well as others, and some explanation is required. Consequently, there is a psychological—rather than any objective—distinction which differentiates minor maladies from major afflictions: the latter generate emotional overtones; the former do not. The latter have moral implications, while minor ailments do not. This is because any serious illness is associated with some prior conduct which involved an infraction of moral rules: the illness is explained as a penalty for bad conduct. It is a consequence of behavioral deviation from expected patterns of interpersonal relations, whether between human persons or between a human being and an other-than-human person. "Because a person does bad things, that is where sickness *(ákwazīwin)* starts," is the way one informant phrased it. Bad conduct, the Ojibwa say, "will keep following you"; sooner or later, you or your children will suffer for it by becoming ill, or even dying. Thus, causes of illness are sought by the Ojibwa within their web of interpersonal relations, rather than apart from it. This is consistent with a world view in which the interrelations of *persons* are of paramount importance.

In their chapter on "Sanctions and Moral Feelings", Edel and Edel point out that any consideration of sanctions "carries us on the one hand into the macroscopic social or public procedures of reward and punishment, on the other into the microscopic or deeper-level layers of motivation to ask what internal stimuli or play of feelings operate effectively in guiding paths of choice," i.e., "those motivations and pressures which operate to help maintain conformity." Later they observe that "negative sanctions have their roots in a host of negative emotions—fear, guilt, shame, and so on" (17, pp. 163; 183).[15] It is in these latter terms that the explanation of illness as a penalty for bad conduct operates as a general negative sanction in Ojibwa culture.[16]

Within Ojibwa society, macroscopic—social or public procedures—for punishment are absent. No institutionalized means exist for the public adjudication of disputes or conflicts of any kind. There is no council of elders or any forum in which judgment can be passed upon the conduct of individuals. There is no way in which publicly sanctioned punishment can be initiated in cases of incest, murder, or any other offense. Children, it is true, are disciplined by their parents, but corporal punishment is rare.[17] But in the social world of adults there are no superordinate modes of social control, no institutionalized means of punishment.

"Our grandfathers", unlike ancestral spirits in some other cultures, do not afflict human beings with illness. By and large, they are not characterized by any punishing role. Their attitude toward ánicinàbek is one of helpfulness; they are willing to share their power with human beings, and come to their assistance when in trouble. It is true that if men do not treat game animals properly, the "persons" who are their "masters" will not allow these animals

---

[15] I have used the term sanction in a broad sense, i.e., with reference to the functioning of beliefs, attitudes and responses to events which, by affecting the motivations of individuals promote conformity in behavior in accordance with culturally constituted values. (Cf., Ladd [31], for a discriminating analysis of the concept of sanction and B. B. Whiting and John Whiting [50; 51] for a discussion of mechanisms of social control.

[16] Cf., Dunning: "One of the major sanctions of Ojibwa society is the belief in retributive justice in the form of illness and even death resulting from wrongdoing" (16, p. 180).

[17] Dunning, discussing the relations of fathers and children writes: "Corporal punishment is never needed to establish or re-establish the father's authority. Mild teasing and laughing are sometimes used by the father, and are more than sufficient to control the son" (16, p. 92). He goes on to say that "no cases of corporal punishment of sons were disclosed, but there were two cases of corporal punishment of daughters" (16, p. 93). Both cases, it is interesting to note, were protested openly by others.

to be caught. But the human offenders are not afflicted with sickness on this account.

In the absence, then, of public procedures with sanctioning functions, or a belief in the punishing roles of other-than-human persons, it is apparent that if social sanctions are to operate at all, they must be intimately linked with motivations that are connected with a sense of moral responsibility for conduct mediated through ego and superego functions.[18] In order to understand how a disease sanction effectively reinforces the basic values of Ojibwa culture, there are several factors that must be taken into account, besides the affective states provoked by the illness.

Every individual is not only assumed to be morally responsible for his conduct: in disease situations that arouse anxiety, he is also forced to become the judge of his own past conduct. Feelings of guilt become particularly acute when it is understood that infants, too young to be penalized for their own bad conduct, may be suffering because of the past misconduct of their parents. Thus, whether I become ill or my children do, the question arises: What have *I* done that was wrong? With the help of a doctor, I have to answer this question concretely. I have to reflect on my past behavior. I have to think about my relations with other persons, both human and other-than-human. It is necessary that I identify the bad conduct that has followed me, even if I have to go back to my childhood. I have to pass judgment on my own conduct.

It is useless to withhold anything, because the doctor, with the aid of his other-than-human helpers, will probably find out what kind of bad conduct has followed me. Consequently, the discovery and articulation of it become equivalent to a *confession* of wrong-

---

[18] In what follows I have drawn upon my previous discussion of the social function of anxiety in Ojibwa society (*See* 22, chap. 14). My point of departure was that "this social function of anxiety is definitely linked, in principle, with the biological role which Freud stresses as a generic function of anxiety," namely "that an affective reaction to danger situations, as culturally defined, may motivate behavior on the part of individuals which is as significant in terms of societal values as comparable reactions are valuable in terms of biological utility. Anxiety-preparedness in the face of any danger is a very adaptive reaction."

doing. This is an essential step, necessary to promote recovery.[19] Medicine can then do its work. Thus, confession adds considerable psychological force to the disease sanction. In order to get well, the individual has to suffer not only guilt, but the shame of exposure involved in confession—although this may relieve some of his anxiety.

Confession is also the means by which knowledge of concrete cases of bad conduct is put into social circulation. For, among the Ojibwa, there is no isolation of a patient; on the contrary, the wigwam is always full of people. Any statement on the part of the patient, although it may be made to the doctor, is actually *public* knowledge, and may very quickly become a matter of common gossip. Under these conditions, to confess a transgression is to publicly reveal what may be a secret "sin". To the Ojibwa, however, this public exposure is important. The very secrecy of misconduct is bad in itself, as, for examples, covert aggression through witchcraft, or sexual transgressions. Once misconduct has been publicized, it is washed away, or, as the Ojibwa phrase it, "bad conduct will not follow you any more." When one participant in sexual misconduct confesses, the other person will not subsequently become ill or have to confess.

Confession, by making secret misconduct public, places the sick person on the road to recovery. This is its ostensible purpose, as viewed by the Ojibwa themselves. But confession also has a wider, *social* function: children growing up in Ojibwa society come to *sense,* even if they do not fully understand, the general typology of

[19] Dunning points out that medicine men "were experts in the mytho-theological field of knowledge, who exploited and manipulated the situation on the basis of vision-acquired power . . . the basis of their authority lay in the general belief in retributive justice. If a man transgressed the mores of his society and did not become ill or die, he felt lucky and might tempt fate again by a repetition of the deed. Should he become ill, this would be clear evidence for himself and everyone that he had done wrong, and the social norms would be thus reinforced by his example. It was the duty of the medical specialist to probe the wrong behavior of the patient. And by public confession, not only did the patient recover from his illness, but the social norms of the society were upheld" (16, pp. 180-81).

disapproved conduct. At the same time, since patients who confess often recover, the publicity given to such cases supports both the Ojibwa explanation of serious illness and the efficacy of confession itself. So, while most individuals are motivated to avoid the risk of illness, there is, perhaps, consolation in the fact that even if bad conduct does follow you, there still is an available means of regaining health.

Ojibwa Moral Values

The close associations of confession with illness enabled me to supplement information from other sources with a considerable amount of case material. I sat down with a few Ojibwa doctors and reviewed some of their cases with them. One old man recalled many of his father's cases, too, so that some of the material collected must antedate this century, and the more severe pressures of recent acculturation. From these concrete examples of what individuals under the stress of anxiety-laden disease situations thought they were being punished for, it is possible to obtain direct clues to moral standards which we do not find articulated or codified.[20]

In this section I wish to document the nature and range of the moral values which are reinforced by a disease sanction in Ojibwa culture with reference to selected cases. At the same time, I have maintained the framework of the two previous sections by ordering the discussion of values with reference to the two basic categories of "social" relationship which are implicit in the Ojibwa world view: (a) interpersonal relations between human beings and other-than-human persons; (b) interpersonal relations between human beings. Considered in this way, it will be noted that while there are some differences in behavioral focus between the values that may

[20] In a chapter devoted to "Values and Value-Orientations", Parsons and Shils note that "acts regarded as 'deviant', 'abnormal', and 'psychotic' provide clues to conduct valued by a group," and that "sanctions and values are linked in the concrete motivational system of each individual actor. Also, they are involved in the determinism of selection: external as well as internal consequences follow upon choice. Sanctions and values are inextricably linked. It is from group values that rules are derived and sanctions justified" (40, pp. 403, 432).

be inferred from the infraction of expected behavior between human beings and other-than-human persons, as compared with those expected between human persons, there are interesting convergencies in emphasis. These overlapping areas point, I think, to primary moral value in the Ojibwa ethos.

My intention here, however, is not to deal with Ojibwa values systematically, but, chiefly, to show how the disease sanction operates in the reinforcement of the moral values which are reflected in samples of case material.[21] The central role the sanction plays in the functioning of the socio-cultural system of the Ojibwa is evident. Elsewhere, I have dealt briefly with some of the central values of Ojibwa culture in relation to the personality readjustment of the Lac du Flambeau people under the impact of acculturation (22, chap. 20). In an unpublished manuscript, Dr. James R. Leary, who subsequently did field work there, has analyzed cultural variation, personality and values in the frame of reference developed by the Laboratory of Social Relations at Harvard (33, chap. 7).

Interpersonal relations between human beings and other-than-human persons ("our grandfathers;" *ätisokànak* [characters in myth]; *pawáganak* [dream visitors]), *as sources of sickness.* I have pointed out that persons of the other-than-human class are expected to share their knowledge and power with human beings, so that their "social" role in the Ojibwa universe is defined as essentially rewarding, rather than punitive. It is particularly important that men obtain "blessings" from the persons of this class; that is the purpose of the aboriginal puberty fast, in which boys come

---

[21] In terms of the classification of values presented by Ethel M. Albert, I am dealing with a "focal value" (health) and "directives", i.e., "rules of conduct, taboos, obligations and duties, rights and privileges, and any other rules or standards which are intended to regulate conduct" (8, p. 226). I have also dealt with "Premises and Value-Orientations" in the section on *The Ojibwa World View,* above. In Albert's view "the logical and functional relations between values and the general cultural conceptual system (world-view, ethnophilosophy) are so close, the delineation of the world-view is an appropriate adjunct to the description of the value system" (8, p. 222). "To relate metaphysics and value premises," she says, "it is probably sufficient to indicate only the most general principles of the cultural conceptualization of the universe as a whole" (8, p. 223).

"face to face" with other-than-human persons *(pawáganak)* in dreams or visions. The blessings gained range from invulnerability to bullets to the acquisition of specialized curing powers.[22] What kind of bad conduct then, can become the source of illness, and what kinds of values are reinforced by the application of a disease sanction to the relationship between human and other-than-human persons?

The power and knowledge shared by "our grandfathers" with human beings, and which the Ojibwa speak of in English as "blessings", are conceived of in terms of the social interaction of persons, because a reciprocal obligation is imposed on the human beings who are thought to benefit from them. Consequently, there is operative a reciprocal principle, equivalent to the basic patterning of social interaction between human persons, in which both rights and duties obtain. Furthermore, an obligation to share what one has with others is a primary value in the relations between human beings, and, as we shall see, it too falls under a disease sanction. Power and knowledge which an individual receives from other-than-human persons is, therefore, made contingent upon the fulfillment of a personal obligation, which has a primary moral force.

The commands of the *pawáganak* are absolute, though the obligations they impose may take various forms. There may be a food tabu in cases where the "masters" of particular species of game animals share their power; e.g., one man was forbidden to kill or eat porcupine by the "master" of the porcupines. (This is an example of "individual totemism", reported by Long from the Ojibwa during the 18th century, and the source through which the word *totem* entered anthropological literature [cf. 16, p. 79].) In another case, a man was commanded to wear the kind of headgear attributed to a certain mythical character, so it was inferred that this "person"

---

[22] E.g., the ability to remove magically projected lethal objects from the body of a patient; the use of medicine acquired directly from *memengweciwₐk*, a reified type of other-than-human person living in rocky escarpments; conjuring by means of the "shaking tent", where no *materia medica* is involved (for the latter, *see* 21).

was one of his "guardian spirits". Another man was forbidden to speak to, or have sexual intercourse with his wife for a defined period after marriage.

Such obligations are never talked about because there is a general tabu on any references to the relations of a man and his "dream visitors", except under unusual circumstances. So, the observances of the imposed commands often require the firmest self-discipline, for behavior that is not always intelligible to others, and cannot be explained to them, is involved. The man who was not permitted to sleep with his wife or even talk to her, did not succeed in fulfilling his obligation. His wife did not understand his conduct, and left him after one winter of married life. He married again and this time broke the tabu. One of his children became sick and died; later his wife died. He married a third time and the same thing happened. It was useless for him to expect *pīmädazīwin*; he had received a "blessing", but had not been able to exercise sufficient self-control to benefit by it.

Food tabus are interpreted so rigidly that inadvertent, or unconscious violations do not modify the penalty for their infraction. In these cases, as in others, I not only lose my "blessing", but endanger my health and that of my family. Furthermore, the wrongdoing that follows me when I have violated an obligation to other-than-human persons eventuates in illness that cannot be cured. The linguistic term applied to such infractions means: "failure to observe an obligation earnestly entered into" *(kizasīpi'tam).*[23]

Penalization of failure to meet such obligations not only emphasizes the moral relations between human and other-than-human persons; I think we can infer that it also underlines the generic importance of the moral responsibility which the Ojibwa individual is expected to assume for his conduct in *all* interpersonal relations. In the case of men, it also epitomizes the relation between the vital need that is felt for the help of other-than-human persons in the

[23] Jenness refers to the same penalty as "disobedience", without giving any native term (26, p. 52).

Ojibwa world, and the need for the self-discipline that is required to achieve *pīmädaēīwin,* not only for one's self but for one's family.

There is a connection between the psychological reinforcement of self-discipline, moral responsibility, and the stark realities that inhere in a hunting and fishing economy. Self-discipline underlies the self-reliance that is required of the hunter. An illness which is thought to eventuate from the violation of moral obligations to "our grandfathers" cannot be interpreted as stemming from their anger. *They* have done what they could for me; they have fulfilled their role. On my side, I must be able to accept obligations and fulfill them if I wish to reap the benefit of the help I have been offered by them. Among other things, self-discipline is necessary. The severity of the disease sanction in such cases is psychologically sound, if it is interpreted as a means of reinforcing motivations connected with self-discipline, for the Ojibwa are a people for whom life is fraught with objective hazards, which are inescapable. At the same time the sanction lends support, in principle, to moral responsibility for conduct in *all* interpersonal relations. Interdependence and cooperation is vital for survival. Human beings *can* obtain vital help in meeting the hazards of life from other-than-human persons so long as they fulfill the obligation imposed by "our grandfathers". Knowing this, a sense of security is fostered.

What are the limits to the knowledge and power an individual may acquire from other-than-human persons? A case I was told about indicates that there are certain traditional limits recognized. Greediness for power, to the extent that it might enable an individual to far outclass his fellow men, is negatively sanctioned. The case in point involved the puberty fast of a boy who was not satisfied with his initial "blessings". He wanted to dream of all the leaves of all the trees in the world so that absolutely nothing would be hidden from him. While the "dream visitor" granted his desire, the boy did not live to benefit by it. He was told that "as soon as the leaves start to fall you'll get sick, and when all the leaves drop to the ground, that is the end of your life."

"Over-dreaming", or "over-fasting", as it has been called,[24] is evaluated as particularly selfish. Trying to obtain more power than is actually necessary for living is the moral equivalent of hoarding material things, like food. It violates the principle that no one should have too much of anything. All that one really needs is what can be put to use in the foreseeable future. On the other hand, sharing what you have with others is a moral good; it shows that you are acting on the right principle. The fact that you *can* share demonstrates that you actually have more than you need for yourself and family in the foreseeable future. But to have more than others and be unwilling to share is morally bad. (We shall see below how this value receives emphasis in the social relations of human beings.)

A moral disapproval of cruelty, it is interesting to discover, emerges from a consideration of the disease sanction in cases involving the relations between human and other-than-human persons, as well as those between human beings. Cruelty to animals, too, is subject to retribution. While it is necessary, of course, for men to kill animals in order to live, what is wrong is to cause them unnecessary suffering. I believe that the disease sanction is applicable to the treatment of animals because cruelty to individual animals is offensive to the "persons" who are their "masters."[25] Thus, the breadth of the sanction against cruelty is as wide as it is deep in the Ojibwa ethos.

A most conclusive demonstration of the wide range of the sanction against cruelty is indicated by a case in which a boy became ill because his father had caused a cannibal monster *(windigo)* unnecessary suffering. While all such cannibal monsters are conceptualized as terrifying anthropomorphic beings, who must be killed,

---

[24] Radin points out that "throughout the area inhabited by the woodland tribes of Canada and the United States, overfasting entails death" (41, p. 177). W. Jones gives two cases of overfasting (27, pp. 307-311).

[25] This statement refers to wild species of animals only. The domestic dog is an exception. The often brutal treatment of dogs is notorious among the northern Indians.

some of them are human beings who have turned into cannibals, and others are other-than-human persons, who lead an independent existence (cf., 48; 39). To kill a *windigo* of the latter type is considered a feat of the utmost heroism. It is a sure sign of greatness, because it is impossible to accomplish it without the aid of powerful "helpers". Therefore, it was somewhat a surprise to me to discover that the illness of the son of a *windigo* slayer was attributed to the fact that his father had been cruel to one of these cannibal monsters.

I was told about the case by Adam B., a doctor himself, and the son of a doctor. He had accompanied his father when the latter had been called in to treat Flatstone's, the slayer's, son. When they arrived, the boy was spitting blood.[26] "My father talked for a little while. Then he took the rattle in his hand and began to sing. While he was singing he suddenly stopped. 'I can't go on', he said. Then he tried again. After singing some more he suddenly stopped again and said, 'I don't think "my grandson" is going to get better. This blood does not come from nothing. I guess it is your fault,' he said to Flatstone. The latter did not reply. Then my father said, 'Do you remember that *windigo* that overtook you once when you were traveling?' 'Yes,' said Flatstone. 'What did you do to him?' my father asked.

Flatstone then told how he tried to hold the *windigo* down with his own strength, but failed. He then called on one of his other-than-human helpers to come to his aid. The latter held him while Flatstone pulled out his hunting knife. He stabbed the *windigo* in the back. 'I kept on stabbing him. The blood burst from his mouth. I kept at it. He did not last long after that. I killed him at last. But he suffered a long time before I killed him. He kept moving but I knew he was going to die.' My father said, 'Now you have told this, in two days your child will be better.' And the boy did get better," Adam B. added.

Adam B. also told me that it would have been all right if Flatstone had cut off the cannibal's head with an axe (a weapon that appears in other narratives about *windigowak*). What was wrong was the suffering caused, and the fact that in telling about his encounter, originally, Flatstone did not give a complete account: he was secretive about what had actually happened. It was also pointed out to me that Flatstone's daughter, who was an old woman at the time, spit up blood now and then.

Since power to cure illness that is a threat to health and life cannot be acquired by human beings solely through their own efforts, the ultimate validation of any kind of curing procedure is rooted in the interpersonal relations between a healer and other-than-human persons. And, just as the human recipient of the knowledge and power to cure has to fulfill obligations to "our grandfathers" in order to successfully practice his art, the human patient, in turn, cannot obtain a doctor's advice for nothing. The healer must be compensated for his services. Consequently, it is understandable why it is shocking to the Ojibwa when, occasionally, a healer, under the stress of illness himself, confesses that he never received any power from other-than-human sources. He reveals himself as a charlatan; he has been practicing medicine without a "license". Deception of this kind falls under the disease sanction. And, as some measure of the seriousness with which the Ojibwa view this offense, I should like to point out that, on the basis of the case material that came to my attention, it would appear that the types of illness believed to be the consequence of "deceit", fall into the general category of what we would classify as nervous and mental disorders.

One summer I heard that an old man whom I had met inland was suffering from an apoplectic stroke. Shortly afterward he died. Simultaneously with the news, came gossip that the old man's illness and death were probably due to the fact that he had long been deceiving people about the powers which he claimed and exercised. Whether this was based on a confession I do not know. In another case, W. G., a conjurer, began to suffer from acute insomnia, and developed a phobia. He found that he could not go into the woods alone, not even for 200 yards. One can readily comprehend how abnormal this kind of a phobia is, granted the context of a hunting culture. W. G. confessed "deceit", and, it is said, he subsequently recovered from his phobia.

Another man (J. D.), similarly afflicted, whom I knew personally, and to whom I have referred elsewhere (22, p. 261ff.), was a well-known conjurer, and leader of the *wábano*. He suffered from phobias for many years. Darkness disturbed him profoundly. Once, in winter, when J. D. was traveling with some other men, they attempted to reach camp late at night because they had no blankets or bedding with them. Before darkness fell, J. D. insisted that they help him collect birch bark so that they could make torches to carry with them during the rest of the journey. They did this, but every now and then the wind would blow the torches out. I was told that when this happened, and they were plunged in darkness, J. D. would fall to the ground and writhe and scream like a "crazy" man. J. D. also suffered from a kind of agoraphobia. When paddling a canoe, he would never head directly across any large body of water if he could avoid it, but would always skirt the shore.

When he was an old man, J. D. suffered a physical and mental collapse, and was placed in a mental hospital by the Indian agent. Even before his breakdown, however, doubt was being expressed about the validation of his curative, clairvoyant and ceremonial activities. "If he is such a strong man as he claims to be," one Indian said to me, "and he has so many *pawáganak,* why is he afraid to do so many things?" Doubt was even expressed about his conjuring. In fact, all the Indians I talked to about J. D. expressed the view that he suffered because of some bad conduct. One acculturated Indian said that if he had any ordinary disease, the white doctors would have cured him. In this man's opinion, it was too late for anyone to do anything for J. D. Neither medicine nor confession would help him. He suggested that J. D. had tried to do "too many things." What he meant was that he had exceeded the prerogatives that were legitimately validated through his contacts with other-than-human "helpers". Otherwise, he would not have acted so "scared".

J. D. was a man who had offered curative and clairvoyant services to the people of his community for many years. Despite the symptoms he exhibited, he at no time confessed to any wrongdoing. His final collapse provoked the kind of speculation that helps document the basic orientation of Ojibwa thinking in cases of illness. The fact that J. D.'s symptoms were mental rather than physical, and that no one maintained that he was wholly a charlatan, made the case all the more perplexing. It was generally admitted that he had cured many people, yet full confidence in him was lacking. Some kind of wrongdoing must be following him. Ojibwa speculation could follow no other course than to suggest that the services he had been offering were not as firmly validated by his relations with other-than-human persons as they should have been.

While in theory the doctor's role in Ojibwa society is primarily validated by dream experiences which he alone can know about, there is also a pragmatic validation, insofar as he achieves success as a healer. And, since the disease sanction is directed against deception in regard to the kind of validation required, probably most individuals do have the necessary validating dreams or, in retrospect, believe that they have had them. If they did not, the burden of anxiety they would have to tolerate in the face of the sanction would be too heavy to bear. If this is so, the disease sanction itself may be said to have genuine pragmatic value in the support which it gives to the conceptual validation of curing power which characterizes Ojibwa culture.

Interpersonal relations between human beings as sources of illness. We already have emphasized the importance of the disease sanction, not only as a means of reinforcing specific obligations imposed by "our grandfathers", but as supporting the values of self-discipline, self-reliance and, in general, the principle of moral responsibility in interpersonal relations. These are values which are characterological; they have to be rooted in personality organization. When we turn to the relations of human beings with each other, we find that the naming ritual, in which infants are made "grandchildren" to their namers, is the source of a parallel emphasis upon the same values, reinforced by the same sanction in a special relationship which is set up between children and their *human* "grandfathers". The term "grandfather" has a conventional usage which transcends actual genealogical connections. Having an honorific connotation, it is applicable by human beings to any old man of my father's father's generation, and to other-than-human persons. Thus other-than-human "grandfathers" address their suppliants as "grandchildren" when they appear in the latter's dreams, and the old men in the anecdote cited above, addressed Sun as "my grandfather".

In a naming ceremony, infants are always given a name by a "grandfather", who may or may not be a close relative. The bestowing of this name is, at the same time, an act in which a "grandfather" shares with a "grandchild" a "blessing" which the namer, in turn, has received from an other-than-human "grandfather" earlier in his own life. The name given alludes in some way to a dream, which was the source of power. But the namer does not explain the connection, and the name given may be so vague and elusive in meaning that the child's parents, or other persons present, may not understand what is referred to. Specific examples from my genealogies are: Between the Clouds *(nèwadànakwap)*; Going Straight Through the Air *(kepeäs)*. These are names given to boys, and Going Right Through from One End of the World to the Other *(cäbakamägok)* and, Thing That Comes from Above *(mizaki)* are samples of names given to girls. The child may never be addressed by these names, since nicknames and other forms of appellation are common. Without prodding, a person may never mention this type of name, although it is the most vital he bears because it carries a "blessing" with it, useful in achieving *pinädazïwin.*

In order to realize the name "blessing", some obligation must be met, and violation of tabus imposed by human grandfathers fall under the same sanction as those imposed by other-than-human grandfathers. One man was forbidden to eat the flesh of birds with hawk-like claws. He told me that he had never done so for fear that he might get sick and die. In due course, a child is made aware of such personal tabus by his parents, and they become an integral part of the total pattern of prohibitions with which each child is indoctrinated in the socialization process.

Personal tabus, of course, assume qualitative distinctiveness because they are so intimately connected with one's own personal welfare. The self-discipline necessary to maintain them acquires a special saliency, as in the case of a woman who was forbidden by her namer to eat sturgeon, a fish greatly relished and eaten by everyone in bygone days. In later life, this woman broke the tabu, became "bloated" (dropsy?) and died. A young man whom I knew was forbidden to cut his hair. He wore it long until he was about nineteen. Then he became self-conscious about it because he was teased, and cut it. He told me that ever since he had had "bad luck", although he never suffered any serious illness. It was the opinion of his father, however, that if he had observed his namer's tabu he would not only have had better luck, but some great "blessing" would have come to him.

In the case of Ojibwa boys, the self-discipline involved in maintaining tabus imposed by human "grandfathers" in the naming ceremony is a preparation for obligations imposed in the puberty fast by other-than-human "grandfathers", which may be even more difficult to fulfill. Personality traits, embodying basic characterological values, receive reinforcement from the traditional patterning of interpersonal relations with "grandfathers" of both categories. As I have pointed out elsewhere, evidence of firm inner restraint and control can be seen in Ojibwa Rorschach protocols as features of a highly introverted personality organization. Behind the façade represented by this severe control is wariness and caution, and a preoccupation with people can be inferred from the content of Ojibwa Rorschach responses (22, pp. 71, 149).

The characterological evidence can be directly linked, I believe, with a world outlook in which primary emphasis is placed upon the interaction of persons. Since the "persons" of the Ojibwa world differ widely in the power they are able to exercise, and may act capriciously and unpredictably at times, caution and restraint is necessary in all interpersonal relations. This is particularly true with respect to human social relations, where, for various reasons, my fellow men may become hostile towards me. While other-than-human persons may be characterized as beneficent, in the abstract, and I can, of course, always depend upon the help of my own *pawáganak*, human persons hostile to me may set their helpers against me. Nevertheless, it is assumed by any Ojibwa individual that, with the cooperation of both human and other-than-human persons, it is possible to achieve a good life.

Pīmädazīwin is the Ojibwa term that embodies this concept. It is asked for in ceremonies in which all the other-than-human persons in the universe are addressed in a smoke offering in which a pipe is turned ritually in all directions. I believe that *Pīmädazīwin* implies an equitable balance in interpersonal relations, the recognition that the interdependence of "persons" is a necessary condition of a good life. What is unarticulated is the *right* of all human persons to share equally in a good life if their conduct is good. This is why the achievement of *Pīmädazīwin* depends upon normatively oriented social behavior, and why bad conduct becomes a threat to *pīmädazīwin*.

In the daily round of life, therefore, amiable social relations and approved modes of cooperation need to be maintained. I cannot afford to endanger my welfare and that of my family by bad conduct. Even though I may feel inwardly secure in some respects because of the "blessings" I have obtained from my *pawáganak*, I have need of my fellow human beings, too. If I fail to share a good life equally with my fellow men, bad conduct must be following me. I can only blame myself. Any serious illness reminds me of this fact.

This is what makes the disease sanction intelligible and acceptable within the world outlook of the Ojibwa. Viewed from the outside, it has an equilibrating function: it reinforces the primary group organization of a hunting and gathering culture where no economic competition exists, where the circulation of goods does not depend upon a market, where there is a minimum of social stratification and no social machinery for ajudication of disputes, and where it is believed that whatever differences in power exist are due to other-than-human persons. What the disease sanction does is to support the independence and equality in status which individuals enjoy by discouraging deviations or innovations which would undermine and disrupt the Ojibwas' relatively simple form of social organization.

For purposes of illustrative exposition I shall discuss several groups of selected cases. In the first, equalitarian values are upheld by promoting the circulation of material goods through hospitality, lending and sharing. Related in principle to these expressions of equalitarian values are cases in which resentment, envy or jealousy may be aroused as a consequence of rivalry in competitive situations. It is the *winner* who feels guilty and interprets his illness as a penalty for his success!

The second group of cases are some in which individuals suffer illness because of behavior which is considered hostile, insulting, threatening or aggressive.

The third category involves cases of penalties for disapproved sexual behavior, with respect to the choice of a sexual partner and/or the modes of sexual gratification adopted.

1. One of the most obvious features of Ojibwa society is the ease with which various kinds of food and other economic goods circulate—through sharing, borrowing or mutual exchange, rather than by purchase. To a large extent, the principle of reciprocity

explains this. Dependence upon hunting, fishing and trapping for a livelihood is difficult, at best, and it is impossible to accumulate food for the inevitable rainy day. If I have more than I need today, I share it with you because I know that you, in turn, will share your surplus with me tomorrow. Children learn this principle very early in life. I remember still how much impressed I was on my first visit to Lake Pekangikum by an instance of this: I gave a child of six or seven some candy. There were some other children nearby, and I intended to treat them, too, but before I had a chance to do so the first child began sharing her candy with them.

Some articles of clothing are used by more than one member of a family, and, in particular, pipes may be shared. One of my interpreters left his own pipe at home for his wife to use one morning. When he arrived at my camp, he asked me to lend him mine. He profited by this request, as I had an extra pipe which I gave him as a present. I also found that my possession, in the field, of considerable amounts of tea and flour, periodically brought Indians to my tent to borrow, "a little" of them. Sometimes there were return "gifts". Missionaries have had the same experience, and sometimes found their supplies dangerously depleted during the winter months because of their responses to the Indians' importunities. I solved the problem by stocking more goods than I needed for my own use. At a more formally organized level, the emphasis upon sharing and exchange explains the former popularity of the so-called Give-Away Dance, forbidden in Canada by the Indian Act.

It might be inferred from all this that such behavior was self-sustaining in terms of mutual interest, or that it might even be motivated in some cases by "generosity" or "altruism". That this is only an incomplete explanation is demonstrated by the fact that in a number of instances we find that individuals were motivated to be hospitable because they were afraid of retaliation by witchcraft. Others believed that they had suffered illness because they had offended someone with whom they failed to share, or refused to lend something, upon request.

With regard to hospitality, for example, the generalization made by Jenness about the Parry Island Ojibwa applies equally well to those whom I observed: "He sets food before chance visitors of his own race, whatever the hour of the day or night, *lest they resent any semblance of inhospitality and later cast a spell on himself and his household*" (Italics added.) (26, p. 88). Refusal of hospitality, in other words, may be interpreted as a personally directed hostile act. Mediated by sorcery, illness, as a penalty for not sharing what you have with others, lurks in the background here as a sanction for traditional values. The cautious man, whatever his actual motives may be in any particular case, will always be hospitable, and thus will avoid any chance of provoking illness through bad interpersonal relations. By the right kind of conduct, anxiety is avoided, the goodwill of others is enhanced, the equalitarian value of food sharing is maintained and reciprocal food sharing insured in times of adversity. Realistically viewed, "good behavior" does promote *pīmädazīwin*.

Some years ago, an Ojibwa friend of mine was suddenly afflicted one day with a pain in his leg. The leg began to swell, and he could not walk. He was not on the reservation at the time but in the town of Selkirk, Manitoba. He thought himself bewitched by a man with whom he had not shared some whiskey he had bought. In short, he had discriminated against this man in a situation which required that he share his liquor with him. There is no evidence in this case that the man actually was offended. Psychologically, this is all the more significant, since it shows how the guilt experienced by an individual in such circumstances is a form of self-accusation. He is forced to accept responsibility for some disapproved conduct, in this case the transgression of the important canon of sharing. In telling me the story, this man went to great length to explain why he had happened to forget the man he failed to treat. But even his excuses did not shake his firm conviction that he had been bewitched.

An example of how the fear of offending others, who may retaliate by witchcraft, can motivate what appears on the surface to be extremely generous conduct, is illustrated by an episode told by S., about himself. He had accumulated a winter stock of goods, with, among other things, quite a lot of brown sugar. Another Indian came along who wanted his brown sugar. S. gave it all to him, in exchange for practically nothing. The explanation was very simple: S. was a half-breed, who had married into the Little Grand Rapids Band. When he first settled among them, his father-in-law told S. that if any of the sons of a certain old man, with a reputation for being a sorcerer, ever asked him for anything, to be sure to give them what they wanted. It was one of these sons who asked S. for the brown sugar, and his apparent "generosity" was due to his not wishing to risk offending him.

Jenness gives the following case, which shows how sickness may be interpreted as a penalty for refusal to lend money when requested to do so.

> Johny Angus, who is a member of the Grand Medicine Society ... tried to borrow some money from me a few summers ago to take him home. I refused to lend him any, for I knew he would probably never return the loan; and he left me very angry. Late in the fall, ... something hit me in the ear, and by the time I reached home I felt very ill. I was laid up all that winter; my hair turned white and my teeth began to fall out, for the "medicine" Angus shot into me circulated all over my body. My wife, who was alive at that time and was also a member of the Grand Medicine Society, gave me remedies that finally cured me. She met Angus five years later and openly accused him of bewitching me. "It would serve you right if I killed you by witchcraft," she told him. Angus backed off from her without saying a word, and finally walked away [26, p. 87].

Here again we see how the guilty feelings of an individual determined the selection of a sorcerer. If an individual could not accept moral responsibility for an act in violation of the deeply rooted evaluation of the necessity of sharing, illness as a penalty for bad conduct in interpersonal relations would be unworkable.

The same unarticulated equalitarian values that are exhibited in customary habits of sharing, the exchanges in the aboriginal Give-Away Dance, and in cases of illness thought to be a retaliation for failure to be hospitable, to lend, or to share, are likewise implicit in cases where illness is believed to have afflicted the *winner* in some competitive situation. In this type of case, sickness is interpreted as a hostile act of sorcery perpetrated by the loser; no objective evidence is required. The afflicted person may even retaliate in kind in order to protect himself. The evidence that the illness is a consequence of bad conduct is psychological. The victim's anxiety about his illness stimulates feelings of guilt, and when he discovers or recalls that he has worsted some rival in a competitive situation, he may attribute an act of sorcery to him. The implication is that out-doing someone, or "getting out ahead" of someone, is offensive. It is bad conduct, and consequently dangerous, since the offended person may get "mad" and retaliate through sorcery. But it is the original victor who provoked him by his victorious act, so that in the final analysis he is morally responsible for his own illness. This is the source of his guilt, and the connecting link with the equalitarian values just mentioned.

In one case a sick young man, P., had won a dog team race, against seven other contestants. One of the others got mad, and openly threatened P. with trouble. Later P. became ill. He was thought to be suffering from "Indians' disease": Some material object had been projected into his body by sorcery, so that a special type of doctor *(nïbɑkïwininï)* had to be called in.[27] Although at first it seemed that he would recover, P. had a relapse and died. P. firmly believed, and in this he was supported by the doctor, that the man whom he had beaten in the dog team race was responsible. The latter's threat was considered important evidence for that fact.

[27] In Sigerist (46; pl. XXI, fig. 44) there is a photograph of a sculptured group in the Wellcome Historical Medical Museum (London) showing this kind of Ojibwa doctor at work. It was made by Miss Jane Jackson, after a pencil drawing by Dr. Eric Stone, author of *Medicine among the North American Indians*.

P's grandfather had also suffered illness, as a consequence of a competitive situation of another kind. When the Dominion of Canada made a Treaty with the Indians of the Lake Winnipeg region in 1876, a system of elective chieftainships was inaugurated so that the government could deal with representatives of the local Indian groups which adhered to the Treaty. This was a novelty, since institutionalized chieftainships were not characteristic of the aboriginal culture. Two men were rivals for the chieftainship of the Berens River Band. Jacob Berens, a recent convert to Christianity was one. *Sagɑtcīweäs,* an influential medicine man was the other.

Jacob Berens won. The day after the election he put on his new uniform and felt fine. But that very night he began to feel sick. He was convinced that *Sagɑtcīweäs* had bewitched him because of the defeat he had suffered. Although Jacob recovered, even in later years, when he suffered from a skin disease, he thought that *Sagɑtcīweäs* was still trying to "get him".

Jacob Berens may be considered to have won a double victory. He demonstrated his own special strength: he not only won the election, but he believed that the Christian faith he had adopted helped him to recover from his illness. His son told me that although he did suffer considerable anxiety when he became ill—for he knew he had been bewitched—he was confident that he would recover. Apparently he did not suffer a great deal of guilt. He knew what to expect when he ran against *Sagɑtcīweäs,* and was willing to take the consequences. In part, he may have been able to assume this attitude because he was already sloughing off his aboriginal values.

Men who are believed to have acquired much power from other-than-human sources occupy a special position in Ojibwa culture. Since they have both the power to cure, as well as the power to kill, people's attitudes towards them are ambivalent: they may exercise a great deal of personal influence because they are feared, and may

outrank other men in power, though not in material wealth or
formal social ranking.

It is clearly recognized that although all men share equally the
opportunity to secure power from other-than-human persons in
the puberty fast, the actual power secured varies greatly among
individuals. (It may be recalled here that what was interpreted as
greediness for power on the part of the boy who wished to dream
of all the leaves on all the trees in the world, was followed by illness
and his death.) The exhibition of too much power, like hoarding
of food or display of prowess is frowned upon by the Ojibwa. The
fact that J. D., the phobic conjurer, tried to do "too many things"
raised the question of the validation of such diversified powers.
Even the great "medicine men" of the Ojibwa cannot escape the
emphasis given in their culture to equalitarian values. The acquisition or display of too much power is menacing to other human
beings; it disturbs the equalitarianism that is felt to be basically
good. And, for the individual, it is dangerous to outdo others in
this as in other activities.

2. In the interpersonal relations between human beings, the disapproval of acts of cruelty and murder, of overtly hostile and
threatening acts such as verbal insults or gestures, is illustrated in
a series of cases where conduct of this kind is punished by illness.

With respect to cruelty, as I have already pointed out, sickness
may follow cruelty to game animals, and I have cited the case of a
boy who suffered because of his father's treatment of a *windigo*.
Here, I would like to refer to a case of infanticide, in which it
would appear that the subsequent illness of the mother was due
mainly to the *suffering* of the child she had killed.

"My father was called to treat the sick child of a young married
couple," my informant said. "They had two children and this was
the younger one. When he arrived, they took some of the old birch
bark covering from the wigwam and laid down a clean piece for
him to sit on. That night, after he had been singing awhile, he said
to the mother: 'Did you ever have a child before you were married,

and do away with it? The child you killed must have suffered a lot
before it died. This baby here is suffering now like that child did.'
For a long time the woman would say nothing, but she knew it was
true, and finally she had to tell. 'Why did you do it, and why did
you keep it secret?' my father asked her. 'You should have kept that
first child.' The woman said she wanted to marry her present husband and did not want him to know about the other child. My
father told her everything would be all right now that she had told
all. 'What you did will not follow you anymore. Your child will
get well.' And it did."

While it is impossible to say how prevalent infanticide was
among the Ojibwa, Dunning (16, p. 150) thinks the incidence must
have been low and, from a variety of sources, which I cannot cite
here for reasons of space, it would seem that adult homicide, except
when drunkenness was involved, was equally infrequent. While
there was no judicial machinery for dealing with murder, illness
subsequent to it was considered to be inevitable for the slayer. The
case of infanticide just mentioned may perhaps be considered a
double penalty.

Murder was culturally defined in such a way that the Ojibwa
excluded some cases which we, in Western society, would consider
as homicide. When human beings were thought to be developing
cannibalistic proclivities, for example, they were killed.[28] In one

[28] In the summer of 1906 two Ojibwa Indians (Jack Fiddler and Joseph Fiddler) of the Sandy Lake Band (then in the North West Territories) were ar-
rested by two constables of the Royal Northwest Mounted Police for strangling
a woman to death. They were taken to Norway House and held on a charge of
murder. But what they had done in Ojibwa terms was to execute a woman who
was believed to be a *windīgo*. Jack Fiddler escaped from custody and hanged
himself. Joseph was tried for murder by a special jury of six white men and
found guilty. But the jury recommended mercy "on account of the prisoners'
ignorance and superstition." Joseph was sentenced to life imprisonment. He died
of tuberculosis in the prison hospital about two years later. This case received
wide publicity in Canada at the time, and sharply dramatizes differences in the
cultural definition of murder. While some sympathy was expressed for Joseph,
one headline in a Winnipeg newspaper read: "Horrible Cruelties—Twenty
Similar Crimes in 25 years by the same chief."

case, a woman was executed by her three sons. But this was not bad conduct; it was an act of self-defense, and in the interests of the community, so no sickness followed. In actual cases of cannibalism, moreover, extenuating circumstances were sometimes taken into account. For example, a man, his wife, their two children and an adopted son faced starvation. Finally, the man became so weak that he could no longer leave camp in search of game. So the adopted child, said to have been fatter than the other children, was killed and eaten. I was told that no disease sanction operated in this case for three reasons: (*a*) these people were starving and it was better that one of them die rather than all; (*b*) they made no secret of what they had done; (*c*) they developed no cannibalistic proclivities. In this instance, it appears that the sanction gave way before biological realities. *Survival* became the primary value.

In several of the cases already referred to, the ostensible cause of death was sorcery. My guess would be that, in former days, the number of persons believed to have met death by sorcery greatly outnumbered actual cases of homicide by physical violence. What is interesting about cases of sorcery is that there can be no direct evidence that a sorcerer performed an act of sorcery. Initially, there can be only an *inference* on the part of the reputed victim, or others, that sickness or death is the consequence of a hostile act assumed to have taken place. There is also verbal evidence of a feeling of guilt on the part of some individual who believes that a person *he* has wronged has sorcerized him. Indeed, the most convincing evidence of sorcery, even from an Ojibwa point of view, are the cases of "Indians' disease", of which a case has already been cited, in which some material object believed to have been projected into the body of the victim is removed and exhibited by a "sucking doctor" (*nibαkīwininī*) as the "material" source of the trouble. Consequently, the operation of the disease sanction in cases of physical homicide only finds a parallel in covert acts of aggression, insofar as sorcery is *actually* practiced.

While I am not prepared to argue that acts of sorcery are entirely the fantasy projections of guilty minds, since I once obtained an example of a so-called medicine doll, of the type said to be used in sorcery,[29] I cannot escape the impression that such procedures were rare among the Ojibwa. In terms of objective analysis we can see how the belief in the possibility of sorcery made it possible to rationalize sickness or death as a punishment for personal wrongdoing. The actual function of the disease sanction in relation to aggression was to mute overt hostile acts in everyday life by making individuals feel guilty about them.

An overtly aggressive act—shaking a fist, pointing a finger, some insulting remark—which *I* initiate may lead me to think later that the person towards whom I directed open hostility has bewitched me in retaliation. Children are, in fact, warned against aggressive behavior.

Ridicule of deformed or crippled persons is another type of aggressive conduct that is disapproved. One man's father had cautioned him thus: "Don't laugh at old people. Don't say to anyone that he is ugly. If that person has power, he will make *you* ugly." Another informant told me that if you insult an old person he may cause your face to become twisted, as a sign of what you have done. One boy said he thought he was ill because he had made fun of a hunchback by imitating his peculiar gait. The father of the cripple was a conjurer, and the boy dreamed that his "soul" was "stolen" while he slept and taken into his conjuring tent. Fortunately, he was able to escape, but he was very ill for several days afterwards. He told his father what had happened in the dream and the latter was convinced that the conjurer was trying to kill him. (Elsewhere, I have cited an anecdote to show the circumstances under which it is possible for a person to be accused of sorcery when he is not guilty in fact. In that case I knew the accused man, who was an accultured Indian. His reputation as a sorcerer was built on the

[29] It is in the Museum of the American Indian, Heye Foundation, N. Y. A photograph may be seen in Dockstader (15, no. 225).

fact that a pagan Indian, believed to have attacked *him* through sorcery, became ill in turn [22, pp. 284-5].)

In all of the case material on sorcery which came to my attention, there was only one instance in which a person, an old man, mortally ill, confessed to murder by witchcraft. In view of the general disapproval of overtly aggressive acts of so many different varieties, it is not to be supposed that covert aggression, represented by sorcery, often would be confessed. No one in Ojibwa society wants to be labelled a witch, so lack of evidence need not imply that actual acts of sorcery, however secret, do not occur. It is particularly interesting, therefore, to note the fate of an old man who *did* confess, and how he rationalized his behavior. He confessed that he had killed two people a year for half a century! He said he was commanded to do this by his *pawáganak*; otherwise he would have lost his own life. Since there is no appeal from the commands of "our grandfathers" the old man had an excellent defense. However, his confession did not prolong his life. He died soon afterwards. So this case, too, can be interpreted as a punishment for bad conduct, however delayed.

The cases reviewed here enable us to understand how the disease sanction against hostility and aggression works. Theoretically, it penalizes murder by sorcery as well as by physical violence, but, as already noted, in many cases no aggressive acts can be literally attributed to a sorcerer. What the sanction actually does is to induce feelings of guilt in persons who become sick after they have overtly expressed some kind of hostile or aggressive impulses in face-to-face contact with other people. The main function of the sanction, then, is not to penalize sorcery or physical violence, but to motivate amiable social relations by reinforcing the suppression of aggressive impulses. The outwardly mild and placid traits of character which the Ojibwa exhibit, and the patience and self-restraint they exercise in personal relations, are a culturally constituted façade that often masks the hostile feelings that actually exist.[30] Individ-

[30] Duncan Cameron, referring to the Ojibwa of Lake Nipigon (Ontario) of

uals *wish* to harm others, but fear retaliation through sorcery should they expose their aggressive impulses.

3. Man's sexual activities are everywhere subjected to moral evaluation. In addition to the biologically rooted and intrinsically rewarding values of sexual stimulation and gratification, human sexual behavior involves an inevitable compromise between instinctual impulses and the moral appraisal of their expression that is characteristic of a given society. For the individual, psychosexual adjustment is fraught with all sorts of possibilities for conflict. The balance that results between biological determinants, traditional cultural values and the operation of social sanctions, is intimately related to both societal organization and personality structure.

In the case of the Ojibwa, sexual behavior is one of the major seedbeds of bad conduct that is believed to be penalized by sickness. The disease sanction reinforces the choice of approved sexual or marital partners, in accordance with the basic pattern of the kinship structure, while, at the same time, it supports positive moral evaluation of a single mode of gratification between sexual partners and negative evaluation of deviant techniques.

Ojibwa social organization is of the Dakota type, according to Murdock's scheme of classification.[31] Kinship terms are used in a widely extended sense, and are not indices to actual blood relationship, except in the case of father and mother. They are not simply verbal means of classification, address or reference; they are direct guides to the organization of interpersonal relationships in the Ojibwa social world. Prescribed attitudes and reciprocal patterns of behavior are implied in their use. All "persons", in the social

more than a century ago, says: "When sober they are of very gentle and amiable disposition towards their friends, but as implacable in their enmity, their revenge being complete only by the entire destruction of those against whom they have a spite. They very seldom take that revenge when sober, as few people disguise their minds with more art than they do, but, when in the least inebriate all they have in their mind is revealed and the most bloody revenge taken" (Quoted in 22, p. 142. For further discussion of *aggression, see* 22, chap. 15).

[31] Actually the sub-type he calls *Bi-Dakota* (38, p. 237).

world of the Ojibwa, fall within the kinship structure. For example, a myth recounts the adventures of a young man, the youngest of 10 brothers, who fell in love with a Thunderbird girl and followed her above to Thunderbird Land. There, the same kinship
terms were used between himself and the girl's relatives as were
customary between human beings. After a time, the young man
brought his wife and her nine sisters back to earth, where they
become metamorphosed into human beings, and the sisters married his brothers.

Only those persons who are *ninαm* to each other can have sexual relations, or marry, without risk of illness. In the Ojibwa system such persons are cross-cousins to each other, i.e., the children of
siblings of the opposite sex. This mating and marital limitation
narrows down sexual choice to persons of the same kinship generation, and, within this generation to persons of one of two classes.
For, within one's own kinship generation, persons of the opposite
sex who are *not ninαmαk* (sweethearts) are sisters to a male ego
(*see*, 22, chap. 16). Since brothers always are *ninαmαk* to the
same class of girls, the marriages between the Thunderbird girls in
the myth and their human sweethearts follows this pattern.

All the other terms in the Ojibwa kinship system carry a connotation of sexual avoidance. Sexually approved behavior, then, is
defined in terms of the position which individuals occupy in the
social structure, and between whom a certain term is used. Since
kinship terms are extended throughout the social world of the
individual there can be no equivocal cases.

By logical deduction from the kinship system, we can easily infer
the types of sexual partners that are disapproved. However, instances of them, exposed by confession under stress of sickness,
demonstrate the persistent force of instinctual drives, and the conflict between these drives and sanctioned moral values (described
in [20]).

(a) Bestiality is *a priori* ruled out by the kinship system. The
cases which came to my attention include men's relations with

freshly killed moose, caribou, bear, a bitch, and a woman's relations with a dog.

(b) Since persons of the same sex do not use the term *ninɑm* between them, homosexuality is excluded from approval. But in a few cases, both men and women confessed homosexual relations. One girl said: "After we became women, another girl and I used to be together all the time. She used to get on top of me like a man and use a sucker bladder" (comparable in size and shape to a man's penis).

(c) All persons in the incestuous category, as narrowly defined, are ruled out as possible sexual partners, as well as many individuals *not* related by blood. Incest prohibitions in the narrow sense function within a much wider range of tabued sexual relations. Since *ninɑm* is only applicable between people of the same kinship generation, this fact alone makes legitimate sex relations between any persons of different kinship generations impossible. Case material includes sex relations between father and daughter; mother and son; a man and his step-daughter; brother and sister; father's sister and brother's son; mother's brother and sister's daughter; man and his mother's sister; grandfather and granddaughter.

(d) Sexual intercourse with a corpse is also disapproved. In all three cases about which I was told men had had intercourse with their dead wives.

Considered in relation to the maintaining of Ojibwa social organization, the disease sanction does not eliminate all sexual deviations. When confession occurs, what it does is to remind everyone in the community of the consequences of any departure from the choice of a sexual partner who is not addressed as *ninɑm*. At the same time, good sexual conduct is accentuated. Dynamically viewed, a society can well tolerate a few breaches of the mores if a knowledge of such cases is a constant reminder to all to live a good life and thereby avoid illness and possibly death. The only real danger to the social order would stem from an accumulative trend in a deviant direction of actual conduct, or from a direct challenge to primary values that might influence actual conduct.

The one case in my notes of actual brother-sister marriage is particularly interesting in this connection. It obviously runs directly counter to the sanctioned rules of sexual relationship, in or out of marriage, and it was not a casual affair, as are all other cases of incest of which I have knowledge. *Sagaskī,* or Creeper, as Dunning (16, pp. 112-13) calls him, lived for many years with his younger sister, had three children by her, and when she died, married again. Of course, it was said by some that her death and that of one or two of his children was a penalty for bad conduct. If we stopped there, however, the deeper significance of this case for an understanding of the dynamics of Ojibwa society would be lost. *Sagaskī* was an outstanding man; he was acknowledged to have obtained great power from other-than-human persons. In one sense, he may be said to have flouted Ojibwa values. But this is not literally true because he did not challenge the validity of Ojibwa mores. He claimed he had had a dream in which the "master of the Beavers" *commanded* him to do as the beavers do, that is, to mate with his sister.

Sagaskī must have felt just as guilty about his incestuous desires as anyone else. But he was able to rationalize them in culturally intelligible terms. And I have no doubt that he actually dreamed what he said he dreamed. He was able to tolerate the burden of guilt and anxiety and justify his morally deviant behavior by appealing to the moral obligation he owed his *pawágan.* Since obedience to the commands of other-than-human persons is of such vital importance to a human being's welfare, the rationalization of *Sagaskī* was not only intelligible, but defensible as a validation for his conduct. A man who felt less confident of his own power and security, however, might not have dared to act as *Sagaskī* did. Under the circumstances, his conduct was not viewed by anyone, and certainly not by himself, as a challenge to traditional mores. And, since I was told that this case became notorious as an example of what *not* to do, it shows how concrete instances of the violation of the sexual code, even when confession is not involved, may be used to lend support to approved sexual conduct and primary values.

Elsewhere (22, pp. 274-5), I have given details of a case in which sexual relations between a young man of seventeen or eighteen and a fairly young woman who was his father's sister, was *not* followed by illness. It is a particularly interesting case, not only because these individuals were not *nīnamak* to each other, but because persons in their relationship address each other by terms equivalent to mother-in-law and son-in-law, and are under a severe avoidance tabu. In this instance the woman had adopted the young man a number of years before, and the sexual episode occurred during one winter when he was hunting and they camped alone together for a long period. The extenuating circumstances turned on the fact that sexual intercourse occurred only once; the woman resisted the young man's advances, and refused to continue the relationship. Besides this, the affair was not kept secret, and both married shortly afterwards. The boy's "mother-in-law" was a very sensible woman, my informant said. In my opinion what we have here, then, is a parallel to the case of cannibalism previously mentioned. For, to the Ojibwa, the satisfaction of sexual impulses are equivalent to the satisfaction of the demands of hunger, and, under the circumstances of isolation mentioned, the violation of the tabu seems to have been condoned.

In addition to limiting the choice of a sexual partner, the moral code of the Ojibwa places severe limits upon modes of sexual stimulation and gratification, even with approved types of mate. However, confessed cases of oral-genital contacts, the use of artificial phalli, anal intercourse and masturbation occur in my notes.

In summary, in Ojibwa society sexual activity is only approved between persons of opposite sex, occupying a defined position in the social structure, and only genital gratification receives full moral sanction.

Summary

The key to the world view of the Ojibwa is to be found in the conceptualization of "persons", and their "social interaction", as the dynamic core of the universe. All persons, moreover, are assumed to be morally responsible for their conduct. Consequently, their behavior is predictable within narrow limits. Order in the world of the Ojibwa is rooted in social organization, in a society of interacting persons with differentiated characteristics and roles, and between whom traditionally established rights and obligations obtain. Ideas of causation, therefore, assume a personalistic guise. Impersonal forces are not operative. What threatens the orderly and predictable interaction of persons and the achievement of *pimädαziwin* on the part of the individual, is the deviant behavior of human beings.

Serious cases of illness, whose actual etiology is unknown, are considered to be the consequence of behavior which departs from expectations. Since individuals are morally responsible for their conduct, deviant and unpredictable behavior is bad conduct, and illness is the penalty for it. The occurrence of illness as an empirical phenomenon thus becomes the focus of a negative sanction because it is a constant reminder of the existence of conduct which is an implicit threat to the social imperatives and primary values of Ojibwa culture, as well as an immediate danger to the life and health of individuals.

But sickness could not operate effectively as a social sanction if the emotional responses to disease situations did not become linked with motivational patterns that reinforce approved conduct, while discouraging deviant conduct. Since disease may, in fact, endanger health and life itself, it can readily generate fear and anxiety on the part of afflicted persons as well as their associates. In the case of the Ojibwa, such emotional responses become qualitatively sharpened, and are made poignant by their belief that sickness is a punishment for wrongdoing.[32] Sickness becomes ego-involved. Feelings

---

[32] On the basis of systematic cross-cultural sampling, Whiting (51) has dis-

of guilt are generated (superego), and shame is experienced when confession of bad conduct has to be made as a first step towards recovery. It is through confession that bad conduct in such highly private relations as those between a man and his *pawáganak*, or in human sexual acts, comes to light. Private, too, are the hostile acts that may have provoked sorcery which, although not confessed, may also generate guilt. From the Ojibwa point of view, there is no escape from the penalty for bad conduct. Children may suffer the consequences of the bad conduct of their parents. An analysis of case material, however, shows that there may be extenuating circumstances.

While we cannot accept either the intellectual content or the objective validity of the world view of the Ojibwa, we cannot fail to recognize the psychological validity of channelling personal conduct in accordance with social imperatives by motivations rooted in anxiety and guilt, and functioning through superego processes.

The unrecognized fallacy in the thinking of the Ojibwa is their conceptualization of illness as a dependent variable in a "lawful" sequence that follows, more or less regularly, from types of interpersonal relations defined by them as bad conduct. They are ignorant of the fact that disease is an independent variable when considered in relation to the social life of man, and human moral values. The intellectual consequences of the discovery of this fact by Western science lie at the core of the difference between the cognitive orientation of the Ojibwa, and that of modern Western civilization.

---

criminated three types of social control, which he relates to three independent motivational systems and the child-rearing processes and conditions required to produce and maintain them. The Ojibwa system—although he has not included these Indians in his study—would appear to conform to his *Type 3,* which is characterized by "the sense of guilt and readiness to accept blame deriving from a sense of personal responsibility for one's actions" (51, p. 194).

REFERENCES

1. Ackerknecht, Erwin H.: Problems of Primitive Medicine. *Bull. Hist. of Med., 11*:503-521, 1942.
2. ———: Primitive Medicine and Culture Pattern. *Bull. Hist. of Med., 12*:545-574, 1942.
3. ———: Primitive Medicine. *Transactions, N.Y. Academy of Sciences* (Series II), *8*:26-37, 1945.
4. ———: Natural Diseases and Rational Treatment in Primitive Medicine. *Bull. Hist. of Med., 19*:467-497, 1946.
5. ———: Primitive Medicine: a contrast with modern practice. *The Merk Report,* July, 1946.
6. ———: *A Short History of Medicine.* New York: Ronald, 1955.
7. ———: Primitive Medicine's Social Function. *Miscellanea Paul Rivet Octogenario Dicta, 1*:3-7, 1958.
8. Albert, Ethel M.: The Classification of Values. A Method and Illustration. *Amer. Anthropologist, 58*:221-248, 1956.
9. Bates, Marston: *The Prevalence of People.* New York: Scribners, 1955.
10. Bidney, David: *Theoretical Anthropology,* New York: Columbia University Press, 1953.
11. Caudill, William: Applied Anthropology in Medicine. In: *Anthropology Today,* Ed. A. L. Kroeber. Chicago: University of Chicago Press, 1953.
12. Clements, Forrest E.: Primitive Concepts of Disease. *University of California Publications in American Archeology and Ethnology,* 32, pp. 185-252, 1932.
13. De Laguna, Grace A.: Cultural Relativism and Science. *Philosophical Rev.,* March, 1942, pp. 141-166.
14. Densmore, Frances: Uses of Plants by the Chippewa Indians. *44th Annual Report, U.S. Bureau of American Ethnology.* Washington: 1928, pp. 275-347.
15. Dockstader, Frederick J.: *Indian Art in America.* Greenwich, Connecticut: New York Graphic Society, 1961.
16. Dunning, R. W.: *Social and Economic Change Among the Northern Ojibwa.* Toronto: University of Toronto Press, 1959.
17. Edel, May and Edel, Abraham: *Anthropology and Ethics.* Springfield, Ill.: Thomas, 1959.
18. French, David: The Relationship of Anthropology to Studies in Perception and Cognition. In: *Psychology: A Study of a*

446   Ojibwa Culture and World View

Science. (Study II, Empirical Substructure and Relations with Other Sciences. Vol. 6, Investigation of Man as Socius.) New York: McGraw-Hill, 1963.

19. Hallowell, A. Irving: The Bulbed Enema Syringe in North America. *Amer. Anthropologist, 37*:708-710, 1935.
20. ———: Sin, Sex and Sickness in Saulteaux Belief. *Brit. J. Med. Psychology, 18*:191-197, 1939.
21. ———: *The Role of Conjuring in Saulteaux Society.* Philadelphia: University of Pennsylvania Press, 1942.
22. ———: *Culture and Experience.* Philadelphia: University of Pennsylvania Press, 1955.
23. ———: Self, Society, and Culture in Phylogenetic Perspective. In: *Evolution After Darwin* (Vol. II, The Evolution of Man, Ed. Sol Tax). Chicago: University of Chicago Press, 1960.
24. ———: Ojibwa Ontology, Behavior, and World View. In: *Culture in History: Essays in Honor of Paul Radin.* New York: Columbia University Press, 1961.
25. Horton, Robin: A Definition of Religion and Its Uses. *J. Royal Anthropological Inst., 90*:201-226, 1960.
26. Jenness, Diamond: *The Ojibwa Indians of Parry Island: Their social and religious life.* Ottawa: Canada Department of Mines, National Museum of Canada, Bulletin 78, Anthropological series 12, 1935.
27. Jones, William: Ojibwa Texts. New York: *Publications of the American Ethnological Society,* vol. 7, part II, 1919.
28. Kluckhohn, Clyde: Universal Categories of Culture. In: *Anthropology Today,* Ed. A. L. Kroeber. Chicago: University of Chicago Press, 1953.
29. Krech, D.: Psychological Theory and Social Psychology. In: *Theoretical Foundations of Psychology,* Ed. H. Helson, New York: Van Nostrand, 1951.
30. ——— and Crutchfield, R. S.: *Theory and Problems of Social Psychology.* New York: McGraw-Hill, 1948.
31. Ladd, John: *The Structure of a Moral Code, A Philosophical Analysis of Ethical Discourse Applied to the Ethics of the Navaho Indians,* Cambridge: Harvard University Press, 1957.
32. Landes, Ruth: *The Ojibwa Woman.* New York: Columbia University Press, 1938.
33. Leary, James Russell: Cultural Variation, Personality, and

Values. *Doctoral Thesis,* in Depart. of Anthropology, Harvard University, 1960.
34. Leeuw, G. van der: *Religion in Essence and Manifestation.* London: Allen and Unwin, 1938.
35. Long, John: *Voyages and Travels of an Indian Interpreter and Trader.* London: 1791.
36. Lovejoy, Arthur O.: *Essays in the History of Ideas.* Baltimore: Johns Hopkins Press, 1948.
37. —— and Boas, George: *Primitivism and Related Ideas in Antiquity.* A Documentary History of Primitivism and Related Ideas (Vol. I). Baltimore: Johns Hopkins Press, 1935.
38. Murdock, George Peter: *Social Structure.* New York: Macmillan, 1949.
39. Parker, Seymour: The Wiitiko Psychosis in the Context of Ojibwa Personality and Culture. *Amer. Anthropologist, 62*:603-623, 1960.
40. Parsons, Talcott and Shils, E. A. (Eds.): *Towards a General Theory of Action.* Cambridge: Harvard University Press, 1951.
41. Radin, Paul: *Primitive Man as Philosopher.* New York: Appleton, 1927.
42. Rather, L. J.: Towards a Philosophical Study of the Idea of Disease. In: *The Historical Development of Physiological Thought.* Eds. Chandler McC. Brooks and Paul F. Cranefield. New York: Hafner, 1959, pp. 351-373.
43. Redfield, Robert: The Primitive World View. *Proceedings, Amer. Philosophical Soc., 96*:30-36, 1952.
44. Ritzenthaler, Robert E.: Chippewa Preoccupation with Health: Change in a Traditional Attitude Resulting from Modern Health Problems. *Bull. Pub. Mus. of the City of Milwaukee, 19*:175-258, 1953.
45. Rivers, W. H. R.: *Medicine, Magic and Religion.* New York: Harcourt, Brace, 1924.
46. Sigerist, Henry E.: *Primitive and Archaic Medicine.* A History of Medicine (Vol. I). New York: Oxford University Press, 1951.
47. Swanton, John R.: Some practical aspects of the study of myths. *J. Amer. Folklore, 23*:1-7, 1910.
48. Teicher, Morton I.: *Windigo Psychosis, A Study of a Relationship between Belief and Behavior among the Indians of*

Northeastern Canada (American Ethnological Society). Seattle: University of Washington Press, 1960.

49. Warren, Howard C.: *Dictionary of Psychology.* Boston: Houghton-Mifflin, 1934.

50. Whiting, Beatrice B.: *Paiute Sorcery.* Viking Fund Publications in Anthropology No. 15, 1950.

51. Whiting, John W. M.: Sorcery, Sin, and the Superego. A Cross-cultural Study of Some Mechanisms of Social Control. In: *Nebraska Symposium on Motivation* (1959), (Ed., Marshall R. Jones). Lincoln, Nebr.: University of Nebraska Press, 1959, pp. 174-195.

52. —— and Child, Irwin L.: *Child Training and Personality: A Cross-Cultural Study.* New Haven: Yale University Press, 1953.

53. Willey, Basil: *The Seventeenth Century Background.* New York: Doubleday (Anchor), 1953.

The Role of Dreams in Ojibwa Culture
1966

While dreaming has long been taken for granted
as a commonplace human phenomenon, recent experimental observations in the, laboratory have supplied
firmer empirical evidence of its universality, particularly
since objective quantitative measures of the frequency
and amount of time consumed by dreaming in laboratory subjects are now available. Among other things, it
has been demonstrated that the total amount of time
devoted to dreaming during any single night is much
greater than previously realized. Dreams reported following a night of sleep offer no precise measure of
dreaming time since most of the dreams experienced of
individuals are never recalled.[1] On the other hand, a
high percentage of dream recall is possible when subjects
under experimental observation are awakened. Dement, moreover, has advanced the hypothesis that since
experimental curtailment produces such phenomena as
anxiety, irritability, and so on, "a certain amount of
dreaming each night is a necessity."[2] If this hypothesis
is substantiated, it may turn out that we can assume

[1] See Dement and Kleitman, 1957; Kleitman, 1960; Wolpert and
Trosman, 1958.
[2] Dement, 1960.

that dreaming is not only a universal human experience but that it is vitally linked with man's psychobiological functioning and his distinctive level, perhaps, of behavioral adaptation.[3]

Since *Homo sapiens,* as contemporarily observed, is the end product of a long process of hominid evolution, it may be possible in the future to consider the phenomenon of dreaming in this wider evolutionary perspective. Although direct observations of early hominids can never be made, it would be interesting to know whether systematic observations on living infrahuman primates would yield any of the objective indicators of dreaming which have been observed in man. I should like to suggest, speculative though it may be, that a consideration of dreams in an evolutionary frame of reference has important anthropological implications that are closely related to a revitalization of interest in man's behavioral evolution. For it is becoming increasingly clear that the problems presented by hominid evolution no longer can be focused exclusively in the area concerned with the study of the structural changes that occurred. It is necessary to take into account all the complex and interrelated variables that made possible not only the emergence of *Homo sapiens* considered as a zoological species, but concomitantly to consider the development of language and the cultural mode of adaptation which distinguish the behavior of the euhominids (i.e., the subfamily Hominidae) from earlier hominid species and other primates. Linguistic communication and cultural adaptation may be interpreted as the culminating stage of anciently established modes of organized social living in which protolinguistic and protocultural levels of social organization represent earlier evolutionary levels. A fact often overlooked is that structural changes, such as the erect posture that distinguishes the earliest hominids from related primate groups, and the expansion of the brain that characterizes the later hominids, occurred in animals typified by the fact that they lived in discretely organized social groups. Consequently the interplay and cumulative effects of such structural changes must have been fed back into the systems of social action that existed and, in time, modified social behavior and prepared the way for later developments.[4]

[3] In the course of the Fifth Conference on Problems of Consciousness, held in 1954, Kleitman said at one point in the discussion (1955, p. 114): "I am quite sure you need a cortex for dreaming." If this is so, the question may be asked whether the *expansion* of the cortex in the course of hominid evolution did not introduce a differential factor of importance with respect to the level of dream functioning that we find in the later and more evolved hominids. Early hominids, or other primates, may have experienced dreaming but, if the cortex is given special emphasis, it would be interesting to know how its expansion influenced dreaming.

[4] For a more detailed discussion of the behavioral evolution of man, see Hallowell, 1960.

I have made this brief excursion into the behavioral evolution of man because it seems to me that the same condition that made possible the development of a new behavioral plateau, characterized by language and fully developed forms of cultural adaptation, was also that which enabled dreams, visions, and products of imaginative processes to be articulated, and thus to assume the social significance we find in *Homo sapiens*.[5] Dreaming may have occurred in the early hominids, but, without the psychological potentialities fully released only with the expansion of the hominid brain, it would not have been possible for the content of dreams or the products of imaginative processes to have been communicated to others. It will be recalled that Mrs. Hayes observed the homebred Viki playing with an imaginary pull toy. This was inferred from Viki's overt behavior. "Viki was at the pull-toy stage when a child is forever trailing some toy on a string . . . dragging wagons, shoes, dolls . . . [Viki's] body assumed just this angle." Viki herself had no means of representing and articulating the content of her imaginative processes and communicating them to Mrs. Hayes.[6]

The development and elaboration of cultural adaptation in the hominids implies a psychological restructuralization. It led to the development of a personality structure in which ego-centered processes and self-awareness became prime characteristics. Until this psychological level was reached memories of dreams could not be recalled and integrated with other self-related experiences. But, once in possession of psychological capacities, which made symbolic modes of personal expression and communication possible, the inner life of individuals could take on a new personal significance and be communicated to others through verbal and graphic means. The inner world of private experience and the outer world of publicly shared experience now became intricately meshed through symbolic representation. Unconscious psychological forces, hitherto latent in hominid evolution, but now mediated through dreams, visions, and other imaginative processes, intruded themselves upon man, because of

[5] Beres (1960), departing from the everyday usage "which makes imagination a phenomenon associated with creativity and unreality, beyond the realm of ordinary thought processes," defines it as a "process whose *products* are images, symbols, fantasies, dreams, ideas, thoughts, and concepts." He considers imagination to be "a ubiquitous component of human psychic activity unique to man. . . ." He views it as "a complex psychic function, itself the resultant of a group of ego functions, that enters into all aspects of human psychic activity—normal mentation, pathological processes, and artistic creativity. . . . Reality is a relative, indeterminate concept, influenced by the imaginative processes in man." Thus "imagination is not opposed to reality, but has as one of its most important applications, adaptation to reality."

[6] See Hayes, 1951, chap. 11, p. 81, and comments in Hallowell, 1960, p. 354.

his evolving capacity for self-awareness and the knowledge he could acquire of the inner life of other persons. Dream experiences could become the object of reflective thought and become socially significant. Varied interpretations of the meaning of dreams could become an integral part of the diversified world views that arose and became embedded in traditional cultural systems.

When we assume that contemporary individuals in our society are able to recall and report dreams, we are postulating psychological capacities and an evolutionary level of communication and cultural adaptation that did not exist at the earliest levels of hominid evolution. The capacity for recalling, communicating, and identifying "more or less coherent imagery sequences during sleep" as a "dream" not only implies complex psychological functions, but a culturally defined attitude toward a particular kind of subjective experience. We assume the existence of a sense of the continuity of a self in time and a capacity for objectifying self-related experience. We take it for granted that the subject associates memory images recalled from his period of sleep with a continuing self in the same way that memory images from past experience when awake can be recalled and self-related.

While dreams in our culture are recognized as self-related, the manifest content of dream experiences is not fully integrated with memories of past experiences while awake. Dream experiences are not considered to be of the same order. A dichotomy exists in our thinking. The world of dreams is considered to be a world of unreality, imagery, and fantasy, as compared with the "real" world of perception. The dreams I report are recognized as mine, but they are not considered the equivalent of other personal experiences. In the cognitive orientation of individuals in other cultures, however, such a sharp dichotomy may not exist, or may exist only to a lesser degree. Dream experiences may be interpreted, in some cases, as the literal equivalent of the experiences of individuals when fully awake. Indeed, the psychological depth of this attitude is attested by the fact that even in acculturated individuals, the "reality" of dreams may persist.

Devereux, for example, refers to the case of a highly educated Plains Indian who was once a patient of his. When this man "realized that the florist's delivery wagon of which he had dreamed represented the counselor, he quite spontaneously, though with an air of half-humorous shamefacedness, asked the counselor where he went after he disappeared from the patient's dream." Devereux also mentions a group of Papuan natives who, having been converted to the Catholic faith, were "sufficiently well indoctrinated to know that they were not 'morally' responsible for the content of their dreams." Nevertheless, their priest discovered that when they frequently confessed adultery, "the adultery occurred merely in dream." [7]

Dorothy Eggan has pointed out that, viewed in cross-cultural perspective, dreams "can be considered both a projection of the personality and a reflection of the culture," so that in this frame of reference depth analysis of dreams is only a single facet of the area of dream study. Dreams may "not only [be] remembered and told," she says, but likewise may become "an active force in cultural conditioning and personality expression." And, functioning in response to varying cultural concepts, they "can operate in one direction as a sanction for witchcraft, murder and cannibalism, and in the opposite direction to maintain group unity and individual equilibrium. . . ." [8]

What I wish to do here is to show how the dream experience of a group of North American Indians, the Ojibwa, interpreted as actual experiences of the self, functioned as a positive factor in the operation of their aboriginal sociocultural system. In this case we have an interesting example of a mode of cultural adaptation in which man's capacity for dreaming has been made an integral part of the life adjustment of a people who faced the harsh realities of a northern environment in which subsistence depended upon hunting, fishing, and gathering. If dreaming may be considered to be a necessity at the individual level of psychobiological adjustment, here, at the level of group adaptation, the Ojibwa interpretation of dreams may be seen as a positive and necessary factor in the maintenance of the sociocultural system that gives meaning to their lives. Imaginative processes linked with traditional values play a vital role in psychocultural adaptation.

The northern Ojibwa represent a regional branch of a widely distributed group of Algonquin-speaking Indians in the United States and Canada, perhaps numbering 50,000 in all. When first reported in the Jesuit *Relations* of 1640, they appear to have occupied a much more restricted area in the region north of the Great Lakes. Their association with the Sault Sainte Marie led to their designation as Saulteurs by the French fur-traders, a name which, in its Anglicized form, Salteaux, is still applied to them in Canada. A form of the term Ojibwa is an equally early name for them. In the United States their designation as Chippewa is derived from the fact that the Bureau of American Ethnology officially adopted this term, a corruption of Ojibwa.

What I say here applies primarily to the northern group of Ojibwa I have studied at first hand. Located east of Lake Winnipeg along the

[7] Devereux, 1951, p. 86.
[8] Eggan, 1961, pp. 552, 554.

Berens River in the eastern part of the province of Manitoba and western
Ontario, at approximately 52° N. Lat., these Ojibwa retained much of
their aboriginal system of beliefs until recent years. During the period
of my fieldwork (1930–1940) for example, there was one band that had
not yet become entirely Christianized. The relative conservatism of the
Ojibwa east of Lake Winnipeg is partly the result of the fact that, unlike many other North American Indians, they were able to retain their
native ecological adjustment as hunters and fishermen. The physical environment inhabited by them was not fitted for agriculture or settlement,
and the white population has remained extremely sparse.

I shall not deal with the changing aspects of their culture here
but endeavor rather to present the substantive aspects of their outlook
upon the world as it was constituted for them by their aboriginal culture.[9]

Man's cultural adaptation everywhere embodies a cognitive orientation that makes life meaningful and establishes a blueprint for action. A
psychological field, or behavioral environment, is structured for the individual. Traditional beliefs, knowledge, concepts, and values mediate personal adjustment to a culturally defined world.[10] It is in these terms that
events become intelligible to human individuals. A world view is created
which establishes the ultimate premises for all that is involved in any
comprehensive explanation of the nature of events in the universe and
man's relation to them. "Of all that is connoted by 'culture,'" says Redfield, "'world view' attends especially to the way a man, in a particular
society, sees himself in relation to all else. It is the properties of existence
as distinguished from and related to the self. It is, in short, a man's idea
of the universe. It is that organization of ideas which answer to a man
the questions: Where am I? Among whom do I move? What are my
relations to things?"[11]

The culturally defined attitude toward dreams which we find
among different peoples is often a direct clue to the basic premises of their
world view. Among other things, it provides insight into how what we
are accustomed to designate as "objective" and "subjective" phenomena
are sharply differentiated, fused, or blurred. It will be recalled that
Tylor, in his *Researches into the Early History of Mankind* spoke of the
life of primitive man as resembling "a long dream."[12] And, in his *Primitive Culture,* he referred to the "vivid and intense belief in the objective
reality of the human spectres" which peoples at lower levels of culture
"see in sickness, exhaustion, or excitement. . . . Even in healthy waking

[9] See Hallowell, 1955, chap. 5, "The Northern Ojibwa."
[10] See Hallowell, 1955, chap. 4, "The Self and Its Behavioral Environment."
[11] Redfield, 1952, p. 30.
[12] Tylor, 1878, p. 137.

life," he says, "the savage or barbarian has never learned to make that rigid distinction between imagination and reality, to enforce which is one of the main results of scientific education." [13]

What I should like to emphasize here is the fact that it is inconceivable that man could have evolved without making *some* distinction between dreams, or visions, and the objective realities of his actual physical environment. Man could not have developed the tools and techniques for which we have ample evidence in the archaeological record if this were not so. What should not be overlooked is that the intrusion of dreams upon man's consciousness and the exercise of imaginative processes of all kinds did not overwhelm him or submerge him in a totally subjective world. Early man became endowed with capacities that enabled him to absorb such experiences and, through his creative imagination, to integrate them with an apprehension of the actual properties of the objects in his actual environment. This human capacity is reflected in the world view of different peoples when we examine and compare the cultural patterning of the polarity we characterize as "objective-subjective." Too often conceived as a simple linear continuum, I believe that the basic principle involved has been stated by MacLeod. He points out that "subjectivity and objectivity are properties of an organized perceptual field in which points of reference are selves (subjects) and objects, and the degree of articulation in this dimension may vary greatly." [14] This variation is a function, in part, of the outlook upon the world provided the individual by his culture. It is through concepts pertaining to the nature of the self, and to the nature of the objects in the universe other than self, that the individual receives his basic psychological orientation.

Ojibwa culture defines a psychological field of conduct for individuals in which their cognitive orientation—in the dimension of self to other—is elaborated with particular emphasis upon the interaction of "persons" in a "society" that is cosmic in scope. The participating individuals of this "great society" manifest differential personal characteristics and play various roles, but they are unified by traditionally established rights and obligations. There are two categories of the "person" class which can be differentiated: human beings and other-than-human persons. While animals, plants, and inanimate objects constitute other classes of being in the Ojibwa world, "persons" are the focal point of their ontology and the key to the psychological unity and dynamics of their outlook. This aspect of their metaphysics of being permeates the content of their cognitive processes; perceiving, remembering, imagining, conceiving, judging, and reasoning. Nor can the motivation of much of

[13] Tylor, 1874, I, 445.
[14] MacLeod, 1947.

their conduct be thoroughly understood without taking into account the relation of their central values and goals to the constant awareness they have of the existence of other-than-human as well as human persons in their world. "Persons," too, are so inextricably associated with notions of causality that, in order to understand their appraisal of events and the kind of behavior demanded in situations as they define them, we are constantly confronted with the role of "persons" as loci of causality in the dynamics of their universe. For, by and large, the Ojibwa make no cardinal use of any of the concepts of impersonal forces as major determinants of events. Thus it is within an intricate web of social relations with other-than-human, as well as human persons, that the Ojibwa individual strives for *pimädazïwin*, life in the fullest sense.[15]

Whereas social relations with human beings belong to the sphere of waking life, the most intimate social interaction with other-than-human persons is experienced chiefly, but not exclusively, by the self in dream. Social interaction in terms of the Ojibwa outlook involves no vital distinction between self-related experience when awake and experiences during sleep which are recalled and self-related. There is no sharply defined differentiation between subjectivity and objectivity here. The culturally accepted patterning overrides any such polarity. At the same time, dream experiences are not confused with events when awake. Qualitative differences are recognized as well as the fact that the kind of persons who play the major role in dreams are not those with whom the individual is most concerned in waking life. On the other hand, it should be noted that the Ojibwa are expert hunters whose reliable knowledge of the "real" properties of the fauna of their physical environment, as well as other resources, is highly impressive. Important as dreams are when considered with reference to their world view and the functioning of their sociocultural system, the Ojibwa cannot actually be said to live in a world of dreams.

What kind of entities, then, comprise the other-than-human class of persons of the Ojibwa world? I have used this somewhat awkward term in order to avoid applying the label "supernatural" to them. The concept of the "natural," ambiguous as it often is when used in Western culture,[16] is certainly not indigenous to Ojibwa thought. Consequently, the use of the term "supernatural" doubly distorts their outlook. Supernatural is an easily applied cliché but its descriptive accuracy, when introduced into discussion of the cognitive orientation of non-Western peoples, is highly

---

[15] Cf. Hallowell, 1961.
[16] Many years ago Lovejoy observed that the "word 'nature' is probably the most equivocal in the vocabulary of the European peoples . . ." (see Lovejoy and Boas, 1935, p. 12; Lovejoy, 1948, p. 69).

questionable.[17] Bidney, among others, has pointed out that "the dichotomy of the natural and supernatural implies a scientific epistemology and critical, metaphysical sophistication which must not be assumed without reliable evidence." [18]

A few selected examples must suffice to illustrate the *types* of *other-than-human* objects or personified natural objects. They are thought of as persons; they may be addressed as such, and interaction with them is cast in a personal mode. In an anecdote I recorded, it is recounted how two old men at dawn vied with each other in influencing the sun's movements:

> The first old man said to his companion: "It is about sunrise now and there is a clear sky. You tell Sun to rise at once." So the other old man said to Sun: "My grandfather, come up quickly." As soon as he had said this, Sun came up into the sky like a shot. "Now you try something," he said to his companion. "See if you can send it down." So the other man said to Sun: "My grandfather, put your face down again." When he said this, Sun went down again. "I have more power than you," he said to his companion, "Sun never goes down once it comes up."

In a myth, an other-than-human person once set a snare in the path that Sun regularly traveled. Sun was caught and could not move; darkness continued until Sun was released by an animal sent by human persons who could not carry on their daily activities in the darkness. In this myth, the movements of Sun are those of a person, not a natural object subject to impersonal forces. In the anecdote, the "natural" movement of the sun is reversed by the command of a human being. When Sun appears in the dream of a human person he addresses the dreamer by the reciprocal term used by the old men, that is, my grandchild. These brief examples give the flavor of the Ojibwa outlook; they illustrate the occurrence of "social" interaction between the "persons" of the Ojibwa universe,"[19]

[17] With respect to the general applicability of the natural-supernatural dichotomy to primitive cultures see van der Leeuw, 1938, pp. 544–545. Ackerknecht (1958, p. 53) says: " 'Supernaturalistic,' though often used by the best authorities, is quite obviously a misnomer for these primitive representations, as it presupposes the notion of the predictable natural which primitives characteristically do not have. This notion of natural is a much later invention. I have been as prone to use 'supernatural' in some of my earlier writings as others have."

[18] Bidney, 1953, p. 166.

[19] Radin (1924, p. 518) records an anecdote that refers to a man who had dreamed of the "thunder-spirit." "When he wanted to make lightning he used to sing a song praising the thunder-spirit. Then when he had finished singing, he would cut up some tobacco, put some into the fire and some into his pipe. Then he would shout in the direction of the south, 'Let thunder come!' The next day there would be a tremendous thunder storm."

and they demonstrate the unity in thought which prevails in anecdote, myth, and dream.

The Winds are conceptualized as siblings, and there is a myth referring to their birth from an anthropomorphic mother. The directions of the Ojibwa cosmos are defined by their dwelling places, that is, the homes of these other-than-human persons. Another typical subcategory of other-than-human person comprises the "owners" or "masters" of what we term natural species of plants and animals. There is a "master" of birch trees, and of bears. If animals, like the bear, are not treated properly after being killed, the master may take offense and retaliate by withholding members of the species from the hunter.

The Thunderbirds represent another type of personage. They live in a land above the flat earth that is the dwelling place of human persons, that is, *änicinabék* (the Ojibwa). The Thunderbirds are classified with the hawks, of which there are several natural species known to the Ojibwa. In a myth, a human being reaches Thunderbird Land where he immediately finds himself at home. These creatures hunt and talk and dance. Besides this, the young man is enabled to find his place in their kinship system at once because it is precisely the same as that of the Ojibwa. He marries a Thunderbird girl. Later she and her sisters return to earth with him and her sisters marry his brothers, a pattern that often occurs among the Ojibwa. In one case in my genealogies six blood brothers were married to a sorority of six sisters.

Although the Thunderbirds are primarily conceived as avian in form, their outward appearance is not constant. In the myth, metamorphosis occurs as part of the plot. Some of them become anthropomorphic in appearance. Here we come close to the metaphysical core of the Ojibwa conception of being. Outward appearance is actually superficial. Although the Thunderbirds, like other entities of the other-than-human category, have distinctive attributes of their own, they have the same basic, enduring essence as do human persons. It is this vital core that is constant in both categories of persons. Human persons, too, have a constant and enduring essence (*òtcatcákwin*) and a bodily form (*mìyó*) which, under most circumstances, is an identifying characteristic. But in neither category of the person class is the inner essence accessible to *visual* perception under any conditions. What can be perceived visually is only the aspect of being that has form. As we shall see later, metamorphosis, under certain conditions, is also possible for human beings. Change in outward appearance is potentially inherent in individuals belonging to both categories of persons. Consequently, the metamorphosis of the Thunderbird girls in the myth, and their marriage to human beings, can be accepted by the Ojibwa as an actual event in the kind of world to which they are culturally oriented. It is not a fanciful event attributable only to fictitious characters in an alien world of myth. I was once told of an Ojibwa woman (identifiable in my genealogies) who claimed that North Wind was the father of one of her children. My informant said he did not believe this; nevertheless, he thought it would have been accepted as a possibility in the past.[20]

The kind of social interaction possible between human and other-than-human persons in the context of daily life is illustrated by another anecdote. An informant told me that once on a summer afternoon during a storm he was sitting in a tent with a very old man and his wife. There was one clap of thunder after another. Suddenly, the old man turned to his wife and asked, "Did you hear what was said?" "No," she replied, "I didn't catch it." My informant, an acculturated Indian, told me that at first he did not know what the old man and his wife referred to. It was, of course, the thunder. The old man thought that one of the Thunderbirds had said something to him. He was reacting to this sound in the same way as he would respond to a human being whose words he did not at once understand. The casualness of the remark demonstrates the psychological reality of the social relations with other-than-human persons that may become explicit in the behavior of the Ojibwa as a consequence of the cognitive "set" induced by their culture. I may add that, implicit in this anecdote is the assumption that the old man must have had previous contact with a Thunderbird in the dreams of his puberty fast. This explains why he thought he was addressed. By and large, the Ojibwa do not attune themselves to receiving messages every time a thunderstorm occurs!

Another occasion when social interaction becomes possible between human and other-than-human persons is at a conjuring performance (ḳosábandamowin). Its purpose is to secure help from other-than-human persons by invoking their presence and communicating human desires to them. A barrel-like framework of poles is built and covered with birchbark or canvas. The conjurer enters the structure after dark; the audience gathers outside. The conjurer invokes his particular benefactors among the host of other-than-human persons. They manifest themselves vocally, the voices issuing from the lodge being distinguishable from each other and from the voice of the conjurer who kneels within. These invoked entities may sometimes sing a song and name themselves. The Master of the moose may say: "Moose I am called." The lodge is in almost constant movement from the time the conjurer enters it. The Winds are responsi-

---

[20] This may have been a rationalization of mother-son incest. But, if so, the woman's "bad conduct" was never punished by sickness, nor did she ever confess her wrongdoing. These circumstances may have lent credence to her claim, when considered in the context of the Ojibwa world view.

ble for this. Direct communication sometimes takes place between members of the audience and some of the other-than-human persons present. At one performance I attended several members of the audience called for Mikīnák, the Great Turtle. Anyone may speak to Mikīnák and he always has a witty answer ready. He talks in a throaty nasal voice not unlike that of Donald Duck. His popularity with the audience was manifested throughout the evening by the intermittent stream of repartee that took place between Mikīnák and members of the audience. He strikes a note of levity in performances that are basically very serious in purpose.

One of the major sources of information about other-than-human persons, both to the Ojibwa themselves and to the investigator, are the myths. From the Ojibwa point of view they are not fiction. On the contrary, they narrate the past activities of well-known other-than-human persons who are their chief characters. The attitude toward myth exemplified in Ojibwa culture is essentially generalized by Eliade when he says that "it is the foundation of a structure of reality as well as a kind of human behavior. A myth always narrates something as having *really happened,* as an event that took place, in the plain sense of the term. . . . Myths reveal the structure of reality, and the multiple modalities of being in the world. . . . They disclose the *true* stories, concern themselves with the *realities*." [21] In the context of their aboriginal culture, myths among the Ojibwa were only told during the long winter evenings by a narrator who dramatized them by gestures and other appropriate actions. These occasions were, in fact, a kind of invocation. The characters of myth, immortal living persons, were thought to come and listen to what was being said. In ancient times, one of these entities (Wisekedjak) is reputed to have said to the others: "We'll try to make everything to suit the *änicinabék* as long as any of them exist, so that they will never forget us and will always talk about us." Whereas we are inclined to think of myths as a special class of stories, the Ojibwa term for them—*ätisokának*—has no such connotation. It refers, rather, to the characters themselves, so that as William Jones said many years ago, "Myths are thought of as conscious beings, with powers of thought and action." [22] Consequently there is conclusive linguistic evidence of the category to which the characters in these belong. Along with other persons of the other-than-human category they are collectively referred to by the Ojibwa as "our grandfathers." This attests both to their psychological status as persons while, at the same time, it brings them within the boundaries of a social system in which everyone is given a kinship status. On account of the repeated recitation of myths winter after winter, children growing up in Ojibwa society be-

[21] Eliade, 1960, pp. 14–15.
[22] W. Jones, 1919, Part II, p. 574 n.

came almost as familiar with their other-than-human grandfathers as they did with their human grandfathers.[23] They also heard the voices of the former at conjuring performances.[24] Furthermore, the individuality of other-than-human beings became reinforced by the fact that a character like Mikīnák always was heard to speak in the same characteristic manner whether in the narration of myths or in the shaking tent. Thus the reality of these characters did not depend upon conceptualization alone; their image was strongly reinforced by actual perceptual experience.

Any members of the other-than-human category of persons might appear in the dreams of Ojibwa individuals. In this context they were usually referred to as *pawáganak*, which may be rendered "dream visitors." Their appearance in the dreams was, of course, not as strangers or unfamiliar figures but as well-known living entities of the Ojibwa world. It is scarcely to be expected, then, that interpersonal relations with them in dreams could be dissociated from the knowledge of them which already existed in other contexts. Such relations could not be interpreted as other than experiences of the self. But dream experiences brought the individual into intimate personal contact with particular other-than-human persons. Besides this, the role that this category of persons played in those experiences was culturally defined as immensely vital to the welfare of the individual.

DREAMS, MOTIVATION, AND
THE SOCIOCULTURAL SYSTEM

Having considered the world view of the Ojibwa, I now analyze the relations between dreams, the motivation of individuals, and the functioning of their sociocultural system. I already have indicated that, for the Ojibwa, social relations with other-than-human persons are not metaphorical but intimately meshed in their thought and experience with interrelationships between human beings. I have referred to a few examples which show how social relations with other-than-human persons

[23] I was told that on the winter evenings when myths were narrated children were encouraged to dream about their other-than-human grandfathers. That they may well have done so is suggested by the fact that C. W. Kimmis has called attention to the influence of stories read to children before going to sleep upon the content of their dreams. See quotations from Kimmis in Woods, 1947.

[24] I once asked an informant who was about seventy years old to name all the other-than-human persons he had heard speak, or sing, in conjuring performances (see Hallowell, 1942, for the list). They included five characters who play a prominent role in myth; four other personages semihuman in form; and almost two dozen of the "masters" of various animal species.

may enter the waking consciousness of human beings. Dreams, however, assume a special significance in any analysis of the functioning of the Ojibwa sociocultural system because the dream imagery that is interpreted as bringing the individual into direct face-to-face contact with other-than-human persons becomes so intimately linked with the motivation of individuals, traditional values, and social behavior. Contacts with other-than-human entities are highly motivated and sought by individuals as a means of achieving a personal life adjustment consonant with the characteristic values of the Ojibwa world. At the same time, dream experiences have significance with relation to the social system and community life because they are not only influential components of actual conduct but because they validate specialized services, like curing, which become available to other persons.

It must likewise be noted that interpersonal relations between human and other-than-human beings involve reciprocal rights and obligations, in the same way that social relations between human persons do. And these obligations are reinforced by the same sanctions that apply to social relations between human beings. Failure to fulfill them, in either case, is one variety of "bad conduct," bad conduct being culturally defined as any unpredictable or deviant conduct that fails to conform with the traditional normative standards of interpersonal relations. The penalty for bad conduct is illness. Any kind of bad conduct on my part is said to "follow me." I will inevitably become ill, or my children may get sick, or my wife may die. The fear of becoming ill and the anxiety engendered by any serious sickness is the major sanction of the Ojibwa sociocultural system. What is particularly characteristic is the fact that the bad conduct of human beings is believed to be the major source of illness. Consequently in every case of serious sickness an individual must reflect upon what kind of misdeeds he may have been responsible for in the past. Even in cases of sorcery the reputed act of the sorcerer is interpreted as retaliation for some previous bad conduct on the part of the *victim* in his interpersonal relations with the sorcerer.[25]

In this society no institutionalized means exist for the public adjudication of disputes or personal conflicts of any kind. There is no way in which publicly sanctioned punishments can be initiated in cases of incest, murder, or other offenses. For adults there are no superordinate modes of social control. Nor do other-than-human persons, any more than human beings, sit in judgment upon the acts of the latter and initiate punishment. Other-than-human entities exercise no punishing role; their relations to man are benevolent. If a human being fails to fulfill any obligation to them, sickness "follows him" as a matter of course. Social control

---

[25] For a detailed discussion of Ojibwa world view and disease, see Hallowell, 1963.

in Ojibwa society conforms to the type that Whiting describes as operating through the mechanism of conscience or superego.[26] It involves a highly developed sense of personal responsibility for one's own conduct, sensitivity to guilt, and readiness to accept blame for one's actions. Consequently, it is necessary that the Ojibwa individual be groomed for independent action, associated with the capacity for bearing a heavy burden of moral responsibility, acquired through self-discipline. At the same time he needs to develop an inner sense of personal security in order to face the vicissitudes of life. This applies particularly to males who, being the hunters, are responsible for supplying the daily needs of their families.

A central value correlative with the Ojibwa food-gathering economy is the emphasis laid upon what may be called "equalitarian" values; these serve to equilibrate the distribution and consumption of goods in a system where purchase in a market is absent. They are expressed through sharing, borrowing, and mutual exchange. Dependence upon hunting, trapping, and fishing for a living is precarious at best and, even though the individual hunter may exercise his best skills, it is impossible to accumulate food for the inevitable rainy day. As a result, if I have more than I need today, I share it with you because I know that you, in turn, will share what you have with me tomorrow. In Ojibwa society there are no culturally structured incentives that induce individuals to surpass their fellows in the accumulation of material goods. No one is expected to have much more than anyone else, except temporarily.

It is particularly important to recognize that sharing what one has with others is a value that permeates the "great society" in which the Ojibwa live. This is the reason why the Ojibwa expect that powers possessed by other-than-human persons will be shared with them. Beings of the other-than-human category, considered as persons, are believed to be oriented to the same values and to be motivated like themselves. Other-than-human beings have more power than they need. From the Ojibwa point of view they may be said to have a surplus of power, so that it is legitimate to induce them to share it with human beings in order to meet the latter's needs.

The Ojibwa believe that a good life, free from illness, hunger, and misfortune (i.e., *pīmǎdazīwin*) cannot be achieved through relations with other human beings alone, cooperative as they may be. The help of powerful persons of the other-than-human category is a necessity, especially for

---

[26] On the basis of systematic cross-cultural sampling, Whiting (1959) has discriminated three types of social control, which he related to three independent motivational systems and the child-rearing practices and conditions required to produce and maintain them. Although he did not include the Ojibwa in his study, they would appear to conform to Whiting's Type 3.

men. Women may obtain such help but men cannot get along without it. Since the Masters of the game animals, for instance, control the most vital source of food supply, a man needs contact with them. His own acquired skill as a hunter and trapper is not all that is required. With the help of powerful other-than-human persons a man can also defend himself against human beings hostile to him. Besides this, every special aptitude—such as curing and conjuring—exercised by men, depends upon the help of other-than-human entities, rather than upon their own individual talents or efforts. Furthermore, other-than-human persons of any functional significance were males, a fact correlative with patrilineal descent in Ojibwa culture and the subordinate role that women played in ceremonial life, and in such specialized activities as conjuring and curing.

THE DREAM FAST

The help that men needed from males of the other-than-human category was primarily obtained in a lonely vigil through personal face-to-face contact with them in dreams. The grandfather of one of my informants said to him: "You will have a long and good life if you dream well." In aboriginal days it was customary to send boys between the ages of ten and fifteen out to fast for six or seven nights. They became suppliants in need of help; they were said to provoke the "pity" of their other-than-human grandfathers.[27] Coming to their aid these *pawáganak* "blessed" them, as English-speaking informants phrase it, by offering to share their knowledge and power.

A boy undergoing a dream fast was called *k̇igúsämo*. The essential condition for this experience was that he be *pékize,* that is, pure, clean. He must never have had sexual intercourse. Even less intimate relations with women before, during, and immediately after fasting were considered contaminating and were to be avoided. If he had not met these conditions

---

[27] Blumensohn, in his survey, points out that "the use of fasting in a personal relation with the supernatural was peculiar to the Central Algonkian" (1933, p. 468). "They believed that by fasting the suppliant underwent such suffering, made himself so weak, that the spirits were overcome with pity, and so granted him whatever he desired" (p. 451). Kohl, visiting the Lake Superior Ojibwa over a century ago, was fascinated with the dream fast. "I found this subject most remarkable," he writes (1860, p. 228), "in fact, could it be possible to hear any thing stronger, or, I might say, more wonderful, than these stories of unheard of castigations and torments, to which young boys of thirteen or fourteen subject themselves, merely for the sake of an idea, a dream, or the fulfillment of a religious duty, or to ask a question of fate. . . . What courage! What self control! What power of enduring privation does this presuppose!"

no other-than-human person would bless him or even approach him. Anecdotes are told to illustrate the importance of keeping such taboos. Boys
were sent out in the spring to some distance from the camp. One informant said he was about thirteen years old at the time. A boy's clothes
were carefully washed beforehand and he was provided with a new
blanket. A moose or caribou skin, dyed with red ochre or sometimes
painted with pictographs, was given him to lie on. Prior to his departure
the boy slept in the "cleanest" place in the dwelling, that is, toward the
rear, in the area reserved for the men. Before this he had slept nearer the
front with his mother and other prepuberal children. This shift in sleeping quarters symbolized his segregation from the women and his approach to manhood.

When a boy is ready to depart for his dream fast he is accompanied
into the bush by his father, grandfather, or other male relatives. When
they arrive at a desirable spot a "nest" (*wázisan*) is built. In the case of
the informant mentioned, an older brother built it. The *wázisan* is a
platform made by laying poles across the branches of a tree, about 15 feet
from the ground. The *kigúsämo* climbs the tree and seats himself, or
stretches out, on this platform. It was forbidden to descend to the ground
during the dream fast except to urinate and defecate. No food or drink
must pass his lips. My informant said that his dream fast had lasted ten
nights. "While I was there," he said, "I only thought of the good things
I wanted for myself. I thought of nothing evil."

During the period when a boy was fasting alone in the forest, his
father or grandfather might drum and sing continually in order to
strengthen and help him. It may be mentioned in passing that many songs
of the Ojibwa are not composed in the ordinary sense, but are the consequences of dream experiences.[28] Thus, older male relatives of the
kigúsämo may invoke, or communicate with, their own other-than-human
tutelaries at the same time that the boy is undergoing his first personal
contacts with such entities. When the fast is ended the *kigúsämo* usually
returns to camp shortly after daybreak. He hides in the bushes nearby and
signals his presence by a whistle, or call, his father knows. The latter goes
immediately to him and brings him to camp. The purpose of this procedure is to avoid being seen by a woman first. This would endanger the
boy's blessings.

Many years ago Paul Radin published a sample of dreams from the
dream fasts of Ojibwa boys. It should be emphasized, as Radin pointed
out, that all the dreams of this type which we have on record were told
by adults in later life, in some cases, filtered through another person. We

---

[28] Densmore, 1910, p. 118.

have no information whatever on dreams obtained immediately or even a short time after the dream fast itself.[29] I believe, nevertheless, that the general outlines of the basic cultural patterning of such dreams is known to us. Since recounting experiences in a dream fast violated an obligation to *pawáganak*, no investigator who had been present when aboriginal culture was flourishing could have obtained such material. Although I was not able to add very much to the scanty corpus of published examples, discussion with informants confirmed the general pattern exhibited by Radin's sample. There are, however, a few points with regard to the content of dream experience on which I wish to comment.

In one dream I collected, a *pawágan* first appeared to a boy in anthropomorphic guise. Later, this being said, "Grandchild, I think you are strong enough now to go with me." Then the *pawágan* began dancing and, as he danced, he turned into what looked like a golden eagle, that is, the Master of this species. Glancing down at his own body, the boy noticed that it was covered with feathers. The Great Eagle spread its wings and flew off toward the south. The *kigúsämo* then spread his wings and followed.[30] In this case we find the instability of outward form in both human and other-than-human persons succinctly dramatized. Individuals of both categories undergo metamorphosis. In later life the boy will recall that in his dream fast he himself became transformed into a bird. This does not imply that subsequent to his dream fast the boy can transform himself into a golden eagle at will. But it does demonstrate by personal experience that such a metamorphosis is possible for a human being. In this instance, the dream itself does not inform us whether the boy's blessing included power to transform himself. There are, however, many anecdotes told where it is believed that a human individual has appeared in the guise of a bear.[31] The assumption is that power to do this does exist in exceptional cases and that it was obtained in a dream fast. In the

---

[29] See Radin's discussion (1914, pp. 7–10) regarding the transmission of the patterns of the dreams reported. Not all of the Ojibwa material in Radin (1936) is new. Dreams to be found in the earlier article are republished in a different wording but with no reference to previous publication. Lincoln (1935, pp. 271–293) gives a selection from Radin's material.

[30] For a fuller account of this dream see Hallowell, 1955, p. 178.

[31] For a more detailed discussion of this kind of metamorphosis see Hallowell, 1961, pp. 36–38. Peter Jones, a converted Ojibwa, who became famous as a preacher and author says (1861, pp. 145–146) that "sorcerers can turn themselves into bears, wolves, foxes, owls, bats, and snakes. . . . Several of our people have informed me that they have seen and heard witches in the shape of these animals, especially the bear and the fox. They say that when a witch in the shape of a bear is being chased all at once she will run around a tree or hill, so as to be lost sight of for a time. . . . Then, instead of seeing a bear they behold an old woman walking quietly along or digging up roots, and looking as innocent as a lamb."

dream cited what we do know is that the Master of the Golden Eagles became one of the boy's tutelaries, or "guardian spirits," for life.

Even in the dreams of acculturated individuals who never underwent a dream fast, we find a manifest content that is interpreted as a great blessing, so that the significance of certain dream experiences remained the same for individuals long after the period when the aboriginal culture flourished. An example of this is a dream of my friend W. B. He entered a house and there he found a small boy wearing a red toque. This boy had a bow and two arrows, one red and the other black. "I'm going to find out how strong you are," he said to the dreamer. The latter took up a position in the middle of the room and when the boy shot his arrows he managed to dodge them. Then the boy exchanged places with the dreamer. My friend managed to hit the boy with the second (red) arrow, but it did not kill him. He said it was difficult because the boy seemed to be constantly moving, yet remaining in the same place, which was about a foot above the floor. The boy acknowledged that he had been beaten in the contest. The *pawágan* identified himself as an insect, "one of those which are so quick in their movements that they never seem to be at rest." The narrator called them "flies." [32] They have a yellow body and red marks on the head. The latter feature he associated with the red toque worn by the boy in his dream. Finally, this boy said to the dreamer: "If at any time in your life you are in a fight, think of me. Your body will always be quivering like mine." The dreamer was then directed to enter the next wigwam he came to on the trail. The moment he did so a man pointed a gun at him and fired. But W. B. felt no bullet enter his body. "This proved to me," he said, "how I had been blessed. Later I told my wife I would not be killed if I went to war. She asked me how I knew that, I told her it was none of her business." W. B. recognized this dream as a very special kind of dream. And it was. It falls within the type that is traditional in the dream fast. Other dreams of this man, of which I have more than a dozen, were not all of this type. W. B. was absolutely confident with respect to his invulnerability to bullets and if he had gone to war I am sure this would have given him unusual courage.

Another dream of this same man likewise illustrates the kind of manifest content associated with the dream fast. W. B. said it would have enabled him to become a *manáo* if he had so desired. A *manáo* is a doctor who dispenses medicine, which he obtains from the *memengwéciwak*. The latter look very much like human beings, but they belong to the other-than-human category. They travel in canoes and make their home in the rocky escarpments that border some of the lakes. W. B. dreamed that

---

[32] He said they did not sting. But I never was able to make a positive identification of the species.

he was out hunting and met one of the *memengwécī*. He asked W. B.
to visit his home. "On the northwest side of the lake there was a
very high steep rock. He headed directly for this rock. With one stroke
of the paddle we were across the lake. The fellow threw his paddle down
as we landed on a flat shelf of rock about level with the water. Behind this
the rest of the rock rose steeply before us. But when his paddle touched
the rock this part opened up. He pulled the canoe in and we entered a
room in the rock." In this dream the geographical details are extremely
precise. W. B. said that some time later, when *awake* and out hunting, he
recognized the exact spot he had visited in his dream. He could go back
any time in the future and obtain the special kind of medicine for which
the *memengwécīwak* are famous.[33] The fact that W. B. said he could act
this way in the future with reference to a dream experience of the past
indicates clearly enough that in the Ojibwa world there is a unified
spatiotemporal frame of reference for *all* self-related experience.

While the personal motivation of the boy who undergoes a dream
fast is to secure "blessings" that will augment his limited human powers
and enable him to achieve *pimădazīwin,* exceptional powers can be obtained which may be exercised for the benefit of other human beings. If
W. B. had been a pagan instead of a Christian, he would have become a
manăo. All specialized forms of curing, such as the ability to remove
from the body lethal objects that have been projected there by sorcery,[34]
depend upon dream revelation. The boy destined by his dream fast to become a conjurer is blessed by the Master of conjuring who lives in the
West, but not on earth; he also must dream of the Winds, who are responsible for the movements exhibited by the conjuring lodge, and the
Great Turtle, who acts as a messenger. I was told that four dreams are
required before the instructions of the neophyte are completed. In the last
dream he is told what kind of wood to select for the poles of the conjuring
tent, which differs from conjurer to conjurer. The Master also designates
the "moon" in which his initial performance must take place. The neophyte is told that he must not conjure too frequently, or to show off.
There must be a real need for his services. In practice the occasions when
there is a resort to conjuring are quite varied. If game is scarce and
famine threatens, a conjurer, with the aid of his other-than-human helpers,
may be able to direct hunters to the place where game can be found. By
similar means it is possible for him to receive news about the health or
circumstances of absent persons which will alleviate apprehension. A
powerful conjurer is also able to protect a whole community for malevo-

[33] For the full text of this dream, see Hallowell, 1955, p. 97.
[34] See Densmore, 1910, pp. 119 ff., where the songs used by this type of doctor, as
well as other details, are recorded.

lent influences, such as the approach of a cannibal monster (*windīgo*).

The knowledge and power acquired by human individuals in their dream experiences vary greatly. One man may acquire a great many more tutelaries than another, but only a relatively few individuals acquire exceptional powers. In these cases, there is no sharp line that divides human from other-than-human persons. Exceptional men may be able to make inanimate objects behave as if they were animate.[35] They are able to transform one substance into another, such as ashes into gunpowder, or a handful of goose feathers into birds or insects. In such manifestations they are elevated to the same level of power as that displayed by other-than-human persons. We can, in fact, find comparable episodes in the myths. It must also be observed, however, that despite wide variation in the powers obtained from other-than-human sources, "equalitarian" values prevail in this sphere, too. Although other-than-human persons are willing to share their knowledge and power with human persons, greediness is discountenanced, as is the hoarding of material goods among human beings. I was once told about the dream fast of a boy who was not satisfied with his initial blessing. He wanted to dream of all the leaves of all the trees in the world so that absolutely nothing would be hidden from him. This was considered greedy and, while the *pawágan* who appeared in his dream granted his desire, the boy was told that "as soon as the leaves start to fall you'll get sick and when all the leaves drop to the ground that is the end of your life." Overfasting is considered as greedy as hoarding. It violates a basic moral value of the Ojibwa world and is subject to a punitive sanction.

The knowledge and power that other-than-human persons share with the suppliant who seeks their help is not a free gift. The dream fast introduced a boy to a new set of moral obligations. The full benefit of the power and knowledge obtained was made contingent upon the fulfillment of obligations to other-than-human entities that assumed a primary moral force in his life. A reciprocal principle, equivalent to the basic patterning of social interaction between human persons, where rights and duties obtain, was operative. Besides this, the commands of *pawáganak̯* were considered absolute. The obligations they imposed took various forms. There might be a food taboo in the case of relations with the Masters of game animals. One man was forbidden to kill or eat porcupine by the Master of the porcupines.[36] In another case a man was commanded to wear the kind of headgear attributed to the mythical character who had blessed him in a dream. Another man was forbidden to speak to, or to

---

[35] For example, the animation of a string of wooden beads, or animal skins (Hoffman, 1891, pp. 205–206).

[36] This is an example of what was called "individual totemism" by older writers.

have sexual intercourse with, his wife for a defined period after marriage.

Such obligations are never talked about because there is a general taboo directed against any reference to the relations of a man and his *pawáganak*, except in a highly allusive manner or under unusual circumstances. It is equivalent to the taboo against narrating myths in summer, which is not considered the proper time to talk about "our grandfather." All children are given a personal name by a human grandfather and this name contains an allusion to some dream event in the namer's experience. But no one is given further information. We can see, then, that the obligations imposed by the *pawáganak*, which individuals must fulfill in order to obtain great blessings, often involve firm self-discipline, because the behavior they involve cannot be explained to anyone. The man who was not permitted to sleep with his wife, or even talk to her, did not succeed in fulfilling his obligation. She did not understand his conduct and left him after one winter of married life. He married again and this time he broke the taboo. One of his children became sick and died; later his new wife died. He married a third time and the same thing happened. It was useless for him to expect *pīmádazīwin*. He had received a blessing, but had not been able to exercise sufficient self-control to benefit by it. Food taboos were interpreted so rigidly that inadvertent or unconscious violations did not modify the penalty for their infraction. The linguistic term for such infractions means "failure to observe an obligation earnestly entered into."

The seriousness of the failure to fulfill obligations to *pawáganak* is exemplified by the belief that the sickness that inevitably follows as a penalty cannot be cured. Other-than-human persons have done what they could for me; they have fulfilled their role. If I have been unable to fulfill my obligations to them it is my own fault, and I can only blame myself. The severity of the disease sanction in such cases is psychologically sound if it is interpreted as a means of strongly reinforcing self-discipline and personal independence among a people for whom life is fraught with objective hazards that are inescapable. At the same time the sanction lends support, in principle, to a readiness to accept personal responsibility for one's conduct in all interpersonal relations in a society where any organized superordinate forms of authority are absent.

The existence of the dream fast undertaken by boys in aboriginal days receives explanation as a necessary institution when considered in the perspective of the world view of the Ojibwa. It served to validate, through direct personal experience, the existence of other-than-human persons. It served to engender, at an early age, self-confidence in meeting the vicissitudes of life as defined by Ojibwa values. The dream fast was the most crucial experience of a man's life: the personal relations he established with his *pawáganak* determined a great deal of his destiny as an individual. He met the "persons" on whom he could most firmly depend in the future. He also acquired knowledge of the specialized powers that would be of potential benefit to his fellow human beings. The dream fast was recognized as the ultimate source of their validation. If a doctor or a conjurer offered his services without dream validation, this was considered "deceit" and illness would surely follow. One such conjurer began to suffer from acute insomnia and a phobia. He found he could not go into the woods alone, not even for 200 yards. He confessed "deceit" and recovered from his phobia. Finally I believe we can say that the obligations, imposed in the dream fast, were the source of psychological effects which were of characterological importance. They reinforced a type of personality structure that, functioning primarily with emphasis upon inner control rather than outward coercion, was a necessary psychological component in the operation of the Ojibwa sociocultural system.

This system exploited a generic human experience—man's capacity for dreaming. Individuals, through appropriate socialization processes and institutions, were given a cognitive orientation toward the universe and themselves which required participation in a greater-than-human society in order to fulfill their personal needs. Dreaming was a means to this end. But dreaming was always linked to conduct. Thus, the role that dreaming played in the sociocultural system of the Ojibwa exemplifies the complex, coordinate, yet variable factors that may become structurally and functionally related in man's adjustment to a world in which his own imaginative interpretation of it is fed back into his adaptation to it.

References

Ackerknecht, Erwin H. 1958. "Primitive medicine's social function," in *Miscellanea Paul Rivet Octogenario Diata*. Mexico City: Universidad Nacional Autónoma de México. I, 3–7.

Beres, David. 1960. "Perception, imagination, and reality," *International Journal of Psycho-Analysis,* 41:327–334.

Bidney, David. 1953. *Theoretical Anthropology.* New York: Columbia University Press.

Blumensohn, Jules. 1933. "The fast among North American Indians," *American Anthropologist,* 35:451–469.

Dement, William. 1960. "The effect of dream deprivation," *Science,* 131: 1705–1707.

Dement, William, and Nathaniel Kleitman. 1957. "Cyclic variations in EEG during sleep and their relation to eye movements, body motility, and dreaming," *Electroencephalography and Clinical Neurophysiology* (Amsterdam), 9:673–690.

———. 1957. "The relation of eye movements during sleep to dream activity: An objective method for the study of dreaming," *Journal of Experimental Psychology,* 53:339–346.

Densmore, Frances. 1910. *Chippewa Music.* Bureau of American Ethnology. Bulletin 45. Washington.

Devereux, George. 1951. *Reality and Dream.* New York: International Universities Press.

Eggan, Dorothy. 1961. "Dream analysis," in Bert Kaplan, ed., *Studying Personality Cross-Culturally.* Evanston: Row, Peterson.

Eliade, Mircea. 1960. *Myths, Dreams and Mysteries.* Trans. Philip Mairet. London: Harvill.

English, Horace B., and Ava Champney. 1958. *A Comprehensive Dictionary of Psychological and Psychoanalytical Terms.* New York: Longmans, Green.

Hallowell, A. Irving. 1942. *The Role of Conjuring in Saulteaux Society.* Philadelphia: University of Pennsylvania Press.

———. 1955. *Culture and Experience.* Philadelphia: University of Pennsylvania Press.

———. 1960. "Self, society, and culture in phylogenetic perspective," in *Evolution after Darwin,* vol. 2 of *The Evolution of Man,* ed. Sol Tax. Chicago: University of Chicago Press.

———. 1961. "Ojibwa ontology, behavior, and world view," in *Culture in History: Essays in Honor of Paul Radin.* New York: Columbia University Press.

———. 1963. "Ojibwa world view and disease," in Iago Galdston, *Man's Image in Medicine and Anthropology.* New York: International Universities Press.

Hayes, Cathy. 1951. *The Ape in Our House.* New York: Harper and Brothers.

Hoffman, W. J. 1891. *The Midēwiwin or "Grand Medicine Society" of the Ojibwa.* Bureau of American Ethnology. Seventh Annual Report. Washington.

Jones, Peter. 1861. *History of the Ojibwa Indians.* London.

Jones, William. 1919. *Ojibwa Texts.* Publication of the American Ethnological Society. Vol. 7, Part II. New York.

Kimmis, Charles W. 1920. *Children's Dreams.* New York: Longmans, Green.

Kleitman, Nathaniel. 1960. "Patterns of dreaming," Scientific *American,* 203:82–88.

———. 1955. "The role of the cerebral cortex in the development and maintenance of consciousness," in *Problems of Consciousness.* Transactions of the Fifth Conference sponsored by Josiah Macy, Jr., Foundation, 1950–1954. New York.

Kohl, J. B. 1860. *Kitchi-Gami: Wanderings Round Lake Superior.* London: Chapman and Hall.

Leeuw, G. van der. 1938. *Religion in Essence and Manifestation.* London: Allen and Unwin.

Lincoln, Jackson Steward. 1935. *The Dream in Primitive Cultures.* London: Cresset.

Lovejoy, Arthur O. 1948. *Essays in the History of Ideas.* Baltimore: Johns Hopkins Press.

Lovejoy, Arthur O., and George Boas. 1935. *Primitivism and Related Ideas in Antiquity,* vol. 1 of *A Documentary History of Primitivism and Related Ideas.* Baltimore: Johns Hopkins Press.

MacLeod, Robert B. 1947. "The phenomenological approach to social psychology," *Psychological Review,* 44:193–210.

Radin, P. 1914. *Some Aspects of Puberty Fasting among the Ojibwa.* Canada Department Mines. Museum Bulletin no. 2, Ottawa.

———. 1924. "Ojibwa ethnological chit-chat," *American Anthropologist,* 26: 491–530.

———. 1936. "Ojibwa and Ottawa puberty dreams," in *Essays in Anthropology Presented to A. L. Kroeber . . . June 11.* Berkeley: University of California Press. Pp. 233–264.

Redfield, R. 1952. "The primitive world view," *Proceedings of the American Philosophical Society,* 96:30–36.

Tylor, E. B. 1878. *Researches into the Early History of Mankind.* New York. (1st ed., 1865.)

———. 1874. *Primitive Culture.* 2 vols. New York. (1st ed., 1871.)

Whiting, John W. M. 1959. "Sorcery, sin and the superego: A cross-cultural study of some mechanisms of social control," in *Nebraska Symposium on Motivation.* Lincoln: University of Nebraska Press. VII, 174–195.

Wolpert, Edward A., and Harry Trosman. 1958. "Studies in the psychophysiology of dreams. I. Experimental evocation of sequential dream episodes," *American Medical Association Archives of Neurology and Psychiatry,* 79:603–606.

Woods, Ralph L. 1947. *The World of Dreams: An Anthology.* New York: Random House.

VI | CULTURAL CHANGE

INTRODUCTION

Wilcomb E. Washburn

Just as Professor Hallowell moved so easily in his professional
career from sociology to anthropology, so he moved readily
in his research into the fields of psychology and history, combining profound theoretical insight with thorough reading in
the sources. The two papers that follow represent this interest
and achievement. In "The Impact of the American Indian on
American Culture," published in the *American Anthropologist*
in 1957, Hallowell boldly confronted a subject that had, in his
words, "fallen between two academic stools." Historians like
Frederick Jackson Turner had conceived of the frontier as a
primarily nonhuman force to be acted against and transformed
by the white frontiersman: the Indian provided a shadowy background to the historians' story, if not serving simply as a sur-
rogate of nature. Anthropologists, on the other hand, had been
concerned primarily with the description and analysis of Indian
culture before its alteration by white contact. (Literary figures
like James Fenimore Cooper had dealt extensively with the
influence of the Indian on white culture, but their work tended
to be outside the scope of scholarly inquiry.) Into this rich but
neglected area Hallowell stepped, skillfully blending his knowledge of anthropology, psychology, history, and literature,
developing particularly the theme of mutual acculturation
which he was to define in more precise terms in his 1963 essay
in *Current Anthropology*, "American Indians, White and
Black: The Phenomenon of Transculturalization." In his 1957
essay Hallowell had not yet coined the word he was to select
so perceptively in 1963 to indicate the process by which whites
and blacks were not merely influenced by, but became actual
members of, Indian societies. In 1957 Hallowell took favorable

Wilcomb E. Washburn is director of American Studies at the Smithsonian
Institution.

note of the Cuban scholar Fernando Ortiz's use of the phrase "transculturation" to emphasize the reciprocal character of the contact situation. In 1963 Hallowell had progressed to the newer phrase and correlative terms such as "transculturite." Hallowell's 1957 essay in the *American Anthropologist*, while incorporating most of the author's argument, referred interested readers "for a more comprehensive survey of the various facets of Indian influence than is possible here" to his essay "The Backwash of the Frontier: The Impact of the Indian on American Culture," which first appeared in *The Frontier in Perspective*, edited by Walker D. Wyman and Clifton B. Kroeber (Madison, 1957) and which was shortly afterward reprinted in the Smithsonian Institution's *Annual Report* for the year ending 30 June 1958 (Washington, 1959), pp. 447–72. Among the comments from the longer article ommited in the *Anthropologist* article were Hallowell's observation that the development of anthropology in its modern form and the closing of the frontier coincided and his development of the theme that the investigation of the Indian as a subject had given American anthropology "a distinctive coloring as compared with British, French, and German anthropology" (p. 469).

One of the most praiseworthy aspects of Hallowell's writing was his candid, personal style. He did not claim dignity or authority or attempt to create distance between himself and the reader. (In this approach he mirrored his personal warmth and openness.) In his *Current Anthropology* article, for example, he noted (p. 520) that while visiting a St. Francis Abenaki community near Quebec as a graduate student, he was surprised to hear about a white man, Joseph-Louis Gill, who was for fifty years of the eighteenth century an Abenaki chief. "I had never given any thought to the circumstances under which a white man could become an Indian chief," Hallowell wrote. "Indeed, nothing had led me even to conjecture that the impact of European culture on Indian culture would produce white Indian chiefs." By emphasizing his own surprise at the phenomenon, Hallowell helped his readers, particularly those from outside the discipline of anthropology, to understand better the complex, subtle distinctions he then proceeded to make. His refusal to sheath his insights in cold, impersonal, scientific dress is an important reason why his influence has spread far beyond the field of anthropology. Scholars in Indian history, like Robert Berkhofer and James Axtell (and certainly myself) owe him a debt of gratitude. But perhaps anthropologists owe him even more respect; for he helped move a discipline that had virtually turned its back on history and rejected moral judgment to a more sophisticated awareness of the validity of both these approaches to the study of cultural interaction.

The Impact of the American Indian
on American Culture

1957

THE global expansion of European peoples, beginning in the fifteenth century, initiated a series of events whose fateful character for modern history scarcely can be overestimated. Among other things, the historical setting was provided in which Europeans came into contact with the primitive cultures of the world, which led, in time, to the accumulation of the kind of empirical knowledge on which a science of man could be soundly based.

If we look at anthropology today, we find increasing attention being paid to the changes taking place in the primitive cultures which still flourish in the contemporary world. What we now observe are later stages in processes that began during the great age of exploration and colonization. As cultural anthropologists we have been concerned with only one side of this continuing process of social interaction, cultural readjustment, and transformation. For the most part we have ignored what happened to European culture as a consequence of contacts with primitive cultures. Attention has been focused on the effects upon them of contact with Europeans. Yet we know that Europe itself was profoundly affected by the discoveries overseas, particularly by the discovery, exploration, and settlement of the New World. Besides new dreams of wealth and power there were many other effects: new food plants, new drugs, new dyes, tobacco, unheard-of languages, novel modes of life that provoked moral and political disputation and challenged the authority of old traditions, fresh subject matter for original themes in literature. Yet a comprehensive history and appraisal of the total effects of this impact upon European culture, in all its aspects, remains to be written. Only a few highly specialized studies of selected topics by a handful of scholars come to mind.[1]

Across the ocean in the Americas, where Europeans met the Indians face to face and direct social interaction took place, a more complex culture-historical situation developed. Settlement and conquest did not eliminate the indigenous populations. They remained as potential sources of influence during the period when the nations of the Americas were achieving political maturity and differentiation. Aboriginal populations varying in racial composition and in the retention of native languages and cultures have persisted down to the present in almost all the nations of the New World.

What, then, have been the cultural consequences in the Americas of both the initial and the continuing presence of these native populations upon the European cultural tradition in the New World? How have these influences varied from nation to nation? Can we explain the differential effects? The picture presented is complex, but an unusual opportunity is afforded for the analysis of the impact of the New World aborigines upon the European heritage transplanted here because so many phases of it can be documented from written sources.

The greatest density in the aboriginal population was to be found in Hispanic America. In the modern nations of these same regions the percentage of the Indian population still remains highest, amounting to fifty percent or more in some cases. At the opposite extreme we have the United States, where the Indian population is less than one percent, and Canada, where it is a little higher (Brand 1943).

Anthropologists working in Latin America have long been aware of the interchange of cultural influences and their subtle mixture (Gillin 1955). Foster (1951) says, "Even in non-Indian areas of Mexico, for all the influence of Spain and the modern world, one is impressed with how thoroughly native American culture has left its imprint." He concludes, "Hispanic American culture cannot be described as Indian any more than it can be described as Spanish. It is a new, distinctive culture, with roots deep in two separate historical traditions, but with a unique and valid ethos of its own." This is the *tertium quid* that Malinowski so frequently referred to in his discussion of culture contact. It has no precise parallel in the United States and Canada. Does this mean that in the case of the United States the impact of the Indian on our culture has been altogether absent or negligible? Or has the historical setting been so different that discernable influences have been of a different kind, perhaps manifested in less obvious ways? There is one basic fact, however, which makes our situation directly comparable with Latin American countries: although the Indian population in the United States has never been large and has become relatively smaller as our national population has rapidly increased, in this country, too, we have had the continuing presence of the Indian throughout our colonial and national existence. Thus the question of the impact of the Indian on our culture cannot be reduced to the problem of influences that can be derived from frontier contacts alone.

The influence of the Indian on American culture is by no means a novel topic. Yet there is no over-all integral account of how our speech, our economic life, our clothing, sports and recreations, our indigenous religious cults, our pharmacopeia as well as curative practices on the vernacular level, to say nothing of our folk songs, our concert music, literature, and certain aspects of our intellectual history, have been affected through interaction with the American aborigines.[2] When the topic has been discussed it has usually been considered piecemeal: Maize may be considered apart from the vocabulary of corn foods, or as a decorative motif; concert music apart from folk music and the popular song; place names as place names; the "Indian guide" in American Spiritualism apart from the special treatment of the Indian in the Book of Mormon; the popularity of the *Leatherstocking Tales* and *Hiawatha* apart from the phenomenal success of *Metamora* on the American stage in the nineteenth century and the Indian in twentieth century American literature. In particular, various types of impact at different historical periods and their relation to the changing patterns of American culture have not been differentiated, nor later borrowings from those made on the frontier.

Alexander Francis Chamberlin was the first to deal comprehensively with the topic of Indian influence on western culture in an article published in 1905 (Chamberlin 1905). It is a classic article and later writers on the same subject have borrowed freely from it. He ranged from New World plants of economic importance to the Indian as a subject in American, English, and German literature. He himself made early contributions to the subject of linguistic borrowings. What Chamberlin did not do was to distinguish systematically between the influences that could be attributed to direct contact between Europeans and Indians in the United States and those mediated to us via Europe, or those mainly characteristic of Latin America. His article was entitled "The Contributions of the American Indian to Civilization" and this indicates its primary orientation. Chamberlin was concerned, as he says, with "the world's debt to the Red Man, what we owe to the race from whom we have snatched a continent." The same frame of reference was adopted by a number of subsequent writers, both anthropologists and others. It is clearly indicated by the titles of articles or chapters in books ranging in date from 1914 to 1955.[3] The attitude implied is inescapable. The Indians—savage or barbaric as they may appear to be in the ascending scale of cultural evolution—nevertheless had something to offer the more advanced and civilized newcomers from Europe. In none of these discussions is there an exclusive focus upon the United States or a serious attempt to relate the acquisition of this item or that to particular regions or periods of contact, to identify the tribal or linguistic groups who were the donors, to analyze the circumstances under which borrowing took place, or to take account of the subsequent fate of borrowed traits, their elaboration and integration with the changing values and new configurations of American culture.

It may be that as a subject worthy of detailed scholarly investigation, the influence of the Indian on American civilization has fallen between two academic stools. The influential historian Turner and his disciples made little point of it, even though the frontier was conceptualized as "the meeting point between savagery and civilization" and "the line of most rapid and effective Americanization." It was not contact with Indians on the frontier, however, that was in any way crucial to the development of American democracy and nationalism, as Turner conceived them. The earliest stages of frontier experience always had to be transcended—again and again. At first ". . . the wilderness masters the colonist. It finds him a European in dress, industries, tools, modes of travel, and thought. It takes him from the railroad car and puts him in the birch canoe. It *strips off* [italics ours] the garments of civilization and arrays him in the hunting shirt and the moccasin. It puts him in the log cabin of the Cherokee and Iroquois and runs an Indian palisade around him. Before long he has gone to planting Indian corn and plowing with a sharp stick; he shouts the war cry and takes the scalp in orthodox Indian fashion." But he does all these things only temporarily and in order to survive; when he does, "there is a new product that is American" (Turner 1920). According to this view, "Indianization" on the frontiers involved a cultural step downward in order to make possible a cultural leap ahead on a higher progressive level.[4]

If this epitomizes all that needs to be said about the Indian in American historical experience, the subject can indeed be treated briefly. So far as I can see, there is no hint in Turner's writings that inherent in frontier borrowings from the Indians there were potentialities for cultural elaboration and development that were to give certain aspects of American civilization a distinctive flavor.

On the other hand, Bernard de Voto complains that the role of the Indian has been shockingly neglected by American historians. He writes: "Most American history has been written as if history were a function solely of white culture—in spite of the fact that till well into the nineteenth century the Indians were one of the principal determinants of historical events. Those of us who work in frontier history—which begins at the tidal beaches and when the sixteenth century begins—are repeatedly nonplussed to discover how little has been done for us in regard to the one force bearing on our field that was active everywhere. Disregarding Parkman's great example, American historians have made shockingly little effort to understand the life, the societies, the cultures, the thinking, and the feeling of the Indians, and disastrously little effort to understand how all these affected white men and their societies" (De Voto 1952b:8). As for American anthropologists, De Voto's impression (1952a:XV) is that "archeological and ethnological inquiries" have received preference over historical ones. "In most of their treatises" he says, " 'the period of white contact' is likely to be the one most perfunctorialy explored." Personally, I see no reason to dispute this observation. Traditionally, the anthropologist has not considered it his business to deal with historical facts and events in the same manner as the professional historian. Systematic inquiries by trained students, instituted early in this century, were mainly concerned with securing information from Indians on reservations which would permit the reconstruction of aboriginal cultures as they had existed in the past. The use of historical documents was a secondary consideration; information obtainable from living informants was given primary emphasis. It was only in the thirties that the study of culture contact, or acculturation, was defined as a special subject for investigation. Once begun, such studies have been focused upon the various ways in which the cultures of the Indians have been affected by their contacts with white men. Despite the fact that in the well-known memorandum of Redfield, Linton, and Herskovits (1936), acculturation was conceived as potentially a two-way process, in practice, American anthropologists have investigated it as a one-way process. Beals has called attention to this fact and likewise points out that Ortiz, in 1940, introduces the term "transculturation" in order "to emphasize the reciprocal character of the contact situation." Malinowski greeted the term with enthusiasm in his preface to Ortiz' book but, says Beals (1953), "one finds no serious consideration of the reciprocal aspects of culture in any of his own publications."

Within the widening framework that has been developing in acculturation studies, which relates them more closely to the broad problems of culture change, it would seem that a closer study of the impact of the Indian on Amer-

ican culture invites attention. Many of the points in the process of acculturation that have been emphasized in recent discussions, but which are often
difficult to demonstrate in nonliterate cultures, can be historically documented in our contacts with the Indians.

Forty years ago, Clark Wissler (1916) published a famous essay in which
he demonstrated that, trait for trait, "the white colonist took over the entire
material complex of maize culture" from the Indians, omitting only its social
and ceremonial associations. Subsequently, this example has been used over
and over again as a classical case of cultural borrowing or diffusion. But Wissler
was not writing in the intellectual climate of acculturation. He did not think it
necessary to discuss the actual circumstances surrounding the borrowing process, localized in time and place. (For the role of the individual, see Barnett
1953.) In the case of corn, however, we do have some facts which are well
known to historians and easily accessible. In the spring of 1609, for example,
forty acres of maize were planted in Jamestown under direct Indian super-
vision and instruction. It was (Bruce 1896:199) "the first maize produced in
any quantity in the boundaries of the United States by people of English blood
of which we have any authentic record." Up until this time maize had been
traded from the Indians, but in precarious quantities. Captain John Smith
induced two Indian captives to supervise the planting, which was done in
complete accord with Indian practice. We do not know the names of these
Indians, but we do know their linguistic and tribal affiliation. In New England,
of course, Squanto has become immortal because of his comparable role in
teaching immigrant Englishmen how to plant corn. Thus, in the case of maize
we are not compelled to limit ourselves to abstract statements about the maize
complex being borrowed from the Indians and let it go at that.

One of the points given considerable emphasis in the report of the Social
Science Research Council Seminar on Acculturation is "cultural creativity."
Acculturation is "neither a passive nor a colorless absorption. It is a culture-
producing, as well as a culture-receiving process." And, "when not forced, is
essentially creative." It is this aspect of acculturation that is not always so
easy to evaluate in nonliterate societies where we do not have documentation
over considerable time periods. It is otherwise in the case of American culture.
So far as corn is concerned, it is a commonplace to refer to the expanding
role which this plant and its products came to play in our national life when
considered purely in its economic aspects. But should we stop here if we wish
to understand the total effects upon our culture of the corn that we borrowed?
When we look at Peruvian culture we pay some attention to the fact that
maize was used as a decorative motif in art. But corn has likewise been used
in this way in American culture. There are a few well-known examples, but
are there others?[5] In the United States in the nineteenth century there were
Americans who might be called "apostles of corn." For these individuals, the
origin of the maize-complex was unimportant; an attitude toward the plant
was assumed which made it an ostensible symbol of a personalized Americanism that could be acted on. From such attitudes there arose an active

movement to make corn our national emblem.[6] Could this have been predicted from Turner's statement that before long the backwoodsman "has gone planting Indian corn and plowing with a sharp stick," or any abstract statement about borrowing a maize complex from the Indians? And, although maize did not become our national flower, in the highly industrial phase of American culture found in this century, corn-husking became one of our recognized national sports. In 1935, over 130,000 Americans attended the championship contest. "It was the sixth or seventh largest crowd to see any sport contest [up to that time] in the United States."[7]

Wissler said that the borrowing of the maize-complex was "one of the few cases of culture transmission from a lower to a higher form of civilization." In the framework of acculturation it seems to me that the mere fact of borrowing is the least important point, and that Wissler did not sufficiently appraise the facts of cultural creativity.

If we wish to thoroughly understand the role which maize has played in American culture as a whole, reductive explanations that make reference only to the period of initial borrowing or a maize-complex are inadequate. Although it is true that the earliest frontiers were the seed-beds in which many influences derived from contacts with the Indians first began to sprout, we also need to consider the subsequent history of these early borrowings and their relation to later developments in American culture. Another question also suggests itself which transcends in importance Wissler's point about borrowing being from a "lower" to a "higher" culture. What qualitative aspects of American culture made it possible for corn to play the role it has? Were these qualities inherent in the transplanted European culture of the colonial frontiers, or were subsequent events and the development of new American culture patterns responsible? If we could answer questions like these, perhaps we could better explain some of the noncreative effects of contacts with Europeans on native Indian cultures.

The history of the humble moccasin is less well known than corn, and presents special problems of its own. For here, too, although we need to consider the frontier situation and the conditions under which direct borrowing occurred, there are considerations other than purely pragmatic ones to be evaluated. Among them is the fact that the moccasin was a fitted type of footgear belonging to the same area of tailored clothing in the Northern Hemisphere from which Europeans came. Perhaps this fact is related to the later transformation of the moccasin into the commercialized moccasin-type shoe in present-day American culture.[8]

One of the most interesting aspects of the general question of Indian influences on American culture is that all of them did not originate on the frontier. This fact in itself suggests different kinds of influences at successive periods of American history. If acculturation be conceived in terms of continuing first-hand contacts between the peoples involved, Indian influences can be discriminated as a function of changing patterns, interests, and values in American culture.

In the last decade of the nineteenth century, for example, there was a conscious effort to develop national qualities in American music. Unlike the situation in Europe, there was no older tradition of folk music in America on which composers might draw (Howard 1931; Chase 1955). Following this, the "modern" type of musical idiom began to gain ground and some American composers discovered that Indian music had anticipated some of the devices that were being exploited by composers of modern music.[9] It was in this historical context that American composers turned to the Indians. But how did they acquire direct knowledge of aboriginal music? The frontier was closed; the Indians were now settled in reservations.

Just as Longfellow had turned to Schoolcraft's *Algic Researches* (1839), the first collection of Indian myths to be published, so Edward McDowell turned to the first published collection of American Indian melodies. These had been obtained in the field by Theodore Baker in 1880 and published in 1882.[10] The outcome was McDowell's famous *Indian Suite* (composed 1891–92; first performed, 1896),[11] which, along with Skilton's *Indian Dances* (1915), were among the twenty-seven compositions of twelve American composers which had the greatest number of performances in the United States during the seven years following World War I.[12] Following the lead of McDowell, an increasing number of American composers became interested in American Indian music, and in the early years of this century a number of them made excursions to the Western reservations (Burton, Cadman, Farwell, Jacobi, Arthur Nevin, Skilton, Troyer). Thus Indian songs were harmonized and arranged for performance by white musicians and Indian themes were handled freely in the composition of original works; an excellent example of the principle of selective borrowing and adaptation of culture elements. The most extreme form of this process is represented in two of America's most popular songs: Cadman's *Land of the Sky Blue Water* (1909) and Lieurance's *By the Waters of Minnetonka* (1921).[13] Both composers had direct contact with the Indians; Cadman visited the Omaha reservation in 1909 with Francis La Flesche, and Lieurance visited various reservations as early as 1905.

A striking example of the direct borrowing of Indian songs without adaptation also occurred in this century. This was by the Boy Scouts of America. How amazed the frontiersman of yesterday would be to read in the Scout Handbook of today that it "is a pity that most boys think of head-dresses, war whoops, tomahawks and scalps the instant Indians are mentioned . . . there are so many thousands of beautiful and desirable things in their lives that it is safe to say that they can offer boys a mighty good code of sport and happiness." What a revolutionary change of attitude this represents! On the New England frontier the Indians had been called "tawny serpents," in Kentucky they became "red niggers," while on the trans-Mississippi frontier of the sixties they were once characterized as "a set of miserable, dirty, lousy, blanketed, thieving, lying, sneaking, murdering, graceless, faithless, gut-eating skunks as the Lord ever permitted to infect the earth . . ." (Taft 1953:66). But in the twentieth century, the Boy Scouts of America instituted a Merit Badge in Indian Lore. In order to win this it is necessary, among other things, to learn to "sing three Indian songs, including the Omaha Tribal Prayer and tell something of their meaning." The source of two of the songs, printed in the pamphlet *Indian Lore*, goes back to the pioneer collection of Omaha songs published by Alice C. Fletcher in 1893.[14] In the past six years approximately 47,000 copies of *Indian Lore* have been printed, and since 1911 there have been 18,719 American boys who have qualified for the Merit Badge in Indian Lore.[15]

Willard Rhodes (1952) has recorded the impression that, so far as art music is concerned, "we have accepted more from the Indian than he has accepted from us," and Gilbert Chase (1955) has observed that "it may be true, as W. Rhodes suggests, 'that the time has arrived when the composer can safely reconsider American Indian music as a source of material'—now that the romantic and picturesque exploitation of the American Indian is a thing of the past . . . "

While borrowings of the type noted in the case of music represent one of the most familiar kinds of acculturative influences, two other categories that likewise apply to the arts in America need discrimination. The first of these is the acquisition and use of Indian-made objects, distributed through ordinary commercial channels. In this century Navajo rugs, silverwork, pottery, and so on, are familiar examples. In principle, this is the same kind of phenomenon so familiar on the frontier when iron knives, axes, and guns manufactured by us were traded to the Indians. And when the frontiersman obtained Indian-made moccasins and snowshoes for his own use,[16] or corn before he had thoroughly mastered the techniques of planting and cultivation, the same process was in operation; the consumable goods simply were of a different class. The key to the dynamics of this kind of phenomenon is the conditions that give rise to the demand for ready-made goods of a particular kind on the part of one, or both, peoples in contact.

However, the full significance of the impact of the American Indian on American civilization may be qualitatively underestimated if we confine ourselves exclusively to exchanges of objects in trade or more complex cultural borrowings in the narrowest and most literal sense. Throughout our history, consciousness of both the contemporary presence and our past relations with the Indians has continued to exert an influence upon the American mind. The Indian has had a long history as a subject in our painting and sculpture, as well as in our fiction, poetry, and drama.[17] It has been said that more statues have been erected to Sacajawea than to any other American woman (Dictionary of American Biography). In the nineteenth century probably more Americans saw *Metamora* than have seen *Tobacco Road* or *Abie's Irish Rose* in the twentieth century.[18] *Hiawatha* is *the* poem of the American Indian. *The Leatherstocking Tales* conquered the international literary world besides establishing Cooper's reputation as an American novelist. As a subject of the American folk song, the Indian long antedated the musical borrowings that have influenced American art music and the popular song.[19] Who in America

has not heard Burl Ives sing "Little Mohee," "The Sioux Indians," or "Tobacco's but an Indian Weed"? We have come to take the Indian so much for
granted that he can be freely drawn upon in American advertising and car-
toons. And, with the modern proliferation of cards for all possible occasions,
the Indian asserts his presence on birthdays and on Valentine's Day, when a
new house is acquired ("I see, said the Sioux, that your tepee is new"), when
a baby is born ("a brand-new papoose? How!"), when one goes on a vacation
trip ("Happy Hunting") or to the hospital ("Pale face gottum bug? Ugh!").

Although the Indian as a subject in American literature is far too complex
to discuss here, its initial flowering in the first half of the nineteenth century
does appear to bear a direct relation to the conscious efforts that were being
made just after the war of 1812 to find nationally distinctive themes for exploitation by American writers.[20] Consequently there is an earlier parallel to
what occurred in American music at the end of the nineteenth century. But
so far as literature, and particularly fiction, is concerned, the continued interest of the reading public requires an explanation that has not been forth-
coming. The Indian as a subject in fiction has survived the passing of the long-
prevailing traditon—Romanticism—which gave him literary birth. Referring
to novels and stories about the Indians in the first four decades of this century,
the authors of *America in Fiction* (1949) write: "Now that he is on reservations, not a military foe, and generally not an economic competitor, the Indian
is a subject of great interest, so much so that more fiction has been written
about him in recent years than about any other ethnic group except the Negro.
In many works of fiction he has been given central prominence, his cultural
complex has been detailed, and much attention has been paid to his problems
of adjusting himself to the dominating white civilization which surrounds
him. Where once we had melodrama about the Indian with his bloody toma-
hawk, we now have clear-cut realism."

However, the fact should not be overlooked that, although nut written in
the spirit of contemporary realism, some nineteenth-century writers did
handle one theme which is paramount in twentieth-century fiction written
about reservation Indians: the psychological effects of continued social interaction between Indians and whites. Fenimore Cooper, the "first effective
novelist of the frontier," was likewise the first to dramatize the psychological
consequence of the acculturation process (Jones 1952). In *The Pioneers* (1823),
the old Delaware warrior, Chingachgook, who has survived his bellicose past,
is shown "as a relic of a broken and dispersed people, living in his own country with the status of a 'displaced person': lonely, frustrated, drunken, proud.
His dignity, what remains of it, stems from the consciousness that his own
personal tragedy is but a symbol of the tragedy wrought on his race by 'war,
time, disease, and want' " (Wallace 1954). In *Wyandotté* (1843), Saucy Nick,
a detribalized Tuscorora who has attached himself to the whites and loves
their rum, is caught up in a tremendous inner conflict because he cannot entirely relinquish the image of himself as the warrior *Wyandotté* and the code of
revenge it entails. *The Oak Openings* (1848) shows how Scalping Peter, whose

hatred of the white man was once his ruling obsession, becomes a devoted Christian.

In nineteenth-century fiction, too, we find treated the reverse effects of the acculturation process—the Renegade theme—white men who, by becoming Indianized and finding Savagism good, in effect symbolize the rejection of Civilization and Progress (Pearce 1953). Already in the eighteenth century, Colden (1747), Peter Kalm (1770–71), Crevecoeur (1782) and others, had commented on the contrast between the attitude of the whites who, having sojourned with the Indians, so often refused to return to the mode of life into which they were born, and the eagerness of Indians to return to·their tribal life after having been brought into close contact with whites.[21] This theme, rooted in the stories of actual captivities (Ackerknecht 1944) beginning in the seventeenth century, is continued and elaborated in various ways in fiction of the nineteenth and twentieth centuries. "Captivated" whites, "white Indians," and "squaw-men" have retained their fascination as fictional characters for American readers.[22]

The consequences of these intimate relations with the Indians in historical reality involved many complex gradations of psychological identification. In Natty Bumppo, the internationally famous Leatherstocking, who has been called "the most memorable character American fiction has given to the world" (Van Doren 1917), Cooper was the first writer to give literary expression to an American character who embodied intimate association with the Indians. What is particularly noteworthy is the generally accepted fact that Leatherstocking appears to be "Cooper's spokesman for what he feels to be most worthwhile in life, the proto-type of the self-reliant American democrat, reverent in religion, fearless in danger, always calm and just in his relations with his fellows" (Spiller 1951). And only recently Perry Miller (1955), in a broadly gauged discussion of the "shaping of the American character," says that "for years Cooper more than any single figure held up the mirror in which several generations of Americans saw the image of themselves they most wished to see . . . " and "persuaded not only thousands of Americans that he was delineating their archetype but also Europeans."

This is an arresting observation. For Natty Bumppo was of course a semi-Indianized white man. By one contemporary reviewer he was called a "demi-savage." Although white by "natur' " (i.e. heredity), he had Indian "gifts" (i.e. acquired traits). His early life was spent among the Delaware and, long before they called him "Deerslayer," he had successively borne three other Indian nicknames. He is said to have "acquired some knowledge of most of our Indian dialects." On occasion, he identified himself with the Delaware and their aboriginal values. When contemplating torture by the Hurons, he says he will strive "not to disgrace the people among whom I got my training." (Quotations from *The Deerslayer*.)

Thus we find depicted in Cooper's saga of the frontier the *beau ideal* of an American character type which dramatizes in a fictional image the psychological effects of the reverse side of the acculturation process which American anthropologists have been studying. Cooper simply takes it for granted that there were psychological consequences which affected the backwoodsman as a result of his contacts with the Indian. Natty Bumppo personifies these. In this semi-Indianized white man, who has managed to acquire the best "gifts" from each side, Cooper projected a literary image acceptable to Americans themselves. Leatherstocking, however, was not a renegade to savagery; he was not a squaw man; he did not reject civilization. In a preface to *The Pathfinder* written in the year of his death (1851), Cooper says that "it appeared to the writer that his hero was a fit subject to represent the better qualities of both conditions, without pushing either to extremes."

Past discussions by historians or anthropologists of the "contributions" to the Indian to American civilization have not included any reference to a characterological "gift." Yet Jung (1928) thought he could discern an Indian component in the character of some of his American patients. So we may ask: Was there, in fact, a period in America when along with the early cultural borrowings from the Indian that occurred, there were concomitant psychological effects? In the light of present-day knowledge does Leatherstocking, as a literary character, offer a cue to a problem rather than an answer to one? If there ever comes a time when we are able to grapple with such a complex question as the historical development of an American national character, the psychological effects of frontier contacts with the Indians need to be more fully explored and evaluated.

This is only one of a number of problems which a re-examination of our relations with the Indians in the perspective of acculturation suggests.[23] At the same time, the consequence of our historical experience with the Indians in the United States is only a provincial phase of the total processes of cultural change which, following the discovery of the New World, affected the European cultural tradition both at home and abroad.

NOTES

[1] E.g., Laufer's pioneer studies of the spread of New World plants to other parts of the world (1929, 1938); Salaman's subsequent study of the influence of the potato (1949); Gillespie's broadly gauged treatment of overseas contacts on England (1920); Chinard's classical monographs on the impact of the discovery of America on French literature (1911, 1913, 1918); Bissell's treatment of the Indian theme in English literature (1925); and Frederici's compilation of 1,550 Indian words that have been incorporated into Spanish, Portuguese, French, and English (1947).

[2] Williams asks (1956: ix-x), "Is it necessary to continue the study of the American Indians?" His answer is that "he is more than an exhibit in a museum, more than a vendor of trinkets, more than an extra in a Hollywood western. The American Indian has left an indelible mark upon the culture of America, upon its customs, its habits, its language, and even upon its mode of thought . . . there are more ways to study the Indian than to botanize on the grave of his dead past. History and literature have too long done no more than that. To discover his ever-living impact on the society that we call modern is the function of anthropologists, ethnologists, sociologists and folklorists. Add to these the social psychologist and the instrumentalists and we get a half-dozen intellectual disciplines with which to study the totality of American culture, a culture in which the Indian has had and still has a very significant part."

[3] The only general discussion of the topic I have been able to find which antedates Chamberlin is in a section ("Lessons Learned from the Barbarians") of an article by Edward Eggleston (1883).

Following Chamberlin we have, chronologically, Frachtenberg (1914) who draws heavily on Chamberlin; Wissler (1929; 1937); Emily Davis (1931); Winifred Hulbert (1932); Edwards (1934) who owes a great deal to Chamberlin; Brown and Roucek (1937) contains a chapter by Wissler; Embree (1939) contains a section on Indian contributions; Jenness (1939) on contributions to Canada; Cohen (1952); Heizer (1952) whose chapter replaces that of Wissler in this third edition of Brown and Roucek; Carter (1955). (On the dust jacket of the Carter book it is stated that the author has "learned that their [the Indians'] culture, old when the first white men came to the continent, has not been lost, but has been poured generously into the mainstream of American life and has so thoroughly mingled with the white that most of us have forgotten the source of the bright tributary.")

For the large literature dealing particularly with native American plants and their relation to Western culture, see Edwards and Rasmussen (1942).

⁴ Turner, like many anthropologists and others of his period, made the a priori assumption that there were regular sequences to be gone through in man's social evolution. Mood (1943) says that the theory of social evolution was the "fundamental unifying concept" of Turner's early writings.

⁵ For information on maize in relation to the arts in America, see Weatherwax (1928). He writes (p. 219), "The maize plant has thus far inspired few works of art, literature, or architecture, but these fields offer promising possibilities. These are the products of the maturity of a nation, and America is still in the period of growth and development. . . . Maize has ornamental properties that will in time give it a place in decorative art." Cf. Kempton (1937:385–408) for an illustration (Plate 2) of the famous Latrobe corn capitals, which he says are "the oldest known replicas of maize wrought by Europeans." Plate 3 is of a cast iron fence with a corn motif from New Orleans.

⁶ See Our National Flower (1893). Daniel Lothrop arranged the corn "in his dining-room in festoons of the long red and golden ears hanging in the corners and along the fireplace; tassels were put over the pictures, and the long spathe-like leaves were draped above windows, drooping over the curtains, where the light and shade gave out new tints to add to the glory of the corn." The Lothrops lived at "Wayside," Old Concord, the former home of Hawthorne. On the occasion of a garden party in honor of Mrs. General Logan, a huge American flag was hung along the piazza which was festooned with corn and had sheaves of corn stacked at the ends of it. "The effect was startling, as many had never seen the conjunction of corn and the flag. It was voiced by all: 'It is our emblem. Long wave the corn, as our flag has waved, and ever shall'." President Harrison's wife once visited the Lothrops and was "delighted at the beauty of the corn decorations. She searched for perfect ears of corn to sketch from for artistic effects at the White House; for she was an enthusiast on the subject, and a most ardent adherent to the cause of maize." Of William Cobbett, another enthusiast, it is said, "he wrote Indian corn, planted Indian corn, raised Indian corn, made paper of Indian corn husks, and printed a book on Indian corn paper." Elihu Burrett, visiting in England, wrote to a friend from Birmingham in 1869, "I only consent to be any man's guest, that his wife shall serve up a johnny-cake for breakfast, or an Indian pudding for dinner."

⁷ Menke (1947) says that although there had been county and sectional championships, corn-husking "did not take on national importance until 1924, when Henry Wallace, editor of 'Wallace's Farmer,' Iowa periodical, arranged a tournament which became a national affair."

⁸ Although this type of shoe seems to have increased in popularity during the past decade, it is not a recent development in American footwear. While it requires further investigation, there is evidence that what were called "wigwams" were being advertised in the Middle West as early as 1887 (Milwaukee), and that "wigwam slippers" were "invented" and first manufactured at Orono, Me., in the eighteen eighties (see "Wigwam" in Mathews 1951, Vol. 2).

On the frontier there was a close association between snowshoes and moccasins. Loosley (1942) says, "Although the European forced his type of dress upon the Indian, he, in turn, was compelled to borrow from the savage. In the deep snows of winter, the European, if he wished to travel, must use the snow-shoe evolved by the Indian. To walk comfortably on snow-shoes, it is necessary to add the moccasin." In some parts of the country, lumbermen also adopted the moccasin. (See the description of Tidd's lumber camp in Tuttle 1866.)

⁹ Skilton (1939) writes, "Many devices of the ultra-modern composers of the present day

have long been employed by Indians—unusual intervals, arbitrary scales, changing tune, conflicting rhythm, polychoral effects, hypnotic monotony."

[10] An article on Northwest Coast music by Eells (1879) probably was not known to McDowell, nor the transcription of Bella Coola melodies published by Stumpf (1886). For further reference to the pioneer period in the study of Indian music, see Herzog (1949).

[11] Gilbert (1912), a pupil of McDowell, writes, "McDowell became somewhat interested in Indian lore and curious to see some real Indian music. He asked me to look up some for him, so I brought him Theodore Baker's book. . . . 'Oh yes,' he said, 'I knew this book, but had forgotten about it.' From Baker's book the main themes of his Indian Suite are taken. . . . "

[12] Based on the programs of the thirteen most important orchestras in the United States, Howard Hanson compiled a list of orchestral works of American-born composers having the greatest number of performances between 1919 and 1926 (Scholes 1950).

[13] Cadman's song vied with *The Rosary* in popularity and, at midcentury, *By the Waters of Minnetonka* appeared in the Victor album, *Twelve Beloved American Songs.*

[14] The songs are *Shupida* and *Omaha Tribal Prayer.* The source cited in *Indian Lore* is a 1911 Bureau of American Ethnology Report (see also Fletcher 1893). The three other songs included in the Boy Scout publication are from other bulletins and reports of the Bureau of American Ethnology.

[15] Letter from Lex R. Lucas, Director, Editorial Service, Boy Scouts of America, December 23, 1954.

[16] Turner noted (1920), "In 1703–4 . . . the General Court of Massachusetts ordered 500 pairs of snowshoes and an equal number of moccasins for use in specified counties 'lying Frontier to the Wilderness'."

[17] For a parallel in the plastic and graphic arts of nonliterate peoples, see Lips (1934). He maintains that up until the later years of the nineteenth century, "the representations made by white artists of the native (in various parts of the world) showed less gift of observation and far more purely of artistic result than the plastics and drawings which the savage produced of the white man." This is applicable to the art of "the Melanesians, Bushmen, Australians, Eskimo, and Plains Indians, of the plastics from West Africa and Melanesian races, and of the carvings from the north-west coast of North America." It is not only that Europeans are clearly represented, it is possible to distinguish individuals of different nationalities. Besides human beings, various objects of material culture appear in native art.

[18] *Metamora or The Last of the Wampanoags*, in which King Philip was the leading character, was in the repertoire of Edwin Forest for almost forty years. With the exception of two years, it was played regularly in Philadelphia for a quarter of a century. Forest had advertised in 1829 for a play in which "the hero, or principal character, shall be an aboriginal of this country." William Cullen Bryant was the chairman of the committee which selected *Metamora* from the fourteen plays submitted. A radio version was broadcast in 1939 (Clark 1943).

[19] See Fife and Redden (1954). In one group of songs the Indian appears merely as an incidental personality, and the attitudes toward him are vague. In the second group, negative attitudes are sharply defined since many songs of this class are long narrative ballads which depict actual frontier conflicts. Folksongs about historic events, "including songs about dramatic episodes in the relationships of Indian and White, have been sung regularly since the earliest days of colonization and have faithfully reflected changing relationships between the two culture groups at least down to the present century when modern techniques for the commercialization of popular songs may have beclouded the issue." A third category of songs reflects a positive attitude toward the Indian varying "from vague references to good Indians or Indians with heroic qualities, to songs and ballads exclusively about romanticized Indians, who were admired for their stamina and other heroic qualities."

[20] For documentation of the "call" issued in various American periodicals for the exploitation of Indian material, see McCloskey (1935) and Sedgwick (1935).

[21] Crevecoeur wrote (1782: Letter XII): "By what power does it come to pass, that children who have been adopted when young among these people [Indians] can never be prevailed on to readopt European manners?" Again he commented (1925:193): "What a strange idea this joining

with the savages seems to convey to the imagination; this uniting with a people which nature
has distinguished by so many national marks! Yet this is what the Europeans have often done
through choice and inclination, whereas we never hear of any Indians becoming civilized Europeans."

   [22] A few examples that have circulated in the past five years in paperback form are: Conrad
Richter, *The Light in the Forest* (the story of a captive white boy who is adopted and becomes
identified with the Delaware); Charlton Laird, *Thunder on the River* (a captive is adopted and marries an Indian girl; divided loyalties); Jefferson Cooper, *Arrow in the Hill* (the main character
was raised from childhood by the Mohawk; the villain is a renegade Englishman who disguises
himself as a Huron and spies for the French); James D. Horan, *King's Rebel* (an English lord is
a "white Indian"); Janice Holt Giles, *The Kentuckians* (the villian is a white man identified with
the Indians; he hates his own white blood and the settlers of Kentucky), also a movie; Caroline
Gordon, *Green Centuries* (a white captive marries an Indian girl and becomes completely identified
with the Cherokee).

   [23] For a more comprehensive survey of the various facets of Indian influence than is possible
here, see my essay "The Backwash of the Frontier," in the *Frontier in Perspective*, University of
Wisconsin Press, 1957.

REFERENCES CITED

ACKERKNECHT, ERWIN H.
   1944   White Indians. Bulletin of the History of Medicine 15:15–36.
BAKER, THEODORE
   1882   Über die Musik der Nordamerikanischen Wilden. Leipzig, Breitkopf and Härtel.
BARNETT, HOMER G.
   1953   Innovation: the basis of culture change. New York, McGraw-Hill.
   1954   Comments on the Social Science Research Council Seminar on Acculturation.
            American Anthropologist 56:1000–1002.
BEALS, RALPH
   1953   Acculturation. *In* Anthropology today, ed. A. L. Kroeber and others. Chicago,
            University of Chicago Press.
BISSELL, BENJAMIN
   1925   The American Indian in English literature of the eighteenth century. Yale Studies
            in English, Vol. 68. New Haven, Yale University Press.
BRAND, DONALD D.
   1943   The present Indian population of the Americas. New Mexican Anthropologist
            6–7; 161–170.
BROWN, FRANCIS J. and JOSEPH S. ROUCEK (eds.)
   1937   Our racial and national minorities. New York, Prentice-Hall. (Revised edition,
            new title: One America, 1945, 1952).
BRUCE, PHILIP A.
   1896   Economic history of Virginia in the seventeenth century, Vol. I. New York, Mac-
            millan.
CARTER, E. RUSSELL
   1955   The gift is rich. New York, Friendship Press.
CHAMBERLIN, ALEXANDER FRANCIS
   1905   The contributions of the American Indian to civilization. Proceedings of the
            American Antiquarian Society, n.s., 16:91–126.
CHASE, GILBERT
   1955   America's music: from the Pilgrims to the present. New York, McGraw-Hill.
CHINARD, GILBERT
   1911   L'exotisme Américain dans la littérature française au XVI siècle. Paris, Hachette.
   1913   L'Amérique et le rêve exotique dans la littérature française au XVII et au XVIII
            siècle. Paris, Hachette.
   1918   L'exotisme Américain dans l'oeuvre de Chateaubriand. Paris, Hachette.

CLARK, BARRETT H. (ed.)
1943　Favorite American plays of the nineteenth century. Princeton, Princeton University Press.

COAN, OTIS W., and RICHARD G. LILLARD
1949　America in fiction, an annotated list of novels that interpret aspects of life in the United States. Third edition. Stanford, Stanford University Press.

COHEN, FELIX S.
1952　Americanizing the white man. The American Scholar, spring issue.

COLDEN, CADWALADER
1747　History of the Five Indian Nations. London. (Later edition New York, Morrell, 1866.)

CRÈVECOEUR, ST. JEAN DE
1782　Letters from an American farmer. London. (Later edition New York, Fox, 1904.)
1925　The Wyoming massacre. In Sketches of eighteenth century America, more "letters from an American farmer," ed. by H. L. Boundin, R. H. Gabriel, and S. T. Williams. New Haven: Yale University Press.

DAVIS, EMILY
1931　Ancient Americans: the archeological story of the two continents. New York, Holt. (Chap. 18, "We owe these to-the Indian").

DE VOTO, BERNARD
1952a　The course of empire. Boston, Houghton Mifflin.
1952b　Introduction to Strange Empire, by Joseph K. Howard. New York, Morrow.

EDWARDS, EVERETT E.
1934　American Indians' contribution to civilization. Minnesota History 15:255–72.

EDWARDS, EVERETT E., and WAYNE D. RASMUSSEN
1942　A bibliography on the agriculture of the American Indians. Revised edition. United States Department of Agriculture, Miscellaneous Publications No. 447.

EELLS, MYRON
1879　Indian music. American Antiquarian 1:249–53.

EGGLESTON, EDWARD
1883　The aborigines and the colonists. Century Magazine, May.

EMBREE, EDWIN R.
1939　Indians of the Americas: historical pageant. Boston, Houghton Mifflin.

FIFE, AUSTIN E., and FRANCESCA REDDEN
1954　The pseudo-Indian folksongs of the Anglo-Americans and French-Canadians. Journal of American Folk Lore 67:239–251, 379–94.

FLETCHER, ALICE C. and J. C. FILLMORE
1893　A study of Omaha Indian music. Papers of the Peabody Museum of American Archeology and Ethnology. Harvard University, Vol. 1, No. 5.
1911　The Omaha tribe. Smithsonian Institution, Bureau of American Ethnology Report 27, Washington, D. C.

FOSTER, GEORGE M.
1951　Report on an ethnological reconnaissance of Spain. American Anthropologist 53:311–25.

FRACHTENBERG, LEO J.
1914　Our indebtedness to the American Indian. Society for American Indians Quarterly Journal 2:197–202. (Reprinted in Wisconsin Archeologist 14:64–69.)

FRIEDERICI, GEORGE
1947　Amerikanistisches Wörterbuch. Hamburg, Cram, De Cruyter.

GILBERT, Henry F.
1912　Personal recollections of McDowell. New Music Review 2:132.

GILLESPIE, J. E.
1920　The influence of overseas expansion on England to 1700. New York.

GILLIN, JOHN
    1955   Ethos components in modern Latin American culture. American Anthropologist
            57:488–500.
HEIZER, ROBERT F.
    1952   The American Indian: background and contributions. *In* One America, ed. by
            Francis J. Brown and Joseph S. Roucek. Third edition. New York, Prentice Hall.
HERZOG, GEORGE
    1949   Salish music. *In* Indians of the urban Northwest, ed. by Marian W. Smith. New
            York, Columbia University Press.
HOWARD, JOHN T.
    1931   Our American music . New York, Crowell.
    1944   Our contemporary composers. New York, Crowell.
HULBERT, WINIFRED
    1932   Indian Americans. New York, Friendship Press.
JENNESS, DIAMOND
    1939   Canada's debt to the Indians. Canadian Geographical Journal 18:268–75.
JONES, HOWARD MUMFORD
    1952   Prose and pictures: James Fenimore Cooper. Tulane Studies in English, 3:126–37.
JUNG, CARL G.
    1928   Contributions to analytical psychology. London, Routledge and Kegan Paul.
KALM, PETER
    1770–71   Travels into North America. English translation. London.
KEMPTON, J. H.
    1937   Maize—our heritage from the Indian. Annual Report, Smithsonian Institution,
            Washington, D. C.: 385–408.
LAUFER, BERTHOLD
    1929   The American plant migration. Scientific Monthly 28:239–51.
    1938   The American plant migration. Part I: The potato. Field Museum of Natural
            History, Anthropological Series, Vol. 38, No. 1.
LIPS, JULIUS E.
    1934   The savage hits back. New Haven, Yale University Press.
LOOSLEY, ELIZABETH W.
    1942   Early Canadian costume. Canadian Historical Review 23:349–62.
MATHEWS, MITFORD W.
    1951   A dictionary of Americanisms. 2 vols. Chicago, University of Chicago Press.
McCLOSKEY, JOHN
    1935   The campaign of periodicals after the War of 1812 for a national American litera-
            ture. Proceedings of the Modern Language Association 50:262–73.
MENKE, FRANK G.
    1947   The new encyclopaedia of sports. New York, S. A. Barnes.
MILLER, PERRY
    1955   Shaping of the American character. New England Quarterly 28:435–54.
MOOD, FULMER
    1943   The development of Frederick Jackson Turner as a historical thinker. Publications
            of the Colonial Society of Massachusetts 34:304–7.
OUR NATIONAL FLOWER: a symposium advocating the claims of the maize.
    1893   The Arena 8:92–114.
PEARCE, ROY HARVEY
    1953   The savages of America: a study of the Indian and the idea of civilization. Balti-
            more, Johns Hopkins Press.
REDFIELD, R., R. LINTON and M. J. HERSKOVITS
    1936   Memorandum on the study of acculturation. American Anthropologist 38:149–52.

RHODES, WILLARD
    1952   Acculturation in North American Indian music. *In Acculturation in the Americas,* ed. Sol Tax. Chicago, University of Chicago Press.

SALAMAN, REDDIFFE N.
    1949   The history of the social influence of the potato. New York, Cambridge University Press

SCHOLES, PERCY
    1950   The Oxford companion to music. Revised edition.

SEDGWICK, WILLIAM ELLERY
    1935   The materials for an American literature: a critical problem of the early nineteenth century. Harvard Studies and Notes in Philology and Literature 17:141–62.

SKILTON, CHARLES S.
    1939   American Indian music. *In* International cyclopedia of music and musicians. New York, Dodd, Mead and Co.

SOCIAL SCIENCE RESEARCH COUNCIL SUMMER SEMINAR ON ACCULTURATION, 1953.
    1954   Acculturation: an exploratory formulation. American Anthropologist 56:973–1002.

SPILLER, ROBERT E.
    1951   Introduction to *The Last of the Mohicans,* by James Fenimore Cooper. New American edition of Everyman's Library. New York, Dutton.

TAFT, ROBERT
    1953   Artists and illustrators of the Old West. New York, Scribners.

TURNER, FREDERICK JACKSON
    1920   The frontier in American history. New York, Holt.

TUTTLE, J. M.
    1868   The Minnesota pineries. Harper's New Monthly Magazine 36:409–23.

VAN DOREN, CARL
    1917   Chapter 6 (Brown, Cooper) *In* Cambridge history of American literature, Vol. 3.

WALLACE, PAUL A. W.
    1954   Cooper's Indians. New York History, October.

WEATHERWAX, PAUL
    1928   The story of the maize plant. Chicago, University of Chicago Press.

WILLIAMS, MENTOR L. (ed.)
    1956   Schoolcraft's Indian legends. East Lansing, Michigan State University Press.

WISSLER, CLARK
    1916   Aboriginal maize culture as a typical culture-complex. American Journal of Sociology 21:656–60. (Reprinted *in* Readings in the economic history of American agriculture, ed. by L. B. Schmidt and E. D. Ross. New York, Macmillan, 1925.)
    1929   The influence of aboriginal Indian culture on American life, with reference to traces of Oriental origins. *In* Some Oriental influences on Western culture. New York, American Council of the Institute of Pacific Relations. (Reprinted in part *in* When peoples meet, eds. Alain Locke and B. J. Stern. Revised edition. New York, 1946.)
    1936   The universal appeal of the American Indian. Natural History 30:33–40. (Reprinted *in* Indians at Work, 1936, No. 11:19–24.)
    1937   Contributions of the American Indian. *In* Our racial and national minorities, eds. Francis J. Brown and Joseph S. Roucek. New York, Prentice-Hall.

THIRTEEN

American Indians, White and Black:
The Phenomenon of Transculturalization

1963

My first acquaintance with Indians "at home" was in the twenties when, as a graduate student under the tutelage of Frank G. Speck, I began visiting the St. Francis Abenaki at Odanak, Quebec, Canada. In this little Indian community an Algonkian language could still be heard, but the dominant speech was French-Canadian, and many persons could also speak English. There were a few old-timers left who occasionally hunted and trapped, although there was little ostensible evidence of an aboriginal mode of life. The Abenaki had been Christianized for generations, the majority of them being devout Roman Catholics. Across the railroad track was a typical French-Canadian village. In short, the St. Francis Abenaki were a highly acculturated group of Indians.[1] I did not go there to study acculturation, however, for this was a decade before studies of acculturation had been "legitimatized" in American anthropological research. My purpose was to secure information about the vanished culture of their aboriginal past. Being very green in cultural anthropology, and knowing even less about Indian-white relations in American history, I was surprised to learn about their famous white chief, Joseph-Louis Gill, who had served in this capacity during fifty years of the eighteenth century. I had never given any thought to the circumstances under which a white man could become an Indian chief. Indeed, nothing had led me even to conjecture that the impact of European culture on Indian culture would produce white Indian chiefs.

Joseph-Louis Gill was white only in a biological sense. In the early eighteenth century the Abenaki had captured two English children, a boy and a girl, in one of their raids across the border. These children had been adopted into Indian families and raised in Indian fashion and also as Catholics like their adoptive parents. Later, these captives married each other and remained with the Abenaki for the rest of their lives. Joseph-Louis, born in 1719, was the eldest son of his "captivated" father and mother who raised a family of seven children. His first wife was an Indian who was killed by Rogers' Rangers; his second wife was French. He became chief in 1747. (See Maurault 1866 and Huden 1956).

Here, then, in the history of the Abenaki we have epitomized all of the complex relations of whites and Indians that arose in the frontier areas: the intrusion of Europeans, trade, warfare, white captives, Christianization of the Indians, interracial marriages. Although changes were initiated in the mode of life of this Indian group, there were resistant tendencies toward linguistic and cultural conservatism. Fitting into the old pattern was the "Indianization," the cultural assimilation, of captured individuals.

Problems of historical research derived from the consequences of such complex events on American frontiers have long engaged the attention of historians, linguists, anthropologists, and others. Many American writers, too, have been fascinated by this historical material. Cooper's romances of the frontier, the historical novel and the dime novel, the western, have been immensely popular since the beginning of the nineteenth century. Interestingly enough, it has been mainly the American novelist, rather than the scholar, whose interest has been caught by the phenomenon of "Indianization." Possibly it was due to the immense popularity of actual accounts of captivities in the eighteenth century that early writers took up the theme.

"Indianize," in the sense of "to adopt the ways of Indians," is an Americanism dating back to the late seventeenth century. Cotton Mather asked: "How much do our people Indianize?" While the word has sometimes been used in a collective sense, in its later usage it seems to have been employed primarily with reference to individuals who adopted the ways of Indians (Mathews 1951). In his article entitled "White Indians," in which eight cases of captured children who became Indianized are analyzed in detail, Ackerknecht (1944) uses the term only for individuals. I am using Indianization in this old American sense.

Probably the earliest introduction of the Indianization theme in American literature occurs in the poem published in 1790, *Ouâbi*, or *The virtues of nature*, by Mrs. Sarah Wentworth Morton writing under the pen name Philena. Celario, a white man, falls in love with Azakia, an Illinois girl who is already married. He becomes identified with her people, leads a war party and rescues her husband, Ouâbi. He finally is able to marry Azakia when Ouâbi recognizes their love and his debt to Celario for saving his life. Mrs. Morton must have felt the novelty of her theme because she says in the Introduction:

> I am aware it may be considered improbable, that an amiable and polished European should attach himself to the persons and manners of an uncivilized people; but there is now a living instance of a

like propensity. A gentleman of fortune, born in America, and educated in all the refinements and luxuries of Great Britain, has lately attached himself to a female savage, in whom he finds every charm I have given my Azakia, and in consequence of his inclination, has relinquished his own country and connections, incorporated himself into the society, and adopted the manners of the virtuous, though uncultivated Indian.

(For further information see Bissell 1925:207 ff.).

In two early American novels white girls marry Indians. In *Hobomok: a tale of early times* (1824), by Lydia Maria Child, the young chief, for whom the novel is named, marries Mary Conant after her fiancé is thought to be dead. They have a child. The lover returns, and Hobomok, a noble savage, magnanimously disappears in the forest leaving Mary a newly killed deer. In *Hope Leslie* (1827), by Catherine M. Sedgwick, Faith Leslie is abducted by the Indians, marries a brave, and chooses to remain with him. N. M. Hentz attempted to draw the character of a white girl brought up among the Indians in *Tadeukund, the last king of the Lenape* (1825).[2]

It was Cooper, however, who was the first American writer to dramatize the Indianization theme in any psychological depth, to come to grips with the actual consequences of intimate identification of whites with Indians. In *The wept of Wish-ton-Wish* (1829), Ruth Heathcote was captured as a child of seven or eight and lived a decade with the Indians as Narra-mattah (Driven Snow), before she returned to her Puritan family with her Indian husband to face tragedy. Confronting her white relatives after so many years, Cooper writes (p. 348):

In air, expression, and attitude, (she) resembled one who had a fancied existence in the delusion of some exciting dream. Her ear remembered sounds which had so often been repeated in her infancy, and her memory recalled indistinct recollections of most of the objects and usages that were so suddenly replaced before her eyes, but the former now conveyed their meaning to a mind that had gained its strength under a very different system of theology, and the latter came too late to supplant usages that were rooted in her affections by the aid of all those wild and seductive habits that are known to become nearly unconquerable in those who have long been subject to their influence.

Leatherstocking, of course, was a semi-Indianized white man. Carl Van Doren (1917) has declared him "the most memorable character

American fiction has given to the World." His early life was spent among the Delaware, and long before they called him "Deerslayer" he had successively borne three other Indian nicknames. He acquired "knowledge of most of our Indian dialects," and absorbed Indian values. When contemplating torture by the Hurons, he says he will strive "not to disgrace the people among whom I got my training." (Quotations from *The Deerslayer*.)

In nineteenth century fiction we also find the renegade theme—the white man who, becoming Indianized and finding "savagism" good, symbolized the rejection of progress, civilization, and Christianity, and was easily cast as a villain. *Shoshone Valley* (1830), by Timothy Flint; *The renegade* (1848), by Emerson Bennett; *Old Hicks the guide* (1848), by Charles Webber, are all early novels of this type. Among the later dime novels, for example, *The jaguar queen, or the outlaws of the Sierra Madre* (1872) by Frederick Whittaker, characters like the latter's Count Montriche who became an Apache chief and a renegade, often appeared. (See Pearce 1953:244-25 and Smith 1950:114-15).

Despite the radical changes in intellectual climate from the eighteenth century, when the colonists were confronted with the disturbing realities of capture and many accounts of captivity experiences were published, up until the present day—a period of two hundred years—Indian captivity, the renegade, and Indianization have never lost their fascination for the American public. These themes have as much vitality in popular fiction as they ever had. In the early years of this century *The squaw man* (Royle 1905) was a very popular sentimental play. In it an Englishman marries an Indian girl who has saved his life. When she discovers that he has inherited an earldom she leaves him and their children and commits suicide. First staged in 1905, this play is historically noteworthy since it later became the first full-length motion picture, directed by Cecil B. DeMille (Blum 1953).

Currently, more than an occasional story is woven about the white man, woman, or child who, whether "captivated" or not, has been Indianized to some degree and is sometimes a renegade. Without any systematic search, I have picked up over a dozen of these in paperbacks that have appeared within the past decade or so. The leading character in *Arrow in the hill* (Jefferson Cooper 1955) was raised from childhood by the Mohawk; the villain is a renegade Englishman disguised as a Huron who leads war parties and spies for the French. *Thunder on the river* (Laird 1950) deals with divided loyalties in an adopted captive who marries an Indian girl. In *Green centuries* (Jordan 1953) a white

captive boy becomes completely identified with the Cherokee. Conrad
Richter's *The light in the forest* (1954), later transferred to the screen,
is concerned with a captive boy who is formally adopted by the
Delaware but develops a conflict in values and leaves them. An English
lord appears as a "white Indian" in *King's rebel* (Horan 1955). *The
Kentuckians* (Giles 1955) contains a villain who is a white man who
hates the settlers and identifies himself with the Indians. The hero of
Roanoke renegade (Tracy 1955) finally chooses to make his life
among the Indians. In *White warrior* (Patten 1956), a story told in the
first person, the narrator is captured by the Arapaho at the age of nine
when his mother and father are killed. He is formally adopted by an
Indian family in place of a lost son. The manner in which his foster
parents train him to be an Arapaho, the affection with which they treat
him, the way he gradually indentifies himself more and more fully with
the Indians is convincingly portrayed. *The searchers* (Le May 1956),
made into a moving picture, is concerned with a six-year search for
Debbie, a white child captured by the Comanche at the age of ten.
When the hero finds her it is a nightmare for him. "Behind the surface
of this long-loved face was a Comanche squaw." Her Comanche speech
was fluent, but her English almost forgotten. She did not wish to leave
"her people." The author says it was as if they had taken out her brains
and put in an Indian brain instead. "You—you are Long Knives," she
said, "We hate you—fight you—always, till we die." Another Indianized white girl is one of the main characters in *Pemmican* (Fisher
1957).[3] *The double man* (Pryor 1957) and *Cherokee* (Tracy 1957) both
portray divided loyalties. Tsani, the hero of the former, becomes war
chief of the Cherokee at eighteen. But he is not an Indian; his parents
were English, ambushed and killed when he was an infant. *Comanche
captives* (1960) by Will Cook, is a highly realistic account of the
pressure brought upon the army to redeem captured whites. The plot
turns on the lack of understanding by relatives and others of the
psychological depth of the emotional ties Indianization may bring
about and the consequences of a blind demand for captives' redemption. One boy had become completely identified with the Comanche
and fought against his rescuers, saying over and over again, "I am a
Comanche!" When his white mother "cooked a meal for the boy, a
homecoming meal that had been long planned and was the best she
had, . . . he picked up the laden tin plate and threw it in her face." His
father "did not know whether to hit the boy or forgive him; he touched
him and the boy seized his arm and bit it deeply . . ."[4]
Although Indianization has been a distinctive feature of American

historical experience and the Indianization theme still strongly appeals to readers of light fiction, why is it, then, that (like so many other aspects of the impact of the Indian upon us) it has remained a neglected topic of scholarly research? Dr. Wilcomb Washburn has pondered the same question and thinks it has been too simply passed over. In a paper contributed to the American Indian Ethnohistoric Conference in 1956 and published in 1957 (4:51-52), he observes:

> Most of us know that an extraordinary number of whites preferred Indian society, while almost no Indians preferred White society. Why did the Spanish report in 1612 that forty or fifty of the Virginia settlers had married Indian women, that English women were intermingling with the natives, and that a zealous minister had been wounded for reprehending it? Why were there, at this time in Virginia, such severe penalties for running away to join the Indians? Some have dismissed the evidence as showing merely that White civilization is so fragile and sophisticated that men tend to revert to the primitive when given the opportunity.

The problem is further complicated if American Negroes as well as whites are taken into account. Negro slaves in the South ran away and took refuge with the Seminole, Cherokee, Creek, Choctaw and Chickasaw, the so-called Five Civilized Tribes (Hodge 1907, 1910. *Handbook of American Indians* 2:600). While in the colonial period of our history some Indians shared the status of slaves with Negroes (Crane 1956: 113-14),[5] basically the relations of the Indians with whites was structured in a totally different way from white–Negro relations. Despite the vicissitudes of contact, the indigenous Indians managed to maintain a high degree of cultural autonomy in organized communities. This was particularly true in the case of the Five Civilized Tribes in the South. On the other hand, whatever their retention of Africanisms may have been, groups of Negroes never constituted autonomous sociocultural units in the United States. Forcibly detached from various tribal groups in their homeland and transported to the New World, it was solely in their individual roles as slaves that they became an integral part of socio-economic systems in the United States. Primarily they were slaves of the whites but in some cases they subsequently became slaves of the Indians when several Southern Indian nations acquired the institution of slavery from their white neighbors. Under these circumstances Negroes were assimilated to the same role in an Indian culture that they had played in white society. However, there appears to have been a notable difference, for Negro slaves continued to run away from their white masters and offer themselves as slaves to the Indians. Negro freedmen, too, often chose to cast their lot with the Indians. Furthermore, the Indians intermarried with both slaves and freedmen. Thus like some whites there were Negroes who became completely Indianized.[6]

Outside the South, the Indianization of Negroes occasionally occurred but it did not involve slavery. To mention a few examples: in the West the famous Negro, Jim Beckwourth, was a Crow chief. An active participant in the Sioux massacre of 1862 was an Indianized Negro named Godfrey.[7] When Henry R. Schoolcraft made his journey through the Great Lakes country to the source of the Mississippi River, he discovered a Negro living in an Ojibwa village of sixty people near the mouth of the St. Louis River. This Negro, a freedman, had been in the service of the Hudson's Bay Company for many years and had married an Ojibwa woman by whom he had had four children (Schoolcraft 1953:139). Swanton early in this century noted the fact that the richest man among the Skidegate Haida on the Northwest Coast was a Negro (See "Negro and Indian," Hodge, 1907, 1910. *Handbook of American Indians* 2:53) Dr. Ruben Reina tells me that today there is a Caribbean Negro from Belize (Honduras) who married an Indian woman from San Jose in Peten and has been living in her village for the past quarter of a century. She is a midwife and he is recognized as having an expert knowledge of the forest and "good power." They have raised a family of six children.

So far as I am aware, the experience of Negroes in Indian cultures has been almost completely neglected in fiction. The only examples I know of are Tarquinous, a minor character in *Alabama Empire* (1957) by Wellbourn Kelley, and Spence in Dale Van Every's *The Voyagers* (1957).[8] The period of the former novel is the late eighteenth century and the famous Creek chief Alexander McGillivray, who was himself mixed Indian and white, is a major figure in it. Tarquinious speaks Creek fluently. Perhaps racial attitudes in the United States have made the Indianization of Negroes a less romantic theme for the general reader. The same racial attitudes have made it a sensitive subject from the point of the Indians who in many parts of the country have struggled to achieve the social status of whites.

A further question now arises. The term Indianization has a provincial ring. Is it a phenomenon unique to American history, or is it only a particular manifestation of a far wider phenomenon? I believe the latter to be the case.

First of all, is it simply one aspect of acculturation? What American anthropologists have called *acculturation*, British anthropologists, *culture contact*, and the Cuban scholar Ortiz, *transculturation* (1947: 98 ff. and Introduction), refer primarily to the effects of contact upon the subsequent cultural attributes of organized *groups*. While individuals belonging to these groups are, of course, involved and play a variety of mediating roles in the process, the characteristic focus in acculturation studies is upon the changes induced in the mode of life of either, or both, groups. From the beginning, acculturation has been recognized as one aspect of the study of cultural dynamics. The pioneer memorandum of Redfield, Linton and Herskovits in 1936 (38:149–52) and the Social Science Research Council, Summer Seminar on Acculturation, which reviewed this field of study in 1953 (56:973–1002) delineated the fundamental problem in much the same terms. The Summer Seminar defined acculturation as "culture change that is initiated by the conjunction of two or more autonomous cultural systems" (56:974).

While sometimes occurring in the same historical context as acculturation, Indianization can be categorically distinguished from it and requires conceptual and terminological differentiation. It is a phenomenon that involves the fate of *persons* rather than changes in sociocultural systems. The fact that the indentification of these persons with the group to which they formerly belonged has been broken, or modified, distinguishes them as a class from persons undergoing readjustment who remain functioning members of an organized group undergoing acculturation. Since I have not found a generic term already in use that characterizes this phenomenon, I have had to coin one. *Transculturalization* seems appropriate. It is the process whereby *individuals* under a variety of circumstances are temporarily or permanently detached from one group, enter the web of social relations that constitute another society, and come under the influence of its customs, ideas, and values to a greater or lesser degree. A correlative term, *transculturite*, can then be used to designate those individuals who have undergone transculturalization.

In transculturalization, at one polar extreme are individuals who become permanently identified with the second culture. In such cases there is more than a cultural readaptation—typically, there is a psychological transformation. At the other extreme, readjustment may be relatively superficial and have little psychological depth. Manners and speech may be affected, but not basic attitudes and values. In between, we have cases where historical circumstances combined with unusual personality characteristics have motivated some individuals to

play a dual role effectively. For example, on the American frontier we
have the unusual double identification of Sir William Johnson. His
most recent biographer, James T. Flexner (1959:38), refers to:

> ... Johnson's "singular disposition" which included a quality
> much rarer than the appreciation and practice of Indian skills—
> throughout American history thousands of white men joyfully
> exchanged breeches for breechcloth. His unique gift was his ability
> to feel simultaneous loyalty to both Indian and white institutions ... [9]

The degree of transculturalization depends, of course, on a number
of different variables: the age at which the process begins; the previous
attitude toward the people of the second culture; length of residence;
motivational factors; the nature of the roles played, and so on.
Indianization is thus a specific example of the wider human phenomenon of transculturalization. The same process has occurred in other
parts of the world.

In the Pacific, for instance, some of the first missionaries sent out by
the London Missionary Society in the late eighteenth century became
transculturites (Wright and Fry 1936: chapter 1). They were among the
earliest "squaw men" of the South Seas. There were also other white
men who married native women but became more than squaw men in
the narrow sense. Churchill of the "Bounty" became a Tahitian chief;
John Young and Isaac Davis, British seamen captured in Hawaii,
married into the native aristocracy and achieved chiefly rank. (Furnas
1947:121, 215). William Mariner, a boy under sixteen when his life was
spared in Tonga in 1806, became Chief Toki Ukamea and a landowner.
His sojourn as a transculturite was temporary, however. He did not
marry a native girl, but after four years returned to England where he
married and raised a family of eleven children. These few selected
cases illustrate the varying degrees of transculturization which
took place in the Pacific and the differing conditions under which it
occurred. To appreciate the importance of the transculturites in the
Pacific Islands in the late eighteenth and the nineteenth centuries we
must realize that even the many recorded cases are only an insignificant
sample; their numbers reached the proportions of a migration. Ernest
S. Dodge says, "No one knows how many runaway sailors settled in the
various Polynesian islands and became absorbed in the native population, but there were literally thousands" (1963:106).

While the expansion of European peoples since the fifteenth century
has tremendously accelerated contacts between all varieties of the
culture of Europe and all other cultures of the modern world, neither

acculturation nor transculturalization has been limited to this period. The historical setting for acculturation is provided whenever peoples of different socio-cultural systems come into contact, and transculturalization is possible whenever conditions arise which permit an individual to become detached from one cultural group and temporarily or permanently to become affiliated with another. In principle this also applies at the sub-cultural level, for example, between nations or between religious or caste groups. At this level we have many instances of transculturalization. I will only give one of them here.

A distinctive feature of the Ottoman state, perfected by Murad I (1359–89) and continued by successive Sultans for three centuries, was the systematic transculturalization of Christian children drawn from dependent provinces. The aim of this high policy, based upon a form of human tribute, was to insure the active cooperation of the vast Christian population over which the Turks were politically dominant. Thousands of boys were taken regularly from their native villages and trained for the Sultan's service. Every three or four years agents were sent to subject villages where lists of all youths of adolescent age were obtained from the priests. These boys were personally examined, and the handsomest and strongest selected. They were removed from their villages and indoctrinated with Moslem values by being rigorously trained in special schools or in Turkish families of the highest status, even in the Sultan's seraglio itself. "Their early duties as pages were connected with all branches of the palace service, four favored ones being designated to keep watch with dagger and torches in the Sultan's chamber." Particularly interesting is the fact that for all these transculturites "possibilities of advancement, based on merit, were almost unlimited. Here was a democratic practice of promotion where it would be least expected . . . a simple page might become grand vizier through sheer ability . . ." Indeed, transculturalization was so effective that many of the former Christian boys became fanatical members of the Turkish elite corps, the *Yeni Cheri* (New Troops) or Janissaries as they became known in the West. (Rouillard 1941:13–14, 173, 210, 225).[10]

Although the conditions under which transculturalization has occurred have not yet been studied systematically on a wide comparative scale, the American material on Indianization provides clues to the kind of analysis that is needed and possibly to the kind of generalizations that may emerge. In America, two specific conditions initiating the detachment of an individual from his primary cultural affiliation can be distinguished: involuntary detachments and voluntary ones.

We know, of course, that involuntary detachment—capture—did not

necessarily lead to transculturalization. But in the case of children it
seems to have been the major condition that led to the most complete
transculturalization, even without any systematic indoctrination such
as that adopted by the Ottoman Turks. What aroused the astonisment
of the early American colonists was the fact that captives often refused
to be redeemed. One of the earliest and best known of such cases was
Eunice Williams, the daughter of a Deerfield pastor, who was "captivated" in 1704 when she was seven. In an Indian raid her mother was
killed and her father and brother shared the fate of Eunice. The latter
were redeemed a year later, but Eunice, formally adopted by a
Caughnawaga woman, refused to leave her foster parents. She had
forgotten how to speak English by the time she was seventeen; she
married an Indian and lived to be ninety years old. Although we shall
never know how many captive children remained with the Indians,
Barbeau (1950:529) refers to the fact that:

> In his investigations among the Wyandots of Oklahoma, in 1911,
> 1912, [he] heard that the familiar names among them of Dawson,
> Walker, Brown, McKee, Boone, Johnson, Young, Armstrong,
> Clarke, etc., had originated among them through captive children of
> Virginia. After they had grown up, they were given the choice of
> returning to their white parents or of staying with their adopted
> kinsmen. And they preferred to stay.

On the other hand, it would be hard to imagine the captured Mrs.
Mary Rowlandson becoming Indianized under any circumstances. She
was too firmly entrenched in Puritan beliefs. Her seventeenth century
editor concluded, "None can imagine what it is to be captivated, and
enslaved to such atheistical, proud, wild, cruel, barbarous, brutish (in
a word) diabolical creatures as these, the worst of the heathen" (quoted
by Pearce 1952:205).

Even more astonishing to many "civilized" Americans and Europeans were the cases where individuals Indianized by choice. It was
particularly shocking to the Puritans, convinced as they were that the
Indians were indeed Satan's children, that the religion of the aborigines was literally Devil worship, and that "wherever the Indian opposed
the Puritan there Satan opposed God" (Pearce 1952:204).[11] To the
Puritan mind it was only right in the cosmic scheme of things that the
Indian should become civilized and Christianized or perish. No
wonder, then, that to Indianize voluntarily was tantamount to a crime.
Yet there were such cases among the Puritans. In 1677, two years
following the capture of Mary Rowlandson, William Hubbard
denounced a man who, during King Philip's War, "renounced his

religion, nation, and natural parents, all at once fighting against them."
This man had gone off with an Indian woman. Captured later he was
subjected to examination and condemned to die (Pearce 1952:209).

In the less constricted cultural outlook of the eighteenth century
cases of voluntary Indianization apparently became more common,
although they were still considered a puzzling phenomenon.[12] Particularly perplexing was the fact that transculturalization seemed to
operate in only one direction. We find the repeated comment that
whites who had been brought up among Indians, or lived with them,
chose to remain, whereas the reverse was true in the case of Indians
who had sampled a "civilized" existence. Crevecoeur (1957:208-9) in
his famous *Letters from an American farmer* wrote:

> By what power does it come to pass, that children who have been
> adopted when young among these people, can never be prevailed on
> to readopt European manners? Many an anxious parent I have seen
> after the last war, who at the return of peace, went to the Indian
> villages where they knew their children had been carried in captivity;
> when to their inexpressible sorrow, they found them so perfectly
> Indianised, that many knew them no longer, and those whose more
> advanced ages permitted them to recollect their fathers and mothers,
> absolutely refused to follow them, and ran to their adopted parents
> for protection against the effusions of love their unhappy real
> parents lavished on them! Incredible as this may appear, I have
> heard it asserted in a thousand instances, among persons of
> credit.... It cannot be, therefore, so bad as we generally conceive it
> to be; there must be in (the Indians) social bond something
> singularly captivating, and far superior to anything to be boasted of
> among us; for thousands of Europeans are Indians, and we have no
> examples of even one of those Aborigines having from choice become
> Europeans![13]

To appreciate fully the phenomenon of Indianization in America it
needs to be set within the historical context of an expanding frontier
and basic contemporary American values and attitudes, on the one
hand, and of the values and characteristic institutions of the Indians
with whom social interaction was taking place, on the other. For one
thing, the implicit, if not always explicit, moral evaluation of Indianization on the part of the whites directly reflected the increasing
consciousness of the eighteenth century European of the meaning of
"civilization" which arose along with the term itself (cf. Smith 1950:
218 ff. and Cohen 1947:231). The values inherent in "white" culture
were necessarily "higher" than those which prevailed in any aboriginal
culture because they embodied the consequences of a progressive

improvement in the life of mankind which "led up to" the contemporary "civilization" of the European peoples (Pearce 1953:155-59). In the New World this was all a contemporary reality. "Looking at the Indian in his relation to the whole of their society, Americans could see manifest the law of civilized progress" (Ibid.:155). More than this, the graded steps of progress did not have to be abstractly conceived; they were geographically visible. In his later years, Jefferson wrote in a letter to a friend (quoted in Smith 1950:219):

> Let a philosophic observer commence a journey from the savages of the Rocky Mountains, eastwardly towards our seacoast. These he would observe in the earliest stage of association living under no law but that of nature, subsisting and covering themselves with the flesh and skin of wild beasts. He would next find those on our frontiers in the pastoral state, raising domestic animals to supply the defects of hunting. Then succeed our own semi-barbarous citizens, the pioneers of the advance of civilization, and so in his progress he would meet the gradual shades of improving man until he would reach his, as yet, most improved state in our seaport towns. This, in fact, is equivalent to a survey, in time, of the progress of man from the infancy of creation to the present day.

"The theory of the progressive stages of history," says Pearce, "and of the relationship of character to circumstance explained the savage's essential inferiority, the final inferiority of even his savage virtues" (1953:95). Thus, regardless of individual needs or motives, and despite the romantic treatment of the Indian in literature, for a white person to become Indianized was necessarily a retrograde step. If the frontier farmer was "a rebellious fugitive from society" (Smith 1950:218), the squaw man was doubly indictable. Wissler (1938:185-86) writing of early twentieth century squaw men on western reservations, says:

> Almost without exception ... if I called at the home of a white man with an Indian wife, my host sooner or later offered apologies.... The squaw man was aware of the contempt in which he was held by those of his kind married to white women. One only needed to sense the "emotional slant" of the term as used in speech to understand the social position of these white derelicts....

The special opprobrium attached to the white renegade—those who not only became identified with Indians, but actively *opposed* "civilized" white men in trade, politics or war—is easily understood. Such individuals had plunged into the deepest pit of social degradation.

An evaluation somewhat similar to that accorded transculturites was also applied to frontier communities in the late nineteenth and early twentieth centuries by scholars who fully recognized the direct impact of Indian culture on these marginal segments of American civilization, and sought to fit the events into a unilinear sequence of cultural development. Frederick Jackson Turner conceptualized the frontier experience as "the meeting point between savagery and civilization ... [It] strips off the garments of civilization and arrays [the frontiersman] in the hunting shirt and the moccasin" (1920:2-3). It is a cultural step downward which, although necessary for survival, must always be transcended.[14] A. G. Keller (1915:276-77) in his *Societal evolution* took a similar position.

> [The frontier group, or colony,] is a reversion. But that means no more than that it is an adaptation to a set of conditions out of whose range old societies have passed. Reversion is as much adaptation as is progression ... [The frontier society sacrifices much] of the civilization which it had, in favor of forms of adaptation which ... are successfull as they resemble those of the natives. Acculturation takes place, strange to say, from the *lower* toward the *higher* race; thus the colonists in New England ... "Indianized."[15]

Both Turner and Keller were writing at a time when anthropologists were beginning to question and reject unilinear theories of cultural evolution, but more than a decade before intensive studies of acculturation were undertaken. With the abandonment of the theory of regular progressive stages in the cultural history of all peoples, we are now free to examine processes of acculturation and transculturalization more objectively and without moral prejudice. We do not have to ask whether transculturalization is a "reversion" to a more "primitive" level, or an "escape" from "civilization." Like other non-literate peoples of the world, the aborigines of America lived in societies which were as regularly patterned in terms of their own value systems as the culture of the European intruders. Whether there was "in their social bond something singularly captivating, and far superior to anything boasted of among us" that lured and held so many whites, is a psychological question to which we cannot give a final answer.[16] There are other and related questions, however, which a reexamination of cases of transculturalized whites and Negroes suggest. They are not primarily what their motives were, nor a moral evaluation of their choices, but rather: What cultural factors were present in Indian societies that made it possible for alien individuals—so often enemies— to become functioning members of them? Why were the Indians motivated to accept them? What social mechanisms and values in Indian societies mediated the acceptance and assimilation of these strangers? What roles did whites and Negroes play in Indian cultures? Conversely, what values and attitudes prevailed in American culture that limited the roles which it was possible for Indians to play among us?

From the very beginning white intruders in North America repeatedly commented upon the hospitality of the Indians. Many years ago, James Mooney pointed out, "The narratives of many pioneer explorers and settlers, from DeSoto and Coronado, Amidas and Barlow, John Smith and the Pilgrims, down to the most recent period, are full of instances of wholesale hospitality toward white strangers, sometimes at considerable cost to the hosts" (Hodge, 1907, 1910 *Handbook* 1:571). In the seventeenth century some of the Jesuits were very much surprised by the hospitality with which they were received. Father Le Jeune, for example, wrote (Thwaites 8:94–95):

> As soon as I was perceived in the village someone cried out ... and at once everyone came out to salute and welcome me.... I lodged with a man who was one of the richest of the Hurons. You can lodge where you please; for this Nation above all others is exceedingly hospitable towards all sort of persons, even toward strangers; and you may remain as long as you please, being always well treated according to the fashion of the country.

Among the Indians, moreover, there was the well-known custom, antedating white contact, of adopting persons captured in war. There were special rites involved. Indians formally adopted in this manner could not return to their own tribal group. This custom, then, must have led to the transculturalization of Indians by Indians. The same practice was carried on in the period of white contact, but there was a modification. The Indians found they could profit materially in many cases. Whether adopted or not, white captives could return to their own society if they were ransomed. (*Handbook* 1: "Captives"; 2: "Slavery.")

In some tribes adoption was specifically motivated by the desire to replace a dead child or other relative. This involved the building up of all the affective ties of Indian family life, the social integration of the individual into the kinship system, and his orientation to all the values and social sanctions of the group. Functionally, it was equivalent to the normal processes of socialization in all societies, on which the psychological structuralization and personal adjustment of the human individual depends. No wonder, then, that many white children who had been subjected to this process found it impossible to leave the Indians. The result is predictable. Not that in every case the old white personality quickly faded into the new Indian one. Writers like Conrad Richter in *The light in the forest* and Lewis B. Patten in *White warrior* (rather than social psychologists or anthropologists) have attempted to depict for us the conflicts that may also arise.

In contrast to the institutionalized pattern of adoption in Indian cultures, consider the picture presented in the society of the white European settlers. There was no comparable institution of adoption. The few Indians who became associated with the whites must have found themselves confronted with a social situation in which intimate personal contacts were narrowly restricted. They might be offered a formal education, but not acceptance as fully fledged members of a family group. The social isolation of the Indian boy in Cooper's *The wept of Wish-ton-Wish*, living among whites in a household rigidly molded by Puritan values, is a fictional example which is close to the reality. It was not that the Indian could not be raised "up" to the level of civilization but rather, the lack of an equivalent desire on the part of whites to welcome and assimilate the Indian, and the absence of any established cultural means that would mediate the transition from one culture to the other in a manner that was psychologically sound. Swanton quotes from a report written by some New England missionaries which documents this (1926:502):[17]

> An Indian youth has been taken from his friends and conducted to a new people, whose modes of thinking and living, whose pleasures and pursuits are totally dissimilar to those of his own nation. His new friends profess love to him, and a desire for his improvement in human and divine knowledge, and for his eternal salvation; but at the same time endeavour to make him sensible of his inferiority to themselves. To treat him as an equal would mortify their own pride, and degrade themselves in the view of their neighbours. He is put to school; but his fellow students looks on him as a being of an inferior species. He acquires some knowledge, and is taught some ornamental, and perhaps useful accomplishments; but the degrading memorials of his inferiority, which are continually before his eyes, remind him of the manners and habits of his own country, where he was once free and equal to his associates. He sighs to return to his friends; but these he meets with the most bitter mortification. He is neither a white man nor an Indian; as he has no character with us, he has none with them.

There is a further point to be made. The Indian institution of adoption entailed the fullest kind of socialization of the white child. It prepared him for *all* the various roles which were open to him in Indian society. I have already mentioned several cases of whites and Negroes becoming Indian chiefs; in their review of cases of Indianization both Ackerknecht and Swanton cite a number of other instances. Old White Boy, who was captured in 1760 when he was about four years old, could never remember his name. "Not only he himself but all his sons ... became famous Seneca chiefs. When his youngest son was elected chief, he feared that the jealousy of the Indians might be aroused by his continued success and therefore he wanted to leave; but they begged him to stay, so he did" (Ackerknecht 1944:17). Of the thirty cases of captivity, fifteen male and fifteen female, examined by Swanton (1926: 501), three or four of the men became chiefs and a similar number of the women became chief's wives.[18] The fact that white or Negro men could become chiefs in Indian societies is one indication of the complete receptiveness of these cultures to transculturites. This basic receptiveness was mediated to a large degree by the nature of their social organization and kinship structures. It explains why it was that *adult* whites and Negroes could by choice, and with relative ease, become assimilated to an Indian manner of life. Squaw men, for example, did not all become transculturalized in equal degree; nevertheless marriage with an Indian woman, residence with her people, and the acquisition of an Indian tongue mediated the social roles of these individuals in such a manner that they inevitably were drawn into the web of interrelations of the society. Indeed, the use of kinship terms alone prescribed patterns of conduct as well as rights and obligations in daily social interaction that were inescapable. This is undoubtedly the reason for the often heard complaint of squaw men that "when you marry an Indian girl you marry the whole damn tribe!"

On the other hand, what roles were open to an Indian in white society? Even if educated, the presumption was that he would return to his people as a missionary. Samson Occum (1723-92), "the pious Mohegan," is a case in point. He became transculturalized, achieving great fame as a preacher in America and England. Clad in a black suit and knee breeches, an *Indian* clergyman "with the garb, mannerisms, and habits of thought of the Puritan divine," Occam was a novelty in England (C. T. Foreman 1943:87). Most of Occam's life, however, was spent in missionary work among Indians in this country. He *spoke* from many pulpits, but he received no call to *occupy* a pulpit in America. Despite his education, his personal talents, the money he had raised for Dartmouth College, and the evident success with which he had adopted the way of life of his Christian contemporaries, the missionary role was the only one open to him.[19]

In the case of the Negroes, certain other conditions were added to their transculturalization. Once the southern Indians had borrowed the institution of slavery from Europeans, they *wanted* Negro slaves. The system being less rigid than among whites, it is intelligible why some Negroes ran away to join the Indians. It might be thought that having an African background in the first place, they were seeking to escape the more rigorous demands of "civilization," but this is more ironic than illuminating. Under the circumstances, they were inexorably caught in a role from which there was no immediate escape; they simply chose to play it under better conditions. The Seminoles, for example, "held their vassals in a form of benevolent bondage, exacting only their fealty and a small amount of corn, stock or peltries" (G. Foreman 1932:315). Speck writes of the Creeks in general (1908:107):

> It is said among the descendants of these slaves today that the Indians were easy masters, and that the servitude to the Negro was more like a form of hired service, where they were supported and protected by the Indians to whom in return they tendered their aid in agriculture and household labor. [Adding from Colonel Benjamin Hawkin's observations in 1789-99] Where the Negroes were there was more industry and the farms were better.... During the Seminole War, Negro slaves and their mixed offspring played an important part in the ranks of the Indians. Even Osceola, the Seminole leader, is believed to have had Negro blood in his veins.

Furthermore, those who were transculturalized and remained with the southern Indians until after the Civil War were able to transcend their earlier formal status as slaves. Foster says (1935:65-66):

> Seminole Negroes continued to live among their Seminole relatives, friends and former masters. The Indians adopted their former slaves and also the Negro freedmen among them, making them citizens of their country. They were given equal rights to land and annuities. Those now living [1929-30] who remember these times have informed the author that they scarcely knew the difference between being free and being in slavery. They maintain that the Seminole Negroes continued to live an "Indian life," and that many of the older ones were "Indian" in their religion as well as in their social and economic practices. Instances have been cited ... of three Seminole Negroes who were religious leaders among the Seminoles. The Seminoles and the Negroes continued to intermarry, as they had done in former years. The Negroes continued also to form a

part of the Seminole Council. There were even Seminole Negroes connected with the "Crazy Snake Rebellion."

Whatever choices were involved in the course of their personal readjustment as transculturites, there is no reason to suppose that these Negroes weighed in any abstact fashion the values of "savagery" versus "civilization."

Turning to the South Pacific, even a superficial examination of a few cases of transculturalization illuminates the motivations of chiefs as well as the institutional basis of the process. The Tonga chief Finau II found Mariner and other white seamen of particular use in enhancing his political ambitions through the conquest of additional islands. Furnas (1947:215) says that in the forties of the last century,

> Wilkes found well-fed beachcombers, on several islands in the Gilberts, treated with respect and long married to young women of standing; they usually wanted to go home, but had little to complain of. In the early days many Fijian chiefs had such tame white men, regarding them as mannerless but useful; to have one was part of a chief's prestige.

CONCLUSION

From this brief survey of Indianization in America, it is obvious that not all socio-cultural systems are equally receptive to the assimilation of alien individuals, and that the degree of receptivity of a culture depends, not primarily on individual good or ill-will, but on *social* values and attitudes, and on institutions to mediate the induction of alien individuals into it. In studies of diffusion and acculturation it has always been assumed that selective factors were at work which were a function of the organization or patterning of the culture. The same seems to be true of the reception of transculturites. In some societies, such as these Indian ones highly receptive to transculturites, it is difficult for an alien individual to remain peripheral except as a guest, or visitor, or trader. To live *in* them he must in a sense be "reborn" into them. On the other hand, aware of their "advanced" European heritage, the small communities of Europeans in America erected a defensive wall of heightened consciousness of superiority against the surrounding Indians. To condescend to "raise up" the Indians was the greatest magnanimity. In the case of the Puritans' religious communities, their fierce opposition to Indianization was only an extension of their antagonism to all of different belief—witness their persecution of the Quakers. Their somberness and rigidity of outlook was also the antithesis of that of the Indians who, for the most part, must have been repelled by it. An Indian transculturite in such circumstances, even if he had loyal friends among them, remained an alien. At a level of social organization transcending the tribal or family group, such as a political community where an alien can become a citizen with legal rights, his assimilation in the society may be extensive or limited, depending on the nature of these legal rights, on circumstances, and on the individual. The trader may be permitted a limited role; special groups may be permitted to live in restricted areas, but not be members of the community. If all such factors were known in particular cases, they might explain the varying degrees of assimilation it is possible for alien individuals to achieve in different cultures, and to rate cultures on a scale of receptivity.

The role of transculturites in the promotion of culture change in the group with which they become affiliated is another question that might be investigated. So far as America is concerned, it is clear that, in the nature of the case, abducted children who became tranculturalized did not play such a role. Old White Boy, for instance, became converted to Christianity in the same acculturation process that led to the Christianization of his fellow Seneca. In the South Seas, on the other hand, although I have not examined these cases in detail, my impression is that some of the captured seamen did play a role in acculturation. Hypothetically, the role of transculturites as agents in the acculturation process may be a function of the degree to which they explicitly reject the culture of their natal group and become identified with the central values of their adopted culture. The Baptist missionary, Isaac McCoy, writing in the nineteenth century, thought the squaw men were obstacles to "organizing an Indian territory and of rendering the Indians secure in their possessions. [These white men] who identify themselves with the Indians as much as possible ... [and] who have preferred savage to civilized society do not desire the improvement of the former" (1840:529). Psychological and cultural identification, however, does not exclude the influence of transculturites on culture change. Many years ago Speck (1908:109) was convinced that

> in mythology the culture of the Creeks and other southeastern tribes has been subjected to modification by the Negroes [who] being more amenable to white influence than the Indians ... have been the entering wedge in the past century for many new ideas and new interpretation of old ones.[20]

Swanton (1926:512) in his examination of thirty cases of white captives concluded his essay by saying:

The number should be very much increased, [and] similar studies of white captives among other peoples of the world should be made, and the whole checked by reciprocal cases of captives from the various primitive races held by white.

This task still remains to be done. Our perspective might be further expanded by including a careful examination of the consequences of the policy adopted by the Ottoman Turks, or other comparable cases, and by collecting and analyzing cases of voluntary transculturalization of various kinds. The comparative investigation of transculturalization as a human phenomenon, the conditions under which such cases have occurred, the motivation of the individuals concerned, and the relation of differential cultural values and patterns to their readjustment would greatly enrich our knowledge of crucial psychological and cultural factors underlying the functioning of group identification and alienation, as well as culture change.

NOTES

A. Irving Hallowell is Professor Emeritus of Anthropology at the University of Pennsylvania, Philadelphia, Pennsylvania, and curator of Social Anthropology at the University Museum. He received his M.A. and Ph.D. from this University and an Honorary Sc.D. (1963). With the exception of three years at Northwestern University (1944–47) he has been an active member of the Anthropology Department there from 1923–63. In addition, he has taught at Swarthmore College, Bryn Mawr, Columbia, and the Universities of California (Berkeley) and Washington. Currently he is conducting a seminar for selected graduate students at Temple University, as Adjunct Professor of Sociology. Dr. Hallowell is a member of the Permanent Council of the International Congress of Anthropological and Ethnological Sciences and a past president of the American Anthropological Association, the American Folklore Society, and the Society for Projective Techniques. He was chairman of the division of Anthropology and Psychology of the National Research Council, 1946–49, and has been chairman of the Board of Directors of the Human Relations Area Files since 1957. From 1950–55 he was editor of the Viking Fund Monographs in Anthropology (Wenner-Gren Foundation for Anthropological Research). He is a member of the National Academy of Sciences, the American Philosophical Society, and in 1955 was the recipient of the Viking Medal and Award in General Anthropology.

Dr. Hallowell's field work has been principally conducted among the Northern Ojibwa of Canada and other Algonkian peoples. His focal points of professional interest, as represented in papers published in journals and symposia, have included kinship and social organization, folklore, culture and personality, the psychological dimension of human evolution and the history of anthropology. A collection of selected papers is to be found in *Culture and Experience* (1955). Monographic publications are *Bear Ceremonialism in the Northern Hemisphere* (1926) and *The Role of Conjuring in Saultean Society* (1942).

A. Irving Hallowell's paper is the fifth in a series, edited by Francis L. K. Hsu and Alan P. Merriam, specially prepared to honor Melville J. Herskovits. The entire series, when completed, will constitute a new type of *Festschrift* (CA 4:92).

1. For information on the history and ethnography of this group see Leger (1929), Maurault (1866), and Fried (1955). Gordon M. Day, in a recent article on the relations of the St. Francis Abenaki to Dartmouth College (1959), writes:

"These were the Abenakis whom the Jesuits extolled for their native mildness, their exemplary piety, and whom Canadian historians lauded for their loyalty and military qualities in the service of New France. These were the model converts whose conversion consoled the Fathers for the destruction of the Huron Nation by the Iroquois and the debauching of the Algonquins of Three Rivers by the fur traders."

From this village, too,

"came the war parties which raided the New England frontier and warriors who ambushed Braddock; from it came Hannah Dustin's captors and the attackers of Fort Number Four, now Charlestown, New Hampshire. This is the village where John Stark was captive and which was burned by Rogers' Rangers. And oddly enough, this is the village which provided one of Eleazar Wheelock's strongest motives for locating his Indian school at Hanover...."

The purpose of the school was to train Indians and missionaries to the Indians. After Wheelock lost his Six Nations pupils and the cooperation of Sir William Johnson, most of the Indian recruits over the next 80 years came from St. Francis, thus reinforcing the Protestant tradition in the Canadian village. "At the present time," says Day, "about 130 Indians live at Saint Francis, but the band numbers over 500 registered members. There is in addition a sizable number of persons of Saint Francis descent who have given up formal connections with the band and live in other parts of Quebec, in Ontario, and in the Northeastern States, often not known as Indians by their neighbors. In all this number there remain only about fifty persons who can speak the native language fluently. The native speakers are mostly over 65 years of age, and with few exceptions the children are not learning the language."

2. Long before these American novels appeared, Smollett in *Humphrey Clinker* (1771) had introduced an episode in which the Scot, Lismahago, fighting on the early American frontier, had been captured

and adopted by an Indian sachem to replace his lost son. Lismahago marries the betrothed of the latter and has a son by her. He becomes a sachem and is "acknowledged first warrior of the Badger tribe (clan)." Then his wife dies, he is exchanged for an Indian and returns to Britain after the war. Still earlier, in France, Voltaire had published *L'Ingénu* (1767), a witty little tale about an Indianized French boy who had been raised by a Huron foster mother after his parents had been killed in the New World. Returning to France as a young man he declares himself a Huron, but is identified by his uncle and aunt as their nephew. For the purposes of the story, which is a vehicle for satirizing French attitudes, customs and institution, what are purportedly Indian attitudes are given The Simple Soul. But these are superficial and have no psychological depth. While this story is historically important so far as the Indianization theme is concerned, it does not come to grips with the actual consequences of early association with Indians on the part of white children. For the literary background of Voltaire's story see, Eugene E. Rovillain, "L'Ingénu de Voltaire: quelques influences." *Pub. Modern Language Association of America* (1929), 44:537-45.

3. In his *Foreword* the author, Vardis Fisher, writes:

If any reader thinks it unlikely that a white girl could have been on the scene as an Indian, I would refer him to John Henry Moberly, an HB (Hudson Bay) factor of a little later time, who says in his *Journal*: "Quite a number of women among the Indians who came to the trading posts in those days had no sign of a drop of Indian blood. Their hair was light, they had blue eyes and good figures and, except for sunburn, were as fair as any white woman. For this there was an explanation: when the Indians raided an immigrant train on the American side they killed all grown people and boys but preserved the female children, who grew up perfect Indians in their ways. Rarely could they be persuaded to leave their Indian friends."

4. I have omitted reference to short stories in which the Indianization can also be found. In this genre Dorothy M. Johnson's *Indian country* (1953) is an outstanding contemporary example. It contains three distinguished stories dealing with captivity and Indianization which first appeared in *Argosy* and *Colliers* prior to the date of publication in book form. "Flame on the Frontier," for example, is concerned with two sisters who are captured. One of them marries an Indian and refuses redemption. The other goes back and marries a white man by whom she has two children. One of her Indian suitors never forgets her and after an interval of ten years makes a long journey to see how she is. Her husband says, "What's that bloody Injun doing here?... If I ever set eyes on that savage again, I'll kill him. You know that, don't you, you damn squaw."

5. In Charleston there were markets in which both types of slaves

were sold. In 1708, when the total population of South Carolina was 9,580, the slave population was more than 44 percent of this figure; the Negro slaves numbered 2,900, the Indian slaves, 1,400. At this time there was a market for Indian slaves in New England. Crane says, "In the early eighteenth century the Boston News Letter printed frequent advertisements of runaway Carolina Indians."

6. Johnson (1929) calls attention to the fact that in 1832, when the first census of the Creek nation was taken, the commissioners were confronted with questions concerning the status and rights of individuals with Negro blood for which they sought authoritative decisions. They reported (1) cases in which an Indian has "living with him as his wife a Negro slave, the property either of himself or of another," and (2) the existence of "free black families that seem to be in every way identified with these people and the only difference is color." The decision in such cases was:

(1) An Indian, whether full or half blood, who has a female slave living with him as his wife, is the head of a family and entitled to a reservation; (2) free blacks who have been admitted members of the Creek nation, and are recognized as such by the tribe, if they have families are entitled to reservations of land under the second section of the Creek treaty.

Herskovits says (1930:279):

"Although the Indian element is not readily discernible in the analysis of traits within the genealogical classes, there is no reason to doubt the statement of 29% of the persons measured who claim to have partial Indian ancestry, partly because of known historical contacts between the Negroes and the Indians, and particularly because the statements as to the amounts of Negro-White ancestry check so satisfactorily with the results of anthropometric measurements."

7. See Bonner 1931; Heard 1863: Chapter 13. Godfrey's father was French Canadian and his mother was a Negro. At the time of the Sioux uprising he was 27 years old. He had been married four years to a Sioux woman, daughter of Wakpadoota. Godfrey's father-in-law was later executed, but his own part in the massacre was never fully clarified. Although the commissioners found him guilty of murder, they recommended that the penalty be commuted to ten years imprisonment.

8. In a more recent historical novel, Trask (Berry 1960), the scene of which is laid in Oregon Territory in the forties of the last century, Don Berry has introduced a character who is a descendant of a Negro. The latter, a blacksmith, was a castaway from a wrecked ship who married a Killamook (Tillamook) woman. Kilchis (his son or grandson?) who was tyee of the Killamook at the time of the story is a major character. He "stood several inches over six feet" and his face was like "an ebony mask." Trask says to his Indian companion: "That man's a

nigger! He's no more Indian than I am." The reply is: "He is a Killamook. What color doesn't matter. He was born a Killamook and lives and will die a Killamook."

9. Reconstructing Johnson's participation in an Indian dance in his younger days, Flexner writes (p. 54):

"Round and round Johnson went, yelling as he drove an imaginary hatchet into an imaginary skull, and gradually his mind was washed clean of every European thing. No longer was he an ambassador on a ticklish mission from another world: he was one with his fellow dancers, one flesh, one heart, one brain. And when he too sank to the ground in exhaustion, his war-painted body was hardly distinguishable from the bodies that lay around him. But when he awoke the next morning, his mind awoke with him, and he returned to his scheming for English ends."

And speaking of George Croghan he says: "He became second only to Johnson as the most powerful white Indian on the continent." (p. 126).

10. In the seventeenth century changes were occurring which, according to the French observer Deshayes, were weakening the Ottoman Empire. Turkish children in larger numbers were being substituted for transculturalized Christian boys, and the merit system was being corrupted by graft. In the opinion of this observer "native Turks can never have the singleness of interest and loyalty to the Sultan that the trained renegades had" (1624:247-48).

11. Dorson points out, "If the English accepted a personal Devil and his human consorts, they could not very well deny practice in the black art to the red heathen, especially ones so gifted in necromancy" (1950:5).

12. Crevecoeur, referring to the period of the Revolution when loyalty to the English or to the "Rebel" government came up, wrote (1925:23):

"Many of those who found themselves stripped of their property took refuge among the Indians. Where else could they go? Many others, tired of that perpetual tumult in which the whole settlement was involved, voluntarily took the same course; and I am told that great numbers from the extended frontiers of the middle provinces have taken the same steps,—some reduced to despair, some fearing the incursions with which they were threatened. What a strange idea this joining with the savages seems to convey to the imagination; this uniting with a people which Nature has distinguished by so many national marks! Yet this is what the Europeans have often done through choice and inclination, whereas we never hear of any Indians becoming civilized Europeans. This uncommon emigration, however, has thrown among them a greater number of whites than ever has been known before."

13. The same point of contrast is made by Peter Kalm (Kerkkonen

1959:184) and by Colden (1922:203-4). Voluntary Indianization is referred to by Lawson (1860:302). In his chapter on "The American Captives" Henry Beston observes (1942:47),

"The Indian path had its own gods; it was strong medicine. Those who had followed it, and were later returned to their own white inheritance, often heard the shaking of the Indian rattle and the voices of Indian ghosts. I remember the man from Wells who all his life long sat on the floor like an Indian and maintained that they were 'better people than the whites.'"

14. Mood (1943) points out that the theory of social evolution was the "fundamental unifying concept" of Turner's early writings.

15. Keller, op. cit., 276-77. This author's use of the term *acculturation* in 1915 is worth noting. *Indianized* is used correlatively for the general influence exerted.

16. When Crevecoeur, referring to the Indians, says:

"Without temples, without priests, without kings, and without laws, they are in many instances superior to us. And the proofs of what I advance are, that they live without care, sleep without inquietude, take life as it comes, bearing all its asperities with unparalleled patience, and die without any kind of apprehension for what they have done, or for what they expect to meet with hereafter,"

and then asks: "What system of philosophy can give us so many necessary qualifications for happiness?" (1957:210), he reflects the literary tradition of the Noble Savage, rather than any precise, ethnographic knowledge of Indian life. Fairchild (1928:103-4) has pointed out that later Crevecoeur reversed his earlier attitude towards the Indians expressed in the *Letters*. The evidence is to be found in *Voyage dans La Haute Pennsylvanie* ... published in 1801, but never translated into English. In this book the author says he has been an eye-witness of such brutalities as devastating war parties, tortures, and scenes of drunkenness among the Indians.

17. In her short story "Back to the blanket," Alice Marriott dramatizes the situation (1945:247, 250). Leah, a Kiowa child had been sent east to school at nine. Leah thought it would be easy to go home, "go to the mission, work to uplift her people. Then she would marry some good young man, not an Indian, a missionary, and go away and do good all her life." But when she got home it was not so easy. "Here was her own sister calling her Indian." And when the local missionaries called and wanted her to go live with them, she refused.

"What good would it do to live at the mission? There was no warmness for her to Mr. and Mrs. Gaines. There was respect, that was all. Here there was warmness towards the people around her and towards her, anyway. Yes, and there was the beginnings of respect."

18. Simon Girty, the famous "white savage" renegade of the Revolutionary period, told Oliver Spencer, a white captive, that although he would never see home, if he turned out to be a good hunter

and a brave warrior, he might someday be a chief (Boyd 1928:211-12).

19. There are, of course, a few individual exceptions. As early as 1504 a Brazilian Indian was taken to France by Captain de Gonneville and became completely transculturalized. He was converted to the Catholic faith, married the captain's daughter, founded a family which long flourished in France (Lee 1929:242). Since many Elizabethan voyagers had made it a practice to bring a few American Indians back to England, it was thought by some that the number should be increased, with the aim of making such individuals "into civilizing instruments among their own people." This idea came to a head in 1620 when

"a serious proposal was ventilated to extend the practice by importing into England a large number of Indian lads to be educated on English lines. It never reached fruition, however, the chief argument against it being that the Indian who had lived in England awhile tended to assimilate the vices rather than the virtues of civilized life (Lee 1929: 242; see also C. T. Foreman 1943:28)."

The most famous Indian to undergo transculturalization in the seventeenth century was the world-renowned Pocahontas. And her son, Thomas Rolfe, returning to America, became the progenitor of distinguished descendants. Yet all these cases were exceptional and incomparable in numbers with the whites and Negroes on the other side of the Atlantic who became Indianized.

20. Some Americans, debating "the Indian question" in the second half of the nineteenth century, thought the problem could be solved by a very strict segregation of the Indians on reservations. In the opinion of one writer, F. A. Walker, whose statements undoubtedly reflect more widely held views, the abiding presence of Indians in our midst was complicated by the evil influence of white transculturites who, backsliders as they were from civilization and sunk to the lower level of Indian culture (conceived as practically anarchical), were likely to corrupt the latter rather than to improve it (1813:385). "White men will still be found," he says, "so low in natural instincts, or so alienated by misfortunes and wrongs, as to be willing to abandon civilization and hide themselves in a condition of life where no artificial wants are known, and in communities where public sentiment makes no demand upon any member for aught in the way of achievement or self-advancement. Here such men, even now to be found among the more remote and hostile tribes, will, unless the savage customs of adoption are severely discountenanced by law, find their revenge upon humanity, or escape the tyranny of social observance and requirement. Half-breeds bearing the names of French, English, and American employees of fur and trading companies, or of refugees from criminal justice, 'in the settlements,' are to be found in almost every tribe and band, however distant. Many of them grown to man's estate, are among the most

daring, adventurous, and influential members of the warlike tribes, seldom wholly free from suspicion on account of their relation on one side to the whites, yet by the versatility of their talents and the recklessness of their courage, commanding the respect and the fear of the pure-bloods, and, however incapable of leading the savages in better courses, powerful in a high degree for mischief."

REFERENCES CITED

Ackerknecht, Erwin H. 1944. White Indians. *Bulletin of the History of Medicine* 15:18-35.

Barbeau, Marius. 1950. Indian captivities. *Proceedings of the American Philosophical Society* 94:522-48.

Bennett, Emerson. 1848. *The renegade*. Cincinnati.

Berry, Don. 1960. *Trask*. New York: The Viking Press.

Beston, Henry. 1942. *The St. Lawrence*. New York: Farrar and Rinehart.

Bird, Robert Montgomery. 1939. *Nick of the woods*. American Fiction Series, ed. by Cecil B. Williams. New York: American Book Co. (First edition 1837).

Bissell, Benjamin. 1925. *The American Indian in English literature of the eighteenth century*. New Haven: Yale University Press.

Blum, Daniel. 1953. *A pictorial history of the silent screen*. New York: Putnam, pp. 53, 54, 172.

Bonner, T. D. (Ed.). 1931. *The life and adventures of James P. Beckwourth*. New York: Alfred A. Knopf, Inc.

Boyd, Thomas. 1928. *Simon Girty: The white savage*. New York: Minton, Balch & Co.

Child, Lydia Maria. 1824. *Hobomok: A tale of early times*. Boston.

Cohen, Morris R. 1947. *The meaning of human history*. La Salle: Open Court.

Colden, Cadwallader. 1922. *History of the Five Nations*. New York (First ed. London 1747).

Cook, Will. 1960. *Comanche captives*. New York: Bantam Books Inc. (Serialized in *The Saturday Evening Post* 1959).

Cooper, James Fenimore. 1883. *The wept of Wish-ton-Wish*. New York: Appleton (First ed. 1829).

———. 1952. *The Deerslayer*. New York: Dodd, Mead & Company (First ed. 1841).

Cooper, Jefferson. 1955. *Arrow in the hill*. New York: Dodd, Mead & Company, and Pocket Books Inc.

Crane, Verner U. 1956. *The southern frontier, 1670-1732*. Ann Arbor: University of Michigan Press (First ed. 1929).

Crevecoeur, J. Hector St.John de. 1957. *Letters from an American farmer*. New York: Dutton (First ed. 1782).

———. 1925. *Sketches of eighteenth century America: More letters from an American farmer.* Ed. by H. L. Bourdin, R. H. Gabriel and Stanley T. Williams. New Haven: Yale University Press.

Day, Gordon M. 1959. Dartmouth and St. Francis. *Dartmouth Alumni Magazine,* November, 1959.

Deshayes, Louis (Baron de Courmenin). 1624. *Le voyage de Levant fait par le commandement du roi, l'année 1621.* Paris (Republished 1629, 1632, 1645, 1664).

Dodge, Ernest S. 1963. Early American contacts in Polynesia and Fiji. *Proceedings of the American Philosophical Society* 107:102-6.

Dorson, Richard M. 1950. *America begins.* New York: Pantheon.

Fairchild, Hoxie Neal. 1928. *The noble savage.* New York: Columbia University Press.

Fisher, Vardis. 1956. *Pemmican.* New York: Doubleday & Co., Inc. (Pocket Books, Inc. 1957).

Flexner, James Thomas. 1959. *Mohawk baronet: Sir William Johnson of New York.* New York: Harper and Brothers.

Flint, Timothy. 1830. *Shoshone Valley.* 2 vols. Cincinnati.

Foreman, Carolyn Thomas. 1943. *Indians abroad, 1493-1938.* Norman: University of Oklahoma Press.

Foreman, Grant. 1932. *Indian removal.* Norman: University of Oklahoma Press.

Foster, Laurence. 1935. *Negro-Indian relationships in the Southeast.* Ph.D. dissertation, University of Pennsylvania. Philadelphia: privately printed.

Fried, Jacob (Ed.) 1955. *A survey of the aboriginal populations of Quebec and Labrador.* Eastern Canadian Anthropological Series, number 1. Montreal: McGill University.

Furnas, J. C. 1947. *Anatomy of paradise.* New York: William Sloane Associates.

Giles, Janice Holt. 1954. *The Kentuckians.* New York: Houghton Mifflin Company (Bantam Books, Inc., 1955).

Gordon, Caroline. 1941. *Green centuries.* New York: Charles Scribner's Sons (Bantam Books, Inc., 1953).

Hallowell, A. Irving. 1957. "The backwash of the frontier: The impact of the Indian on American culture," in *The frontier in perspective.* Ed. by Walker D. Wyman and Clifton B. Kroeber. Madison: University of Wisonsin Press (Reprinted in *Annual Report of the Board of Regents of the Smithsonian Institution, 1958.* Washington: Government Printing Office, 1959).

————. The impact of the American Indian on American culture. *American Anthropologist* 59:201-17.

Heard, Isaac V. D. 1863. *History of the Sioux War and massacres of 1862 and 1863.* New York: Harper and Brothers.

Hentz, N. M. 1825. *Tadeuskund, the last king of the Lenape*. Boston.

Herskovits, Melville J. 1930. *The anthropometry of the American Negro*. New York: Columbia University Press.

Hodge, F. W. (Ed.). 1907, 1910. *Handbook of American Indians*. Parts I and II. Bureau of American Ethnology, Bulletin 30. Washington: Government Printing Office.

Horan, James D. 1953. *King's rebel*. New York: Crown Publishers (Bantam Books, Inc., 1955).

Huden, John C. The white chief of the St. Francis Abenaki—Some aspects of border warfare: 1690–1790. *Vermont History* 24:199–210.

Johnson, Dorothy M. 1953. *Indian country*. New York: Ballantine Books.

Johnson, J. Hugh. 1929. Documentary evidence of the relations of Negroes and Indians. *Journal of Negro History* 14:21–43.

Keller, A. G. 1915. *Societal evolution: A study of the evolutionary basis of the science of society*. New York: Macmillan.

Kelley, Wellbourn. 1957. *Alabama empire*. New York: Rinehart & Company, Inc. (Bantam Books, Inc., 1958).

Kerkkonen, Martti. 1959. *Peter Kalm's North American Journey, its ideological background and results*. Helsinki: The Finnish Historical Society.

Laird, Charlton. 1949. *Thunder on the river*. New York: Little, Brown & Company (Bantam Books, Inc., 1950).

Lawson, John. 1860. *The history of Carolina*. Raleigh (First ed. London, 1714).

Lee, Sir Sidney. 1929. *Elizabethan and other essays*. Ed. by F. S. Boas. Oxford: Clarendon Press.

LeMay, Alan. 1954. *The searchers*. New York: Harper and Brothers. (First serialized as *The avenging Texans* in *The Saturday Evening Post*, 1954; Popular Library, 1956).

Leger, Sister Mary Celeste. 1929. *The Catholic Indian missions in Maine (1611-1820)*. The Catholic University of America Studies in American Church History 8.

McCoy, Isaac. 1840. *History of the Baptist Indian missions*. Washington and New York.

Mariner, William. 1817. *An account of the natives of the Tonga Islands, by John Martin, M.D.* London: privately printed.

Marriott, Alice. 1945. *The ten grandmothers*. Norman: University of Oklahoma Press.

Mathews, Mitford M. (Ed.). 1951. *A dictionary of Americanisms on historical principles*. 2 vols. Chicago: University of Chicago Press.

Maurault, L'Abbe J. A. 1866. *Histoire des Abenakis depuis 1605 jusqu'à nos jours*. Sorel, Province of Quebec.

Mood, Fulmer. 1943. The development of Frederick Jackson Turner as a historical thinker. *Publication of the Colonial Society of Massachusetts* 34: 304-7.

Morton, Sarah Wentworth. 1790. *Ouâbi, or The virtues of nature.* Boston.

Ortiz, Fernando. 1947. *Cuban counterpoint: Tobacco and sugar.* Introduction by B. Malinowski. New York: Alfred A. Knopf, Inc.

Patten, Lewis B. 1956. *White warrior.* New York: Fawcett Publications.

Pearce, Roy Harvey. 1947. The significance of the captivity narrative. *American Literature* 19:1-20.

———. 1952. The "ruines of mankind": The Indian and the Puritan mind. *Journal of the History of Ideas* 13:200-17.

———. 1953. *The savages of America: A study of the Indian and the idea of civilization.* Baltimore: Johns Hopkins University Press.

Pryor, Elinor. 1957. *The double man.* New York: W. W. Norton & Company, Inc.

Redfield, Robert, Ralph Linton and Melville J. Herskovits. 1936. Memorandum on the study of acculturation. *American Anthropologist* 38:149-52.

Richter, Conrad. 1953. *The light in the forest.* New York: Alfred A. Knopf, Inc. (First serialized in *The Saturday Evening Post* 1953; Bantam Books, Inc., 1954.).

Rouillard, Clarence Dana. 1941. The Turk in French history, thought, and literature (1520-1660). *Etudes de Littérature Etrangère et Comparée.* Paris: Boivin.

Rovillain, Eugene E. 1929. *L'ingénu de Voltaire: quelques influences. Publications of the Modern Language Association* 44:37-45.

Royle, E. M. *The squaw man.* Play, first produced in 1905; in 1908 produced in England as *The white man.* James D. Hart. 1944. *The Oxford Companion to American Literature.* New York; London; Toronto.

Schoolcraft, Henry R. 1953. *Narrative journal of travels through the northwestern regions of the United States extending from Detroit through the great chain of American lakes to the sources of the Mississippi River in the year 1820.* Ed. by Mentor L. Williams. East Lansing: Michigan State College Press.

Sedgwick, Catherine M. 1827. *Hope Leslie, or early times in Massachusetts.* 2 vols. New York.

Smith, Henry Nash. 1950. *Virgin land: The American West as symbol and myth.* Cambridge: Harvard University Press.

Smollett, Tobias G. 1929. *Humphrey Clinker.* New York: Modern Library Edition (First ed. 1771).

Social Science Research Council Seminar in Acculturation, 1953. Acculturation: An exploratory formulation. *American Anthropologist* 56:973-1002.

Speck, Frank G. 1908. The Negroes and the Creek nation. *Southern Workman* 37:106-10.

Swanton, John R. 1926. Notes on the mental assimilation of races. *Journal of the Washington Academy of Sciences* 16:493-502.

Thwaites, Ruben Gold (Ed.). 1896-1901. *The Jesuit Relations and allied documents*. Cleveland.

Tracy, Don. 1951. *Cherokee*. New York: Dial Press (Pocket Books, Inc. 1958).

————. 1954. *Roanoke renegade*. New York: Dial Press.

Turner, Frederick Jackson. 1920. *The frontier in American history*. New York: Holt.

Van Doren, Carl. 1917. "Fiction: Brown, Cooper," in *Cambridge History of American Literature*, Vol. 3, Chapt. 6. Cambridge: Cambridge University Press.

Van Every, Dale. 1957. *The voyagers*. New York: Henry Holt and Company (Bantam Books, Inc., 1959).

Voltaire, F. M. A. de. 1926. "The simple soul [*L'ingénu*]," in *Zadig and other romances of Voltaire*. Translated by H. I. Woolf and Wilfred S. Jackson. New York: Dodd, Mead & Company (First ed. of *L'ingénu*, 1769).

Walker, F. A. 1873. The Indian question. *North American Review* 116: 329-88.

Washburn, Wilcomb E. A moral history of Indian-white relations: Needs and opportunities for study. *Ethnohistory* 4:47-61.

Webber, Charles. 1848. *Old Hicks the guide*. New York.

Whittaker, Frederick. 1872. *The jaguar queen, or The outlaws of the Sierra Madre*. Beadle's New Dime Novels, number 389.

Wissler, Clark. 1938. The enigma of the squaw man. *Natural History* 41:185-89.

Wright, Louis B. and Mary Isabel Fry. 1936. *Puritans in the South Seas*. New York: Holt.

SUPPLEMENTARY BIBLIOGRAPHY
OF WORKS BY A. IRVING HALLOWELL

This supplements and updates the previous bibliography provided in A. I. Hallowell, *Culture and Experience* (1955, pp. 430-34). A bibliography of Hallowell's writing through 1965 appears in M. E. Spiro, ed., *Context and Meaning in Cultural Anthropology* (New York: Free Press, 1965, pp. 417-25). No effort has been made to collate translations of Hallowell's work or to track down articles that have since found their way into anthologies. I acknowledge the help of Maude Hallowell and Jean Adelman in locating some stray references. This bibliography, plus the one that appeared in *Culture and Experience*, may be taken as a definitive list of Hallowell's writings.

R. F.

1920.   "The Problem of Fish Nets in North America." Master's thesis, University of Pennsylvania.

1924.   "Bear Ceremonialism in the Northern Hemisphere." Ph.D. dissertation, University of Pennsylvania.

1941,   ed. *Language, Culture and Personality: Essays in Memory of Edward Sapir* (with Leslie Spier and Stanley S. Newman). Menasha, Wis.: Sapir Memorial Publication Fund.

1943.   Discussion of "Nativistic Movements," by Ralph Linton. *American Anthropologist* 45:240.

1951.   "Frank Gouldsmith Speck, 1881-1950." *American Anthropologist* 53:67-75.

1953.   Discussion, with others, of *An Appraisal of Anthropology Today*, edited by Sol Tax et al. Chicago: University of Chicago Press.

1954a.   "Daniel Sutherland Davidson, 1900-1952" (with Erna Gunther). *American Anthropologist* 56:336.

1954b.   Review of *The Philosophy of Psychiatry*, by Harold Palmer. *American Anthropologist* 56:336.

1955.   *Culture and Experience*. Philadelphia: University of Pennsylvania Press.

1956a.   "The Structural and Functional Dimension of a Human Existence." *Quarterly Review of Biology* 21:88-101.

1956b.   "The Rorschach Technique in Personality and Culture Studies." In *Developments in the Rorschach Technique*, vol. 2, edited by Bruno Klopfer et al. Yonkers, N.Y.: World Publishing Co.

1956c. Preface to *Primary Records in Culture and Personality*, vol. 1, edited by Bert Kaplan. Madison, Wis.: Microcard Foundation.

1957a. "The Impact of the American Indian on American Culture." *American Anthropologist* 59:201-17.

1957b. "The Backwash of the Frontier: The Impact of the Indian on American Culture." In *The Frontier in Perspective*, edited by W. D. Wyman and C. B. Kroeber. Madison, Wis.: University of Wisconsin Press.

1957c. "Rorschach Protocols of 151 Berens River Adults and Children and 115 Adults from Lac du Flambeau." In *Microcard Publications of Primary Records in Culture and Personality*, no.6, edited by Bert Kaplan. Madison, Wis.: Microcard Foundation.

1957d. Review of *Theories of Personality*, by Calvin S. Hall and Gardner Lindzey. *American Anthropologist* 59:936-37.

1957e. Review of *American Indian and White Relations to 1830: Needs and Opportunities for Study*, by William N. Fenton et al. *American Anthropologist* 59:1118-19.

1958. "Ojibwa Metaphysics of Being and the Perception of Persons." In *Person Perception and Interpersonal Behavior*, edited by R. Tagiuri and L. Petrullo. Stanford, Calif: Stanford University Press.

1959a. "Behavioral Evolution and the Emergence of the Self." In *Evolution and Anthropology: A Centennial Appraisal*, edited by B. J. Meggers. Washington, D.C.: Anthropological Society of Washington.

1959b. "The Backwash of the Frontier: The Impact of the Indian on American Culture." *Smithsonian Institution, Annual Report for the Year Ended June 30, 1958*. Washington, D.C.: Smithsonian Institution.

1960a. "Ojibwa Ontology, Behavior, and World View." In *Culture in History: Essays in Honor of Paul Radin*, edited by Stanley Diamond. New York: Columbia University Press.

1960b. "The Beginnings of Anthropology in America." In *Selected Papers from the American Anthropologist, 1888-1920*, edited by Frederica de Laguna. Evanston, Ill.: Row, Peterson and Co.

1960c. "Self, Society, and Culture in Phylogenetic Perspective." In *Evolution after Darwin* (vol. 2, *The Evolution of Man*), edited by Sol Tax. Chicago: University of Chicago Press.

1960d. Discussion, with others, of *Issues in Evolution* (vol. 3 of *Evolution after Darwin*), edited by Sol Tax and Charles Callender. Chicago: University of Chicago Press.

1960e. "Algonkian Tribes." *Encyclopaedia Britannica*.

1960f. "Frank G. Speck." *Encyclopaedia Britannica*.

1960g. "Ojibwa." *Encyclopaedia Britannica*.

1961a. "The Protocultural Foundations of Human Adaptation," in *Social Life of Early Man*, edited by S. L. Washburn. Viking Fund Publications in Anthropology, no. 31. New York: Wenner-Gren Foundation for Anthropological Research.

1961b. "To Nigeria!" *Philadelphia Anthropological Society Bulletin* 14(1): 7–11.

1961c. Review of *The Phenomenon of Man*, by P. Teilhard de Chardin. *Isis* 52(3):439–41.

1961d. Review of *Aristotle and the American Indian*, by Lewis Hanke. *American Quarterly* 11:536–37.

1962a. Review of *From Ape to Angel*, by H. R. Hays. *American Anthropologist* 64:174–76.

1962b. Review of *Psychology: A Study of a Science*, vols. 1, 2, 3, edited by Sigmund Koch. *American Anthropologist* 64:204–7.

1962c. Review of *The Clinical Application of Projective Drawings*, by Emanuel F. Hammer. *American Anthropologist* 64:207–8.

1962d. Review of *Ishi in Two Worlds: A Biography of the Last Wild Indian in North America*, by Theodora Kroeber. *Annals, American Academy of Political and Social Science* 340:164–65.

1962e. "Anthropology and the History of the Study of Man" (unpublished manuscript prepared for the Social Science Research Council's Conference on the History of Anthropology).

1963a. "Personality, Culture, and Society in Behavioral Evolution." In *Psychology: A Study of a Science*, vol. 6, edited by Sigmund Koch. New York: McGraw-Hill.

1963b. "The Ojibwa World View and Disease." In *Man's Image in Medicine and Anthropology*, edited by Iago Galston. New York: International Universities Press.

1963c. "American Indians, White and Black: The Phenomenon of Trans-culturalization.." *Current Anthropology* 4:519–31.

1963d. Review of *The Teaching of Anthropology* and *Resources for the Teaching of Anthropology*, edited by D. G. Mandelbaum, G. W. Lasker, and E. M. Albert. *Science* 141:144–45.

1963e. Review of *Culture and Behavior: The Collected Essays of Clyde Kluckhohn*, edited by Richard Kluckhohn. *Journal of Higher Education* 34:237–38.

1964a. Review of *Primitive Social Organization: An Evolutionary Perspective*, by Elman R. Service. *American Sociological Review* 29: 314–15.

1964b. Review of *Essays in Social Anthropology*, by E. E. Evans-Pritchard. *American Sociological Review* 29:424–25.

1964c. Review of *Human Nature and the Study of Society: The Papers of Robert Redfield*, vol. 1. *American Sociological Review* 29:464.

1965a. "The History of Anthropology as an Anthropological Problem," *Journal of the History of the Behavioral Sciences* 1:24–38.

1965b. "Hominid Evolution, Cultural Adaptation, and Mental Dysfunctioning." In Ciba Foundation Symposium, *Transcultural Psychiatry*, edited by A. V. S. de Reuck and Ruth Porter. London: J. and A. Churchill.

1966*a*.   "The Role of Dreams in Ojibwa Culture." In *The Dream and Human Societies*, edited by G. E. von Grunebaum and R. R. Caillois. Berkeley: University of California Press.

1966*b*.   Review of *A Hundred Years of Anthropology*, by T. K. Penniman. *American Anthropologist* 68:267-68.

1966*c*.   Review of *Letters from Edward Sapir to Robert H. Lowie. American Anthropologist* 68:774.

1966*d*.   Review of *Indian Culture and European Trade Goods*, by G. I. Quimby. *Michigan History* 1966 (Sept.):225-56.

1967*a*.   "Anthropology in Philadelphia." In *The Philadelphia Anthropological Society: Papers Presented on Its Golden Anniversary*, edited by Jacob W. Gruber. Philadelphia: Temple University Press.

1967*b*.   Preface to the paperback edition of *Culture and Experience*. New York: Schocken Books.

1967*c*.   Review of *Men and Apes*, by Ramona Morris and Desmond Morris. *American Anthropologist* 69:783.

1968*a*.   "Speck, Frank G." *International Encyclopedia of the Social Sciences*, edited by D. L. Sills. New York: Macmillan Co. (Free Press).

1968*b*.   Review of *Origins of the American Indian*, by Lee Eldridge Huddleston. *American Anthropologist* 70:1185.

1968*c*.   "Bear Ceremonialism in the Northern Hemisphere: Reassessment" (unpublished manuscript in the possession of Frederica de Laguna).

1969.   Review of *One Hundred Years of Anthropology*, edited by J. O. Brew. *American Anthropologist* 71:725-26.

1970.   Review of J. G. Herder on *Social and Political Culture*, edited and translated by R. M. Barnard. *American Anthropologist* 72:861-62.

1971*a*.   *The Role of Conjuring in Saulteaux Society*. New York; Octagon Books (reprint of the 1942 University of Pennsylvania Press edition).

1971*b*.   Review of *Missionary Linguistics in New France*, by Victor E. Hanzeli. *American Anthropologist* 73:408-9.

1972.   "On Being an Anthropologist." In *Crossing Cultural Boundaries*, edited by S. T. Kimball and J. B. Watson. San Francisco: Chandler Publishing Co.

1974.   *Culture and Experience*. Philadelphia: University of Pennsylvania Press (paperback reprint of the 1955 University of Pennslyvania Press edition).

1976.   "Northern Ojibwa Ecological Adaptation and Social Organization"